FRANCE

THE AXIS OCCUPATION OF EUROPE
THEN AND NOW

*This book is dedicated to the millions of civilian casualties
of the Second World War throughout occupied Europe,
killed by military action, slaughtered in reprisals,
executed as political prisoners or extinguished by starvation.*

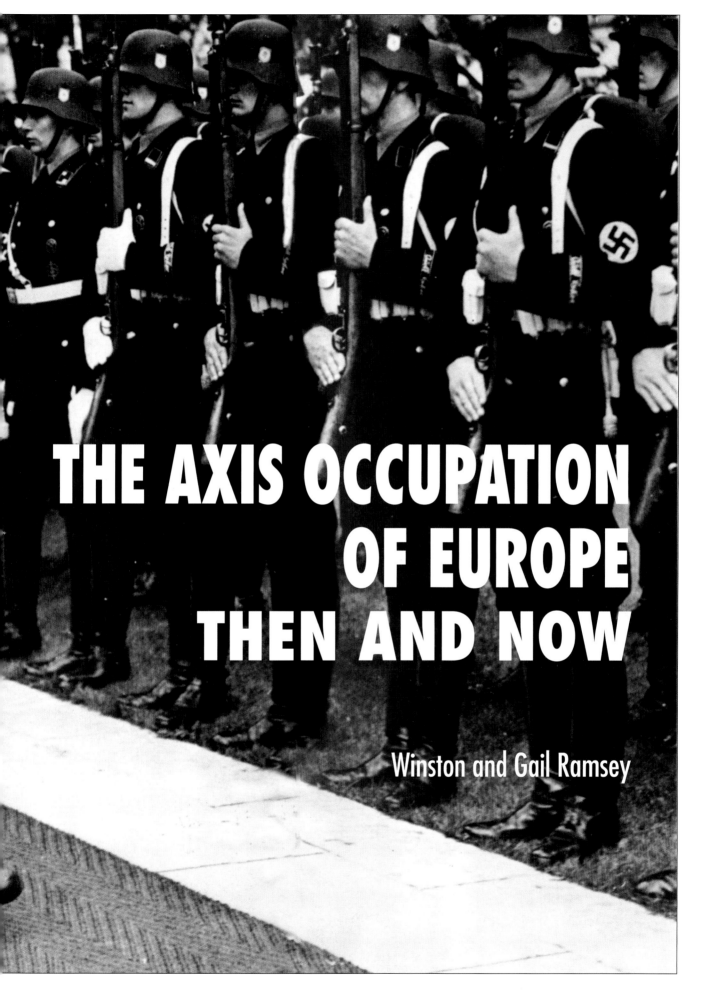

THE AXIS OCCUPATION OF EUROPE THEN AND NOW

Winston and Gail Ramsey

Credits

ISBN: 9 781870 067 935
© *After the Battle* 2018

PUBLISHERS
Battle of Britain International Ltd
The Mews, Hobbs Cross House,
Hobbs Cross, Old Harlow,
Essex CM17 0NN

Telephone: 01279 41 8833.
Fax: 01279 41 9386
E-mail: hq@afterthebattle.com
Website: *www.afterthebattle.com*

PRINTERS
Printed by Ozgraf S. A., Olsztyn, Poland.

ACKNOWLEDGEMENTS
Our sincere thanks are extended to the many individuals listed below who gave of their time to make this book possible. We also appreciate the expert assistance provided by Karel Margry, Editor of *After the Battle* in Holland, and Jean Paul Pallud in France.

Pages included with updated stories from *After the Battle* are presented within boxed borders in this book.

PHOTOGRAPHS
Alamy: 204 top, 305 bottom. **Esther Ancoli-Barbasch:** 285 bottom. **Sergio Andreanelli:** 14 all, 221 bottom left. **Byelorussian State Museum of the History of the Great Patriotic War:** 292 top right and bottom. **Ardit Bicaj:** 271 top right. **Phillip Birnbaum:** 260 top and bottom. **James Blevins:** 285 top, 295 centre. **Charles E. Brown:** 213 centre, 215 top. **Yelena Brusilovsky:** 290 top left. **Bundesarchiv:** 81 centre (101I-012-0022-23 LANZINGER), 82 top left (RH 82-00079 MENSING), 87 bottom left (695/412/12), 181 (1983-1985-1216-524), 219 centre (101I-185-0412-14A), 224 top (101I-166-0525-19) and bottom left (101I-166-0525-08), 225 top left (101I-166-0525-39), top right (101I-166-0525-29), centre left (101I-166-0525-30), centre right (101I-166-0525-36) and bottom left (101I-166-0527-04), 247 top (121-0726), 248 top (121-0723), 252 top (101I-185-0116-02A), 252 centre (F016229-0014), 324 top left (101I-312-D983-16), 324 top right (101I-312-D83-0983-15), 325 centre (101I-312-0983-10), 326 top left (101I-312-D983-25), 326 centre (101I-312-D983-24), 327 top (101I-312-D983-03), 327 centre (101I-312-0983-05). **George Birman:** 277 top and bottom left. **Peter Chamberlain:** 26 bottom left and right. **CTK:** 47 top, 52 centre left, 53 top, 56 top, 57 top, 58 top left, 59 top, 64 centre, bottom left and right. **Bernard Debruyne:** 194 top left and right, centre, bottom left. **Ada Dekhtyar:** 293 top, 294. **Millicent Diamond:** 347 top left and right. **ECPAD:** 81 top left (DAT 3112 L22), 275 top. **Ekebergparken:** 115 bottom right. **Rebecca Green:** 103 bottom, 105 bottom. **Peter Gunn:** 201 top, 202 bottom left. **Hadassah Bimko Rosensaft:** 348 top. **Douglas Hinton:** 106 bottom. **Hochschule für Musik und Theater München:** 20 bottom. **Egon Horvat:** 249 bottom. **Thomas Hughes:** 171 bottom. **Instytut Pamieci Narodowej:** 289 top left. **Nikola Jelenkovic:** 262 bottom right, 263

bottom, 273 centre. **Jewish Historical Museum, Belgrade:** 268 bottom right, 269 top left. **Joachim Joachimczyk:** 87 top. **Boris Kosic:** 267 bottom right. **Hubert Kuberski:** 304 top left. **Henry Landman:** 263 top and centre. **Karel Margry:** 135 bottom, 137 bottom, 139 centre, 140 bottom, 141 centre and bottom, 142 bottom, 143 top right and bottom, 145 centre and bottom, 146 bottom, 147 bottom, 148 both, 149 both, 150 all, 151, 152 top left and right, centre, bottom, 153 top, 154 top and bottom left, 155 bottom right, 162 bottom, 163 bottom right, 164 top right and bottom, 167 bottom, 168 bottom, 169 centre, 170 top right and bottom, 276 bottom. **Harry Marsh:** 11 bottom left, 23 bottom, 24 top right, 34 bottom both, 45 bottom right, 47 bottom right, 48 top, 52 centre right, 58 bottom right. **Memorijalni muzej Jasenovac:** 257 bottom, 265 bottom left, 267 top and bottom left, 268 top 270 top left and rights. **Craig Morfitt:** 207 bottom. **Alessandra Mori:** 315 bottom right, 316 bottom right, 317 bottom, 318 top and bottom right, 319 bottom, 320 bottom, 321 top right and bottom. **Dan Mouritsen:** 102 top both and bottom. **Museum of Danish Resistance:** 106 top right. **NIOD:** 317 centre (19508) **Julius Norwilla:** 279 bottom. **Muzej Revolucije Narodnosti Jugoslavije:** 254 bottom left, 257 top, 258 top right, 259 top left, 268 bottom left, 273 top. **Norwegian Industrial Workers Museum:** 124 bottom left and right. **Václav Novák:** 33 bottom, 45 bottom left, 57 bottom left. **Terry O'Brien:** 212 top right, centre and bottom. **Tony Oliver:** 123 bottom, 124 top left, 125 top and bottom right. **Patrick Ott:** 224 bottom right, 225 bottom right, 226 bottom right. **Jean-Paul Pallud:** 126, 127 top and bottom left, 156 top, 172 top right, 174 bottom, 177, 178 top both, centre left, bottom both, 179 all, 180 centre, 184 top left and right, 185 top, 187 top and bottom right, 188 bottom, 189 bottom, 190 bottom, 195 bottom, 207 top right, 204 bottom, 226 bottom left, 339 top

left, 342 bottom left. **George Pararas-Carayannis:** 223 top left and right. **Colin Partridge:** 208 bottom right, 210 bottom right, 214 centre right, 265 bottom. **Tony Pike:** 209 centre, 210 top right, 213 bottom. **Robert Porter:** 37 top, 38 bottom, 39 top, 40 bottom, 46 bottom right, 52 top both, 55 bottom right, 59 bottom right. **Brana Radovic:** 196 all, 197 centre and bottom, 201 centre and bottom. **Gail Ramsey:** 16 top right, 223 bottom right, 229 both, 230 top left and right, 231 all, 233 centre and bottom right, 243 bottom, 309 top, 328 top right and bottom, 331 bottom. **Pauline Robinson:** 350 top right. **Kylie Rogers:** 53 bottom, 56 bottom. **Royal Court Guernsey:** 214 top, centre left and bottom. **Eugene Shnaider:** 289 bottom left and right. **Societé Jersiaise:** 209 bottom right. **Society for the Study of the ETO:** 12 bottom left and right, 15 top left, right and bottom, 16 top left and bottom, 17 bottom left, 27 top and bottom left, 28 top left, 30 centre, 32 top, 39 bottom, 40 top, 42 all, 43 all, 46 top left and right, 58 top right, 61 top, 62 top left, right and centre, 73 top, 108 top, 109 top, 116 top, 117 bottom, 121 bottom, 145 top left, 165 all, 166 top right and bottom, 167 top right, 168 top, 169 top and bottom, 170 top left and centre, 198 both, 202 top right, 287 top and bottom both. **Nikita Tiepliszczew:** 181 bottom. **Alan Tomkins:** 123 top right. **United States Holocaust Memorial Museum:** 255, 256 top, 259 bottom left, 261, 271 top left, 274 top, 280 top, 282 bottom, 283 top. **United States National Archives:** 89 bottom, 155 top right, 195 top, 288 bottom left, 289 top right, 299 top right, 302 bottom, 315 top. **Yad Vashem:** 280 bottom, 298 top. **Thomas Wartenberg:** 288 bottom right. **Warsaw Uprising Museum:** 80 bottom left. **YIVO Archives:** 32 bottom both, 36, 37 bottom, 38 top, 41, 44 top left and bottom, 45 top, 50 both, 51 top, 64 top. **Fred Yvonne:** 200 bottom. **Samuel B. Zisman:** 344 bottom.

Preface

The story told in this volume is not for the faint-hearted. Its pages are full of accounts of untold cruelty to innocent people, the recounting of horrendous treatment meted out to men, women and children, and religious massacres of wholesale proportions. From the outbreak of war in September 1939, 17 countries in Europe were progressively occupied and subjugated, but umpteen millions of their peoples never came through to witness the final victory in 1945.

The 'Axis' was formed by the three signatories of the Tripartite Pact, a defensive military alliance signed by Germany, Italy and Japan in the Reich Chancellery on September 27, 1940. Also known as the Berlin-Tokyo-Rome Axis, it was later expanded with the addition of Hungary (November 20, 1940), Romania (November 23, 1940), Slovakia (November 24, 1940), Bulgaria (March 1, 1941), Yugoslavia (March 25, 1941), and Croatia (June 15, 1941).

Bearing in mind the tens of thousands of Axis personnel involved in turning the repressive wheels of the occupation machine, relatively few of the perpetrators were ever brought to justice. Certainly, trials were held for those who could be found, and firing-squads and hangmen carried out their grisly tasks but, for so many of the guilty, retribution passed them by.

Although three-quarters of a century have passed, and the events described occurred over two generations ago, we felt that this was still a story that had to be told before the memories fade. We also acknowledge the invaluable contribution by Dr Raphael Lemkin which was first published while these events were still taking place.

It has not been pleasant journey but we hope that in some small measure it will help bring a spotlight upon one of the most shameful periods in the history of the 20th century. We dedicate our work to all those who had to endure it.

WINSTON AND GAIL RAMSEY, 2018

Contents

Introduction by Raphael Lemkin

During the Second World War, and the period immediately preceding it, the European Axis powers comprising Germany, Italy, Hungary, Bulgaria and Romania, occupied by means of duress and/or force, a large part of Europe. Moreover, by assuming the role of supreme arbiters in European territorial problems, Germany and Italy determined territorial changes in central and south-eastern Europe.

In the course of the war, Germany occupied Poland, Danzig, Denmark, Norway, the Netherlands, Belgium, Luxembourg, France, the Channel Islands, Yugoslavia, Greece, the Baltic states of Lithuania, Latvia and Estonia, and parts of Russia. In several instances occupation was followed by incorporation of parts of the occupied territory into the Reich. Previously, by bloodless war, Germany had entered and annexed Austria, and then the Sudeten part of Czechoslovakia. Later it completed the dismemberment of Czechoslovakia by creating the Protectorate of Bohemia and Moravia and the separate state of Slovakia. In March 1939, Memel Territory was ceded to Germany by Lithuania under pressure and was incorporated into the Reich.

Following the armistice with France of June 24, 1940, Italy occupied the Mentone district. Later on, during the course of the occupation of all of France in November 1942, the Italian occupation was extended to the Rhône valley and to Haute-Savoie. After the downfall of Mussolini in July 1943, the Italian zone of occupation in France was taken over by Germany. In 1941, after the Greek resistance was crushed by Germany, Italy, which had waged an unsuccessful war against Greece since October 1940, occupied north-western parts of Greece, the Ionian Islands, Corfu and part of Crete. The Albanians were permitted to occupy the provinces of Yanina, Thesprotia and Prenza.

Fluctuations in the military situation led to frequent changes as between the German and Italian occupation forces. However, following the downfall of Mussolini, all the Italian-held areas were taken over by Germany and Bulgaria. After the invasion of Yugoslavia in 1941, Italy had occupied the province of Ljubljana and Dalmatia, later annexing them, and had occupied Montenegro. Previously in April 1939, Italy had occupied Albania and created a union between the two states but following the dismemberment of Yugoslavia, Albania, which was under the control of the Italian vice-regent, occupied parts of Yugoslavia, namely, Kosovo, Dibrano and Struga.

Raphael Lemkin was born on June 24, 1900 in Bezwodne, a village near the town of Wolkowysk in what was then the Russian Empire. During the First World War the Lemkin farm was destroyed by German troops, the family taking shelter in the nearby forest. At Kazimierz University in Lwów (now Lviv in the Ukraine) he studied linguistics, becoming fluent in nine languages and having the knowledge of 14. From 1929 to 1934 Lemkin was the Public Prosecutor for the district court in Warsaw and also the secretary of the Committee on Codification of the Laws of the Republic of Poland. He left Warsaw on September 6, 1939, barely evading capture by the Germans advancing to the east and the Soviet Army moving westward into Polish territory. Reaching Stockholm, he arrived in the United States in 1941 where he joined the law faculty at Duke University in North Carolina. In 1943 he was appointed a consultant to the US Board of Economic Warfare and largely due to his experience in international law, became a special adviser to the War Department. His book *Axis Rule in Occupied Europe* was published by the Carnegie Endowment for International Peace in 1944, including an extensive legal analysis of German rule in countries occupied by Nazi Germany during the course of the Second World War. Lemkin had lost 49 members of his family during the war, a factor no doubt leading him to coin a new word to describe the wholesale slaughter: 'genocide'. This became one of the legal bases in the Nuremberg Trials for which Lemkin served as an adviser to the Supreme Court of the United States Justice and trial chief, Robert H. Jackson. After the war, he lectured on international law defining and forbidding genocide, a resolution being placed before the General Assembly of the United Nations in 1948, being ratified by 20 nations in 1951. Lemkin died in 1959, aged 59, and was buried in Mount Hebron Cemetery in New York.

Hungary occupied the following Czechoslovak territories: the southern part, called by the Hungarians the Highland Regions, was occupied in November 1938 and March 1939, and Sub-Carpathia in March 1939. After the dismemberment of Yugoslavia, Hungary occupied the Yugoslav territories of Prekomurje, Medzumurje and the provinces of Baranja and Backa in the Voivodina region. In addition, in accordance with the German-Italian arbitration award of August 30, 1940, the northern part of Transylvania, belonging previously to Rumania, was occupied by Hungary. All of these territories were subsequently incorporated into Hungary.

In the course of the war against Greece, Bulgaria occupied eastern Macedonia, the Aegean region of Thrace and the islands of Thasos and Samothrace. Previously, following the treaty with Romania of September 7, 1940, Bulgaria had occupied southern Dobruja that had been taken from Bulgaria and given to Rumania by the Treaty of Neuilly in 1919.

After the dismemberment of Yugoslavia, Bulgaria occupied western Macedonia, the Skoplje and Bitolia regions and part of the Yugoslav province of Morava.

During the war against Russia, Romania occupied Bukovina and Bessarabia that it had ceded to Russia at the latter's request in June 1940. In addition, it occupied the territory between the eastern border of Bessarabia and the lower Bug river with the main city of Odessa, an area later called Transnistria.

Concerning the territories of the dismembered Czechoslovakia and Yugoslavia, two new states were established: Slovakia under the protection of Germany, and Croatia, initially under the protection of Italy but actually always under the predominant control of Germany. For strategic reasons, Germany held under military occupation certain areas within the boundaries of these puppet states, for example a western portion of Slovakia and the Zemun area in Croatia.

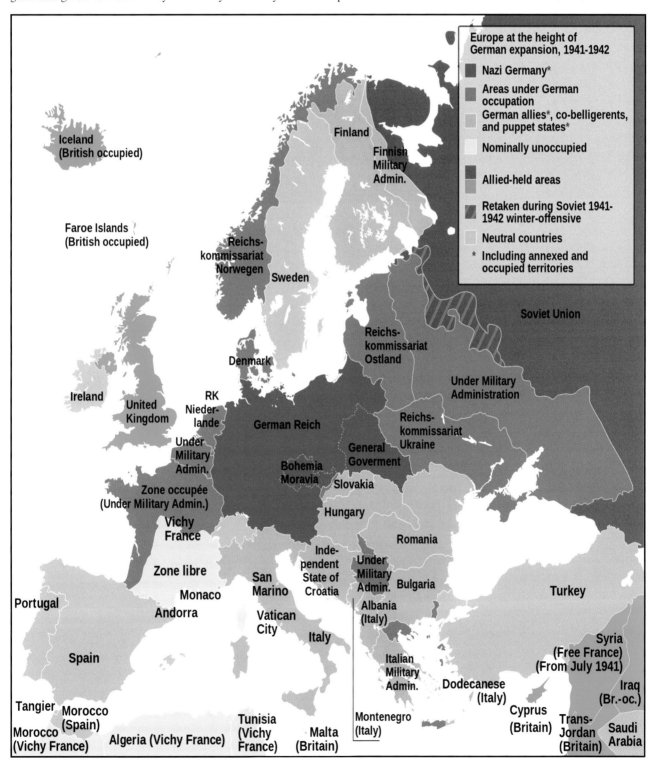

7

Benito Mussolini — Il Duce — had been the fascist dictator in Italy since the 'March on Rome' by the Blackshirts in 1922. Italy then began flexing her muscles in North Africa, colonising Libya that had been ceded to her in 1912. In 1929 Mussolini joined Tripolitania and Cyrenaica into one colonial province, his appetite for expansion now being focussed on Ethiopia which he wanted to invade as early as 1932.

In January 1933, Adolf Hitler — Der Führer and leader of the Nazi Party — achieved a similar dictatorial role in Germany, and top of his wish-list was to incorporate Austria into a Greater German Reich. Being the place of his birth, it was a personal ambition close to his heart and Nazi supporters were already preparing the way by causing trouble there with organised riots on the streets.

The Administration of the Occupied Countries

As stated in the introduction, Germany occupied the following countries during the war: Poland, Danzig, Denmark, Norway, the Netherlands, Belgium, Luxembourg, France, the Channel Islands, Yugoslavia, Greece, the Baltic States, and parts of the Soviet Union. Previously Germany took over Austria on March 9, 1938; the Sudeten on October 1, 1938 and the remainder of Czechoslovakia on March 15, 1939. Memel Territory was ceded by Lithuania to Germany by treaty of March 22, 1939.

INCORPORATED AREAS

Some of these territories occupied before the war and in the course of military operations were expressly incorporated into Germany, these being Austria, the Sudeten, Danzig, the Polish provinces of Posen, Upper Silesia, Teshen, Pomerania, Lódz (the city of that name was renamed Litzmannstadt), Ciechanow, Suwalki, Bialystok; the Belgian districts of Eupen, Malmédy, and Moresnet; and the northern Yugoslav provinces of Carniola, Carinthia and

Lower Styria. Memel was also incorporated into the Reich. Other territories like Alsace-Lorraine and Luxembourg were attached to the Reich by including them within the German customs frontier, by making them separate parts of the German districts, and by introducing into these areas political institutions of the Greater Reich.

NON-INCORPORATED AREAS

The non-incorporated territories included the following: the central and southern part of Poland which were administered as the Government General with headquarters in Krakow, and the territories occupied in the war with the Soviet Union which were under the administration of the Reich Minister for the Territories Occupied in the East. The Reich Ministry for these latter areas created the following sub-divisions: (a) the Reich Commissariat for Ostland and (b) the Reich Commissariat for the Ukraine. The Reich Commissariat for Ostland consisted of four general commissariats, namely a general commissariat for Estonia with

headquarters in Tallinn; for Latvia with headquarters in Riga; for Lithuania with its headquarters in Kaunas, and for White Russia with headquarters in Minsk. The General Commissariat for White Russia comprised the eastern Polish territories occupied by Russia in September 1939, and Russian territories to the north-east of the Polish frontier. The Reich Commissariat for the Ukraine consisted of the Ukraine proper, the whole of the Polish province of Wolhynia, and the southern part of the Polish province of Polesie.

Besides the above-mentioned territorial divisions, four of the countries occupied in the west — Norway, Denmark, the Netherlands and Belgium (excluding Eupen, Malmédy and Moresnet) — were administered within their original boundaries.

The non-incorporated German-held part of France was divided into four zones: (1) Northern France and Pas de Calais under the German commander in Brussels which one can call the northern zone; (2) the central western zone limited in the south and south-west by

The two dictators had yet to meet but, at the instigation of German diplomats who wanted to try to moderate Hitler's obsession with Austria, a meeting was arranged for June 1934. The plan was for Hitler to fly to Italy for discussions that were to be held in the 18th-century Villa Pisani at Stra, near Padua, which had been bought by Napoleon in 1807. Mussolini wanted to impress his visitor so parts of the Royal Palace were refurbished specially for the occasion.

the German-French armistice agreement; (3) the so-called Vichy zone, and (4) the prohibited zone along the coast which had a special regime of military control because of the fortifications built there.

In addition to the loss of the Sudetenland, Czechoslovakia had undergone the following partition: Bohemia and Moravia were occupied by the German forces and formed the so-called Reichsprotektorat Böhmen und Mähren, and the third part of the country was treated as a separate state under the name of Slovakia and was put under the protection of Germany.

In Yugoslavia, Germany established the puppet state of Serbia, as well as Croatia (the latter in collaboration with Italy). The Yugoslav part of Banat, where there was a considerable German minority, was given a special status and was attached to the puppet state of Serbia. After the downfall of Mussolini, and especially after the signing of the armistice agreement between Italy and the Allies, Germany took over the control of the greater part of Yugoslavia and Albania.

In Greece, Germany occupied Central Macedonia, including Salonika, parts of the Aegean region, and the islands of Lemnos, Mytilene and Chios. After the armistice, the Germans extended their zone of occupation to the area previously occupied by Italy.

When Hitler stepped from his Ju 52 in Venice in civilian clothes carrying a grey felt hat, Mussolini was not impressed. Dressed in uniform with shiny boots, spurs and a dagger, he upstaged the German leader and, we are told, Mussolini said of Hitler: 'I don't like the look of him', and after their first conversation he commented: 'He's quite mad'.

The following year Mussolini's forces invaded Ethiopia. The seven-month war began on October 2, 1935 during which poison gas was employed in defiance of the fact that Italy had signed the Geneva Protocol seven years earlier. The League of Nations quickly declared Italy the aggressor; nevertheless, Ethiopia was annexed and united with Italy's other colonies to form the new colony of 'Italian East Africa' with Victor Emmanuel III of Italy adopting the title: 'Emperor of Abyssinia'. In September 1937, Mussolini was invited to Germany for what would now be called a state visit. One of his conditions of acceptance was that he would not have to wear civilian attire in which he did not appear to his best advantage, and a uniform was specially designed for the occasion. His train had to cross Austria through the southern Tyrol which had been awarded to Italy at Versailles so there was a real fear of an assassination attempt. Consequently the track-side was lined with troops. This was the welcome as the train arrived at the German frontier with Kiefersfelden station dressed for the occasion.

POLICIES

In regard to dealing with the local population, three different policies were adopted by the Germans.

Absorption. The policy of absorption was adopted with respect to the incorporated areas such as western Poland, Eupen, Malmédy and Moresnet, Luxembourg, and the Yugoslav provinces of Carinthia, Carniola and Lower Styria, with the aim of achieving complete assimilation with the political, cultural, social and economic institutions of the Greater Reich. Indoctrination of National Socialism was employed to a great extent, especially in areas where the German cultural pattern pre-existed, as in Austria and the Sudeten.

Forced Co-operation. Forced co-operation was used in Norway, France, Belgium, the Netherlands, Greece, Czechoslovakia, and to a certain extent also in Estonia, Latvia and Lithuania. This comprised full economic co-operation and in part as to certain groups, political co-operation as well. Denmark represented a type of forced 'co-operation', mainly in the economic field.

Despoliation. The Government General of Poland, the General Commissariat for White Russia (as part of Ostland), and the administration of the Ukraine and other Russian territories represented a type of despoliation policy. The occupant considered these territories as being areas to supply raw materials, food and labour. The Germans were not able to find in these areas people who would be willing to co-operate in organising central governments.

TYPES OF ADMINISTRATION

There were two basic methods for governing occupied areas. First by German administration as carried out by the occupiers, and secondly by using local administration as exercised by authorities created by the local population under German control. There were three types of German administration

District Administration by Gauleiters. This type of administration was introduced into the incorporated areas which were absorbed as a part of the Greater Reich. According to the German pattern of administration, the incorporated areas were divided into administrative districts (the Gau), which also formed the administrative units of the National Socialist Party. The head of the National Socialist Party in the given district, the Gauleiter, was at the same time governor (Reichsstatthalter) of the district. The districts were then subdivided into counties and communities. For special purposes of imposing a German pattern upon these areas, an agent of the Reich Commissioner for the Strengthening of Germanism was attached to the office of the Gauleiter. This was the system of administration carried out in the incorporated Polish territories, in the Sudeten, in Austria, in Luxembourg and Alsace-Lorraine, in Eupen, Malmédy and Moresnet, and in the northern Yugoslav districts of Carinthia, Carniola and Lower Styria.

The station remains virtually unchanged since the day when the banner proclaimed: 'Deutschland grusst den Duce'.

Administration by Reich Commissioners and Governors. The non-incorporated areas, for example Norway, the Netherlands and central Poland, were handed over for administration to civilian Reich Commissioners. In central Poland (Government General) the civilian head of administration was called the Governor General.

In the same areas there are also military commanders who deal with questions of military security and military operations. A division of jurisdiction is thus created between the Reich Commissioners and military commanders, the Reich Commissioners handling matters which relate to the civil domain and the military commanders those which relate to the military domain.

Administration by Military Commanders. Countries that were of strategic importance, such as Belgium, France (within the borders delimited by the armistice agreement), Yugoslavia and Greece, were put under the administration of military commanders. The military commanders exercise their authority through field and local military commanders throughout the specific country.

The military commanders and the Reich Commissioners in the occupied countries were directly responsible to Hitler indicating the importance that he attached to the problem of administering the occupied countries.

Prominent in the welcoming committee were (L-R) the German Ambassador in Rome, Ulrich von Hassell; Generalleutnant Wilhelm List (later responsible for integrating the Austrian Armed Forces into the Wehrmacht); Rudolf Hess; the Italian Ambassador in Berlin, Bernardo Attolico, and Hans Frank who could converse in Italian and was to act as the Duce's personal escort during the visit.

The visit lasted five days, encompassing troop reviews in Mecklenburg, a visit to Krupps in Essen, banquets and parades in Berlin, and a visit to Göring's residence at Carinhall. This wreath-laying took place on September 25 at the Ehrentempel in Munich — the tombs of the Nazi casualties in Hitler's abortive putsch in 1923.

In January 1947, American army engineers demolished the columns as part of the de-Nazification programme. The base still remains next to the Führerbau building.

In 1938 Austria was just 20 years old. Formed out of the collapse of the Austro-Hungarian Empire at the end of the First War, the coming to power of Hitler in 1933 led to an increasingly vociferous campaign for Anschluss (union) with Germany. In 1934 civil war broke out between the Social Democrats and the authoritarian government of Englebert Dollfuss and although the uprising was crushed after four days, five months later Dollfuss was murdered after a group of Nazis seized the Chancellery. This attempt to install a Nazi Government also failed and the new Austrian Chancellor, Dr Kurt von Schuschnigg (left), was assured by Hitler that 'Germany neither intends nor wishes to interfere in the internal affairs of Austria, to annex Austria or to conclude an Anschluss.' Italy had historically always been aligned with Austria but when Mussolini allied himself with Hitler in 1936, the Austrian leader realised that a formal agreement with the German dictator was the only insurance policy possible to try and preserve his country's independence. In the Austro-German agreement signed in July 1936, Germany reaffirmed its recognition of Austrian sovereignty and assurance not to interfere; in return Austria had to promise to conduct its foreign policy on the principle that it was was a German state. Secret clauses also allowed an amnesty for Nazi political prisoners and the appointing of representatives to positions of political responsibility. This agreement to allow a Nazi element in Austria led to a terror campaign of bombings and demonstrations throughout 1937, and a police raid on January 1938 uncovered plans for an outright revolt that Spring. In order to sort out with the Austrian Chancellor 'such misunderstandings and points of friction as have persisted' since the 1936 agreement was signed, Hitler invited von Schuschnigg to the Obersalzberg for talks. The meeting on February 12 was not so much a discussion as a tirade by Hitler and an ultimatum that the Austrian government be turned over to German control within a week with the installation of Dr Arthur Seyss-Inquart as Minister of the Interior. Brow-beaten into submission with threats of massive military intervention if he wavered, von Schuschnigg signed.

Puppet Governments and Puppet States. In countries where active groups of pro-Nazis, even in minor numbers, were to be found, puppet governments were created. The puppet government was organised as a cabinet with a prime minister or a president as the head but its activities were still controlled by the occupier. Essentially the puppet governments retained the same local authorities (with the exception of agencies whose members were elected by the population), using them for the administration of the country. Puppet governments functioned in Norway, in Serbia, in Greece, in France under Pétain and Laval, and, with certain special restrictions, in the Protectorate of Bohemia and Moravia.

Left: The next four weeks marked the political and economic decline which ensued as inflammatory speeches, demonstrations, and acts of violence struck an Austria bereft of any sign of the support of the major powers. In a last-minute effort to forestall the Nazis, on Wednesday, March 9, 1938, von Schuschnigg produced his trump card: he would appeal direct to the country in a referendum, asking for a simple 'Ja' or 'Nein' for or against union with Germany, in much the same way as Général Charles de Gaulle asked for support for his policies in post-war France. A plebiscite was something that Hitler could not allow and the unexpected news sent the Führer into a fit of rage. With voting day announced as Sunday, March 13 — four days hence — Hitler issued immediate orders for the military occupation of Austria by Saturday. This was followed by a demand to von Schuschnigg that he must cancel the arrangements for the vote and resign. Under the excuse of preventing further bloodshed — which German newspapers headlined 'German Austria saved from Chaos' — German troops crossed the frontier at daybreak on Saturday, March 12 (right).

Having left Austria for Germany in 1913, Hitler (save for a few quick visits) did not return to his native country until after the Anschluss. First stop on his victorious journey to the capital Vienna, where he was to announce the 'return of his Heimat into the German Reich', was his birthplace, Braunau. Following in the wake of the troops, on Saturday March 12, he drove across the bridge over the Inn river that formed the border between the two countries and which leads directly on to the town's central Stadtplatz where he received a rapturous welcome from the ecstatic population. Hitler's motorcade slowly made its way past the house where he had been born, although it did not stop.

Puppet states were different to puppet governments as they were entirely new entities created by the Germans like Slovakia and Croatia.

Headless or Sub-cabinet Governments. Before the occupation of Belgium and the Netherlands, the secretary-general was the highest public civil servant in a given ministry with the exception of the minister himself. He was second only to the minister. Whereas the minister's tenure of office was subject to political changes, the secretary-general was a permanent part of the civil service and not subject to change to the same extent. Because of their professional skill and sometimes long experience, the secretaries-general represented a valuable element in government. The Germans retained them in office and put them in charge of the administration of their ministries.

A special kind of headless government had also been introduced in the three Baltic States. Here the heads of the departments are called councillors (in Lithuania) and directors (in Estonia and Latvia). However, the authority and scope of activities of the councillors and directors were less than those of the secretaries general.

Utilisation of Services of Minor Authorities. In countries where the Germans received no collaboration, for example in the Government General of Poland, in the Polish territories included in the General Commissariat for White Russia, and in the Russian territories, the services of only minor authorities and lower officials were used.

Normally, belligerent occupation of a country does not transfer sovereignty over the occupied territory. The occupant merely holds the territory in trust for any future peace conference to decide upon its ultimate disposition. Therefore, the occupier has no right to perform such acts as would indicate that he has usurped sovereignty. However, during the Second World war, the Germans usurped sovereignty over the occupied areas by the following acts:

(1) By the incorporation of parts of Poland, Belgium, France and Yugoslavia, and all of Luxembourg and Danzig, and using in decrees the word 'former' in regard to states whose territory they occupied. This was especially true with to Poland where the expression 'property of the citizens of the former Polish State' was regularly used.

(2) By introducing a German pattern of administration in the incorporated areas.

(3) By changing the customs frontiers.

(4) By changing basic laws of the occupied countries and introducing German law and German courts, and by compelling the courts to render justice in the name of the German nation, not in the name of law.

(5) Granting the local German population of the incorporated areas representation in the Reichstag of Greater Germany. This was granted on the basis of one representative to every 60,000 Germans living in these areas. The representative had to be over 25 years of age, the act being promulgated for Eupen, Malmédy and Moresnet by the decree of February 4, 1941.

(6) Germans living in the incorporated areas became German citizens or German nationals. According to the German Nationality Code, there were two types of nationality. The superior type, called 'Bürger', embraced those of German origin who were in every respect loyal to the Nazi regime. The second type of nationality, 'Staatsangehörige', was merely a conception of legal relationship with the Reich, consists mainly of the right to possess a German passport and all the privileges deriving therefrom. Persons of non-German blood could not be Bürger but they could be Staatsangehörige.

Military conscription was introduced in the Polish territories by a decree issued by the Supreme Commander of the German Armed Forces on April 30, 1940. It was also introduced into Alsace-Lorraine. However, the above-mentioned acts regarding citizenship and representation in the Reichstag, as well as military conscription, implied necessarily taking an oath of allegiance to the occupying power, which was contrary to Article 45 of the Annex to Hague Convention IV of 1907, and military conscription in occupied territory is expressly prohibited by Article 52 which states that the inhabitants of an occupied territory cannot be compelled to take part in operations of war against their country.

The steel bridge, blown in 1945, has been replaced by a modern concrete span and the Inn river once again marks the border between Germany and Austria.

Two days before the Germans marched into Austria, Hitler sent a letter by personal courier to Mussolini, explaining that 'I am now determined to restore law and order in my homeland. I wish now solemnly to assure your Excellency, as the Duce of Fascist Italy: (1) I consider this step only as one of national self-defence. (2) In a critical hour for Italy I proved to you the steadfastness of my sympathy. Do not doubt that in the future there will be no change in this respect. (3) Whatever the consequences of the coming events may be, I have drawn a definite boundary between Germany and France and now draw one just as definite between Italy and us. It is the Brenner. This decision will never be questioned or changed.' Mussolini had once declared that Italy 'could never permit Austria — the bastion of Mediterranean civilisation — to be a victim of Pan-Germanism', so when the Duce responded to the Anschluss in a very friendly manner, Hitler was greatly relieved. Now was the time for him to take up the invitation extended to him the previous September to visit Rome.

Mussolini was determined to equal, if not outdo, his own visit to Germany and six months were spent on the planning, the Duce personally spending hours supervising the arrangements. He even had a new railway station built — the Stazione di Roma Ostiense *(top)* — with the new approach road to it named the Viale Adolf Hitler.

OCCUPATION LAW

In occupying every new country, the Germans made it a practice to declare in a first proclamation to the population that local law would remain in force unless contrary notified otherwise. Because the aims of German occupation were not limited to military considerations, but were directed toward the integration of the occupied countries into the 'New European Order' under German hegemony, it was obvious that most of the laws of the occupied country were incompatible with the aims of the German occupation. Therefore many important changes in law were introduced.

In the Free City of Danzig, and in Memel, and in the incorporated Belgian districts of Eupen, Malmédy and Moresnet, practically the entire body of German and Prussian law was introduced. This was possible because these cities were governed before the occupation by a great body of Prussian law. With Eupen, Malmédy and Moresnet,

Adolf Hitler's street has now been renamed Via delle Cave Ardeatine in memory of the massacre there (see page 320).

Hitler's party numbered some 500, arriving at Ostia Station aboard three trains. The Führer was escorted by Party officials, diplomats, security guards and journalists. Dr Paul Schmidt, Hitler's interpreter, was one of them and he commented that the most exhaustive part of the visit was the frequent changes of dress to suit each occasion, from civilian into uniform and then evening attire. 'By the end of the journey, any one of us could have got a job at any average music hall as a quick-change artist'.

the Germans were eager to return to the situation existing before the 1914-18 war when these districts belonged to Germany.

In Austria and in the Sudetenland, it was declared that German laws promulgated after a specified date following the occupation (for Austria, March 13, 1938, and for the Sudeten, October 10, 1938) applied also to these territories unless a provision to the contrary was made in the given law. Earlier German laws were, after these dates, individually introduced in those countries as these territories had never belonged to Germany.

In western Poland (incorporated into Germany), in Alsace-Lorraine, and in Luxembourg, no provision was published to the effect that laws promulgated in the Reich after the occupation should apply directly to these territories. On the contrary, they had to be individually introduced in each case. However, an extensive volume of law was thus introduced into these areas, such as the German Commercial Code, German extradition law, the German organisation of courts, and the German Lawyers' Code of November 1, 1936. The German Criminal Code was made applicable to western Poland by the decree of June 6, 1940 as were a great number of laws of a political and administrative character.

In the last group of countries embracing all the other occupied territories and the Protectorate of Bohemia and Moravia, a great body of German law was introduced pertaining mainly to economy and labour. However, in these countries the law of the 'protection of blood and honor' (as limited to Germans only) was also made applicable, and laws pertaining to Nazi indoctrination and the protection of German political institutions, as well as particular German administrative decrees, were introduced.

Technically Hitler was the guest of King Victor Emmanuel and staying with him at the Quirinal Palace.

Wreath-laying was an important part of both visits and in Rome the venue was the Tomb of the Unknown Soldier which had been built under the statue of the goddess Roma in front of the 'Altar of the Fatherland', the huge monument built in honour of Victor Emmanuel, the first king of unified Italy.

When the unknown soldier was chosen in October 1921 by Maria Bergamas, whose son was missing in action in the war, the monument still had not been finished. Begun in 1885 amid much controversy as it destroyed the ancient Capitoline Hill, it was finally completed in 1925.

In the Protectorate of Bohemia and Moravia, the introduction of German law was originally checked by the provisions of the legislative authority of the Protectorate. But later on the Reich Protector made extensive use of the measures giving him the right to change local law.

The Dutch law on citizenship was altered. According to Dutch law as it existed prior to the occupation, a Dutchman serving in a foreign army lost his citizenship but as the Germans were eager to see the Dutchmen form an anti-Bolshevik legion, the Reich Commissioner published a decree to the effect that Dutchmen taking part in the fight against Russia would not lose their Dutch citizenship. Also in Holland, Articles 92-98 of the Netherlands Civil Code, requiring that a girl of Dutch nationality who is under age must have the consent of her parents, grandparents, or local guardian to marry, were modified by the Reich Commissioner to the effect that if such a person wishes to marry a German, the consent of the Reich Commissioner was now sufficient. Overriding the rights of the parents by the Reich Commissioner was an example of a flagrant disregard of family rights protected under Article 46 of the Hague Regulations.

Six months before his visit to Rome, Hitler had disclosed to his generals that his next intention was to overthrow Czechoslovakia, if necessary by war, and incorporate it with the Reich. The Czech republic, as it existed since 1918, included large German, Polish, Hungarian and Ukrainian minorities. The 3½ million German-speaking Czechs lived largely in the Sudetenland, the borderlands of Bohemia and Moravia. This horseshoe-shaped region was vital to the Czech state both economically and militarily. It contained much of the country's industry and, perhaps even more important, in it lay the strong frontier fortifications which were the backbone of the whole of the Czech defence system. The Sudeten Germans were organised in 1933 in the Sudetendeutsche Heimatfront, founded by Konrad Henlein, seen here *(left)* on the terrace of the Berghof on the Obersalzberg. Supported from the Reich, both financially and with propaganda, it was a useful tool in Hitler's scheme for conquest. His policy was to have the Sudeten Germans demand ever-increasing minority rights hoping to create so much tension and unrest that he could intervene and act as saviour of his fellow Germans. In 1935, looking for allies against possible foreign aggression, Czechoslovakia had joined the French-Russian defensive Alliance but France was unwilling to go to war without Britain. Russia would only come to assist if France initiated help and would have to negotiate with other countries — Poland or Romania — for passage of troops. In April 1938, on Berlin's instructions, Henlein, in a speech at Karlsbad, proclaimed his latest demands: full self-government for the Sudeten Germans within the Czech state and freedom to adhere to Nazi ideology. The Czech government, headed by President Edvard Beneš and Prime Minister Milan Hodža, had negotiated on and off with the Sudeten Germans since 1936 and tried its best to reach a settlement. But on May 20, when exaggerated reports of German troop movements led to a partial Czech mobilisation, Henlein immediately suspended negotiations.

POLICE

German police played an essential part in maintaining political life in Germany and in the occupied countries in particular. They provided the main striking power for National Socialism, and the political efficiency of the German police and their faithfulness to Nazism may be explained by their history.

The force began with the SS (Schutzstaffeln), or Elite Guard of the National Socialist Party. These guards originally gave assistance at party meetings in protecting physically the members of the party against political opponents. On January 6, 1929, Hitler, as the head of the National Socialist Party, appointed Heinrich Himmler as Reich Leader of the SS and when Hitler came to power, the fusion of the SS with the police was started. Between March 9, 1933, and April 1934, Himmler was appointed Chief of the State Police (Reichsführer der SS und Chef der deutschen Polizei) suc-

cessively in each of the Länder outside Prussia. On February 10, 1936, the State Secret Police (Geheime Staatspolizei, abbreviated to Gestapo) was created for Prussia by Hermann Göring, the Minister-President for Prussia, and Himmler became the Deputy Chief of the Gestapo. This law specified that 'the State Secret Police has the task of investigating and fighting against all movements dangerous to the State in all spheres of State existence, of collecting and exploiting the results of investigations, of reporting to the Government and of keeping other authorities informed on all current issues of importance to them, and providing them with the requisite conclusions'. Since Himmler acted in a dual capacity as Deputy Chief of the Prussian Gestapo and as commander of the political police of the Länder outside Prussia, later he extended the Gestapo organisation (which had existed previously only in Prussia) to the other

Länder. Thus Göring started the Gestapo in Prussia and Himmler expanded it throughout all the German Reich including the occupied countries.

In his capacity as Reich Leader of the SS, Himmler created a very intimate connection between the SS and the Gestapo. As mentioned above, the SS originaly consisted of small groups of Nazi Party guards but, on the assumption of power by Hitler, the SS became the most powerful unit in Germany. Himmler endeavoured to supplant the idea of the former Prussian Junker caste by the conception of the SS organisation and special training was established in the SS Junker School. The selection of candidates was restricted and the Aryan origin of the candidates was investigated as far back as 1800. To be accepted for training, they also had to have reached a certain stage in the Hitler Youth organization and had to have the reputation of devout National Socialists.

The crisis that was to hold Europe in its grip for 18 days began on September 12, 1938. On that day, at the Nuremberg party rally, Hitler made a brutally abusive speech, denouncing the Czech government and demanding 'justice' for the Sudeten Germans. For the first time, he openly spoke of cession of the region to Germany. Two days later, the British Prime Minister, Neville Chamberlain, on his own initiative, sent a message to Hitler, asking for a meeting to discuss the current danger to peace in Europe. The proposal took Hitler completely by surprise, but he accepted. Chamberlain flew to Munich on the 15th and was received by Hitler at the Berghof on the Obersalzberg in their first-ever meeting. *Left:* Here, Chamberlain leaves his hotel, the Berchtesgadener Hof, in Berchtesgaden for the short drive up the Obersalzerg to see 'Herr Hitler'. *Right:* The Nazis had purchased the hotel in 1936 to be used to host important visitors. In May 1945 it was taken over by the US Army but closed in 1995 and it was demolished in 2006.

The SS constituted the reservoir from which the ranks of the German police, especially of the Gestapo, were filled. Although not every member of the SS was a member of the police, generally every German policeman — and in particular every Gestapo agent — belonged to the SS.

The German police force was divided into two main groups: Ordnungspolizei (Public Order Police) and Sicherheitspolizei (Security Police). In the main the Ordnungspolizei embraced the uniformed branch, i.e. the Schutzpolizei (not to be confused with the Schutzstaffeln), and the Gendarmerie (administrative police), while the Sicherheitspolizei comprised the criminal police and the Gestapo. In addition, Himmler headed the Security Service of the Reich Leader of the SS (Sicherheitsdienst des Reichsführers-SS), which acted as an espionage organisation for the party and state. In this field it also assisted the Sicherheitspolizei. The Security Service collaborated with all the authorities which were duty bound to provide information to it. Its membership was secret and the operatives did not wear uniforms.

Members of the police were initially appointed on a temporary basis, with the right of cancellation of the appointment, and later on a permanent basis. In order to be appointed on a permanent basis, quite long probationary periods were required: for officers, five years; for minor members of the Gestapo or criminal police, 12 years. These unusually long probationary periods had the purpose of inspiring and confirming the devotion of the person to the Führer.

On Chamberlain's return, he and his Cabinet conferred with the French government of Premier Edouard Daladier and, on September 19, London and Paris produced a proposal which they put to Prague. If Czechoslovakia co-operated in a cession of the German-majority districts of Sudetenland, Britain and France would guarantee the country's new frontiers. This ultimatum-like proposal presented the Czech Cabinet with a cruel dilemma as a refusal would mean war with Germany. The Czech general staff was consulted and advised fighting only if France stood by her commitments. Trusting that she would, Beneš and Hodža turned down the proposal but in a night of diplomatic frenzy, it was made clear to them that France was not perpared to go to war. Bitterly disillusioned, they accepted the Anglo-French proposal. Immediately, mass demonstrations broke out in Prague, forcing the Hodža Cabinet to resign. The new government, quickly formed by General Jan Syrový, was clearly more prepared to defend the country. The next day, September 23, after border incidents at Asch and Eger, it ordered the general mobilisation of the Czech armed forces. Meanwhile, on the 22nd, Chamberlain had returned to Germany for his appointment with Hitler. This time they met at Bad Godesberg, on the banks of the Rhine near Bonn. The British stayed at Hotel Petersberg but the talks were held at Hotel Dreesen *(above)* on the opposite bank, the delegation being ferried across by motor launch.

The appointment of any official in Germany was based upon the Reich's confidence in him and the assurance that the official would always endeavour to justify this confidence and would be conscious of his high mission. The Führer and the Reich demanded from him real love for the country and readiness to sacrifice everything for it. The relationship of the police to the Führer was not simply of a legal and administrative character but rather more of an emotional nature, finding expression in the words: 'Faithfulness to the Führer till death'.

The police, particularly the Gestapo, were the most active fighters for National Socialism being trained carefully in its doctrines. Such matters as racial theories, history of German ideas of hegemony, the Jewish problem, Catholicism as a political problem, Communism, relations with the Anglo-Saxon world, etc were basic subjects in the programme for indoctrinating the police.

In the occupied countries the role of the police and SS was of primary importance. In particular, the experience of the Gestapo in foreign countries before the war enabled that organisation to make a special contribution to the German administration in every country later occupied. These pre-war activities of the Gestapo in foreign countries were widespread, reaching into such fields as politics, economics, culture, Press and racial relations. On one hand, the Gestapo gathered information while on the other hand it was active in playing off different elements in the political life of foreign countries against one another. The weak spots in the social and economic structure of these countries were used for the benefit of Germany. By spreading Nazi ideology in foreign countries, the Gestapo paved the way for the creation of fifth columns which assisted in the military conquest of the respective countries. This was true with Norway.

The first session took place on the afternoon of September 22 at which Chamberlain was shocked to discover that, since their previous meeting, Hitler had now decided to move the goalposts and introduce new demands. To his astonishment and chagrin, the Czech acceptance of cession of the Sudetenland to Germany now no longer satisfied Hitler as he now insisted on a settlement of the Polish and Hungarian claims on Czech territory in connection with the Sudeten question. Next morning, Chamberlain sent a letter across the river from his own hotel on the eastern bank proposing a traditional British compromise. This Hitler rejected out of hand, again playing the war of nerves by keeping the Prime Minister waiting all day for a reply. Not until late evening did Chamberlain return with Sir Neville Henderson (left), the British Ambassador in Berlin. (In the background on the left is Dr Paul Schmidt, Hitler's interpreter.)

In every central administration of the occupied countries the police and SS exerted a predominant presence in the headquarters of the administration chief. The Chief of Police, who was a ranking SS officer, was technically a member of the administration and was regularly head of the section of public safety. The police and SS were represented in the headquarters by an officer with the title of Höhere SS- und Polizeiführer (Higher SS and Police Leader). This officer commanded not only the units of the Schutzstaffeln, the Gestapo, and the Sicherheitsdienst, but also the German Ordnungspolizei, as well as the police units recruited from among the local population. Because of the special functions he had to fulfill, particularly in such a non-collaborationist country as Poland,

the officer in that country was appointed the Deputy of the Governor General of Poland, with the title of Staatssekretär für das Sicherheitswesen (Secretary of State for Security Matters). Only with respect to questions of great importance was it necessary for him to obtain the consent of the Reich Commissioner or the Governor General of the area.

One of the main functions of the police and SS was the liquidation of politically undesirable persons and of the Jews. The Gestapo administered the concentrtion camps and organised executions. The rounding up of the Jews in all the occupied countries and the deportation of them to Poland for physical extermination was also one of the main tasks of the Gestapo and SS units.

The police were also mainly responsible for mustering the labour manpower in the occupied countries and deporting it to Germany. They would round up people for work in the streets using physical force and carry out the registration of persons at the Reich Labour Office.

The extent to which the local police were used by the Germans depended on whether there was a puppet or a headless government in the country, or whether neither of these two types of government had been established. In the first case, the services of the local police were utilised to a greater extent than in the second. In the Netherlands for example, the maintenance of public peace, safety and order was entrusted to the Netherlands police 'unless the Reich Commissioner calls on German SS or police

The second meeting began at 10.30 p.m., the somewhat heated exchanges going on for three hours, until Chamberlain declared that 'there was no point in continuing the conversation'. He told Hitler that 'he was going away with a heavy heart for the hopes with which he had come to Germany were destroyed'. He immediately returned to London to deliberate with his Cabinet and with the French. Hitler's Godesberg memorandum was put to Prague and categorically rejected on the 25th. Next day, Hitler delivered a fanatical speech at the Berlin Sportpalast, full of hate against the Czechs and declaring that the Sudetenland would be in German hands, by 'peace or war', on October 1.

With German troops deploying for attack along the Czech border and the Czech Army mobilising, war now seemed inevitable. For the many millions of people in western Europe, this was the peak of the crisis. French reserve units were dispatched to man the Maginot Line and the mobilisation of the British fleet was ordered. At this point, Mussolini stepped in and, in response to an official British request, the Duce proposed to Hitler a Four Power Conference to solve the crisis. When Mussolini agreed to represent Italy in person Hitler accepted and invitations were sent to Britain and France to attend. Mussolini was met by Hitler at Kiefersfelden station and the two dictators travelled to Munich together in Hitler's personal train. On the journey, Hitler explained his demands to the Duce using an ethnographic map of Czechoslovakia.

However, Czechoslovakia was not invited. The news of a conference was everywhere in Europe received with great relief. Everywhere, except in Prague. As a result of Beneš anguished pleas that his country should be heard, the Czechs were, at the last hour, advised by London to send two 'observers' to Munich. The French and British delegations came to Munich by air, the British arriving last and being driven through throngs of cheering crowds, directly to the conference. The meeting was held at the Führerbau, Hitler's newly completed party headquarters facing the Königsplatz. Seated anti-clockwise around the fireplace are: British Prime Minister Neville Chamberlain, his advisor Sir Horace Wilson, Hitler, Mussolini, Italian Foreign Minister Galeazzo Ciano, French Premier Edouard Daladier, German Foreign Minister Joachim von Ribbentrop and his State Secretary Ernst von Weiszäcker.

forces for the enforcement of his orders'. In general, the Reich Commissioner appointed and dismissed the Chief Police Commissioners. This was particularly true in countries of a non-collaborationist type like Poland, where, for example, the local Polish police carried out minor functions such as traffic control, protection of buildings, maintenance of patrols and police posts. The Polish criminal investigation police investigated crimes committed by Poles, within the sphere of jurisdiction of the Polish courts but had no right to act if one of the parties involved was German. In such case the Polish police had to cede the investigation to the German police.

RAPHAEL LEMKIN, 1944

Now a simple classroom of Munich's State High School for Music.

With an agreement signed over the heads of the Czechs, the fate of their country had been sealed within 12 hours. The following morning the British Prime Minister called on Hitler at his private apartment on the Prinzregentenstrasse for an unscheduled meeting. Dr Schmidt, who had worked non-stop for some 13 hours at the session at the Führerbau, was the sole witness. Chamberlain, exuberant in the thought that he had just secured the peace of the world, was anxious to add a final full stop to the proceedings. Hitler, 'pale and moody, listened absent-mindedly to Chamberlain's remarks about Anglo-German relations, disarmament and economic questions, contributing little' wrote Schmidt in 1951. 'Towards the end of the conversaiton Chamberlain drew the famous Anglo-German declaration from his pocket.' Chamberlain later said that Hitler eagerly assented to this, but Schmidt felt that he only agreed to the wording 'with a certain reluctance, and I believe he appended his signature only to please Chamberlain'. This was the piece of paper waved aloft when he returned to Heston. The paper 'bears his name upon it as well as mine', declared Chamberlain, little realising the contempt with which Hitler viewed the whole matter.

When Foreign Minister von Ribbentrop complained to Hitler about signing the document, Hitler replied scornfully: 'Don't take it so seriously. This paper has no importance at all!' Hitler later confided to the Hungarian Foreign Minister that he had not thought it possible that 'Czechoslovakia would be served up to me by her friends'. In fact the victory had been won too easily for him and Chamberlain's complaisance had taken him 'by surprise'. On October 3, Hitler crossed the frontier personally to celebrate his bloodless conquest, while many in Britain lauded Munich with thanksgiving. One voice spoke out; that of Winston Churchill who declared it to be 'a total, unmitigated defeat'.

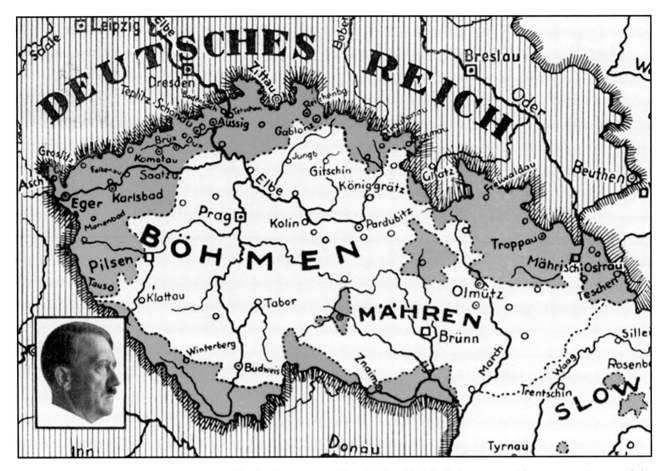

Czechoslovakia

The Sudeten areas of Czechoslovakia (shaded green on this propaganda map of the period) were acquired by Hitler via the agreement signed in Munich by Britain, France and Italy. It was, he said, his last territorial claim in Europe.

During the course of 1938 and 1939, the territory of the Republic of Czechoslovakia was disposed of in the following way but one must bear in mind that after Munich the Republic of Czechoslovakia continued as a federative state consisting of three autonomous divisions.

In accordance with the Munich Agreement, the Sudetenland was incorporated into Germany. Moreover, Germany also took over two areas in the neighbourhood of Bratislava that dominated the strategic position of this city, namely Devin and Petrzalka, inhabited by Slovaks.

The Protectorate of Bohemia and Moravia was created within the boundaries of the German Reich as an autonomous area comprising these two divisions, while Slovakia was made a separate state and a special Treaty of Protection between Germany and Slovakia put the latter under the protection of Germany. According to this treaty, the area delimited on its western side by the frontiers of the state of Slovakia and on its eastern side by a line formed by the eastern rims of the Lower Carpathians, the White Carpathians and the Javornik Mountains, was put under the 'military sovereignty' of the German armed forces.

Parts of the following districts were ceded to Poland on October 2, 1938. From Moravia: Frystát, Frydek, Cesky Tesin; from Slovakia: Cadca, Kezmarok, Stará Lubovna and Spisska

Stará Ves. After the occupation of Poland by Germany, the first group was incorporated into Germany, namely into the district of Silesia, while the second group was turned back to Slovakia.

SUDETENLAND

The Sudeten were incorporated into the Greater German Reich following the Munich Agreement of September 29, 1938, which was signed by Germany, Italy, Great Britain and France under threat of a German invasion of the Sudeten. Under the terms of this agreement, the Sudeten were incorporated into Germany and the new boundaries of the Czech State were to have been guaranteed by the four signatory powers. This guaranty however, was given neither by Italy nor by Germany. During the war of nerves which preceded the Munich Agreement, Hitler declared that the Sudeten represented the last territorial demand that he had to make in Europe.

The Munich Agreement was never recognised by the United States and Russia, and it was subsequently denounced by Great Britain and the French National Committee for the following reasons:

1. The guaranty of the new Czechoslovakian boundaries, which was an essential element of the agreement, was not given by Germany and Italy.

2. This agreement was violated by the German invasion of Czechoslovakia.

3. No consent of the Czechoslovak Parliament was obtained for the cession

of the territories, as is required by Article 64 of the Czechoslovak Constitution of February 29, 1920.

ADMINISTRATION

In matters of administration, the Sudeten were disposed of in the following manner: From the main part was created a special district (Reichsgau Sudetenland); the parts in the neighbourhood of the districts of the Upper Danube (Oberdonau) and Lower Danube (Niederdonau), formerly part of Austria, were incorporated into these districts, while other parts were incorporated into Prussia and Bavaria, respectively.

The district of Sudetenland was headed by a Reich Governor (Reichsstatthalter) having his official residence in Reichenberg. He was under the supervision of the Reich Minister of the Interior and also subject to the instructions of the several Reich ministers for the respective branches of administration. All agencies of the special administrative services of the Reich within the Reich District Sudetenland were under the Reich Governor with the exception of justice, railways and postal services. The Reich Governor was empowered to promulgate law with the consent of the Reich ministers involved. The Governor had two deputies: for general administrative duties a so-called Government President, and for autonomous administration of the district, a District Chief (Gauhauptmann).

Although the agreement was signed in September 1938, it was not until the Wehrmacht invaded the rest of the country on March 15, 1939, occupying Bohemia and Moravia, that Hitler had the opportunity to inspect his prize. He travelled to the border in his special train, the Sonderzug, on the morning of the 15th and, after lunch, he and his party transferred to a ten-vehicle convoy to drive through a heavy snow storm to the capital Prague.

REPARATIONS TO GERMANS

After the incorporation of the Sudeten, the Germans in the Sudeten who were active under their leader Konrad Henlein, and who had brought about the Munich crisis, were rewarded in the form of reparations. A law signed by the Führer on October 20, 1939 provided reparations for any Germans who incurred physical or property damages because they belonged to the Sudeten German party or because of their National Socialist convictions, or if the damages occurred in connection with the fight for the incorporation of the Sudetenland into the Reich. Such damages must have been caused through action of members of the armed forces or officials of the Czechoslovak State or of political adversaries before January 1, 1939.

The parade was lined up for Hitler to inspect in the courtyard of Hradcany Castle.

Dating from the Middle Ages, Prague Castle is the largest ancient castle in the world and in 1918 it became the seat of the President of the Czech Republic which had been carved out of the old Austro-Hungarian empire. On March 15 Hitler spent the night in the castle, we are told 'proudly surveying his new possession', even being portrayed in a special postage stamp.

PROTECTORATE OF BOHEMIA AND MORAVIA

On March 16, 1939, a Führer decree was published concerning the Protectorate of Bohemia and Moravia, the preamble to which stated that 'the Bohemian-Moravian countries belonged for a millennium to the living space (Lebensraum) of the German people', and that there was danger that out of this area 'would arise a new, stupendous menace to European peace'. Moreover, the Czechoslovak State was declared to have 'demonstrated its inherent inability to exist and therefore now has fallen into actual dissolution'. Since 'the German Reich cannot tolerate everlasting disturbances in these areas', it was held to be 'only an act of compliance with the law of self-preservation if the German Reich is resolved to take decisive action for the re-establishment of the foundations of a Central European Order'. Moreover, 'the millennial historic past of the German Reich has proven that it alone is chosen by virtue of its greatness and the qualities of the German people to solve this problem'.

Under Article 3 of the decree, the Protectorate of Bohemia and Moravia was declared to be autonomous, and it was described as possessing certain 'sovereign rights'. These sovereign rights, however, were to be exercised 'in conformity with the political, military and economic interests of the Reich'. Provisions were included to the effect that the Protectorate could act through its own government and that it could even have the right to accredit a minister to the Government of the Reich, but it was also provided that the German Government would appoint as guardian of its interests an official with residence in Prague whose title would be 'Reich Protector of Bohemia and Moravia'. Thus the autonomous status was in fact a mere illusion since the Reich Protector had almost supreme power in the Protectorate.

The Reich maintained police and military forces in the Protectorate and supervised directly such essential agencies as traffic, posts and telegraphs. The members of the Czech 'autonomous' government were also subject to confirmation by the Reich Protector.

The castle is once again the seat of the Head of State of the new Czech Republic created with the peaceful separation from Slovakia in January 1993.

The overlord of the Reichsprotektorat Böhmen und Mähren was titled the Reichsprotektor with his headquarters also located in the castle, Konstantin von Neurath being appointed the first incumbant. He had been a diplomat before Hitler came to power and in fact did not join the Nazi Party until 1937. The following year he was sacked as Foreign Minister when he made it clear that he did not support Hitler's plans for war, but he remained a minister without portfolio to try to allay concerns abroad about his removal. In March 1939, Neurath was chosen as Reichsprotektor of Bohemia and Moravia, in part to try to pacify the international outrage over the German occupation of Czechoslovakia. However, by Nazi standards, Neurath's rule was too lenient and in September 1941 Hitler stripped him of his day-to-day duties.

Reinhard Heydrich was named as Neurath's deputy but in reality he wielded the real power. He had joined the German Navy in 1922, rising to the rank of Oberleutnant zur See but was dismissed the service in 1931 for conduct unbecoming an officer as he had broken an engagement promise. Heinrich Himmler took Heydrich under his wing in 1932 to develop ideas he had in mind for establishing an SS intelligence service. Heydrich was appointed head of the new security service, the Sicherheitsdienst (SD). In September 1941 Heydrich was sent to Prague to enforce Nazi policy and also to maintain maximum production of vehicles and armaments from Czech factories that was now vital for the war effort. On May 27, 1942, he was the target of an assassination attempt by Czech patriots.

With Heydrich's death, a new hard-line replacement had to be found, the man chosen being SS-Oberstgruppenführer Kurt Daluege who had been the SS chief in northern Germany. He had been in charge of all the country's uniformed police since 1934, being appointed head of the Ordnungspolizei by Himmler in 1936. Daluege signed deportation orders for Jews from Germany, Austria and the Protectorate, and had attended mass shootings of Jews by police. After Heydrich succumbed to his wounds, Daluege ordered that all the men in the villages of Lidice and Lezáky were to be executed as a reprisal and the buildings razed to the ground (see page 32). The women and children were destined for deportation to the death camps. At the end of the war he was put on trial in Czechoslovakia and hanged on October 23, 1946.

It was stated in the decree of March 1939, that the Reich may undertake any changes it deems necessary in the Czech administration, and a further decree of May 7, 1942 delegated to the Reich Protector powers which enabled him to make further limitations on the rights of the Czech administration. It was broadly stated that the Reich Protector was empowered 'to undertake measures in order to make possible the adaptation of the administration of Bohemia and Moravia to any situation which may arise'.

In execution of the decree of March 1939, two central authorities were established in Prague: the office of the Reich Protector (German) and the government of the Protectorate (Czech). The German Protector acted through 19 German district prefects for the 12 districts in Bohemia and the seven districts in Moravia. These German prefects, each of whom had authority over one district, controled German administrative agencies and handled matters relating to general administration and citizenship, as well as other matters concerning Germans living in their districts. The Czech administration carried out its functions through local authorities but on every level the Germans controlled the Czech authorities.

In May 1943 Daluege suffered a major heart attack so had to be medically retired. Wilhelm Frick, seen here on the left with Konrad Henlein, the Reichsstatthalter (Governor) of the Sudetenland since 1939, was brought in as the new Reichsprotektor. Frick had been instrumental in formulating the racial policy in Nazi Germany, and had drafted the notorious Nuremberg Laws in 1935 which facilitated deportation. He was also influential in the programme of forced sterilisation and euthanasia. Henlein cheated justice by committing suicide on May 10, 1945, but Frick met his end at the hands of the hangman at Nuremberg on October 16, 1946.

Czechoslovakia had a long track record for the production of armaments — from guns for dreadnaughts of the Austro-Hungarian Navy to tanks for the Wehrmacht — so the country was a very valuable asset to the German war machine. One of the best-known arms companies was Skoda which made what the Germans called the Panzerkampfwagen 35 and 38(t), the 't' indicating that it had been manufactured in Tschechoslowakei, the German name for the country. This photo shows the PzKpfw 35(t) in the factory at Pilsen.

CITIZENSHIP

Citizens of German origin were granted citizenship of the German Reich, whereas the Czechs became citizens of the Protectorate. Czech patriots who were abroad were deprived of the citizenship of the Protectorate. The decree of the Reich Protector of October 3, 1939, stated that citizens of the Protectorate who were abroad and who had committed acts detrimental to the interests or reputation of the Reich, or who did not comply with an order to return to the Protectorate, would lose citizenship of the Protectorate and their property would be confiscated for the benefit of the Reich.

COURTS

The judicial system was based upon the principle of extra-territoriality for Germans. As a rule Germans could not be tried by Czech courts. Czechs, however, were subject not only to the criminal law of the Protectorate but also to the Criminal Code of the Reich in cases in which the political interests of Germany were involved, for example cases involving treason, attacks against the Führer, disrespect for German national emblems, and libel of the National Socialist Party or similar National Socialist organisations.

CONTROL OF INDUSTRIES

As the areas included in the Protectorate were highly industrialised, the Reich Protector was eager to take over control of all industries. On June 23, 1939, a decree was published creating a framework for the totalitarian reorganisation of the economy of the Protectorate, the order implementing it being dated August 29. Twenty-three groups were covered, which included all persons engaged in specific industries, the acquisition of raw materials by these groups, as well as the production and sale of their products, being controlled. The industries were (1) mining, (2) production of sugar, (3) production of alcohol, (4) production of beer, (5) malt industry, (6) flour mills, (7) food industry, (8) meat and poultry industry, (9) metal industry, (10) electrical works, (11) timber mills, (12) timber manufacturing, (13) paper and graphic industry, (14) chemical industry, (15) ceramics, (16) construction industry, (17) glass industry, (18) textile industry, (19) clothing industry, (20) leather industry, (21) film industry, (22) gas and water works, (23) manufacture of precious metals and precious stones.

CONTROL OF TRADES AND OCCUPATIONS

The most efficient instrument for subduing the Czechs to the will of the German ruler was provided by a decree in which the government of the Protectorate was forced by the Reich Protector to promulgate. It was dated November 4, 1939, and entitled, 'Government decree concerning temporary restrictions on trade and other gainful occupations'. It specifically stated that the authorities could deny permission to exercise a trade or occupation, even if all the necessary requirements had been met, so practically, no Czech could make a living without being compelled to comply with the new order.

PROPERTY

A great part of Czech property, as well as almost all Jewish property, was taken over by the Germans. A decree of October 4, 1939, gave the Reich Protector the right to confiscate property of persons and associations which had promoted 'tendencies inimical to law' (Rechtsfeindliche Bestrebungen). As political pressure on and persecutions of the Czechs and Jews increased, many of them endeavoured to obtain permission to leave the country. Such permission was granted only when the applicant agreed to pay a high tax, amounting to a substantial part of his property, for the benefit of the Reich. Such an 'emigration tax' amounted in practice to a profit

Of the 424 PzKpfw 35(t)s produced between 1935 and 1938, the Wehrmacht appropriated 219 in March 1939, many being used in the invasion of Poland and later in France.

The BMM company produced 150 of the 38(t) between May and November 1939. Fifty-nine saw service in Poland and 15 went to Norway in 1940. This tank went through several updates.

The Skoda factory was a prime target for RAF Bomber Command even though the round trip from Britain would be close on 1,500 miles. This photo was taken before the raid carried out on the night of October 20/21, 1940 when a mixed force of Blenheims, Hampdens, Wellingtons and Whitleys ranged over the occupied countries. One notable loss on the raid to Pilsen was that of a Whitley from No. 58 Squadron based at Linton-on-Ouse. It was shot down by Hauptmann Karl Hulshoff of I./NJG 2, this is believed to be the first known success against a Bomber Command aircraft by a German intruder over mainland Britain.

taken by Germans on persecutions they organised against the inhabitants of the invaded country. Moreover, many of the Czechs, especially those possessing larger industrial undertakings, were compelled to sell their property to persons indicated by the Reich Protector.

THE PRIVILEGED SITUATION OF THE GERMANS

Czechoslovak citizens of German origin (Volksdeutsche), who before the invasion played the role of fifth colum-

nists, became a privileged element in the Protectorate. They were entitled not only to dual citizenship but also to a great many other privileges. They were granted rewards for their pre-invasion activities on behalf of Germany in the form of reparations for damages incurred by them when they were fighting the Government of the Czechoslovak Republic. In order to increase the number of Germans in the Protectorate, the German laws on subsidies for marriages and children were extended to

German officials, members of the Gestapo and of the SS and those of the Reichsarbeitsdienst.

Moreover, the Protectorate became a vacation ground for Germans and men on leave from military service. They looked to the Protectorate for better food and better beer so the Minister of Agriculture of the Protectorate issued a decree on January 15, 1941 to the effect that ration cards of Germans on leave or on vacations should be valid in the Protectorate.

By 1945, over a third of the factory had been destroyed, the last raid coming on April 25 when the US Eighth Air Force was running out of targets to attack. Falling within the Soviet bloc, Skoda was nationalised and manufactured heavy machinery and locomotives and later trolley buses. Following the fall of Communism in 1989, several changes in ownership and activity have taken place.

Formerly the offices of the Bank of Petschek, this building at No. 20 Bredovska (now Politickych veznu) in Prague was taken over by the Gestapo and secret police. Jews and Czechs were brought here for interrogation and torture, and on November 24, 1939, 120 students accused of anti-Nazi plotting were executed here.

JEWS

The status of the Jews in the Protectorate was established both by legislation of the Reich Protector and by the puppet Czech government. On June 21, 1939, all Jewish property was ordered to be registered, and Jewish employees were eliminated from enterprises by decrees of October 23, 1939 and September 14, 1940. On January 26, 1940, the Reich Protector issued a decree concerning the elimination of Jews from the economy of the Protectorate. Two orders of January 26 and February 7 that year implemented this elimination decree. Jews were, in fact, excluded from economic enterprises of every kind. Even peddling was prohibited. On February 16, 1942, another decree was published concerning measures for the allocation of Jews in closed settlements. As a result, thousands of Jews were concentrated in the prison fortress town of Terezin (Theresienstadt).

RESISTANCE

The German language was introduced as a compulsory subject to be taught in schools and the revision of Czech textbooks was required. Czech teachers were forbidden to refer to Czech national heroes, and books by authors representing the national spirit were prohibited. Books which empha-

sised national elements were initially burned but later the Germans changed this practice and pulped them to provide material for papermaking.

Plays and operas were censored. Dvorak's opera *Jakobin*, which had been first performed in 1889, was prohibited on the ground that it contained a tune starting with the words 'Adolf, you are mad!'

Because of the patriotic feelings and activities of Czech students, all universities were closed.

SLOVAKIA

The Germans took advantage of some difficult population problems within the Czechoslovak Republic in order to foster the dismemberment and division of that country. For this purpose they directed their attention particularly to Slovakia, a nation of about two and a half million people. The Slovaks and Czechs were of the same ethnic group, but political differences arose between them during the period of the Czechoslovak Republic, the Slovaks claiming that they were not duly represented in the public affairs of the republic. At the time of the Munich crisis, Hitler, through his agents, played upon these political differences. The majority of the Slovaks, however, seemed to prefer to remain within the framework of the Czech Republic; thus the Germans found supporters only among the extremists of the Slovak population.

Autonomous status was granted to Slovakia by the government in Prague on November 19, 1938. The Slovak Diet opened at Bratislava on January 20, 1939 with Monsignor Jozef Tiso being appointed Premier by the President of the Republic.

The Germans who swarmed over Slovakia worked against the consolidation of the good relations between the two federated countries. Especially active in this field was the German leader Franz Karmasin. On March 10, 1939, the

Their deaths are commemorated today by a plaque on the corner of the building which is now the HQ of the Czech Trade Office.

After visiting Prague on March 15/16, Hitler paid a flying visit to Brno (Brünn in German), the capital of Slovakia, on March 17.

The trip was in response to a request by Monsignor Jozef Tiso to Hitler on March 16 to take Slovakia under his protection.

The Führer travelled to Brno by train, and he inspected the Guard of Honour outside the railway station on Nadrazni.

The Germans installed Jozef Tiso, a Roman Catholic priest, to head the Slovak Republic which became an autonomous satellite of Nazi Germany. He was captured by the Americans in June 1945 and extradited to stand trial in the reconstituted Czechoslavakia. One of the many crimes of which he was accused was for decorating Karl Hermann Frank with the Grand Cross for his involvement in the students' murders and the Lidice massacre. He was hanged in Bratislava in April 1947.

Prague government, being aware of the separatist activities in Slovakia, dismissed Monsignor Tiso, and the next day appointed Karol Sidor as the new Premier.

On March 13, Monsignor Tiso was summoned to Berlin by Hitler and was accompanied on his visit by Karmasin. On his arrival in Berlin the former was given the honours due a prime minister. At the same time a Vienna broadcasting station was used by members of the Slovak faction advocating the separation of Slovakia from Czechoslovakia. On March 14 the Slovak Diet, which had functioned as the federal Diet of the Slovak part of the Czechoslovak Republic, after hearing Monsignor Tiso's account of his visit to Hitler, voted for the creation of an independent State of Slovakia. By the same vote, the Slovak Diet was transformed into the legislative Diet of the State of Slovakia.

After the occupation of Bohemia and Moravia and the proclamation regarding a protectorate for those territories, the German Army occupied the western part of Slovakia, its arms and munitions factories, hydro-electric plants and the most-important railways, linking the capital, Bratislava, with the rest of the country and with Bohemia-Moravia. Thus Germany controlled the railway communications between Bratislava and the eastern part of Slovakia, as well as the communications with Poland, Romania, and Hungary. Afterward it sought to legalise this unlawful occupation by a treaty between it and Slovakia.

On March 24, 1939, a declaration was issued by the Reich Minister of Foreign Affairs announcing that the German and Slovak governments had signed a treaty extending protection by the German Reich to the State of Slovakia, the treaty stating that the Slovak State 'has placed itself under the protection of the German Reich'.

In 1939 Franz Karmasin was appointed State Secretary for German Affairs and Führer of the German residents of Slovakia the following year. Here he is pictured reviewing one of his armed units in Bratislava's Mostová Street on March 30, 1940. He was Konrad Henlein's deputy and contributed to the 'cleansing of the population from racially inferior and anti-social elements'. Ending the war an SS-Sturmbannführer, he fled to West Germany under an assumed name and died in June 1970.

THE VIENNA AWARD

During the Munich crisis, Hungary renewed its claims to the territories situated in Czechoslovakia to the north of the mountainous Hungaro-Czech frontiers. As Germany and Italy had taken over the factual control of Central Europe, they decided to settle this claim of Hungary against Czechoslovakia by arbitration.

Accordingly the Foreign Ministers of Germany and Italy met in Vienna and issued the so-called Vienna Award on November 2, 1938 under which a number of districts were allotted to Hungary. These regions, referred to as the 'Highland Territories' were incorporated into Hungary by the law of November 12, 1938, enacted by the Hungarian Royal Parliament. In this law, the doctrine of the Holy Crown found its full expression in the solemn words: 'The Hungarian Parliament devoutly expresses its gratitude to Divine Providence that after 20 years' separation, trial and heroic resistance against foreign rule, one part of the torn-away Highland Territories returns to the realm of the Hungarian Holy Crown. The Hungarian fatherland greets with the deepest joy, and clasps to its heart with the affection of a loving mother, these returning children who have suffered so much.'

Through the Vienna arbitration award, Hungary incorporated the following Slovak areas: the entire districts of Stará, Dala, Feledince, Královský, Chlumec, Komárno, Kosice (city), Parkan, Dunajská, Streda, Zeliezovce; parts of the districts of Bratislava, Galanta, Modrý Kamen, Velké Kapusany, Kosice, Krupina, Levice, Lucenec, Michalovce, Moldava nad Bodrou, Nitra, Revúca Roznava, Rimavská Sobota, Sala, Samorín, Tornala, Trebisov, Trstená, Váble and Nové Zámky.

Hungary regained southern Czechoslovakia in the First Vienna Award in 1938 but this did not satisfy a territorial dispute with Romania which had been forced to surrender land to the USSR and Bulgaria.

In implementation of the award, the frontiers between Slovakia and Hungary were rectified, and it was announced by order of the Hungarian Royal Ministry of the Interior on March 13, 1939, that the following communities 'shall hereafter come under the authority of the Hungarian Holy Crown: Vága, Alsójattó, Nagycétény, Kalász, Nagyhind, Bori, Hévmágyarád, Felsözellö, Alsopokorágy, Pádár, Felsö-falu, Rekenyevitálu, Andrási, Aifalucska, Jászov, Jászomindszent, Rudnok, Aranyida-Reka, Mészpest and Bajánháza'. Moreover, the Vienna arbitration allotted to Hungary the following entire districts or parts of districts belonging to Carpathian Ruthenia or Sub-Carpathia:

the entire district of Berehovo; the city districts of Mukacevo and Uzhorod; parts of the districts of Irsava, Mukacevo, Sevlus and Uzhorod. The rest of Sub-Carpathia was also occupied and incorporated by Hungary in March 1939.

By the incorporation of the Highland Territories, Hungary acquired land totalling 11,927 square kilometres (4,605 square miles) and a population of 1,044,438. Of these inhabitants, the main groups consisted of the following: 587,692 Hungarians, 51,578 Jews, 288,803 Slovaks and 35,261 Sub-Carpathian Ruthenians (figures from the 1930 census).

RAPHAEL LEMKIN, 1944

To solve the problem, the German and Italian governments offered to arbitrate and Foreign Ministers Joachim von Ribbentrop and Galeazzo Ciano met on August 30, 1940 at the Belvedere Palace in Vienna. They agreed that an equitable solution would be to reduce the Hungarian demand to 43,492 square kilometres, something which was amicably accepted. Here Foreign Minister István Csáky signs the Second Vienna Award for Hungary.

The Razing of Lidice and Lezáky

Reinhard Heydrich (right) assumes command in Prague. His deputy, Karl Hermann Frank, stands on the left.

On September 27, 1941, SS-Gruppenführer Reinhard Heydrich arrived in Prague as Acting Reichsprotektor of Bohemia and Moravia. This was the new name for that part of Czechoslovakia (less Slovakia) that had been declared by Hitler following his take-over of the country in stages during 1938-39. At first, Hitler had installed the moderate Baron Konstantin von Neurath as Protektor but, after the Czechs proved an unwilling and un-cooperative element in Hitler's new empire, Heydrich was appointed his replacement as the new hard-line governor.

As Chief of the Security Police (which included the Gestapo), the ambitious Heydrich was already aspiring to oust his superior Himmler and, proudly, Hitler had even named him as being groomed as his own successor. When he arrived at Hradcany Castle in Prague, Heydrich began a clever campaign to win the co-operation of the people.

On the one hand, the velvet glove offered extra rations, holidays and even the world's first social security programme as rewards for hard work, but the new measures were backed by the iron fist for those that rebelled: imprisonment, the concentration camp and the firing-squad.

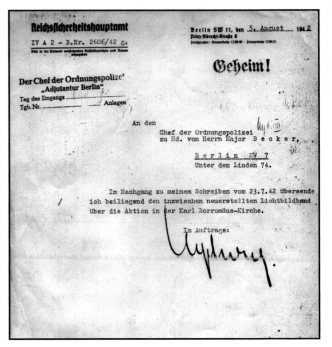

The Germans produced a fully-documented report on the assassination of Reinhard Heydrich, and we are indebted to the YIVO Institute for Jewish Research in New York for permission to reproduce material from their copy. The investigation was carried out by Section IV-A-2 of the Sipo/SD office in Prague, and was finalised within three months of the attack on May 27, 1942. Forwarded to the Reichssicherheitshauptamt in Berlin, it comprised 180 pages in nine short volumes with 85 'scene of crime' photographs, some of which have been included in this chapter.

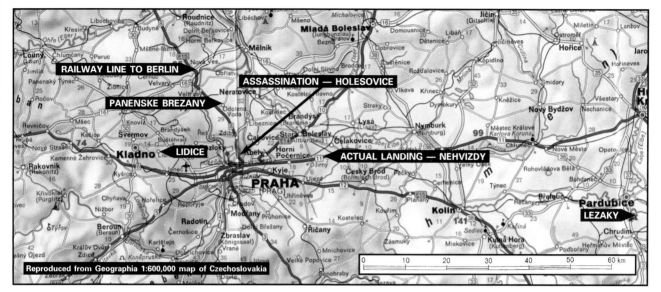

The London-based Czechoslovakian Government-in-exile was deeply divided over what action should be taken by them. On the one hand, there were those who pressed for immediate action against the Germans but there were also those who said that the reprisals, which would surely follow any attack, would have severe repercussions on the civilian population and that, even if Heydrich was eliminated, his successor might be much worse.

Nevertheless, fearful of the apparent success of Heydrich's insidious new measures to counter the rebellious spirit of the Czechs, the Government-in-exile, backed by British Intelligence, decided to prepare a counter-stroke.

The conference initiating the proposal was held in London on October 3, 1941. At this meeting, Colonel Frantisek Moravec, Chief of the Czech Intelligence Service, described the worsening conditions in Czechoslovakia heralded by Heydrich's declaration of a State of Emergency immediately on his appointment six days earlier. A swift blow to the Nazis was essential, explained Moravec, and it could either be directed against Karl Hermann Frank, the Nazi Secretary of State, or against Heydrich. The death of either would be an example and an encouragement to those suffering under the German yoke. The ideal date for an attack would be later that month, on October 28, when the nation celebrated the founding of the Czechoslovakian republic. The plan, if successful, would not only free the Czechs from their overlord but strike a tremendous psychological blow to the over-confident Nazis riding the crest of their victorious wave over Europe. Present at the meeting were the two Czechs selected for the task: Sergeants Jozef Gabcik and Karel Svoboda. Their departure date was fixed for October 10.

When Hitler had overrun Western Europe in 1940, the remnants of those armies that had fought with the Allies against Germany and were fortunate enough to reach England, were formed into various Free corps. There were the Free French, the Free Poles, the Free Norwegians . . . and the Free Czechs. The latter were based in the grounds of Cholmondeley Castle (pronounced Chumley), six miles north of Whitchurch in Cheshire. It was from here that the two men had been selected for the almost-suicidal mission; two men who were not hastily-trained killers or professional assassins but patriots prepared to carry through their task regardless of the odds. However, before the planned departure date arrived, Sergeant Svoboda was injured in a training exercise and Jan Kubis was appointed to take his place.

Jan Kubis had been stationed with Jozef Gabcik at Cholmondeley for more than a year, both having met in a Warsaw refugee camp and had reached England via a round-about route by joining the French Foreign Legion. They were close friends and spent most of their weekends staying with the Ellison family in their red-brick house on the edge of Ightfield, a small village four miles south-east of Whitchurch. Mrs Jessie Ellison had befriended the two boys in Whitchurch one day and invited them to her home although perhaps it was her two pretty teenage daughters who provided an additional attraction for the lonely young Czechs singled out for the special mission.

The delay in the mounting of the operation gave a few more weeks for the organisation of the operation code-named 'Anthropoid'. The two Czechs finally took off from Tangmere airfield at 10 p.m. on December 28, 1941. Together with them in the Halifax, piloted by Flight Lieutenant R. C. Hockey, were two other groups, 'Silver A' and 'B'.

'Silver A' comprised First Lieutenant Alfred Bartos, Sergeant Josef Valcik and Jiri Potucek and 'Silver B', Jan Zemek and Vladimir Skadna. They had the task of getting in touch with the Czech underground movement as contact with London by the resistance had been broken by the Germans.

The Halifax crossed the French coast at 10.49 p.m. and, two hours later, was successfully avoiding German fighters over Darmstadt in Germany. Continuing almost exactly due east, the route then ran via Bayreuth (1.32 p.m.) to Pilsen which was reached at 2.15 a.m. Nine minutes later Kubis and Gabcik parachuted to earth. On his return, the pilot reported that the original dropping zone was covered with fog and that the 'Anthropoid' group had been dropped about eight kilometres south of Pilsen.

The ground was covered in deep snow as Jan and Jozef made their landing. Although they were unaware of it at the time, they had been dropped some 115 kilometres north-east of the planned spot and were now just 20 kilometres from Prague. Their landing had also not been unnoticed. A local gamekeeper at Nehvizdy, Antonin Sedlacek, woken by the sound of a low-flying aircraft, looked out to see a parachute floating down behind the cemetery. Next morning he found trampled snow and hidden parachutes and footprints leading away to a hill 1½ kilometres away

The cave in the quarry at Nehvizdy where Jan Kubis and Jozef Gabcik sheltered after the first night landing by parachute. In 2015, local stonemasons produced a memorial dedicated to all the Czech airmen, serving the RAF, who returned to Czechoslovakia in 1945. It was unveiled in a small park opposite Prague's Ruzyne airport on August 24.

that was crowned with a copse. Following the trail to the trees surrounding an old quarry, he came across the two men standing outside a cave in the rocks. Jan and Jozef, although wary of the stranger, decided the best policy would be to trust the visitor. He told them where they were and of their luck in discovering the best hiding place for miles. Sedlacek offered to bring them food and to find out if their arrival had been noticed by anyone else.

As they had jumped from only 900 feet, it was inevitable that other villagers would have been woken by the low-flying four-engined bomber, and the fact that parachutists were in the area soon became common knowledge. The local miller, Bretislav Baumann, soon discovered their hiding place independently from Sedlacek for, although it was ideal, it was also the first place anyone would search. Warning Jan and Jozef of their vulnerability, Baumann contacted the local resistance movement and by January the pair had made their way to Prague.

There they were hidden in a variety of places until they reached the safe house of the Moravec family — in reality a second-floor flat on Biskupcova Street. When in Prague they made contact with underground leaders, notably Jan Zelenka, a local schoolmaster known as 'Uncle Hajsky', to formulate a successful plan for the attempt on Heydrich's life.

During February Jan and Jozef made contact through 'Uncle Hajsky' with Josef Valcik of the 'Silver A' group who had established cover for himself as a barman at the Veselka Hotel in Pardubice, 80-odd kilometres east of Prague, an ideal place to gather information as it was frequented by high German officials. Another source of information on Heydrich's movements was provided by one of the Czech staff in Hradcany Castle, overlooking the River Moldau (now called the Vltava) where the Reichsprotektor had his office. However the castle itself was heavily guarded and Jan and Jozef were forced to look elsewhere for a place to mount their operation.

One idea they examined was to attack Heydrich in his private train during one of his frequent visits to Berlin. The line to Ger-

Jan Kubis, born in 1913, joined the Czech army in 1935 but following the Munich Agreement and demobilisation of the armed forces, he was discharged in October 1938. The following year, he joined a Czech unit in Poland and then fought in France, being awarded the Croix de Guerre, before he reached Britain to train as a paratrooper. The photos were taken at the Czech Military Intelligence Service HQ in Porchester Gate Building in London.

Jozef Gabcik, born in 1912, served in the Czech army between 1934-37. Like Jan, he crossed into Poland in 1939, then went to Algeria where he joined the Czech Foreign Army. When he arrived in Britain he was assigned to the Czech Mixed Brigade as 2 i/c of No. 2 Platoon of No. 3 Company. He was among the first to volunteer for assignments in occupied territory and was dropped in Czechoslovakia on the night of December 28/29, 1941.

many followed the River Vltava northwards and two possibilities presented themselves. First they discovered that the train always had to stop at the station in the Royal Park, in the northern suburbs of Prague, where the branch line joined the main route north, waiting for a clear signal. Just 400 metres beyond the station, thick trees provided excellent cover for a man with an anti-tank rifle to fire a shell at Heydrich's carriage. However when they carried out a rehearsal of the plan, they found the train gathered speed so quickly that it passed in a blur, too

fast to recognise the correct compartment. Then further north in the mountainous border region beyond Liberec, where the train was certain to be travelling slowly, another spot was reconnoitred. This time it was planned to place explosives on the line to blow up the train and, although a dummy run was carried out on a troop train, this was only derailed with light casualties. It was obvious that attacks on Heydrich's train would be a hit-and-miss affair so Jan and Jozef began looking for an alternative place for an ambush.

Having made contact wtih the underground in Prague they were hidden in a variety of safe houses. *Left:* **The main one was a second-floor flat at No. 1745/7 on the corner of the** **building in Biskupcova Street, the home of the Moravec family.** *Right:* **On the opposite side of the road was apartment No. 4 of Jan Zelenka ('Uncle Hajsky'). Photos by Harry Marsh.**

Heydrich lived in a château at Panenske Brezany when he took over as Stellvertretender Reichsprotektor (Deputy/Acting Reich Protector) in September 1941. In the spring of 1942 he was joined by his wife Lina and their children Klaus (killed in a car accident in 1943), Heider and Silke. Following Heydrich's death on June 4 that year, his family continued to live at the château until the end of the war. It was later owned by the Czech Metals Research Institute but then lay abandoned for 25 years until it was offered for sale in 2016. In poor shape, the asking price was $17 million.

Heydrich lived with his wife Lina and his children, Klaus, Heider and Silke, in a country villa in Panenske Brezany, a village 14 kilometres north of Prague, from where he commuted daily to the city in a Model 320 Mercedes driven by his personal chauffeur, SS-Oberscharführer Johannes Klein. The car would come to fetch him at around nine o'clock each morning. It then drove through Panenske Brezany village (where Frank also had a house), climbed a hill and then entered a dense wood for about one hundred metres before reaching open country. There an escort car would be waiting for the Mercedes and the convoy would drive at speed along the tree-lined road before joining Route 8 for the city. The journey took 45 minutes.

The villa, like the castle in Prague, was closely guarded but the daily car journey, during which time Heydrich sat in the front seat of the open touring car, could possibly be used to advantage. Exploring the whole route on bicycles, Jan and Jozef found that the straight tree-lined road leading to the main road offered distinct possibilities although Heydrich's love of speed meant that the car often reached 100 km an hour on this stretch, leaving the escort car far behind. The trees by the road could easily support a steel cable across the road to stop or wreck the car and they would be on hand to finish off the occupants with their pistols. However the location offered no chance of subsequent escape. Their bicycles would easily be overtaken by the escort car and the open countryside provided no form of concealment.

Nevertheless, although the plan was rejected, the car journey seemed to provide the key and Jan and Jozef persevered with their examination of other likely spots. It was during their return to Prague on a recon-naissance trip of the route, as they descended the Kirchmayerstrasse (since renamed the Rude Armady) in the northern suburbs, that they came upon the perfect location. Here the cobble-stoned road turned sharply right as it joined Klein Holeschowitzerstrasse (now V Holesovickach) on its way down to the river. Although the road was wide and double tram lines ran down the centre, cars negotiating the hairpin bend had to slow down to at least 15 or 12 km an hour. Additionally, a nearby tram stop would provide an excellent reason for them to be standing near the corner. The German's own edict, issued when they occupied Prague, changing the traffic from the left to the right, would also mean the car would be close to the inside bend of the hairpin. It was a perfect location, almost made for the job, and excitedly the two set about planning the attack in detail.

This sharp bend where Kirchmayerstrasse joined Klein Holeschowitzerstrasse was selected for the attack as Heydrich's open-top Mercedes would have to slow right down to make the right turn. Heydrich would be sitting in the right-hand front seat and another advantage would be that he would be close to the curb as, following their take-over of the country, the Germans had switched traffic to driving on the right. The picture shows the bend as it appeared in 1977.

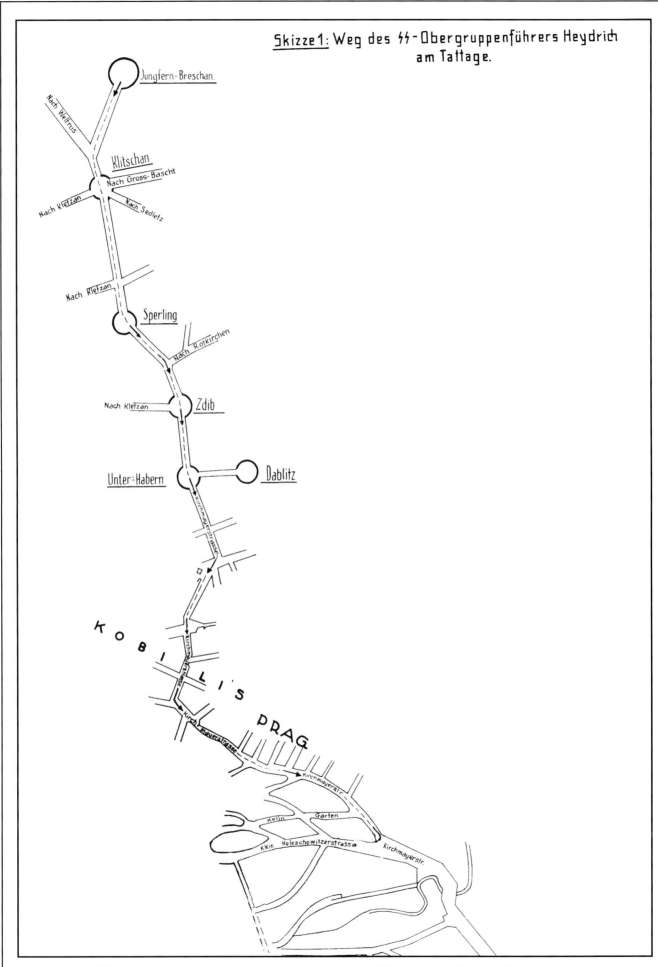

Skizze 1: Weg des SS-Obergruppenführers Heydrich am Tattage.

Plan from the official report showing the route as it entered the suburbs of Prague towards the fatal corner.

In 1979, the road junction could be seen exactly as it was in 1942 but soon afterwards it was completely changed to eliminate the sharp bend (see Google Earth view on page 38). In this comparison by Robert Porter, who has made an extensive study of the assassination, the same yellow building can be seen in the background of the Gestapo picture below, but the road in the foreground is the new bypass, the original carriageway being hidden beyond the trees.

In all, four men would be involved in the actual assassination. Josef Valcik's cover had been blown in Pardubice so he joined Kubis and Gabcik in Prague together with Adolf Opalka who had been dropped by parachute on March 28 as one of the three-man 'Out Distance' Group. (Altogether, 17 Czechs were flown from England and parachuted into the country during March and April 1942 for various missions.)

It had now been four months since Jan and Jozef had arrived in Czechoslovakia and the underground's informer in Hradcany Castle had already told them that Heydrich's duties in Bohemia and Moravia were shortly to end. He was due to be sent to France following a meeting with Hitler in Berlin on May 27 so there was no time to lose.

Final approval for the operation was radioed from London to Prague on May 20 and the date for the attempt fixed for seven days later. Although the time of Heydrich's departure for Berlin on the 27th was not known, it was assumed he would follow his usual routine and drive to his office early that morning before leaving.

At 8 a.m. Jan Kubis and Jozef Gabcik set out to cross the city for the Holesovice junction. Each was carrying a leather briefcase containing the weapons for the attack. Jan had two primed grenades converted from British No. 73 anti-tank hand-grenades. The standard grenade had a tinplate body 9.5in long and 3.25in in diameter containing 3.25lbs of Polar Ammon Gelatin Dynamite — a nitro-glycerine-based explosive. The grenade was fitted with the No. 247 fuze made of black bakelite which is often referred to as the 'all-ways fuze' designed to function on impact irrespective of how the grenade landed. Total weight was 4lbs. The grenade had been declared obsolete in October 1941, two months prior to the parachute drop in December, but the weapons that Jan was to use were a conversion of the standard device made from the upper third portion only. The filling was prevented from falling out by covering the open end with adhesive tape and then binding the whole with tape for added security. The effect of the conversion was to cut the size and the weight to just over one pound which would make the device more easy to

throw and conceal. Jozef had a disassembled Mk II 9mm Sten (No. FF209) with one spare magazine and, for some unknown reason, a No. 73 grenade without the detonator. Both men, in addition, carried .32-calibre Model 1910 Colt semi-automatic pistols.

Collecting their bicycles en route, by 8.30 a.m. they had reached the junction. Valcik was already waiting for them at the tram stop. It was his job to stand further up the road and to signal to Jan and Jozef on the corner when Heydrich's car was approaching. Opalka was to keep a look-out from the

opposite side of the road. Propping their bicycles on the opposite side of the road against two lamp posts, they all took up their positions. Gabcik, with the assembled Sten now under his raincoat, stood near the corner and Kubis a few metres further downhill.

The tension at the Holesovice bend was unbearable as Heydrich should have been along by now. Opalka crossed the road to talk to Jan and Jozef. Trams continued to grind up the hill to the nearby hospital. Opalka returned to his post. If Jan and Jozef stood there much longer without catching a

Photo from the SD report showing 'the women's bicycle (Jozef had borrowed it from the Moravec family) and brief-case, left behind at the crime scene'. Heydrich's Mercedes can be seen stopped on the far side of the road on the left.

The escape routes: Jan Kubis pedalled furiously straight down Kirchmayerstrasse while Jozef Gabcik ran the opposite way.

tram, someone in the experimental institute opposite might get suspicious. What had gone wrong? Suddenly Valcik's mirror flashed. Heydrich was coming. As Gabcik moved forward with the Sten, he heard a tram rumble up the street behind him. He flung aside his coat covering the sub-machine gun, raised it to his shoulder and as the Mercedes rounded the bend aimed at the front seat passenger and pulled the trigger.

Kubis watching from a few metres further down the road heard the tram approaching. As it neared the corner he saw Jozef step into the road and aim at the green Mercedes as it came into view. At the same instant Opalka ran across the road in front of the car. Waiting for the burst of fire, he gripped his own grenade inside the brief-case. To his utter amazement the car passed Jozef without a shot being fired. The vehicle with its

two occupants continued past him absolutely unscathed.

Moving with lightning speed, keeping hold of the tape which automatically pulled the pin as it unwound from the grenade, Kubis flung it at the rear of the car. It exploded as it touched the rear nearside panel, bursting the tyre and blowing a huge hole in the bodywork. At the same time Jan felt splinters strike his own chest and face.

Robert Porter's plan clearly shows the extent of the alteration: 'The red arrow indicates where the road and bend would have been in 1942. The white arrow indicates the bend as it is today. The black rectangle is where Heydrich's car came to a halt after the assassination attempt. The electricity sub-station [1] is still there today and can be clearly seen in most photographs taken of the incident in 1942, looking across the road from the car.'

The remaining piece of the original road near where Josef Valcik, the look-out, must have stood to flash the signal by mirror.

One can imagine the silence that followed the explosion, the action frozen in the minds of those present. Then, suddenly, everything came to life like a still frame of a film suddenly set in motion. Heydrich and Klein emerged from the car, seemingly untouched, the latter's pistol already freed from its holster. The tram with its windows shattered disgorged its screaming, shouting passengers. Jan ran across the road and mounted his bicycle just as a second tram ground to a halt. Pedalling like mad down the hill, Jan shot down Kirchmayerstrasse and disappeared from view.

Jozef Gabcik, impotently aiming the silent Sten gun at the Mercedes as it passed him, was rooted to the spot. Some frustrating, mechanical malfunction had completely negated all the planning of the past months. Transfixed to the spot, his finger pulling the trigger for all he was worth, it was only the explosion of Jan's grenade that freed him for action. Throwing down the useless gun he prepared to make his escape. Heydrich and Klein emerging from the shattered car barred the way downhill and passengers emerging from the tram blocked the other side of the road. There was only one way to go and that was back up the road, the way the Mercedes had come.

Abandoning his bicycle, he turned about and ran around the corner. Although Heydrich had his pistol unholstered, the German was staggering holding his back and it was Klein who gave chase. Unable to catch the first man who had escaped on the bicycle, the driver had immediately turned his attention to Jozef. Pounding after him pistol in hand, a wild west-style shooting match ensued as each exchanged shot for shot. Realising he was bound to be hit if he ran straight up the road, when Jozef reached the first turning on the left (then called Kolingarten by the Germans, and Na Kolinske by the Czechs but now fittingly renamed Gabcikova), he sped round the corner. He saw a small, suburban street lined with houses with front gardens that conveniently led downhill. Reaching the first crossroad, he decided to continue straight on as a turn to the left would only bring him back to the scene of the attack. Jozef must have realised that by now the Germans and local police would be stirring into action; road-blocks would be set up and unless he could shake off Klein, his ammunition would soon be exhausted.

Robert Porter's quest for ultimate accuracy is demonstrated in this comparison: 'Within a few feet I am standing on the bend, putting myself in the front seat of the Mercedes, where Heydrich would have been sitting'.

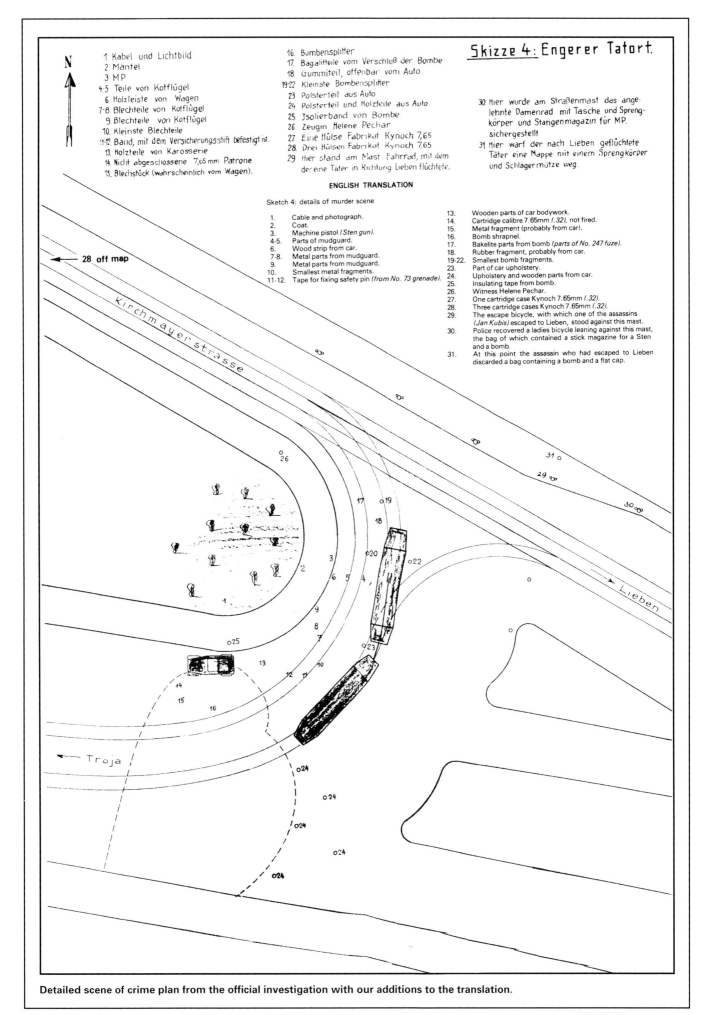

Detailed scene of crime plan from the official investigation with our additions to the translation.

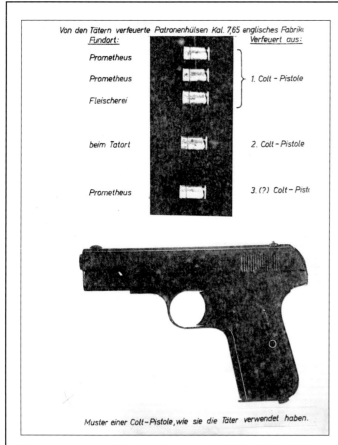

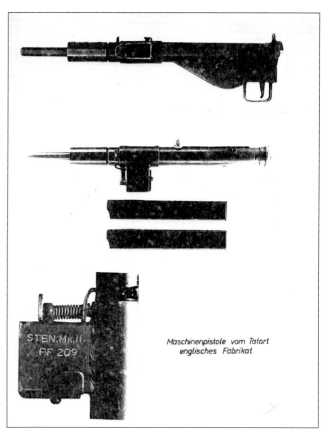

Weapons recovered by the Germans. *Left:* The .32 Colt left at the scene, either No. 539370 or 540416. *Right:* The Mk II Sten gun, serial FF 209, which failed to fire when Jozef Gabcik pulled the trigger. Stens were notorious for stoppages due to the fact that the double column of rounds had to merge at the top of the magazine to form a single column.

When the gun failed to fire, Jan Kubis hurled one of his modified grenades at the rear of the Mercedes. *Left:* This photograph included in the report shows an unmodified British Type 73 anti-tank hand-grenade — the device painted buff with a red band indicating high explosive. *Right:* The unprimed grenade recovered from Jozef's briefcase.

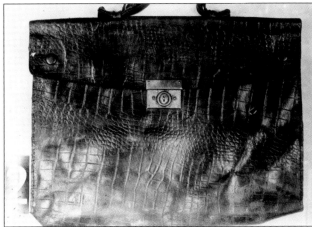

Brief-case 1 'found hanging from woman's bicycle with bomb without blasting cap'. Brief-case 2 'containing primed bomb'.

Below left: **'Security pin on cloth ribbon with lead strip from an explosive device.'** *Above and below:* **The coat and cap.**

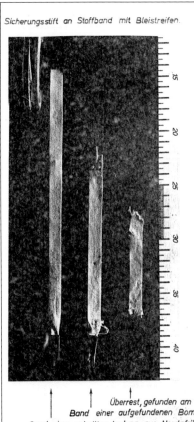

Sicherungsstift an Stoffband mit Bleistreifen.

Überrest, gefunden am
Band einer aufgefundenen Bomb
Band einer geballten Ladung aus Nordafrik

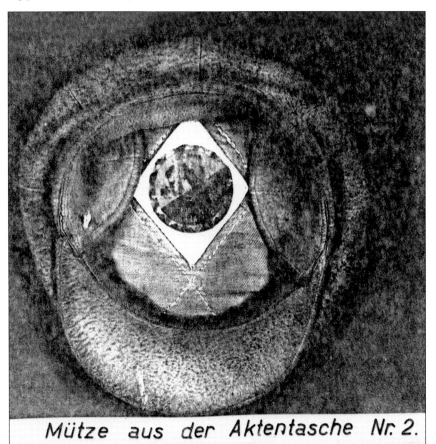

Mütze aus der Aktentasche Nr. 2.

'Escape route of the machine gunner.' Scene of crime photograph at the lower end of Kolingarten, now symbolically renamed Gabcikova.

A few yards further on another road, Pomezni, crossed from left to right. On the corner stood a butcher's shop. A local coalman, Jan Zavazal, was watching and later described what happened:

'Here, at this crossroads the young chap stopped; he probably didn't know where he was any more. Then suddenly he saw the butcher's shop. I must tell you about this butcher's shop. It was a little place and you went into it down some steps. The butcher was called Brauner: he had a relation who worked for the Gestapo. And this young chap, all out of breath, saw the shop and darted in. How could he have known the butcher was a fascist?

'Brauner came out of the shop and looked round and at this moment up comes Heydrich's chauffeur and a carter with him. They say the chauffeur had seen him in the street and forced him at pistol-point to run after the young chap along with him. Brauner pointed to the shop, to tell them he was inside.

'And now it all began again. The chauffeur sheltered behind a little post in the garden and blazed away like mad. But the man hidden in the shop opened fire too and he fired better than Heydrich's chauffeur because the next moment the chauffeur fell, holding his leg. He had a bullet in his thigh. The young chap came out of the shop and started running again with the carter and Brauner the butcher after him as the chauffeur had given Brauner his revolver, but he didn't know how to use it.

'And the boy ran along this street towards me. I made myself small. A young chap, good-looking, his hair dishevelled went right by me and vanished between the houses.'

Having wounded Klein it was easy for Jozef to out-distance the half-hearted chase by the butcher who gave up as soon as he was out of the sight of the German. However by continuing down Na Zapalci (the lower part of the road now renamed Valcikova after the third member of the team who had already made good his escape), Jozef re-entered Klein Holeschowitzerstrasse. There Mrs Milada Matulova, sunbathing in her garden, was alerted by the noise:

'People were coming and going along our street, and up the hill we heard a few shots, but from our place you can't see as far as the corner. At that moment Gabcik came running from the side street. How best to describe him? Rather short, staring eyes, a revolver in his hand pointing in front of him, his tie flying in the wind. He was out of breath. At that time I had no idea of his name, of course, and I didn't know he had taken part in the killing, but that came to my mind at once. His strange look drew your attention. Brauner's butcher's shop was in the street he had just run along,

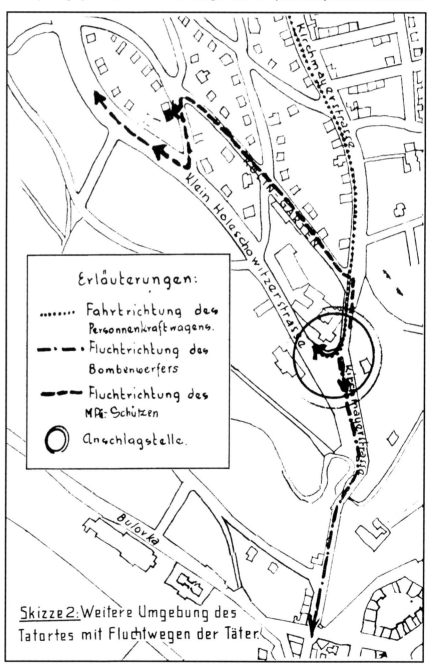

Erläuterungen:

.... Fahrtrichtung des Personnenkraftwagens.

—·—· Fluchtrichtung des Bombenwerfers

——— Fluchtrichtung des MPi-Schützen

◯ Anschlagstelle.

Skizze 2: Weitere Umgebung des Tatortes mit Fluchtwegen der Täter.

Sketch 2 from the investigation showing what the Germans knew at the time — the escape routes of Jan ('Bombenwerfer') and Jozef ('MPi-Schütze').

Klein hinter dem
Pfeiler in Deckung

weiterer Fluchtweg

Fluchtweg

Nach dem Verlassen
des Fleischerladens schoß
der Täter auf seinem weiteren
Fluchtwege auf den Fahrer Klein

30: Fleischerladen, in den der MPi.-Schütze flüchtete

The 'Battle of Brauner's Butcher's Shop' where the driver, SS-Oberscharführer Johannes Klein, was shot in the leg.

and afterwards people said there had been a positive gun-battle between him and Klein, Heydrich's chauffeur.

'For a few seconds Gabcik stopped there at the corner of our street and it seemed to me he didn't know where to go on running. He stood for two or three seconds perhaps. He looked up the hill and he must have realised that he was right by the place of the ambush — that he had turned a circle in escaping. Then he set off again, running down the hill along the tram tracks. I could still see him as he went round by the inn but then he vanished among the surrounding gardens.'

Since we were there in 1977 (left) the forecourt has seen considerable change. Right: Harry Marsh's comparison is as it appears today.

The blast from the explosion had driven a piece of bodywork into Heydrich's lower back, shattering his 11th rib, puncturing his stomach and lodging in his spleen. Horsehair filling from the seat back had also been carried ino the wound.

Meanwhile at the scene of the accident, all was confusion. A Zetka car, driven by Karel Duben, was halted and a blonde German woman, who had chanced on the scene and taken things in hand, ordered him to unload his load of sweets and take the wounded Heydrich to Bulovka Hospital. While Duben and his mate were so doing, a Tatra van approached the crossroads. Shouting and waving the blonde woman brought it to a halt and commandeered it instead of the car. As the back was loaded with crates of floor polish, Heydrich was helped in beside the driver, Frantisek Sitta. Sitta set off down the hill only to realise when he reached the bottom that the quickest way to the hospital was via the crossroads at the top. When he turned the van round Heydrich, obviously in great pain holding his bleeding back with one hand and waving his pistol in the other, sharply questioned Sitta in German. Sitta shrugged an answer but stopped when he reached the scene of the attack where the blonde was still waiting. Explaining the change of route she translated for Heydrich's benefit. At this stage, Heydrich said he would prefer to travel lying down and he was helped out by a policeman and placed flat on his stomach on top of the smelly crates in the back of the van.

At Bulovka Hospital the duty doctor in the surgical department was Vladimir Snajdr:

'Heydrich was alone in the room, stripped to the waist, sitting on the table where we carried out the first examination. I greeted him in Czech; he raised his hand but did not answer. I took forceps and a few swabs and tried to see whether the wound was deep. He did not stir, he did not flinch, although it must have hurt him. Meanwhile a nurse had telephoned Professor Walter Dick, a German, asking him to come to the theatre.

'At first sight the wound did not seem dangerous — unfortunately. Sometimes, you know, doctors find themselves in a complex situation. Take this case, for example. Since I was a decent Czech I was delighted that Heydrich should be in a bad way. All it needed was for him to have been wounded a few centimetres lower down, in the kidneys, or for the spinal column to have been affected and everything would have been straightforward. But since I was also a doctor, my duty was to cure, not kill. But should you cure fascists? He was a murderer and killing a tyrant is an act that benefits mankind as a whole. Before I could make up my mind Professor Dick hurried in. He was a German doctor who the Nazis had appointed to our hospital.

'"What's the matter?" he asked. It was only at that moment that he caught sight of Heydrich. He cried "Heil!", clicked his heels and began to examine him. He tried to see whether the kidney was touched: no, all seemed well for Heydrich. And the same applied to his spinal column. Then he was put into a wheel-chair and taken off to the X-ray room. Heydrich tried to behave courageously and he walked from the chair to the X-ray machine by himself.

'The X-ray showed something in the wound, perhaps a bomb splinter or a piece of coachwork. In short, there was something there inside. Dr Dick thought the splinter was in the chest wall and that it could be extracted by a simple local operation. We had a theatre in the basement for operations of that kind. Dick tried it, but without success. The patient's state called for a full-scale surgical operation. One rib was broken, the thoracic cage was open, a bomb splinter was in the spleen and the diaphragm was pierced.

'"Herr Protektor", said Dick to Heydrich, "we must operate", but Heydrich refused. He wanted a surgeon to be brought from Berlin. "But your condition requires an immediate operation", said Dick. They were speaking German, of course. Heydrich thought it over and in the end he agreed that Professor Walter Hollbaum of the German surgical clinic in Prague should be called in.

'He was taken to the theatre but I was not there as I had to stay in the room where the instruments were sterilised. Dr Dick was the only one who helped Professor Hollbaum during the operation. The wound was about eight centimetres deep and it contained a good deal of dirt and little splinters. Karl Hermann Frank, Emil Hácha, the President of the Protectorate, and members of the government waited in the corridor outside the theatre.

Bulovka Hospital still stands on Bulovka Street, not far from where the attack took place (see map page 48).

'After the operation Heydrich was taken to Dr Dick's office on the second floor. The Germans had emptied the whole floor, turning the patients out or sending them home, and they transformed the dining room into an SS barracks. They set up machine guns on the roof and SS, armed to the teeth, paced about the entrance below.

'No Czech doctor and no Czech member of the staff was allowed on the floor where Heydrich was. I tried to go up there to ask how he was doing. I said that I was on duty and that I was looking for Dr Puhala but they told me openly that I had no business there.

'So I have no exact information on Heydrich's condition after the operation. Perhaps they had to remove his spleen. I did not see him again. But Dr Dick said that he was coming along very well. His death surprised us all. Up to the last moment of his life, not one of the Czech doctors working at the Bulovka knew the truth.

'During the last days of Heydrich's life we lived in a kind of dream. Every day visitors appeared, wearing black uniforms, the cream of the SS with bunches of flowers. His own doctor flew in from Berlin and Frau Heydrich came to see him up until the day of his death.

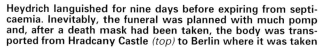

Heydrich languished for nine days before expiring from septicaemia. Inevitably, the funeral was planned with much pomp and, after a death mask had been taken, the body was transported from Hradcany Castle *(top)* to Berlin where it was taken **through the Ehrenhof (Courtyard of Honour) *(left)* of the new Reich Chancellery to lie in state in the Mosaiksaal (Hall of Mosaics) *(right)* surrounded by the flaming urns which were part and parcel of the Nazi ideology.**

'Septicaemia, they said. Blood transfusions could do nothing. Professor Herwig Hamperl, head of the German Institute of Pathology, and Professor Günther Weyrich, head of the German Institute of Forensic Medicine, drew up a joint report on their medical conclusions. Among other things, it reported that death occurred as a consequence of lesions in the vital parenchymatous organs caused by bacteria and possibly by poisons carried into them by the bomb splinters and deposited chiefly in the pleura, the diaphragm and the tissues in the neighbourhood of the spleen, there agglomerating and multiplying.'

Following his death on June 4, eight days after the attack, Heydrich's body lay in state in the forecourt of Hradcany Castle before being transferred to Berlin. There on June 8, amid much pomp and demonstration of mourning, he was buried in the Invaliden Cemetery.

Left: **Buried with German 'heroes' in the Invaliden Cemetery, there has been much debate and controversy as to where the grave lies today. For 40 years after the war, the burial ground was bisected by the Berlin Wall and by the time that came down in 1989, few of the Second World War headstones remained in situ.** *Right:* **'Anthropoid' historian Harry Marsh has it on good authority that this is the site of the grave.**

Kubis had been wounded in his left eye by the explosion and was almost within sight of the Novak's house at No. 5 Stranskeho Street when he nearly knocked a pedestrian over due to blood in his eye. In order not to draw any more attention to himself, he abandoned the cycle outside a Bata shoe shop on Rude Armady. Today the same building is occupied by a chemist shop called Teta.

When Jan Kubis descended the hill on his bicycle, he found refuge in the house of the Novak family. Mrs Novak was at home when Jan, wounded in the face, chest and hand from splinters, knocked at the door. He had left the bicycle, a blazon piece of evidence with bloodstains on the handlebars, propped outside the nearby Bata shoe shop. Mrs Novak sent her 14-year-old daughter, Jindriska, to fetch it but, in doing so, several passers-by spotted her and asked her if she had been in an accident. (Later this was to lead the Gestapo to trace and arrest the Novak family.)

Jozef Gabcik reached the house of another resistance family, Mr and Mrs Fafek; Adolf Opalka had reached the flat of Mrs Tereza Kasperova and Josef Valcik the house of Frantisek Sulek.

Meanwhile Nazi Secretary of State Karl Frank had telephoned Hitler at 12.15 p.m. informing him of the attack. Hitler flew into a rage, the more so when he learned that Heydrich had been travelling without an armed escort. Hitler immediately appointed Frank to take over the duties of Reichsprotektor, to begin an immediate search for the criminals responsible, and to offer a reward of one million marks for their capture or for information leading to their arrest. He also ordered that any persons found helping the attackers were to be shot together with their whole families and, additionally, 10,000 Czechs were to be taken as hostage and executed.

Immediately the manhunt for the attackers swung into top gear and Prague became the focus of attention throughout German-occupied Europe. Frank issued his first proclamation to the populace by radio at 4.30 p.m. and announced that a curfew would be in operation from 9 p.m. to 6 a.m. that night during which time all cinemas, restaurants, theatres and other places of entertainment were to close and all traffic was to leave the streets. The ordinance was broadcast by both German and Czech radio with increasing frequency during the afternoon and evening.

At 8 p.m. Frank informed Himmler of the measures already taken and, at 9.32 p.m., a State of Siege was proclaimed throughout the whole country. As darkness fell, 4,500 men of the Gestapo, SS, NSKK and Czech national police together with three German Army battalions began a huge dragnet operation throughout the city which was completely sealed off with sentries in every street. In all, 541 people were arrested and 111 taken into custody for further questioning. Although the sweep failed to unearth any of the attackers, Mrs Kasperova had a nasty moment when her house was searched. There was just time for Opalka to secrete himself in a small broom cupboard before the SS burst in but fortunately they did not move aside the sofa which stood in front of the hiding place.

The following day Frank flew to Berlin to confer with Hitler. While the Gestapo had failed to make any positive arrests during the night's city-wide search, they were not totally without leads. During the apprehension of a resistance worker some time before, a briefcase had been found containing names and photographs of Czech agents which had been prepared for false identity papers. On May 28, the Germans distributed posters showing one of these photographs of Jozef Gabcik (although they incorrectly named him as Miroslav Valcik) offering a reward of 100,000 Czech crowns for his arrest. Purely by chance, the Gestapo had stumbled on more than they realised.

At the same time all the witnesses in the tramcars, surrounding houses and passers-by were taken in for detailed questioning. The articles left at the scene had already been minutely examined and were put on display in the Bata shoe shop at No. 6 Wenceslas Square in central Prague from 9 a.m. on May 28. A full description of the objects found was also given on striking red and black posters.

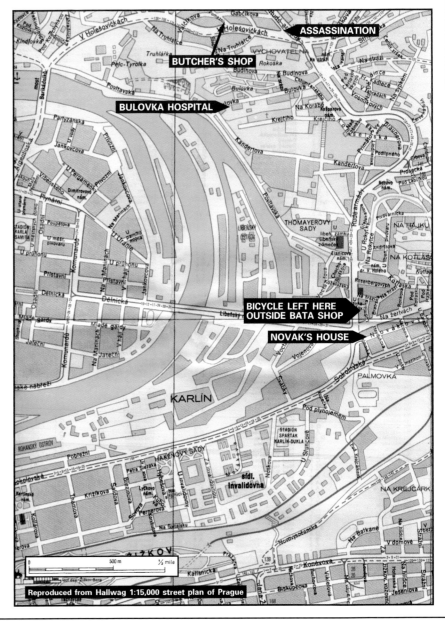

Reproduced from Hallwag 1:15,000 street plan of Prague

The official police report states that on the night of May 27/28, a force of over 2,000 police were deployed on the manhunt: 600 Ordnungspolizei, 1,200 Protektoratspolizei and 300 Gestapo operatives. These numbers had been increased to nearly 10,000 men by the time Heydrich died. It was inevitable that the assailants would be discovered in their 'safe' houses so a more secure hiding place had to be found. An ideal sanctuary was suggested as the crypt of St Cyril and St Methodius on Resslova Street and arrangements were made with the priest, Dr Vladimir Petrek *(right)*, to secrete the men there.

However, in spite of an efficient start to their investigation, the Gestapo failed to uncover the whereabouts of the four assailants. They were all still in the city being constantly moved from house to house but increasing Gestapo pressure made it essential to find a completely safe place where they could hide, if necessary, for weeks until the furore died down. It was at this point that the underground leader 'Uncle Hajsky' approached the Dean of the Orthodox Church in Prague, Jan Sonnevend, for help. The latter suggested that the crypt of St Cyril and St Methodius Church on Resslova Street would make an ideal sanctuary and arrangements were made with the Priest, Dr Vladimir Petrek, to receive the fugitives. Jan Kubis arrived first on May 30 to be followed by Josef Valcik, Adolf Opalka, Jaroslav Svarc of the 'Tin' group, Josef Bublik and Jan Hruby of the 'Bioscop' team and finally Jozef Gabcik who arrived on June 1. Seven men in all.

As the men sheltered in the church crypt, the Germans intensified their investigations; Prague became a hot-bed of arrests with daily proclamations of executions of innocent hostages as the Nazis vented their wrath on the Czechs. However, to the seven men in the crypt, not knowing at that stage that their target was on his deathbed in Bulovka Hospital, it seemed that their futile action had only brought death and suffering to their own countrymen.

For a week following the attack and two weeks after the death of Heydrich, in spite of the most stringent measures against the Czech population, the Gestapo investigation was no nearer finding the culprits. Then, on June 16, Karel Curda of Adolf Opalka's 'Out Distance' group called at the Gestapo HQ in the Petschek Palace at No. 20 Bredovska (today Politickych veznu) in Prague to betray his fellow Czechs. The official report, written on June 25, 1942 by the Chief of the Prague Gestapo, SS-Standartenführer Dr Hans Geschke, describes in detail the depth of his treachery:

'Curda stated that he recognised one of the briefcases left behind at the place of the outrage. During the interrogation, the results of which agreed with those of the technical criminal investigation, it at once became apparent that we were dealing with a clue of the first importance and that Curda's statements were true. Later he admitted that he was a parachutist and that he had landed in Protectorate territory during the night of March 28/29, 1942 together with five other agents. He recognised the briefcase immediately, saying that he had seen it in the possession of another parachutist at the flat occupied by the Svatos family and he confirmed that this briefcase contained an English light machine gun with which he was familiar.

'As his description of this parachutist agreed with the description of one of the criminals, Jozef Gabcik (cover-name Zdenda Vyskocil), formerly domiciled at Poluvsie near Zilina, was set down as a suspect. Curda did not know Gabcik's present dwelling place. The head office of the state police worked upon this clue with the utmost energy and, employing all possible means, it discovered a direct lead after no more than 36 hours of the most concentrated activity. This clue pointed to the criminals and in the subsequent five hours it led to their discovery.

'Curda mentioned his suspicion that the second criminal might be Jan Kubis (cover-name Ota Navratil), Gabcik's best friend; but he was unable to confirm this. The two parachutists named by Curda were unknown to us as enemy agents; their names too were unknown. The weapons of English manufacture found at the place of the attack showed that parachutists had certainly taken part in the outrage. When at last Curda, in the

Today the church is the 'National Memorial to the Heroes of the Heydrich Terror'.

49

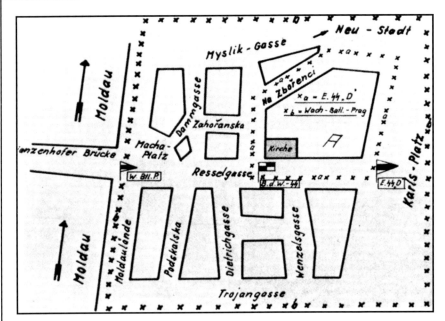

Sadly it was one of the Czech parachutists, Karel Curda from the 'Out Distance' group, who went to the Gestapo to betray the seven now sheltering in the church, although it appears that Curda himself was not aware of their actual hiding place. However, his treachery led to more arrests and by June 17 someone had been broken under torture. Immediately the SS-Ersatz-Bataillon 'Deutschland' and the SS-Wach-Bataillon Prag were ordered to surround the church, this plan of the double cordon which was thrown up coming from the German report.

At 2 a.m. on June 18, the first orders were issued and by 4.15 a.m. SS troops had formed two cordons around the church. Ten minutes later Kriminalkommissar Heinz Pannwitz, one of the Gestapo chiefs leading the investigation, entered the church with his team and interpreter.

For more than 14 days the little church on Resslova Street had been a refuge for the seven Czechs. They took it in turns to keep watch from the balcony above the rood screen that separated the altar from the congregation while the others slept in the crypt. The latter was reached through a 60 cm-square hole covered by a thick flagstone set with an iron ring, normally covered by a coconut mat. It led down to a chamber some 15 by 3.5 metres with a series of empty, square-shaped niches set in the walls which, in former years, had been the repository for coffins, end on. On the far side, a set of stone stairs led up to the nave of the church but this opening was permanently sealed by a heavy stone slab. A small, barred opening, high up in the wall, provided ventilation from the street. As the only way to enter the crypt was one man at a time, the place was virtually impregnable to assault. A bucket containing lime and chlorine provided the only WC.

Because the sacristan's wife, presently on holiday, could not be relied on to keep her mouth shut, it was decided on June 16 to move the seven men before she returned to new hiding places in the countryside on Friday, June 19, from where it was hoped they could eventually get back to England.

course of subsequent interrogations, betrayed part of the clandestine shelter network used by enemy agents and known to him, these shelters were discreetly watched according to our tactical methods, all at the same time and as rapidly as possible. This investigation finally resulted in the identification of the Svatos family, the owners of the second briefcase found at the place of the outrage, and of Mrs Maria Moravcová, the owner of the woman's bicycle.

'The bicycle had in fact been lent to Zdenda, alias Gabcik, and the Svatos family's briefcases to Ota, alias Kubis; from the criminal point of view this entirely proved these persons' complicity in the attempt on the life of SS-Obergruppenführer Reinhard Heydrich.'

Curda's traitorous act led to a series of arrests throughout June 17, one of the Gestapo's first calls being at the home of the Moravec family (where Jan and Jozef had first stayed when they reached Prague) which was raided at dawn. As the Gestapo prepared to take the family away, Mrs Moravec made an excuse to visit the toilet where she swallowed poison. 'Uncle Hajsky' living in the same street was next on the list; he too committed suicide as the Gestapo smashed down his front door. The arrests continued throughout the day to be followed by the torture of those taken alive. By midnight someone had broken and the hiding place of the seven was known. SS-Gruppenführer Frank was immediately informed who, in turn, roused SS-Brigadeführer Karl von Treuenfeldt who was instructed to mount an immediate operation to seal off the church.

Skizze über Lage wichtiger Punkte in der Karl-Borromäus-Kirche Prag (ohne Massstab) = Sketch indicating the location of important points in the Karl Borromäus Church in Prague (not to scale). [1] Trapdoor to the crypt used by the assassins. [2] Entrance to the crypt that had been sealed with a flagstone. [3] Spiral staircase to the choir balcony. [4] Side entrance. [5] Window from which iron grating had been removed as an escape route. [6] Entrance to office. [7] Disused entrance closed off. [8] House of the church assistant.

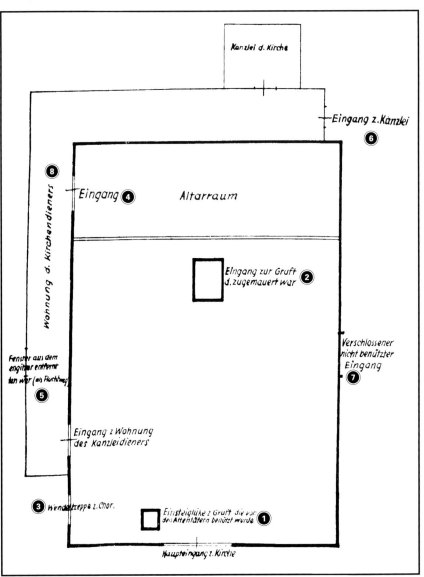

On entering the church the Germans were greeted by a hail of gun-fire from the balcony where Jan Kubis was mounting guard together with Adolf Opalka and Jaroslav Svarc. The Germans annotated this photo with the direction of fire.

Robert Porter found that the balcony railings still bear the marks of the battle.

As dawn was breaking on Thursday, June 18, Lieutenant Opalka, the most senior of those present, Kubis and Svarc were mounting guard on the balcony. Perhaps they had already been alerted by the noise of the troops arriving in the street but, nevertheless, when Kriminalkommissar Pannwitz entered the church, they were ready and waiting. As the Germans approached the altar, shots crashed out from above, one of the Gestapo men, Obersekretär Kurt Kahlo, immediately being wounded. Pannwitz shouted for them to retire and it was more by luck than judgment that there were no more casualties as they crowded back to the door.

On hearing the firing the SS, who had set up a machine gun in a window of the school opposite, opened up on the large church windows. The battle had begun. Detachments of storm troopers were ordered into the building but the excellent vantage point for the three defenders on the balcony routed every attack. The only way up was via a spiral staircase, impossible to ascend except in single file. During the next two hours, the three Czechs held off every attempt by the SS to storm their position, the interior of the church becoming a shambles of broken wood and stone. The crash of grenades and gunfire must have been agonising for the other four, impotent in the vault below, knowing their comrades were fighting for their lives. The end came about 7 a.m. Pannwitz's interpreter, Josef Chalupsky, was on hand and later described what happened:

'Suddenly there was silence up there, an agonising silence throughout the church. The SS waited a moment and then they went up; they

The windows facing Resslova Street were shattered by machine gun fire.

found three parachutists covered with blood. They came out of the church carrying one body and two dying men. They laid the dead man on a church carpet outside on the pavement. They took the two others to hospital, but they died without having recovered consciousness.

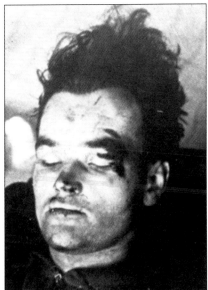

Killed on the balcony: Adolf Opalka and Jaroslav Svarc. Jan Kubis was mortally wounded and bled to death.

'This was at about seven o'clock in the morning. The Gestapo brought the traitor Curda and Ata Moravec, Mrs Moravec's son who had been arrested on June 17. They showed them the dead man and asked his name. Pannwitz did not know who was hidden in the church: perhaps he was thinking only of Kubis and Gabcik. Curda was silent, confused, ashamed, but at last he muttered: "Opalka".

'Meanwhile they were searching the inside of the church for the way into the crypt. The nave was almost destroyed, the windows were broken and the altar overturned. Through loudspeakers set up in the street the Germans called upon the besieged men to surrender, promising that they would be treated as prisoners of war. The men hidden in the crypt said nothing. I do not know how the Gestapo learnt they were there — possibly from clues inside the church. No sound had come from the crypt during the battle. [*An extra set of clothing had been discovered in the church. Ed*]

'But now they began to fight: and they knew how to fight. It is said the Germans brought Curda to the only window to tell his former friends to stop firing. It seems that Ata Moravec refused to do so. The parachutists replied with a burst of fire. From that moment on they knew who had betrayed them.

'The loudspeakers and the machine guns were no use. Either someone suggested it to him or Pannwitz himself had the idea of calling for the fire brigade. About eight o'clock, a Nazi officer came to the switchboard where I was waiting and telephoned for the pumps to be sent to Resslova Street. As he left, the officer said to me: "We shall need you in a few minutes. As soon as the firemen get here."

When the fire brigade arrived at the church it was the intention of the Germans to flood the crypt by hosing water through the small barred ventilation slot. Much against their will, the Czech firemen were forced to help. The SS were already firing into the crypt through the small barred window but without effect.

Once it was known that there were others below in the crypt, an attempt was made to smoke out the defenders by introducing a pipe through the 15cm by 105cm ventilation opening. When this failed the fire brigade were called to pump in water.

One fireman was ordered to smash in the bars with a hammer; when this was done tear gas cannisters were tossed inside. However, the four Czechs had a ladder and, as fast as the bombs were thrown in, they were returned to the street. They also did not stop firing from inside which made any direct approach to the opening a hazardous operation.

The Germans then set up a floodlight to attempt to blind the defenders but this was shot out before the light had even been switched on.

An attempt was then made to introduce smoke into the vault but each time the pipe was inserted through the slot it was pushed out from inside.

Having tried direct gun-fire at the slot, and attempts to introduce smoke followed by water, an alternate way of getting into the crypt had to be found.

Entry to the crypt was via a small trapdoor (see plan page 50) sealed with a flagstone.

Those inside had used a ladder to descend but the first German who was lowered by rope got shot.

All the time, attempts were being made inside the church to reach the four defenders as Josef Chalupsky explains:

'The firing could be heard in the street. I did not want to think about it but I knew the parachutists in the crypt were fighting a hopeless battle unless they could escape by a tunnel. But I knew the Germans had lined the banks of the Vltava and that they were watching the outfalls of the drains. Even if the parachutists succeeded in finding a way out, death was waiting for them at its mouth.

'The SS came for me. "Come to the church." Once again I went in by the priest's corridor. To one side there was the sacristan's flat: through a small window in the kitchen one could see the inside of the church. An earthquake could not have caused more damage. The door through which Pannwitz and his men had passed, and through which they had fled from the fire of the parachutists hidden in the gallery, was no more than a blackened hole. This door led to the altar, which was separated from the nave, as it is in all Orthodox churches, by a high wooden screen. Now the screen and the altar were overturned and riddled with bullet holes. The ground was strewn with paintings and books and other religious objects.

'It was a baroque church, and it measured roughly 45 by 15 metres with the main door opposite the altar. Close to this entrance a group of SS were leaning over a hole, quite a narrow hole; one of the Gestapo said that the men used it for getting in and out, probably with the help of a ladder.

'An SS man said to me, "You're too late". I saw what he meant; by the dark hole there stood a man; he was translating what Pannwitz said into Czech. Leaning forward a little, but not too much, so as to avoid the bullets, he called down the hole, "Surrender! You will not be harmed".

'Silence below: then the parachutists began firing again. The answer was clear. Pannwitz beckoned to a man with a black beard, wearing handcuffs, Dr Petrek, the priest of the church. The superintendent ordered him to tell the men in the crypt to surrender. The priest hesitated. His eyes had a feverish light and his pain-racked face showed they had tortured him. "Hurry up. We haven't much time to spare", cried Pannwitz ironically.

'Dr Petrek looked at us all, took a step towards the hole, and said, "I am ordered to tell you that you must surrender. Therefore I do so. And that nothing unpleasant will happen to you — that you will be treated as prisoners of war".

'Now for the first time voices were heard from below. "We are Czechs! We shall never surrender: never, do you hear? Never! Never!"

'Once more a voice from the crypt cried "Never!" and there was a burst of fire.

'The men in the crypt were still holding out. Once again the loudspeakers in the street called upon them to surrender. An ultimatum was delivered: if they did not surrender, the whole church would be destroyed and they would die in the ruins. But the parachutists' only reply was a burst of fire.

'The SS officers called for volunteers. The group formed with no great haste. At first no one at all came forward; then after a fresh appeal a few men made up their minds and then the commanding officer picked the rest. They were taken into the church. Kriminalkommissar Pannwitz addressed them with a few well-chosen words. He spoke of the call of honour and showed them the black hole. A rope was brought; one end was put round a "volunteer's" chest, and he was lowered into the hole. A howl of pain. He had been hit by the parachutists and had to be hauled out with a wounded leg. The hole was so narrow that it did not allow for the smallest movement.

Today the crypt of the church where the men fought for their lives has been transformed into a memorial-cum-museum.

Realising that there must be another larger entrance to lower coffins into the crypt, the carpet in front of the altar steps was pulled back to reveal a large slab. Explosives were called for and when the smoke cleared, a flight of steps could be seen leading down.

'The superintendent and the SS commander were completely at a loss: they saw they could lower one volunteer after another without achieving anything. And outside, in the street, K. H. Frank was stamping up and down.

'So now in their baffled fury they gave orders for the carpets to be rolled back and the whole floor of the nave examined. In a few minutes the ground was bare; one SS watched the hole and the others searched feverishly. Pannwitz hurried to and fro: there must certainly be a way into the crypt — in former times the coffins of the monks had been laid there. How were the coffins taken down? There must be stairs, but where were they? Somewhere at the place where a stone sounded hollow. At last to their delight they found it, a heavy slab concealed beneath the altar.

'The Kriminalkommissar sent for the firemen and ordered them to break it. Behind them stood the SS, their rifles in their hands. But the slab held firm, and after 20 minutes a fireman tried to explain in pidgin German that it was impossible to deal with it with the tools they had there. The firemen were sent away and the SS ordered in with dynamite. They did something round the slab, then we were told to leave the church. They blasted the slab, and the heavy stone broke in two. An eager, inquisitive Gestapo man pulled away part of the wreckage and peered in to

The precise moment when Czech firemen got hold of the ladder. With their means of reaching the ventilator slot (some 3.5 metres from the cellar floor) denied them, it was the beginning of the end for Valcik, Gabcik, Bublik and Hruby.

see what was inside as bullets whipped past his head. Pannwitz grinned with satisfaction: there were steps leading into the crypt; this was the way down.

'Once again the SS were called upon. They were to go down the steps, and this time they were sent group by group, in waves of attack. How I admired those men in the crypt: for hours now they must have known that their

struggle was hopeless, that sooner or later they would be killed; but they did not give in. They fought like lions.

'The first SS attack failed. When they had gone a few steps down a burst of fire stopped them dead and some of them fell; they could not see clearly, and the stairs being so narrow and steep the wounded men threw the others into disorder. They had to retreat.

The battle is over. Once the water was pumped out, this photograph was taken of the detritus.

'Meanwhile, in the street, a fireman was ordered to get hold of the ladder the besieged men used for pushing away the hoses. Frank wanted to flood them out — the fireman obeyed. He went along the wall of the church and, just as a parachutist was thrusting at the hose, he grasped the end of the ladder and pulled it out.

'Now the parachutists' position was becoming critical. Water was flowing into the crypt and they no longer had anything to push the hose away with, for the little barred window was too high. At the same time the SS launched another attack, throwing grenades, and steadily the water flooded into the crypt.

'Yet the parachutists went on firing. They hit back without a pause, resisting ferociously. And then suddenly, at about noon, four isolated shots rang out below. After that, a great silence.

'Pannwitz stiffened. He looked at the way into the crypt and beckoned to an SS officer.

The SS hesitated, then sent two soldiers, who went cautiously down: one step, two steps, three. Still silence. They looked back at the officer, who waved them on. They moved down further still, everyone in the church watching them, hardly breathing. They vanished into the crypt and then called up: the officer hesitated no longer; with his revolver in his hand he rushed down. A moment later he re-appeared, wet above the knees, and cried, "Fertig!" It was over.

In the communist era, access to the crypt was by the opening the Germans had used in 1942. However, as Prague grew in popularity following the fall of the Iron Curtain, it became impractical to continue to use this for access as it was directly in front of the altar. So this was sealed and a section of stonework removed at the front of the church to provide a new entrance for visitors.

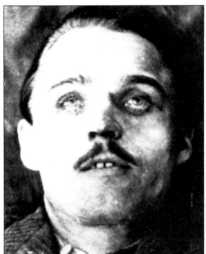

Above left: The Czech informer, Karel Curda, circled, who had been trained in England with the others, examines the results of his handywork as the bodies are laid out on church carpets on the pavement. *Above right:* Jan Hruby (foreground) and Josef Bublik played no part in the attack on Heydrich but chose to die in the crypt with the others. *Left:* Josef Valcik was the look-out man further up the street who signalled the approach of the car (see page 38). *Lower left:* Detailed for the operation from the beginning, Jozef Gabcik was the one who had Heydrich in his sights only to have his gun misfire at the critical moment. He held out with the other three men in the crypt until all the ammunition was exhausted — except for one round each.

'It was no longer dramatic: it was deeply sad. The firemen took their hoses and went away; the Nazis laid the bodies on the pavement — K. H. Frank wanted to see them. Before they were taken out of the church I looked at their faces. You must certainly have seen the photographs. I did not know their names; they were soaking and covered with blood. Each had kept his last bullet, had killed himself with it and had fallen in the water. There they lay beside one another, in civilian clothes, their eyes open. The vanquished or the victors? Later the Gestapo took them away to the Pathological Institute and brought witnesses to identify them there.

Harry Marsh pictured the corner where the bodies were laid.

'I went down into the crypt, dimly lit by the little window, the one the water had come through. The place was bigger than I had expected. I had to stay on the steps — the floor was quite hidden under the water: half a metre deep or rather more. I was too overwhelmed to attend to details of that kind.

'I lit a match. There were scraps of paper floating in the water — money and identity papers torn to shreds: they had thought of everything. Bloody marks on the walls; bloody marks on the steps. And water everywhere. But the ceiling of the crypt was high, and they could have held out for a long time, probably for a whole day before it was completely flooded. No, it was not the water that beat the parachutists.

'What was it then? There is only one likely explanation — lack of ammunition. Later the crypt was cleaned out: underclothes were found, stoves, tins of food; but not a single round of ammunition. It is true that the Gestapo report speaks of the flooding but there is not the least foundation for it. No, the parachutists fought to the death. It was only lack of ammunition that put an end to their struggle.

'A heap of bricks was found near the little window. They had vainly tried to pierce the wall of the church: there was no way out. From that moment on they had known they were condemned.

'I left the church. A German band was marching down Resslova Street, playing a strident Nazi victory march. It was attempting to conceal the Germans' immense disappointment that the parachutists should have chosen their own death. Not one of them would ever speak now.'

A desperate attempt had been made to try to break through to reach a reputed secret tunnel but to no avail.

The German's horrific wave of vengeance began from the moment the attack was perpetrated. Athough Hitler had ordered the immediate execution of 10,000 Czechs as a reprisal, this was seen by the new acting Protektor Karl Frank to be a counter-productive move at that time when every effort had to be directed towards capturing the assassins. Nevertheless scores of civilians were arrested and tortured in a frantic attempt to get information.

Even before the siege of the church had begun, retribution was being exacted on a little mining village 15 kilometres north-west of the city. The Gestapo had intercepted a letter which appeared to indicate that there was some connection between Heydrich's assassination and the Horák family living in Lidice as they had a son serving in the RAF in Britain. Although house-to-house searches produced no evidence, the Nazis were hell-bent on carrying out an act of vengeance for the death of 'an outstanding man of the German nation', and the total obliteration of the village began a few hours after midnight on June 9/10.

Then, at dawn on June 10, six days after Heydrich had expired, German police surrounded a small village 15 kilometres northwest of Prague . . . its name: Lidice. All the 88 children living there were taken from their parents and were subsequently put to death. Their mothers, 60 in all, were shipped to the concentration camps at Ravensbrück, Auschwitz and Mauthausen where they were executed. The men were lined up in the village and summarily shot and buried in a pit on Horák's farm. The whole of Lidice was then dynamited, bulldozed flat and the rubble carted away to leave a completely barren site which was then grassed over so that no trace of the village remained. The following day this prepared statement was then broadcast:

'In the course of the search for the murderers of SS-Obergruppenführer Heydrich, it was ascertained that the population of this village supported and assisted the perpetrators. Apart from the help given to them, the population also committed other hostile acts, such as the keeping of an illegal dump of munitions and arms, the maintenance of an illegal transmitter and hoarding of an extraordinary large quantity of goods which are controlled. The male inhabitants have been

shot, the women taken to concentration camps, the children put into suitable educational establishments. The buildings have been razed to the ground; the name of the community has been erased.'

Later, the same fate befell the smaller village of Lezáky; 17 men and 16 women were shot and 14 children gassed; just two little girls survived. Afterwards the village was completely obliterated.

Show trials were held in Prague and, on September 3, 1942, Dr Petrek, Bishop Gorazd and two representatives of the Orthodox church were sentenced to death for providing the building as a refuge for the attackers. Later that month, on the 29th, 252 other Czechs were condemned to death for supporting or sheltering the attackers including Mr Moravec and his son Ata, the Novaks with their little daughter Jindriska, and the Fafek family. The entire families and all the relatives of Valcik and Kubis were rounded up from all over Czechoslovakia including Opalka's father and aunt and taken to the little fortress of Terezin en route for the Mauthausen concentration camp in Austria where they all disappeared in October 1942. Only Gabcik's family escaped as they lived in Slovakia which

was an independent Fascist State where the Germans had little direct contact.

From information received from Karel Curda, the Germans began a massive roundup of the Czech underground network and dozens of operators were arrested and executed. Revenge was also taken with the systematic murder of thousands of Czech political prisoners already held in concentration camps. The price of the assassination of Reinhard Heydrich was very high.

German records state that 19 officers and 740 other ranks were involved in the battle in Resslova Street but to this total one must add the forces of the security services. Fourteen Germans were killed and 21 wounded in the six-hour battle.

Eleven weapons were found in the church two of them being nickel-finished .32 Colt pistols Nos. 539370 and 540416 which the Germans proved, after forensic tests, to have been used by Jan Kubis and Jozef Gabcik at the scene of the attack. Jan had shot a policeman during his escape on the bicycle. (We wrote to Colt's in America and established that both pistols were part of a shipment of 50 supplied to the British Purchasing Commission in New York on April 28, 1941.)

No sooner had the funeral eulogies for Heydrich finished in Berlin than Hitler ordered SS-Grüppenführer Frank 'to make up for his death'. Any village found to have harboured the killers was to be burned down and levelled completely while all the male inhabitants were to be executed. At Lidice, on June 10, the men were taken to the rear of the Horák farm where they were lined up and shot in groups of five or ten. Mattresses taken from local houses provided protection to the shooters from splash back. By afternoon 173 lay dead. A total of 203 women and 105 children were first taken to the village school and then into the nearby town of Kladno where they remained for three days. Four pregnant women were subjected to forced abortions before being despatched to different concentration camps. The rest of the women were sent to Ravensbrück. Eighty-eight Lidice children went to Lódz where they were examined by officials from the Reich Race and Settlement Office which selected seven for Germanisation. The remaining 81 children were sent by the Gestapo to Chelmno extermination camp where they were gassed. After the war only 17 surviving children were traced.

June 1945: British and American soldiers and war correspondents stand at the mass grave of the murdered men. The sign reads 'Here lie the citizens of Lidice murdered June 10, 1942 by German occupation forces'. The town lay in the background with the church and school near the centre between the two trees; all was completely wiped from the face of the earth.

The bodies of the five defenders who died in the church — Opalka, Gabcik, Valcik, Bublik and Hruby — were laid on the pavement outside the church to be photographed. Kubis and Svarc, severely wounded in the first battle on the balcony, were taken to hospital where they died without regaining conciousness. The Svatos family which had sheltered Gabcik were brought to the church and forced to identify the bodies; they named two, Gabcik and Valcik. Mrs Moravec's son Ata, who had already been hideously tortured also identified the two Josefs. The five bodies were then taken to the Prague Pathological Institute for autopsies to be performed. There the heads of the two men who had mounted the actual attack on Heydrich, Kubis and Gabcik, were severed from the bodies which were then cremated. The heads were then preserved in alcohol and retained in Gestapo headquarters in the Petschek Palace on Bredovska. At the end of the war the flasks with the heads disappeared.

After the war Pilot Officer Josef Horák returned to Lidice but as he was killed in a flying accident in 1948 after he had returned to Britain, he never lived to see the foundations of his family home emerge from the ground.

This young child was pictured in 1945 perched on the stump of what once was a well-known cherry tree in the school playground at Lidice, the school being across the road from the town church. The destruction was so complete that even trees and shrubs were cut down and burned.

Local people marked the site where the executions had taken place with this birchwood cross.

The Memorial to the Children Victims of the War by Marie Uchytilova was erected on the site of the school.

Two weeks later another Czech village, Lezáky, some 90-odd kilometres east of Prague (see map page 33), was similarly destroyed although this time a radio set belonging to the 'Silver A' group led by Alfred Bartos was discovered by the Gestapo. Bartos committed suicide and on June 24 SS troops raided the village to execute all 33 adults (men and women) and send 14 children to the gas chambers, before razing the houses to the ground. Lezáky was never rebuilt and only memorials remain today.

The turncoat Karel Curda changed his name to Jerhot, married a German woman and became a trusted associate of the Gestapo which had rewarded him well for his treachery. However his change of name did not deceive the Czech authorities. He was arrested in June 1945, brought to trial and was hanged in 1947.

After the June 18 battle, SS-Oberst-gruppenführer Kurt Daluege replaced Karl Frank as Reichsprotektor. At the end of the war, Frank was arrested and convicted by a Czech court for the reprisal against Lidice and publicly hanged near Prague on May 22, 1946.

After the war the Czech government erected a memorial and museum on the site of Lezáky although the village itself was not rebuilt. The rebuilding of Lidice, however, was begun in 1948 on a new site a few hundred metres from its original position. As Lidice had been a miner's village, contributions were received from British, Swedish and French trade unionists and the British Union of Mineworkers collecting £32,374 for the 'Lidice shall live' campaign. By 1949 the construction of the new village had been completed and the houses in New Lidice were given to every woman and child who had survived the Nazi concentration camps.

The Czechs did not delay convicting Karl Frank and hanging him in front of an invited audience in Pankrác Prison on May 22, 1946. Karel Curda followed him to the gallows in 1947.

Also no time was lost in demolishing the memorial which the Germans had erected on assassination corner. *Below:* **Here Heydrich's widow Lina and her two sons, Klaus and Heider, pay their respects on the first anniversary of his death in 1943. Klaus was run over and killed later that year on October 24.**

Although the road layout was drastically altered during the communist years, the Czechs unveiled their Operation Anthropoid Memorial there on Wednesday, May 27, 2009 at precisely 10.35 a.m. which was exactly 67 years to the minute when the attack took place. A bronze slab set into the ground in front of the memorial bears the inscription: 'Here on this spot on May 27, 1942 at 10.35, the heroic Czechoslovakian paratroopers Jan Kubis and Jozef Gabcik carried out one of the most significant resistant acts of the Second World War — the assassination of acting Reich Protector Reinhard Heydrich. They could never complete their mission without the help from hundreds of Czech patriots who paid for their bravery by their own lives.'

The memorial was designed to symbolise the resolve and bravery of the paratroopers and to illustrate the danger of their actions in 1942. The monument was chosen after a competition opened to artists and architects, announced by the City Hall of the Municipal District of Prague 8, winner of which was the joint submission by sculptors David Mojescik and Michal Smeral and architects Miroslava Tumová and Jiri Gulbis. Basic concept of the nine-metre-high monument is the steel pillar in the form of the triangular wedge of the Czechoslovakian flag. Two of the silhouettes represent Czechoslovak soldiers and the third is a representative of the civilians, who played their integral role in the resistance. The shape of the bronze-cast figures is inspired by the famous drawing *Vitruvian man* by Leonardo da Vinci of a man with outstretched arms and legs, and is at the same time an allusion to the code-name of the agents' mission — 'Anthropoid' — i.e. man.

There is never an absence of floral tributes at the church. The plaque reads: 'On June 18, 1942, in this Orthodox Church of the Saints Cyril and Methodius, fighters of the Czechoslovak army abroad Adolf Opalka, Jozef Gabcik, Jan Kubis, Josef Valcik, Josef Bublik, Jan Hruby and Jaroslav Svarc died in defence of our freedom. Bishop Gorazd, the priest Cikl, Dr. Petrek, the President of the religious community, and other Czech patriots who provided a haven to the soldiers were executed. We will never forget them.'

In Prague itself the church of St Cyril and St Methodius was opened as a memorial shrine to Czech resistance in July 1966 although the Communist government played down the fact that the operation was mounted from England (i.e. the West). High Mass is celebrated each year on June 18. The crypt is open to visitors daily and one now descends through a new entrance made in the outer façade of the church to a small museum with photographs and personal effects displayed in showcases. The damage inside the church has been repaired but the wall around the ventilator slot still bears the marks of German bullets. An inscribed plaque has been mounted just above and flowers are in evidence all the year round.

DR. MIROSLAV INVANOV, 1972

It was somewhat ironic that when Hitler visited his next conquest, the one-time capital of East Prussia that had been taken from Germany by the Treaty of Versailles, he came in a capital ship, the size of which had also been determined by the terms of the Treaty. The *Deutschland* was a battleship that had been launched in May 1931 but the Treaty restricted its size to 10,000 tons with a maximum armament of 11-inch guns whereas normally a full-blown battleship like the *Bismarck* would weigh in at over 40,000 tons and be armed with a multitude of guns up to 21 inches.

Memel Territory

Under Article 99 of the Treaty of Versailles, Germany renounced in favour of the Principal Allied and Associated Powers the port of Memel, with a small territory surrounding it.

Upon the ratification of the Treaty, the Allies occupied and administered this territory for three years. Meanwhile, the suggestion had been made that Memel might be given a status in regard to Lithuania similar to that which had been accorded Danzig in relation to Poland. The administration of Memel was in the hands of a French High Commissioner, with the old German Direktorium retained as the executive organ, which, according to Lithuanian claims, pursued a policy hostile to the Lithuanians. Then on January 9, 1923 the Lithuanians seized Memel in a surprise attack.

After negotiations between the Lithuanian Government and the Conference of Ambassadors, and action taken by the League of Nations, a convention was signed in Paris on May 8, 1924, between Great Britain, France, Italy and Japan on the one side, and Lithuania on the other, by the terms of which Memel Territory was placed under the sovereignty of Lithuania. An annex was attached to the convention constituting the statute for Memel Territory, which provided that Memel was to enjoy 'legislative, judicial, administrative and financial autonomy' within the limits prescribed in the statute, with a governor appointed by the President of the Lithuanian Republic. In a second annex to the convention the port of Memel was described 'as a port of international concern' to be placed under a Harbour Board, which was to include among its members a technical expert of neutral nationality appointed by the League of Nations.

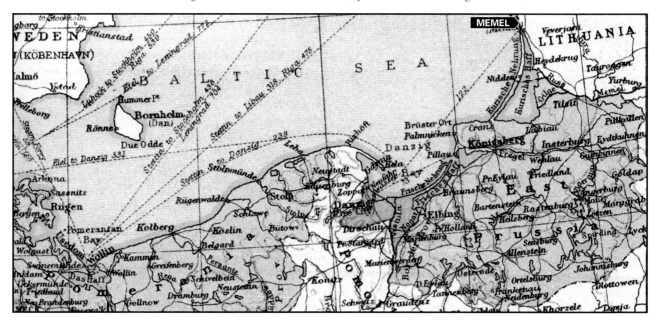

Memel (also known by its Lithuanian name of Klaipeda) in the Baltic, dated from 1252, later being included in the Kingdom of Prussia. The first verse of the old German National Anthem even included the line: 'Von der Maas bis an die Memel' referring to fact that the country stretched from the River Meuse to the River Memel, the town of that name being the most northerly after the unification of Germany in 1871. Under the Treaty of Versailles, Memel Territory was detached from Germany and made a protectorate, the French becoming the provisional administrators. When it was mooted that it might become a Free City like Danzig, the Lithuanians staged a revolt in January 1923 to take the territory by force, the League of Nations reluctantly accepting the annexation. As tensions in Europe increased, Lithuania anticipated that Germany would make a move to try to regain its possession, and sure enough on March 20, 1939, German Foreign Minister Joachim von Ribbentrop delivered an ultimation demanding the surrender of Memel. Unable to raise international support, two days later Lithuania peaceably gave in, while retaining the use of the harbour.

Hitler could not wait to make his entrance and the *Deutschland*, accompanied by Germany's Baltic Fleet, arrived on March 23.

She was later renamed the *Lützow* and reclassified as a heavy cruiser which the Royal Navy referred to as a 'pocket battleship'.

INCORPORATION

In the atmosphere of international terror created after the sudden occupation and dismemberment of Czechoslovakia by Germany, Hitler made a request to the Lithuanian Government that it cede Memel to Germany. Lithuania complied with this request, and on March 22, 1939 a treaty was signed with Germany regarding the cession of this territory.

On March 23, Hitler arrived in Memel on board the battleship *Deutschland*, and the whole of the German Baltic fleet entered the harbour. In a speech in the city, Hitler thanked the Memellanders for their loyalty during the separation from Germany. He also said that 'we know what we have to expect from another part of the world. We have no intention of imposing suffering on that other world, but merely of making good the suffering which it has imposed on us, and I believe that to a great extent we have come to the end of this unique reparation.'

After the war Memel ditched the German name and, as Klaipeda, was incorporated into Lithuania, the Soviets making good use of the foremost ice-free port in the Baltic, building new docks and shipyards. In March 1990 Lithuania was the first of the Soviet republics to declare that it was independent, later being admitted as a member of the North Atlantic Treaty Organisation. A popular watering hole for cruise ships, the contrast with 1939 could not be greater, and in 2014 the port surpassed the Latvian capital Riga for the first time with visits by 64 cruises, including that by the Italian-flagged 114,000-ton *Costa Pacifica*.

Aboard the *Deutschland*, Hitler signed the 'law concerning the reunion of Memelland with the German Reich. Under the terms of this law, Memel Territory was incorporated into the German Reich and included within the province of East Prussia, namely, in the district of Gumbinnen. Inhabitants of Memelland were declared German citizens if they were German citizens on July 30, 1924, and if on March 22, 1939 they had their domicile in the territory of Memel or in the German Reich. According to this law, the whole body of German law, and also Prussian law, was to be enforced in Memel Territory as from May 1, 1939 with such exceptions as the proper German ministers might decide. The Reich Minister of the Interior was authorised to carry out the incorporation.

On March 23, 1939, a decree was published by which the Reichsmark was made legal tender and Lithuanian currency was replaced by the Reichsmark at the rate of one Lithuanian lit to 40 Reichspfennigs.

RAPHAEL LEMKIN, 1944

69

Albania

When Italian troops occupied Albania after a short but stubborn resistance during which King Zog I fled abroad, the occupiers immediately started to organise a puppet regime to function under Italy's guidance. On April 12, 1939, a National Constituent Assembly was convened which decided (1) to proclaim the abrogation of the political regime previously in force as well as the abrogation of the constitution of December 1, 1928; (2) to create a government vested with full powers; (3) to express the desire for the creation of a union between Italy and Albania, and to offer the Crown of Albania to the King of Italy and to his successors in the form of a personal union.

On April 13, 1939, the Fascist Grand Council (Gran Consiglio del Fascismo) gave its approval to this union, and a law was published in Italy proclaiming the acceptance by the King of the Crown of Albania and the consequent creation of a union between the two states. This was formally effected when a special Albanian mission, consisting of members of the Provisional Albanian Government, officially presented the Crown of Albania to the King of Italy.

By the royal decree of April 18, 1939, an Under Secretariat for Albanian Affairs was established in the Italian Ministry of Foreign Affairs, and in the further development of relations between Italy and Albania, a convention was signed in Tirana on April 20. This stated that citizens of Albania in Italy and citizens of Italy in Albania would have all the same civil and political rights that they enjoyed in their respective countries. On the same day, a treaty on economic matters as well as matters pertaining to customs and exchange established a customs union between the two states.

By another treaty signed in Rome on June 3, 1939, Italy assumed management of the foreign affairs of Albania and the representation of that country abroad.

Spending some 500 years under Turkish domination, Albania enjoyed a brief period of independence from 1912 to 1939. Bounded by Yugoslavia on the north and east, and Greece to the south, Italy lay less that 80 kilometres to the west across the Adriatic. In 1912 as one of the Albanian representatives, Ahmet Zogolli *(left)* signed the Declaration of Independence, and during the 1920s he went on to serve as Minister of the Interior and Chief of the Albanian armed forces. In 1922 Zogolli changed his name to Zogu, a more Albanian sounding name, being shot and wounded in Parliament in 1923. After a period of enforced exile, he returned to become the Prime Minister and was elected as the first President of Albania in January 1925. Three years later Albania was transformed into a kingdom and President Zogu became King Zog I, and at the same time raised to the rank of field-marshal. Although he was a self-proclaimed monarch, he also accorded royal status to the members of his family. Italy had already been rebuffed in trying to occupy Albania in 1920 and the Duce was anxious to redress the situation. He had supported Zog since he was President and Italian influence in Albania increased as a result. The timing of Italy's first major aggressive action since the invasion of Abyssinia was undoubtedly influenced by Hitler's occupation of Czechoslovakia. Italians had been allowed to settle in Albania, and the Albanian military was trained and led by Italians; consequently, when Italy invaded on April 7, 1939, the Albanians were no match and the defence came largely from the gendarmerie and the general population. That same day King Zog, his wife Queen Geraldine, and their two-day-old son Prince Leka fled to Greece, taking with them part of the gold reserves from the Albanian National Bank. On hearing the news, an angry mob sacked the King's residence. The following day Italian troops entered the capital Tirana. By April 12 it was all over and the Albanian Parliament voted to depose of Zog and unite with Italy.

In addition, the union between the two states was carried out mainly through the creation of the office of a Vicegerent of Albania through the Albanian Fascist Party, and the permanent Italian counselors with Albanian ministries. The Vicegerent was appointed by royal Italian decree of April 22, 1939 to represent in Albania the absent King and to exercise in his name the rights of sovereignty.

A fusion of the Albanian and Italian armed forces was effected by Italian law No. 1115 of July 13, 1939, and by the decree of the Vicegerent of Albania of December 11, 1939.

By the decree of the Vicegerent of June 2, 1939, permanent Italian counselors were established with the various Albanian ministries and also in municipalities.

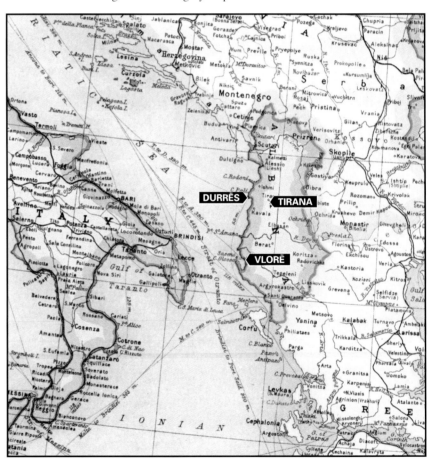

Three days later the country withdrew from the League of Nations from which Italy had left in 1937. The Albanian military was formally absorbed into the Italian Army in 1940, Albania serving as a base for Mussolini's next target: Greece. One attraction for the acquisition of Albania was that Italy would then have the use of the port of Vlorë, strategically located at the entrance to the Adriatic Sea.

Under the overall command of Generale Alfredo Guzzoni, the invasion force was built up from ad hoc units with the operational title of Corpo di Spedizione Oltremare-Tirana (Overseas Expeditionary Corps-Tirana). The First Group landing on April 7 was made up of four contingents. Force 1 landing at Shëngjin comprised three battalions of the Bersaglieri (the III, VI and XXVIII) and two companies of the San Marco Marine Battalion. Force 2 landing at Durrës *(left)* had five more Bersaglieri battalions (the II, X, XIV, XVII and XXVII), the I/47th Infantry Battal-

ion, the VIII and X Light Tank Battalions, a 65/17mm artillery battery, and an AA battery. Two Grenadier battalions, the I and II, were airlifted in. Force 3, consisting of the I and XVI Bersaglieri Battalions and the XL and LXXVI Blackshirt Battalions, landed at Vlorë, and Force 4 at Sarendë with the XX and XXXIII Bersaglieri Battalions, the San Giorgio Fast Tank Group and two companies of the San Marco marines. *Right:* Today Durrës, transformed with high-rise blocks of apartments, is a popular destination for cruise ships.

BASIC STATUTE

On June 3, 1939, King Victor Emmanuel III conferred a Basic Statute upon the Albanian people to replace the constitution of 1928 then in force. Under this statute, the Albanian State was to be ruled by a constitutional monarchic government. The Italian throne was hereditary in the dynasty of Victor Emmanuel III; the executive power belonged to the King and was exercised by him through a Council of Ministers who were appointed and dismissed by him. The King could appoint a Vicegerent to exercise the royal powers, with the exception of those that the King expressly reserved to himself.

The role of the former Parliament was assumed by the Fascist Upper Corporative Council composed of the Central Council of the Albanian Fascist Party and of members of the Central Council of Corporative Economy. The Fascist Upper Corporative Council was

convoked by the King, and he, together with the Fascist Upper Corporative Council, exercised legislative power. When reasons of urgent and absolute necessity required it, the King could issue decrees having the force of law. In this case, however, the royal decree had to be presented to the Fascist Upper Corporative Council for conversion into law. Civil rights were granted the Albanians by this statute but every article of the statute in this respect was qualified by such reservations as 'except in cases otherwise provided for by law'.

ITALIAN ADMINISTRATION

The supreme authority (under the King) was the Vicegerent, who represented the King in Albania. The Vicegerent promulgated decrees called Vicegerent's decrees (Decreti Luogotenenziali).

Control over the Albanian Government was carried out by the exercise of

the appointive power on the part of Italy, but the Albanian Government was also controlled from within by the permanent Italian counsellors mentioned above, who were active in every ministry.

A decree of September 18, 1939, defined the functions of these Italian counsellors as advising the ministry on the one hand and the control of it on the other. The counsellors were appointed by the Albanian Government but the government had to be authorised to do so by the Italian Vicegerent. The permanent counsellors had a civil service rating in the Albanian administration and were paid from the Treasury of the Albanian State.

Beside this form of control of the Albanian administration through permanent Italian counsellors, the Italian Government exercised an effective influence on Albanian administration by establishing Italian authorities in

The Second Group, landing at Durrës (known as Durazzo by the Italians) on April 8, brought ashore the headquarters of the 47th Infantry Regiment plus battalions of infantry, cavalry,

machine gunners and heavy artillery. Here Carro Veloce 33/IIs are unloaded at the modern harbour which had been constructed in 1927 under the auspices of King Zog.

The Third Group landed the HQ of the 23rd Infantry Division, the 48th Infantry Regiment, the III/47th Infantry Battalion, the XCII Blackshirt Batallion and the 14th Field Artillery Regiment.

Albania. These authorities were controlled by the Under Secretary for Albanian Affairs in the Ministry of Foreign Affairs in Rome. In this way, various Italian offices were created in Albania, such as those for civil engineering, for highway, tramway and automobile transportation, for railways and for public works. There was also an office of Director of the Italian Day Dispensary of Tirana, for Albanian Youth, and for After-Work Recreation Centres. The salaries of such officials were paid by the Italian Treasury.

ALBANIAN ADMINISTRATIION

The Albanian Government was directed by a Council of Ministers consisting of a President, the Minister Secretary of the National Fascist Party, Minister of Justice, Minister of the Interior, Minister of Public Works, Minister of Finance, Minister of Public Instruction, and Minister of National Economy. To these ministries a Ministry for Redeemed Territories was added when Albania annexed certain territories after the dismemberment of Yugoslavia by the Axis. Every minister was assisted by one or more under-secretaries of state. The ministers and the under-secretaries were nominated by the Vicegerent.

The country was divided into prefectures but the provincial administration was not essentially changed. Among other new authorities there was one for the confiscation of property and another for police internment.

In the field of finance the same unit of currency remained in force. The Albanian franc, divided into 5 lek, was equivalent to 6.25 lire.

FASCISTISATION

The fascistisation of Albania was carried out mainly through the Albanian Fascist Party, the Fascist Upper Corporative Council, and the Central Council of Corporative Economy.

The Albanian Fascist Party — the only political party in Albania — was organised in the first month after the occupation of Albania by Italy. It was not constituted as a separate organisation but as a branch of the Italian Fascist Party. The unity of the two parties was indicated by the subordination of the Albanian branch to the Duce of Fascism. The members of the Albanian Fascist Party took an oath to obey the orders of the Duce.

The organisation of the Albanian Party provided that its secretary be appointed and dismissed by the Vicegerent on the recommendation of the President of the Council of Ministers, after consultation with the Secretary of the National Fascist Party in Rome. The Secretary of the Albanian Fascist Party was to have the title and function of Minister of State, and to receive orders of the Duce from the secretary of the party in Rome. The latter party was represented in the Albanian Fascist Party 'by a National Fascist Party Inspector assisted by a Federal Secretary and by Federal inspectors of the National Fascist Party'.

ITALIAN PROPAGANDA

In order to carry out Italian propaganda in Albania, a special institution called the 'Skanderbeg Foundation' was established with headquarters in Tirana. The Foundation was composed of two autonomous sections. The first, called the Institute for Albanian Studies, had as its object the development of 'philosophical, literary, artistic and historic culture in Albania'. The second section was the Italo-Albanian Skanderbeg Club and had as its purpose the establishment, improvement and furtherance of social relations between Albanians and Italians. The Foundation was based upon an endowment of eight million Italian lire granted by the Minister of Foreign Affairs of the Kingdom of Italy.

ECONOMIC CONTROL

By the treaty of April 20, 1939, a customs union between Italy and Albania was established. By the terms of this treaty the territory of both countries was considered as one territory. All trade restrictions between the two countries were abolished. Italian customs laws applied in both countries. Under the treaty, Albania was to receive 15 million Albanian francs from Italy per year as compensation for the customs duties that Albania expected to lose because of the tariff union.

CRIMINAL LAW

A considerable part of the Italian Criminal Code of 1930, namely, the chapter on 'crimes against the personality of the state', was introduced into Albania by a decree of the Vicegerent of January 6, 1940. The Italian Criminal Code dealt with all forms of offences against the state for both internal and international relations. A considerable part of the Italian Criminal Code of 1930 covering 'crimes against the personality of the state' was introduced into Albania by a decree of the Vicegerent of January 6, 1940. The Albanians were called upon to be faithful to both states, Albania and Italy, to the same extent as Italians were obliged to be faithful to Italy. As a rule, treason was punished by the death penalty.

One of the striking features of Durrës, which is located 30 kilometres west of the capital Tirana, is its Roman castle which dates from 500 BC.

Foreign Minister Count Ciano and the commander of the Italian occupying forces Generale Guzzoni read together a telegram from Mussolini congratulating them on the successful operation to subjugate Albania.

Italian transport rolls into Tirana in 1943

POLICE INTERNMENT

Judicial guaranties as to personal freedom did not exist in the regime introduced by Italy. A person could be deprived of his freedom by way of police internment — equivalent to confinement in a certain type of concentration camp.

In a country like Albania the safety of the roads was an important problem, as it was here that Albanian patriots struck most frequently in their struggle against the Italians. Therefore a special additional sanction for such acts was introduced in a decree of November 13, 1942. This order did not specify the exact nature of the offences but specified acts that constituted 'a menace to public safety on the roads and to telecommunications services'. According to this decree, all inhabitants of villages included within a radius of five kilometres from the spot where any of the acts were committed were made collectively responsible for such acts. A collective fine of from 1,000 to 20,000 Albanian francs was to be imposed on such inhabitants, and heads of all families residing in the area were to be interned for one year. If the fine was not paid, the land produce, sheep, and other cattle of the inhabitants was to be sold in order to cover the sum of the fine.

RAPHAEL LEMKIN, 1944

Since then, Skanderberg Square has undergone a major transformation.

73

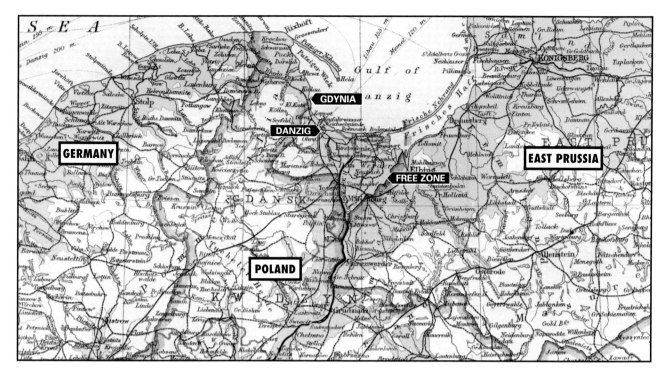

The Treaty of Versailles included the outright cession of most of West Prussia to Poland and the creation of an access corridor to the Baltic at Danzig. The 'Free City of Danzig' was officially declared in November 1920 under the protection of the League of Nations but the redrawing of the boundaries in eastern Europe after the First World War led to discontent on both sides. Although the Free City had been re-created on paper, the Poles were still subservient to the local legislature which was German-dominated and this forced Poland to develop a rival port on her own territory at Gdynia (Gotenhafen). For her part, Germany was equally annoyed about her loss of unrestricted access to East Prussia so Hitler used what he called the 'Diktat' of Versailles as one of his main political platforms for the re-unification of the two portions of Germany.

Danzig

The port of Danzig, founded by the Poles, was for centuries a goal in the German Drang nach Osten. In 1308 it was conquered from Poland by the Teutonic Knights who carried out a mass slaughter of the Polish population. On June 19, 1310, Pope Clement V denounced the massacre of more than 10,000 people in the city of Gdansk (the Polish name for Danzig), the procurators of the Teutonic order alleged that 'the mentioned citizens destroyed the houses of the town of their own free will and went to live in other parts'.

About the middle of the 15th century, a Prussian League that included Danzig appealed to the ancient Polish sovereign against the Teutonic Order of Knights, and after a 12-year war Danzig was restored to the Polish Crown. The city received full self-government from the Polish king and entered on a period of great economic prosperity because it served as the only port for all the exports from Poland.

After the Peace Conference of 1919, the economic interdependence of Poland and Danzig was recognised. The Conference initially intended to incorporate Danzig into Poland, but finally decision was reached to make it a Free City (together with an area of over 2,000 square kilometres and a population of 400,000) under the protection of the League of Nations and with special rights for Poland. The provisions for the establishment of the Free City were contained in Articles 100 to 108 of the Treaty of Versailles, and these provisions were further implemented by two

In October 1938, Hitler had begun to campaign for the return of the Free City of Danzig and in March 1939, as Czechoslovakia disintegrated and German troops marched into Prague, Hitler ordered his military high command to draw up the plans to take care of the 'Poland problem' militarily. On May 1, 'Fall Weiss' (Plan White) was presented as part of 'Instructions for Operations in the East' designed for the invasion of Poland. Rebuffed in his demand for the immediate return of Danzig, Hitler rescinded Germany's 1934 Non-Aggression Treaty with Poland on April 28, 1939. German troops massed along the border; Poland mobilised 1.5 million, then 2.5 million into military service. Atrocity stories heated up tensions on both sides. British Prime Minister Neville Chamberlain, embarrassed by the result of the Munich pact, publicly committed his nation to the protection of Poland against Nazi aggression. German preparations for aggression were then stepped up.

On August 25, 1939, the battleship *Schleswig-Holstein* sailed into the port of Danzig to a cheering crowd on a so-called 'goodwill visit'. The tug *Albert Forster* was named after the Gauleiter of Danzig.

On August 11, Hitler met with Professor Carl Burckhardt, the League of Nations High Commissioner in Danzig. He did not mince his words: 'If there's the slightest provocation, I shall shatter Poland without warning into so many pieces that there will be nothing left to pick up.' He added that where his generals may have been hesitant in the past, he was now having difficulty holding them back. On August 22 Hitler gathered his armed forces commanders on the Obersalzberg to announce his plans for the invasion of Poland: 'I will give propagandistic cause for the release of the war, indifferently whether convincing. The winner is not asked later whether he said the truth or not.' Now assured of Russian neutrality through the German-Soviet Non-Aggression Pact signed in Moscow the following day, and confident of Western weakness, Hitler decided that 'Fall Weiss' would

proceed on August 26. Hope for peace between Germany and Poland faded as the world's attention turned to the ratification of the Molotov-Ribbentrop Pact on August 23/24. Within 12 hours of signing, Germany was only thinly veiling its plans for a partition of Poland between herself and the Soviet Union. A mobilisation order was issued across England. On the night of August 31/September 1, 1939, the German Sicherheitsdienst (Security Service) staged a series of fake border incidents in Upper Silesia designed to give Nazi Germany an excuse for invading Poland. *Above:* The most prominent of these provocations was the seizure of the German radio station in the town of Gleiwitz, five kilometres from the border, by a band of seven 'Polish rebels' who proceeded to broadcast a message of Polish insurrection.

conventions between Poland and the Free City which were signed, one in Paris on November 9, 1920, the other in Warsaw on October 24, 1921.

The mutual rights of Danzig and Poland as formulated in these provisions were that the Free City was included within the Polish customs frontiers and a free area was established in the port. Poland received the free use and service of the whole railway system, the waterways, docks, basins, wharves and other works within the territory of the Free City necessary for Polish imports and exports. The railways and docks of the port were to be administered by a commission of Poles and Danzigers with a neutral chairman. Poland received also the control and administration of postal, telegraphic and telephonic communication between Poland and the port. The Polish Government was granted the right to conduct the foreign affairs of the Free City of Danzig and was entrusted with the diplomatic protection of the citizens of that city when abroad. No discrimination could be undertaken within the Free City to the detriment of Polish citizens.

At the mouth of the Vistula, a spit of land called Westerplatte lay on the northern bank while Danzig itself lay to the south. In 1924, Poland was given the right to establish a 'Military Transit Depot' on Westerplatte, sealed by a gate through which a railway line serviced the depot. Five guardrooms were built forming a ring around a central barracks although actual fortifications were prohibited. *Left:* Westerplatte railway station just beyond the railway gate. It was here that the station master,

reserve Company Sergeant-Major Wojciech Najsarek, was killed in the very first minutes of the assault — possibly the first victim of the Second World War. The station building survived almost intact up to the end of the six-day battle, (which we recounted in detail in *After the Battle* No. 65) when it was blown up by German pioneers. *Right:* The attack came up the road on the right, the gate being situated roughly where the group of posts now stand.

The shooting war had in fact begun earlier than 5.45 a.m. In the pre-dawn hour of 4.47 a.m., the battleship *Schleswig-Holstein* opened fire on Danzig's Westerplatte fortress. At the same time, the Luftwaffe launched the opening attack upon the Polish town of Wielun, destroying about 75 per cent of buildings in the town centre and killing 1,200 civilians.

At 8 a.m. the Wehrmacht launched its offensive near Mokra where the Polish Army on horseback held off the Germans. Hitler did not specifically mention Gleiwitz in his Reichstag speech later that day but he did cite frontier incidents: 'Recently in one night there were as many as 21 frontier incidents. Last night there were 14, of which three were quite serious.'

In spite of the fact that the Germans had a battleship supporting the ground troops firing almost at point-blank range, it still took them six days to overcome the defenders on Westerplatte. The heaviest single piece of armament available to the Poles was their 75mm field gun which had been dismantled and smuggled into Westerplatte early in 1939. *Left:* It was put out of action here on the first morning by an 88mm shell from the *Schleswig-Holstein* and became a much-prized trophy of war being taken on board the ship when finally captured *(right)*.

A constitution was drawn up for the Free City of Danzig, providing for a popular Assembly (Volkstag) as a parliament, and for an executive body called the Senate, which was elected for a period of four years by the Volkstag. Danzig had its own currency (gulden), and its own courts. The official language was German.

It seems almost impossible to believe, but in the whole of the week-long siege of Westerplatte, under almost constant attack from the land, sea and air, of the 200 men manning the Polish defences, only 15 were killed. Seven of those men lost their lives here on the second day when Guardhouse V received a direct hit during a Stuka attack. Only three out of the ten-strong crew survived, those killed including Sergeant Adolf Petzelt, the post commander.

The League of Nations was represented in Danzig by a High Commissioner whose main task was to co-ordinate and maintain good relations between the Free City and Poland. For the safeguarding of Polish interests, the office of a Polish Commissioner was established in Danzig.

Westerplatte fell on September 7. The base of the demolished guardhouse was therefore a fitting location to establish the first memorial on Westerplatte which was erected here in 1946 together with a T-34. The tank has since been removed

Built in 1934-35, these are the shattered remains of the barracks located right in the centre of Westerplatte, pictured after the fighting looking south-west.

Adolf Hitler addressed the Reichstag at 10 a.m. on the morning of September 1, 1939: 'For months we have been suffering under the torture of a problem which the Versailles Diktat created — a problem which has deteriorated until it becomes intolerable for us. Danzig was and is a German city. The Corridor was and is German. Both these territories owe their cultural development exclusively to the German people. Danzig was separated from us, the Corridor was annexed by Poland. As in other German territories of the East, all German minorities living there have been ill-treated in the most distressing manner. More than 1,000,000 people of German blood had in the years 1919-20 to leave their homeland.

'It is impossible to demand that an impossible position should be cleared up by peaceful revision and at the same time constantly reject peaceful revision. It is also impossible to say that he who undertakes to carry out these revisions for himself transgresses a law, since the Versailles

Diktat is not law to us. A signature was forced out of us with pistols at our head and with the threat of hunger for millions of people. And then this document, with our signature, obtained by force, was proclaimed as a solemn law.

'*I am determined to solve (1) the Danzig question; (2) the question of the Corridor; and (3) to see to it that a change is made in the relationship between Germany and Poland that shall ensure a peaceful co-existence. In this I am resolved to continue to fight until either the present Polish Government is willing to bring about this change or until another Polish Government is ready to do so. I am resolved to remove from the German frontiers the element of uncertainty, the everlasting atmosphere of conditions resembling civil war. I will see to it that in the East there is, on the frontier, a peace precisely similar to that on our other frontiers.*

'*This night for the first time Polish regular soldiers fired on our own territory. Since 5.45 a.m. we have been returning the fire, and from now on bombs will be met with bombs.*

After the war, the entire right-hand, or northern wing was demolished to make room for the building of an access road to the memorial.

Possibly the most well-known photograph of the entire series taken on Westerplatte shows Hitler examining the effect of the shelling on the entrance to the barracks.

'*For six years now I have been working on the building up of the German defences. Over 90 milliards have in that time been spent on the building up of these defence forces. They are now the best equipped and are above all comparison with what they were in 1914. My trust in them is unshakable. I am asking of no German man more than I myself was ready throughout four years at any time to do. There will be no hardships for Germans to which I myself will not submit. My whole life henceforth belongs more than ever to my people. I am from now on just first soldier of the German Reich. I have once more put on that coat that was the most sacred and dear to me. I will not take it off again until victory is secured, or I will not survive the outcome. As a National Socialist and as German soldier I enter upon this struggle with a stout heart. My whole life has been nothing but one long struggle for my people, for its restoration, and for Germany. There was only one watchword for that struggle: faith in this people. One word I have never learned: that is, surrender.*'

Albert Forster was born in Fürth, Bavaria, on July 26, 1902 and became a member of the SA in 1923 and within seven years he had been appointed the Nazi Party Gauleiter of the Free City of Danzig. In the spring of 1933, at Hitler's prompting, he began spearheading the Nazi take-over of the city which at the same time embroiled him in a feud with the Nazi President of the Danzig Senate, Arthur Greiser. He tried but failed to gain control of the organisation dedicated to the interests of the ethnic German population in the adjacent Polish Corridor, so that after the invasion when this territory was annexed into Reichsgau Danzig, he filled the administrative posts with his own people. Admired by Hitler, Forster was awarded Honourable Citizenship of Fürth and Danzig, and in May 1934 was married in the Reich Chancellery in Berlin with Hitler and the Deputy Reichsführer Rudolf Hess as witnesses. By 1937 he was already boasting about his fight against 'sub-humans and Communists' and, reacting to orders from Berlin, stepped up the agitation in Danzig in parallel with Hitler's demands for it to be incorporated into the Reich. After Poland was defeated, Forster became both the Gauleiter and Reichstatthalter (Governor) of the province of Danzig-West Prussia. It was his aim to fully Germanise the area yet he was willing to accept as German any Poles who claimed to have German blood. This policy was against Nazi racial theory and President Greiser complained about it to Himmler. Nevertheless the outcome was that two-thirds of the Polish population in Forster's Gau were Poles classified as German under the Deutsche Volksliste. Forster had also been given carte blanche by Hitler to oversee the extermination policy in the region and as early as November 1939 he stated that the province was already 'Judenfrei'. In February 1940 he reported that 87,000 people had been 'evacuated'. At the end of the war, Forster was handed over by the British to be dealt with by the People's Republic of Poland and he was hanged on February 28, 1952.

Hitler had left Berlin in his personal train on September 4 — the day after Britain had declared war against Germany in support of Poland. He then began a two-week tour of the Eastern Front and on the 18th his train was at Goddentow-Lanz, 65 kilometres north-west of Danzig. The following day he entered the city.

the Danzig statute and making it an 'Act of the Reich'. Under this statute, citizens of the Free City of Danzig were to become German citizens and provision was made for 'the entire body of Reich law and Prussian law to take effect as of January 1, 1940'. The Reich Minister of the Interior was entrusted with all matters connected with the incorporation of Danzig into the German Reich.

Later, on October 8, 1939, Danzig was incorporated into the District (Gau) of Western Prussia and served as headquarters for the Reich Governor. Poles living in Danzig, even if they were formerly citizens of the Free City, were treated just as were the Poles in the incorporated parts of western Poland. They were excluded from German citizenship and their property was sequestrated in Danzig in the same way as in the Polish Incorporated Territories.

The German Reichsmark was made exclusive legal tender and the local Danzig gulden were exchanged into Reichsmarks at the rate of one Reichsmark to 1.43 Danzig gulden.

RAPHAEL LEMKIN, 1944

INCORPORATION

On April 28, 1939, Hitler declared that Danzig must return to German sovereignty. After four months of great political tension, Germany launched an attack on Poland on September 1, 1939, and occupied Danzig.

On the same day, the Gauleiter of the Nazi Party in Danzig, Albert Forster, signed a statute abolishing the Constitution of the Free City of Danzig and declaring the city, with its territory and its citizens, incorporated into the German Reich. All legislative and executive power was vested exclusively in the Head of the City. On the same day an act was passed by the Reichstag embodying

A tumultuous welcome awaited the Führer in Danzig, for so long a bone of contention. Driving in his Mercedes, the route ran down the city's main street (now called Dluga) to the historic Artushof where he was to give a speech in which he stated that 'I have no war aims against England and France'.

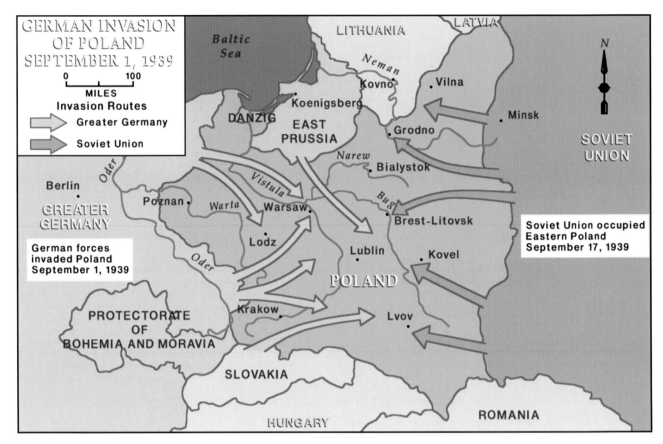

GERMAN INVASION
OF POLAND
SEPTEMBER 1, 1939

0   100
MILES
Invasion Routes

⇒ Greater Germany

⇒ Soviet Union

German forces
invaded Poland
September 1, 1939

Soviet Union occupied
Eastern Poland
September 17, 1939

GREATER
GERMANY

Berlin

Poznan

Warsaw

Lodz

Lublin

Krakow

Lvov

POLAND

PROTECTORATE
OF
BOHEMIA AND MORAVIA

SLOVAKIA

HUNGARY

ROMANIA

DANZIG

EAST
PRUSSIA

Koenigsberg

Baltic
Sea

LITHUANIA

LATVIA

Kovno

Vilna

Minsk

Grodno

Bialystok

Brest-Litovsk

Kovel

SOVIET
UNION

Heralded by the surprise attack on Danzig, early on the morning of September 1, 1939, five German armies crossed the Polish frontier from three different directions — north, north-west and south-west. The invasion, under the code-name 'Fall Weiss' (Plan White), introduced to the world the concept of 'Blitzkrieg' or Lightning War in which a concentrated spearhead comprising tanks, artillery and motorised infantry, supported by dive-bombers, cuts right through enemy lines at high speed without regard to its flanks. Within a week German forces had reached the gates of Warsaw but the Poles were able to stave off defeat for three weeks in what became known as the 'Siege of Warsaw'. Danzig had already fallen and, two days before Hitler made his visit there, Poland had been dealt a mortal stab in the back when Soviet forces crossed her eastern border.

Poland

POLISH INCORPORATED TERRITORIES

Through an order of October 8, 1939, the western parts of Poland (referred to in German legislation as Incorporated Eastern Territories — Eingegliederte Ostgebiete — because of their geographical position in regard to Germany), were incorporated into Germany creating the following administrative units.

(1) The Reich district of Danzig-West Prussia embracing the Free City of Danzig and the Polish districts of Pomerania, Lipno and Ripin, as well as the German district of Marien-werder (formerly a part of the province of East Prussia) and some counties belonging formerly to the province of West Prussia.

Left: Warsaw's defences included 86 AA guns and numerous detachments of AA machine guns. Here a crew poses with their weapon on the corner of Aleja Jerozolimskie (Jerusalem Avenue) and Ulica Marszalkowska (Marshal Street). *Right:* Warsaw is one of those cities whose appearance has completely altered since pre-war days. Three times during the war there was wholesale destruction in the capital: first as a result of the German bombing and shelling in September 1939; then in May 1943 when, in the aftermath of the failed uprising in the Jewish ghetto, the Germans blew up the entire Jewish quarters in the city centre, and then finally in August-October 1944 when the Polish underground army in Warsaw rose in rebellion against the Germans. Post-war reconstruction of the devastated city by the Communist regime led to the loss of the distinctive tower along Marshal Street seen in the background of the wartime photo. The building that replaced it is the Palace of Culture and Science, built in 1952-55 and cynically known by the Poles as 'Stalin's gift to Warsaw'.

Left: **With German forces rapidly approaching the capital, the city authorities called upon the population to assist in constructing barricades and defensive positions. This improvised pillbox lay on the corner of Targowa and Wilenska Streets in** the suburb of Praga. *Right:* **The same building, seen in the background, still stands today, its façade pockmarked by bullet strikes from the 1944 uprising and dilapidated by years of neglect.**

(2) The Reich district Wartheland, embracing the Polish province of Poznan (Posen) and the Polish city of Lódz (renamed Litzmannstadt) with surrounding areas.

(3) The northern Polish district of Ciechanów was incorporated into the province of East Prussia. The eastern Polish district of Suwalki was also incorporated into East Prussia as part of the county of Gumbinen. The Polish industrial city of Bialystok, with large surrounding areas, as well as most of the Polish district Grodno, was attached to East Prussia as a separate administrative unit (Regierungsbezirk).

(4) The industrial city of Katowice with a large surrounding area and also the Cieszyn district were incorporated into the district of Silesia.

Every Reich district (Gau) was administered by a Reich governor (Reichsstatthalter) and was divided into government districts, which in turn were divided into counties and municipalities. The governor was at the same time head of the Nazi Party in each district (Gauleiter).

The office of the Reich governor was divided into the following sections: General Financial and Organisational Matters; Public Health and Hygiene; Education, Instruction, Furtherance of Cultural and Communal Life; Agriculture, Settlement, Reallocation of Realty and Waterways; Economics and Labour; Forestry and Hunting; Private and Public Construction.

To the office of the Reich governor was attached the ranking SS and Police Leader, who was at the same time the agent of the Reich Commissioner for the Strengthening of Germanism. This officer was mainly responsible for the destruction of Polish nationhood and its supplanting by German elements.

The Reich Minister of the Interior was designated as the responsible agency for the reorganisation of the incorporated territories. These areas were subjected to an especially severe regime involving genocide for the Polish population. On short notice Poles were removed from their homes and replaced by German settlers. Institutions of Polish administration were abolished and replaced by German

agencies. Polish cultural institutions were closed, and the German language

was made the language of education in the schools.

Panzers advance down Grojecka Street, the main thoroughfare entering Warsaw from the south-east and leading into the borough of Ochota, at its intersection with Siewierska Street.

Grojecka Street has changed out of all recognition since 1939 and none of the buildings visible then remain standing. Today, the entire length of Grojecka is lined by high-rise apartment blocks built in the Communist era. Practically the only common feature between then and now are the tracks and overhead masts of the tram line to Okecie. This is the view looking south-west and out of town, at the point where Siewierska used to connect with Grojecka.

Left: German forces officially entered Warsaw on October 1 and, to celebrate their victory, each division held its own parade through the city. Here, the 10. Infanterie Division lines up for the march on Plac Polytechniki (Polytechnic Square) in Mokotow in southern Warsaw. *Right:* The main auditorium building of the University of Technology remains unaltered.

The series of march-pasts culminated in a massive victory parade held on October 5 attended by Hitler and his commanders. Generalmajor Erwin Rommel, who had just been appointed the commander of the Führer-Begleit-Bataillon (the Führer's Escort Battalion), had flown in to Warsaw three days earlier to oversee arrangements. Hitler arrived from Berlin during the morning, being met at Okecie airport by Generaloberst Walther von Brauschitsch, the Commander-in-Chief of the Army, together with Generals Johannes Blaskowitz, (8. Armee), and Walther von Reichenau (10. Armee). Hitler first made a tour of the city in his open-top Mercedes before alighting at the saluting base that had been set up on Aleja Ujazdowskie, the grand avenue running through the diplomatic quarter of Warsaw. The streets were lined with German troops but it was noticable that there was an almost complete absence of civilians. The parade lasted two hours and was certainly the largest ever held in the capital of any of the countries conquered by Nazi Germany.

Today a bus stop marks the location of the Führer's saluting base.

On August 23, 1939, the German and Soviet Foreign Ministers concluded a secret agreement for the dismemberment of Poland in the so-called Molotov-Ribbentrop Pact. Sixteen days after the Germans invaded Poland from the west, the Red Army came in from the east without a declaration of war, just with a simple statement that 'the Polish State has ceased to exist'. The outcome was a foregone conclusion and, in spite of a gallant fight by the Polish forces, by October 6 it was all over. Here Soviet cavalry parade through the streets of Lwów.

THE LEGISLATIVE SET-UP

The Reich Minister of the Interior was instructed to introduce German law in the incorporated territories. He, in turn, delegated some of his powers to the governors and even to the police. He also gradually introduced a great body of German statutes in these territories, starting with the Conscription Law for military service, the Nuremberg Laws, and the Four-Year Plan. A great many German decrees were also declared applicable in the territory.

The replacement of civil law was difficult because in these incorporated areas there already existed a variety of civil codes. In the districts that belonged to Germany before 1918, a great part of the German Civil Code (Bürgerliches Gesetzbuch) was still in force. In other parts which did not belong to Germany before 1918 but which formed the so-called 'Congress Poland', the Code Napoleon was in force, and in the districts of Suwalki and Bialystok, the Russian Civil Code of 1864 still had effect.

THE JUDICIARY

A decree of June 13, 1940 introduced in the incorporated eastern areas the German basic law on organisation of courts as well as subsidiary laws concerning the judiciary. Polish courts thereby ceased to exist. German judges were appointed instead and Polish judges were used only as clerks in the transitional period for translating Polish records in cases still pending in the courts. By the introduction of the decree concerning qualifications for attorneys of January 4, 1939, Polish barristers were practically barred from the courts.

CURRENCY AND FOREIGN EXCHANGE

By a decree of November 22, 1939, the Reichsmark was declared the sole legal tender. By the same decree, the German Treasury and Reichsbank offices which had been established in these territories, and other delegated agencies, were directed to exchange the notes of the Bank Polski and the Polish Government coins for all residents at a rate of exchange of two zlotys for one Reichsmark.

Poland was dismembered by Germany by incorporating western and northern Poland, as well as the Bialystok area in the east. The Government General was established for territories of central and southern Poland, and other eastern territories were made part of the General Commissariat of White Russia. The south-eastern province of Wolhynia and parts of the province Polesie were incorporated into the Reich Commissariat of the Ukraine. The Soviets annexed over 200,000 square kilometres east of a line formed by the Pisa, Narew, the western Bug and San rivers.

The odd term 'General Government' (a throw-back to an area created by the German Empire in the First World War) was used to describe that area of central Poland and later Ukraine occupied by Nazi Germany. For logistical purposes, it was run as a separate adminstrative area. It came into being through a Führer decree of October 12, 1939, putting Hitler's personal lawyer, Hans Frank *(left)*, in place as Governor General. The area was divided into four adminstrative districts with seats at Warsaw, Radom, Lublin and Krakow where Frank ruled from Wawel Castle *(right)*.

THE GOVERNMENT GENERAL

The Government General (General-gouvernement) of Poland was established by the decree of the Führer of October 12, 1939. The Governor General had the title of Reich Minister and was responsible directly to the Führer. The headquarters of the government were located in Krakow with the office divided into six sections (chancellery, legislation, territorial organisation, personnel, organisational matters, business), and 15 divisions (finance, economy, interior, labour, agriculture and food, justice, enlightenment and propaganda, foreign exchange, education, health service, building, forestry, post, railways, and trustee administration). In addition there was a liaison office for relations with the army and with the administration of the Four-Year Plan. The Chief of Police co-ordinated his activities with those of the office of the Governor General.

The Government General was divided into the following districts: Krakow, Warsaw, Radom and Lublin. After Lwów was occupied in 1941 (up to then it had been held by the Russians), an additional district was formed consisting of Lwów and Eastern Galicia. Each district was under a governor although the title of 'Governor' was complimentary so a district under a governor was not called 'government'.

The districts in turn were divided into counties and municipalities. The municipal administration was in the hands of mayors, the Governor General appointing those officials in communities of over 20,000 inhabitants, while in smaller communities they were appointed by the governor of the district. In communities of less than 10,000 inhabitants, the mayor selected five advisers, and in communities of over 10,000 inhabitants he selected ten advisers to assist him in the administration of the municipalities. The district governor could, at his discretion, appoint a special commissioner to act with the mayor. This commissioner was empowered to suspend, change or invalidate any order of the mayor and to issue orders of his own.

COURTS

There were two main types of courts, German courts and Polish courts. Germans could only be tried by German courts but Poles were regularly tried by Polish courts unless a case against the interests of the German Reich or of a German was involved.

(1) German courts of original jurisdiction tried criminal cases if one of the parties was a German, or if the offence involved 'the security and authority of the German Reich and people', or if the offence was committed on the premises of a German authority or in connection with activities of German authorities. The German courts had jurisdiction in civil cases if a German was involved or if the case pertained to matters concerning German commercial records.

(2) German Superior Courts mainly heard appeals from the court of original jurisdiction. They functioned in Krakow, Rzeszow, Lublin and Lwów.

The Higher SS and Police Leader was SS-Obergruppenführer Friedrich-Wilhelm Krüger *(left)*, appointed by Himmler on October 4, 1939. He was responsible for setting up forced labour camps, the deportation of Jews and anti-partisan operations. Also he supervised many crimes against humanity. He was replaced in November 1943 by SS-Obergruppenführer Wilhelm Koppe *(right)*. He was responsible for numerous atrocities against Poles and the Jews including operations at Chelmno, the extermination camp in the Wartheland incorporated territory. While Krüger committed suicide in 1945, for some reason the West German government refused a request from Poland for Koppe's extradition and he died in Bonn in 1975.

Although there were many ghettos established for Polish Jews throughout the area administered by the General Government, it was SA-Gruppenführer Ludwig Fischer *(left)*, the Governor of Warsaw, who was responsible for the one in the capital.

Right: Sometimes a main street was so important that it had to be left out of the Jewish area, hence in Chlodna Street a bridge was provided so that trams could still run impeded through the ghetto.

(3) German Special Courts. Every district has one special court whose jurisdiction was defined in every case by orders and decrees promulgated by the Governor General. For example, it tried cases involving offences against banking, against the order of confiscation of private property, or against the order requiring Jews to wear special signs, etc.

(4) Polish Courts. The jurisdiction of Polish courts was permitted with respect to those cases that did not come within the jurisdiction of a German court. These courts applied Polish law.

ECONOMY AND TAXATION

The Four-Year Plan was introduced in the incorporated territories by orders of October 30, 1939 and July 9, 1940. These territories were thereby integrated into the economy of the Greater German Reich. Poles were in great part expelled from economic life, such as trade, handicrafts, banking and especially from agriculture. Special divisions in the offices of the respective Reich governors were responsible for uprooting Poles from economic life and putting Germans in their place.

To induce Germans to settle in the Polish territories, numerous tax incentives were offered to them. An order concerning tax abatement was issued on December 9, 1940 introducing a great number of tax exemptions for German

In January 1943, the Jewish underground rose up against the Germans, attacks continuing for three months until Himmler decided enough was enough. He brought in SS-Brigadeführer Jürgen Stroop with simple orders: destroy the ghetto and its inhabitants. Consequently, his force of Waffen-SS and police set about reducing the ghetto to rubble *(right)*. Over 13,000 Poles had been killed in the uprising and at least 50,000 Jews shipped off to the death camps, four of which had been built in the territory of the General Government.

Above: This is the same corner today; fortunately the building in the background survived the subsequent demolition of the ghetto, as did St Augustine's Cathedral *(below)*.

Left: **In the last week of August 1944, with the German front in eastern Poland collapsing, the occupation authorities started evacuating Warsaw in a state of haste and panic. Here lorries are being loaded with goods from the Zacheta art gallery on Malachowski Square, which during the German occupation** was known as the Haus der deutschen Kultur (House of German Culture). *Right:* **With the original Latin inscription — 'Artibus' (To the Arts) — restored on its sculpted pediment, the Zacheta is today a State Art Gallery and once again one of Warsaw's prime exhibition centres.**

nationals and persons of German origin in the incorporated Eastern Territories. This order began with a blunt statement of its purpose: 'In the effort to establish and promote Germanism (Deutschtum) in the incorporated Eastern Territories through taxation measures we order that . . .' Thus, Germans with an income of 25,000 Reichsmarks or less could deduct 3,000 Reichsmarks from their income when calculating and paying income taxes. The exemption of 3,000 Reichsmarks was increased by 300 Reichsmarks for each minor child belonging to the household. Also the regular tax exemptions provided for in the German property tax law were tripled for Germans. Germans were released from property acquisition tax, while a person selling property to a German was released from the sales tax. There were also provisions for release from inheritance and gift taxes if the acquisitor was German.

For the calendar years 1940-50, German retailers and partnerships were told that they may claim exemption from income tax on as much as 50 per cent of the net profit or 20 per cent of the gross profit of the enterprises. Corporation tax was lowered for Germans to 20 per cent of incomes not exceeding 300,000 Reichsmarks and 30 per cent for incomes above that amount. Property of Germans belonging to a farm or timber business, or to an industrial

enterprise or plant, was to be taken into account in the assessment of property tax only in so far as its value exceeded 250,000 Reichsmarks.

Another source of looting is taxation. Despite the economic distress of the inhabitants, taxes were raised. Thus the Polish property tax for the fiscal year 1940 was increased by 50 per cent, and registration fees were raised to 200 per cent. A new head tax was introduced which communities were required to collect from their inhabitants.

The Germans also drew heavily in other ways on the meagre finances of the population. The budget for Poland, a country of 35 million inhabitants, in normal times amounted to around 2,500 million zlotys. However the budget of the Government General for 1940 shows that it alone had a budget of 1,004,004,440 zlotys for a population which then numbered hardly a third of the former population of all Poland.

Through the Four-Year Plan introduced into the Government General by the decree of October 12, 1939, practically all raw materials and agricultural products were seized and administered by German authorities.

The anti-German attitude of the Polish population led the Germans to use special devices to get agricultural products from the Polish farmers. At first the Germans began to destroy private trade with Polish currency as their first target.

A decree was published inviting every Pole to deposit for six months with certain banks under German control all Polish currency with the exception of 200 zlotys. After the six months had elapsed, the money was to be stamped and returned to the depositors. There was also a provision that any money that had not been deposited should lose its value. The Germans knew that the Poles mistrusted them and would not deposit their money and there were, in fact, very few deposits so after six months the greater part of the Polish currency in circulation was destroyed. With the destruction of the currency, no trade could be carried on.

Then the Germans proceeded toward their intended goal. There were in Poland special co-operative agricultural societies for trade with the peasants. The Germans took these societies under their control, and provided them with manufactured goods that any peasant could buy upon presentation of a certificate from one of the co-operative associations testifying that he had sold a part of his agricultural products to that association. Through the destruction of Polish currency, and through the lack of manufactured goods in the towns, private trade was thereby destroyed, the peasants being compelled to trade with the German-controlled agricultural associations. Thus the Germans came into control of the agricultural products of the country.

Then on August 1, 1944, the Polish underground army in Warsaw rose in rebellion against the Germans. The leaders of the Home Army had decided to undertake the operation, not only so that Poland could be seen to liberate its own capital, but also as a statement of Polish independence vis-à-vis the Soviet Union. With the Red Army having reached positions just kilometres from the city, the Poles expected that fighting would only last a couple of days before the Russians would arrive and seal the fate of the Germans. However, Soviet dictator Stalin had other plans for Poland and, on his orders, the Red Army stopped its offensive, giving the Germans ample opportunity to concentrate on brutally suppressing the uprising. The Polish insurgents — out-gunned, out-numbered and only sparingly re-supplied by Allied airdrops — fought on for an incredible 63 days until they were finally forced to capitulate on October 2.

SEQUESTRATION AND CONFISCATION

According to the decree of September 17, 1940, the property of Polish citizens was subject to sequestration, trustee administration, and confiscation although this did not apply to the property of persons who had acquired German nationality. Sequestration was required to be ordered in regard to the property of Jews and those persons who had fled or were not merely temporarily absent. Sequestration could be ordered if the property was required 'for the public welfare', particularly in the interests of Reich defence or the strengthening of Germanism, or if the owners had immigrated after October 1, 1918 into territory which had belonged to the Reich up until the end of the First World War. Excluded from such sequestration were movable objects for personal use and cash, bank or savings balances, or securities of less than 1,000 Reichsmarks.

All measures concerning sequestration, administration and confiscation under this decree were carried out through a special trustee agency under the authority of the Commissioner for the Four-Year Plan or, if concerning agriculture, through the Reich Commissioner for Strengthening Germanism.

In the first days of the uprising, barricades went up right across the city, ordinary citizens joining with the underground fighters to erect obstacles blocking streets. This is the barricade sealing off the western end of Chmielna Street in the city centre.

Although Warsaw was 85 per cent destroyed in the war, much has been repaired or painstakingly restored. Here and there, individual buildings have survived the massive redevelopment of the post-war decades so it is still possible to find meaningful comparisons in the present-day city. Chmielna Street today is a pedestrian area.

Left: During the first days of the uprising, German troops advancing through western suburbs acted with the utmost savagery, rounding up and shooting every Polish person they came across. Thousands of men, women and children were slaughtered in the boroughs of Wola and Ochota, the main perpetrators being the men of SS-Brigade RONA and SS-Brigade Dirlewanger. *Right:* This is Welska Street — then and now.

One of the Polish strongholds in the Old Town was the Bank Polski (Polish Bank). Units of the Home Army occupied this massive building on Bielanska Street. Fighting for it started on August 20 and lasted until September 1.

EDUCATION AND CULTURAL MATTERS

Education was completely re-organised and controlled by a special section under the Governor General in Krakow. In several cities and counties, the administration of schools was now directed by an educational council. The officials of the school administration had to be Germans, although the city and county educational councils could appoint Poles and Ukrainians as school supervisors for a period of two years.

German and Polish children had to be educated in different schools. German children could only attend German schools and be taught by German teachers. In places where there were at least ten German schoolchildren, a German school had to be opened. Polish grammar and professional schools were to a certain extent re-established but private Polish schools required a licence from the district governor before they could be re-opened.

The procedure of expropriating the property of Poles and Jews was considered as a primary matter of policy and severe penalties were imposed for interfering with such procedure: 'If the culprit acts from opposition to the new political order, or if the case was particularly serious for some other reason, then the death penalty shall be imposed'.

A comparison of the decree on sequestration of private property issued in the Government General with the analogous decree issued in the incorporated territories is worthwhile. In the decree on sequestration in the incorporated areas, one of the chief reasons given for confiscations and sequestrations was the 'strengthening of Germanism', whereas the decree in the Government General stated that sequestration might be ordered in connection with the performance of tasks 'serving the public interest'. In particular, in the Government General property might be liquidated because it was 'financially unremunerative' or 'anti-social'. Since the German authorities had the right to define these terms, they could likewise use the opportunity to loot.

The ruined building was never repaired and it became a symbol of the uprising. In 1984 it was decided to set up an Uprising Museum in the building but this never materialised and the plan was finally abandoned in 2002 in favour of another location.

The universities and liberal art schools were closed but on the Führer's birthday in 1940 the Governor General opened an Institute for German Eastern Work at the Polish University in Krakow. The Governor General stated in his opening speech that 'the establishment of the Institute means the resumption of the historical mission that Germanism is to fulfill in this place' and the 'restitution of all that which the Poles took away from the German spirit and German influences in this place'.

The uprising in Warsaw in 1944 was the largest rebellion to occur in any of the countries occupied by Nazi Germany. It had lasted precisely three months and by the time the Poles capitulated on October 2, between 130,000 to 180,000 civilians had lost their lives. The Home Army had suffered 18,000 casualties killed or missing and 25,000 wounded, 6,500 of them seriously. Thousands more were marched into captivity . . . the cost had been high.

On September 14, units of the Soviet Army had entered Praga, the suburb of Warsaw of the east bank of the River Vistula, but there they stayed for six weeks, restrained by orders from Josef Stalin not to come to the aid of the Polish insurgents. In the meantime, the Germans now began to follow Hitler's orders to completely demolish the city and over the following weeks more than 30 per cent of Warsaw was razed to the ground. The Soviets did not finally cross to the west bank until January 17, 1945 — over three months after the end of the uprising. *Left:* As the Germans had blown all the bridges across the river, this convoy had to cross using a wooden bridge which had been built alongside the demolished Poniatowski Bridge.

Right: Looking east along the rebuilt bridge today. Where the Poles had fought to liberate their country from the Germans, they now found it reduced in size and locked in behind the Iron Curtain. The Communist regime lasted for the next 37 years until it collapsed in 1982. During that time, military courts issued almost 6,000 death sentences, and carried out over half of them. Two million persons experienced arrest, torture and imprisonment, and six million were investigated by the secret police. The life and fate of Poles was now totally in the hands of the all-powerful Ministry of Public Security. Even as late as 1989, former members of the Home Army were still under surveillance by the security services.

RESISTANCE

From the first days of the occupation, the Polish population displayed an attitude of stubborn and uncompromising resistance to the occupiers. The Germans not only failed to organise a puppet or sub-cabinet government in Poland but they feared this resistance so much as not to allow Polish agencies to function in the middle tier of administration. The services of Poles were used only in the lowest branches of administrative agencies in the cities and communes.

Occupied Poland was covered by a network of Gestapo and SS units whose task it was to trace Polish patriotic activities, particularly in the strong underground movement. This movement was headed by a Directorate of Civilian Resistance that organised the underground press and propaganda, as well as conducting acts of sabotage, and even open hostilities carried on by the units of a secretly organised Home Army. The Directorate of Civilian Resistance organised special Polish tribunals to try Germans and occasional

Polish traitors. The sentences were issued in the name of the Polish Republic and they were normally communicated to the culprit before the penalty was executed, even if the person was tried in absentia.

The distrust and the fear of patriotic conspiracy went so far that no opportunity was given for Poles to assemble, even for social events. An order was even published on April 9, 1941 covering the prohibition of dancing in the Government General. This was absolute and no exceptions were made, even for private parties.

THE EASTERN POLISH TERRITORIES

The Eastern Territories of Poland were different from the Incorporated Eastern Territories discussed earlier.

The Wilno area was occupied in September 1939, and handed over to Lithuania by Russia the following month. In June 1941, the same area was occupied by Germany. The city of Wilno, together with the western part of the province of Wilno, was administered as part of the General Commissariat of Lithuania.

Other territories between the pre-war Polish-Russian frontier and the area of Bialystok (which was incorporated as a separate unit into East Prussia) were administered as part of the General Commissariat of White Russia. Bialystok with its surrounding area, as well as the province of Wolhynia, was occupied by Russia in September 1939 but later on in June-July 1941 by Germany in the course of the Russo-German war.

The south-eastern Polish province of Wolhynia and the southern part of the province of Polesie were administered as part of the Commissariat for the Ukraine.

RAPHAEL LEMKIN, 1944

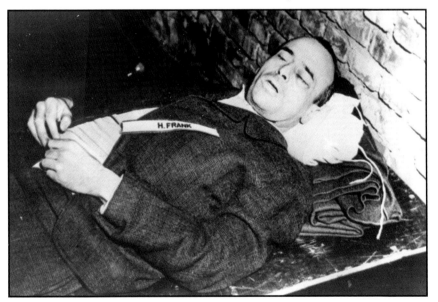

In January 1944, an attempt to assassinate Gauleiter Hans Frank by trying to blow up his train near Krakow failed, and after he was captured by American troops in Bavaria he tried to commit suicide twice. In the end it was left to the International Military Tribunal sitting at Nuremberg to convict him of carrying out 'a common plan or conspiracy to seize power and establish a totalitarian regime to prepare and wage a war of aggression; violation of the laws of war, and crimes against humanity, persecution and extermination'. He went to the gallows on the night of October 15/16, 1946.

In 1941, the Soviets attempted to blame the Nazis for an atrocity of horrendous proportions, yet it was not until 1990 that Mikhail Gorbachev finally admitted the culpability of the Soviet Union in the killing of many thousands of captured Polish servicemen. For 50 years after the war, the authorities in the Soviet Union maintained this Polish cemetery in a wood at Katyn, just west of Smolensk, as a 'Memorial to the victims of Hitler-Fascist Terror'. This chapter describes what really took place, and is included to illustrate the cover-up of an event attributed to the Axis forces.

A Soviet Massacre blamed on the Nazis

On September 17, 1939, two weeks after beginning of the Second World War, the Soviet Union invaded Poland from the east. Battling now against an invasion from east and west, the Polish Army was soon overcome. Several Polish units surrendered to the Soviets induced by a pledge that all officers and men would be released and given a choice either to return home or cross the frontier into Romania or Hungary so that they could join the Polish forces which were being formed abroad to continue the fight against the Germans. However, units that did so, like the garrison of Lwów, were taken prisoner and deported to camps in Russia. In all, the Soviets took some 250,000 Polish soldiers prisoner, among them at least 8,500 officers

After Germany and the USSR had carved up Poland between them, Stalin set about to systematically liquidate all of Poland's potential leaders of opposition, both military and intellectual. Having captured a large part of the Polish officer corps, he had the NKVD (the Soviet secret state police), concentrate these officers in three special camps in the western part of the Soviet Union: Kozielsk, Starobielsk and Ostashkov. The total number of prisoners detained was around 15,000.

In all three camps, the Soviets started a programme of 're-education'. They bombarded the prisoners with Soviet propaganda, by means of lectures, posters, Soviet newspapers printed in Polish, loud-speaker radio broadcasts, film shows, etc. They also tried to stamp out religious practices among the Poles, forbidding communal evening prayers and arresting chaplains for conducting mass. The Poles proved particularly recalcitrant here and they continued to practice their religious beliefs in secret. To determine which of the prisoners could possibly be of use to the Soviet Union, every man was interrogated by the NKVD. Each prisoner was photographed and his personal dossier was sent to Moscow for evaluation. This screening campaign lasted six months, from October 1939 to March 1940.

In early April 1940 news of the impending dissolution of the camps reached the prisoners. Rumours were rife as to what would happen to them: many expected that they would be handed over to the Western Allies; others that they would be sent back home, i.e. to territories now occupied by Germany, Lithuania or the USSR; the more pessimist ones thought they would simply be transferred to other camps, or handed over to the Germans and interned by them.

Although the camps were located in widely-separated administrative districts, their clearing was evidently based on a single plan, prepared beforehand by the highest Soviet authorities. The disbandment was started simultaneously, and the procedure was the same in each camp. The prisoners were sent away in groups of between 100 and 300 men. The groups were not made up at random, but according to lists of named prisoners. At about 10 a.m., a telephone call would come from Moscow ordering the camp commander to organise a transport for that day and giving the names of the people that were to be included. The groups left more or less regularly, sometimes on successive days, sometimes at intervals of several days, departing in rail wagons. At Kozielsk, the first group left on April 3, 1940 and it took 21 convoys to clear the camp. The liquidation of the camps took some five to six weeks and by mid-May all three had ceased to exist.

On June 22, 1941, Germany invaded the Soviet Union. Under the new political-military situation, diplomatic relations between the Russia and Poland were resumed. The Polish government-in-exile in London made no special reservation, nor asked for any compensation from the Soviets, but only for a return to the status quo of before the Soviet aggression. And it requested an immediate release of all Polish prisoners held on Soviet territory. This was granted in the Polish-Soviet Agreement which was signed on July 30,1941, and the Polish-Soviet Military Agreement signed on August 14. From that moment, Polish prisoners of war

and civilian internees deported from Poland by the Soviets, were released from camps and prisons to join the Polish units that were being organised on Soviet territory. General Wladyslaw Anders (himself released from Lubianka Prison in Moscow on August 4), was appointed Commander of Polish Forces in the USSR where he set up a Polish Army headquarters.

Very soon, however, the members of Anders' headquarters realised that many officers whom they knew personally, and who according to their own most reliable intelligence had been taken prisoner by the Soviets in 1939, were still missing. Among them were nearly all the officers of General Anders' own command group of 1939. The Polish authorities then learned of the three special camps where some 15,000 had been held, and of the camps' dissolution in April-May 1940.

As early as August 16, at his first official meeting with the Soviet military authorities, General Anders asked about the men from these three camps. The Soviets replied they were unable to answer the question but would try to obtain exact information. When pressed, the Soviet liaison officers attached to the Polish HQ stated they also were unable to supply any further details, and repeated the old semi-official story that many Polish officers had been released in 1940 and sent back to Poland.

The Polish HQ in the USSR set up a special department tasked with drawing up a list of the missing officers. These lists were compiled with great difficulty from memory and, at the same time, the Polish authorities asked the Underground Army in Poland to investigate the Soviet claim that the missing prisoners had been sent home. Their reports confirmed that these officers had definitely not returned home, and also that they were not being held in German POW camps.

Meanwhile, the Polish Ambassador in Moscow, Professor Stanislaw Kot, made strenuous efforts to get the Soviet government to abide by its pledges to release all

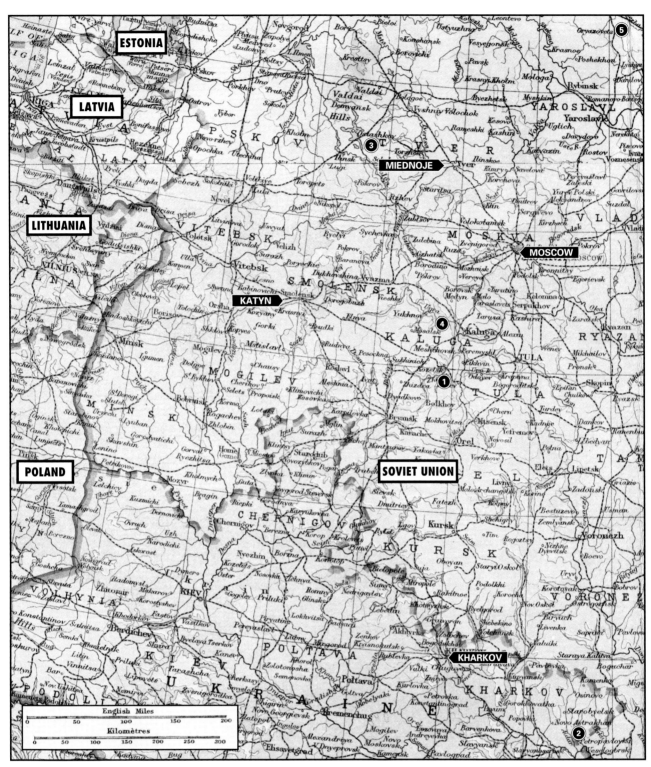

Polish citizens, requesting permission to contact those who were still unable to leave their camps, and asking about the whereabouts of the missing prisoners. Between September 20 and November 12, he had five meetings with the Soviet Deputy Commissar for Foreign Affairs, Andrei Vyshinsky, at which he brought up the subject. Each time, Vyshinsky only came with vague and non-committal answers, saying that the figures of missing persons quoted by the Poles were incorrect and much too high, or that the matter was being looked into but that administrative problems had caused delays, or repeating the claim that all prisoners had been released. Twice, on September 27 and again on October 13, Kot handed the Soviet government a formal note stating that it was not abiding by its pledges.

After Germany and the USSR had carved up Poland between them in September 1939, Stalin set about to systematically eliminate potential opposition, both military and intellectual. Having captured a large part of the Polish officer corps, he had the Soviet secret police, the NKVD, concentrate these men in three special camps in western Russia: [1] Kozielsk. [2] Starobielsk. [3] Ostashkov. Between September 1939 and March 1940 the prisoners were interrogated to discover if any of the Poles might be of future use to the Soviets, and any suitable candidates were sent to Pavlishchev Bor [4] or Griazovietz [5]. Early in April, groups of prisoners in batches of 100 to 300 were despatched from each of the three camps for an unknown destination in western Russia.

On October 22, Kot had a meeting with the Soviet foreign minister, Vyacheslav Molotov, at which he raised the question again. Molotov replied that all Polish citizens had been released but that owing to a great shortage of transport and administrative difficulties they were still in the places where they had been detained.

On November 1, Kot handed Molotov yet another note about the prisoners, and on November 3, at a Polish request, the British government queried the Soviet authorities on the same matter. This precipitated a note sent by Molotov on November 8 that declared that all Polish citizens in Soviet custody had now been released. A note delivered by

Arriving at Gniezdovo railway station, the prisoners from Kozielsk were off-loaded into buses and driven down a small road to the main Smolensk-Vitebsk highway.

Alexander Bogomolov, the Soviet Ambassador to the Polish government in London, on November 14 specifically added that all Polish officers detained on USSR territory had also been released and that the Polish assumption that they were still somewhere in the northern areas was based on inaccurate information.

Eventually, after three and a half months of vain attempts to find the missing men, Kot was able on November 14 to obtain an audience with Stalin. Molotov was also present. In answer to Kot's queries, Stalin too said that all Poles had been released, suggesting the missing ones had gone to Romania. In the course of the interview, Stalin picked up a phone, requested to be put through to the NKVD: 'Stalin here. Have all Poles been released from prison? Because I have with me here the Polish Ambassador who tells me not all have been.' After a few minutes, he received an answering call, but did not say what had been reported. Presumably, it was all an act staged to give the impression that Stalin himself had not been properly informed about, or personally involved in the fate of the Polish prisoners.

Meanwhile, not handicapped by diplomatic protocol, General Anders had approached the NKVD directly. On November 4, he sent a letter in which he estimated the number of missing officers at 8,722, adding the list was not complete. There was no reply.

As a final attempt, General Wladyslaw Sikorski, the Polish Prime Minister and C-in-C of the Polish Armed Forces, flew from London to Moscow for a personal interview with Stalin. The meeting took place at the Kremlin on December 3, with Anders and Molotov present. Sikorski handed Stalin a list of 3,845 officers of whom the Poles had confirmed that they were not at home nor in German POW camps. Stalin at first suggested they must have escaped, possibly to Manchuria, then repeated the old excuse that some might not yet have made it back from their faraway detention places, and promised that special instructions would be issued to settle this.

At first, the Polish civilian and military authorities were prepared to believe the Soviet explanations but, as time went on, they became more and more suspicious. They no longer believed the Soviet excuses, and supposed that the missing prisoners had been sentenced to imprisonment. The Polish government still hoped that if a conciliatory attitude was taken towards the Soviets they would be released, and therefore tried to prevent this question from gaining too much publicity. Nobody in Polish circles suspected that not one of the missing POWs remained alive.

In January 1942, Anders appointed Captain Josef Czapski as officer in charge of the search for the missing prisoners. He had meetings with General Viktor Nasyedkin, Chief Commander of the GULAG (Directorate of Labour Camps), and with General Leonid Rajchman, Assistant Deputy Head of the NKVD, but again he got nowhere.

On March 18, General Anders and his Chief-of-Staff, Colonel Leopold Okulicki, had another audience with Stalin and Molotov, at which he handed over two lists containing 800 additional names of missing officers, offering them as instruments to help the Soviets in their search. Stalin said he did not know where the missing men were. 'It may be that they were in camps in territories which have been taken over by the Germans and came to be dispersed', he said. This was the first mention of what later became the official Soviet version of the fate of the disappeared Polish POWs.

The summer of 1942 passed without any of the missing men surfacing. When the Polish Forces in the USSR left for the Middle East in the autumn, new rumours began circulating that they were still in the arctic northern regions. On October 19, the Polish Defence Minister in London, Lieutenant-General Marian Kukiel, referred to these new rumours in a conversation with the Soviet Ambassador, Bogomolov. At this, the latter suddenly broke off the conversation looking so 'disturbingly helpless' that an alarmed and worried Kukiel concluded that Bogomolov knew that they had all perished.

Lageskizze der Ausgrabungsstelle

Sipatschi

NowoBateki

Sofiewka

zur Autobahn MOSKAU-MINSK

Dnjepr

Ausgrabungsstelle

0   1   2 Km

Kuprino

Olscha

Dubrowjenki

van Witebsk

Katyn

Gniesdowa   Dnjepr

SMOLENSK

Wonlju-rowo

Katyn

Lugawtzy

Dnjepr

Übersichtsskizze

Eisenbahnen   Straßen   0   5   10 Km

Three kilometres further on the transport turned left into the forest at Katyn.

On April 13, 1943, Berlin radio broadcast the following news: 'A report has reached us from Smolensk to the effect that the local inhabitants have mentioned to the German authorities the existence of a place where mass executions had been carried out by the Bolsheviks and where 10,000 Polish officers had been murdered by the GPU [the predecessor of the NKVD].

'The German authorities accordingly went to a place called Kosygory [i.e. 'Goats Hill' — a small hill inside the Katyn Wood], a Soviet summer rest resort situated 12 kilometres west of Smolensk, where a terrible discovery was made. A ditch was found, 28 metres long and 16 metres wide, in which the bodies of about 3,000 Polish officers were piled up in 12 layers. They were fully dressed in military uniforms, some were bound, and all had pistol shot wounds in the back of their heads. There will be no difficulty in identifying the bodies as, owing to the nature of the ground, they are in a state of mummification and the Bolsheviks have left on the bodies their personal documents. It has been stated today that General Smorawinski from Lublin has been found amongst the murdered officers. Previously, these officers were in a camp at Kozielsk near Orel and in February and March, 1940, were brought in cattle wagons to Smolensk. Thence they were taken in lorries to Kosygory and were murdered there by the Bolsheviks. The search for further pits is in progress. New layers may be found under those already discovered. It is estimated that the total number of officers killed amounts to 10,000, which would correspond to the entire cadre of Polish officers taken prisoner by the Bolsheviks. The correspondents of Norwegian newspapers, who were on the spot and were thus able to obtain direct evidence of the crime, immediately sent their despatches to their papers in Oslo.'

The news about the Polish graves in the Katyn forest had reached the German authorities in February 1943, and Sekretär Ludwig Voss of the Gruppe Geheime Feldpolizei 570 was appointed to lead the investigation. Preliminary excavations, carried out during the February frost, proved the existence of mass graves. At the same time, Voss began collecting sworn evidence of numerous witnesses, and on March 1 the Germans brought in Professor Dr Gerhard Buhtz, Professor for Forensic Medicine and Criminology at Breslau (Wroclaw) University, for the forensic medical investigations. Systematic and large-scale excavations were then begun on March 29. Little by little the appalling scope of the mass murder was revealed.

Witnesses described how between March and May 1940, trains, consisting of three to four carriages with gratings over the windows, had arrived almost daily at Gniezdovo station, nine kilometres west from Smolensk and three kilometres east of the forest, bringing loads of between 100 and 300 prisoners of war in Polish uniforms. Their personal belongings would be taken from them and be thrown on lorries while the prisoners themselves would be put into three prison buses and driven towards the NKVD rest-house in Katyn forest. The buses were of a closed type especially adapted for transporting prisoners. A narrow corridor ran up the centre, on both sides of which were many low and narrow doors. When a prisoner stepped into the corridor, an NKVD man ordered him to step backwards into one of the cabins which were unlit and so small the prisoners had to crouch. Sometimes, the buses repeated the journey between Gniezdovo station and the NKVD rest-house ten times a day.

The German announcement about the mass graves at Katyn made a tremendous impression and caused deep dismay in Polish circles. However as the rest of the world knew nothing about the Poles missing in Russia, or the Polish behind-the-scene attempts to find them, they found it all hard to believe. Many thought it was just another German propaganda stunt designed to turn opinion against Germany's largest enemy.

On April 15, Radio Moscow broadcast a vehement rejection of the 'vile fabrications' made against the USSR which it said served only to cover up the fact that the Germans themselves had murdered the Polish prisoners who — so the report claimed — 'in 1941 were engaged in construction work in areas west of the Smolensk region and who fell into the hands of the German-Fascist hangmen in the summer of 1941'. The BBC bulletin broadcast on the 15th flatly accepted the Soviet denial, and spoke of 'German lies'.

Realising the free world would be hesitant to accept the German revelations at face value, Germany sought a neutral and competent international body to confirm her findings. On April 16, the German Red Cross requested the International Red Cross (IRC) in Geneva to send a delegation to participate in the investigation on the spot.

In London, the Polish government was in a difficult position: it knew that both the Nazi and Soviet dictatorships were capable of the crime, but the overwhelming evidence pointed to the murders having been committed by the Soviet Union. Next day, April 17, the Polish government, too, instructed its representative in Switzerland, Prince Stanislaw Radziwill, to request the IRC to send a delegation to Katyn to investigate the German revelations.

Left: **The Polish soldiers were first marched to this 'datcha' (Russian for villa) that was used by NKVD officers as a summer rest-house. It stood at the far end of the wood overlooking the** gorge of the Dnieper river. *Right:* **This ruin is all that remains of the original building and even that has not been preserved and has now been replaced.**

Since similar proposals had now come from two parties between whom a state of war existed, according to the rules laid down by the IRC, the matter would have to be put before its Executive Council, a special session of which was announced for April 20. However, before that took place, and also as a result of Soviet opposition, the IRC changed its mind. The IRC rules stipulated that it could only take part in an investigation of this kind if all the parties agreed to it. The IRC therefore suggested to the German Red Cross and the Polish government to obtain the consent of the USSR, either directly or through an intermediary.

Instead of consenting to an independent international inquiry, the USSR now began attacking the Polish government for 'collaborating' with Nazi Germany. On the night of April 25/26, the Polish Ambassador was summoned to the Commissariat for Foreign Affairs, where Molotov read out a note expressing Soviet indignation over the Polish behaviour, behind which they suspected a Polish scheme to wrest territorial concessions from the USSR, and announcing the Soviet Union's immediate severance of all relations with the Polish government. (Shortly before, the Soviets had set up a 'Polish Committee' in Moscow made up of Polish communists, and this they now recognised as representing Poland.)

This action by the USSR surprised public opinion in the West and revived fears that Russia might make a separate peace with Germany. Worried that the unity of the Allies was threatened, the British government immediately tried to appease both parties. The Soviet Union, however, persisted in its stand.

The Soviet reaction, both its refusal to consent to an IRC investigation and its cutting of relations with Poland, was not lost on the world. Many who at first had been sceptic about the German revelations, discarding it as propaganda, now began to have second thoughts.

The prisoners were then led some 300 metres to the execution site where grave pits had already been prepared. Taken in 1942, this is the earliest known photograph showing one of the mass graves marked with a simple birch-wood cross.

Meanwhile, the excavations in Katyn forest continued. To confirm the fact that Kosygory Hill had already been used for executions before the war by the GPU and its predecessor, the Cheka, the Germans carried out several experimental excavations. In the wooded area to the north-east of the Polish graves, on the opposite site of the track to the NKVD house, and also in the woods to the south, several graves were discovered containing bodies of Russian civilians of both sexes who, without exception, had been killed by a neck shot. Many had their hands tied behind their backs. From documents found, it appeared they were prisoners from the NKVD jail in Smolensk, the majority being political prisoners. Their state of decomposition varied but in all cases was such that they must have lain buried for many years.

Although the Germans had attacked the Soviet Union in June 1941, the true horror of what had taken place at Katyn only came to light in February 1943. A German war photographer was present throughout the excavations, Russian labourers being used for the actual digging.

The main excavations, however, concentrated on the Polish mass graves. By late April, seven separate grave pits had been laid bare. They covered a relatively small area in a clearing in the wood and were all on the south-western side of a small sandy hill sloping down to a marshy area. They were fairly easily recognisable because of the young fir trees which had been planted on top of them. The average depth of the pits was about 2.3 metres and the graves were filled with bodies up to 1.5 metres of the surface. By April 26 some 900 bodies had been exhumed of which some 600 had been identified.

The exhumations were well organised. The actual grave-digging was done by 35 Russian civilian workmen recruited locally. The autopsies and identifications were done by Dr Buhtz and his specially trained, 13-strong team of doctors, analysts, autopsy assistants and photo lab workers. Polizeisekretär Voss had arranged for stretchers, autopsy tables, surgical instruments and a water cart to be brought to the site. A wooden shed in a nearby village was taken down and rebuilt next to the graves, fitted with a stove and roof windows to serve as all-temperature autopsy room where frozen corpses could be macerated. The Wehrmacht field laboratory at Smolensk was available for laboratory tests. The Feldpolizei were responsible for cordoning off the site, assisted by Polish policemen and Russian auxiliary guards.

Each exhumed body was given a serial number (stamped on a metal disc which was attached to the victim's clothing) and then searched for documents. Papers and personal effects were put in special paper bags marked with the same serial number.

The bodies were in various stages of decay. In a few cases, notably at the top and at the sides of the graves, mummification of the uncovered parts of bodies had taken place, but elsewhere and with bodies nearer the centre a humid process had taken place. Adjacent bodies were stuck together with a thick putrid liquid, as if glued to one another. Moreover, the weight of the mass of bodies had completely flattened those in the lower layers. The grave workers had great difficulty wrenching the corpses out, having to wedge each body carefully and then tear it away from the others.

The uniforms left no doubt that the victims were Polish officers. Supporting this were Polish eagles on the buttons, badges of rank, awards and medals, regimental badges, Polish-type long boots, field caps, belts with field flasks, aluminium cups, and markings on the linen.

There were several clues as to the period that the executions had taken place. Letters and postcards with post office stamps from the German-occupied and Soviet-occupied zones of Poland pointed to a time after September 1939. All bodies wore winter clothing, mostly military greatcoats, leather or fur jerkins, pullovers and sweaters. No insects were found in the graves, which pointed to execution and burial in a cool season. Various Russian and Polish newspapers were found on the bodies, all dating from March or the first half of April 1940.

Excavation of the burial pits began in earnest at the end of March. A number of 'autopsy' tables had been prepared to examine and, hopefully, identify the corpses.

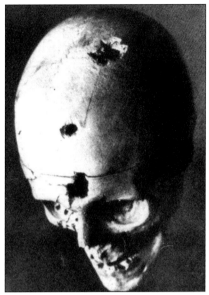

Left: **The victims had all been despatched by shots to the head, sometimes more than one.** *Right:* **The many 7.65mm cartridge cases found were all of German manufacture by the Gustav Genschow Company of Durlach, near Karlsruhe. These rounds were later confirmed as coming from batches supplied to both Poland and the Soviet Union between the wars.**

Without exception, all victims were killed by a shot in the back of the head, the bullet entering below the protrusion on the back of the skull and exiting in the forehead above the eye. A few victims had a double neck shot; two had been shot three times. In many instances, the bullet had been fired through the raised-up collar of the greatcoat. In many cases, it had not left the skull, or was found lodged between the forehead and the inside of the cap. Apart from one 6.35mm bullet, all were of 7.65mm calibre. A number of spent pistol cartridge cases stamped 'Geco 7.65 D' were found in the area of the graves or among the bodies, and one live cartridge. There was a great surprise, followed by a short period of panic among the German authorities, when it was discovered that these bullets were of German manufacture, having been produced by the firm of Gustav Genschow & Co in Durlach, near Karlsruhe. The panic only subsided when the German Army HQ confirmed that ammunition for pistols of that calibre, and actual pistols, had been supplied to the Soviet Union and Poland before the war, notably between 1922 and 1931. The bullets could either be from Russian dumps or from Polish equipment captured in 1939.

A great number of the bodies had their hands tied behind their backs. The ropes had apparently been prepared beforehand as they were cut in identical lengths of 1.75-1.95 metres, and a uniform method of binding had been used. In addition, several of the victims had their heads wrapped up in their overcoats, the greatcoat or service dress having been pulled over the head and tied around the neck with cords, so tight it must have virtually choked the victims. The head and hand bindings were then tied together tightly. Some victims in addition had their mouths stuffed with sawdust. Again, these were evidently men who had shouted or resisted at the moment of execution. All these methods were identical — so it was noted — to those used on the Russian civilian victims found in the pre-war GPU graves nearby. Also, both the expert and uniform neck shot and the uniform way of tying the victims' hands and binding their heads pointed to executions by men skilled and experienced in this kind of work.

Prevented by the USSR from obtaining an investigation by the International Red Cross, the Germans decided to do the next best thing: they invited distinguished professors of forensic medicine from 12 neutral European countries to join an International Medical Commission to conduct an investigation on the spot. The term 'neutral' meant only that the countries had no direct interest in the matter for of the 12 countries, four were

German-occupied, seven allied to Germany (Bulgaria, Croatia, Finland, Hungary, Italy, Romania, Slovakia), and only one (Switzerland) really neutral.

In their final report, the International Commission confirmed the findings of the German investigation, concluding that the executions had taken place in March and April 1940.

When the commission left on May 1, 982 bodies had been exhumed. The excavation continued. After identification and forensic examination, the bodies were reburied with the help of members of the Polish Red Cross in newly-dug pits situated just to the north-west of the original graves. The new graves were numbered 1 to 6. The two identified generals were buried in single graves.

On June 3, the German police ordered the exhumation work to be stopped for sanitary reasons on account of the summer heat and the flies. The work came to an end on June 7. The Germans planned to resume the exhumations at a later date, but owing to the flux of war it never came to that. By late summer 1943, the Red Army was inexorably pushing the Wehrmacht back westward, and by the end of September the Soviets had freed Smolensk and pushed beyond Katyn.

In a way, the loss of the massacre site helped the Germans to dispose of a difficult problem. In all of their reports, they had upheld their initial claim that the Katyn

graves contained an estimated 10,000 to 12,000 Polish officers, i.e. the full cadre of the Polish Army, but by now they had about emptied the gravepits and knew there were far less than that, only about 4,300. Worried that this lower figure would jeopardise their propaganda, they kept silent about it, hoping perhaps to find the remaining corpses when diggings could be resumed. The loss of the site solved this problem for them.

As soon as they retook the region of the Katyn graves in September 1943, the Soviets launched their own counter-investigation. They set up an 'Extraordinary State Commission for Ascertaining and Investigating the Crimes committed by the German-Fascist Invaders and their Associates'. This in turn set up a 'Special Commission for Ascertaining and Investigating the Circumstances of the Shooting of Polish Officer Prisoners by the German-Fascist Invaders in the Katyn Wood'. A Russian team went to Smolensk on September 26, 1943, and conducted an alleged four months of study and investigation into the massacre. The Soviets dug up more bodies to carry out their own post-mortems, inviting a score of Allied journalists in Moscow to look at the bodies. Most journalists were prepared to believe the Soviet version that they had been killed by the Germans in late summer 1941, although several began having doubts when they noticed most corpses were clad in winter clothes.

A considerable number of the bodies still had their hands tied behind their backs.

The Germans were convinced that the Russians were responsible for carrying out the massacre in 1940, but the Soviets refuted this saying that the Germans had perpetrated it in 1941. The Germans made great efforts to sway international opinion their way, even taking Allied officers from German POW camps to view the massacre site, but suspicion that it was all a propaganda exercise to discredit the Russians was hard not to accept. These two American prisoners have been identified as Lieutenant Colonel John H. van Vliet and Captain Donald B. Stewart, both of whom had been captured in North Africa.

The report of the Special Commission, released on January 24, 1944, concluded that the Katyn murders had been committed by the Germans in September-December 1941. They even named the German unit that did it: Nachrichten-Regiment 537. The sudden departure from the earlier Soviet claims of 'August-September 1941' was probably caused by the need to explain the victims' winter clothes.

Although the Soviet exhumations had been insufficient to warrant proper calculations, their report very cleverly agreed with the German estimation of 1943 that the graves contained some 11,000 corpses. By doing so, the Soviets conveniently solved the disappearance of many more Polish prisoners than the 4,300 that had actually been found, and avoided awkward questions about what had happened to the others.

In general, the Soviet report did not stand up to careful scrutiny but the Western allies, needing the Soviet Union in the common fight against Nazi Germany, were unwilling to query the Russian story. US President Franklin D. Roosevelt played an important part in suppressing the truth about Katyn. Roosevelt thought it was all a German plot and was convinced the Soviets had not done it. In the post-war era, with the world divided into two blocks, it was still not in the interest of the Western powers to irritate or provoke the Soviet Union, and further mention of Katyn would have done just that.

After the 1945 Yalta Conference, the Western nations opted to recognise the Soviet-sponsored Communist government of Poland, withdrawing recognition of the Polish government-in-exile in London in July. Indefatigably, the exiled Poles continued to fight for their cause, and for the perpetrators of Katyn to be punished. In December 1944, the Polish government-in-exile had appointed a special committee to conduct its own investigation into the disappearance of the 15,000 officers and intellectuals and its findings were published in February 1946.

On April 2, 1949, the Polish Association of Former Soviet Political Prisoners was founded. On April 28, 1950, at a press conference called on the occasion of what the Poles were sure was the 10th anniversary of the Katyn murder, General Anders called for the appointment of a new International Tribunal to judge the case that had been ignored at Nuremberg and condemn the culprit which the Poles were positive was the Soviet Union.

At the 1946 Nuremberg trials, the Soviet Union had brought in the Katyn massacre as part of its war crimes indictment against Germany, but by failing to pin the blame on the Germans, the Russians had only strengthened the suspicion against themselves. However, the court chose to drop the case.

For over 35 years, there was no memorial anywhere in the world to the 14,500 Poles murdered under Soviet terror. In Poland, the Communist regime did not allow any Katyn memorial to be set up, let alone one that would date the crime to 1940. To correct this,

a Katyn Memorial Committee was set up in Britain. It took several years to achieve its goal, Soviet diplomatic protests frightening Her Majesty's government from giving the committee its wholehearted support, but a Katyn Memorial was finally unveiled in Gunnersbury Cemetery in Hammersmith, London, on September 18, 1976.

For nearly 50 years, notwithstanding de-Stalinisation under Khrushchev, Moscow continued to uphold Stalin's version of Katyn. After the war, the Katyn wood grave-site was made into a monument to the 'Polish officers murdered by the German-Fascist invaders'. For nearly 50 years, and all through the Cold War, Katyn continued to cloud the relations between Poland and the Soviet Union, yet the subjugated Poles did not forget Katyn. In October 1956, demonstrators in the streets of Warsaw chanted 'Katyn, Katyn, Katyn'.

In the late 1970s, things began to shift in Poland with the rise of the Solidarnosc movement. In Warsaw, a birch grove in Powazki Military Cemetery was baptised a symbolic grave of Katyn victims. Known as the 'Katyn Hollow', it became a place of pilgrimage to dissidents and a symbol of opposition to the government, especially after the new Polish leader, General Wojciech Jaruzelski, declared martial law on December 13, 1981. Then, at Easter 1985, the Polish authorities sprang a surprise move. Overnight, they erected a granite cross in the cemetery with the text: 'To the Polish soldiers, victims of Hitlerite fascism who rest in the Katyn soil'. The inscription caused widespread indignation and in protest people wrote 'NKVD 1940' in the sand around the cross.

On June 4, 1989, the Solidarnosc democrats defeated the Communists in the Polish general elections. The new government immediately increased the pressure on Moscow concerning the Katyn issue. At home, the Poles could at last talk freely about Katyn. Signs that the subject was no longer taboo were immediately evident. The inscription on the granite cross at Powazki Cemetery, already changed in April, was finally given a year: '1940'. In October, millions of people watched a documentary about Katyn, the first programme on Katyn ever broadcast by Polish television. That same October, the Russian authorities for the first time allowed a group of Polish relatives of Katyn victims to visit the memorial in Katyn wood.

The approach of warmer weather led to a profusion of flies so in June exhumations had to be halted and the bodies reburied, watched here by Allied officers.

Katyn remained in German hands only for another three months and just ten days before the fall of Smolensk a delegation of Vichy French officers and journalists, led by the French Ambassador Fernand de Brinon, visited Katyn. Here they are pictured at the graves of Polish Generals Mieczyslaw Smorawinski and Bronislaw Bohatyrewicz, whose remains had been identified. They were the only victims to be accorded individual graves. By the end of September 1943 the advancing Red Army had retaken Smolensk, leaving the Katyn Wood area out of bounds to western visitors.

At last, on the 50th anniversary of the crime — April 13, 1990 — the USSR for the first time admitted that it was responsible for the Katyn murders. Chairman Mikhail Gorbachev ordered a judicial inquiry into the Katyn case, calling upon the prosecutor's office to search KGB and Interior Ministry archives for files to reveal the truth.

Then, within a very short time, the two massacre sites of the Poles from the other two POW camps were found. First, in May 1990, the Russian Memorial association, a private organisation founded in the wake of 'glasnost' and dedicated to the memory of the victims of Stalinism, announced that it had discovered a mass grave of Polish officers in a wood near Kharkov. Researchers of the local Kharkov branch had been looking for graves of Ukrainian victims and accidentally stumbled upon the Polish graves. It soon became clear that it contained the remains of the 3,891 prisoners from Starobielsk, whose trace had ended at Kharkov station. Then in June 1990 the Soviet Military Attorney-General's office announced that it had found another mass grave of Polish officers at Miednoje near Tver (Kalinin), about 160 kilometres north-west of Moscow. This contained the remains of the Ostashkov prisoners, 6,287 in all in 30 separate pits.

Then, 52 years after the crime, came the final disclosure and admission of guilt. On October 14, 1992, Russian President Boris Yeltsin sent the director of the Russian State Archive, Rudolf Pikhoya, to Warsaw as a personal envoy to hand over to Polish President Lech Walesa copies of documents which finally proved Soviet responsibility. One was a proposal by Lavrenti Beria, chief of the NKVD, to the Politburo, dated March 5, 1940, and signed for approval by Stalin, Molotov, Voroshilov and Mikoyan, to execute 25,700 Polish officers, policemen, landowners, clergymen, state officials, and other members of the intelligentsia as 'mortal enemies of the Communist power'. Another document was a 1959 KGB report stating that 21,857 Poles had actually been executed.

Thus, the documents revealed that, if anything, all Polish and Western historians so far had underestimated the scope of the massacre: Stalin had not just ordered the elimination of the 14,700 from the three camps, but also of 11,000 others detained in Ukrainian and Byelorussian prisons; and many more graves remained to be discovered.

The documents also revealed deliberate actions of the post-war Soviet leaders to hide the truth. One document, dated March 4, 1970, recorded a decision by the Politburo, then headed by Leonid Brezhnev, that the Katyn file should be placed in a super-secret archive marked 'Do not ever open'.

The last document, dated as late as December 24, 1991, was an instruction from Gorbachev confirming that the file should remain closed. According to Pikhoya, all successors of Stalin, from Khrushchev to Gorbachev, had known of these documents, and the file had been found in the secret personal archive of the secretary of the Central Committee of the Soviet Union, i.e. Gorbachev.

Yeltsin's move was generally seen as an attempt to discredit his predecessor and rival for power Gorbachev by exposing him as a man who only paid lip-service to the truth, and to expose the Russian Communist Party as a criminal organisation.

The controversy finally laid to rest, both governments embarked on reconciliation. On August 25, 1993, during his first state visit to Poland, Yeltsin laid flowers at the Katyn monument in the Powazki Cemetery.

However, even though Russia admitted its guilt, the Katyn case was still a delicate matter. For one thing, Moscow was afraid that Poland would demand financial compensation, and many Poles were still angry that the Russians had never made an official apology for their crime. Also, other Eastern European countries — Hungary, Finland and the Baltic countries — mourn similar victims of Soviet terror and might demand similar enquiries which could lead to more mass graves being located.

Since the discovery of the graves at Miednoje and Kharkov, Polish efforts have been directed at getting permission to turn them into proper cemeteries. At Katyn a high steel fence, which the Soviets had erected closely around the Polish Memorial to keep visitors from exploring the rest of the wood, ran right across the site of the original graves and blocked access to other possible grave-sites.

After prolonged negotiations with the Russians, Polish investigative teams of the Rada Ochrony Pamieci Walk i Meczenstwa (Council for the Preservation of the Memory of the Struggles and Martyrdom) left for Russia in September 1994 to conduct surveys and earth soundings at the three sites. The work was continued in June-September 1995, resulting in extensive written, photographic and cartographic documentation. At Katyn, the steel fence was removed and the exact position of the original graves plotted.

On June 4, 1995, Walesa travelled to Katyn wood to lay a memorial plaque in memory of the victims buried there and elsewhere in Russia. In his message to Walesa, Yeltsin noted that Stalin's henchmen had also buried more than 10,000 other victims of various nationalities in the forest declaring that 'we consider this forest a memorial for the victims of totalitarianism, where a monument to all the innocent victims should be created'.

KAREL MARGRY, 1996

On a cold November day in 1995 Karel Margry visited Katyn only to find that winter had come early and the two Polish graves were covered with snow. (Karel's full report on the Katyn massacre appears in *After the Battle* No. 92.)

It was only in 1989 when the Communist regime in Poland was ousted that the ban on correctly dating memorials to the massacre — hence giving a clear sign as to who was responsible — was lifted. Also, in October that year, for the first time ever, the Russians permitted a group of Polish relatives to visit Katyn. Six months later, on the 50th anniversary in April 1990, Mikhail Gorbachev admitted that the Soviet Union was responsible and on October 14, 1992 the new Russian President Boris Yeltsin ordered copies of formerly secret documents to be handed over to the Polish President Lech Walesa. In June 1995, he travelled to Katyn wood to place a memorial plaque to the victims there and elsewhere in Russia. Yeltsin declared that Stalin's henchmen had buried more than 10,000 other victims of various nationalities in the wood. Then, in October 1996, Russia agreed to create a formal memorial at Katyn jointly with Poland which was opened in July 2000. A museum and exhibition centre was added in 2008.

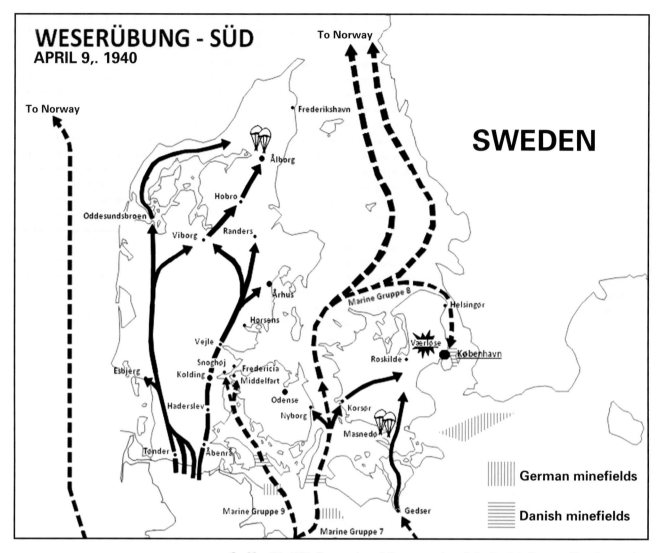

WESERÜBUNG - SÜD
APRIL 9,. 1940

To Norway

To Norway

SWEDEN

Frederikshavn

Ålborg

Hobro

Oddesundsbroen

Viborg

Randers

Århus

Horsens

Helsingør

Vejle

Marine Gruppe 8

Værløse

Snoghøj

Fredericia

Roskilde

København

Esbjerg

Kolding

Middelfart

Haderslev

Odense

Korsør

Nyborg

Masnedø

Tønder

Åbenrå

German minefields

Marine Gruppe 9

Danish minefields

Marine Gruppe 7

Gedser

Denmark

Without warning, and in violation of the Non-Aggression Pact between Germany and Denmark signed less than a year before on which the Government of Denmark strongly relied, German troops marched into Denmark and took possession of the country in the early morning hours of April 9, 1940. At the same time German cruisers entered the harbour at Middelfart on the west coast of Fyn. Other ships landed troops on the east coast of Fyn and at the Korsor.

At the very moment when the German Army began its invasion of the country, the German Minister to Denmark informed the government that German troops had occupied Denmark's most important military objectives. He then handed over a memorandum that stated that the territory of Denmark had been occupied in order to forestall violations of Denmark's neutrality by the Allies. In this memorandum the Danish Government was requested to co-operate with the German troops and a solemn promise was given by the German Government that neither the territorial integrity nor the political independence of Denmark would be challenged.

On May 31, 1939, Denmark and Germany signed the Danish-German Non-Aggression Pact which stated in Article 1: 'The Kingdom of Denmark and the German Reich will in no case resort to war or any other use of force against each other'. Less than 12 months later, the surprise invasion of Denmark on April 9, 1940 was one of the shortest military operations of the Second World War. Code-named 'Weserübung-Süd', it was all over in six hours and it also included the first-ever attack made by paratroopers.

After receiving notice of these events, as well as the memorandum, King Christian met with his government to consider the situation. The conclusion was reached that since a large part of the military objectives had already been occupied, resistance would result only in bloodshed and destruction.

A protest was presented to the German authorities against the invasion. The King gave orders to Danish troops everywhere to cease resistance but, before orders were received, some fighting had already taken place along the border.

On the same day a proclamation was issued to the people of Denmark signed by the King and Prime Minister:

'To the Danish People! German troops last night crossed the Danish frontier and have landed in various places. The Danish Government have decided under protest to arrange the affairs of the country with a view to the occupation which has taken place, in pursuance whereof the following announcement is made:

'The German troops which are now present in the country enter into contact with the Danish defence force, and it is the duty of the population to refrain from any resistance to these troops. The Danish Government will endeavour to safeguard the Danish people and our country against the disasters resulting from war conditions and therefore urge the population to adopt a calm and restrained attitude to the conditions which have now arisen. Quiet and order must prevail in the country and a loyal attitude must be displayed to all who have authority to exercise.'

The King added the following personal warning: 'Under the present conditions which are so momentous for our fatherland, I beg you all in town and country to maintain a perfectly correct and dignified behaviour, remembering that any ill-considered deed or word may entail the gravest consequences. God keep you all! God keep Denmark!'

On the same day, both houses of the Rigsdag met in joint session. The Prime Minister made a full report on the situation and the Rigsdag approved the government's action.

Commanding the operation was the career soldier-cum-aviator General Leonhard Kaupisch (left). Seeking to allay the fears of the Danes, he justified the invasion with a leaflet drop and an appeal over the radio: 'Strong German military forces have this morning taken possession of the principal military points in Denmark and Norway. These measures are the subject of agreements which are at present being made between the German Government and the Royal Danish Government to secure the continued existance of the Kingdom, the maintenance of the Army and Navy, respect for the freedom of the Danish people and the full security of the future independence of this country.' Right: The Danish border was breached in several places, the first clash with the Danish Army coming at 4.50 a.m. when a Danish anti-tank platoon opened fire on German armoured cars approaching Lundtoftbjerg. Other clashes took place at Hokkerup, Bjergskov, Bredevad, Rabsted, Aabenraa, Haderslev, Abild and Sølsted. These panzers are passing through Horsens having just left the port.

ADMINISTRATION

That same day, April 9, the commander of the German troops, General Leonhard Kaupisch, issued a proclamation to the Danish Army and the Danish nation stating that England and France had declared war on Germany without reason and in opposition to the sincere wishes of the German Government and people. He accused England of violating Danish as well as Norwegian neutrality and of preparing for a battle off the Danish and Norwegian coasts. In order to 'forestall' the English attack, the German armed forces assumed 'the protection of the neutrality of the Kingdoms of Denmark and Norway'.

The proclamation also referred to the agreements in course of negotiation with the Danish Government, the purpose of which was 'to make sure that the Danish Kingdom shall continue to exist, that the fleet shall be maintained, that the liberty of the Danish people shall be respected, and that the future independence of that country shall be secured'. The Danish military and civil authorities were then asked to enter into contact with the German commanders and the people were requested to continue to work and to preserve order.

In the first stage of occupation as it developed from April 9, 1940 until August 29, 1943, the structure of the occupation was that Danish governmental institutions remained essentially unchanged. The King carried out his royal functions and even elections to Parliament took place on March 3, 1943. The administration of the country and legislation remained in the hands of the Danish Government. Requests by the German Government, or from the occupation authorities, were presented to the Danish Government by the German Minister or by the commander of the German forces in Denmark. The Danish Government tried, through negotiations, through meeting some requests of the occupation authorities and rejecting others, to make the occupation as little of a burden as possible to the population.

In their negotiations, the German representatives used mainly the threat that if their requests should not be complied with they would not be bound by the promise of April 9, 1940 as to safeguarding the Danish Government and institutions. Also, as Denmark was dependent on German coal and fuel, they threatened to cut off the importation of these essential commodities.

Although the administration was left to the Danish Government, the Germans displayed a particular interest in the police. They required that the Danish police force be increased and trained according to German methods. In the autumn of 1941 the Polizeiverwaltung Dänemark was established. The army of occupation also succeeded in having appointed a police minister acceptable to it. The Gestapo assumed control of

The Jorgensens Hotel, now a Best Western, still stands on Sondergade.

Kaupisch served as the commander in Denmark only for two months, being replaced on June 1 by General Erich Lüdke. However he was relieved of his command in September 1942 because Hitler felt that he was not being strong enough to deal with the increasing attacks by the Danish resistance. General Hermann von Hanneken took over and it was he that imposed martial law on August 29, 1943. In November that year he moved the headquarters from the school that it had occupied in Copenhagen to a new purpose-built complex of underground bunkers in a forest at Silkeborg. General Georg Lindemann replaced von Hanneken on February 1, 1945 until the surrender on May 5.

news and information channels. Censorship was established, but handled by Danish authorities under German guidance. Movement into and out of the country was also controlled. In the summer of 1940 the Germans suggested a customs and currency union and a kind of common citizenship but the Danish Government rejected this proposal.

At the end of 1940 the Germans asked the Danish Cabinet for the retirement of Premier Thorvald Stauning and five other members of the cabinet. This request was also rejected.

When the German Minister made a demand for ten of the modern torpedo boats which formed the larger part of the Danish fleet, the demand was refused and attention called to the German promise of April 9, 1940 that the Danish Navy was to be maintained. The answer of the German Minister was that Germany wished to hire the boats for use in training crews for patrol in the Baltic but the Danes replied that their Navy was not for hire. Then the German Minister declared that if the demand was not complied with, the boats would be expropriated and delivery of German coal would cease. Under these circumstances, the boats were delivered after being disarmed and partly dismantled by the Danes.

The German military headquarters comprised 12 large and 30 smaller bunkers in the grounds of the old sanatorium at Silkeborg Bad. After the war it was used to house refugees and more recently those from Yugoslavia and Iran. In 1995 a bunker museum was opened in one of the former personel shelters.

Christian X was the King of Denmark from 1912 to 1947 and also King of Iceland between 1918 and 1944. In contrast to his brother, King Haakon VII of Norway, Queen Wilhelmina of the Netherlands, King George II of Greece, Grand Duchess Charlotte of Luxembourg, King Peter II of Yugoslavia, President Edvard Beneš of Czechoslovakia and President Wladyslaw Raczkiewicz of Poland, all of whom went into exile in Britain following the Nazi occupation of their countries, King Christian remained in his capital, becoming a popular symbol of resistance. He rode through the streets of Copenhagen every day on his horse *Jubilee*, unaccompanied by guards, claiming that 'Denmark was his bodyguard'. Until the imposition of martial law in August 1943, his policy and that of his government was peaceful co-operation with the occupying forces. However, Hitler fell out with him in 1942 after receiving only the briefest acknowledgment to a gushing telegram from the Führer congratulating the King on his 72nd birthday.

ANTI-COMMUNIST LEGISLATION

Since the beginning of the occupation the German authorities applied strong pressure upon the Danish Government to introduce anti-Jewish legislation and regulations for deporting the 5,000 Danish Jews from Denmark, and for anti-Communist legislation following Denmark's accession to the Anti-Comintern Pact. The Danish Government, especially King Christian, categorically opposed the first request so that no anti-Jewish legislation was ever enacted.

The pressure regarding anti-Communist legislation was continuous. Hitler succeeded in getting accessions to the Anti-Comintern Pact by his Axis partners Italy and Japan, and also by Hungary, Spain, Finland, Bulgaria, Croatia, Romania, Slovakia, Manchukuo, and puppet China. This pact, signed initially November 25, 1936, provided that common action should be taken by the signatory parties against communism, and that they

The Anti-Comintern Pact concluded by Germany and Japan in November 1936 was designed to oppose the expansion of the Communist International which was also known as the Comintern. Other countries were invited to join the pact and Italy and Spain signed up in November 1937, thereby forming a group later known as the Axis. In June 1941, when Germany attacked the Soviet Union, the pact was renewed with ten additional signatories: Bulgaria, Croatia, Finland, Hungary, Manchukuo, China, Romania, Slovakia, Turkey, El Salvador and also Denmark. At the same time, the German authorities in Denmark demanded the arrest of all members of Danmarks Kommunistiske Parti (DKP). The Danish government complied, rounding up 339 Communists including the three communist members of the Danish parliament. Then, on August 22, the Danes passed a law to outlaw the Communist Party and its activities, driving many into the Danish resistance movement.

In the wartime photograph, Danish police stand guard in front of the Communist Party headquarters which was located here at No. 50 Griffenfeldtsgade in Copenhagen.

Denmark had its own version of the Nazi Party, the National-socialistiske Arbejderparti (DNSAP), modelled on the German version with even a translated version of the Nazi anthem, the *Horst-Wessel-Lied.* Although it had three members in parliament it was not party to the coalition government, its main claim to fame being recruitment for the Danish Free Corps created in June 1941. This was the Frederiksberg district office at No. 135 Gammel Kongevej in Copenhagen.

should furnish one another with information as to the activities of the Communist International. Under the terms of the Anti-Comintern Pact, a permanent Executive Committee for its implementation was provided with headquarters in Berlin. After Germany marched into Russia the pressure on Denmark was increased and it finally acceded to the pact on November 25, 1941. As a result of this signature, a law was issued prohibiting Communist associations and activities in Denmark. All such associations were dissolved and conduct or propaganda in favour of communism was prohibited. Communist activities were made punishable by fines, detention or imprisonment up to one year. Of particular interest was Section 2 of this law, which provided for taking into custody any persons who had given reason to believe that 'they intend to take part in communistic activities or propaganda'. Those who were charged with such acts or intentions could be interned by decision of the Minister of Justice when it is deemed necessary 'for the sake of the security of the state or of its relations with foreign states'. However, every person taken into custody under these provisions had to be brought before the City Court of Copenhagen within 24 hours to decide whether custody should be continued. Internment could last as long as was deemed 'necessary for the security of the state or of its relations with foreign states'. The Minister of Justice was required to report every third month to a special committee created within the Rigsdag concerning those persons interned and the reasons for such action.

LABOUR

There was no law on compulsory labour or conscription, but Danish workers were compelled to accept work in Germany because of pressure upon the Danish Government, exerted chiefly through the requirement that the government would withhold unemployment relief from those Danes who would not accept offers of work in Germany.

SELLING POLICY

From the beginning, the occupation of Denmark resulted in the draining of the natural resources and stocks of commodities from the country by Germany. As a result the Danish Government felt compelled to enact a law regulating the sale of merchandise to the the German armed forces. By this means the Danes, who were not strong enough to completely prevent German purchases, endeavoured to organise sales through inter-governmental channels, wherein they could maintain a certain amount of control over such transactions. This law stated that the German armed forces in Denmark 'as a rule receive all supplies of food, forage and all other commodities from Germany'. However, the statement was somewhat illusory as the same law provided among other things for the sale of butter, meat, lard, milk, eggs and cheese without restriction except that such sales had to be made through Danish export agencies controlled by the Danish Government.

Other goods were able to be sold by the Danes to the German armed forces only by special permission issued by the Ministry of Foreign Affairs, although such permission was not required if the price of the commodities did not exceed 200 kroner per shipment. Under pressure from the Germans, the Danish Government was forced to agree that in sales to the German armed forces or to individual units, 'the Danish seller is entitled only to receive payment in the form of cheques'. In sales involving less than 200 kroner, however, payments could be made in cash. This specific regulation as to payment by cheque for larger transactions was a special form of forced long-term borrowing from the Danes.

Now the old DNSAP office is occupied by the Bambi cheese shop.

As the war continued, the curtailing of German buying became one of the main concerns of the Danish Government because the Germans wanted to purchase everything they could lay their hands on. They tried to buy or lease Danish merchantmen and smaller transport ships from Danish shipping firms, and the Danish Government was thereby compelled to issue several laws making such sales or leases dependent on the permission of the government.

After the Nazi occupation of the Ukraine, which was stripped by the retreating Russian armies of all agricultural implements, the Germans sought to buy agricultural implements from Denmark. The Danish Government then promulgated a law to the effect that sale to foreign countries of agricultural machinery or implements without permission of the Danish Directorate for Supply of Commodities was prohibited.

In order to further reduce German purchases, a law was enacted prohibiting the Danes, without the permission of the Danish National Bank, from receiving payments in any form from persons who were not residents of Denmark. Also, because of the German efforts to penetrate Danish companies, the transfer of Danish securities to foreigners was forbidden.

CLEARING ARRANGEMENTS

The main exploitation of Denmark was carried out through the institution of financial clearing arrangements. Under this measure with the Danish National Bank, all trade settlements between Germany and Denmark had to be made through the Verrechnungskasse in Berlin and the Clearing Insti-

On November 17, 1940, the fledgling Danish Nazi Party held a rally on Copenhagen's Rådhuspladsen seeking representation in the government, something that King Christian quickly rejected.

tute in Copenhagen. Through the clearing mechanism, the balances of imports and exports had to be equal, even though Germany was constantly over-importing from Denmark without exporting goods to the equivalent value. For example, in 1942 Germany owed Denmark on account of the clearing trade 'two and one-half billion kroner, equivalent to nearly one-fourth of the national wealth'. In order to continue the exports from Denmark, the Germans forced the Danish National Bank to advance sums to the Danish exporters, but to meet the increasing currency requirements, the volume of Danish currency had to be expanded and this, in turn, led to inflation.

Copenhagen's City Hall Square has undergone a huge change since the war with a major redesign. The statue is *The Foot Soldier and the Little Hornblower* by H. P. Petersen-Dan.

After Hitler took offence at the King's reply to his birthday telegram, and General Hanneken was brought in as the new military commander, SS-Obergruppenführer Dr Werner Best was appointed as the German plenipotentiary in Denmark. His curriculum vitae was impressive: Police Commissioner in Hessen; Chief Section I of the Reich Security Main Office (RSHA); Chief of Civil Administration in occupied France, and a close advisor to Reinhard Heydrich. Hitler said that Germany's behaviour towards the country must become harsher and change from friendly co-operation to governing Denmark as if it was a German province. 'Rule with an iron hand', Hitler told Best. *Left:* Here he stands on the right with the pro-German Danish Foreign Minister Erik Scavenius for an audience with the King. *Right:* German guards on duty outside the Royal Palace.

ADMINISTRATION OF JUSTICE

The problem concerning the administration of justice in Denmark was of particular importance and was the cause of strained relations between the Danish Government and the army of occupation. The question arose as to which courts, German or Danish, should try Danish citizens accused of sabotage and attacks upon the German Army. One of the German commanders agreed that a group of Danish citizens should not be tried by German justice provided alterations were made in the Danish Penal Code. With some exceptions, these cases were tried by Danish courts under a law of January 18, 1941.

PRESSURE ON LEGISLATION

As the occupation authorities did not legislate at all in Denmark, pressure was brought on the Danish Government to introduce legislation that would meet the requirements of the Germans. Accordingly, the following Danish enactments were published: a law requiring deposit of certain naval and radio apparatus; a law prohibiting the photographing of German military establishments; a law to control the private possession of firearms; a law on importation of or trade in firearms and munitions; a law concerning movement in military zones, and a law prohibiting photographing of bombed areas or damaged ships. The Penal Code was supplemented by provisions establishing penalties for giving information on military establishments and military forces, and for aiding opponents of the military forces occupying Denmark.

Another addition to the Danish Penal Code provided that Danish courts could impose sentence of imprisonment of from one year to life for sabotage, espionage, and other acts which might prejudice relations between Denmark and Germany. Under a proclamation dated June 9, 1941, any acts or demonstrations which could disrupt relations with the occupying power were punishable by imprisonment of up to two years if more severe penalties were not already provided by law. In May 1942, the maximum penalty for the dissemination of rumours was increased to three years' imprisonment or, if military information was involved, life sentence could be imposed. As regards prosecutions under these provisions, a law of May 1941 provided that documents could be withheld; the choice of counsel denied; lay assessors could be excluded from the lower court, and appeals could be made directly to the Supreme Court, thus avoiding trial by jury. In order not to stir up public opinion, the Germans insisted that such cases were tried secretly.

Although time marches on, the face of Amalienborg Castle remains unchanged.

With the rise of the Danish Borgerlige Partisaner (BOPA) resistance group, armed by weapon drops from the Special Operations Executive and the US Office of Strategic Services, it launched a hugely successful strike on the Globus munitions factory on June 6, 1944. Two weeks later, BOPA blew up another munitions plant, the Dansk Riffelsyndikatet works. In retaliation, the pro-Nazi Danish Schalburgkorps targeted places dear to the hearts of the Danes and two days later set fire to the Royal Danish Porcelain Factory and placed incendiary bombs in the famous Tivoli Gardens. Berlin became very concerned with the unrest in a country that had largely been easy to manage, and Best was ordered to deal strongly with acts of sabotage. A curfew was introduced but the Danes replied by going on strike. The Danish police were deemed unreliable so the force was disbanded and replaced by the SS and German police. Men were rounded up and deportations to Germany began. This riot took place in July 1944, the barricade having been erected in Norrebro in Copenhagen.

THE REVOLT OF AUGUST 1943

As acts of sabotage increased during the summer of 1943, the German Minister to Denmark, Werner Best, made a demand that those concerned had to be tried by German military courts. The Danish Government did not accept this ultimatum and resigned. In the meantime the population, backing the government, showed signs of unrest; acts of sabotage continued, and in the first days of September open clashes occurred between the German armed forces and Danish patriots. The German commander, General Hermann von Hanneken, thereupon declared martial law and interned the government and the King. The German Army took over control of various localities in Denmark and at the same time von Hanneken assumed control of the administration of the country. He made an appeal to the different agencies of government to continue work under threat of penalties should any strike take place, but when the Germans tried to take over the Danish Navy, some vessels escaped to neutral Sweden while others were scuttled.

The hated Schalburgkorps was a Danish volunteer unit of the German SS, named in honour of Christian Frederick von Schalburg, the commander of the Danish Free Corps who had been killed in action on the Eastern Front in 1942. In July 1944, it was incorporated into a training battalion, the SS-Ausbildungs-Bataillon Schalburg. Their headquarters was located in the Freemasons' Hall at No. 23 Blegdamsvej in Copenhagen.

Fritz Tillisch, a chief organiser of the resistance, was concerned that his operatives in Jutland were at great risk of being identified so he wanted the Gestapo records held at their headquarters in Aarhus University destroyed. He contacted London with a request that the RAF bomb the building. The low-level raid by the Second Tactical Air Force took place on October 31, 1944 which just by chance turned out to be a day when Gestapo officials from various parts of Jutland had assembled at Aarhus for a confefence. The pinpoint raid by low-flying Mosquitos killed over 150 as well as incinerating all the index cards. (See also *After the Battle* No. 54.)

ICELAND

In accordance with the Danish Act of Union of November 30, 1918, Iceland and Denmark were two fully sovereign states united by a common King but with complete equality with Denmark.

After Denmark was occupied by German forces, on April 10, 1940 the Iceland Parliament (Althing) conferred upon the Icelandic Government the powers of the King with respect to Iceland, in the following resolutions:

'Having regard to the fact that the situation created makes it impossible for the King of Iceland to execute the royal power given to him under the Constitutional Act, the Althing declares that the Government of Iceland is for the time being entrusted with this power.

'Having regard to the situation now created, Denmark is not in a position to execute the authority to take charge of the foreign affairs of Iceland, nor can it carry out the fishery inspection within Icelandic territorial waters. Therefore the Althing declares that Iceland will for the time being take entire charge of these affairs.'

This was done in conformity with Article 4 of the Constitution of Iceland of May 18, 1920 in which is stated that should the King be unable to discharge his constitutional functions, the Althing could take over governmental functions and carry on the government as long as the King of Denmark was unable to do so.

The Act of Union of 1918 also gave each country the right to demand the commencement of negotiations for revision of the agreements on the expiration of the year 1940 and, in the event that agreement was not reached within three years from the date of the petition, the law could be annulled by action of the Danish Rigsdag and the Icelandic Althing respectively.

On May 17, 1941, the Althing took further steps toward gaining independence by the passage of the following resolution:

'The Althing considers that Iceland has acquired the right to sever entirely the Act of Union with Denmark, as Iceland has had to take into its own hands the conduct of all its affairs, Denmark not being in a position to conduct such affairs as it undertook to deal with on Iceland's behalf under the Danish-Icelandic Act of Union of 1918.'

On June 17, 1941, the Althing elected the Regent of Iceland in the person of Sveinn Björnsson.

A similar low-level raid followed in March 1945 when the Gestapo headquarters in the Shell House in Copenhagen was targetted.

In the meantime, while these constitutional changes were taking place in Iceland, the Allies were taking military steps in order to forestall an extension of the German occupation to Iceland, and on May 10, 1940, British forces occupied the island. Later, on July 1, 1941, an exchange of messages took place between the Prime Minister of Iceland and the President of the United States. It was stated that it would be in the interest of Iceland if the United States would undertake the protection of that country during the war by sending troops to Iceland to supplement and eventually replace the British forces, which were required elsewhere. Iceland was ready to entrust such protection to the United States subject to the conditions, among others, that the United States would promise to withdraw these forces on conclusion of the present war, and would promise to recognise the absolute independence and sovereignty of Iceland. A further condition was that the United States would not interfere with the Government of Iceland, either while the armed forces remained in the country or afterwards. In his reply the President of the United States accepted all the conditions and forces of the United States Navy arrived in Iceland on July 7, 1941.

Unfortunately, one of the Mosquitos in the first wave struck a lighting pylon in the railway goods yard with its tailplane causing it to veer off course, dropping two bombs before crashing near a school. The conflagration led two of the aircraft in the second wave to bomb the crash thinking it was the target. Eighty-six children were killed and 67 injured. This shot was taken from one of the Mosquitos which was fitted with a still camera facing rearwards. The Shell House is on the extreme right. (For more on this raid, see *After the Battle* No. 113.)

Seen from the opposite direction, the repaired building is in the foreground.

GREENLAND

Greenland, the largest island of the world, with a native population of approximately 17,000 people (including 400 Danes), was also cut off from its mother country in 1940.

A year later, on April 9, 1941, an executive agreement was signed in Washington by the Secretary of State of the United States of America, Cordell Hull, and Henrik de Kauffmann in his capacity as Envoy Extraordinary and Minister Plenipotentiary of the King of Denmark to the effect that the government of the United States was entitled to establish military bases in Greenland. The United States Government reiterated its recognition of and respect for the sovereignty of the Kingdom of Denmark over Greenland.

However, when Minister de Kauffmann informed the Danish Government, Copenhagen replied that it did not approve of the agreement which he had made with the United States and that he was recalled as Danish Minister to Washington. This act of the Danish Government under occupation was considered both by Minister de Kauffmann and the United States Government as having been performed under duress, so the State Department declared that it continued to recognise him as the duly authorised Minister of Denmark in Washington.

In the course of the execution of this agreement, an American-Danish Greenland Commission was created in New York in order to carry on economic relations between Greenland and the United States.

RAPHAEL LEMKIN, 1944

Although the German campaign to subdue neutral Norway lasted nine weeks, the occupation of the country can be said to have begun on the very first day — April 9, 1940 — when troops were pictured marching down Oslo's main street. The Norwegian military forces were totally ill-equipped to defend their country against the massed attack (Operation 'Weserübung-Nord' which targeted seven objectives from Oslo in the south to Narvik in the very north). Even when British and French troops were belatedly sent to help Norway, the end was still inevitable.

Norway

THE INVASION

In connection with the invasion and occupation of Norway certain governmental acts of the occupying power and of the King and Government of Norway must be considered, since they influenced to some extent the institutions of military occupation.

It was apparently Germany's intention to occupy Norway rather by using threats than by actual fighting. In order to create a menacing atmosphere, on April 5, 1940, the German Minister to Norway, Dr Curt Bräuer, invited a group of distinguished guests, including members of the Norwegian Government, to the legation to watch a German film. The guests were horrified as the film showed the German conquest of Poland with gruesome pictures of the bombing of Warsaw, accompanied by the caption: 'For this they could thank their English and French friends.'

The invasion of Norway began on the night of April 8. Several hours later Dr Bräuer presented to Halvdan Koht, the Norwegian Minister of Foreign Affairs in Oslo, an ultimatum stating that Great Britain and France were violating Norway's neutrality and intended to occupy that country; that the German Government had therefore begun 'certain military operations which will result in the occupation of strategically important points in Norwegian territory'; and that the 'German Government therewith takes over the protection of the King-

dom of Norway during this war'. Dr Bräuer expressed the hope that Norway would not resist, using the words of the film showing the bombing of Warsaw: 'For such horrors you would have to thank your English and French friends'.

The document ended with certain demands. The Germans insisted that all places — in particular, all the coastal forts or military establishments — which the German troops wanted to take should be surrendered to them without any resistance. Norwegian troops were requested to co-operate and were told that if they behaved well

they might be permitted to keep their arms. Under the conditions laid down in this ultimatum the Germans would have at their disposal, in addition to military installations, the railways and steamers, the pilots and the lighthouses, the mail, telegraph and telephone services, the wireless, the radio, and the press. The whole country was to be blacked out and the publication of weather reports was to cease. In addition, it was demanded that all communications between Norway and the countries to the west, including America as well as Europe, be severed.

At this point, Karl Johans Street runs past the University Square.

The victorious German commanders on parade (photo taken looking in the opposite direction) L-R: Kurt Bräuer, the German Minister in Oslo; Admiral Hermann Boehm, Commanding Admiral Norway, and General Nikolaus von Falkenhorst, the commander of Operation 'Weserübung-Nord'.

The invasion of Norway was the first campaign of the Second World War jointly planned and executed by combined ground, sea and air forces although von Falkenhorst did not have direct authority over the Luftwaffe and Kriegsmarine (see *After the Battle* No. 126).

The reply of the Norwegian Government was in the negative. In the midst of the bombing of Oslo, the Government and the King, as well as the Storting (the Norwegian assembly), left the capital. At the last moment the gold assets of the Bank of Norway were saved.

On April 9 the Storting held meetings at Hamar at which all but five of the 150 members were present. The government under the Prime Minister, Johan Nygaardsvold, informed the King that they placed their resignations at his disposal in order to permit a new government to be formed representing all the political parties. The Storting summoned the Nygaardsvold government to remain in power, giving the government complete authority to safeguard the interests of the Norwegian kingdom, such authority to continue in effect until the government and the Presidential Board of the Storting should agree to call the Storting into session again. The President of the Parliament, Carl Joachim Hambro, also stated that if the then existing government should be compelled to establish itself in a foreign country, that government alone would remain 'the legal Government of Norway, and the international symbol of the independence of the kingdom'.

In the meantime, Major Vidkun Quisling, the head of the pro-Nazi fifth columnists in Norway, formed a cabinet in Oslo.

On April 10 Dr Bräuer asked for an appointment with the King and, on being received by King Haakon and Foreign Minister Koht, he proposed that the fighting cease and that the King

appoint Quisling as his Prime Minister. After consulting the government and members of the Storting, the King refused.

On April 11 Captain Kjeld Irgens, an emissary from Quisling, appeared at Nybergsund (where the King had taken refuge after the bombing of Hamar), and invited the King to come to Oslo. On the same day a message was received from Dr Bräuer that he would like to see the King again, but he decided that if

any new German proposals were to be made, they should be conveyed to Foreign Minister Koht. Word to that effect was sent to Dr Bräuer. No reply was received from the German authorities, but instead Nybergsund, a small village without military significance where the King and government had taken refuge, was bombed. During the air raid the King and his party, together with the population took refuge in the neighbouring forest.

Johan Nygaardsvold of the Norwegian Labour Party had been the Prime Minister since 1935, this picture being taken after the government relocated to Britain in June 1940.

Vidkun Quisling had founded the Norwegian fascist party, the Nasjonal Samling (NS), in 1933 and his invitation in 1939 to the Germans to take over his country quickly led to his name being added to the dictionary of traitorship. German troops had barely set foot in Norway before he came on the radio: 'Norwegian men and women. England has violated the neutrality of Norway and the Government has fled. Under these circumstances it is the duty and the right of the Nasjonal Samling movement to assume the powers of government with Vidkun Quisling as its head and as Minister of Foreign Affairs.' Bräuer telephoned the news to Foreign Minister von Ribbentrop in Berlin who was not impressed with Quisling's arbitrary announcement so ran it past Hitler. He caught the Führer in an ecstatic mood due to the positive news on the invasion and, having met the Norwegian in December 1939, he swept aside Ribbentrop's reservations: 'Why not Quisling?' he replied.

Once Quisling's treachery became known, what little support he had enjoyed quickly evaporated. Norwegians despised his actions, and when Hitler discovered how few members there really were in the NS, even he decided to drop him. Quisling's reign as Prime Minister had lasted a mere six days. Over the following months he campaigned to raise the membership of the NS and by January 1942, with the total at 40,000, Reichskommissar Josef Terboven decided to give Quisling another chance, giving him the title of Minister President, effective from February 1. Quisling took over the Villa Grande in Oslo as his residence.

ADMINISTRATION

When the fifth-column activities of Quisling were displayed in the form of open treachery, public opinion in Norway was so strongly opposed to him that the Germans felt it necessary to dismiss the puppet government formed by Quisling and to look for other forms of collaboration with Norwegians.

In the latter part of April 1940, an Administrative Council was established with the collaboration of the Supreme Court of Norway, and Ingolf Elster Christensen was chosen as its president. The duty of this Council was to carry on the current administrative functions of government in the occupied areas, while the northern part of Norway was still defending itself under the leadership of King Haakon. In a letter approved by the Cabinet Council on April 19, King Haakon made it clear, however, that although the Administrative Council was necessary

under the circumstances, it could not represent the King or his government, because the Council was controlled by the occupying power.

On April 24 the Führer promulgated a decree in which he appointed a Reich Commissioner to administer the occupied Norwegian territories. By this decree the Reich Commissioner was made 'guardian of the interests of the German Reich and, within the domain of civil administration' and was 'vested with supreme governmental authority'. He was also authorised to call on the Norwegian Administrative Council and the Norwegian civil authorities for collaboration in the administration of the country. The law and statutes theretofore in force were declared to continue in effect 'in so far as is compatible with the fact of occupation'.

The Reich Commissioner set up offices in Trondheim, Bergen, Harstad, Hammerfest and Kirkenes. He was assisted by his staff, the Reich Commissariat, which was divided into three main sections: Administration, Economy and Propaganda. In addition, a ranking SS police officer supervised the police forces within Norway.

Today the building houses the Centre for Studies of the Holocaust and Religious Studies.

Josef Terboven, seen here alongside Quisling in the courtyard of Akershus Fortress built to defend Oslo (Quisling faced a firing-squad here in October 1945), had been appointed Reichskommissar on April 24 when Hitler's decree was released setting down the 'rules' for the governing of Norway. Born in Germany he served in the German military in the First World War, being awarded the Iron Cross. He joined the NSDAP and marched in the abortive Beer Hall Putsch in 1923. By 1936 he had been promoted to the rank of Obergruppenführer in the SA. As the civilian administrator in Norway, Terboven was widely disliked, not only by the Norwegians but even by many Germans. He had control of a personal force of around 6,000 including the secret police. He established concentration camps and ordered a number of reprisals. He also attempted to coerce the Storting to depose the King.

DECREE OF THE FÜHRER CONCERNING THE EXERCISE OF GOVERNMENTAL AUTHORITY IN NORWAY, APRIL 24, 1940

In order to safeguard public order and public life in the Norwegian territories placed under the protection of the German armed forces, I hereby decree:

SECTION 1. The Reich Commissioner for the occupied Norwegian territories shall administer these territories. His official residence shall be at Oslo. The Reich Commissioner shall be guardian of the interests of the German Reich and, within the domain of civil administration, shall be vested with supreme governmental authority.

SECTION 2. The Reich Commissioner may, for the enforcement of his orders and the exercise of his administrative functions, call on the Norwegian Administrative Council and the Norwegian civil authorities.

SECTION 3. The laws and statutes heretofore in force shall continue in effect in so far as is compatible with the fact of occupation. The Reich Commissioner may issue laws in the form of orders. These orders shall be published in the *Verordnungsblatt für die besetzten norwegischen Gebiete.*

SECTION 4. The Commander of the German Forces in Norway shall be vested with supreme military authority; his orders, in so far as they relate to the domain of civil administration, shall be enforced by the Reich Commissioner exclusively. In so far as, and as long as, military considerations demand, he shall be authorised to take all measures necessary for the execution of his military orders and for the military security of Norway.

SECTION 5. The Reich Commissioner may employ members of the German police forces for the execution of his orders. The German police forces shall be subject to the orders of the Commander of the German Forces in Norway in accordance with military requirements and with due regard to the duties of the Reich Commissioner.

SECTION 6. The Reich Commissioner shall be directly responsible to me and shall be subject to my instructions as to general policies, and to my orders.

SECTION 7. I hereby appoint President Terboven Reich Commissioner for the occupied Norwegian territories.

SECTION 8. In accordance with my instructions, rules and regulations for the enforcement and implementation of this order shall be issued for the domain of civil administration by the Reich Minister and Chief of the Reich Chancellery, and for the military domain by the Chief of the Supreme Command of the German Armed Forces.

ADOLF HITLER, Führer

Dr. Lammers, Reich Minister and Chief of the Reich Chancellery
Keitel, Chief of the Supreme Command of the Armed Forces
Frick, Reich Minister of the Interior

Although the central Norwegian administration passed through various stages (having been directed, first, by the Quisling Government; second by the Administrative Council; third by the State Council; and fourth, again by a government with Quisling as Minister-President), the Norwegian administration remained essentially the same except that control by the Nasjonal Samling was gradually tightened.

The country was divided into 20 districts known as Fylke, of which Oslo and Bergen were city Fylke (Stadt-Fylke). Every Fylke was headed by higher administrative officials called Fylkesmenn. Under these Fylkesmenn were subordinate Lensmenn. The Norwegian police force was under the direc-tion of the Norwegian Minister of Police. Directly responsible to him were 55 Chiefs of Police (Politimester). The higher administrative officers were pre-dominantly members of the Nasjonal Samling Party that had its headquarters in the Villa Grande in Oslo.

Beside the Reich Commissioner, Josef Terboven, who was vested with supreme civil authority, the Comman-der of the German Forces in Norway was vested 'with supreme military authority'. The jurisdiction was divi-ded between the Reich Commissioner and the military commander — ini-tially General der Infanterie Nikolaus von Falkenhorst. If it was necessary for the military commander to issue orders relating to the civil domain, these orders were to be enforced exclusively by the Reich Commis-sioner. Both the Reich Commissioner and the military commander in Nor-way were to be supervised by, and received orders from, their respective authorities, i.e., the Reich Commis-sioner by the Reich Minister and Chief of the Reich Chancellery, and the mili-tary commander by the Chief of the Supreme Command of the Wehr-macht. The Reich Commissioner was declared to be directly responsible to the Führer and, as the military author-ities were also responsible to the lat-ter, so any conflict of jurisdiction between the Reich Commissioner and the military commander had to be decided by Adolf Hitler.

King Haakon (left) and Crown Prince Olav (right) left the capital on April 9 for Hamar, a town 150 kilometres north of Oslo, moving on to Elverum. The German Minister to Norway, Curt Bräuer, went to see the King to press him to end all resistance and follow the example of the Danish government — and that of his brother Christian X — and surrender. The King reported the meeting to his Cabinet, explaining that he was 'deeply affected by the responsibility laid on me if the German demand is rejected. The responsibility for the calamities that will befall the people and country is so grave that I dread to take it. It rests with the government to decide, but my position is clear. For my part I cannot accept the German demands. It would conflict with all that I have considered to be my duty as King of Norway since I came to this country nearly 35 years ago.' With the knowledge that the King and his government were now at Nybergsund, on April 11 the Luftwaffe mounted a raid on the little town in the hope that their deaths would solve the problem but the party was unscathed and it continued to travel north reaching Molde on the west coast. From there, on April 29 the King and government were taken on board HMS *Glasgow* to be moved another 1,000 kilometres to the town of Tromso near the Arctic Circle. There a provisional capital was established on May 1. It was only after much agonising, that the King finally agreed to leave Norway for Britain together with the Norwegian government. They sailed abord HMS *Devonshire* on June 7, spending the next five years in exile.

ATTEMPTS TO DETHRONE THE KING

The fact that King Haakon enjoyed great popularity with the people, and that he was continuing resistance from London after he departed for the United Kingdom on June 7, was a disturbing element to the German administration of the country. Terboven therefore endeavoured to bring about the dethroning of the King by the Storting. Under pressure from him, the Presidential Board of the Storting (a kind of Speaker's Committee, which had no constitutional functions) notified the King of its request that he abdicate. The King replied on July 3 saying that he declined to resign his royal duties for the reason that the request emanated from a body that was subject to the control of the occupying authorities and was not the free expression of the will of the Norwegian people.

Later on the members of the Storting were summoned to meet in September (those who had left the country being expressly excluded) for the purpose of dethroning the King, which by statute required a majority of two-thirds. Two texts of resolutions were proposed, one in Norwegian, the other in German. (During the voting procedure it was discovered that the two texts differed substantially.)

The Board of the Storting advised the members that an agreement had been reached with the German authorities to the effect that in consideration of their dethroning the King, a Norwegian National or State Council (Riksraad) would be formed to carry on independently the administration of internal affairs without interference by German authorities. In the trial vote, the highest total reached for suspension — not dethroning — was 92 votes for and 52 against. Under these conditions, the efforts of the German authorities to bring about the dethronement of the King failed.

However, on September 25, Terboven announced that the Royal House of Norway had been repudiated by a two-thirds majority of the Storting; that the King had no further importance and would not return to Norway. The Supreme Court of Norway declared the dethroning of the King unlawful, and the action of the Reich Commissioner aroused great sympathy for the King with the result that his popularity rose even higher. Terboven therefore issued an order on October 7, 1940 prohibiting any activities on behalf of the Royal House of Norway. Violations of this order were to be punished by forced labour for a period up to three years, or by imprisonment, as well as by fine.

From the point of view of the Hague Regulations, this attempt by the Germans to dethrone the King was a violation of international law. While an occupier has the right and the duty to restore order and safety in an occupied territory, this right does not include measures for dethroning the local sovereign such as was attempted in Norway.

The final insult came when Terboven took over the King's Skaugum Estate for his personal residence. It was also there that he committed suicide on May 9, 1945 by blowing himself up.

The Hirden was the uniformed paramilitary organisation that was part of the Nasjonal Samling. They are parading where we saw the Germans on page 111.

IMPLEMENTATION OF THE NEW ORDER

Following these measures designed to divest the King of his office and authority, the Reich Commissioner terminated the activities of the Administrative Council and appointed a State Council (Riksraad) in its place. The latter consisted of 13 members, six of whom had been members of Quisling's original cabinet, Quisling himself not being included. An order was issued to the effect that all political parties and any other political organisations, with the exception of the Nasjonal Samling (the Quisling Party), were dissolved. Under this order the Reich Commissioner was authorised to appoint trustees for the liquidation of the affairs of the organisations so dissolved. However, as the order did not apply to the Nasjonal Samling, a one-party system was thus created in Norway in harmony with the Nazi pattern. At the same time political persecutions were begun against members of the pre-existing political parties who were opposed to the New Order.

A special role under the New Order was given to the party guards of the Nasjonal Samling. These party guards, who considered it their duty to punish members of the opposition by measures outside the law, were called Hirden, and were protected by the police authorities.

In the further evolution of events, Quisling was made Minister-President of the Norwegian puppet government, and ostensibly proceeded to integrate Norway into the New Order. He organised a Norwegian Legion and an SS-Standarte 'Nordland' consisting of Norwegian volunteers serving in co-operation with the German Army. In order to induce Norwegians to join these militaristic organisations, various privileges were granted to them. One decree published by Quisling on February 26, 1942 postponed foreclosure sales of the property of such volunteers.

In January 1941, Heinrich Himmler visited Norway. His declared purpose was to reorganise the struggling Quisling regime that was becoming beset with increasing acts of sabotage, but we are told that he was also led by his fascination for the 'racial purity' of the Nordic people. The Reichsführer-SS therefore felt that Norwegians were prime candidates for the expansion of the Waffen-SS, the fighting arm of the SS of which he was the head. The first 200 volunteers were recruited during this visit. *Left:* Here Himmler, accompanied by von Falkenhorst, is pictured visiting the German Cemetery in Ekeberg Park, Oslo. The Ehrenfriedhof (Graveyard of Honour) was the largest in Norway containing over 3,000 graves in two plots. In between was a set of monumental stairs used for ceremonial purposes. *Right:* The graves were moved in the 1950s to a permanent cemetery established at Oslo-Alfaset to include the concentration of other dead from southern Norway. The stairs remain in what is now Ekeberg Sculpture Park with statues gifted by Christian Ringnes on the site of the old burial ground.

On July 19, 1940, Hitler addressed the Reichstag in Berlin, offering Britain a choice between peace with Germany or 'unending suffering and misery'. When Churchill was asked if he wished to respond, he commented: 'I do not propose to say anything in reply to Herr Hitler's speech, not being on speaking terms with him'. Nevertheless, the Prime Minister had already had taken steps to make sure the Germans suffered from continuing acts of sabotage and subversion, ordering Combined Operations, and a new secret fighting force — the Special Operations Executive (SOE) — to 'set Europe ablaze'. As far as Norway was concerned, the first major operation took place soon after Himmler's visit when in March 1941 British commandos raided four ports in northern Norway. Blowing up fish oil factories on the Lofoten islands, they sank six ships and returned safely to Britain with 225 prisoners (including a dozen NS members) and 315 Norwegian volunteers.

The Germans reacted with reprisals including arrests, deportations to the Grini concentration camp, and the burning down of private homes.

GENOCIDE LEGISLATION

The Norwegians, as representatives of the Nordic race, were declared to be of related German blood, and therefore Norwegian blood was declared to be a 'racially valuable' contribution to German blood — hence the interest of the occupiers in promoting procreation by Germans in Norway. A decree was published by the Führer on July 28, 1942 to the effect that children begotten by members of the German armed forces in Norway and born of Norwegian women should be granted special subsidies through the office of the Reich Commissioner for the occupied Norwegian territories. These benefits were to include costs of delivery of such children; payment to the mothers of maintenance benefits for the time before and after delivery; payment of maintenance benefits for the children; the sheltering of mothers in clinics or homes, and similar care. As an additional means of encouraging such unions, it was declared that the mother of a child begotten by a member of the German armed forces should be given suitable employment.

Undesirable books were banned from libraries. Among others, all books by Jewish and Polish authors and all books on psychoanalysis were included.

COURTS

The New Order was especially protected by two courts, a Norwegian Special Court and a German Court. The Norwegian Special Court was established to try cases concerning the prohibition of political parties in Norway and activities in behalf of the Royal House of Norway. This court was composed of a presiding judge and two associate judges appointed by a commissioner of state for the Department of Justice. No appeal could be made from the decision of the Special Court.

The German Criminal Court had an almost unlimited jurisdiction, since the

Resistance was also slowly developing in Norway where patriotic young men wanted to do something against the invader. Individual groups — as yet with no overall leadership — gradually came together under the title of the Milorg. However, they were without arms and lacked formal training so a supply line for both men and materials came into being using fishing boats sailing across the perilous North Sea to make landfall on the Shetland Isles, hence the name the 'Shetland Bus'. Many thousands escaped by this and other routes to join the Allies but in Norway there remained a large body of men from the disbanded army, disorganised but still willing to make every effort to drive the German forces from their country. It became of paramount importance for the exiled Norwegian government to maintain communications with the potential leaders of this army and, under British direction, to reorganise, train and equip it to harrass the common enemy. The first necessity in attempting this task was to arrange for regular transport between Britain and Norway. In 1941 British resources had still not recovered from the crippling losses at the beginning of the war and neither aircraft nor naval vessels could be used for any work that did not bring immediate results. It was also questioned whether aircraft or naval vessels would be suitable for this type of work.

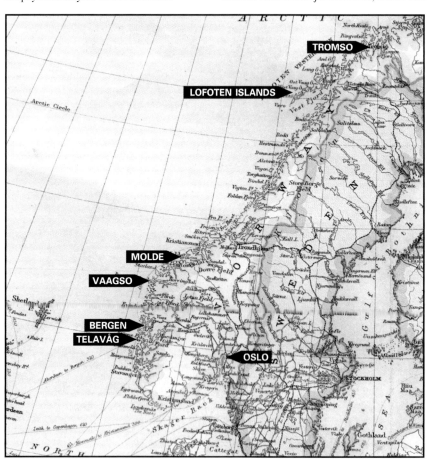

Bergen is situated 300 kilometres to the east of Shetland and from there the coast runs north for 190 kilometres and then north-north-east for nearly 1,600 kilometres to the Arctic zone. It was estimated that any part of this coastline could be reached by fishing boats using extra fuel and water tanks where necessary and it seemed, at least in theory, that having reached the enemy coast a fishing boat could easily mingle with the local craft without detection. Those that had arrived with refugees were certainly seaworthy; they were small, reliable and it would be difficult for the Germans to distinguish them from similar boats. Since the job was to land men and materials in secret, it followed that the occupying forces should be avoided wherever possible. However, the crews were always eager to try their hands at defending themselves against chance encounters and for this reason armament that was invisible except at close quarters was installed in the boats. This still comes from *Shetlandsgjengen*, a Norwegian film reconstruction made in 1954.

In the film, original members of the SOE 'Shetland Bus' played their own parts: this is William Enoksen. In 1943 due to the loss of five boats and 42 men out of the hundred men regularly sailing, it was decided that more suitable vessels for the changing requirements of the war were needed. With the assistance of Admiral Harold Stark, the Commander-in-Chief US Naval Forces in Europe, who was advised of the difficulty in procuring suitable replacement craft, three US submarine chasers were obtained. Much bigger than the fishing boats they replaced, the vessels were nearly four times faster at 17 knots. Top speed was 22 knots and they were armed with a Bofors gun forward, two twin Oerlikons in power-operated turrets, a two-pounder and two .5in Colt machine guns on the upper bridge. Crews were amazed to find that they came complete with hot and cold showers, refrigerators, electric toasters, typewriters and fur-lined coats and boots.

On December 27, 1941, British commandos carried out another raid on the coast of Norway when they landed on two small adjacent islands — Vaagso and Maaloy — located about halfway between Trondheim and Bergen. It was the first operation to be mounted under the newly-appointed Director of Combined Operations, Admiral Lord Louis Mountbatten. While the prime aim was to demonstrate that Britain was still capable of offensive action while harassing the German defences, the tactical objectives of Operation 'Archery' were to destroy a German coastal battery; kill or capture as many Germans as possible; demolish fish factories, wharves and a radio station, and arrest some known collaborators. Six war reporters and photographers accompanied the troops as it was intended to use the success of the operation to boost morale. The combined force from the Army, Royal Navy, RAF, RCAF, RAAF, RNZAF and Norwegian Army brought back 98 German prisoners. This battle ensign was taken from one of the four German vessels sunk. (For a detailed account of the raid see *After the Battle* No. 109.)

117

The following year Norway suffered its greatest tragedy of the occupation when Terboven personally oversaw a Nazi reprisal against the little village of Telavåg, rivalling the one that we have already described in Czechoslovakia. The village on the island of Sotra, 40 kilometres south-west of Bergen, played an important part in the clandestine boat traffic across the North Sea, and on April 26, 1942 the Gestapo discovered that two Norwegian SOE officers were being hidden in Telavåg on the farm of the local Milorg leader. When agents of the SD went to arrest Arne Vaerum and Emil Hvaal hiding in a barn, firing broke out and Kriminalrat Gerhard Berns and Kriminalsekretär Henry Bertram were shot dead. Vaerum was also killed but Hvaal was captured wounded. Terboven was so incensed that he travelled to Telavåg by torpedo boat on April 30 *(left)* to witness the demolitions — he can be seen wearing sunglasses on the left in this photo *(right)* of a group of high-ranking officers. With all the villagers watching, he had all the houses destroyed, all their boats sunk or confiscated, and all the livestock taken away. The men of the village were either executed on the spot or sent to Sachsenhausen concentration camp. Women and children were imprisoned, and 18 Norwegians being held at an internment camp for totally unrelated reasons, were also singled out for a reprisal execution. Thirty-one of the 72 men deported from the village were also murdered. Measures were taken to round up all the members of Milorg so that by the autumn of 1942 a viable resistance movement existed only in northern Norway.

president and its members were directly under the supervision of the Reich Commissioner. No preliminary investigation by the court was required, and it could issue notice and summons within so short a time as 24 hours before the trial. There was also no appeal from the decision of the German Court.

The Supreme Court of Norway, which played an important role in the creation of the Administrative Council, hoped to ensure a regular administration under military occupation, but when it became clear that administration by Germany was being carried out in violation of international law, the Supreme Court blamed these practices on the members of the Administrative Council (called 'state councillors'), as well as on the Reich Commissioner himself.

The Supreme Court had already declared that the dethroning of the King was unlawful, but the open conflict between the court and the German

quently the Supreme Court requested that the order of the Department of Justice should not be carried into effect.

The Reich Commissioner replied that neither the Supreme Court nor other Norwegian courts were justified in raising the question of the validity of decrees issued by him or his councillors. To this the Supreme Court replied that it could not accept this point of view, reiterating its former statement that under the Norwegian Constitution the courts have the duty of testing the validity of laws and administrative orders, and adding that in its opinion the courts may, during a military occupation, test the validity under international law of decrees which are issued by the organs of the occupying power. Such being the considered opinion of the Court, it further stated that its members felt themselves unable, in the light of the views

The house belonging to Lauritz Telle where the two agents were captured was singled out for particular attention.

authorities started with the issue of a decree by the Department of Justice. This was to the effect that the State Councillor should have authority to appoint and dismiss members of Conciliation Commissions, to remove jurors, expert witnesses, and assessors, and to appoint others in civil as well as criminal proceedings. The Supreme Court saw in this decree an attempt to interfere in the composition of the courts, and especially a violation of the principle of the independence of courts, which was guaranteed by the Constitution of Norway and which had also been confirmed in the first decree by the Reich Commissioner.

In a letter sent by the Supreme Court to the Department of Justice in November 1940, the Supreme Court set out its concern regarding this violation of international law. It also pointed out that the independence of courts was

enshrined in the Constitution and that the Führer's decree of April 24, 1940 declared that the Norwegian law would continue in force so long as this was consistent with the occupation. Conse-

expressed by the Reich Commissioner, to remain in office, and they accordingly resigned on December 23, 1940.

RAPHAEL LEMKIM, 1944

After the war Telavåg was rebuilt. The North Sea Traffic Museum in the village, opened in 1998, has a permanent exhibition on the tragedy, as well as one on the 'Shetland Bus' operations during the war.

The properties of 'heavy water' had been discovered in 1932 and the following year Leif Tronstad (left) and Jomar Brun, the head of Norsk Hydro Rjukan (right), created a plan for the industrial production of heavy water in Norway. The plant was already producing ammonia for nitrogen fertiliser with large amounts of electrolised water as a by-product. Tronstad was employed as a consultant by Norsk Hydro which was the world's first facility for the mass production of heavy water. Tronstad held the rank of captain from earlier service in the Norwegian Army, and when the occupation of the country became a reality he became involved in resistance work. Even before the war the Germans had shown interest in the heavy water plant, which was required to be used to moderate the energy of neutrons in nuclear fission, so early in 1940 the total inventory at the plant (185kg) was taken by French agents of the Deuxième Bureau for safe keeping in a vault in France. Unfortunately, the German chemical firm IG Farben was a partial owner of Norsk Hydro and they had already ordered 100kg per month although the maximum monthly production was only 10kg. When Tronstad became aware that production at Vermork had greatly increased, it was a warning sign that Germany was trying to develop atomic weaponry. Accordingly, Tronstad advised the authorities when he escaped to Britain in October 1941.

The Most Successful Sabotage Operation in German-occupied Territories

Heavy water, formed almost entirely of deuterium oxide, is akin to graphite in its neutron absorption properties, and news of its increased production at the Norsk Hydro Electrisk plant at Vermork near Rjukan in central southern Norway (where excess power was used on a routine basis to electrolyse natural water and leave a concentrate of heavy water in the residue) meant only one thing to Allied scientists: their German counterparts were preparing to produce an atomic bomb.

Leif Tronstad, Professor of Physics at Trondheim was the originator of the signal and when Professor R. V. Jones of British Scientific Intelligence requested more information, Professor Tronstad first demanded confirmation that the British interest was genuine and not commercially minded. After all, his message went on, 'remember blood is thicker even than heavy water!' Suitably reassured, the Professor travelled to Britain in the autumn of 1941 to report that Karl Wirtz of the Kaiser-Wilhelm-Institut had inspected the plant — the main source of heavy water in Europe — and a contract had been awarded by the Germans for the supply of 1500 kilograms.

A Norwegian patriot and native of Rjukan, Einar Skinnarland, had already been dropped by parachute in March to find out how far the Germans were advanced and as a result of the information he passed back to England, one of the most daring sabotage acts carried out in the Second World War was planned — Operation 'Gunnerside' — which culminated in a successful attack on the factory on February 27/28, 1943.

On the night of October 18/19, 1942, four Norwegians (Knut Haugland, Claus Helberg, Arne Kjelstrup and Jens Poulsson) were dropped near Lake Songavatn about 80 kilo-metres to the west of Rjukan. The task of the group, which had been given the code-name 'Grouse', was to prepare the ground for the sabotage operation; to maintain radio contact with the United Kingdom, and to collect intelligence on the production of heavy water.

The 'Grouse' group had a hard task reaching their planned base at Sandvatn, just north of Vermork. The four men had to make repeated trips over the next 15 days to move all the supplies a few kilometres each day and it was not until November 6 that they finally reached their destination.

Over the next three years a series of operations were carried out to attack the plant and destroy the supplies of heavy water. The first, code-named 'Grouse', involved the dropping by parachute of four SOE-trained Norwegians: Knut Haugland, Claus Helberg, Arne Kjelstrup and Jens Poulsson. This advance party landed 80 kilometres from Rjukan on the night of October 18/19, 1942, and had the job of reconnoitering the factory and maintaining radio contact with the UK. In this picture, Knut Haugland, the radio operator, joins a team from the 3rd Commando Brigade of the Royal Marines, who restaged the operation to mark the 40th anniversary in 1983.

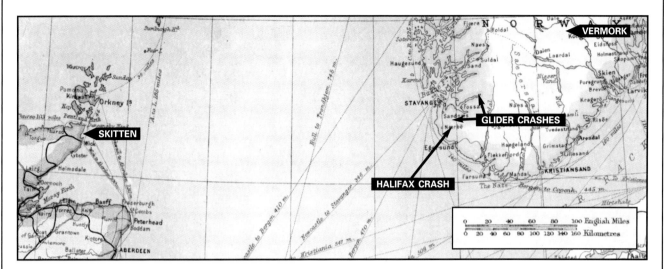

Meanwhile, Headquarters Combined Operations had instructed Major-General Frederick 'Boy' Browning, as Commander Paratroops and Airborne Troops, and Group Captain Sir Nigel Norman, leading No. 38 Wing newly-formed to operate tug aircraft for glider towing, to plan an operation to destroy the installation. After considering various possibilities, the decision was made to use glider-borne troops, the first such operation carried out by British airborne forces in the Second World War. The 9th Field Company (Airborne) and 261st Field Park Company (Airborne) of the Royal Engineers were called upon to provide volunteers and two parties were selected, each comprising one officer (Lieutenant David Methven and Lieutenant Alex Allen respectively), one sergeant, 13 other ranks and two glider pilots. The party was brought together under conditions of great secrecy and as security cover it was given out that they were training to meet the challenge of an American engineer unit for an imaginary 'Washington Cup'.

The Halifax was the only aircraft capable of towing the Horsa glider the required distance (nearly 600 miles), which included a sea crossing of 300 miles, and the two aircrews were specially selected to include an element of Dominion personnel. Squadron Leader A. B. Wilkinson of No. 295 Squadron captained the first tug towing the glider piloted by Staff Sergeant Malcolm Strathdee and Sergeant Peter Doig, both of the 1st Glider Pilot Regiment. The second Halifax, with a seven-man crew under Flight Lieutenant Arthur Parkinson, from No. 297 Squadron of the Royal Canadian Air Force, was towing the Horsa piloted by Pilot Officers Norman Davies and Herbert Fraser, both of the Royal Australian Air Force. In reality each glider contained a completely self-contained party capable of carrying out the operation individually. This duplication was considered a pre-requisite in view of the inhospitable terrain. The troops wore plain clothes under their uniforms to facilitate their escape after the operation. Instructions were issued that any casualties were to be given morphine and abandoned.

The Halifaxes were equipped with the new Rebecca-Eureka radar homing device, the Rebecca set being contained in the aircraft while the Eureka set was delivered to Norwegian agents to set it up on the proposed landing zone near Lake Mosvatn. The operation was code-named 'Freshman'.

On November 17 the whole force moved to Skitten airfield, a satellite of Wick in Scotland, where the extended runway made for a safer take-off, the operation being scheduled for the night of November 19/20. Although the weather forecast was not ideal, it was considered reasonable for the time of year bearing in mind the possibility of deterioration for the remainder of the moon period

Operation 'Freshman' was planned as the main attack on the factory using two 15-man troops from the Royal Engineers towed to Norway in two Horsa gliders. Skitten in Scotland was chosen as the departure airfield being the nearest to the target and also as its long runway would give the Halifaxes a better take-off run. Even so the 600-mile flight on November 19 would be a hazardous undertaking, and so it proved.

which was essential for a safe landing. (A reconnaissance had been carried out on the previous night, under the guise of a leaflet raid on Oslo, although only one aircraft actually reached the area.)

Squadron Leader Wilkinson in 'A' Apple took off first at 5.50 p.m. followed by Flight Lieutenant Parkinson ('B' Baker) 20 minutes later. Nothing was heard from the aircraft until a signal was received at base at 11.55 p.m. from Parkinson's Halifax requesting a bearing for a return course. RDF plotted his aircraft as being over the North Sea at the time and the bearing was transmitted but nothing further was heard from this aircraft.

A few minutes later a signal was received from Squadron Leader Wilkinson announcing that his glider had been 'released in sea' although RDF plotted the Halifax as being over the mountains of southern Norway at the time. When the Halifax returned to Skitten on its last drop of petrol, the crew explained what had happened. They had reached the coast of Norway safely but the

Rebecca set had chosen that moment to go u/s so the run to the landing zone had had to be made through patchy cloud by map reading alone. During a second attempt to locate Lake Mosvatn the aircraft flew into thick ice-making cloud. Unable to climb with both tug and glider icing up, the pair slowly lost height. Back on the coast just north of Stavanger, the tow-line snapped, committing the glider and its 17 occupants to its fate. It crashed on top of a snow-covered mountain at Fylgjesdal.

The other aircraft fared even worse. Because of bad weather encountered over the landing zone, the tug and glider turned back towards Scotland. During the flight towards the Norwegian coast, its tow-rope broke forcing the glider to make an unscheduled landing. The Horsa crashed into a mountainside near Egersund and while the Halifax was circling the area it suddenly banked heavily, lost control and crashed into the next mountain range approximately four kilometres to the south near Helleland.

Contact could not be established with the ground party which were to signal the landing site; both glider tow-lines snapped, and one Halifax came to grief. Eighteen men had lost their lives in the crashes but there was worse to come.

German troops found the wreckage of Halifax W7801 and Horsa HS114 that had crashed near Egersund the following morning. From the position of the two wrecked aircraft, and the distance between them, it was evident that the bomber pilot had set the glider free at the last minute in an attempt to save his own aircraft. All seven crewmen of the Halifax were killed while 14 soldiers had survived the glider crash. German officers found explosives, small arms, and radio transmitters amid the glider wreckage and correctly concluded that the British troops had been on a sabotage mission. The German battalion commander in Egersund followed Hitler's Commando order which stated that: 'On account of the increased number of cases in which aircraft are used for landing saboteurs, who do serious damage, I order that personnel from sabotage aircraft shall be immediately shot by the first persons who come into contact with them.' Consequently the 14 surviving soldiers (not 11 as stated on the plaque) were rushed to Egersund, where, after a brief and superficial interrogation, they were taken out and executed on this spot by a German firing squad.

When news of the executions reached Reichskommissar Terboven and General Wilhelm Rediess (left), the head of the German secret police in Norway, they could not believe that the soldiers had been executed without any attempt having been made to determine the nature of their intended target. Rediess complained bitterly to Berlin: 'A British towing aircraft and its glider have crashed near Egersund at about 3 a.m. on the 20th Cause of accident not yet known. As far as has been ascertained, towing aircraft's crew is military, all dead. There were 17 men in glider, probably agents. Three of them were killed, six badly injured. Glider's crew was in possession of large quantities of Norwegian money. Unfortunately the military authorities executed the survivors so explanation scarcely possible now.' General von Falkenhorst, the German Commander-in-Chief in Norway, was equally infuriated, for the action of the Egersund battalion commander reflected adversely on his command. He immediately ordered all army units to delay any future Commando executions until the men could be interrogated by security police, noting that Hitler's Commando order made specific provisions for delay in execution for the purpose of interrogation. No sooner had Falkenhorst's order been distributed than an Army unit near Stavanger received word that Norwegian police had arrested three British soldiers and were seeking to turn them over to an appropriate German command. Under questioning, the British soldiers confessed that they were survivors of the second glider and gave their captors the location of the downed aircraft. Search parties quickly rounded up six other survivors (four of them badly injured). Given a second opportunity to question British glider troops, the Germans did not repeat their first mistake. Gestapo agents, alerted to the capture, subjected the British soldiers to a lengthy and brutal interrogation. Only after the survivors had revealed all that they knew, including details of their objective, did the Gestapo release them and permit the German Army to execute them in compliance with Hitler's order (the four wounded men were given lethal injections). Right: A memorial now marks the execution site in the Trandum forest just outside Oslo. Von Falkenhorst was pleased with the outcome. 'The interrogation', he proudly reported, 'provided valuable admissions of the enemy's intentions.' Even General Rediess was placated. In a memorandum to his superiors in Berlin, he indicated that before they were killed the British troops had indicated 'that the British placed great importance on the planned destruction of Vemork's heavy water plant'.

Forty-one men had now lost their lives in a vain attempt to knock out the factory; now it was time to send in a elite SOE team of six Norwegian commandos. On February 16, 1943 they were dropped by parachute from a Halifax of No. 138 Squadron flying from Tempsford at a new drop zone closer to the factory. They met up with the four men waiting for them from the 'Grouse' team who by now had been given the new code-name of 'Swallow'. Operation 'Gunnerside' was to take place on the night of

February 27/28 but, as the Germans had been forewarned of a possible assault, they had sown mines, installed floodlights and placed a permanent guard on the bridge, seen *(left)* spanning the ravine over the River Mana during the making of *Heroes of Telemark* in 1965, which was filmed at the original location. This meant that the team would have to descend the ravine, ford the river, and then climb up to the plant. *Right:* The same bridge still spans the ravine today.

Despite the setback, the 'Grouse' group was still intact, though from now on its code-name was changed to 'Swallow'. They had to withdraw into the heart of the Hardanger Vidda (plateau) where they spent the winter, eking out what was left of their food with wild reindeer, which they were lucky enough to track down and shoot. They even had to eat the entrails to keep alive.

On February 16, 1943 a new group known as 'Gunnerside' was chosen by the Norwegian section of SOE and flown to Norway. As a warning had been received from the 'Swallow' base at Sandvatn warning against any more aerial activity over the factory area, the six men (Knut Haukelid, Kasper Idland, Fredrik Kayser, Joachim Ronneberg, Birger Stromsheim and Hans Storhaug) were dropped 45 kilometres to the north near Lake Skrykken. Battling south through blizzards, it was several days before the 'Gunnerside' group was able to join up with the four men of 'Swallow'.

On the evening of February 27 the ten saboteurs were lined up at Fosbudalen, just north of the Vermork installation, ready to strike. They quickly tackled the perilous and difficult descent down the mountain, negotiating the gorge running down to the heavy water plant, and forcing their way with wire cutters through the perimeter gates to the plant. The cover party took up their positions, and the sabotage group made their way swiftly to the target, placing their explosive charges on the vital containers of heavy water, the bulk of which was destroyed. Strangely, the German guards had no idea that anything was afoot in the area.

Following a strenuous trek on skis, the saboteurs reached the safety of the plateau. After resting, they split up into two groups. One, fully armed and in uniform, skied right across Norway to the safety of neutral Sweden, while

the other party remained on the Hardanger plateau, skilfully avoiding capture by the many German patrols which were combing the countryside in an attempt to run them to earth. Meanwhile, radio contact was maintained with the Allied command in London.

The heavy water plant was subsequently repaired and to counter this new threat the Americans decided to try to bomb the factory. On November 16, 1943, 160 Flying Fortresses from seven bomb groups were despatched to attack the Vermork power

Knut Haukelid and Arne Kjelstrup found a path alongside the railway line to the gate. The group first tried to get in through a basement door without success but, following the information they had received from London, they climbed a stairway to an opening in the wall leading to a cable duct which led below the ceiling of the ground floor. Joachim Ronneberg and Hans Storhaug then took the guard by surprise. 'Two of us mounted the explosive charges', said Ronneberg. 'The fuzes were about two minutes long but I cut them down to 30 seconds and lit them.' The film recreation was staged in the original high concentration (HK) building to which the electrolysis process had been moved in the 1950s. Dummy electrolysis cells were used to depict the actual damage.

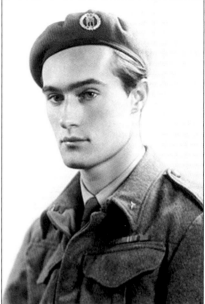

Left: **The hydrogen production factory, which stood just in front of the hydro-electric power station, was decommissioned and demolished in 1977 but fortunately it was still standing when the film was made which featured Kirk Douglas as 'Rolf Pedersen' and Ulla Jacobsson as 'Anna Pedersen' (both fictitious names).** *Right:* **The real team leader for the 'Gunnerside' operation was Joachim Ronneberg. He subsequently went on to lead other raids on various strategic targets.**

station and factory to be followed by 39 B-24s from another four groups. Shortly before midday the first wave dropped over 700 bombs within a two-minute period to be followed 20 minutes later by another 300. However, the raid completely missed the electrolysis plant although it seriously damaged the hydro-electric power plant which ultimately forced the Germans to abandon all plans for future heavy water production in Norway. The raid was carried out at a cost of 20 Norwegian lives.

An amazing discovery took place in September 2017 when an excavation of the foundations of the old hydrogen factory revealed the underground cellar where the electrolysis cells had been found and blown by the 'Gunnerside' team in 1943. These pictures show the work proceeding and it is hoped that the structure will be safe enough to make it available to visitors.

The hydrogen factory lay just in front of the hydro-electric power station complex. The HK, or high concentration plant, is [1] and the new excavated site [2]. (The HK process refers to the final stage in the production of heavy water.)

The saboteurs soon received information that the Germans had decided to move all the stocks of semi-processed heavy water which had survived the raid from Rjukan to Germany and orders were issued from London to sabotage this plan at all costs. The weakest link in the chain was the ferry that carried the railway across Lake Tinn. The night before the ferry was due to sail, the Norwegian saboteur group managed to place a time charge on board and on Sunday, February 20, 1944, the ferry blew up and sank in the middle of the lake, taking its containers of heavy water to the bottom. Apart from the loss of four German guards, 14 Norwegian civilians perished, but the battle for heavy water in Norway was over.

LIEUTENANT COLONEL
IVAR HELLBERG, 1983

As a result, production of heavy water was halted for several months but, as a further commando raid was ruled out, instead the US Air Force were called in to bomb the plant. On November 16, 160 B-17s from the 94th, 95th, 96th, 100th, 385th, 388th and 390th Bomb Groups dropped over 700 bombs although the majority missed the main target, the electrolysis building. Nevertheless, the hydro-electric generating building was badly damaged. The risk of further attacks led the Germans to decide to abandon production at Norsk Hydro.

Knut Haukelid discovered that the Germans were going to transport the remaining stock of heavy water to Germany so he worked out a plan to sink the rail ferry that would have to be used to carry the shipment across Lake Tinn. With the help of one of the crew, he got aboard to place a charge of plastic explosive, triggered by two alarm-clock fuzes timed to explode when the ferry was in transit. On February 20, 1944, the *Hydro* was successfully sent to the bottom of the lake, effectively bringing to an end further German efforts to develop nuclear fission.

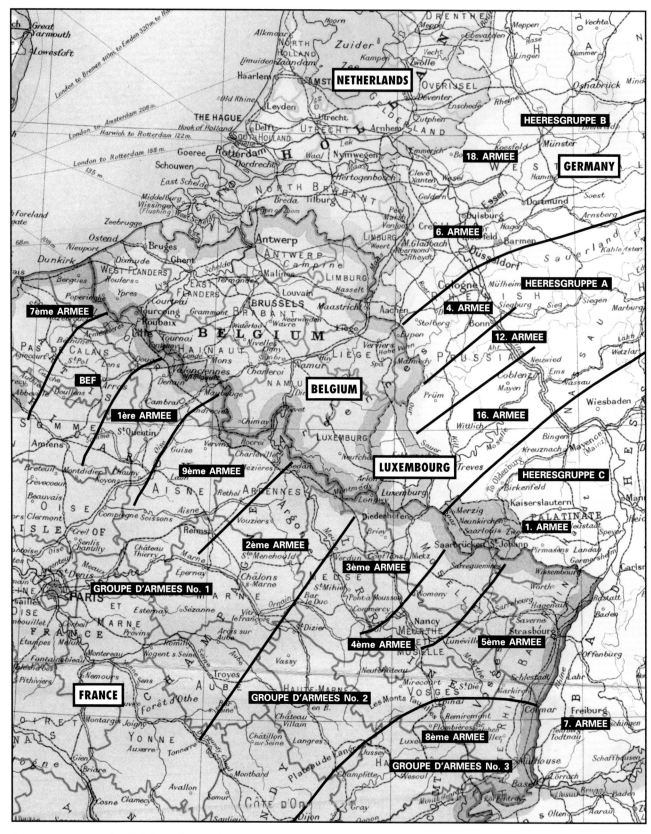

Just over a month after Britain and France had declared war on Germany, Hitler issued his Führer Directive No. 6. Dated October 9, 1939, it stated that he now wanted preparations put in hand for the defeat of the French Army and the Allies fighting on their side. He also wanted to win as much territory as possible in the Netherlands, Belgium and northern France to serve as a base for the successful prosecution of the air and sea war against England. Within ten days an outline plan of attack had been prepared by the Army High Command (the OKH) but Operation 'Fall Gelb' (Plan Yellow) as it was called, was revised several times over the following months, the fifth and final version being issued on February 24, 1940. May 5 was the date set for the attack to begin but postponements delayed this by five days, partly because of the weather. None of this took into account that three of the countries in the firing line — Belgium, Holland and Luxembourg — had declared their neutrality. The map shows the opposing forces on the eve of May 10. Three German army groups, deploying a total of 134 divisions, faced 92 French and ten British divisions. As soon as neutral Belgium and the Netherlands entered the fight, an additional 20 Belgian and ten Dutch divisions were added to the Allied side of the balance sheet. (The military in Luxembourg were confined to barracks.)

Luxembourg

ADMINISTRATION

On May 10, 1940, the Germans crossed the frontier of the Grand Duchy of Luxembourg. After the government left the country, an Administrative Commission was set up by a number of government officials for the purpose of establishing order and for carrying on current administrative affairs, but this was soon abolished by the Germans.

Immediately after the occupation, a German Feldkommandantur, and shortly afterward an Oberfeldkommandantur, took over the administration of the country and early in August the office of a Stadtkommandantur was established. On August 7 a German Civil Administration was set up in the

While Hitler's forces paid scant attention to the small detail of invading neutral territory, British and French forces had to halt at the frontier until they received permission from the Belgian authorities to enter the country. In the Ardennes area, these French troops have arrived at the border with the Grand Duchy of Luxembourg and were pictured waiting at the custom's post for permission to cross into Esch-sur-Alzette.

Grand Duchy and the District Leader, Gauleiter Gustav Simon of Koblenz-Trier, was appointed its chief. Then on August 30, 1942, it was announced by the Gauleiter that Luxembourg had been incorporated into the German District of Moselland.

Since the beginning of the occupation local institutions of administration and communal life were gradually abolished and replaced by German institutions. The Chamber of Deputies and the Council of State established under the constitution of Luxembourg dating back to October 17, 1868, were dissolved and the German Municipal Code of January

30, 1935 was introduced instead. As that Code was based upon the principle of leadership (Führerprinzip), the Luxembourg form of elective government was abolished, and municipalities were thereafter headed by mayors and aldermen who were not elected by the population but appointed by the German authorities. The Mayor constituted the local police authority. Communities were divided into (1) municipal districts headed by mayors, and (2) county districts headed by county chiefs. The mayors and county chiefs were both supervised by the Chief of the German Civil Administration.

Left: Meanwhile, the greater part of the Luxembourg government had already left the capital at 6.30 a.m. that morning, using the same road, and crossed the frontier into France here at Audun-le-Tiche. Little did these two French Army

motorcyclists realise that the Germans were now only five kilometres away! *Right:* Today even this checkpoint, which existed until 1995, has been swept away by the open borders policy of the European Union.

Following consultation with her ministers, the Grand Duchess Char-lotte *(left)* decided to leave the palace with her husband, Prince Felix, mother and other members of the Royal family. They aimed to cross into France a little further to the west at Rodange which they reached at 7.45 a.m. They were then able to link up with the government party at Longwy. The Hereditary Grand Duke and two of his sisters had been held up by German troops near Esch, only escaping when the driver crashed the barrier. By midday the capital was in German hands. Initially, the Grand Duchy was administered from Brussels by General Alexander von Falkenhausen *(centre)*, the Military Commander of Belgium and Northern France, but on July 25 the civil administration was taken over by the Gauleiter of Koblenz-Trier, Gustav Simon *(right)*, who was officially appointed Chef der Zivilverwaltung on August 2. When he entered the Hotel Brasseur on Rue Aldringen, he promptly tore a portrait of the Duchess from the wall, threw it on the ground and stamped on it.

GENOCIDE

For centuries, the Grand Duchy of Luxemburg has been bilingual, speaking both French and German. Nevertheless, on August 6, 1940, Gauleiter Simon issued an order in which he stated that 'the language of Luxembourg and of its inhabitants is, and always has been, German' and that 'the German language shall be the exclusive official language', as well as the language in commercial life. All names of streets and localities were converted into German. Also persons having non-German Christian names were required to adopt the corresponding German first name, or, if that were impossible, to select a German first name. Nationals having a family name of German origin, who later had been given a foreign or non-German form, were required to revert to the original German form. If the person involved did not apply for a change of name before February 15, 1941, the Germans would confer a German name upon him.

An order was also issued concerning legitimation of illegitimate children in which it was declared that an illegitimate child would, in relation to its mother or her relatives, have the legal status of a legitimate child. Although this provision did not expressly mention German fathers, by comparison with other genocide laws issued by the Germans, the order undoubtedly had as its intention the procreation of children by German fathers.

ORDER CONCERNING THE USE OF THE GERMAN LANGUAGE IN LUXEMBURG, AUGUST 6, 1940

The language of Luxemburg and of its inhabitants is, and always has been, German. Pursuant to the authority vested in me as the Chief of the Civil Administration of Luxemburg, I hereby order for the entire territory of Luxemburg as follows:

SECTION 1. The German language shall be the exclusive official language. The language used in judicial proceedings shall be exclusively German.

SECTION 2. The language of instruction in all schools shall be exclusively German. In primary schools the French language shall no longer be taught as a subject of instruction; in secondary schools courses in the French language shall continue to be given.

SECTION 3. Daily papers, weekly publications, and all other periodicals, including any private advertising they may contain, shall be published in the German language only. Likewise, the German language shall be the only one permissible in all other printed matter. It shall be unlawful to display advertisements printed in the French language, in show-cases or in any other offerings to the public.

SECTION 4. In the economic life of the country throughout all its occupations, the German language shall be used exclusively; this applies especially to written communications and advertisements of every description.

SECTION 5. Commercial signs and inscriptions on buildings shall be permissible only in the German language.

SECTION 6. For traffic, street, and road signs, only inscriptions in the German language and with the German versions of local names shall be permissible.

SECTION 7. The term 'German language' for the purpose of this order shall be deemed to refer to 'High German' (Hochdeutsch).

SECTION 8. Violations of this order shall be punishable by imprisonment or fine; in lieu of a sentence imposed by a court, punishment by imprisonment or fine may be imposed by summary order of the police.

SECTION 9. This order shall take effect as of the date of publication. Likewise, changes necessary in commercial signs, inscriptions on buildings, traffic, street and road signs shall immediately be made and completed not later than September 30, 1940.

SECTION 10. The administrative agencies in Luxemburg shall be responsible for the enforcement of this order.

Luxemburg, August 6, 1940.

GUSTAV SIMON,
Gauleiter, Chief of the Civil Administration in Luxemburg

Simon's job was to incorporate 'Luxemburg' (note the German spelling) into the Greater German Reich, the French language being banned with posters proclaiming: 'Your language is German and only German'. In August 1942, Luxembourg was officially made part of Germany which included changing not only street signs but people's own Christian names.

Since the earliest days of the country's existence, both French and German languages have been spoken. Charters written in Latin after the 13th century were later generally worded in French; only 70 charters were written in German while more than 280 were drawn up in French. Because of its affinity with French culture, the French language was the official language of the country. The population also spoke 'Letzeburgesch', a homely dialect based on Teutonic origins, with extensive borrowings from Celtic, Roman and French. Neither Germans nor Frenchmen could understand the Luxembourg dialect so the statement by Simon that German had always been the language of 'Luxemburg' was untrue. French had always been the official legislative, administrative and judicial language. Simon, who was a fanatical anti-Semite, was determined to make his new fiefdom 'Judenfrei' (free of Jews) as quickly as possible. Just two weeks after his installation, on August 16-18, attempts were made to incite the local population to riot against the Jews. Jewish shops were marked with a yellow label for this purpose but the population remained apathetic to the German action and no excesses against Jews were reported. Then on September 5, Simon introduced the anti-Jewish Nuremberg Laws, valid in Germany since 1935, in Luxembourg. A week later, on the 12th, the Gestapo ordered the some 2,000 Jews remaining in the country to leave the country within 14 days. Over the next four months, 13 trains (carrying mainly German Jews who had sought refuge in Luxembourg) left for Portugal and internment camps in France — the first step to the final deportation of the Luxembourg Jews to death camps in Eastern Europe that was to begin in October 1941.

CURRENCY

When the German Army occupied Luxembourg, it was provided with Reich Credit Institute notes (Reichskreditkassenscheine) which the population were compelled to accept in payment for goods purchased by members of the army. By an order of August 26, 1940, the Reichsmark was introduced as additional legal tender, but then on January 29, 1941, the Reichsmark was declared the exclusive legal tender. Consequently, Luxembourg francs, as well as Belgian francs and Reich Credit Institute notes, were withdrawn to be exchanged for Reichsmarks. This exchange procedure closed on March 1, 1941, the rate of exchange being established as one Belgian franc to 0.08 Reichsmark, and one Luxemburg franc to 0.10 Reichsmark. After the above date, francs from Luxembourg and Belgium were considered as foreign exchange. Claims for Belgian and Luxembourg francs by residents of Luxembourg, Alsace-Lorraine, the Protectorate of Bohemia and Moravia, and the Greater German Reich on other residents had to be changed into claims for Reichsmarks. Thus Luxembourg was completely incorporated into the Reichsmark currency area.

STANDRECHT in LUXEMBURG

Nachdem auch in Luxemburg-Stadt Fälle von Streiks und Arbeitsverweigerung eingetreten sind, wird der zivile Ausnahmezustand für den Gesamtbereich des Chefs der Zivilverwaltung in Luxemburg verhängt.

Die Zuständigkeit des Standgerichts wird entsprechend erweitert.

Todesurteile gegen Streikende werden sofort durch Erschiessen vollstreckt

Luxemburg, den 31. August 1942.

Der Chef der Zivilverwaltung in Luxemburg:
gez. Gustav SIMON

The 'New Order' in Luxembourg was displayed in posters like these.

By a proclamation of September 13, 1940, all residents were required to sell their US dollar notes, Swiss francs, Swedish crown notes, French franc notes, gold coins, and gold, pure and unalloyed, to the German authorities acting through specified banks. In addition, claims in foreign and home currency against non-residents were subject to registration.

Gauleiter Simon welcomes German police units just transferred to the Grand Duchy.

LAW AND COURTS

The Supreme Court of Luxembourg was abolished and its functions assigned to chambers of the Provincial Court of Appeals. The courts were also Germanised, and a German Special Court (Criminal Court) was set up with very broad jurisdiction over matters supposedly opposed to German interests, ranging from gatherings in the streets to ceasing work in factories. Moreover, the German prosecuting attorney could always send any case to the Special Court by removing it from the jurisdiction of the local courts. This created an atmosphere of legal insecurity in the country because the jurisdiction was vague and the penalties not defined for specific offences. They were also very severe, ranging from fines and imprisonment to hard labour and even death.

THE BAR

On the continent of Europe, 'honour courts' for attorneys and barristers usually deal with matters involving professional conduct of the Bar, but in Luxembourg not only the judicial system, but also the Bar, was Germanised. In order to make Luxembourg barristers comply with the New Order, a special Honour Court (Ehrengericht) for practising attorneys was established. The jurisdiction of this court was practically unlimited: 'The special Honour Court shall have jurisdiction to try acts which constitute a violation of the duties arising from the organisation of a German administration in Luxembourg'. The person initiating proceedings before the special Honour Court was the Chief of the Civil Administration. The jurisdiction being vague and undefined, Gauleiter Simon had therefore practically unlimited authority over the Bar in Luxembourg. He alone could determine what constituted a 'violation of the duties arising from the organisation of a German administration in Luxembourg'. The aim of this order was to break the resistance of the Luxembourg Bar, to make its members subservient to the German administration, and to deprive the persecuted Luxembourg population of its natural legal protectors and intellectual leaders. However the Luxemburg Bar displayed a stubborn attitude toward the German Administration and, according to the *Luxembourg Grey Book*, 'All the members of the Luxembourg Bar who had, up till May 23, 1941, refused to associate themselves with the activities carried out by the Germans against the independence and the Constitution of the Grand-Duchy were condemned to forced labour.'

ECONOMY

The economy of Luxembourg was organised according to the principle of economic totalitarianism, e.g., the grouping of all persons and enterprises involved in economic activities into professional and regional organisations controlled by the central authority of the Chief of the Civil Administration. Participation in economic life and the right to work and to own property were made dependent upon the willingness of the person concerned to promote Germanism. According to the decree of February 21, 1941, the Chief of the Civil Administration could restrain managers of enterprises from their activities if they are not willing to 'promote Germanism at all times without any reservations', or if they violated duties 'arising from the general principles of a National Socialist Labour Community (Arbeitsgemeinschaft)'. All measures undertaken by the Germans in Luxembourg showed but one aim, namely, the destruction of the Luxembourg nationhood and the promotion of Germanism.

LABOUR

The manpower of Luxembourg was mobilised for German purposes through work-books issued by the Labour Office. By order of February 12, 1941, youths and girls were compelled to enter the Reich Labour Service. Originally they were required to work within the District of Moselland, of which Luxembourg was annexed, but later on they were sent to work in Germany.

Simon reviews another parade drawn up on the Place d'Armes in Luxembourg City on January 7, 1941.

A corner of the capital which has remained almost unchanged since the war.

NAZI PARTY

An order was published on January 15, 1941 placing the National Socialist Party under special protection. By this order, persons who voice utterances against the German Reich or the National Socialist Party and its leading personalities — even though not made in public — were punishable. Not only deliberately malicious but also careless statements of this character rendered the speaker liable to penalties; it was sufficient that the judge found that the person involved had been guilty of negligence. Legal insecurity was augmented by the provision that prosecution under this law was subject to the consent of the Chief of the Civil Administration.

The main instrument of Germanism, aside from the Civil Administration, was the National German Party (Volksdeutsche Bewegung) led by Professor Damian Kratzenberg. Only persons who joined this party were considered as being willing to promote Germanism and as such they achieved privileged status.

Himmler visited Luxembourg in September 1940 for negotiations with Simon. *Left:* This is Rue Aldringen with the Hotel Brasseur on the left where Simon smashed the portrait of Duchess Charlotte. The German Press reported that 'Himmler was on an inspection visit of the occupied territories and accompanied by the Higher SS and Police Leader of the Rhine region, SS-Brigadeführer Erwin Rösener. His first stop in Luxembourg was at the Spa town of Mondorf, where he was welcomed by Simon's deputies Fritz Reckmann and Heinrich Siekmeier. On arrival in Luxembourg city, Himmler first visited the barracks [on Heilig-Geist-Plateau] where the Freiwilligen-Kompanie (volunteer police company) commanded by Oberleutnant Jean Brasseur was out on parade for his inspection. He then proceeded to the Grand Hotel Brasseur where he was greeted by Simon and General Karl Weisenberger, commander of the 71. Infanterie-Division stationed in the region. Afterwards, Simon accompanied Himmler on his continued journey via Diekirch, Vianden to Trier'.

Rue Aldringen has been almost totally redeveloped, the historic Hotel Brasseur being demolished in 1969.

In August 1940, a Sicherheitsdienst (Security Service, SD) Einsatzkommando moved into the Villa Pauly at No. 57 Boulevard de la Pétrusse in Luxembourg City. This then became the nerve centre for the Gestapo and security police in the capital (a plaque on the gatepost unveiled in January 2016 records its former use), although sub-offices were set up in other towns. In command was SS-Sturmbannführer Wilhelm Nölle, ordered to Luxembourg from Trier, but later succeeded by SS-Obersturmbannführer Dr Fritz Hartmann whose term of office — 1941-43 — coincided with most of the expulsions and deportations. A Judenreferat (Jew's Section) was set up under Kriminalsekretär Oskar Schmalz to produce a master card index of Jewish citizens. The Luxembourg authorities were coerced into co-operating, the Administrative Commission and the Luxembourg police providing lists of names. The Jewish Consistory also had to provide additional names so that within a short time the Germans had a register of hundreds of Jews.

In 1940 Luxembourg City had fewer than 100,000 inhabitants, while the population of the entire country numbered around 300,000 which enabled the Gestapo and security police to implement their anti-Semitic measures without much difficulty. In April 1941, Adolf Eichmann, the head of the Jewish section (Abteilung IV-b-4) at the Reichssicherheitshauptamt, summoned the Jewish representatives in Luxembourg to Berlin. At the meeting he made it clear that Luxembourg needed to be 'clean of Jews', and that they had a simple choice: either emigration toward the west or deportation to the east. Before the war there were over 3,500 Jews in the country, with at least another 1,000 from eastern Europe who had found shelter in the Duchy. Attempts had been made by Simon to incite the population against the Jews; Jewish shops had to be marked as such,

followed by instructions for individuals to wear the yellow star. Until mid-October 1941, Jews still had the opportunity to leave Luxembourg for other countries, and an estimated 1,450 Jews had managed to escape the measures of the Nazi state. The last convoy with 120 people left for Portugal on October 15, one day before the first major deportation to the east, but many unsuspecting Jews continued to prepare for their immigration unaware that the deadline had closed as the German authorities had not announced the prohibition. More than 2,500 Jews left, many for the unoccupied zone of France from where deportations would later still lead to the gas chambers in Poland. Between October 1941 and July 1944, Jews were deported to the German Reich from Hollerich station, this group being herded onto a train on September 19, 1942.

RESISTANCE

Despite oppression, however, the Luxembourg people remained faithful to their country and nationhood. During the census of the population on October 10, 1941, forms to be filled in and signed contained the usual entries: surnames, Christian names, age, nationality, language. A special order was issued to the effect that where German nationhood did not apply, foreign nationhood, such as Italian or French, could be indicated, but in no case could Luxembourg be given. The Luxembourg language was excluded under the pretext that the dialect was only a branch of the German language. In spite of these orders, however, 96 per cent of the population in towns and 99 per cent in the country stated their nationality to be that of Luxembourg and their native language to be Luxemburgisch.

RAPHAEL LEMKIN, 1944

In 1996, the station was memorialised to remember the deportations carried out from there.

In 1940 Luxembourg had been overrun in a day but in 1944 it was at the centre of a lengthy battle when Hitler launched his massed attack through the Ardennes. The frontier with France had been crossed early in September, Luxembourg City being entered on September 10 by Combat Command A of the US 5th Armored Division. Here Jeeps can be seen parked outside the Villa Pauly. The Germans retreated without a fight and within two days, 90 per cent of the Grand Duchy had been liberated, the frontier into Germany being crossed on September 11. When the Battle of the Bulge was launched on December 16, much of the northern part of the country was lost again to German forces, although Luxembourg City remained in Allied hands. Gauleiter Simon had fled the country and went into hiding using his mother's maiden name, posing as a gardener in Upsprunge, near Salzkotten, west of Paderborn. It was not until December 1945 that he was traced by a British patrol and taken to Paderborn prison where he died on December 18, although the actual circumstances of his death have never been established with certainty. The official version is that he hanged himself in his cell shortly before he was to be handed over to the authorities in Luxembourg, but a second version describes him being killed by his escort as he was being transferred to Luxembourg. His body was certainly photographed in Grund prison, near Luxembourg, where he was subsequently buried. However, Thomas Harding revealed in 2013 that he believed that his great-uncle, Captain Hanns Alexander, had been involved in Simon's death. He wrote that en route from Paderborn prison, his great-uncle was joined by several Luxembourg partisans who took Simon to a nearby forest and shot him. Having been sworn to secrecy, Captain Alexander covered up the murder by presenting the 'official version' at the press conference the following day.

The Netherlands

GERMAN ADMINISTRATION

After a short but stubborn fight, Germany took over the administration of the Netherlands. Hitler appointed as Reich Commissioner Arthur Seyss-Inquart, the same individual who, as a member of the last 'Austrian Government', had invited Hitler to 'protect' Austria against internal disorders. The Reich Commissioner was made responsible directly to Hitler.

In his first proclamation to the Netherlands population, the Reich Commissioner stated that as a result of 'the magnanimity of the Führer and the power of the German armed forces, an order of public life has been restored within a few days after the catastrophe brought about by the former leadership of the Netherlands'. Because the German people 'are fighting a decisive battle for their survival or destruction, a struggle which the hatred and envy of their enemies have forced upon them', the exigencies of that struggle compelled the German nation 'to exert all its strength' and gave it 'the right to avail itself of all means within its reach'. A reference to the blood kinship of Dutchmen and Germans suggested that Dutchmen were to be treated in a favourable way.

It was stated in the Reich Commissioner's order of May 29, 1940, that 'to the extent required for the fulfillment of his duties, the Reich Commissioner for the occupied Netherlands territories assumes all powers, privileges and rights heretofore vested in the King and the government in accordance with the Constitution and the laws of the Netherlands'.

Dr Arthur Seyss-Inquart *(left)* served in the Austrian Army in the First World War, receiving wounds that left him with a limp. In 1933, now a successful lawyer, he was invited to join the cabinet of Chancellor Englebert Dollfuss in Austria, and when Dollfuss was murdered the following year, his successor, Kurt von Schuschnigg, appointed Seyss-Inquart the Austrian Minister of the Interior. When von Schuschnigg resigned on March 11, 1938, faced with pressure from Hitler (see page 12), President Wilhelm Miklas reluctantly appointed Seyss-Inquart to replace him as Chancellor, a position he retained for two days. Extending an invitation for German troops to enter Austria, he quickly drafted the legislative act reducing Austria to a province of Germany called Ostmark of which he became its Reichsstatthalter (Governor). He was also given the rank of SS-Gruppenführer. The following year, after the invasion of Poland, he was appointed deputy to Governor General Hans Frank, but after the capitulation of Holland in May 1940, he was moved there to become Reichskommissar for the Occupied Netherlands with his headquarters located in the Clingendael estate just outside The Hague *(right)*. Within a few months of his arrival in Holland, Seyss-Inquart began to remove every Jew from public service, the Press, and leading positions in the Dutch industry. A database of Jewish residents was compiled and a ghetto set up in Amsterdam, prior to carrying out forced deportations to concentration camps. A so-called 'voluntary labour recruitment campaign' led to over half a million Dutch civilians working for the Germans, half of those in Germany.

PROCLAMATION OF THE REICH COMMISSIONER FOR THE OCCUPIED NETHERLANDS TERRITORIES TO THE NETHERLANDS POPULATION, MAY 25, 1940

On this day I have assumed supreme governmental authority within the civil domain in the Netherlands.

It is due to the magnanimity of the Führer and the power of the German armed forces that within a few days after the catastrophe brought about by the former leadership of the Netherlands, an order of public life is restored which will interfere with the usual and prevailing state of affairs only to the extent demanded by the special conditions.

As Reich Commissioner I hold supreme governmental authority in the civil domain in the Netherlands territories placed under the protection of German troops, for the purpose of safeguarding public order and public life. I shall take all measures, including those of a legislative nature, which are necessary for the fulfilment of this task. It is my will to leave unimpaired, as far as this is possible, the Netherlands law as heretofore in force, to avail myself of the Netherlands authorities for the fulfilment of administrative tasks, and to preserve the independence of the judiciary. I expect, however, that all Netherlands judges, officials and employees presently active in public service will conscientiously comply with my orders directed toward that objective, and that the Netherlands nation will follow this leadership with understanding and self-discipline.

The Netherlands soldiers have fought well in battle. The Netherlands civil population has adopted a satisfactory attitude toward the fighting troops. There is nothing which should prevent us from meeting each other on a plane of mutual respect.

Under their Führer the German people are fighting a decisive battle for their survival or destruction, a struggle which the hatred and envy of their enemies have forced upon them. This struggle compels the German nation to exert all its strength and gives it the right to avail itself of all means within its reach. This compulsion and privilege will also necessarily affect the life of the Netherlands nation and its economy. It will, however, be my concern that the Netherlands nation, akin in blood to the German nation, shall not be subject to living conditions less favourable than those necessitated by the community of fate and the destructive intentions of our enemies at this time.

As Reich Commissioner I have to safeguard the interests of the Reich in the Netherlands territories placed under the protection of the German troops and I shall safeguard them. The Netherlands nation, in fulfilling the duties resulting from the common task, will be able to secure its country and its liberty for the future.

Headquarters of the Führer, May 25, 1940.
SEYSS-INQUART
Reich Commissioner for the Occupied Netherlands Territories

Left: **The Wehrmachtbefehlshaber was an ex-WWI German naval aviator ace, General Friedrich Christiansen, with a score of 13 kills. He was awarded the Iron Cross Second Class for bombing raids on Ramsgate and Dover, later adding the Iron Cross First Class, the** Ritterkreuz and the Pour le Mérite. He ended the war with the rank of Kapitänleutnant. *Right:* **He was the supreme military commander in Holland from May 29, 1940 to April 7, 1945 at his headquarters at Hilversum. The HQ bunker still survives at Verdilaan/Rossinilaan.**

Himmler, Seyss-Inquart and the Higher SS Police Chief in the Netherlands, SS-Obergruppenführer Hanns Rauter, inspect newly-trained Dutch policemen.

culture, and matters relating to schools and churches; (6) public health and 'cultural and social welfare of juveniles', a euphemism for the Nazi indoctrination of youth.

The Commissioner for Public Safety, who was at the same time Higher SS and Police Leader, commanded the units of the military SS and German police forces stationed in the Netherlands. He also supervised the Netherlands central and municipal police. The General Commissioner of Finance and Commerce supervised all matters relating to: (1) the Ministry of Finance; (2) the Ministry of Economics (Commerce); (3) the Ministry of Waterways; (4) the Postal Administration; and (5) the Ministry of Public Welfare (with the exception of public health and 'cultural and social welfare of juveniles'. The General Commissioner for Special Matters was entrusted with the political aspects of administration. His duties included 'the moulding of public opinion' and the controlling of non-profit associations.

A further decree promulgated on June 3, 1940 stated that the Reich Commissioner would operate through a staff consisting of general and special commissioners. The general commissioners headed the following sections: (a) General Administration and Judiciary; (b) Public Safety (Higher SS and Police Leader); (c) Finance and Commerce (Economics); (d) Special Matters. The section on General Administration and Judiciary embraced matters relating to: (1) general orders and legislation, constitutional law, and the Official Gazette (*Verordnungsblatt für die besetzten niederländischen Gebiete*); (2) planning; (3) civil administration, especially the supervision of municipalities, but with the exception of municipal police forces; (4) administration of justice, with the exception of the Reich police forces; (5)

This took place at the Nazified police school which was set up by the Germans at Schalkhaar, near Deventer in the east of the country, on February 1, 1944.

The leader of the Dutch Nazi Party — the Nationaal-Socialistische Beweging (NSB) — was Anton Mussert (left). A prominent Nazi since the Dutch party was formed in 1931, his foremost aim during the occupation was to get himself appointed leader of a Dutch government. Although this was never in the German plans, it led him to increasing collaboration. In June 1940, he agreed to have his members join the SS-Standarte 'Westland', and in September that year issued instructions for the formation of the Nederlandsche SS (renamed Germaansche SS in Nederland in 1942).

Primarily a political organisation, it also served as a recruiting ground for the 'Wiking' division of the Waffen-SS. However, in July 1941, much to Mussert's chagrin, his rival Arnold Meyer of the Nationaal Front (the Dutch Fascist Party) in the wake of the German invasion of the Soviet Union suggested the creation of a Vrijwilligerslegioen Nederland (Volunteers Legion Netherlands), an idea much applauded by Himmler who wanted to establish a foreign legion of volunteers willing to fight in a 'crusade against Bolshevism'.

DUTCH ADMINISTRATION

For purposes of local administration, a sub-cabinet or headless government was organised consisting of the Secretaries-General of the existing Dutch ministries. Secretaries-General functioned in the Ministry of Trade, Industry and Shipping; Ministry of Agriculture and Fisheries; Ministry of Waterstaat (supervising the waterways, waterworks, ports and generally all communications); Ministry of the Interior; Ministry of Finance; Ministry of Social Welfare (labour matters belonged also to this ministry); Ministry of Justice, and Ministry of General Affairs.

To the Ministry of Trade, Industry and Shipping was attached the office of a Price Commissioner, appointed by the Secretary-General of that ministry. His authority extended especially to prices for 'all articles of everyday need, to rentals for chattels and property, and to tariffs for transportation, gas and electricity, and for rates of interest.' The Price Commissioner was assisted by a board consisting of members representing: (1) the Ministry of Trade, Industry and Shipping; (2) the Ministry of Agriculture and Fisheries; (3) the Ministry of Waterstaat; (4) the Ministry of the Interior; (5) the Ministry of Finance; (6) the Ministry of Justice; and (7) the Ministry of Social Welfare.

Powers and duties relating to food problems were vested in the Director-General for the Food Supply who was assisted by a Commission for Securing the Food Supply. The members of this commission were appointed by the Secretary-General in the Ministry of Agriculture and Fisheries.

For the regulation of transportation and traffic, an office of the Inspector-General of Traffic was established under the supervision of the Ministry of Waterstaat. The Inspector-General of Traffic was appointed by the Secretary-General of the Ministry of Waterstaat to control all matters pertaining to

Recruits for the 'Westland' Regiment of the Waffen-SS practice the art of the 'goose-step' parade march.

The headquarters of the NSB was located at No. 35 Maliebaan in Utrecht. Although in December 1942 Hitler dubbed Mussert the 'Leader of the Dutch People', by the following year his influence was on the decline and, at his last meeting with the Führer in May 1943, he was told that he would never have political control in the Netherlands.

In his decree of August 20, 1940, Seyss-Inquart stated that he would appoint certain categories of Dutch officials (these categories were specified in the order), leaving to the Secretaries-General the right to appoint all others. However this right of appointment of the secondary officials by the Secretaries-General was made illusory by the further provision in the order stating that the Reich Commissioner reserved to himself the right to exercise, if he saw fit, the power of appointment that he was granting to the Secretaries-General in the preceding section of the order.

The following basic institutions of Dutch self-government were suspended by the orders of June 21, 1940, and August 11, 1941, implementing the decree of May 18,1940: (1) the two Chambers of the States-General (Staten Generaal) comprising the parliament of the Netherlands which was divided into upper and lower chambers as in some other countries; (2) the State Council (the advisory body to the Crown whose members were appointed by the Queen); (3) the Provincial States (Provinciale Staten), which were representative bodies for the provinces; (4) the municipal councils (Gemeenteraden) in the cities.

The local administration was reconstructed. Members of the advisory councils, which were previously elected by the population, were now appointed by the mayors who were strictly supervised and acted according with the instructions of the supervising administrative authority.

By the decree of July 4, 1941, political parties were dissolved. The only party allowed to continue was the Dutch Nazi party NSB under its leader Anton Mussert.

transportation. As the transportation of goods for personal use, even on public highways, was prohibited without a permit, one of the functions of the Inspector-General was to deal with applications for such permits. Furthermore, as the unauthorised use of motorcycles or any motor vehicles (with the exception of motor busses) had been prohibited in order to save petrol, it fell within the jurisdiction of the Inspector-General to decide on the granting of permits for the use of such vehicles.

A Netherlands Reconstruction Service (Opbouwdienst) was established by an order of July 30, 1940, with the objective of affording employment to members of the former Netherlands armed forces. This service was headed by a Labour Commandant and by an Administrative Director, both acting under the orders of the Secretary-General in the Ministry of Social Welfare.

To deal with labour problems in general, as well as with public occupational guidance and the apprenticeship placement service, a State Labour Office was created within the Ministry of Social Welfare, headed by a General-Director. As labour procurement had been monopolised for the needs of the German war economy, the continuation of licenses issued to private employment agencies for trade and industry were now dependent on approval from the Ministry of Social Welfare. Favourable decisions were only made with respect to agencies that were collaborating with the German authorities in procurement of labour for Germany.

All these Dutch agencies were under the control of German authorities, especially the four general commissioners who were members of the staff of the Reich Commissioner. Their powers were divided in such a way that each general commissioner controled a different ministry and agency, according to the jurisdictional division set forth in the decree of June 3, 1940.

Today the house is occupied by a children's day care home. Mussert was arrested on May 7, 1945 and convicted of high treason. Exactly one year after his arrest he faced a firing-squad on Waalsdorpervlakte, an area of dunes near The Hague, the same site where over 250 Dutch citizens had been put to death by the Nazis. Of all the German-occupied countries in western Europe, the Netherlands suffered the highest per capita death rate, about 200,000 having lost their lives.

Having experienced over 100 years of peace, and in spite of Hitler's guarantee of observing Holland's neutrality, Operation 'Fall Gelb' provided for a combined assault on the country by ground and airborne troops in the early hours of May 10. Rotterdam also suffered a devastating bombing raid just as a surrender ultimatum had been delivered. The attack, which killed between 600 and 800 civilians, led to the immediate capitulation of the Netherlands on May 15. Here German troops are drawn up on the Binnenhof, the centre of the Dutch government and the office of the Prime Minister in The Hague.

The government and members of the Dutch Royal Family managed to escape to Britain aboard Royal Navy destroyers, although Queen Wilhelmina had to be persuaded to leave as she wanted to remain behind with her people. This comparison shows the Golden Coach leaving from the inner courtyard on September 17, 2013 –- Prinsjesdag (Little Princes Day) — when the King addresses members of the government in the Ridderzaal, the Knight's Hall seen in the background.

CITIZENSHIP

Dual nationality was unknown in the Netherlands, but the Germans were eager to create a privileged class of fifth columnists who would be protected by German nationality and, at the same time, enjoy the rights of Dutch nationals and thus be able to perform political tasks for the benefit of the Germans within the Dutch national community.

Disrespect for the exclusiveness of Netherlands nationality was displayed by Seyss-Inquart who issued an order which provided that a Dutchman acquiring German nationality would not be deemed to have lost his/her Dutch nationality unless it was renounced within one year after acquisition of German nationality.

The law regarding citizenship was also changed further for recruiting reasons. According to Dutch law, a

The anti-Jewish programme with the threat of deportation or worse led to a series of street battles between the action squads of the NSB and Jewish self-defence groups which culminated in a pitched battle on February 11, 1941 on Waterlooplein in Amsterdam. German troops and the Dutch police restored order and cordoned off the area from the rest of the city to deny it to Jews. One of the wounded NSB streetfighters died from his injuries on February 14 which only provoked further disturbances in which several police officers were wounded. *Above:* On the weekend of February 22-23, the Germans took 425 Jewish men hostage (eventually they ended up in Buchenwald and Mauthausen camps), which led to a huge protest meeting being held on Monday morning to call for a general strike. Promoted by the banned Communist Party, this strike stands as the first and only direct action undertaken against anti-Jewish measures by the Nazis in any country in occupied Europe.

Begun by striking tram drivers, it is estimated that over 300,000 people joined the protest, bringing Amsterdam to a complete halt. Although it spread to several other towns, it did not last long and by February 27 the Germans had regained control, executing three of the Communist ringleaders.

Memory of this strike still lives on, and a commemoration is held every February 25, culminating with a march past the memorial on Jonas Daniel Meyerplein by Mari Andriessen erected in 1952.

Dutchman serving in a foreign army automatically lost his citizenship. When the creation of the Anti-Bolshevik Legion was announced by the Germans, the law on citizenship was changed so that service against Russia did not deprive the person of their Dutch citizenship.

DAMAGES AND CIVIL CLAIMS

A decree of February 7, 1941 declared that German nationals were to be indemnified for damages to property that they had suffered, or may suffer, in the occupied Netherlands as a result of the war. A special fund, called the 'Reconstruction Fund' was created for this purpose under the administration of the Secretary-General of the Ministry of Finance. The income and expenditure of this fund were established by an annual budget and financed by funds supplied by the Dutch Government. Thus the Dutch Treasury was made to pay for war damage caused by the German Army to German residents in the Netherlands. If the funds from the Dutch Government proved insufficient, the order provided that the Treasury could incur short- or long-term loans.

Forced moves of the Jewish population from other parts of the country to Amsterdam began in late 1941 and by July 1942, most Jews were concentrated in the capital's so-called Joodsche Wijk (Jewish Quarter).

Another order dealt with the problem of civil claims that might arise from orders of the Reich Commissioner. For example, an order from the Reich Commissioner could undertake the re-allocation of property. The party aggrieved by such an order, or his successor, was thereby excluded from relief in the courts. The person could only appeal direct to Seyss-Inquart. Thus the same authority which issued the order aggrieving the party, also decided upon the right of appeal from such order. Moreover, the same decree stated that suit on civil claims could not be brought against Germans or corporations having their domicile in the Greater Reich if the cause of action had arisen directly or indirectly as a result of the events of war. Thus, Dutchmen were precluded from suing for war damages, yet had to provide money to pay Germans for such damages caused by Germans.

AMERICAN PROPERTY

On September 11, 1941, the Reich Commissioner issued an order concerning the declaration of United States assets in the Netherlands. According to this decree, real and personal property situated in the occupied Netherlands had to be declared if owned or even controlled by the Government of the United States, or by citizens of the United States, or corporations, private associations, foundations, endowments, trusts, or other forms of organisations which had their seat or principal place of business in the United States or which had been incorporated under the laws of the United States. Moreover, the order also covered other persons if, besides the personal property situated in the occupied Netherlands, such persons had business branches in the United States.

Parts of the Jewish area were sealed off with a barbed-wire fence like this one on Nieuwmarkt. The building is a 15th-century former city gate called the Waag.

After Mussert had been appointed by Hitler as the 'Leider van het Nederlandse Volk', he formed a Secretarie van Staat (Secretariat of State), an agency of the NSB that could give advice on various matters to Seyss-Inquart. The new organisation began work on February 1, 1943. One of its members was retired General Hendrik Seyffardt, the commander of the Vrijwilligerslegioen Nederland, seen standing third left in this photograph next to Seyss-Inquart. On his left is SS-Obergruppenführer Hanns Rauter.

Secretaries-General in the Ministry of Trade, Industry, and Shipping, and in the Ministry of Finance, were then compelled by the Germans to issue an order authorising Dutch banks to extend loans to those exporting firms 'which find themselves financially embarrassed through their inability to enforce claims arising out of shipments abroad'. An instrument was thus created whereby the Dutch banks financed further exports to Germany with consequent inflationary effect upon the Dutch currency.

Another peculiar evolution occurred in the field of exchange control. At the beginning of the occupation, the Netherlands was divided from Germany by a customs frontier and by exchange control restrictions. Later on, because of the relatively strong and well-organised Dutch economy, the Germans saw the advantage of incorporating the Netherlands totally into the economy of the Greater German Reich. A logical consequence of such incorporation was the abolition of customs frontier and exchange control restrictions between these two countries, especially concerning the transfer of money from one country to another. Germany, however, had owed large sums of money to individuals in the Netherlands for many

FINANCE

With regard to finance, the same technique was adopted in the Netherlands as in other western countries that had been occupied. Reichskreditkassenscheine were issued which the Bank of the Netherlands had to exchange for guilders. The exchange rate between the Reichsmark and the guilder was established as one guilder to 133 Reichspfennigs.

A clearing arrangement was established between the Netherlands and Germany, as well as between the Netherlands and other countries, through the German Verrechnungskasse (Clearing Institute). As the Germans were unwilling to maintain a balance of trade between the Netherlands and Germany, Dutch exporting firms had difficulties when their claims were frozen in Germany. Disruption of Dutch economic life was the result. The

Mussert was speaking to the NSB at a rally taking place in front of the Ridderzaal (Hall of Knghts) at the Binnenhof (see page 138).

Although there were a number of resistance organisations active in Holland, many concerned with hiding and moving people, there were three that specialised in armed resistance, sabotage and, sometimes, assassinations: the National Assault Groups (Landelijke Knokploegen — LKP); the Council of Resistance (Raad van Verzet – RVV), and the Communist CS-6, its name coming from its address in Amsterdam: No. 6 Corelli Street. One of their leaders was Dr Gerrit Kastein and Seyffardt was second on their assassination list after Mussert. On the evening of February 5, 1943, Seyffardt was shot twice on his doorstep *(left)* by Jan Verleun who had accompanied Dr Kastein to the general's house at No. 103 Statenlaan in Scheveningen. Seyffardt died the following day. Two days later CS-6 shot one of the NSB ministers, Attorney Herman Reydon, and his wife. The attacks led to massive reprisals, Rauter immediately ordering the execution of 50 Dutch hostages, and a series of raids were mounted on universities when it was realised that Verleun was a student. As the net closed in, Kastein committed suicide so as not to be broken under torture.

On the night of September 30/October 1, 1944, members of the Dutch resistance ambushed a vehicle carrying two German officers and two NCOs on the road between Putten and Nijkerk. The two officers were wounded, one dying the following day while the NCOs fled the scene. One of the resisters, Frans Slotboom, was wounded in the clash and he later succumbed from his wounds. When the news of the ambush reached General Christiansen, he ordered a reprisal raid be made on Putten. In the General's order to Oberst Fritz Fullriede, he was quite specific: 'Put them all up against the wall' — words which were to find him accused of a war crime after the war. On October 2, German troops descended on the village, segregating all the men between 18 and 50 who were taken to the concentration camp at Amersfoort. A week later over 600 were transported to Neuengamme of whom only 48 returned in 1945.

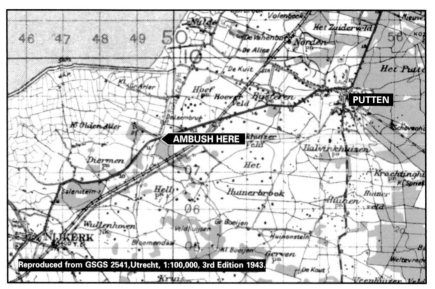

Reproduced from GSGS 2541, Utrecht, 1:100,000, 3rd Edition 1943.

Left: Over 100 houses in Putten village were burned down, the pyre being visible for miles. *Above:* This is the ruin of the Oldenaller Herberg, an inn on the Nijkerk to Putten road. The ambush that led to the reprisals occurred in the background on the left.

years before the war. Since 1931, these sums had been under the protection of the German Exchange Control Law, so that all the demands of Dutch creditors were met with the answer that the German debtor was not allowed to pay because of exchange control restrictions. However, the exchange control restrictions were abrogated on March 31, 1941. Now, theoretically, money could be transferred from Germany to the Netherlands, but on the very same day another decree was published to the effect that every Dutchman withdrawing money from the Greater Reich to the Netherlands must now pay a tax for the benefit of the Dutch Treasury amounting to 72 per cent of the sum withdrawn.

RESISTANCE

The resistance of the Dutch population to the Germans was strong, despite the fact that some Dutchmen were forced into collaboration, especially as regards the German war economy. The activities of Dutch patriots gave rise to the introduction of severe punishments. On October 16, 1941, an order was issued concerning defence against acts of sabotage in which the Reich Commissioner declared that 'Germany is

The same spot today. A silent memorial service is held every year on October 2 to remember the victims. There are no speeches, just a choir singing verses from Psalm 84 . . . exactly the same as the men did in 1944 as they were taken away.

While the reprisal was being carried out, six men and a woman were shot dead. The remainder of the women were held in the church and only released in the evening with the children who had been held separately in the school.

On October 1, 1949, Queen Juliana unveiled a monument of a grieving widow (by Mari Andriessen). 'The Little Lady of Putten' faces the Old Church from where the men were deported. A memorial garden contains 552 symbolic graves.

tion as to the time within which such date may be set'. The indictment also 'may be preferred orally.' In such cases a German Superior Court, acting as a special court, had exclusive jurisdiction.

Not only were the lives and personal liberties of Dutchmen held in pawn against non-compliance, but also their property. By the order of July 4, 1940, the property of persons and associations which had furthered 'activities hostile to the German Reich or Germanism, or of whom it must be assumed that they will further such activities in the future may be confiscated. The same applies to property and rights which have been used for the furtherance of activities hostile to the German Reich or Germanism, or which are capable of being thus used.' This order created an attitude, not only of complete compliance with the orders of the Germans, but also of complete sub-servience. Such a provision was also without parallel in law for, according to well-established principles of criminal law, a person can only be punished for acts that have been committed or attempted, not for acts that may be committed in the future.

RALPHAEL LEMKIN, 1944

engaged in a fight against the enemy powers, on behalf of Europe's future'. Although the death penalty was prescribed for every act of sabotage, the Reich Commissioner did not give an exact definition for the term sabotage. According to his order, any person would be punishable by death as a saboteur who wilfully perpetrated 'an act punishable under existing statutes and intended or liable to endanger public order or security of public life'. If one considers that any violation of administrative regulations pertaining to public order could be interpreted as endangering that order, there was unlimited application of the death penalty, even for offences that were essentially of a purely administrative character. Moreover, an attempt was punishable in the same way as perpetration. No judicial guaranties were given as to trial of such offences; for example, the date of trial could be fixed 'without the usual restric-

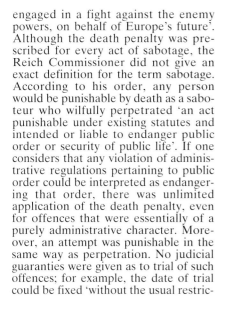

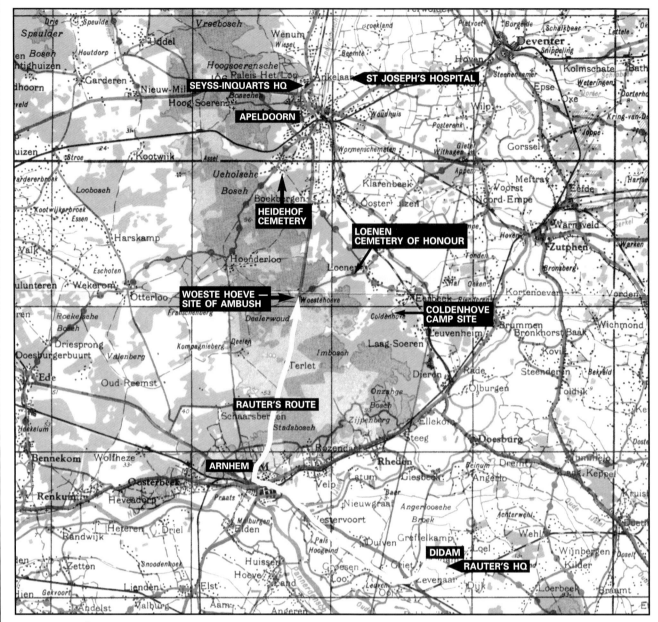

Reprisal at De Woeste Hoevre

By the beginning of March 1945, the forces of British 21st Army Group were stationed along the River Rhine about to cross over and enter the northern half of Holland.

In September 1944, the three largest armed Resistance organisations in the Netherlands were united into the Binnenlandse Strijdkrachten (BS, Dutch Interior Forces) under overall command of Prince Bernhard. The BS was divided into districts and when in November 1944 the front lines stabilised along the Dutch rivers, 14 of the 19 BS districts still lay in occupied territory. One of these was District 6, comprising the Veluwe, an undulating forest region with extensive heathlands and large wooded tracts which was one of the few areas in the Netherlands suited for maquis warfare. The town of Apeldoorn lay in the centre.

The Apeldoorn BS had taken over from the former LKP organisation a small team, called GG-Groep, which was only used for the more risky operations. It was well armed with Sten guns, pistols and grenades and, having somehow got hold of SS uniforms, usually operated disguised as Germans. The team-leader was a dashing young mechanic, Geert Gosens, but the group was plagued by a serious problem as in the preceding weeks, mainly because of intensified searching by the Germans it, had lost all its vehicles. This became acutely relevant on Tuesday, March 6, 1945.

Information was received that a Wehrmacht truck was expected to collect 3,000kg of pork for distribution to the German army from a butcher's in the nearby village of Epe the following morning. In a country that had been systematically starved by the Germans since the previous autumn, such information was of vital importance. If the meat could be seized, it could replenish the BS's own meagre food supplies and the rest could be distributed clandestinely among the hungry population. The local Apeldoorn BS Sabotage Commander ordered Gosens and his team to try and do so.

Gosens saw an easy way of doing it. If the team, dressed in their German uniforms, were to arrive at the butcher's with a truck a short time before the real Germans were due, they could simply load up the meat and drive away with it, but that left another problem: where were they going to find a truck at such short notice? They did not like using private vehicles because of the trouble it could get the owner into, but this time it was also impracticable as it had to look like an army vehicle. What Gosens decided to do was to capture a German truck first, and carry out the theft the same night.

The decision made, Gosens notified his men to meet him at No. 17 Korteweg, a bakery shop of a trusted friend, Jaap Jonker, and one of their secret addresses. Six men were present that evening: four Dutchmen, Gosens, Henk de Weert, Karel Pruis and Wim Kok, and two Austrians, Sepp Köttinger and Herman Kempfer. The presence of Köttinger and Kempfer was remarkable. They had previously been members of the Waffen-SS, but had deserted and joined the Dutch Resistance. Both were trained fighters and of great value to the team. Whenever it operated in German uniforms, Köttinger, the more commanding of the two, took the lead and did all the talking.

Together, the six men sat down to formulate a plan. The discussion centred on the best place to lay an ambush and Wim Kok suggested the Apeldoorn to Arnhem road as it was quiet, the woods through which it ran offered ample cover, and few people lived near it. Furthermore, it was not far from one of the team's hiding places, a camp-site by the name of 'Coldenhove' in the woods near Eerbeek, some seven kilometres to the east.

In September 1944, Resistance organisations in the Netherlands had united as the Binnenlandse Strijdkrachten (BS, Dutch Interior Forces) under the overall command of Prince Bernhard *(left)*. The BS had divided the country into separate districts, the town of Apeldoorn becoming the centre of activity of the GG-Groep, led by a young auto-mechanic, Geert Gosens. *Right:* He lived at No. 6 Molendwarsstraat where the team kept two of their vehicles but both were lost when the Germans raided the premises early in March 1945. The group were desperate to obtain a lorry so on the night of March 6/7 they set out to hijack a replacement.

Shortly after 10 p.m. the team set out on bicycles for the Arnhem road. All were armed with Stens. Reaching the village of Beekbergen, they tried out their credibility as a patrol on traffic-control duty. Flashing a torch, they stopped an oncoming vehicle, which turned out to be a civilian lorry, and demanded to see the driver's papers. The Dutchman at the wheel obviously suspected nothing and obeyed promptly. Their self-confidence thus fortified, the team pedalled on until they reached a roadside inn called 'De Woeste Hoeve'. Two hundred metres further on they stopped, laid down their bicycles on the grass verge, prepared their weapons and waited.

Soon they heard a vehicle approaching, but by the sound of the engine they took it to be a car and not the lorry they wanted, so they let it pass unchallenged. The noise died away in the distance, until they were left once more in total silence. This happened several times with cars from both directions. There was not a lot of traffic at that time of night and slowly the minutes ticked by. It was now close to midnight and, despite the nervous tension, the men could feel the cold entering through their clothes.

Having decided on the best place to set up an ambush to capture a lorry, they left on pushbikes shortly after 10 p.m., five wearing German uniforms and one that of a Dutch military policeman, ready to set up a road-block close to the inn at De Woeste Hoeve on the Apeldoorn—Arnhem road.

After several false alarms, near midnight the sound of another vehicle was heard approaching from the direction of Arnhem.

Left: **SS-Obergruppenführer Hanns Rauter was Generalkommissar fur das Sicherheitswesen (Commissioner General for Public Safety) in occupied Holland and also the Höhere SS- und Polizeiführer Nordwest (Higher SS and Police Leader, 'Nordwest' being the pan-Germanic denomination for the Netherlands). As HSSPF, Rauter commanded all the SS organisations in the country. These included the Ordnungspolizei (the ordinary German police), the Sicherheitspolizei und Sicherheitsdienst (Secret Police and Security Service), and all Waffen-SS**

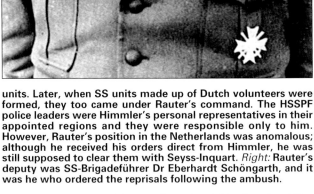

units. Later, when SS units made up of Dutch volunteers were formed, they too came under Rauter's command. The HSSPF police leaders were Himmler's personal representatives in their appointed regions and they were responsible only to him. However, Rauter's position in the Netherlands was anomalous; although he received his orders direct from Himmler, he was still supposed to clear them with Seyss-Inquart. *Right:* **Rauter's deputy was SS-Brigadeführer Dr Eberhardt Schöngarth, and it was he who ordered the reprisals following the ambush.**

An hour and a half earlier SS-Obergruppenführer Hanns Rauter left the house on Kerkstraat in Didam that was his Corps Command Post. A grey-green BMW convertible stood waiting, its roof folded down. Rauter had a suitcase full of laundry that he wanted to have done at Apeldoorn which he tied to the rack at the rear of the car. Then, as he always did, he sat in the front seat next to the driver, Wilhelm Klotz. His orderly, Oberleutnant Erwin Exner, sat in the back.

Leaving Didam, they took the road to Zevenaar and from there the main road to Arnhem. The Rhine bridge, blown by the Germans, lay mangled and broken in the river. Entering the town from the east, Rauter's car passed the buildings down by the northern ramp, ruined and scarred in the September fighting, and turned into Eusebiusbuitensingel on the road to Apeldoorn. The car had black-out lights so that only a few metres of the road ahead were visible.

Suddenly, a white light flashed in the distance up ahead. Peering through the darkness, Rauter saw two uniformed men standing on the road, one of them signalling them to halt. An order had recently been issued forbidding the challenging of traffic in open country because of the increase of attacks on German vehicles by Resistance groups. Patrols, including those of the Dutch police, were allowed to establish check-points only in built-up areas, on the outskirts of towns and villages, and forbidden to do so in open country. So when Rauter saw two uniformed men, one with a torch, he was sure that this could not be an official road-block.

'Achtung! Be ready, probably terrorists in front of us!' he shouted, reaching for his sub-machine gun. 'Don't stop!' he ordered his driver. 'Full speed and drive into them! You defend the rear!' he called out to Exner who also had a sub-machine gun.

In the wake of the German victory at Arnhem, Rauter had also been given a formal military command to guard the Veluwe region and the bridges over the IJssel river from a possible airborne attack. In February 1945, Kampfgruppe Rauter was raised to the status of a provisional corps under the 25. Armee with its command post in this house at No. 12 Kerkstraat in Didam, a village 15 kilometres east of Arnhem. Every week Rauter travelled to Apeldoorn for a meeting with Reichskommissar Seyss-Inquart, departing on this particular week on Tuesday, March 6.

This re-enactment was staged by SD officers the following day to show the positions of Gosens' men, determined from the locations of spent cartrige cases. When the approaching vehicle failed to stop, they opened fire.

Rauter later blamed what happened on the inexperience of his new driver. Instead of accelerating straight through the men in the road, Klotz hesitated, then applied the brakes. As the car slowed down, the man on the left with the torch could be seen pointing the light at the car's number plate and moving to ask for papers. Still not level with the two men, Rauter stuck his gun towards the one nearest to him, the one on the right, and shouted angrily: 'What's the matter, man, don't you know who we are?'

Köttinger and Gosens must have been as surprised as Rauter. They had expected to see a lorry approaching, but what they saw was a car with occupants grabbing for their weapons. They had no time to think. Gosens made a split-second decision and pulled the trigger. His first burst, a short one, went through the windscreen and hit the German sitting beside the driver.

'Don't shoot and get out of the car!' he ordered, as the BMW finally came to a halt, but it was obvious that these Germans had no intention of obeying and were going to fight it out. Everything happened very fast. While Köttinger, still forward of the car, ran to his right and took up a position on the driver's side, Gosens raced along the other side of the car to the rear and shouted 'Fire!'

So far, the other team members, standing on the other side of the road a few metres back, had taken no part in the action. In the darkness, they could only vaguely see what was happening and when they heard Gosens' shout, they feared that he and Köttinger might be in their line of fire. Nonetheless De Weert and Pruis let loose with their Stens. Köttinger opened up too and a murderous cross-fire raked the BMW and its occupants. Within a few seconds it was all over. No movement came from the car and the firing stopped. From the number of used Sten magazines, the men later calculated that they must have fired at least 234 rounds. Incredibly though, neither Gosens nor Köttinger had been hit.

In the hail of fire, Oberleutnant Exner, facing rearwards with his gun, was riddled with bullets and killed instantly. One bullet hit driver Klotz behind the right ear and he slumped dead, his hand still clasping the hand-brake, his body against Rauter, who had slumped forward, bleeding profusely. However, Rauter, who had been hit first when Gosens fired his opening burst through the windscreen, was not dead. Those first bullets had gone through the fingers of his right hand, through his lower jaw (smashing his jaw bone) and through one of his lungs. Being furthest away from

the attackers after the car came to a stop, he may have been a little more shielded than the other two when the shooting broke out after that. Still, a bullet from the rear went through his neck vertebrae and flung his body forward into the windscreen. Then, as he raised his left arm to push his dead driver aside and pull himself up by the windscreen frame, a bullet went through his left armpit and, finally, another grazed his left arm.

After the firing stopped, the six men, shaken and disconcerted, cautiously approached the car and, by the light of the torch, glanced inside. The only sound coming from any of the bodies was a deep rattling. They were convinced that the occupants must all be dead or dying. 'We've got them, the bastards', one of the team let out. It was spoken as a natural release of pent-up tension, but to Rauter, lying semi-conscious in the car, it served to confirm that the ambush had been especially set up to assassinate him. To him it was unthinkable that he had been attacked by accident, by coincidence. Yet that was what had happened. The BS men had set out to capture a truck, not to kill Germans. They had absolutely no idea who their victims were, still less that they had shot the highest SS official in the Netherlands.

Although his driver and orderly had been killed, amazingly Rauter survived the fusillade although severely wounded.

Inevitably the ambush led to reprisals with 117 hostages being shot at the spot where it had occurred.

Suddenly, the BS men heard another vehicle approaching from the direction of Arnhem. Their Sten magazines were empty and there was no time to move the BMW off the road. Grabbing their bicycles, they quickly hid in the ditch on the west side of the road. A Wehrmacht truck pulled up beside the BMW. For a few seconds, it stood there, engine running. Then someone slammed a door and it rumbled off at speed towards Apeldoorn. (Rauter, who could only hear, not see, thought this was his attackers' vehicle leaving.)

For the second time, the Resistance men ventured out to the car. By now the light of the torch, its batteries almost flat, was fading. When again a vehicle was heard coming from Arnhem the team decided the time had come to withdraw. As planned, they did not return

to Apeldoorn, but went to their secret hide-out at Coldenhove camp-site, a few kilometres to the east. At the entrance to Loenen village, at the turn-off to Eerbeek near the De Eikelboom Hotel, a German sentry, mistaking them for men of his own unit, asked unsuspectingly: 'Are you cold, Franz?' Assuring him that he need not worry, the men quickly turned into the Eerbeek road and cycled on. Around 2 a.m. they arrived safely at their quarters at Coldenhove.

Meanwhile, back at De Woeste Hoeve, Rauter had still not been found. He was too weak to get out of the car. Blood was coming from his mouth and chest wounds and he was sweating profusely. All night he waited. Three times he heard lorries driving past and twice he tried to attract attention by firing his pistol.

It was early morning, around 6 a.m., before he was found by troops with horse-drawn transport on their way to the Harskamp training grounds. A few minutes later the inhabitants of the De Woeste Hoeve inn were awakened by agitated Germans demanding to use the telephone. Their call was the first news of Rauter's ambush to reach the German authorities at Apeldoorn. Immediately, the Reserve-Kriegslazarett, housed in the buildings of the St Joseph-Stichting Hospital on Deventerstraat, was alerted and an ambulance sent to De Woeste Hoeve. Rauter, who had handed over his maps and papers to the men who had found him, was by now very weak from loss of blood and almost frozen from cold. He finally reached the hospital at 8.30 a.m.

Scene of crime photos were taken by Dutch Police Inspector Jan Muda, many from the vantage point of the roof of a lorry. In this shot the BMW has been pushed to the side of the road, the chalk marks to the right of the men indicating the original position. It was Gosens' first burst that shattered the windscreen.

148

The ambush was not discovered until 6 a.m. Rauter, by then weak from loss of blood, was rushed to the St Joseph-Stichting Hospital on the outskirts of Apeldoorn. When the photos were taken of the car, the body of Oberleutnant Erwin Exner was still lying in the rear seat while that of the driver, Wilhelm Klotz, was slumped over the steering wheel.

The investigation of the crime scene was begun by SS-Hauptsturmführer Arthur Thomsen and SS-Untersturmführer Willy Bühe from the SD at Arnhem. Other officers arrived from the SD office at Apeldoorn and the SD main HQ at Zwolle. All the fired cartridge cases were ringed with chalk. Also, acting on Rauter's recollection that he had heard a lorry stop, plaster casts of tyre tracks were made as it was assumed the attackers had arrived in a vehicle.

THE REPRISALS

Now the Sicherheitsdienst machinery was set in motion. First to arrive at De Woeste Hoeve was a two-man investigation team from the SD office at Arnhem-Velp. Shortly, it was joined by SS-Hauptsturmführer Oscar Gerbig, SD chief at Apeldoorn. The SD men made a thorough search of the car, still with two bodies left in it, and of the ground surrounding it. Examination of the numerous cartridges found showed that they were of British origin and this suggested that organised Resistance was involved. Plaster moulds were made of all the tyre tracks found around the BMW. When Gerbig returned to Apeldoorn later in the morning, he found that another investigation team had been sent especially from the SD main office at Zwolle, and he went back to De Woeste Hoeve with them that afternoon. The Germans brought along some Dutch police detectives, and a police photographer, Jan Muda, was ordered to take a series of crime scene photos.

An interrogation room was set up in the inn and the inhabitants and their neighbours questioned. The civilians, fearing reprisals against them (they had been told by one of the four Germans billeted in the inn, with whom they were on friendly terms, that Rauter was among the victims), denied having seen anything. Only one of them admitted he had heard gun-fire in the night. None of them, however, was arrested.

They were indeed lucky. In taking reprisals, the SD had a habit of including people who lived near to where an attack had taken place. In such cases, houses had been set on fire and the inhabitants executed. The BS team could be justly criticised for the fact that, of all the 30 kilometres from Apeldoorn to Arnhem, it had chosen a spot with three houses close by for its ambush.

With Rauter himself out of action, it fell to SS-Brigadeführer Eberhard Schöngarth, his Befehlshaber der Sipo und des SD and deputy, to take action. As soon as he heard of the attack, Schöngarth drove from his HQ at Zwolle to Rauter's office at Apeldoorn to

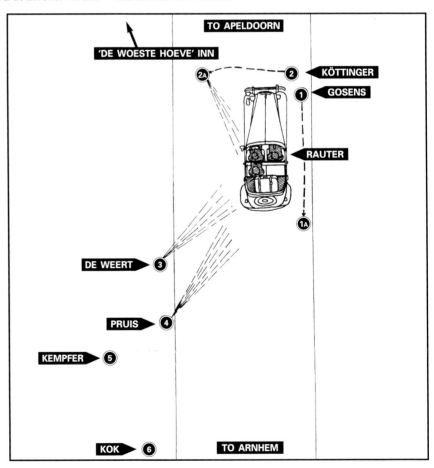

When our Dutch Editor Karel Margry researched this story for *After the Battle* No. 56 in 1986, he experienced incredible difficulties in reconstructing the precise course of events that had taken place at De Woeste Hoeve as the 'official' account, written by the Resistance in 1946, only gave pseudonyms for the six gunmen. It took Karel a long time to establish their real names, and those still alive in 1986 were very unwilling to talk. Fortunately, he traced the police inspector, Jan Muda, in retirement.

learn more of what had happened. He then drove to De Woeste Hoeve and had a short look round there himself. Returning to Apeldoorn, he first went to see Gerbig at his office. Gerbig told him that the investigation was making good progress and was even able to produce a photograph of a probable suspect. Incredibly, it was a picture of Geert Gosens, who was well known to the Apeldoorn SD. In fact, Gerbig said, everything in the ambush pointed to Gosens and his gang and, he assured Schöngarth, his men were putting everything aside to hunt the man down. Taking the photo album of suspects with him, Schöngarth then went to the hospital to see his superior, who had already been visited by Seyss-Inquart earlier that afternoon. Rauter was still very weak and had difficulty talking. He told Schöngarth he was absolutely convinced that the ambush had been laid with the specific purpose of assassinating him. The number of his attackers he guessed at about six, but he could give a description of only one of them: the man whose face he had seen, he clearly remembered, had jutting-out ears. When Schöngarth showed Rauter Gosens' picture, he was sure he recognised the face.

Finally, in the late afternoon, Schöngarth had a meeting with Seyss-Inquart at the latter's headquarters to discuss reprisal measures. To the Germans involved, it was clear that such measures would have to be taken, regardless of whether the actual perpetrators were caught or not. An attack on the highest SS official in the Netherlands called for the severest punishment.

According to Seyss-Inquart at his Nuremburg trial, Schöngarth told him at the meeting that he had received orders from Himmler personally to shoot 500 prominent citizens but that he thought that excessive.

Schöngarth said that he would prefer shooting a smaller number of Todeskandidaten (prisoners who had been sentenced to death) and not innocent hostages.

Earlier, he had already ordered Gerbig to prepare a list of candidates for execution held in Apeldoorn jails. Before leaving Apeldoorn, he now personally telephoned at least two of his other SD commanders, those at Deventer and Groningen, and ordered them to do the same. After returning to Zwolle, he delegated this job to his subordinate, SS-Obersturmbannführer Hans Kolitz. The prisoners from the northern and eastern provinces were to be brought to Apeldoorn and shot at De Woeste Hoeve, the others were to be executed where they were being held.

All through the evening and night of March 7/8, Kolitz made frantic phone-calls to various SD chiefs in the Netherlands. There were not enough Todeskandidaten available and Kolitz had to bargain with the SD chiefs for the number of victims they would provide. In the end, a number of prisoners were included who had not yet been sentenced to death or had only been arrested for petty offences.

SS-Sturmbannführer Willi Lages, the SD chief at Amsterdam, received a demand from Kolitz for 75 Todeskandidaten. Lages, however, had only 59 on hand — 53 in Amsterdam prisons and six in Utrecht — and Kolitz quickly settled for those. In the early morning of March 8, the 53 prisoners from Amsterdam were shot in the grounds of a teahouse by the name of Rozenoord, just outside the capital, beside the Amstel river. Germans wielding rifle butts forced passersby on the dike to watch the slaughter. The six Todeskandidaten from Utrecht were not executed in public but brought to Fort De Bilt, on the outskirts of town, and shot there.

The SD chief at The Hague, SS-Hauptsturmführer Johannes Munt, was ordered by Kolitz to provide 80 victims. Munt had a mere dozen available in Scheveningen prison and he asked for the number to be halved, but Kolitz was adamant: 'It doesn't matter where you get them from', he said, 'it's an order from the top and there's nothing to be done about it.' Munt racked his brains. The day before he had sent 49 of his Todeskandidaten to the Amersfoort concentration camp. At 11 p.m., he had his deputy telephone the camp commandant and order these 49 to be shot. Now he needed another 31 and, in desperation, he finally decided that it would not have to matter whether they were Todeskandidaten or not. He knew there were a number of people in custody who had recently been arrested for looting after the large RAF raid on The Hague of March 3. At midnight, he went to Scheveningen prison and himself selected from this group 11 prisoners to be included in the reprisals. These 11, together with 27 Todeskandidaten which Munt had succeeded in scraping together, were shot on the nearby Waalsdorper dunes the next morning. At about the same time, the 49 inmates of Amersfoort were executed on the firing range just outside the camp. Thus, instead of the 80 prisoners demanded of him, Munt had topped Kolitz's order by seven.

The largest reprisals of all, however, were taken at De Woeste Hoeve itself. From prisons in Apeldoorn, Deventer, Zwolle, Assen and even as far away as Groningen, a total of 117 prisoners were collected. Many were real Resistance workers, but some had been arrested for nothing more serious than a breach of curfew. They were transported to De Woeste Hoeve in three buses and four trucks. Gerbig was in command of the operation.

BEKANNTMACHUNG   BEKENDMAKING

Der Höhere SS- und Polizeiführer Nordwest gibt bekannt:

Wegen eines in der Nacht vom 6. zu 7. März 1945 von einer Terroristengruppe verübten feigen und hinterhältigen Überfalls auf die Insassen eines deutschen Kraftwagens wurden am 8. d. M. mehrere Hundert Terroristen und Saboteure öffentlich standrechtlich erschossen.

De Höhere SS- und Polizeiführer Nordwest maakt bekend:

Tengevolge van een in den nacht van 6 op 7 Maart 1945 door een groep terroristen gepleegden laffen en arglistigen overval op de inzittenden van een Duitsche auto werden op 8 dezer eenige honderden terroristen en saboteurs in het openbaar standrechtelijk doodgeschoten.

ABREISSEN ODER BESCHÄDIGEN DIESES PLAKATES IST STRAFBAR   AFSCHEUREN OF BESCHADIGEN VAN DIT PLAKAAT IS STRAFBAAR

The posters announcing the attack were put up in every municipality although they did not mention Rauter's involvement in the ambush, and its opening sentence implied that he was still in office: 'The Höhere SS- und Polizeiführer Nordwest announces: During the night of March 6/7, 1945 a cowardly terrorist group attacked a German vehicle so on March 8 several hundred terrorists and saboteurs were publicly shot.' In all 263 people were shot at various locations.

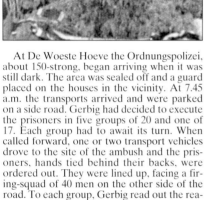

Op 8-3-'45 werden hier 117 Vaderlanders door de Duitsche overweldigers op gruwzame wijze vermoord.

Left: **Immediately after the liberation, a simple memorial was erected at De Woeste Hoevre.** *Right:* **Later the wooden plaque was replaced by a bronze one and bushes and shrubs added.**

At De Woeste Hoeve the Ordnungspolizei, about 150-strong, began arriving when it was still dark. The area was sealed off and a guard placed on the houses in the vicinity. At 7.45 a.m. the transports arrived and were parked on a side road. Gerbig had decided to execute the prisoners in five groups of 20 and one of 17. Each group had to await its turn. When called forward, one or two transport vehicles drove to the site of the ambush and the prisoners, hands tied behind their backs, were ordered out. They were lined up, facing a firing-squad of 40 men on the other side of the road. To each group, Gerbig read out the reason for the execution and a Dutch SD collaborator translated.

Shortly before 8 a.m. the first volley was fired, each group taking about five minutes. Not all the victims died instantly and at least four times SD men went forward and shot men through the head to finish them off.

At 8.15 a.m. it was all over. A long line of men lay massacred by the side of the road. Next to the bodies a notice was set up saying: 'This is what we do with terrorists and saboteurs', and for the next half hour anyone who happened to pass by was forced to get off their bike and read the sign.

When the road was widened and upgraded in the 1970s the memorial was moved further back with a new cross.

In 1992 the whole site was redesigned and a glass panel with the names of all the victims added behind the cross.

During the afternoon, the Germans started cutting the bonds from the corpses. A group of inspectors from the Apeldoorn police then arrived to search the bodies for papers or any means of identification but they had only just started when an order came from the SD at Zwolle that indentification was forbidden. At 3.30 p.m., five lorries pulled up and the bodies were loaded aboard to be taken to Heidehof Cemetery in the village of Ugchelen to be buried in a mass grave.

THE AFTERMATH

A total of 263 people had been shot in reprisal. At first the occupation authorities made no mention at all of Rauter, the note posted on the wall simply informing the Dutch of the execution of 'several hundreds of terrorists and saboteurs' and referring only to 'a cowardly murder assault on the occupants of a German vehicle', without mentioning who the occupants were, or whether they had been killed or not.

Then, probably because the sheer number of people executed indicated that something out of the ordinary had happened, and because rumours of Rauter's shooting could not be stemmed, the Germans decided not to suppress his involvement any longer, and instead present it as if he had died in hospital. This version was widely believed, but not for long. News of Rauter's presence trickled out from the hospital and patriotic policemen passed on the results of the SD investigation to the outside. The Dutch clandestine newspapers were remarkably well-informed: lists of reprisal victims, Rauter's whereabouts, even the fact that his ambushers had been in German uniform and that his driver and orderly had been killed; all this was published in the illegal press within a short time.

The Dutch public was absolutely appalled by the number of deaths. Any joy over the elimination of Rauter was overshadowed by grief and sorrow over the killings.

Yet all this time, even within Resistance circles, it remained a mystery as to exactly who was responsible for the ambush. This lack of information from Resistance sources can be traced back to the high command of the BS. The Dutch Resistance leaders had long since decided that it was no use killing top Nazis, like Rauter or Seyss-Inquart, because they would always be replaced by someone else and murdering them would only cause large-scale reprisals. War criminals were to be brought to trial after the war. Furthermore, when reprisals occurred, the leaders feared the effect these might have on public opinion. People were always quick to call the Resistance 'a bunch of adventurers' who by their 'irresponsible behaviour' endangered the lives of innocent people. It was precisely for this reason that the commander of all the BS forces in occupied territory, Kolonel (Retd.) Henri Koot, had issued an order on February 14 specifically warning against such ill-motivated actions and stipulating that no more be undertaken unless specifically ordered.

Six weeks after the liberation, the bodies were exhumed and Police Inspectors Jan Muda and Sjoerd Adema were given the gruesome task of identifying them from clothing and personal effects. In the end, they were able to positively name all but two.

The families of the dead had the right to bury their loved ones in their local parishes so that today only 16 lie in the National Cemetery of Honour at Loenen, together with one victim *(inset)* who is still unidentified.

Originally there had been two unidentified victims. *Left:* In 2008, after long research by Dutch journalist Richard Schuurman, the one in grave E-1253 was identified as Flying Officer Czeslaw Oberdak, a pilot from No. 306 (Polish) Squadron. His P-51 having force-landed near Ommen in the Netherlands on May 30, 1944, he was picked up by the Dutch resistance and evaded capture until arrested on December 24. Although officially a POW, he was sentenced to death and imprisoned at Doetinchem, and thus came to be included in the Woeste Hoeve reprisals. Identified by DNA, his remains were repatriated to Poland and reburied in Krakow cemetery in December 2009. *Right:* Ten thousand miles away in Australia lies the grave of Geert Gosens, the leader of the ambush. Although it was accepted that the attack on Rauter's car was not deliberately planned, the commander of all the BS forces, Kolonel Henri Koot, was not pleased as he had only just issued an order forbidding such actions which could only result in disproportionate retaliation by the Germans. Much criticised and haunted by the aftermath of his wartime action, Gosens emigrated to Australia where he died in October 1997. He is buried in Bunyip Cemetery, Victoria.

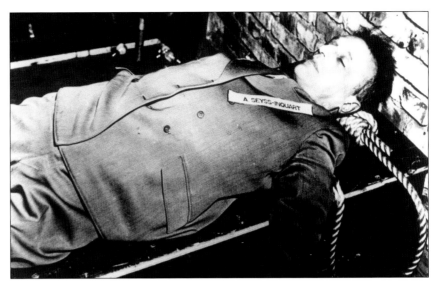

So when the news of the De Woeste Hoeve ambush and reprisals reached BS Headquarters in Amsterdam, Koot and his staff were furious. Like the Germans, they thought that a deliberate attempt had been made to kill Rauter. Enraged, Kolonel Koot immediately sent a special messenger to BS District 6 to ascertain more details.

Geert Gosens, however, had already dutifully reported the exact circumstances of it all to the Geheime Dienst Nederland, one of the largest underground spy and communications networks in the country. But it seems that this initial report never reached Amsterdam.

The second report was made by the District Sabotage Commander, Gijs Numan. It had been one of his subordinates, the Local Sabotage Commander at Apeldoorn, who had given Gosens the fatal order. By now, however, the whole affair was rapidly becoming a controversy, threatening to discredit the Veluwe Resistance. Rather than attempting to explain that it had all been an accident and that nobody could have foreseen the disastrous consequences, the final report simply stated that no blame was attached to the Veluwe BS for what had happened. It failed, however, to make clear whether this applied solely to the reprisals or also to the attack on the car that hap-

Of the German hierarchy in the Netherlands responsible for the deaths, Eberhard Schöngarth was the first to be brought to justice although it was a British Military Court that got to him first. He was accused of murdering a downed Allied pilot on November 21, 1944 and was found guilty on February 11, 1946. The British hangman was brought over to Hameln jail in May 1946 to execute 17 German war criminals, Schöngarth being hung on the 16th together with Erwin Knop. Meanwhile, Seyss-Inquart was facing the International Military Tribunal at Nuremberg as one of the 22 top Nazi criminals. When the verdicts were announced on October 1, 1946, he was found guilty on four counts: waging a war of aggression; violation of the laws of war, and of committing crimes against humanity, persecution and extermination. As Seyss-Inquart had authorised the deaths of between 800 and 1,500 people, including those at the Putten raid (pages 142-143), and the reprisal executions for the attack on Rauter, he was sentenced to death. Upon hearing the sentence, he is reported to have commented: 'Death by hanging, well in view of the whole situation I never expected anything different'. He ascended the gallows in the gymnasium at Nuremberg prison on October 16.

pened to be carrying Rauter, thus it gave a definite impression that the BS was responsible for neither. BS Headquarters in Amsterdam did not ask any further questions and decided to let the matter rest until after the liberation, when the matter was re-examined.

Rauter survived the war. After two lung puncture operations, he was moved to Groningen on April 1 and from there to northern Germany. On May 11, 1945, he was arrested by British Military Police in a hospital at Eutin. During captivity he underwent a bone transplant operation on his jaw. He was still recovering when, on February 6, 1946, he

was turned over to the Dutch authorities to be tried for his four-and-a-half years' reign of terror. He was brought before the Special Court at The Hague on April 1, 1948, and on May 4 he was sentenced to death. He appealed to the Special Court of Cassation which confirmed the sentence and on March 25, 1949, he was executed.

Eberhard Schöngarth, who in the final analysis was responsible for the Rauter reprisals, appeared before a British military court in 1946 on another war crime charge and was hanged.

KAREL MARGRY, 1987

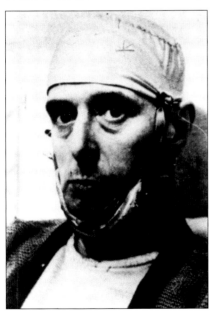

Rauter was still in hospital when he was arrested by British Military Police on May 11, 1945. He was handed over to the Dutch government but his trial dragged on until his death sentence was confirmed on January 12, 1949. After further delays he was executed by firing-squad on March 24 near Scheveningen. The location of his grave remains a state secret.

As we saw on page 126, 'Fall Gelb' included a major attack on Belgium in spite of the fact that King Leopold III had made an open declaration of neutrality in October 1936. Although the Belgians had prepared their own fixed defences, and put great faith in fortresses like Eben Emael, this decision deprived the French and British armies from preparing in advance. Instead they would have to wait until Belgian neutrality had been broken before crossing the Franco-Belgian frontier to a defence line based on the River Dyle. On May 10, what the Belgians refer to as the '18 Days' Campaign', began, heralded by airborne attacks on key targets. Using specialised equipment, Eben Emael fell within 24 hours, opening the eastern door to the country. No sooner had the French entered Belgium than the Germans enacted the second part of their plan: to break through the Ardennes — which had been thought of as unsuitable terrain for a modern army — in a dramatic encircling move across France which had them on the Channel coast within five days. Brussels, the capital of Belgium, fell on May 17 by which time the writing was on the wall. Here, a mixture of transport — two- and four-wheel and horse-drawn — have arrived in Bockstael Square. (Jean Paul Pallud's in-depth account of 'Fall Gelb' is the subject of *Blitzkrieg in the West Then and Now*.)

Belgium

Belgium was invaded by Germany on May 10, 1940. When the King surrendered with his army, his legal status became that of a prisoner of war; thus he could no longer participate in public affairs of the country.

INCORPORATION OF EUPEN, MALMEDY AND MORESNET

Two provinces of Belgium that belonged to Germany before 1918, Eupen and Malmédy, as well as neutral Moresnet, were incorporated into Germany and assigned for purposes of administration to the District of Aachen by a decree of May 18, 1940. Thereafter the institutions of these three districts underwent a regime change of assimilation with German political and cultural institutions. Germans living in these districts were represented in the Reichstag. Inhabitants of 'related blood', i.e. those considered racially akin to Germans, were granted nationality of the inferior type (Staatsangehörige), while German inhabitants were granted nationality of the superior type (Bürger). Gradually the whole body of German and Prussian law was introduced into these districts.

The official language was made German and names were changed to a German form.

King Leopold's residence at the Royal Palace lies barely a kilometre to the north although now he was at his headquarters near Antwerp.

Much controversy surrounds the role of King Leopold *(left)*. On May 24 he assumed command of the Belgium Army, meeting with the ministers of his government for the final time when he was urged to leave the country with the government (as Queen Wilhelmina of the Netherlands had done) but he refused. The King felt that if he were to leave the country he could be seen as a deserter. 'Whatever happens', Leopold said, 'I have to share the same fate as my troops'. However, his decision was misconstrued in that it was perceived that he wanted to stay to form a new government under the Nazis. On May 25 he notified King George VI that his forces were being crushed and a day later, without seeking the advice of his government, Leopold surrendered. With this, the Belgian government left for France before moving to London; meanwhile the Germans banished the King to the palace at Laken *(right)*. In 1944 Himmler ordered Leopold to be sent to Germany. He was freed by American forces in May 1945 only to spend the next few years in exile in Switzerland.

ADMINISTRATION

The remainder of Belgium was put under the administration of a sole military commander for the German armed forces in Belgium and Northern France, including Pas-de-Calais. Because of the strategic importance of the area, the administration was entrusted to the military commander instead of a civilian Reich Commissioner.

The general staff of the Military Commander was divided into two separate staffs: the military staff (Militär- or Kommandostab), and the staff for military administration (Militärverwaltungsstab). The military staff, headed by the Chief-of-Staff, was in charge of purely military matters, while the staff for military administration, headed by a Chief of Military Administration, handled the economic and cultural matters of the occupied areas. This staff was sub-divided into three divisions: (1) Division of the Chief (Präsidialabteilung), (2) Administrative Division (Verwaltungsabteilung), and (3) Division for Economics (Wirtschaftsabteilung).

The Division of the Chief handled general and political matters. The

Left: The Electrobel Building on the Place du Trône was requisitioned by the Germans in June 1940 for the Brussels headquarters for the Oberfeldkommandantur. General Alexander von Falkenhausen was appointed as head of the German military government for Belgium, an interesting choice as his uncle Ludwig had been the Governor-General of the country in 1917-18.

By 1944 von Falkenhausen had come to detest the Nazi regime and, although he played no active part, he was supportive of the conspiritors in the July 20 plot to kill Hitler. He was arrested and spent the rest of the war in various concentration camps. He was replaced by General Martin Grase who lasted for two months until Belgium was liberated.

As with all the occupied countries, the senior Nazi (HSSPF) in charge of the SS, Gestapo and Ordnungspolizei was to be feared more than the military commander, and SS-Gruppenführer Richard Jungclaus *(left)* was no exception. However, the man who has claim to fame in Belgium was not a German but a Belgian aviator in the RAF, Captain Jean de Selys Longchamps *(right)*. He had escaped to Britain and was enrolled in No. 609 Squadron. On January 20, 1943, when based at Manston in Kent, he and a fellow pilot were detailed to attack rail traffic in Belgium, but he left his colleague to carry out a morale-boosting attack of his own on the Gestapo HQ at No. 453 Avenue Louise in Brussels. Flying at low level in his Typhoon, he raked the tall building with cannon fire, reportedly killing a number of Germans. However, on his return he was reprimanded for acting without orders and demoted to Pilot Officer but, at the same time, was awarded the Distinguished Service Order for his exploit. (Artist's impression by Patrick Sadler.)

Administrative Division was divided into sections for political administration, communal administration, social welfare, police, communications, press and radio, finance, justice, schools, culture, health, building of roads, and the administration of waterways. The Division for Economics dealt with all matters pertaining to the economic life of the country.

In the cities of Brussels, Ghent, Liège, and Charleroi chief field commands (Oberfeldkommandanturen) were created for the administration of the respective cities and adjacent provinces. The chief field commanders acted through subordinate field commands (Feldkommandanturen), usually three in number, and the latter in turn also had an average of three local commands (Orts-

kommandanturen) under them. Special city commissioners were appointed for the administration of Brussels, Antwerp, Ghent, Ostend and Liège.

Apart from the German administrative agencies, the Belgian administration was in the hands of the Secretaries-General of the former Belgian ministries, namely those of the Ministry of Justice, the Ministry of Finance, the

Six months later he was killed in a crash-landing at Manston. Meanwhile, in Brussels, the Gestapo quickly moved to a less-prominent building further down Avenue Louise at No. 347. Baron de Selys Longchamps was a native of Brussels and a monument to his memory now stands outside the building he attacked.

Ministry of Labour and Social Welfare, the Ministry of Agriculture and Food, the Ministry of Communications, and the Ministry of Economic Affairs. The local authorities still performed their functions mainly in accordance with the pre-war Belgian pattern. However, the elective element in government was curtailed. A shake-up among officials was undertaken at the beginning by introducing an order that persons over 60 years of age could not hold office. In this order of March 7, 1941, the German military command referred especially to the opening of public offices to demobilised Belgian soldiers who wanted to 'serve their country with energy and in

In Belgium, with the divisive nature of both language and politics, collaboration with the Nazi regime had many different adherents each with their own brand of traitorship, but probably top of the list was a former Walloon politician, Léon Degrelle. He was a member of the Rex group within the Catholic Party and had met with Hitler and Mussolini before the war. Both had supplied funds to Rexism and ideological support as the party embraced Nazi-inspired anti-Semitism. With the surrender, the Rexist Party split over resistance or collaboration, Degrelle being arrested and deported to France but being released when the occupation began. Returning to Belgium he reconstructed Rexism to be in close union with Nazism. When Degrelle left to join the Wehrmacht in July 1941, Victor Matthys was appointed party leader in his place. Here Degrelle and Fernand Rouleau leave the Palais des Arts in Brussels followed by Matthys.

full realisation of their responsibility'. In taking care of the demobilised soldiers of a defeated army, the Germans had two purposes in mind: first to gain popularity, and secondly it gave them

the opportunity to scrutinise politically every candidate for a public office, even though the actual appointments were made through the channels of the Secretaries-General.

In August the Germans formed the Walloon Legion as part of the Wehrmacht to join the battle on the Eastern Front against the Soviet Union. Although Degrelle had to join as a private, he soon rose through the ranks and by June 1943, when the legion was transferred to the SS (becoming the 5. SS-Freiwilligen-Sturmbrigade 'Wallonien'), Degrelle was an SS-Obersturmführer. He was wounded the same year. By April 1945 he had reached SS-Standartenführer and on May 2 Himmler promoted him to SS-Brigadeführer although that rank was

probably not official as four days previously Hitler had stripped the Reichsführer-SS of his authority. Highly decorated, Degrelle fled to Denmark, then to Norway where he commandeered a Heinkel He 111 to fly to Spain. General Franco refused permission to extradite him to the Allies and he was given a name change and Spanish citizenship in 1954. Before his death in 1994 he became a prolific author, and when asked if he had any regrets about the war, his answer was 'only that we lost!'

Probably the most notorious of the Belgian pro-Nazi collaborators was Jef van de Wiele, a Flemish politician who had a staunch admiration of Hitler. In 1936 he had formed the Duitsch-Vlaamsche Arbeidsgemeenschap (German-Flemish Labour Community) known popularly as Devlag. He campaigned for the incorporation of Flanders into the Third Reich, using the Nazi eagle and swastika combined with the black lion of Flanders as its symbol. It is said that de Wiele had been promised the position of Gauleiter by Hitler should Flanders become joined with Germany but that never happened. Due to the complicated nature of the political scene in Belgium, de Wiele clashed with the rival organisations, the Vlaams Nationaal Verbond (VNV) led by Staf de Clercq and Degrelle's Rexist Party, although he got on well with Degrelle with whom he toured Wallonia in 1943. After the liberation, he went to Germany where he gathered Flemish refugees into a cohesive Nazi organisation, the Flemish Liberation Committee. He evaded capture until 1946 when he was recognised dressed in a German uniform. A court-martial in Antwerp sentenced him to death but this was commuted to life imprisonment.

Van de Wiele served 17 years and on his release settled in West Germany. He later returned to Belgium where he died in 1979.

ECONOMY AND FINANCE

The Germans immediately organised a special system for taking over the economic resources of the country. Economic officers (Wirtschaftsoffiziere) followed the troops in order to take possession of the raw materials and factories. Sequestration was ordered of foodstuffs, raw materials, semi-fabricated products, as well as some finished products such as woolen clothing, jute bags, tires, industrial oils, and so on. For purposes of industrial production, commodity control agencies (Warenstellen) were set up with wide powers to issue regulations concerning acquisition, distribution, storing, serving and consumption, and to require the submission of reports. These commodity control agencies provided the factories with materials necessary for the manufacture of their products if and when they were working for the German war economy. The factories also found themselves under the management of factory trustees appointed by the military commander. It was the duty of the factory trustees to see to the maintenance of industrial production and to execute orders of the occupying authorities as well as to undertake all measures for the purpose of increasing output. Moreover, every enterprise in Belgium was made subject to audit by special orders of the Chief of Military Administration in order to keep the production of the enterprises under constant control.

A special device was used in order to provide the Germans with non-ferrous metals. On October 20, 1941, a decree was published to the effect that persons delivering non-ferrous metals were entitled to certain tax exemptions. Thus the Belgian Treasury was compelled to collaborate with the Germans in obtaining non-ferrous metals and yet it was the Belgian Treasury that paid for the scrap.

A number of financial decrees gave the Germans a privileged position in the field of finance. The proclamation of May 10, 1940, established an especially favourable exchange rate of one belga (gold currency worth five Belgian francs) to one-half Reichsmark. The mark was fixed at ten francs at the time of the invasion, after which it was raised to 12½ francs. Occupation currency (Reichskreditkassenscheine) was put into circulation, and later on the Belgian Bank of Issue was compelled to exchange this occupation currency into new Belgian francs.

All Belgian banks were put under the control of a banking supervisory board. This office controlled the business of the banks, especially credit operations. In particular, the banking supervisory office saw to it that credit was given to enterprises working for Germany. A clearing office was established in Brussels in order to carry on trade with Germany and, through German intermediaries, with other countries. The clearing arrangements between Germany and Belgium, and between Belgium and other countries, had to be carried out through Berlin channels arranged by orders of the German military commander. Thus, German authorities decided which commodities Belgium could export and import; what the prices should be, and what exchange rate should apply in every case. Clearing arrangements were established between Belgium and the following countries: the Netherlands, Italy, the Protectorate of Bohemia and Moravia, Switzerland, Sweden, Yugoslavia, Bulgaria, Norway, Hungary, Denmark, the Government General of Poland, France, Romania, Finland and the Union of Soviet Socialist Republics until interrupted by the attack on the USSR.

For the regular functioning of clearing, it was necessary that exports should be equal to imports on both sides, but Germany imported more from Belgium than it exported there. Hence, in order to create a balance, a credit item was entered in the central Clearing Institute (Verrechnungskasse) in Berlin in favour of the clearing office of Belgium. Germany thus became the clearing debtor of Belgium. The trade between Belgium and other countries was likewise carried out through the Clearing Institute in Berlin. However, this central clearing arrangement did not contribute to the unfreezing of Belgian credits, by transferring to Belgium actual payments made to the Berlin Clearing Institute by the countries importing Belgian goods, because Germany was also importing from those countries more goods than she was exporting to them.

These measures were facilitated by the complete control of the entire economic life of Belgium, which was put into effect by the order promulgated by the Secretaries-General on February 10, 1941. This order created the framework for economic totalitarianism in Belgium and furnished a basis for integrating the Belgian economy into the Germany economy. It envisaged the creation of economic associations organised according to trades and regions. These associations were designated as sole official representatives of the trade or region concerned. For example, all mining enterprises in Belgium were organised by one central mining association with headquarters in Brussels. Moreover, all enterprises engaged in any economic activity in a particular area, for example at Charleroi, such as mining, retail and wholesale trade enterprises, handicraft associations, and banks, were all organised through the Economic Chamber of Charleroi. Thus the economic life of Belgium was seized and controlled in a two-fold manner: first, by specific economic control which directly affected the capital structure and, secondly, on a geographical basis.

The Belgian Resistance was equally fragmented between a large number of organisations, separated like the collaborators by political divisions, although its experience of being occupied for four years during the First World War had laid the groundwork for effective resistance. Regional issues also came into play as the underground included men and women from both the Flemish (western) and Walloon (eastern) parts of the country. Among the first members were former soldiers who wished to carry on the fight against the Germans. It is estimated that around five per cent of the population were involved in some form of resistance, be it civil resistance or strikes; aiding shotdown Allied pilots to escape; producing the plethora of underground newspapers; assassination of those believed to be traitors (the brother of Degrelle was killed in July 1944); gathering intelligence and sabotage of military installations, and of the 100,000 persons involved, around a quarter lost their lives in the cause. Today the exploits of the Belgian Resistance are remembered through plaques, road names and memorials scattered right across the country. The Comet Line escape route was set up by a young Belgian woman Andrée de Jongh *(left)* who suddenly appeared in the British Consulate in Bilbao in August 1941 with two Belgian helpers having escorted a British soldier across France and the Pyrenees to Spain. Thereafter, working with British military intelligence, her Comet Line helped 400 Allied soldiers to escape from Belgium, Andrée personally bringing 118 over the Pyrenees herself. She was arrested in January 1943 but survived being held in various concentration camps, and was awarded the George Medal in 1944.

REPARATIONS

During the occupation of 1914-18, Germany tried to disintegrate Belgium by creating and exaggerating differences between the Belgians and the Flemings, and the latter, collaborating with Germany, were given special privileges. When the Germans left the country in 1918, the Belgian Government passed legislation inflicting penalties upon persons who had collaborated with the Germans. During the occupation in the Second World War, the Germans published two orders for the 'restitution of the rights of persons persecuted in Belgium because of their collaboration with the German Army of Occupation during the war of 1914-18'.

To understand this, it is necessary to recall that according to Section 5 of the Belgian Penal Code, a person sentenced to death or to forced labour was deprived forever of 'honour rights', which meant the right of employment in public office, right to be elected, right to decorations and title of nobility, right to be a member of a jury, a court witness, a member of family council, a guardian, a member of the judiciary council, and an administrator of estates, as well as the right to bear arms, to be a member of the civil guard, or to serve in the army.

The German order of September 6, 1940 restored these rights. Moreover, those affected could receive special damages for personal sufferings, for loss of freedom, for expropriations, etc. A special board, as an independent Belgian governmental institution, was created for allotting damages and reinstating such persons their rights. The members of the board were chosen with the consent of the German military commander, and the costs of the reparations, as well as the expenses of the board, were to be borne by the Belgian State. The Belgian Secretary of the Treasury was obliged to hold the amounts currently required for these purposes at the disposal of the board. Thus the Belgian Treasury was compelled to pay compensation for penalties inflicted upon those who had been traitors to the Belgian nation in 1914-18.

RAPHAEL LEMKIN, 1944

Memorial and graves to resistance fighters in the Belgian War Cemetery in Limburg.

CAFE DE LA POSTE

ENTRANCE to BLDG WHERE VICTIMS were MURDERED

Sicherheitsdienst Slaughter at Bande

In September 1944, the Allied armies were sweeping north-eastwards across France and Belgium encountering only light resistance. The Ardennes lay in the path of the US V Corps advancing through southern Belgium and Luxembourg in a dozen or more parallel columns spread over an 80-kilometre front. The main Brussels-Luxembourg highway ran across this line of advance passing through Namur, Bastogne and Arlon. Beside the main road, just south-east of Marche, lies the little village of Bande. In 1944 houses lined both sides of La Grande Route although the main part of the village itself lay on the hillside a few hundred metres to the north.

On September 5, as American forces were approaching the district, a unit of the Maquis camped in the woods nearby attacked a German unit killing three soldiers. At the same time, inhabitants of the village courageously put out their Belgian flags in anticipation of their liberation. As a reprisal for these acts, the following day the Germans set fire to the houses bordering the main road. Two days later the Americans arrived, the Germans retreating eastwards towards the prepared positions of the Siegfried Line.

Just over three months later, Bande lay in the centre of the German Ardennes Offensive launched at daybreak on December 16. A column of German tanks, driving north-westward along the snow-covered road to the River Meuse, arrived at Bande at about 2 p.m. on December 22. The Germans took over the village and it was significant that some of the troops were the same ones that had been there in September. The Mayor, M. Armand Pierre, recognised several soldiers three of whom were officers' orderlies who lodged in the same house they had used three months previously.

Two days later, on the morning of December 24, another group of about 25 men wearing brown and green camouflage suits arrived at the burned-out houses along the main road. They all wore caps with the death's

head emblem and were identified as members of the Sicherheitsdienst by the white letters 'SD' on badges on the left sleeves of their

uniforms. The SD unit immediately set about the systematic arrest of all the men in the village between the age of 17 and 32. That year

Top: **Scene of crime photograph from the report produced by the Belgian War Crimes Commission in February 1945. The original Café de la Poste, burned down by the Germans on September 6, 1944 as a reprisal for killings by the Maquis, lies in the centre of the block.** *Above:* **Now renamed the Café du Monument, its façade has been modernised with only the doorway of the Bertrand house being retained. The new N4 Brussels to Luxembourg highway lies out of the photograph to the left — the old 'Grande Route' in its original width now serving as a convenient parking layby.**

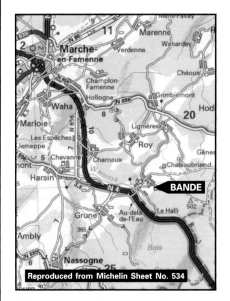

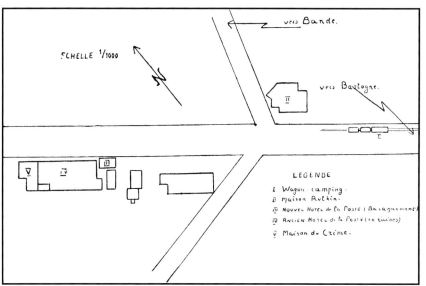

This plan from the Commission's report identifies the relevant buildings but due to the post-war widening of the N4, unfortunately all the buildings on the northern side of the road, including the sawmill, have been demolished. [I] 'Wagon camping' refers to the quarters of the SS-Standgericht. [II] The Maison Rulkin is the sawmill. [III] Nouvel Hotel de la Poste (a wooden building) is where the victims were later laid out for identification. [IV] The burned-out Café de la Poste belonging to M. Marechal. [V] Maison du Crime is the Bertrand house.

Christmas Eve fell on a Sunday and some men were taken from the church during the celebration of High Mass. When questioned as to the reason for the arrests, the villagers were told they were to go to a control post to verify their identity cards. Womenfolk were told that their men would be back for Christmas dinner but were surprised to hear the Germans speaking very correct French; some having a working-class Parisian accent, others using French slang. Walloon and Liège dialects were also detected.

Having assembled a group of some 70 men (including a few outside the age group), they were marched down the hill to 'Control' which had been set up in the remains of the Rulkin sawmill beside the main road. (The mill belonged to M. Rulkin-Tasiaux and had been set on fire in September.) Here they were joined by other Belgians from Grune, a little hamlet lying just to the south of the main road.

At 1 p.m. the SD men began interrogating the prisoners as to the events that had taken place in September. While this was going on, the Mayor of Bande was ordered to collect all the Belgian flags in the village which were subsequently burned in an oven at the sawmill.

During these interrogations, which lasted until 5 p.m., requests were made by the Germans for cognac and wine. Albert Schmitz was 'persuaded' to supply 200 bottles of lemonade in return for his freedom and the Germans offered to free a local farmer, Armand Toussaint, and his son on delivery of 20 bottles of wine and three bottles of cognac. When he returned to the village to get what had been requested, M. Toussaint asked the Wehrmacht officer billeted in his farmhouse to intercede on behalf of the prisoners. This the German officer agreed to do but soon returned saying, 'I cannot do anything for you. Those men are strangers. They must have something to drink for Christmas. Go and bring them what they want, there is nothing else to do.'

Towards evening, the younger men were segregated and led out of the sawmill to be lined up in three rows in the snow. They were relieved of all their possessions. From there, with hands on their heads, the prisoners were marched along La Grande Route to the burned-out Café de la Poste belonging to a M. Marechal. After being called to a halt, the men were ordered to turn to face across the road. There were 33 prisoners, guarded

by seven or eight soldiers armed with rifles or sub-machine guns and commanded by three officers. After a short discussion, two of the officers left to return to the sawmill leaving in charge the one who had led the interrogations and who spoke French with a Parisian accent. He went into the house next door to the cafe — that of M. Bertrand.

A Feldwebel of small stature, aged about 40, then approached the man in the rear rank and laid a hand on his shoulder. At this stage none of the prisoners had any idea of what was planned. They watched the Feldwebel take his man to the door of the Bertrand house. As he entered and disappeared from their view, a shot rang out.

The German returned and placed his hand on the end man in the second row and led him away in the same manner. Another shot followed. By now the remaining 31 men must have realised what was in store for them. As each prisoner entered the door, an SD man, standing inside the entrance so that he could not be seen from outside, fired point-blank into his victim's neck and, with a jerk of his knee, sent the body hurtling into the open cellar. If the prisoner still screamed, a second shot followed instantly.

'La porte de la mort' — the door of the Bertrand house through which the prisoners were escorted to their deaths.

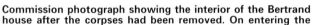

Commission photograph showing the interior of the Bertrand house after the corpses had been removed. On entering the doorway, the victims were each shot in the nape of the neck and then pushed into the cellar in the left foreground.

After 20 men had been executed it was the turn of 21-year-old Léon Praille. He had understood from the very first shot what was to be their fate. He saw what would happen if they all stood meekly awaiting their turn and he tried to incite the others to make a break and attack the guards. He implored them saying that they had nothing to lose but the others were too terrified and in no state to react.

However, Léon was determined not to go like a lamb to the slaughter. When his turn came, he noticed that the Feldwebel was crying. When they were both about two metres from the entrance, Léon gathered all his strength and smashed the German in the face with his right fist. Running for 50 metres, he crossed the main road and scrambled across the River Wamme and into the fields on the other side. The guards were firing at him all the time but failed to score a hit. Although he then tried to escape to the American lines there were too many German patrols so he returned to take refuge in his uncle's barn.

Meanwhile the Christmas Eve massacre continued. When all 32 men had been killed, the Germans covered the bodies with three layers of planks of wood. The cellar was open to the sky and, as night fell, snow soon covered all traces of the dreadful act.

In the late afternoon, the Mayor of Grune and a local language professor, M. Chardonne, had gone to Bande to try to secure the release of the prisoners. When they arrived at the sawmill it was about 6 p.m. and they found only the older prisoners there. Being told to leave, they inadvertently moved off up the road in the direction of the Bertrand house. They heard gunshots coming from somewhere nearby but a German soldier intercepted them and roughly ordered them to go away. This they did but not before they had seen two rows of men standing in front of the Café de la Poste. Leaving La Grande

Route to pass along a small path a hundred metres behind the house, they heard more shots and machine-gun fire.

On the Monday — Christmas Day — another 33 Belgians were rounded up in the village of Roy, two kilometres north of Bande. In the afternoon they were marched to the Rulkin sawmill and interrogated in the same manner as the men from Grune and Bande. About 9 p.m. two men, Georges and Raymond Malempré, were singled out. While the others were set free, the two brothers were taken to the Bertrand house where they were shot and thrown into the cellar.

The following day saw the relief of Bastogne 25 kilometres further down the road towards Luxembourg and the tide of battle turned against the Germans. On January 10 the Germans evacuated Bande which was liberated by British troops the following day. On the arrival of the Allied forces, the mayor reported the massacre to the senior British officer and asked him to accompany him and the sole survivor to the death house. Photographers, Sergeants Bert Hardy, Frank Covey and Bill Lawrie from the Army Film and Photographic Unit, were detailed to record the visit in all its gruesome detail.

Today, the doorway provides a reference point to the same spot which has been transformed into a memorial garden. The cellar has been roofed over (with access down a flight of steps behind the wooden balustrade) and is now a tiny chapel of rememberance.

Twenty-one year-old Léon Praille had tried to persuade the prisoners to revolt and when his turn came, he punched his escort, Ernst Haldimann, in the face and managed to get away in the resulting confusion. The day after his escape from death, he discreetly told his uncle, the Burgomaster of Bande, what had taken place on Christmas Eve, and when the men of the 9th Battalion, The Parachute Regiment, of the 6th Airborne Division arrived on January 11, he informed the commanding officer of the massacre. Together with Léon Praille, the Army photographers visited the scene of the tragedy. These pictures were taken by Sergeant Frank Covey on January 16, 1945.

The snow was several centimetres thick and, having shovelled it aside and removed the boards, the shocking scene of horror was laid bare. The bodies, stiff and frozen, were lifted out and laid in the Café de la Poste for identification. Every victim showed a bullet wound in the nape of the neck, the bullet having travelled in an upward direction as far as the forehead or face

Left: Sergeant Covey also photographed Sergeant Bill Lawrie, his cameraman colleague, as he crouched to inspect the cellar.

Right: Later Sergeant Lawrie interviewed M. Constant Volvert whose 17-year-old son Albert was one of those killed.

After the frozen bodies had been removed, they were taken to the wooden building which replaced the burned-down cafe. There they were laid out for identification by the local priest Jean-Baptiste Musty and Léon Praille.

After the harrowing job of identifying the dead had been completed, the bodies were lined up outside where 34 coffins had been prepared.

It was not easy to identify the bodies which were covered in blood with their hands clenched and it must have been a heart-rending task for their grief-stricken families before the bodies were taken outside to be placed in their coffins.

The final death toll was established as follows:

1. MULLER, Clément Joseph Léon, born in Marcour, age 25.
2. TOURNAY, Xavier Joseph Henri, born in Bande, age 19.
3. MAITREJEAN, Edmond Joseph Gilles, born in Bande, age 18.
4. GOUVERNEUR, André Léopold Léon Ghislain. born in Bande, age 17.
5. MICHEL, Armand Joseph Lambert, age 21.
6. MARÉE, Richard Hubert Georges, born in Bande, age 23.
7. LAMBERT, Gaston Emile Constant, born in Hotton, age 31.
8. MAGONETTE, Fernand Emile Constant, born in Erneuville, age 21.
9. MARCHAL, Albert Fernand Maurice Ghislain, born in Bande, age 28.
10. MATAGNE, René Victor Joseph, born in Bande, age 28.
11. HARDY, Roger Albert Joseph, born in Tenneville, age 20.
12. PONCIN, Joseph Ghislain Arthur, born in Tenneville, age 18.
13. VOLVERT, Albert Maurice Ghislain Joseph, born in Ramont-Tenneville, age 17.
14. DUCHÈNE, Octave Edmond Joseph, born in Berhain (Flamierge), age 18.
15. DUCHÈNE, Joseph Marie Florent, born in Berhain, age 23.
16. GUISSART, Victor Charles Joseph, born in Flamierge, age 20
17. SMITZ, Paul Émile Hubert, born in Grune, age 17.
18. GUISSART, Florent Charles Joseph, born in Flamierge, age 21.
19. LEROY, Alphonse Léon Joseph Gilles, born in Grune, age 18.
20. PETRON, Louis Désiré Joseph, born in Hodister, age 26.
21. GIRS, Fernand Auguste Jean Félicien, born in Vaux (Noville), age 21.
22. GIRS, Georges Albert Joseph, born in Vaux (Noville), age 20.
23. DE GARDE, Jean Henri, born in Liège, age 24.
24. DACO, Donia Armand Joseph, born in Hompré, age 24.
25. PARMENTIER, Joseph, born in Rencheux (Vielsalm), age 19.
26. LAMBERT, Herman, born in Hotton, age 22.
27. LASSANCE, André Pierre Ghislain, born in Amberloup, age 22.
28. LASSANCE, Fernand Elie Ghislain, born in Amberloup, age 18.
29. LAMBERT, Lucien, born in Hotton, age 22.
30. MALEMPRÉ, Georges Jacques Pierre, born in Flémalle-Haute, age 27.
31. MALEMPRÉ, Raymond Victor Joseph Pierre, born in Flémalle-Haute, age 23.
32. HENKINET, Joseph, age 27.
33. NOËL, Jules, age 20.
34. BOURGEOIS, André, age 20.

Only eight were natives of Bande, the others, except for the Malempré brothers from Roy, and Paul Smitz, Alphonse Leroy and Louis Petron from Grune, being refugees from neighbouring villages.

With the men of the 9th Parachute Battalion acting as pall-bearers, the coffins were loaded aboard transport for the short journey to Bande village. There the cortege halted for the next of kin to attend the funeral service.

Although some mordernisation has taken place in Bande, its character still remains as it was on that sad day in January 1945.

The procession then continued up the main street to the cemetery which lies at the western extremity of the village. There graves had been prepared in the frozen ground.

A Commission des Crimes de Guerre had already been set up by Belgian Royal Decree on December 13, 1944 with the task of investigating war crimes committed on Belgian soil and to prepare separate files on each case to help bring the perpetrators to justice. The members of the Commission assigned to the Bande massacre arrived at the village to conduct their investigation on February 9, 1945. Naturally Léon Praille, a bank clerk in Marche, was the most important witness. They were also provided with the report from Lieutenant Valcke, liaison officer from the 51st (Highland) Division, dated December 18, 1944; medical reports from the doctors who had examined the bodies; the report from the ballistics experts; reports of an investigation by the military auditors at Namur and Arlon and the judicial files of the American Army compiled by Captain Victor Darling of the XII Corps.

Although the regular German Army unit in Bande village contained men who had been there three months prior to the massacre, having considered all the evidence, the Commission were firmly of the belief that they were not responsible. Several of the Wehrmacht soldiers billeted in the village had expressed their sorrow over what had taken place and they had explained to the villagers that the unit was unknown to them. When these regular soldiers asked the men on the main road to which unit they belonged they received the answer: 'Special Himmler troops' and 'we don't belong to any unit, we are a Standgericht' (a difficult word to translate having no precise equivalent in English, basically a Security Police squad with the power to arrest and execute on the spot).

When *After the Battle* first researched this story in 1980, the houses opposite the church still stood unchanged, but since then they have been replaced by a whole new development.

January 17: Sergeant Covey records the scene at the cemetery, this shot being taken just inside the entrance.

It was established that the majority of men from the special unit had lived in a railway wagon standing on the line which ran along the edge of the northern side of the main road just beyond the sawmill. The unit was identified as being from the SD (Gestapo). One German officer, a Lieutenant Spaan billeted in Bande, confided to one villager that orders had come directly from Himmler to have 30 men executed to avenge the three Germans killed in September by the underground. Two more were to be shot for the murder of a Belgian collaborator in June 1944.

The preponderance of French accents and dialects in the group linked the unit to similar crimes at Givry and Noville and the Commission was able to establish the identity of at least one man, a German-speaking Swiss born in Pfeffingen.

The mourners were overcome with grief as their loved ones were placed in the ground. The victims were first buried in temporary graves in the central area until relatives could arrange for permanent interment in their individual family graves.

Above: The official ballistics examination of the fired cartridge cases indicated that at least two different weapons had been used, the firing pin being off centre on the primer cap on the left. Note that both rounds are captured ammunition, possibly from the Maquis: US-made by Winchester Repeating Arms *(left)* and *(centre)* from Defence Industries of Canada. *Right:* This photo of Ernst Haldimann, the only perpetrator brought to justice — in his case by a Swiss court — was published in *Le Soir* in April 1948 when he was sentenced to imprisonment for 20 years. He was released in 1960.

Drs. Max Lahaut and Marcel Férir examined all the bodies and established that the victims had also been shot at while lying in the cellar as many had bullet wounds in other parts of their bodies. Cartridge cases, and bullets removed from the corpses, were examined by Captain Commandant Baeten and Major General Mage who established that at least two kinds of 9mm weapons had been used for the killings. Seventeen cartridge cases bore the imprint of one weapon, probably a Schmeisser sub-machine gun, and three had come from another similar weapon. It was not believed that a pistol could have been used and the official report of the ballistics experts stated: 'Although it seems that only one person fired at least on the first prisoners, it is not possible to establish whether a second one fired or whether the isolated shots and the rounds of firing have been fired by one and the same man.'

Ernst Haldimann grew up in Switzerland and undertook an industrial/commercial apprenticeship. After an 18-month prison sentence for theft, he went to work in France in 1938. From June 1942 he worked on the German Army training establishment at Le Valdahon but was jailed again for theft the following year.

On leaving prison, Haldimann joined the SS at Dijon on November 15, 1943 becoming an Unterscharführer in December. He served in various locations in France, mostly in Alsace-Lorraine, and suffered minor wounds during an air attack on Freiburg-im-Bresgau. In December 1944, his unit was integrated with other SD units into 'SS-Kommando zu besonderer Verwendung 8' (No. 8 SS-Commando for Special Duties) numbering some 200 men.

According to Haldimann's indictment, the unit was assigned to the 8. SS-Panzer-Division for the Ardennes offensive but this would seem to be an error and should read 2. SS-Panzer-Division. The detachment sent to Bande was commanded by SS-Untersturmführer Krueger.

When the war was over, Haldimann entered Switzerland illegally on February 3, 1946 and was picked up by the police and jailed. On January 28, 1948, he was charged by a Swiss Army Court with entering a foreign armed service, murder on several counts, assistance with attempted murder and multiple murder.

Haldimann confessed that he had been a member of the SD unit in Bande on December 24, 1944 but that all he had done was to escort each victim, one by one, to the house to be shot. He claimed that two French members of the SS-Kommando actually did the shooting, one holding the prisoner while the other shot him with a machine pistol. He said that the two executioners changed places during the massacre and that other members of the group joined in killing the last few Belgians. Like many others charged with war crimes, Haldimann claimed in his defence that he was only carrying out his orders.

On April 28, 1948 the Swiss Court gave its judgement and found Haldimann guilty on all counts. The court accepted as a mitigating circumstance the fact the accused had not instigated the massacre and had acted under orders. Therefore the court stated it would not pronounce a life sentence but the maximum sentence according to the law:

1) Twenty years imprisonment less 396 days spent in custody before the trial.

2) Exclusion from the Armed Forces for life.
3) No public office to be held for ten years.
4) Payment of costs of 1933.95 Swiss Francs.

Haldimann had already been sentenced to death in absentia on August 21, 1945 by the French Court of Justice at Besançon for espionage and denunciation of French resistance members to the Germans. He served his Swiss sentence in a Liestal Zuchthaus, a severe form of prison. He was released on a four-year parole on June 27, 1960.

According to the Auditorat General of the Military Court in Brussels, Ernst Haldimann is the only member of SS-Kommando 8 that has been brought to trial and convicted for the massacre at Bande.

Personnel of NATO's Allied Rapid Reaction Corps visited the village of Bande in September 2014. They were accompanied by Tom Hughes (right) who was one of the soldiers of the 9th Parachute Battalion at Bande in December 1944. In the dimly-lit cellar where the bodies were found, Tom describes how men of his unit helped the villagers remove them and later acted as pallbearers at the funeral.

Left: The Forêt de Compiègne, November 11, 1918, as the French signatories descend from the Compagnie des Wagons-Lits coach having signed the armistice with Germany ending the First World War. *Right:* Twenty-two years, later a veteran who has lost an arm and a leg has to witness the humiliating sight of a German mounted column passing the Town Hall in Paris. Although the final battles in the defeat of France still had a week to run, on June 14 German troops of the 9. Infanterie-Division entered the capital as the previous day it had been declared an 'open city'.

France

After France signed the armistice agreement with Germany and Italy in June 1940, the following administrative arrangements were set up. Northern France and Pas-de-Calais were placed under the administration of the same German military commander as Belgium. For Alsace and Lorraine, special civil administrations (Zivilverwaltungen) were established within the framework of the neighbouring German Reich districts (Reichsgaue) into which they were incorporated. Thus, Lorraine was incorporated into Westmark and Alsace into Moselland. The district of Menton was occupied by Italian forces. In November 1942, Italian occupation was extended to the Alpes-Maritimes, Haute-Savoie, and the Rhône valley.

Apart from Alsace-Lorraine, the areas included under the armistice agreement in the territory known as Occupied France were administered by a German military commander in Paris. The rest of France (known as Unoccupied France) was administered from Vichy. When German troops occupied all of France in November 1942, the Vichy regime was not displaced, the German authorities exercising only supervision and Gestapo activities.

On the grounds of military security, a special regime was established along the coastline to which outsiders were not permitted access (Prohibited Zone), as well as in the cities of Marseille and Toulon.

In the early morning of June 17 the French made an overture through Spanish channels asking for the terms for an armistice. Hitler was currently touring First World War battlefields in Belgium and Northern France from his field headquarters 'Wolfs-schlucht' (Wolf's Lair) at Brûly-de-Pesche, so the Foreign Office in Berlin immediately relayed the request to him. He had already decided that he was going to turn the tables on the French by arranging that negotiations would take place in the same railway carriage, on the very same spot at Rethondes near Compiègne, where Germany had been forced to capitulate in November 1918. But first he had to consult with Mussolini so a meeting was arranged for the two to meet in Munich, while German engineers began preparing the surrender site, demolishing the end wall of the museum building to drag the coach to the correct spot.

The Alsace-Lorraine Memorial (left) depicting the German eagle being stabbed with the Allied golden sword was covered with the Third Reich flag (right) until it could be dismantled.

L-R: Rudolf Hess, Joachim von Ribbentrop, Admiral Erich Raeder (shaking hands with Hitler), Generalfeldmarschall Hermann Göring and Generaloberst Walther von Brauchitsch.

ALSACE-LORRAINE

The regime in Alsace-Lorraine was directed toward the complete assimilation of the political, cultural and social institutions, as well as the economy of the two provinces, with those of the Greater German Reich. These tasks were in the hands of specially appointed Chiefs of Civil Administration, one for Lorraine and another for Alsace, having the title of Gauleiter. Thus Alsace and Lorraine represented special administrative units incorporated into the normal German administrative districts (Gaue). Alsace was thus incorporated into the District of Moselland and Lorraine into the District of Westmark. Alsace and Lorraine were barred from communication with the rest of France by a customs frontier. Communications between Alsatians and Lorrainers on one side and Frenchmen on the other side of the customs frontier were allowed only within the limits of the so-called small frontier traffic, involving persons living in the immediate neighbourhood of the frontier.

The policies of the Chief of the Civil Administration were designed to promote the complete assimilation of Alsace and Lorraine with the other parts of the German districts, so that a special administration for Alsace and Lorraine was not necessary. However, no express provision of law as to the annexation of Alsace-Lorraine by Germany ever took place, the Germans refraining from any such provision but the treatment of these territories indicated a de facto annexation by Germany. One of the Free French leaders, Général Henri Giraud, stated in his address of March 14, 1943: 'Alsace and Lorraine have been de facto incorporated into Germany. No voice of protest has been heard in France. Here, we protest. All the world must know that France does not accept this annexation. Alsace and Lorraine will again become French in a completely liberated France.'

In carrying out the policies of assimilation, as of January 1, 1941, the Germans introduced into Lorraine the German Municipal Code of January 30, 1935. French citizens of German origin were granted German citizenship. The official language in administration, as well as in courts and business, was declared to be German. A decree was issued requiring that the names of persons be written with the German spelling. German equivalents had to be used for French given names and, where no such equivalent existed, a German given name was to be adopted. Towns were also given equivalent German names.

With the exception of business firms, associations and organisations of all kinds were dissolved in order that reorganisation on National Socialist principles could take place.

The education of the youth was put under Nazi control. In the order of December 6, 1940, the Chief of the Civil Administration in Lorraine stated: 'In order to assure the uniform institution of National Socialist schooling for youth, as well as adaptation to the school system of the Reich, all private schools and school camps shall be closed.' Grammar schools were made public and German, and only persons of German or related blood could be teachers in public elementary schools. Schools also had to be actuated by the spirit of National Socialism in all their work.

Permission had to be obtained to give religious instruction, and such permission would be withheld if the instructor, clergyman or his wife was not of German or related blood. The Reformed

Elsass-Lothringen had been created by the German Empire in 1871 following its victory in the Franco-Prussian War, when it annexed most of Alsace, lying west of the Rhine, and the Moselle department of Lorraine. The German military wanted to shift the border westward for strategic reasons although at the same time the French had a long-standing desire to establish their entire eastern frontier on the Rhine. Many residents who considered themselves French subsequently emigrated westwards, adding to the anti-German feeling in France before the First World War. Victory over Germany in 1918 led to the territory being ceded to France in 1919, a move that caused the German inhabitants to press for home rule and fuelled increasing resentment against what was seen as the punitive penalty clauses of the Treaty of Versailles. However, the French government immediately started the forced deportation of all Germans who, since 1870, had been encouraged by Germany to settle in the area, and by 1921, over 110,000 Germans had been expelled. In 1940 Hitler wanted to reverse the situation and although he drafted an annexation law, it was never put into effect, yet Berlin still took full control, incorporating the area into the German Reich. Beginning in 1942, volunteers were invited to join the German armed forces, while others were impressed, and ultimately well over 100,000 were enrolled, fighting on both the Eastern and Western Fronts.

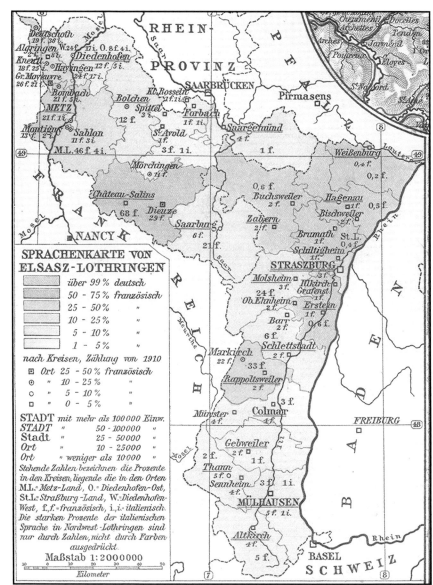

and Lutheran churches were combined with the Pfälzische Landeskirche (United Protestant Evangelical Christian Church of the Palatinate), so that the powers of the Reformed Synod in Alsace-Lorraine, and of the Directorium of the Church of the Augsburg Confession in Alsace-Lorraine, passed to the Protestant Provincial Church Council of the Palatinate.

Victory parade in the Place de la Réunion in Mulhouse, June 19, 1940. Against the backdrop of St Étienne Church, Generalmajor Ferdinand Neuling, the commander of the 239. Infanterie-Division and his staff, together with citizens of the long-disputed territory, await the men of Höheres Kommando z.b.V XXXIII which recaptured the city for Germany.

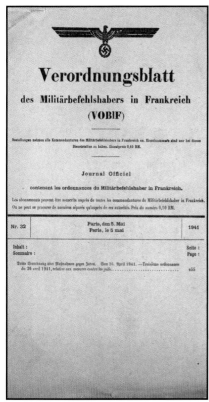

France was no different from the other countries occupied by Germany in that the promulgation of orders and laws were published in the official *Verordnungsblatt*. One of the earliest — No. 3 of June 21, 1940 — read as follows: 'Attention is called to the fact that, for the duration of the occupation, the Military Commanders may issue rules and general orders for their respective command areas which shall have the force of laws. Full familiarity with these rules and orders is therefore of the utmost importance for any resident of the country. They are issued in the *Verordnungsblatt für das besetzte Gebiet der französischen Departements Seine, Seine-et-Oise und Seine-et-Marne*, published by the Military Commander of Paris, and in part they are likewise issued in the form of posters. The rules and orders will also be discussed in the radio and press. The general orders and regulations issued by the German Military Commanders take precedence over the law of the land. Local law not in conflict with these orders and regulations remains in force unless incompatible with the purposes of the occupation. Failure to comply with the orders and regulations issued by the German Military Commanders cannot be justified by ignorance or conflicting local statutes.'

The courts were Germanised, and the requirement laid down that sentences be pronounced 'in the name of the German people'. German criminal law was introduced, and published materials relating to judicial matters appeared only in the *Verordnungsblatt* (Official Gazette of the Chief of Civil Administration).

In order that Germans alone were able to acquire property, a decree was passed on October 10, 1940 to the effect that permission was necessary to acquire a farm, forest or business property, and for buying, renting, starting, building or enlarging enterprises. Moreover, the same decree authorised German authorities to close enterprises without allowing claims for indemnity.

The economy of Alsace and Lorraine was organised according to the totalitarian pattern. Essential goods, foods and products were requisitioned by decree of June 23, 1940, and were administered under German control. Control of prices and wages was introduced by the decree of August 9, 1940.

According to the German genocide philosophy, the imposition of the German cultural and political pattern upon Frenchmen was not sufficient. The Frenchmen themselves were to be removed and replaced by Germans in order to make Alsace-Lorraine German 'forever'. The Germans therefore resorted to mass transfers of the French population. According to an elaborate plan of replacing French population by a German imported population, about 270,000 persons (including 22,000 Jews) were removed from Alsace-Lorraine to unoccupied France, and 200,000 to the Reich.

In 1945, when Alsace-Lorraine reverted to France, the process was reversed once again with another period of 'Francification' to try to eliminate the German influence. There was much controversy over the languages spoken. From 1945 to 1975, in the period known in France as the Trente Glorieuses, the area experienced 30 years of population growth and economic prosperity.

Left: One of the VIP visitors that June was none other than Hitler himself, guided on a three-hour whistle-stop tour by his architect adviser Albert Speer (left) and sculptor friend Arno Breker (right). He was very familiar with the architectural history of Paris and a route had been prepared to take in all the important buildings with Hitler's personal photographer and a military cameraman on board to record the tour which ended, coincidentally, in front of the Sacré Coeur *(right).*

At 5.30 a.m. on June 23, the party arrived at Le Bourget airfield where a convoy of open-top cars was waiting.

Below: This is the only group shot, taken on the Trocadero overlooking the symbolic Eiffel Tower. L-R: General Karl-Heinrich Bodenschatz, C-in-C Luftwaffe; SS-Gruppenführer Karl Wolff, Chief of Personal Staff of Himmler and SS liaison officer; SS-Obersturmführer Max Wünsche, Orderly Officer of the Führerbegleitkommando; Hermann Geisler, Hitler's main architect for the reshaping of Munich and Speer's main rival as most-favoured architect; Generaloberst Wilhelm Keitel, Chief of Oberkommando der Wehrmacht; SS-Obergruppenführer Wilhelm Brückner, adjutant; Albert Speer, Professor Karl Brandt, Hitler's official escort doctor and later co-head of the Nazi euthanasia programme; Hitler, Reichsleiter Martin Bormann, Chief-of-Staff to the Deputy Führer Rudolf Hess; Arno Breker and Dr Otto Dietrich, the Nazi Press Chief.

By 8.15 a.m. the visit was over, Hitler asking his pilot to circle several times over Paris before they departed.

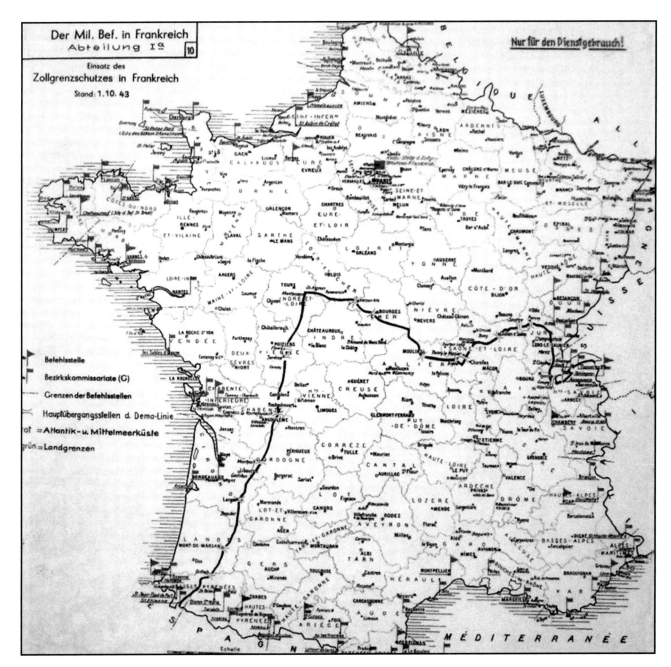

Article II of the Armistice of June 22, 1940: 'To safeguard the interests of the German Reich, French State territory north and west of the line drawn on the attached map will be occupied by German troops'.

THE OCCUPIED ZONE

The Armistice Agreement of June 22, 1940, established the limit of the so-called Occupied Zone as distinguished from the Non-Occupied Zone administered by Vichy. The line mentioned in Article II of the Armistice agreement began in the east on the French-Swiss border at Geneva and ran thence nearly over the villages of Dole, Paray-le-Monial and Bourges to approximately 20 kilometres east of Tours. From there it went a distance of 20 kilometres east of the Tours-Angoulême-Libourne railway line and extended through Mont-de-Marsan and Orthez to the Spanish border. A decree of April 28, 1941, provided penalties of imprisonment or fine for persons who without permission crossed the Demarcation Line between the Occupied Zone and unoccupied France, or carried goods from one zone to another.

On the occupation of all of France by Germany on November 11, 1942, the Demarcation Line was retained, but more facilities for traffic between the two zones were introduced. The Vichy zone remained under the administration of Vichy, but the Germans took over the administration of strategic points and acting in other places mainly through the Gestapo.

According to Article III of the Armistice Agreement, 'in the occupied parts of France the German Reich exercises all rights of an occupying power. The French Government obligates itself to support with every means the regulations resulting from the exercise of these rights and to carry them out with the aid of French administration.' This zone had two types of administration. The German administration was in the hands of a German military commander, and for purposes of military administration, the

Occupied Zone was divided into five chief military field commands (Oberfeldkommandanturen). Each of these chief military field commands was divided into field commands (Feldkommandanturen) and every field command was divided into local commands (Ortskommandanturen). Officers of civil sections of the military commands supervised the French authorities.

The German Ambassador to Paris (whose office was continued) co-ordinated the activities of the central German authorities with those of the local German authorities, as well as with those of the central French authorities. The main body of French authorities was retained, these being supervised by the German military authorities, but they also received instructions from beyond the Demarcation Line. Moreover, the legislative power of the Vichy government extended over the Occupied Zone.

The Armistice with Germany was signed on June 22 (a separate agreement was reached with Italy) and all hostilities ceased three days later. The Armistice divided France into two parts: an Occupied Zone which comprised northern France and the length of the Atlantic coast to Spain, while the remaining two-fifths of the country, south of a 'Demarcation Line', would be under the French government with Maréchal Philippe Pétain — the 'Victor of Verdun' of First World War fame — as Head of State. The French government had been evacuated to Bordeaux but as this city now fell within the Occupied Zone, another move was made to Clermont-Ferrand but that town proved to have poor communications and lacked housing and

office space. The cities of Lyon, Toulouse and Marseille were all considered as alternatives but each was rejected, either for political reasons or because of the fear of unrest. The name of Vichy was then proposed. Situated within the Free Zone, but just four hours by train from Paris, it was an ideal location. It was a popular resort with 300 hotels that could be requisitioned, and officials began to congregate there from June 30. The Vichy regime was officially established on July 11 (see *After the Battle* No. 170). Right from the beginning, the Germans occupied the vulnerable Atlantic coast, all the way down to the frontier with Spain. This is the border post at Hendaye where a bridge crossed the Bidassoa river.

Angoulême was one of the towns specifically mentioned in the appendix to the Armistice through which the Demarcation Line ran. This band is marching along what is today Rue René Goscinny having just passed Rue Raymond Poincaré.

Covering 1,200 kilometres, from the Spanish border the Demarcation Line passed through Saint-Jean-Pied-de-Port, Mont-de-Marsan, Langon, Angoulême, Vierzon, Moulins, Paray-le-

Monial, Digoin, Chalon-sur-Saône and Dole before reaching the Swiss frontier. *Left and right:* This border post was located in La Cure, a little village 30 kilometres north of Geneva.

The Germans decreed that the Demarcation Line could only be crossed at a small number of official checkpoints, and only by those who could present the correct Ausweis which would only be issued after many formalities had been approved. This is the checkpoint set up at the bridge over the Valserine river at Bellegarde, near the Swiss border.

PUNITIVE FUNCTIONS OF MILITARY COMMANDERS

Because the German military commanders played such an important role in controlling the country, they were vested with extensive powers, among them judicial powers that in some respects supplemented the functions of the courts. Not only the commanders of the chief field commands but also the heads of the ordinary field commands could issue orders regarding summary punishment against persons not subject to the Military Penal Code, and they were able to impose penalties up to 30,000 Reichsmarks or, in lieu thereof, imprisonment for a term not exceeding

The Germans also pressured the Vichy government by thwarting the return of refugees — the tens of thousands who had fled the invading German armies in May and June 1940 — back to the occupied northern zone. Each person had to obtain a repatriation certificate from the French admini- stration, with access from 1941 onwards being limited to just four crossing points: Langon, Vierzon, Moulins and Chalon-sur-Saône. *Right:* The checkpoint at the latter town was at the eastern end of the Pont des Chavannes, the bridge over a branch of the Saône river.

SERVICES AND LABOUR

Among the other powers vested in military commanders was that of requiring members of the local population to serve as military guards, failure to fulfill such duties being punishable by death. This was a violation of Article 52 of the Hague Regulations (see page 261) that prohibits the requisitioning of services of inhabitants of an occupied country in activities involving military operations.

The personal responsibility of the inhabitants to the occupying power was extended further by the decree of January 31, 1942, under which the failure to perform personal services, or comply with requisitions ordered by the authorities for the German Army, was made punishable by a fine, imprisonment, hard labour or 'in grave cases' even by the death penalty.

Because all economic and industrial enterprises were put into the service of the German war economy, any interference with employment in such enterprises was also made punishable. Thus, for interruption of work or any aggressive actions by workers against employers, penalties of imprisonment, fine,

The first summer months of 1940 saw an influx of troops on sightseeing visits throughout the French capital. It was the Germans' intention to keep Paris alive to entertain soldiers on leave as the reputation of the city and its famed night-life was world renowned. One of the most popular venues was the Basilica of the Sacré Coeur, built between 1876-1919, on the summit of the 135-metre-high Montmartre hill. This transport is parked in Rue Lepic, just short of the church, but one wonders how many of the visitors realised that it had been built by public subscription in memory of the suffering endured by the city during the Franco-Prussian War of 1871.

six weeks. Moreover, the same offence, if it was sufficiently serious, could be tried later by a court. The primary purpose of the order was to give increased authority to the military commanders to enable them to act as the first and main protectors of the established German order.

The view across Paris is timeless having been enjoyed both in peace and war.

The first military commander of France (Militärbefehlshaber Frankreich) was General Otto von Stülpnagel *(left)* appointed in October 1940. His method of dealing between both parts of France was one of rewarding co-operation which initially played a major role in achieving good Franco-German relations. He still discouraged any activities that did not advance the German war effort, complaining specifically to Hitler about the looting of Jewish-owned art. On October 20, 1942, the French Resistance shot Oberst Karl Friedrich Hotz, the commandant of Nantes, and the following day assassinated Dr Hans-Gottfried Reimers, a German military lawyer in Bordeaux. Hitler ordered the execution of 100-150 hostages for each attack but Stülpnagel condemned large-scale reprisals and instead only had 98 shot. When taken to task over this by General Wilhelm Keitel, the head of the Oberkommando der Wehrmacht, Stülpnagel replied by submitting a letter of resignation. He was replaced in February 1942 by his cousin Carl-Heinrich von Stülpnagel *(centre)* who as early as 1938 had been part of the military opposition trying to remove Hitler from power. He was still in touch with the members of the conspiracy when he became commander in France, and on July 20, 1944 he put his part of the plot into operation by arresting all the SS and Gestapo officers in Paris. When the bomb failed to kill Hitler, Stülpnagel was recalled to Germany, a botched attempt to commit suicide en route only succeeding in blinding himself. On August 30 he was found guilty of high treason in the Volksgerichtshof (People's Court) and hanged the same day in Plötzensee prison, Berlin. *Right:* On July 23 Hitler recalled General Karl Kitzinger from the Eastern Front, where he was Wehrmachtbefehlshaber in the Ukraine, and sent him to France where he fulfilled the role of military commander until October 4. Thereafter command in France was transferred to Ob. West.

While the Hotel Majestic on Avenue Kléber was taken over by the Germans to serve as the headquarters for the high command in France, the Hotel Crillon *(above)* on the Place de la Concorde, was used for the office of the Military Governor of Paris

The historic hotel, once frequented by Queen Marie-Antoinette, underwent a four-year renovation and re-opened in the summer of 2017.

In January 1942 Reinhard Heydrich chaired the Wannsee Conference in Berlin to discuss a 'final solution' to the 'Jewish Problem'. To carry this out in occupied France, in March Reichsführer-SS Heinrich Himmler appointed SS-Brigadeführer Karl Oberg as Höhere SS- und Polizeiführer. As head of all the German police forces, including the SD and Gestapo, he was the supreme authority for managing the anti-Jewish policy in the country. Here he is pictured with Pierre Laval, the Vice-Prime Minister under Maréchal Philippe Pétain. The Vichy government had already instituted its own regime of discrimination against Jewish residents in the 'Zone Libre'.

hard labour or even death could be imposed. Even before labour conscription was introduced, the Germans tried to induce French workers to accept work in Germany, and a decree of June 22, 1942, introduced special privileges for persons accepting work there. The courts were required to adjourn cases concerning such persons if the military commander so requested. Moreover, no execution of contracts of rent and no notice thereof could be effected during the absence of workers in Germany. Later on, a labour conscription law was published by Vichy in order to provide Germany with workers.

ECONOMY AND FINANCE

As already mentioned, the whole economic life of France was controlled and channelled into the German war economy. If an enterprise was not important enough for the German war economy, it could be closed down by the military commander, the reason given that it was because of the requirements of 'economic conditions' and 'particularly the supply of raw materials and equipment'.

That local economic life was subordinated to the interests of the Germans can be seen from the decree promulgated on May 22, 1942, which stated that all construction projects exceeding 100,000 francs required the permission of the German military commander. Applications for such permission were to be filed with the French authorities which, in turn, would submit them to the German commander.

In the field of finance, the same instruments were applied as in Belgium, i.e. Reich Credit Institute notes were issued, and clearing agreements with Germany and other countries were arranged through the German clearing office (Verrechnungskasse) in Berlin. Exchange control was introduced, prohibiting the transfer of currency out of the Occupied Zone, and forbidding transactions of an international character. Also foreign exchange and gold had to be surrendered. The exchange control was carried out by a special institute called Devisenschutzkommando Frankreich (Commando France for the Protection of Holdings of Foreign Exchange).

A special Banking Supervisory Board controled French banks, especially the Banque de France, which was compelled to meet the requirements of the Germans.

BOOKS AND ART

Not only was the press regimented and subjected to censorship but also textbooks of history published before the war were suppressed if they contained 'unjustifiable attacks on the German people and its armed forces'.

Works of art, which in France represented a considerable part of the national wealth, immediately attracted the attention of the Germans. On July 15, 1940, an order was issued by the Supreme Commander of the Army freezing such works of art and stating that movable works of art must not be removed from their present location or changed in any manner without the written authorisation of the military commander. Legal transactions involving the transfer or sale of movable works of art were also made invalid without the consent of the military commander. Owners or possessors of such objects of art that were worth more than 100,000 francs were required to

In May, Heydrich came to the Majestic Hotel to confer with Oberg and discuss the anti-Jewish policy. In June the Germans directed that it was now mandatory for Jews in the Occupied Zone to wear the yellow star although Vichy refused to do likewise. A massive round-up of foreign and stateless Jews commenced in Paris the following month and by the end of the year over 40,000 had been deported.

register them with the field commander's office. The purpose of these provisions was to prevent owners in financial difficulty selling works of art to private persons at their real value. Instead, they were compelled to sell at much lower prices to Germans who were able to obtain the required permission.

This decree concerning works of art was in violation of Article 46 of the Hague Regulations (see page 261), which specified that private property had to be respected. Respect for private property implies not only freedom from confiscation but also non-interference with the enjoyment of the full rights of property, including the right to dispose of it.

The occupation brought forth a host of orders and decrees for governing the country — here are just two from 1940.

Meanwhile it was honour for the fallen. The French Unknown Soldier was interred beneath the Arc de Triomphe in January 1921.

Left: **German security agencies occupied 12 buildings in Avenue Foch which became known to Parisians as Avenue Boche. No. 84 was taken over for the Paris headquarters of the Sicherheitsdienst (SD), the counter-intelligence branch. Excruciating methods of torture were inflicted here on captured resistants and SOE agents,** **and in March 1944 Pierre Brossolette, who had already suffered for over two days at the hands of the torturers, threw himself out of a sixth-floor window rather than risk being made to divulge information about his colleagues in the Resistance.** *Right:* **The headquarters for the Gestapo were located at No. 11 Rue des Saussais.**

RESISTANCE

The Germans did not enjoy a feeling of security in the occupied area despite the policy of 'forced collaboration' imposed upon the French population. One example of the Germans' reticence in trusting the French can be seen in a decree of February 5, 1942. This forbade medical personnel, such as doctors, dentists and nurses who were not serving in the German Army, to treat members of the German armed forces or civilians of German nationality in the service of such forces. French medical personnel were allowed to take care of Germans only in emergency.

The security of the occupying force was gravely challenged not only by the well-organised French underground but also by a special type of guerrilla fighter which was prevalent in the south-eastern part of France, especially in Haute-Savoie. Young Frenchmen who had escaped deportation to labour camps in Germany crossed the Demarcation

These inscriptions are preserved on the walls of the cellars of the Gestapo HQ.

Line to hide in the mountains, and German troops attempting to capture them often met with strong resistance. The French population organised a service of clandestine help for these people who were known as the maquis.

It was only when Paris was liberated in August 1944 that other horrors came to light. This is the Balard shooting range situated on the French Air Ministry training area at Issy-les-Moulineaux. On the orders of Karl Oberg, it was used by the Geheime Feldpolizei to torture and then execute prisoners.

Here it is being inspected by members of the French Forces of the Interior (FFI). The range has since been demolished with the construction of the Boulevard Périphérique de Paris. A plaque listing the names of the 143 people who lost their lives here was unveiled in 1961 on the wall of the Air Ministry.

An innocent-looking street in the 16th arrondissement was synonymous with the worst form of French collaboration with the Nazis. No. 93 Rue Lauriston was the base for a group of around 20 French auxiliaries of the Gestapo — most of them convicted criminals — who between 1941 and 1944 tortured and killed dozens of Resistance personnel there. Its leaders were a disgraced policeman, Pierre Bonny, and a gangster, Henri Lafont. Both men were tried after the liberation and sentenced to death. In March 2009 the owner called for the address to be changed. The local mayor appeared willing to renumber it as 91 bis 'in order not to weigh down the current and future occupants with this monstrous past'. This announcement was received with huge opposition by veterans of the Resistance, Maurice Rafsjus, a historian who specialises in the Vichy regime, saying that 'it's an idea that I find unbearable as a historian. It proves that France is still not at peace with its Vichyist past.' The idea was finally dropped and a plaque on the building now pays homage to the victims of the gang.

Another collaborationist organisation, whose headquarters building also had an address change, was the paramilitary Milice created by Vichy in January 1943. Led by Joseph Darnand who was granted the rank of SS-Obersturmführer by the Germans, its purpose was to fight the Resistance and round up Jews for deportation. *Left:* In January 1944 it took over the former Paris HQ of the French Communist Party (PCF) at No. 44 Rue Le Peletier and at the end of the war the PCF reclaimed the building. It was badly damaged in June 1946 when a march celebrating the appeal that Général de Gaulle made from London to loyal Frenchmen in 1940 degenerated into an attack on anyone considered to be 'anti-French'. Another riot causing more damage occurred during the Hungarian uprising in 1956. The following year the address was changed to No. 13 Place Kossuth in honour of a 19th-century Hungarian hero Lajos Kossuth, a symbol of Magyar nationalism. *Right:* With the Communists having moved out in the 1970s, today the occupier is the Turkish Isbank.

On November 1, 1944, Général de Gaulle paid tribute to members of the Resistance who had lost their lives and visited a clearing at Mont-Valérien, on the outskirts of Paris, where many of the victims had been shot. In 1945, now the French President, he ordered that a fitting monument should be built at the site as a tribute to honour those who had refused to yield. It was specifically meant to present the Resistance as part of the armed services and not as revolutionaries from fragmented groupings. On November 11, 1945 the bodies of 15 fighters were interred in a temporary crypt, until the main memorial, comprising a 150-metre-long wall and 12-metre-high Cross of Lorraine, was dedicated by de Gaulle in June 1960.

On June 10, 1940, Italy declared war on Britain and France — an act that President Roosevelt described as a stab in the back. Ten days later the Italian army invaded France, and a brief campaign followed, fought by mainly Alpine troops on both sides in harsh conditions of icy winds, thick fog and falling snow. Two days after the Armistice had been signed between France and Germany, the Franco-Italian Armistice was signed by Général Charles Huntziger at the Villa Incisa all'Olgiata *(left)* on the Via Cassia in Rome. *Right:* Marshal Badoglio reads the Armistice conditions; one of the more outrageous suggestions (not included) was the return of the Leonardo's *Mona Lisa* to Italy!

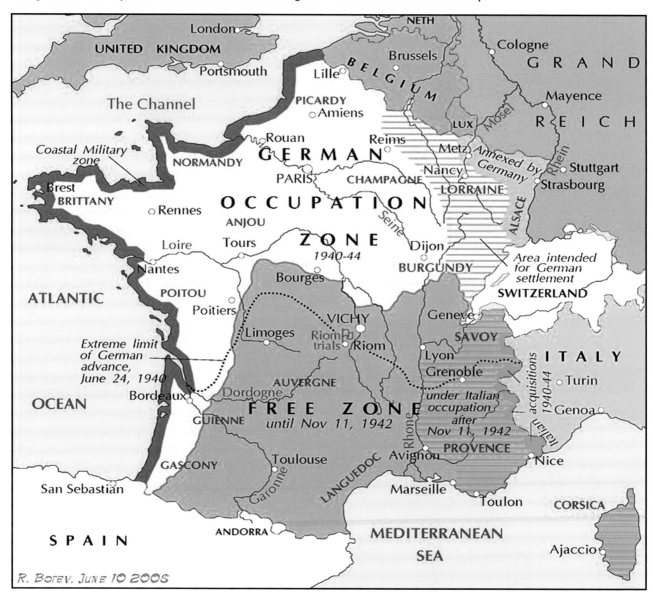

The Armistice specified an Italian Zone of Occupation in southern France although it was to cover no more than what had been captured already. The main town was the city of Menton and its 20,000-odd inhabitants. A demilitarised zone was also specified 50 kilometres deep on the French side of the border. Italy retained the right to French territory as far as the Rhône valley although it did not occupy this area until after the Allied invasion of French North Africa in November 1942. No precise maps appear to have been made, and the actual area of south-eastern France then occupied by the Italians has been disputed. It appears that Italy occupied the eastern part up to a line joining Toulon, Gap, Grenoble, Chambéry, Annecy and Geneva. This map was produced by R. Borev in 2005.

The Italian occupation was very much like that of the Germans in Alsace-Lorraine. Almost immediately the authorities set to work Italianising their zone and removing all traces of the French state. The playing of the *Marseillaise*, listening to French radio, French newspapers were all forbidden. Road signs, shop fronts and even town halls were renamed in Italian. *Left:* These soldiers are lined up outside the Rives d'Azur hotel in Menton. *Right:* Long gone, the site is now occupied by an apartment block.

ITALIAN ZONE

Following the Armistice Agreement, Italy assumed the rights of an occupying power over several localities on the French side of the frontier. In these localities Italian civil commissioners were established for purposes of administration. However, the main institutions of French administration remained. This was also true of the local courts, except that under the law of December 5, 1940, trials for serious offences committed by the inhabitants of the occupied territories could be referred to the Court of Assizes in Turin. The same law provided for appeals from civil or criminal sentences pronounced by French courts to be referred to the Court of Appeals in Turin or to the Supreme Court of the Italian Kingdom. The Italian rules for judicial proceedings were also to be observed in regard to the form of processes before the courts of the Italian Kingdom. The reasons for this provision were due to the comparatively insignificant number of localities occupied by Italy, and the absence of higher judicial French authorities in the occupied area.

The law of December 5, 1940, also empowered the military occupation authorities to extend Italian regulations concerning customs to the occupied territory in order to make them applicable to the passage of goods across the new border.

In the occupied zone, the Italian lira was made legal tender in addition to the French franc by a proclamation of June 21, 1941, the rate of exchange being set at 100 francs to 38 lire.

Because the areas occupied by Italy were cut off from the more important French administrative centres, difficulties arose in dealing with certain activities normally administered under the direction of higher French authorities whose offices were located outside the zone of occupation.

When the Italians moved in in strength in November 1942, their Army of Occupation in southern France comprised four infantry divisions with 136,000 soldiers and 6,000 officers. These two were pictured in Rue Carnot in Annecy.

In late October 1940, Hitler made a personal visit to meet Generalissimo Francisco Franco, the dictator of Spain; Maréchal Philippe Pétain, head of Vichy France, and Benito Mussolini in Italy. The purpose was to decide in which direction the future war in the West should take, and especially to try get active support from Franco whose victory in the civil war had only been achieved with Germany's help. Franco had since declared his country neutral, but it would be a huge bonus if he could capture Gibraltar to seal off the Mediterranean from the Royal Navy. The three-day tour of over 4,000 kilometres was undertaken in the Führer's official train that doubled as a conference room while the train lay stationary in the railway stations. The meeting with Franco took place in Hendaye station on the Franco-Spanish border, although the discussions achieved nothing of value.

VICHY FRANCE

After the collapse of France, the political leaders who supported Marshal Philippe Pétain believed that they could restore the self-confidence of the French people by proclaiming a 'national revolution' in political, social, economic and even private life. The programme of this 'revolution' consisted mainly of such slogans as the strengthening of the executive power; the increase of production through proclaimed solidarity of the classes; a return to the land which amounted to stressing the social importance of agriculture; the strengthening of the family unit; education of the youth in the national spirit, and racialism which resulted in the promulgation of anti-Jewish laws.

DELEGATION OF POWERS TO PÉTAIN

On July 10, 1940, Albert Lebrun, President of the French Republic, promulgated a constitutional law adopted by the National Assembly, to the effect that the National Assembly had vested in Marshal Pétain all authority in the Government of the Republic and empowered him, as President of the Council of Ministers, to promulgate a new constitution. It was stressed that this future constitution should guarantee the rights of labour, of the family, and of the fatherland. It further stressed that the new constitution must be ratified by the nation and applied by the 'assemblies which it shall create', i.e., by a new parliament.

CONSTITUTIONAL ACTS

The Constitutional Law of July 10, 1940, provided for the creation of a new constitution by 'one or several acts'. Pétain chose to promulgate several constitutional acts, directed mainly to the strengthening of the authority of the Head of State and to the abolition of the representative element in government.

By Constitutional Act No. 1, Pétain declared that he assumed 'the functions of Chief of the French State'. In the same act he abrogated Article 2 of the Constitutional Law of February 25, 1875, which provided that the President of the Republic should be chosen by a National Assembly composed of the Senate and Chamber of Deputies.

Little has changed, the same platform was photographed by Jean Paul Pallud for his article on Hitler's diplomatic tour in *After the Battle* No. 178. The next venue was at the French station at Montoire-sur-le-Loir to where Maréchal Pétain had been driven to meet with Hitler.

Although again little was achieved in the discussions with Pétain, it still gave German propaganda an opportunity to take images symbolising French collaboration with Nazi Germany, sealed with the obligatory handshake for the cameras.

By Constitutional Act No. 2 of July 11, 1940, Pétain assumed sweeping powers, not only in the executive branch of the government, but also in the legislative branch. The provisions of the French law of 1875 that 'ministers shall be collectively responsible to the chambers for the general policy of the government, and individually for their personal acts' were made void by the provision that ministers and state secretaries shall be responsible only to the Chief of the French State. Moreover, by the above-mentioned law, the Chief of State assumed legislative power that he exercised only in co-operation with the Council of Ministers. He also promulgated the laws and was able to negotiate and ratify treaties. He could not, however, declare war without the previous consent of the legislative assemblies.

FÜHRER PRINCIPLE
To a certain extent, an imitation of the Führer principle was introduced by Constitutional Act No. 7. Pétain introduced the element of personal leadership, not only in relation to the state but also for officials, especially those of higher rank. Under the above-mentioned act, these officials had to swear allegiance to the Chief of State, and they were made personally responsible to him. This responsibility which, in the language of the act, 'shall apply to their person and their property', was implemented by Pétain himself, and enabled him to institute enquiries concerning any breach of faith on the part of such officials 'by means of a procedure upon which he shall decide'. He could require them to make reparations and could also impose such penalties as 'loss of political rights; surveillance of residence in France or in the Colonies; administrative internment, or detention in a fortress'.

The elements of the personal leadership and authoritarian doctrine were emphasised by the fact that the provision as to the imposition of penalties by the Chief of State for breach of faith in personal allegiance to him was superimposed upon the normal machinery of prosecution and punishment, for the same act provided that persons upon whom such penalties had been imposed might also be punished 'under normal judicial procedure' for crimes or offences which might have been committed by them.

PARLIAMENTARY ISSUES
As mentioned above, the Constitutional Law of July 10, 1940, mentioned the Assemblies which the proposed new constitutional document was to create, and Constitutional Act No. 3 of July 11, 1940, stated that the present Senate and Chamber of Deputies 'shall continue to exist until the Assemblies anticipated by the Constitutional Law of July 10, 1940, have been formed'.

On January 22, 1941, Pétain promulgated a law creating a National Council. Under this law, the Council was to be composed of members appointed by the Chief of State from among representatives of the different legislative assemblies of the departments, municipalities and professions, and from among 'other competent persons or persons who have rendered special services to the state'. However, the sessions of this Council were non-public and were called only for the purpose of expressing opinions on matters submitted to the Council by the Chief of State, so the National Council, as conceived by the law of January 22, 1941, could not be considered as a parliamentary institution representing the French nation.

On August 25, 1942, Pétain promulgated another law by which the bureaux of the Chamber of Deputies and of the Senate were abolished as of August 31, 1942. Thus, the Parliament of France — an institution in which throughout French history the people had taken great pride — was formally eliminated from the public life of France.

TRIAL OF POLITICAL OPPONENTS
From the beginning the new regime fixed its attention on the problem of dealing with political opponents. Since those persons who had left France without permission after the collapse were treated as adversaries of Pétain, a decree was signed on July 23, 1940, to the effect that the property of Frenchmen who, without authority, had fled the country between May 10 and June 30 could be confiscated and their citizenship withdrawn. In addition, Pétain instituted criminal proceedings against members of former governments, the purpose being to not only destroy political opponents, but also to create the impression that the disaster which befell France was due only to the machinations and mistakes of its political leaders. Germany, too, was interested in the removal of French statesmen who were opposed to Hitler.

Today the little station is no longer in use, the building now having been converted into a museum concerning the historic meeting. The brick shelter, seen behind German Foreign Minister von Ribbentrop in the top picture, no longer exists.

For a moment we are back in London from where de Gaulle broadcast on June 18: 'Is the last word uttered? Is the defeat final? No!' Resistance was the refusal to accept the finality of defeat, a refusal to accept that Vichy was the voice of France, and a refusal to accept the Vichy policy of collaboration. The Resistance in France began with the signing of both Armistice documents in June 1940 and only ended in late August 1944 when most of France was freed from the German yoke. 'Resisters' were those men and women who decided to keep on fighting, and an uncompromising hostility towards Germany. An unshakeable faith in the greatness of France was soon to make Général de Gaulle the focal point around which the Resistance movement organised itself. It went into action all over France but one particular operation put it in a special category of its own in the league table of French resistance. The battle that took place in March 1944 at Glières in the Haute-Savoie — a department where the mountainous terrain favoured ambush operations by the maquis — occurred when over 500 resisters came out in open defiance against the occupation forces.

LABOUR

Labour was to become one of the main concerns of the Vichy regime for two reasons. First it was believed that increased production, especially in agriculture, might help to solve the economic crisis and, secondly, the Germans made constant demands for French labour for work in Germany.

Meanwhile the Germans were drawing up their own plans to deal with the situation, bringing in three battle groups of the 157. Reserve-Division. On March 26, with the plateau encircled by the German troops and the French Milice, Capitaine Maurice Anjot, the commander of the largely outnumbered resistance force of 465 men, directed a general retreat that evening. However, around 150 members of the resistance were captured as they tried to escape. Many were summarily shot and the remainder deported to camps in Germany. (See *After the Battle* No. 105.)

Having taken the oath 'Live free or Die', these members of the Armée Secrète are pictured in the high plateau of Glières. A request to London for desperately needed arms and ammunition led to several air drops amounting to nearly 40 tons enabling giving the men a surfeit of weaponry. However, to remove the supplies quickly it would require at least 100 men on the plateau plus more in the valleys below, something that would violate all the basic principles of guerilla warfare.

To this end, a special Supreme Court of Justice — to be seated in Riom from August 8, 1940 — was established by an act of August 1, 1940. This act stated that the court would try persons who had committed offences or had violated their duties 'by acts which contributed to passing from a state of peace to a state of war before September 4, 1939, and also those persons who later on have aggravated the consequences of the situation thus created'.

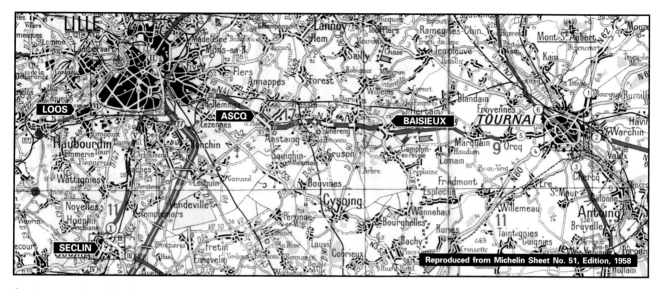

On the morning of April 1, 1944, the 12. SS-Panzer-Division 'Hitlerjügend', stationed in eastern Belgium, entrained ready to proceed to Normandy where it was to cover the coast in anticipation of the Allied invasion that was expected in May or June. The 24 trains were led by the divisional reconnaissance battalion, SS-Panzer-Aufklärungs-Abteilung 12, under SS-Obersturmführer Walter Hauck. Reaching Tournai that evening, the last major town in Belgium, the train had to halt at Baisieux station before crossing the border into France.

CORPORATIVE SYSTEM

The principles of the corporative system were laid down in a report by Admiral François Darlan, Vice-President of the Council of Ministers, which served as a preamble to the law of October 4, 1941, concerning the social organisation of occupations. In this report it was stated that solidarity between workers and industrialists should supplant the old system of the struggle of the classes. In order to further the national interests, the report continued to state that members of occupational groups should collaborate closely among themselves and with other professional groups.

The law of October 4, 1941, created several new institutions for the enforcement of these principles. The most important were the industrial or commercial 'families'; occupational unions; social committees for enterprises and for occupational families, and labour tribunals.

Occupational families were composed of members of various industries and trades. Practically speaking, all French economic activities were to be divided into large 'occupational families', every occupational family representing a separate branch of economic activity. A separate organisation was then to be established for each of these occupational families and also, if necessary, for every industry and occupation within the framework of the occupational family, for example, for the chemical industry; for buildings and public works; for insurance; for banking, finance and exchange, and so on.

The occupational family comprised every person engaged in a given economic occupation, irrespective of his particular role and position, each occupational family comprising both employers and employees. Thus the element of economic solidarity in production was stressed. According to the above-mentioned law of October 4, 1941, the occupational families had as their purpose 'joint administration of

Train derailments were a popular form of sabotage and, six kilometres down the line, a French Resistance team under Paul Delécluse had planted explosive on the line near the little station at Ascq.

191

The bomb had been constructed by Henri Gallois in the cellar of the home of Jeanne Cools at No. 218 Rue Nationale in Ascq.

the occupational interests of their members of every category and contribution to the support of the national economy in accordance with directions given by the public authorities'.

Occupational unions (syndicats professionnels) were reminiscent to a certain extent of the former class organisation in economic life because they were organised according to different categories of members: (1) employers, (2) workers, (3) clerical staff, (4) foremen, (5) engineers and administrative and commercial personnel. A single occupational union was formed in each area for each occupation, industry or occupational family and for each category of members. Since the occupational union had traces of class distinction, its role was made less important and was mainly reduced to technical matters, such as enlistment and representation of its members, execution of corporative decisions, study of occupational questions, and the solving of problems affecting the members of its territorial unit. Any activity of a political or religious nature was expressly excluded. The local occupational unions were represented in regional occupational unions and the regional occupational unions in a national federation of occupational unions.

It exploded as the train passed over it, derailing two flat cars loaded with half-tracks and slightly damaging the engine. The SS troopers immediately jumped down and opened fire on nearby houses on both sides of the track in a spontaneous reaction. This is the precise spot where the charge was placed.

Social committees for enterprises were provided by Article 23 of the law. This required that a Works Social Committee was to be created in every enterprise having a staff of not less than 100 workers or employees, in order to ensure collaboration between employers and employees. Such a committee was to be composed of the head of the enterprise and representatives of every category of personnel. The works social committee had no authority to interfere with the management and operation of the undertaking. Subject to this reservation, however, it had wide functions as regards advising the management con-

The Gestapo, apparently acting on information from an informer, tracked down those responsible and on April 21 arrested six men: Paul Delécluse, Daniel Depriester, Henri Gallois, Louis Marga,

Eugène Mangé and Raymond Monnet. *Left:* They were held in the prison at Loos (it closed in 2011) until June 7 when they were driven south to Fort Duhoux *(right)* at Seclin.

The six men met their deaths here, their bodies buried in a nearby ditch not being discovered until September.

cerning all questions affecting the life and the work of the staff, providing information on the social life of the staff and their families, and organising mutual aid institutions.

Social committees for occupational families or occupations were also provided by the same law. These social committees were local, regional and national in character. Each local social committee consisted of from 12 to 24 members, chosen from among the officers of the occupational union, and divided into three equal groups: (1) employers, (2) workers and salaried employees, and (3) other categories. The regional and national social committees, like the local committees, were tripartite in character. The officers, however, were appointed and through these officers the government maintained control and had the opportunity to shape the policy of the social committees. The functions of social committees were twofold: occupational and social, and political and religious questions were excluded. In the occupational field, they dealt with wages, collective agreements, vocational training, trade practices, and so on, while in the social field they dealt with social security and employment, mutual aid, improvement of living conditions, sport and recreation.

Labour disputes were to be settled, first by the occupational bodies of the respective groups. If it was found impossible to avoid or to settle disputes by this means, then the differences had to be submitted to conciliation boards or, if they did not exist, to Justices of the Peace 'if individual differences are involved'. However, if the differences were of a collective character, then labour tribunals decided the case. These

Meanwhile at Ascq the SS had to take their revenge. Their commander, Hauck, was in a foul mood and 16 people were gunned down in the town while another 70 were marched single file along the railway line for some 300 metres in the direction of Baisieux. As each man reached the appointed place he was shot in the back of the head.

The burial of the dead took place on April 5 — three days after the massacre — when upwards of 25,000 people gathered in Ascq. *Above:* The cortège assembles in Place de l'Église, now Place du Général de Gaulle. *Below:* The crowd outside the Mairie, Rue Marceau having been renamed in honour after one of the victims, Gaston Baratte.

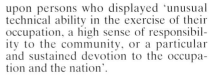

labour tribunals were of two kinds, regional and national. Regional tribunals were composed of two judges — of whom one exercised the functions of the president — and three members of the regional social committee. Appeals from decisions of regional labor tribunals had to be submitted to a national labour tribunal, which rendered final decisions.

In order to foster efficiency, a National Order of Labour was created in April 1942 conferring distinction upon persons who displayed 'unusual technical ability in the exercise of their occupation, a high sense of responsibility to the community, or a particular and sustained devotion to the occupation and the nation'.

At the cemetery a mass grave had been prepared for 49 of the dead, other burials being made in family graves.

On June 5, the BBC broadcast a series of coded messages calling the French Resistance to action on D-Day. On June 8 the maquis in the Vercors area, just south of Grenoble, mobilised over 4,000 men ready to move into action as soon as the Allies landed in Southern France. On July 3 the insurgents even proclaimed the Republic of Vercors and to deal with the uprising, on July 21 the Germans launched the largest operation ever conducted against the Resistance in Western Europe, attacking with airborne and mountain troops. Over 20 DFS 230 gliders were employed to land 200 men in a coup-de-main assault on the maquis positions, this glided being photographed at Vassieux.

Then, on September 4, 1942, a government decree was promulgated relative to the utilisation and organisation of labour. Compulsion was introduced for males between 18 and 50 years of age and for unmarried persons of the female sex between the ages of 21 and 35. Any dismissal of labour or any cancellation of a labour contract, without previous authorisation of labour inspection services, was forbidden in all industrial and commercial enterprises. Every Frenchman between 18 and 50 years of age 'whose physical qualification has been medically recognised' had to be able to prove that he was engaged in work useful to the country. Any person from the above category who could not furnish such proof was subject to employment on any work designated by the Secretary of State for Labour. Under this law, an obligation was imposed upon employers to provide technical and professional educational facilities in order to create skilled manpower for those professions which were short of labour. Severe penalties were introduced for violating the law, namely, imprisonment up to five years and fines up to 30,000 francs. These punishments could be doubled in cases of repetition of such violations.

The law of October 4, 1941, concerning the social organisation of occupations, envisaged an organisation in which all persons engaged in economic activities were to form a pyramid of different groups, controlled and checked one by another and then controlled at the pinnacle by the state. Labour in this pyramid had a clearly subordinate role. The decrees on mobilisation of labour stressed even more this subordinate role, which made it impossible for the workers to defend themselves against the well-established Vichy policy of trading in French labour with Germany.

RAFAEL LEMKIN, 1944

Precise casualty figures are difficult to establish but by the time the battle was over, between 400 and 600 FFI were killed, or executed after the fighting, and also 130 to 200 civilians lost their lives. The Germans casualties numbered 65 killed, 18 missing and 133 wounded. (The full story of the Battle of Vercors is told by Jean Paul Pallud in *After the Battle* No. 174.)

The Destruction of Oradour-sur-Glane

La Grand Rue in Oradour, then and now, courtesy of Brana Radovic. The village remains in a ruined state as a memorial.

Before, but especially following the Allied landings on the Normandy coast, the French resistance movement intensified its efforts to disrupt German communications and supply lines. German military commanders, particularly those who had seen service on the Eastern Front, and whose response to partisan activity had been conditioned by the extraordinary brutality of anti-partisan measures there, intensified responses to real and perceived resistance activity.

On June 8, two days after the Allied landing, the German Commander-in-Chief in the West, Generalfeldmarschall Gerd von Rundstedt, issued orders to 'crush' the resistance 'with swift and ruthless initiative', and expressed the 'expectation that the major operation against the gangs in Southern France will be carried out with the greatest severity and without leniency.' General Carl-Heinrich von Stülpnagel, the Military Commander in France, ordered the redeployment

of a number of units stationed throughout France to reinforce the Normandy front and to crush partisan activity behind the German lines. Among the units redeployed to Normandy was the 2. SS-Panzer-Division 'Das Reich' which had arrived as a reserve unit in the southern French town of Montauban in January 1944.

The Das Reich Division had seen two years of combat duty, including numerous anti-partisan actions on the Eastern Front, before its

The 2. SS-Panzer-Division had its origins in 1939 as the SS-Verfügungs-Division, officially renamed the Waffen-SS in July 1940, although the appendage 'Das Reich' did not appear until 1942. It took part in the invasion of Yugoslavia and Greece, and later fought against the Soviets in the drive on Moscow, at Kharkov and Kursk. From October 1943, the division was commanded by SS-Brigadeführer Heinz Lammerding *(left)*. Following the issuing of his Order of the Day on June 9, 1944, titled 'The position with regard to guerrilla bands and tactics for combatting them', 99 hostages had been hung from lamp-posts in Tulle. The next day came the instructions for the massacre at Oradour. The most senior officer in charge of the death squads in the village on June 10 was SS-Sturmbannführer Adolf Diekmann *(right)*, the commander of the I. Bataillon of SS-Panzergrenadier-Regiment 4. The orgy of death and destruction continued all day and by the time they left, all but six of the villagers were dead . . . and Oradour-sur-Glane ceased to exist.

north-west of Limoges. Led by the commander of the I. Bataillon, SS-Sturmbannführer Adolf Diekmann, the Waffen-SS troops surrounded the village at midday. At that point in time, the village population had almost doubled to about 650 people, swelled by refugees, including some Jewish refugees, from other parts of France.

The SS soldiers rounded up the entire population and concentrated them on the market square. Thereafter they separated the villagers by gender. Members of the 1. and 2. Zugs (platoons) took the 197 men to several barns on the edge of town and locked them in. The 3. Zug locked up 240 women and 205 children in the village church. Then the SS set fire to the barns and threw grenades through the windows of the church, shooting those who sought to escape the flames.

After 642 inhabitants, including seven Jewish refugees, were dead, the company looted the empty dwellings and then burned the village to the ground. The SS finally withdrew from the smoking ruins at about 8 p.m. on the evening of June 10. Only six villagers survived the massacre: five men and a woman, all of them more or less severely injured. About 15 other inhabitants of the village were able to escape the Germans before the massacre started or to evade the round-up by hiding.

transfer to France. Its commander, SS-Brigadeführer Heinz Lammerding, had served from July 1943 to January 1944 as the Chief-of-Staff for SS-Obergruppenführer Erich von dem Bach-Zelewski, whom Himmler had appointed to command and co-ordinate anti-partisan operations behind German lines in the occupied Soviet Union. In this capacity, Lammerding had ordered several retaliation actions against Soviet civilians for real or perceived partisan activities. Such operations involved the murder of tens of thousands of civilians, many of whom had had nothing to do with the partisans, and the torching of dozens of villages.

As the 2. SS-Panzer-Division redeployed to Normandy, French resistance fighters harassed it on its journey. On June 9, Lammerding issued orders for the division to 'cleanse' the area around Clermont-Ferrand of partisans. That same day, members of the division had displayed what the 'cleansing' of partisans would mean when, in retaliation for an attack, soldiers of Das Reich hanged 99 male inhabitants of the town of Tulle, near Limoges.

The next day soldiers of the 3. Kompanie, I. Bataillon of SS-Panzergrenadier-Regiment 4 'Der Führer', a subordinate motorised infantry unit of the 2. SS-Panzer-Division since April 1944, advanced to the village of Oradour-sur-Glane, 25 kilometres west-

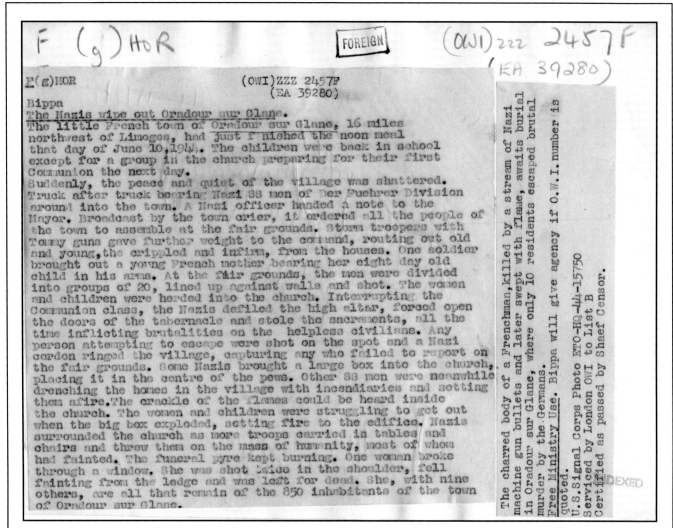

F(g)HOR   (OWI)ZZZ 2457F
                              (EA 39280)
Bippa
The Nazis wipe out Oradour sur Glane.
The little French town of Oradour sur Glane, 16 miles
northwest of Limoges, had just finished the noon meal
that day of June 10,1944. The children were back in school
except for a group in the church preparing for their first
Communion the next day.
Suddenly, the peace and quiet of the village was shattered.
Truck after truck bearing Nazi SS men of Der Fuehrer Division
around into the town. A Nazi officer handed a note to the
Mayor. Broadcast by the town crier, it ordered all the people of
the town to assemble at the fair grounds. Storm troopers with
Tommy guns gave further weight to the command, routing out old
and young, the crippled and infirm, from the houses. One soldier
brought out a young French mother bearing her eight day old
child in his arms. At the fair grounds, the men were divided
into groups of 20, lined up against walls and shot. The women
and children were herded into the church. Interrupting the
Communion class, the Nazis defiled the high altar, forced open
the doors of the tabernacle and stole the sacraments, all the
time inflicting brutalities on the helpless civilians. Any
person attempting to escape were shot on the spot and a Nazi
cordon ringed the village, capturing any who failed to report on
the fair grounds. Some Nazis brought a large box into the church,
placing it in the centre of the pews. Other SS men were meanwhile
drenching the homes in the village with incendiaries and setting
them afire. The crackle of the flames could be heard inside
the church. The women and children were struggling to get out
when the big box exploded, setting fire to the edifice. Nazis
surrounded the church as more troops carried in tables and
chairs and threw them on the mass of humanity, most of whom
had fainted. The funeral pyre kept burning. One woman broke
through a window. She was shot twice in the shoulder, fell
fainting from the ledge and was left for dead. She, with nine
others, are all that remain of the 850 inhabitants of the town
of Oradour sur Glane.

The charred body of a Frenchman, killed by a stream of Nazi
machine gun bullets and later swept with flame, awaits burial
in Oradour sur Glane, where only 10 residents escaped brutal
murder by the Germans.
Free Ministry Use. Bippa will give agency if O.W.I. number is
quoted.
U.S. Signal Corps Photo ETO-HQ-44-15750
Serviced by London OWI to List B
Certified as passed by Shaef Censor.

A series of photographs — some too awful to publish — were released by the Allied Press Censor on July 27. It was declared that the ruins should be left untouched as a memorial to the worst atrocity to have been perpetrated in France. In November 1944 the decision was taken to build a new village on virgin land to the west. A law initiating the project was voted in May 1946, and on June 10, 1947 the President of the French Republic Vincent Auriol came to lay the foundation stone.

AFTERMATH

The Oradour-sur-Glane massacre received significant contemporaneous attention, requiring the German Army command to search for an explanation and the officers of the Das Reich to find one.

On the evening of June 10, after the troops left Oradour-sur-Glane, Diekmann gathered together his officers and non-commissioned officers and ordered them not to speak about the killings. He told them that, if asked, they should say that insurgents attacked the division in the village and the villagers were killed during the firefight. The German Army high command then offered this explanation to the State Secretary in the Vichy Ministry of Defence, Général Eugène Bridoux, after Vichy diplomats had sent a formal protest note that contained an accurate account of the events of June 10. The German explanation stated that 'the men of the village died during the fight; the fight had been initiated from the village, and the women and children had taken refuge inside the church and died as the result of an explosion from a nearby insurgent ammunition supply dump that ignited the inside of the church.'

To quell increasing public outrage, and to try to keep the Vichy government from going over to the Allies, von Rundstedt ordered a criminal investigation of the massacre to be carried out. Since the SS was under a different jurisdiction to the German Army, SS judge SS-Sturmbannführer Detlef Okrent conducted the investigation in which he relied significantly on the testimony of SS-Hauptsturmführer Otto Kahn. Okrent stayed the proceedings in January 1945, concluding that 'military concerns justified the retaliation'.

Général de Gaulle made his first official visit to Oradour-sur-Glane on March 5, 1945. In his speech he mentioned that 'a place like this is something common to all, something in which everyone recognises the common misfortune, the common will and the common hope. Never again, not even once, such a thing must happen anywhere in France.'

This aerial view by Fred Yvonne looks west towards the new Oradour. Six hundred and forty-two men, women and children lost their lives here, and only six persons escaped. Madame Rouffanche, the only woman to survive, managed to climb out of the window behind the altar of the church seen in the left foreground. The other five men, herded with dozens of others into the Laudy Barn [1], feigned death under the bodies of their friends.

POST-WAR

After the war, the massacre in Oradour-sur-Glane also received a great deal of attention. In 1946, the French government declared the site to be a national memorial and mandated its conservation. The French prosecution team presented documentation of the killings at the International Military Tribunal in Nuremberg in 1946.

Why Diekmann and his superiors chose Oradour-sur-Glane, and who gave the order to kill the inhabitants, remains disputed. Neither the International Military Tribunal nor the French authorities at proceedings in Bordeaux in 1953 produced conclusive evidence either linking Oradour-sur-Glane with the French resistance or determining who ordered the massacre. When authorities in the German Democratic Republic prosecuted Heinz Barth, an SS-Oberscharführer who participated in the Oradour-sur-Glane massacre, in 1981, they too could not reach a conclusive answer to these questions.

The evidence presented at the trials and in West German investigations of officers of Das Reich generated a number of theories as to why the SS targeted Oradour-sur-Glane. The most common explanation is that Lammerding and Diekmann received intelligence from SS-Sturmbannführer Karl Gerlach (whom insurgents had kidnapped but who had escaped) that the villagers were assisting the Resistance. A variation of this theory is that French collaborators misled the Germans, perhaps deliberately, into believing that French insurgents were holding another kidnapped German officer, SS-Sturmbannführer Helmut Kämpfe, in Oradour, and that they planned to kill him. This explanation is based on flimsy evidence and flawed logic, for there is no indication that the Germans searched Oradour for Kämpfe. Nor did the soldiers of Das Reich continue the search after the massacre, either in Oradour-sur-Glane or anywhere else. Moreover, survivors stated that one of the German officers, later identified as Kahn, never mentioned Kämpfe, but did inform the villagers that the homes would be searched for weapons and ammunition.

The main road now bypasses the old village; here one enters the silent streets . . .

Marguerite Rouffanche was the only woman to escape from the church. This account in her own words was given at the military tribunal she attended in Bordeaux in 1953. Madame Rouffanche died in 1988.

Shoved together in the holy place, we became more and more worried as we awaited the end of the preparations being made for us. At about 4 p.m. some soldiers, about 20 years old, placed a sort of bulky box in the nave, near the choir, from which strings were lit and the flames passed to the apparatus which suddenly produced a strong explosion with dense, black, suffocating smoke billowing out. The women and children, half choked and screaming with fright, rushed towards the parts of the church where the air was still breathable.

The door of the sacristy was then broken in by the violent thrust of one horrified group. I followed in after but gave up and sat on a stair. My daughter came and sat down with me. When the Germans noticed that this room had been broken into, they savagely shot down those who had tried to find shelter there. My daughter was killed near me by a bullet fired from outside.

I owe my life to the idea I had to shut my eyes and pretend to be dead. Firing burst out in the church, then straw, faggots and chairs were thrown onto the bodies lying on the stone slabs. I had escaped from the killing and was without injury so I made use of a smoke cloud to slip behind the altar.

In this part of the church there are three windows. I made for the widest one in the middle and with the help of a stool used to light the candles — I don't know how but my strength was multiplied — I heaved myself up to it as best I could and threw myself out of the opening through the already shattered window. I jumped about three metres down.

When I looked up I saw I had been followed by a woman holding out her baby to me. She fell down next to me but the Germans, alerted by the cries of the baby, machine-gunned us. The woman and the mite were killed and I too was injured as I made it to a neighbouring garden and hid among some rows of peas and waited anxiously for someone to come to help me. That wasn't until the following day at 5 p.m.

I ask that justice be done with God's help. I came out alive; I am the sacred witness from the Church.

MARGUERITE ROUFFANCE, 1953

This is the Laudy Barn from where six men escaped: Mathieu Borie, Clément Broussaudier, Jean-Marcel Darthout, Robert Hébras, Yvon Roby and Pierre-Henri Poutaraud although the latter was immediately caught and shot. This was the location where over 60 persons were killed. These six lay partly covered by the bodies of the dead. The SS were shooting everyone who was still moving so they pretended to be dead. As the SS set fire to the barn Poutaraud fled to avoid the flames only to be shot down. The other five remained so long under the burning corpses that they caught fire, Robert Hébras explaining that 'my left arm and my hair had already burned. It was a terrible pain, therefore I had to get out of the barn'.

Other explanations seem even less convincing. There is no indication that the Germans ever received intelligence that Oradour was the site of an insurgent headquarters, as SS-Sturmbannführer Otto Weidinger, an officer of Das Reich who had not been involved in the massacre, claimed after the war. There is no information in the German military records that insurgents attacked German troops near Oradour. A war diary entry for the Military Commander in France for June 14 generated the theory that the troops of the 2. SS-Panzer-Division had confused Oradour-sur-Glane with Oradour-sur-Vayres, a village about 25 kilometres to the south-east. This theory is undermined by the absence of any reference to an insurgent attack on the Germans near Oradour-sur-Vayres during this time period.

For all the attention the killings have received, few of the SS men responsible for the massacre ever stood trial. Diekmann fell in combat three weeks after the massacre. German authorities refused to extradite Lammerding to France even though he was convicted and sentenced to death in absentia by the court in Bordeaux in 1953. German lawyers claimed that the German constitution prohibited the extradition of German citizens. The state prosecutor's office in Frankfurt re-opened the Lammerding case in 1961, but stayed the proceedings on grounds of insufficient evidence in 1964. Lammerding died in West Germany in 1971.

In 1953, a French military court in Bordeaux prosecuted 21 former members of the 2. SS-Panzer-Division for crimes committed at Oradour-sur-Glane and Tulle. Fourteen of the defendants were ethnic Germans from Alsace. The court convicted 20 of the defendants; it sentenced two to death and the rest to prison terms between five and 20 years. Amnesties and pardons, however, freed all of the convicts, including the two sentenced to death, within five years of the trial.

In 1981, authorities in the German Democratic Republic arrested and prosecuted Heinz Barth, the former SS-Oberscharführer and platoon commander whose soldiers were among those who shot the men of Oradour-sur-Glane. An East Berlin court sentenced Barth to life in prison. Released in 1997, Barth died in 2007 at the age of 86.

UNITED STATES HOLOCAUST
MEMORIAL MUSEUM

Hébras (left) with Jean-Marcel Darthout pictured in May 2004 in front of the ruined barn from where they escaped. Robert is the last-living witness as Jean-Marcel died in 2016. He regularly takes tours through the ruins and has worked actively at the Centre de la Mémoire since it opened in the village in 1999.

Monaco

The contrast between the wartime years and Monaco today could not be more amazing. Initially occupied by the Italians, then from September 1943 by the Germans, post-war development has ensured its future of the Principality as a prosperous tax haven.

In August 1914, Prince Albert (1848-1922) declared Monaco's neutrality and he suspended the constitution to allow rule by decree. Despite the neutrality declaration, hospitals and convalescent homes were established for Allied soldiers in the principality's hotels. Later that month, Prince Albert's son Louis returned to active duty in the French Army as captain of cavalry in the 5ème Armée under Général Franchet d'Espèrey.

In November 1917, Prince Albert, under pressure from the French press and being now more confident of Allied victory, reinstituted the constitution, which had been suspended in August 1914 to allow rule by decree. Now

Jean Paul took this perfect comparison from a quay of the harbour just north-east of the Rock, packed with luxurious yachts.

Looking north-east towards Monte Carlo, Hauptmann Ralf Buchner and friends during the war and young Simon today.

administrative and judicial powers were separated and the three communes were merged into a single municipality. Also membership on the National and Municipal Councils was limited only to Monégasques, the indigenous inhabitants of the principality.

In July 1918, a new treaty was signed defining relations between France and Monaco. France agreed to uphold the Principality's independence, sovereignty and territorial boundaries, and Monaco agreed to exercise its sovereignty in conformity with the political, economic, military and naval interest of France. It also agreed to consult France before engaging in international relations and grant the French Government right of approval over succession to the throne.

As Prince Louis II had no legitimate heir, in May 1919 he legally adopted his daughter Charlotte (born to Marie Louvet in Constantine, Algeria, on September 30, 1898) to prevent the succession to the throne of Monaco by a German prince. On the death of Prince Albert in June 1922, Prince Louis II ascended to the throne and was promoted to Brigadier-General in the French Army in which had he served in Algeria between 1899 and 1914. Prince Rainier III (Louis Henri Maxence Bertrand Grimaldi) was born to Princess Charlotte in 1923.

When the Treaty of Versailles was signed on June 28, 1919, Article 436 noted that 'The High Contracting Parties declare and place on the record that they have taken note of the Treaty signed by the Government of the French Republic on July 17, 1918 with His Serene Highness the Prince of Monaco defining the relations between France and the Principality.'

In 1939, Monaco's population was 23,154 including 9,724 Italians, 8,540 French, 1,804 British subjects, 1,761 Monégasques and 1,325 nationals of other countries.

On July 4, 1940, Italy declared that the presence of military installations along the coast of Monaco made the officially neutral principality a de facto ally of France. As a result, Mussolini's troops entered the country to the cheers of the resident Italian community. Prince Louis was allowed to remain on the throne and he allied himself with the Vichy regime in France in hopes of staving off annexation by Italy in the event of an Axis victory.

Four small states in Europe declared their neutrality but only Monaco, which followed a pro-Axis line with Vichy, was occupied. (Apart from a German border post at Pas de la Case in Andorra on the border with Spain, that country remained out of the war as did Liechtenstein, closely allied to Switzerland. San Marino was ruled by a Fascist party that had seized power in 1923 but the country had refused to declare war along with its larger neighbour Italy.)

The following year, Jean Eugène Charles, a Swiss Nazi, was dispatched to Paris where he collaborated with Carl Anton Schaeffer, a German administrator in the Bank of France, in organising a money-laundering scheme funneling funds through Monaco.

In March 1942, Radio Monte Carlo was launched with German and Vichy capital to broadcast Axis propaganda to the Mediterranean coast and North Africa. Then, on August 27, Vichy police arrested and deported 66 Jews from Monaco without any protest from the Monégasque administration.

When Italy signed the Armistice with the Allies in September 1943, Monaco was promptly occupied by German forces. Later that month, Adolf Eichmann telephoned the Reich Security Main Office (RSHA) in Berlin to report the escape of approximately 15,000 French Jews into Monaco. Eichmann went on to say that the Government of Monaco had agreed in principle to their capture within Monégasque territory should Berlin request it. The RSHA reported to the German Foreign Ministry with a request for an appeal to Monaco for permission to round up Jewish refugees in the principality. Foreign Ministry Jewish affairs specialist Dr Eberhard von Thadden rejected the request as premature after the German Consulate in Monte Carlo and the Security Police in Nice reported that the number of Jews in Monaco was approximately 1,000, not 15,000.

On September 30, Eichmann met with von Thadden to dispute the consulate's estimate of 1,000 Jews living in Monaco, citing the SD Chief of Southern France

The worst stain on Monaco's wartime history came with the rounding up by Monégasque police of scores of individuals who had fled from France to avoid arrest. At least 66 Jews were expelled on the night of August 27/28, 1942, and altogether about 90 persons were deported of whom only nine survived. On the 73rd anniversary in 2015, Prince Albert II publically apologised saying: 'We committed the irreparable in handing over to neighbouring authorities, women, men and a child who had taken refuge with us to escape persecutions they had suffered in France. In distress, they came specifically to take shelter with us thinking they would find neutrality.' The apology was compared with that made by the French President Jacques Chirac in 1997 which was the first admission by France since the end of the war about its wartime role in the deportation of the Jews. At the unveiling of a memorial in Monaco's cemetery, the Prince declared that 'there is no time limit on true introspection and regret'.

We are told that the Yanks could not resist racing their Jeeps along the Grand Prix circuit but we searched in vain for a photograph. However, this shot taken on the steps of St Charles Church in Monte Carlo is surely a good substitute!

as the source of his estimate of 15,000. Eichmann agreed to telegram the responsible SD unit and request a review of the matter in light of the 'astounding difference' in the two figures. The reply came back on October 22 when Eichmann's deputy, SS-Sturmbannführer Rolf Günther, reported to the Foreign Ministry that 'it has meanwhile been established that there are in the territory of Monaco not, as was formerly believed, 15,000 Jews, but only 1,000 to 1,500 Jews available and ready for deportation.' Thereafter no distinction was made between Monégasque Jews and refugees from France. In July 1944, the German consul in Monte Carlo reported there were no more than 40 to 50 Jews left in Monaco.

That same month, the Swiss Nazi Jean Charles established the Banque Charles in Monte Carlo to facilitate the smuggling of Nazi funds out of occupied Europe with the acquiesence of Prince Louis II.

On August 15, Radio Monte Carlo ceased its broadcasts following the Allied landings in Provence, and on September 3 Monaco was liberated by the US 36th Infantry Division.

On June 26, 1945, Radio Monte Carlo resumed broadcasting under French and Monégasque control.

Motor racing returned to Monte Carlo in August 1945 when American soldiers staged their own races on the track using Jeeps and GMC trucks, although the first post-war Grand Prix did not take place until May 16, 1948 when Giuseppe Farina of Italy won in a Masseratti.

AFTER THE BATTLE, 2017

On September 3, 2014, a rally was held outside the Royal Palace to celebrate the liberation on Monaco. Photo by Craig Morfitt who was on an incredible 23-country tour of Europe. His journey in his Land-Rover took six months and covered over 35,000 kilometres!

A well-known and much-publicised picture taken by Guernsey photographer Charles H. Toms. Lloyds Bank in the background made it a perfect propaganda shot for the occupation forces. The band is marching south on Pollet in St Peter Port.

The Channel Islands

The Channel Islands, situated off the north-west coast of France, are the only portions of the Dukedom of Normandy belonging to the English Crown to which they have been attached since the Norman Conquest. There are four principal islands: Jersey (area, 45 square miles; The 1940 population being 49,701); Guernsey (area, 24.5 square miles; population, 38,283); Alderney (area, 3.06 square miles; population, 1,598); and Sark (area, 2 square miles; population, 614).

ORDER CONCERNING THE LAWS APPLICABLE TO THE ENGLISH CHANNEL ISLANDS, AUGUST 23, 1940

By virtue of the powers vested in me by the Führer and Supreme Commander of the Armed Forces, I hereby order as follows:

SECTION 1. The general orders issued or to be issued by the Supreme Commander of the Army for the area of the Chief Command of the Military Administration in France are applicable, by way of analogy, to the occupied English Channel Islands.

SECTION 2. This order shall take effect as of the day of publication.

On behalf of the Supreme Commander of the Army:

THE CHIEF OF THE MILITARY ADMINISTRATION IN FRANCE

On June 19, 1940, the British Chiefs-of-Staff declared that the Channel Islands could not be defended, and they recommended that they be demilitarised as soon as their aerodromes were no longer required for the evacuations from France. However, the Prime Minister opposed this recommendation saying that 'it was repugnant now to abandon British territory which has been in the possession of the Crown since the Norman Conquest'. Churchill said that he felt that British sea power could prevent an invasion but the Chiefs-of-Staff pointed out that it was impossible to provide either anti-aircraft guns or fighters for the defence of the Islands. The Kriegsmarine was earmarked to capture the Islands in what was hoped would be a bloodless coup as Hitler believed that the Islands were unwilling British colonies, but the Luftwaffe stole a march on June 28 by carrying out bombing raids, the one on Jersey killing ten civilians and that on Guernsey killing 34.

Precautions against air attack at Springfield Stadium in St Helier, Jersey, converted into a First Aid Post.

After the fall of France and the British military reverses, the British Government removed all troops from the Channel Islands and declared them to be demilitarised. A considerable number of the inhabitants — about 40,000 — left on ships sent over from England for their embarkation. The Germans, however, ignored the proclamation of demilitarisation and bombed the harbours of St Helier and St Peter Port, and the next day invaded the islands by air. Guernsey was occupied by German military forces on June 30 and Jersey on July 1, 1940.

The Channel Islands were administered by a German local military commander who was under orders of the military commander in France. On August 23, 1940, an order was published by the Chief of the Military Administration in France to the effect that 'the general orders issued or to be issued by the Supreme Commander of the Army for the area of the Chief Command of the Military Administration in France are applicable'.

The Islands were incorporated into the French Department of Manche as a sub-district of Military Government Area A that had its headquarters at St Germain just outside Paris. On the Islands themselves, the civilian administration was under the control of a Feldkommandant, and on the military side by an Inselkommandant — initially Major Albrecht Lanz on Guernsey and Hauptmann Erich Gussek on Jersey. Above the Inselkommandant was the Befehlshaber der britischen Kanalinseln (Commander of the Channel Islands), this position being occupied by Oberst Graf von Schmettow (left) who set up his HQ on Jersey on September 27, 1940 in 'Monaco', an estate on St Saviour's Road (right). It has since been demolished and replaced by a car park for the Hotel de France.

Soon after the arrival of von Schmettow, a series of instructions were issued for the building of defences that were eventually to absorb one twelfth of the resources allocated to the construction of the entire Atlantic Wall. Hitler issued a directive on October 20, 1941 that specified that the Channel Islands were to be converted into an impregnable fortress. Although the Islands only occupied

the merest fraction of the 2,500 kilometres of occupied coastline, by 1944 they had absorbed eight per cent of the overall supply of concrete. Use was also made of the many existing forts that had been built in the 18th century like this one on Grouville Common in Jersey. Fort Henry was converted into a searchlight platform, ammunition magazine and personnel shelter.

On Guernsey, Castle Cornet, guarding the harbour at St Peter Port, was founded in the reign of Henry II and had formed the cornerstone of the Island's defences for over 500 years. It was captured three times by the French, and a lightning strike in

1672 ignited the magazine, the resulting explosion completely destroying the medieval buildings. The castle was repaired and heavily fortified in the Napoleonic Wars, and again became an important stronghold when the Germans took over.

A large range of artillery was emplaced on the Islands. Jersey had a total of 29 coastal guns of 150mm or larger in eight batteries. Guernsey had no less than 12 field guns of 220mm but the largest battery of all was the four 305mm (12-inch) guns of Batterie Mirus installed at Le Frie Baton at the western end of the Island. The guns themselves were of World War I vintage from the Russian Navy and were destined for Finland when the Germans captured them on the high seas in May 1940 during their invasion of Norway. Mirus was claimed to be the fifth largest battery on the Atlantic coast having a range of 30-35 kilometres. This photograph shows its No. 4 Gun in action some time after April 12, 1942 when the battery was commissioned.

Today the emplacement has found a new lease of life as a paintball venue called 'Festung Guernsey'.

The Mirus guns did not survive the post-war scrap drive, being cut up in 1947. On Jersey, the task of clearing all the ordnance resulted in a team from the British Army gathering all the guns together at Les Landes and simply tossing them all over the cliffs to end up in a tangled mass of metal washed by the sea.

Zimmer and myself which was installed in a replica turret at Noirmont Point *(left)*. Next, in 1993, came the recovery of one of the 220mm K 532(F) barrels weighing nearly ten tonnes. At first the cable slack was caught under several other barrels, but as soon as it was freed, the three large vehicles pulled the barrel up the 240-foot-high cliff in about three minutes! Following this success, the large cable was again lowered down the cliff-side and dragged down the rocks to a 210mm Mörser 18 barrel which was lying in a gully. As soon as we were well clear, the vehicles drove off, the barrel emerged from the water, bounced across the rocks on its breech, climbed the cliff and came to a halt at the top. It is now possible to see the best preserved barrel of each of the five types of coastal artillery gun deployed in Jersey by the Germans. Three are close together at Les Landes, while the other two types are about 400 yards apart at Noirmont Point. It is rewarding to sometimes see school children sketching these guns as part of a history project!'

As far as the authorities were concerned that was the end of the matter . . . but they did not bargain for the ingenuity of latter-day enthusiasts! Back in the 1950s, Terry O'Brien *(above)* spent all his summer holidays on Jersey, exploring and searching for war relics. In those days his souvenirs fitted into his schoolboy pockets but later he became involved in recovering the big stuff! One of the 150mm K18 barrels, which had not fallen right to the bottom, was winched up in 1979, but there followed a series of epic recoveries from the base of the cliff as Terry explains: 'I surveyed the guns on the rocks in 1989 and recovered a 155mm K 418(F) barrel in 1991 (see *After the Battle* No. 73). This was mounted on an original lower carriage complete with wheels (recovered by local enthusiasts). An upper carriage and trail arms were fabricated by Martyn Garnier and the complete gun was installed in an original open emplacement at Les Landes. In 1992, a 150mm SK L/45 barrel was pulled up from the rocks by Mark Anderson, Lou Hulatt, Geoff

Two more barrels were raised for display in Guernsey, a 150mm K 18, and this 220mm K 532(F) seen being installed by Tony Froome at Pleinmont, Guernsey. The carriage is a replica, the emplacement original.

Although there were conscious acts of sabotage, such as the cutting of telephone cables and painting of pro-British slogans like 'V' signs, this was discouraged as with a captive population, reprisals would be easy. People in Guernsey were the most active in this respect, something that led to a proclamation being issued specifically to them by the German HQ in Paris. Then in September 1942, over 2,000 of the Islanders were deported to Germany following Hitler's response for British expulsions of Germans from Iran. Large areas of the Islands had been mined and were out of bounds; a curfew was enforced with a total blackout after 8 p.m. Wireless sets were also banned. *Above:* This minefield protected Jersey's High Tower Hotel which was used for the living quarters for the crew of the nearby defences on St Ouen's Bay.

French having been the official language of the islands before the occupation (although English was the main language of business and religion, and was familiar to all), the orders of the military commander in France were published in both German and French.

The branches of the English banks were evacuated. The Germans recreated a local currency and put into circulation notes of 3d, 6d and 2/6d, and issued an order to open the local banking institutions. Advances equivalent to several million pounds sterling were made by them to the local states.

In the autumn of 1942, a great number of the islanders, men and women of ages up to 70 years, were deported to camps in France and Germany. Due to their insular life, the inhabitants dwelt in closer association than was usual among peoples of the mainland — almost like one big family — so these deportations were a great shock to the population. Farewell services were held in the churches and the deportees were

In 1945 German prisoners were forced to clear mines from all the Islands, this photograph being taken just outside the eastern perimeter of Guernsey's aerodrome. (See also *After the Battle* No. 75.)

After the war, St Ouen's Bay found a new lease of life — or rather nightlife — with a string of discos and bars all along the Five Mile Road but it was an era that has largely disappeared. Most have been closed or demolished for housing, the High Tower Hotel — once the Sands disco — now converted into the Discovery Bay holiday apartments.

With the defeat of the British and French armies, Alderney, being the closest of the Islands to France, received an influx of both escaping refugees and evacuating military. The fear of the 1,000 or so inhabitants as to what lay in store was not helped by a lack of information but, in the end, ships arrived to take off the civilians, just seven people deciding to remain. Included in the evacuation were several hundred cattle so that by the time the Germans arrived, they found the Island virtually abandoned. Nothing much happened until February 1941 when it was decided to fortify the Island, labour gangs from the Organisation Todt being drafted in to carry out the construction work. Four labour camps were set up to house the OT, Lager Sylt being the most notorious, and over 300 workers died during the occupation of Alderney. This parade was held in 1942 on Marais Square in St Anne although spectators are virtually non-existent.

The three main fortifications built by the OT on Alderney were Batteries Annes, Blücher and Elsass, the purpose of which was to close the gap between the Cap de la Hague in France and Guernsey where Mirus and other batteries further south took over. After the landings in Normandy in 1944, Blücher *(above)*, comprising four 150mm K18s in open pits, and having a range of over 25 kilometres, proved a threat to American supply routes on the Cherbourg Peninsula just 13 kilometres to the east. So the battleship HMS *Rodney* was called in to put it out of action. On the afternoon of August 12 she opened up with her 16-inch guns. Guided by a spotter plane, the ship claimed to have hit the target with its second salvo. Allied propaganda made much of the fact that much of the 'Island's defences' had been destroyed although the truth was that only one of the guns had received damage to its carriage. This was repaired on Guernsey and the gun returned to Alderney where it continued to do damage to US fuel dumps near Cherbourg. As the site of the battery lay on prime agricultural land just off the Longy Road at La Basse Corvée, the positions were completely removed after the war and nothing remains to be seen today.

Batterie Annes was built on the south-western headland at the Giffoine at the extreme western tip of Alderney where four 150mm turreted guns (SK C/28s) were mounted in open pits. They had a range of 20 kilometres. Here, after the surrender in May 1945, a group of British Army officers on an inspection tour of the Alderney defences are shown the guns.

Although the guns and their armoured turrets are no longer in situ, the casemates can still be seen.

The Island of Sark was governed by La Dame de Serk, Mrs Sibyl Hathaway, seen here with her American-born husband Robert. She was in Guernsey when the evacuation panic began but her view of the situation was succinct and to the point: 'We stay and see this island through'. Although a few decided to leave, all 471 inhabitants stayed put to await the arrival of the Germans, Major Lanz, the first commander, even signing her visitor's book!

presented with clothing and food by those remaining behind. Among them was the Seigneur of the island of Sark, American-born R. W. Hathaway, who became a British citizen, and acquired the title of 'Seigneur' through his marriage to Dame Sibyl Mary Beaumont, ruler of Sark under charter of Queen Elizabeth.

RAPHAEL LEMKIN, 1944

When in July 1940 Churchill learned that several hundred German troops had landed in the Islands, he immediately said that 'plans should be studied to land secretly by night on the Islands to kill or capture the invaders. It is of the highest consequence to keep the largest numbers of German forces all along the coasts of the countries they have conquered, and we should immediately set to work to organise raiding forces on these coasts. Initially referred to as 'Striking Companies', the new organisation came into being with unusual speed, launching its first operation on June 23, the approved title for the force being 'Commando'. Altogether seven raids were carried out against the Channel Islands over the next three years, two operations to Sark and one each to Guernsey, Jersey and the smaller islands of Burhou, Herm and the Casquets. However, the overall success rate was not great: three Commandos had lost their lives, two had been wounded and six men made prisoner. On the opposing side two or possibly three Germans were killed, one wounded and another eight had been captured.

After D-Day, food and other essentials became increasingly short after the Islands were cut off from France. There were now 23,000 civilians on Guernsey and 39,000 on Jersey but Hitler said that there was no question of either surrendering the Islands or evacuating the population. This in turn led to an increase in crime as some civilians had to resort to theft in order to eat to live. Finally, in December 1944, to alleviate the increasingly desperate situation, the Red Cross were permitted to bring in supplies by ship. Then, on May 9, 1945, it was all over when Vizeadmiral Friedrich Huffmeier signed the surrendered of the Channel Islands. Joyous scenes followed outside the Pomme d'Or Hotel that was formerly the Kriegsmarine headquarters in Jersey. Meanwhile on the beaches landing craft were waiting to ship the German garrison to Britain.

One of the Islanders deported to Germany was the late Michael Ginns and on his return after the war he was in the forefront of studying, researching and recording the Islands' wartime history. This interest, together with that of like-minded individuals, led to the formation of the Channel Islands Occupation Society with branches in Guernsey and Jersey, and the publication of the society's journal every year since 1973. (For more on the occupation, see The War in the Channel Islands Then and Now.)

The New York Times.

"All the News That's Fit to Print."

LATE CITY EDITION

VOL. XC. No. 30,228.

NEW YORK, MONDAY, OCTOBER 28, 1940.

THREE CENTS

ITALY INVADES GREECE, STARTING BALKAN DRIVE, AS ATHENS REJECTS A THREE-HOUR ULTIMATUM; METAXAS ASKS GREEKS TO FIGHT TO THE DEATH

ROOSEVELT TO TOUR 5 BOROUGHS TODAY, MAKING 6 SPEECHES

Due to Cross the City Line at 10 A. M. and End Busy Day With Garden Address

VISIT TO JERSEY IS FIRST

Heavy Police Guard Provided Here—Hunter Is Searched for Reported Egg Cache

Willkie Promises to Place Housing on Efficient Basis

He Says Program Vitally Needed in Nation Has 'Bogged Down' and Offers 6-Point Plan—Campaigns in Midwest Today

By JAMES C. HAGERTY

RUSH AS FAIR ENDS BRINGS OUT 537,952, ITS BIGGEST CROWD

Final Burst of Night Revelry Marks Closing Hours, but Vandalism Is Slight

SOUVENIR HUNTERS BUSY

Exhibits, Pavilions, Cafes and Amusements Are Packed as Throngs Take Last Look

By SIDNEY M. SHALETT

R. A. F. HITS REICH

Key Plants Are Ruined, Nazi Morale Hurt, British State

BERLIN RAIDED AGAIN

Liverpool and Midlands Under Attack—London Defense Effective

By RAYMOND DANIELL

The International Situation

BORDER IS CROSSED

Italians Move In From Albania—Athens Has First Raid Alarm

PREMIER IS DEFIANT

Appeal for Aid Is Sent to Britain—Attacking Force Put at 200,000

By A. C. SEDGWICK

Benito Mussolini, the Italian Prime Minister, had begun his aggressive foreign policy in the 1930s, first by invading Abyssinia in October 1935, then Albania in the spring of 1939. After things had gone badly with his attack on southern France in June 1940, Albania provided a perfect springboard for his next conquest: Greece. In late October that year, Hitler had embarked on a diplomatic tour to meet first with Generalissimo Francisco Franco of Spain, then Maréchal Philippe Pétain of France (see page 188), before travelling to Italy to see Mussolini, but on the morning of the 26th a warning reached Hitler (whose train had just departed from Munich for Florence) that the Italians were about to invade Greece. Hitler was beside himself and ordered full steam ahead to stop 'this crazy scheme of the Duce's'. However, the Prime Minister of Greece, Ioannis Metaxas *(right)*, had already been handed an ultimatum to allow the Italians entry the country at 3 a.m. that morning, giving him just three hours to reply. Without waiting for a response, Mussolini's troops breached the frontier, and by the time Hitler arrived at 10 a.m. he was presented with a fait accompli. The reply given by Metaxas that morning was a simple 'Oxi', something that has since gone down in Greek history as the day that the nation said 'No'.

Greece

At 3 a.m. on October 28, 1940, the Italian Minister handed an ultimatum to the Prime Minister of Greece which demanded that Italy had the right to occupy certain strategic points of Greek territory. The time for the expiration of the ultimatum was set for six o'clock the same morning. Early in the same morning the Italians started the attack against the Greeks.

PROCLAMATION OF THE DUCE OF FASCISM, FIRST MARSHAL OF THE EMPIRE, COMMANDER OF THE TROOPS OPERATING ON ALL FRONTS, ON MEASURES REGARDING THE CIVIL ADMINISTRATION OF THE TERRITORY OF THE GREEK PENINSULA OCCUPIED BY DETACHMENTS OF THE HIGH COMMAND OF THE ARMED FORCES IN ALBANIA, JULY 2, 1941

ARTICLE 1. In the territory of the Greek peninsula occupied by detachments of the High Command of the Armed Forces in Albania, civil authority, as defined in Articles 54 and 66 of the laws of war, shall be exercised by a High Commissioner. The High Commissioner shall be appointed and recalled by order of the Supreme Command.

ARTICLE 2. The High Commissioner shall be responsible to the Supreme Command. The Supreme Command may provide that the High Commissioner in the exercise of particular functions or of all his functions shall be responsible to the High Command of the Armed Forces in Albania.

ARTICLE 3. In emergencies of a political or military nature, or affecting the public welfare, the High Commissioner may order the replacement of civil officials in the occupied territory who have been theretofore retained in office; and he may also appoint civil officials when vacancies occur in the various offices.

ARTICLE 4. The High Commissioner may issue orders regarding buildings, police, sanitation, supplies and consumption, and local finance in urgent cases affecting the public interest and concerning, in whole or in part, the territory under his jurisdiction.

Persons who violate the orders provided for in the preceding paragraph shall be punished, if the act does not constitute a heinous offence, by imprisonment of not more than six months or by fine up to 5,000 lire.

ARTICLE 5. This proclamation shall be published in the *Gazzetta ufficiale* of the Kingdom.

It shall also be posted in the municipal registers of the territory of the Greek peninsula occupied by detachments of the High Command of the Armed Forces in Albania.

General Headquarters of the Armed Forces, July 2, 1941-XIX.

MUSSOLINI

The invasion was a disaster, the 140,000 troops of the Italian Army in Albania being poorly led and equipped. Facing tenacious resistance by the Greeks in the mountainous terrain, by mid-November the Italians had been halted and were being pushed back by a Greek counter-offensive into Albania. Even when the Albanian front was reinforced for an offensive in the spring of 1941, this also failed. In the end, after British ground forces arrived, Hitler was forced to come to Mussolini's aid and Germany declared war on Greece on April 6. By April 20 it was all over yet even Hitler was not short of praise for the way the Greeks had fought. Addressing the Reichstag about the campaign, he stated: 'It must be said, for the sake of historical truth, that amongst all our opponents, only the Greeks fought with such endless courage and defiance of death'. Now both Italian and German troops could pose for photographs in front of the Parthenon.

Today Greeks across the world celebrate October 28 as 'OXI-Day' — the day they said 'No' to Fascism.

Nevertheless, the campaign against Greece was not successful in 1940, although it was in 1941 when Germany joined in the attack. During the Italo-German operations, Bulgaria joined the Axis and, as a result of this common action, Greece was occupied by Italy, Albania, Bulgaria and Germany, and was divided into four Zones of Occupation. The Bulgarians were given Western Thrace (Aegean region), Eastern Macedonia up to the Struma River, and the islands of Thasos and Samothrace. The Germans occupied Central Macedonia, including Salonika, parts of the Aegean region, and the islands of Lemnos, Mytilene and Chios. In addition, the Germans supervised and gave instructions to the Greek Governor of the province of Evros that lay near the frontier of European Turkey. The Italians occupied the remainder of the country and most of the islands, including a small part of Crete, which was in greater part occupied by Germany. The Albanians were allowed to occupy the

The first German commander in Greece was Generalfeldmarschall Wilhelm List who took office as the Wehrmachtbefehlshaber Südost on June 9 but he had to relinquish the post due to illness in October.

provinces of Yanina, Thesprotia and Prenza, an area of 7,821 square kilometres, with a population of 300,573.

Whereas the Bulgarian Zone of Occupation was relatively stabilised, there were frequent changes in the zones occupied by Germany and Italy. Thus, when it seemed that the military situation in Greece was well in hand, and German troops were required for the Russian front, the Italian zone of occupation was extended. During this extension, the German zone was limited principally to strategic points such as ports, communication lines and aerodromes. However, when the military situation in this section deteriorated because of guerrilla warfare, and the menace of an Allied invasion, the Germans took under their control more and more territories. Finally, after the collapse of Italy in the summer of 1943, Germany took over control of the areas previously occupied by Italy. The Bulgarian occupation area was also extended.

ITALIAN OCCUPATION

On Italy's occupation of Greece, a special Office of Civil Affairs was established on the staff of the High Commander of the Troops in Albania.

The first orders on military occupation were issued by the commanding general of the troops in Albania. The proclamation of October 28, 1940, stated that the Office for Civil Affairs was to co-ordinate civilian services and exercise the necessary control over them. The Royal Carabinieri were called on to play an essential role in the administration of the territories in the initial stages of the occupation. They took over the enforcement of the orders and the supervision of the local police. The occupied territory was completely shut off from Albanian territory and only with the permission of the Royal Carabinieri could persons enter the occupied zone.

In 1941, when all Greek territory had been occupied by the Axis, an office of the High Commissioner was established for the civil administration of the territory of the Greek peninsula occupied by units attached to the High Command of the troops in Albania. The functions of the High Commissioner were fixed by the proclamation of the Duce of July 2, 1941. According to this, the High Commissioner was the highest civil authority of that part of the Greek peninsula occupied by Italian forces. He was appointed and recalled by order of the Supreme Military Command and was responsible to that command. However, a provision

When Italy entered the war, Generale Ettore Bastico was Governor-General of the Italian Aegean Islands. These were the islands conquered by Italy in the Italo-Turkish War in 1912. The Greeks referred to them as the Dodecanese (Twelve Islands) but when Mussolini came to power his Fascist regime tried to abolish that term in favour of the 'Italian Islands of the Aegean'.

Left: Here Bastico is pictured on the steps of the Emoupolis City Hall during a visit to the island of Sira (Syros to the Greeks). In July 1941 he went on to become the commander of the Italian forces in North Africa. *Right:* Miaoulis Square takes its name from the statue of the admiral who commanded Greek naval forces in the War of Independence in 1821-29.

On April 27, 1941, exactly three weeks after Germany had invaded Greece, troops of the 2. Panzer-Division reached and occupied Athens. They immediately proceeded to the Acropolis, the great outcrop of rock that towers over the inner city and raised the Reich War Flag marking their conquest of Greece and the capital.

was included which stated that the Supreme Command might specify that the High Commissioner, in the exercise of particular powers or of all his powers, was to be responsible to the High Command of the Armed Forces in Albania. The order also conferred upon the High Commissioner the right to replace local officials and to make new appointments. The area under Italian occupation was divided into civil commissariats with Italian civil commissioners at the head.

Left: Four weeks into the German occupation, two young students Manolis Glezos (left) and Lakis Santas (right), decided to do something about the swastika banner, planning to climb the Acropolis at night and take down the flag and destroy it, probably the first act of defiance in the many years of resistance activities that followed. The Acropolis was heavily guarded, with only one gate providing access, but they learned that a fissure in the rock called the Cave of Aglauros lay on the northern side, and by using this shaft they would be able to reach the top. The bad news from Crete on May 29 only steeled their resolve so they decided to act immediately. The next night, armed with only a torch and a knife, they entered the cave and climbed to the top. No guards were visible although they could hear jovial voices possibly celebrating the victory in Crete. Making their way to the flagpole they found it was 15 metres tall and when they cut the rope the flag snagged on the supporting bracing wire. They tried climbing the flagpole but it was slippery and they could get no purchase on it. Finally, they managed to reach the wire and free the flag that suddenly fell down on top of them. It was too bulky to carry so after removing two pieces as souvenirs they stuffed the rest in a crevice and covered it with rocks. When the Germans realised that the flag had gone they were infuriated. The Gestapo immediately launched a manhunt and announced that the perpetrators would be executed. Although those responsible were unknown, to the Greek people, they immediately became folk heroes. Both men continued to engage in underground resistance activities (see *After the Battle* No. 156) and in 1942 they were betrayed and arrested although the Germans failed to connect them with the theft of the Acropolis flag. *Right:* It was only after the return of democracy to Greece in 1974 that the two men could freely enjoy the fame and recognition they deserved as the pioneer heroes of the Greek Resistance.

In the first few days of the occupation, Lela Carayannis *(left)* began helping the hundreds of Allied and Greek soldiers left behind after the evacuation, organising safe houses where the wounded could be treated. Apart from preparing safe havens, she helped escapes over the mountains and by fishing boats from island to island to enable the men to reach Allied bases in the Middle East. Within a short period Lela had recruited more than 150 Greeks from all walks of life into her resistance organisation that became known as 'Bouboulina' after the exploits of the Greek heroine in the country's War of Independence against the Ottoman Empire in 1821-29. In the months that followed, Lela expanded her activities into form-ing intelligence units and assault teams, even managing to plant members into German offices, including the local Kriegsmarine, Luftwaffe and the German and Italian high commands. Lela carried on her undercover work for the next three years until one of her team was caught and broke down under interrogation. Lela was arrested on July 11, 1944. Torture failed to break her and on September 8, she and 71 of her followers were shot in Chaidari concentration camp, the most notorious camp in Greece where over 2,000 are believed to have met their deaths. *Right:* George Pararas-Carayannis, her adopted grandson, beside Lela's tomb in the First Cemetery of Athens.

ECONOMY

In economic matters, not only the Royal Carabinieri but also the Royal Finance Guards had jurisdiction. It was required under the proclamation of the Commanding General of October 30, 1940, that persons among the local population in the occupied territory owning flour, macaroni products, vegetables, barley, wheat and fodder, beef, poultry, goats and pigs must make and submit an inventory thereof to the Royal Carabinieri or the Royal Finance Guards. The proclamation stated that failure to make such a report or the making of an incorrect report would be punished by arrest and a sentence of from six months to two years, and that the unreported produce would be sequestrated.

The same proclamation introduced penalties of imprisonment up to 15 years for the destruction, damaging or spoiling of food products, fodder, building or firewood, coal or peat, petroleum and other articles of prime necessity to the civilian population or useful to the occupying army. The occupant took over the Greek monopoly services for salt, tobacco, matches, cigarette boxes, automatic lighters and flints.

Left: At the time of Lela's death, the commander of the Ordnungspolizei in Athens was SS-Oberführer Hermann Franz, promoted that month to SS-Brigadeführer as the Higher SS and Police Leader of all Greece. *Centre:* Gestapo headquarters in Athens was located at No. 6 Merlin Street but today the building has been demolished and replaced by a modern department store. *Right:* Nevertheless, one of the original cell doors has been put on display by the entrance as a reminder of the wartime history of this street.

As soon as the Italians had launched their October 1940 attack, British troops had been despatched to the Greek island of Crete, a vital base for the Royal Navy in the eastern Mediterranean. For Germany, the island would serve as an ideal launching point for offensive naval and air operations so, as well as invading the Greek mainland, paratroops of General-leutnant Kurt Student's XI. Fliegerkorps were assigned the task of capturing it. The operation began on May 20 and by the end of the month Crete had fallen.

GERMAN OCCUPATION

As mentioned above, the area of the German occupation varied according to the military situation. Since the beginning of the invasion, Germany held under its administration Central Macedonia, the town of Salonika and the islands of Lemnos, Mytilene and Chios. The Commander-in-Chief of the German Army in Greece had a special staff for civil administration. This staff acted

And it was on Crete that the first major reprisal took place against the civilian population, carried out by German paratroopers and — surprisingly — photographed in detail by Propaganda-Kompanie photographer Franz-Peter Weixler. The village of Kondomari is located near the northern coast of the island just a kilometre or so south-east of Maleme airfield. This was the landing zone for the paratroopers of the III. Bataillon of the 1. Luftlande-Sturmregiment. On landing the Germans were confronted by the 21st and 22nd New Zealand Infantry Battalions, joined by Greek partisans. The paratroopers suffered severe losses including their commander Major Otto Scherber, it being reported that civilians armed with primitive weapons were involved in torture and mutilation. When these stories reached Berlin, Reichsmarschall Hermann Göring ordered General Kurt Student to investigate and carry out reprisals. These measures were to be carried out swiftly by the same units that had been attacked by locals, and as some dead Germans had been found near Kondomari, the village was singled out for attention by Hauptmann Horst Trebes (right).

through local military commands throughout all the occupied military areas with the existing Greek authorities being supervised by German officers.

After the war, Weixler made a statement to the Allies for the trial of Göring at Nuremberg, although at that point his photographs had not come to light. 'The punitive expedition consisted of Hauptmann Horst Trebes, another lieutenant, an interpreter, two sergeants and about 25 parachutists of the III. Batallion. As a photographer assigned to my division I was permitted to accompany this commando. Near the village of Maleme, we stopped and Trebes showed us the corpses of several soldiers, obviously in the process of decay. He incited the men against the civilian population. We continued our drive to the village of Kondomari. The men got off, and ran into the few houses. They got all men, women and children onto the little square. A German soldier brought out the coat of a parachutist which he had picked up in one of the houses and which had a bullet hole in the back. Trebes had the house burned down immediately.'

Weixler: 'One man admitted having killed a German soldier, but it was not possible to convict any of the others of any crimes or plundering, and I therefore asked Trebes to stop the contemplated action and give us orders to return, taking with us only the one man. Trebes however gave orders to separate the men from the women and children; then he had the interpreter tell the women that all of the men would be shot because of having murdered German soldiers, and that the corpses would have to be interred within two hours.' *Left:* Trebes (right) checks that all the houses have been searched. *Right:* The road to the execution site today.

The paratroopers take aim and Trebes gives the order to open fire.

Weixler: 'When Trebes turned his back for a few moments, I made it possible for nine men to get away. Trebes had the men form a half circle, gave the order to fire, and after about 15 seconds, everything was over. I asked Trebes, who was quite pale, whether he realised what he had done, and he replied that he had only executed the order of Hermann Göring, and avenged his dead comrades. A few days later he received the Knight's Cross from Göring for his "braveness" in Crete.'

The following day paratroopers from the same regiment destroyed Kandanos and killed at least 180 of its inhabitants. Later that year Weixler was dismissed from the service being accused of high treason for leaking the uncensored photographs and helping some of the villagers to escape. He was arrested by the Gestapo, court-martialled and imprisoned. His negatives depicting the Kondomari massacre were not discovered until 1980 when a Greek journalist, Vassos Mathiopoulos, was carrying out research at the Bundesarchiv. He could not recognise the location but, after extensive research, another journalist, Kostas Papapetrou, did find where they had been taken although it was rather too late as Trebes had been killed in Normandy in July 1944. General Student, who had ordered the reprisals against Greek civilians, was captured by British forces and brought before a military tribunal in May 1947 but only charged with mistreatment of prisoners of war. He was sentenced to five years but given early release the following year. Greece applied for his extradition but this was refused so he was never brought to justice for his involvement with crimes against civilians.

The mass grave of the victims of Kondomari village has a display of the German photographs.

Left: To mark their victory, the men of the Luftlande-Sturm-regiment built this monument beside the Canae-Maleme road. The swastika which originally appeared on the memorial had already been obliterated when Jean Paul Pallud photographed it in 1985, and by 2000 even the eagle had disappeared. *Left:* In 2017, Patrick Ott checked again after having visited Kondomari and taken the comparison photographs only to find that the eastern side of the hill on which the memorial stands had gone.

The Resistance movement in Greece was like none other in Europe with between 30 and over a 100 separate groupings, and although there was a common enemy, there was constant in-fighting. The largest organisation was the National Liberation Front (Ethniko Apeleftherotiko Metopo, EAM) which claimed the support of up to two million Greeks with more than 150,000 active operatives. It was officially formed in September 1941 from a gathering of several left-wing organisations led by the Communist Party. The Greek People's Liberation Army (ELAS) was the movement's armed guerrilla wing. *Left:* Its leader was 'Aris Velouchiotis', the nom de guerre of Athanasios Klaras, whose group eventually totalled up to 50,000. In Athens, the letters 'EAM' and 'ELAS' began to be seen painted on walls, next to earlier 'OXI' and 'V' for Victory signs. In Major-General Stefanos Sarafis's 1946 history of ELAS, he explained that 'as time went on, the groups were reinforced by the population with all types of supplies and military equipment. They gradually started to build up strength and in some districts were able to carry out various actions against the invader with the help of military equipment received in Allied air drops. These actions were limited at first to attacks on small convoys on the move, isolated outposts and small

enemy forces; later they were mounted against larger convoys, trains and communications. They had the effect of forcing the invader to shut himself up in the towns and larger centres and to take measures to secure his communications. Thus a large part of the country, and paritcularly the mountain area, was gradually rid of the presence of the invader.' General Sarafis estimated that because of their activities, the Germans had to keep at least four to five extra divisions in Greece to try to contain the sabotage being carried out by the partisans. He also listed Axis casualties as German dead 16,062, wounded 6,504, captured 1,878; Italian dead 1,988, wounded 735, prisoners 1,073; and Bulgarian dead 1,305, wounded 1,037, and taken prisoner 2,230. ELAS claimed 30 bridges, 85 railway engines, 957 coaches and 1,007 motor vehicles had been destroyed. Captured weaponry included 100 artillery pieces, over 200 mortars, 400 machine guns, 1,400 sub-machine guns, and nearly 50,000 rifles. The cost in ELAS casualties was approximately 4,500 killed and over 6,000 wounded, but this does not take into account the 70,000-plus civilians killed by Axis forces in reprisals. *Centre:* The monument to the EAM was erected at Anolousia and that commemorating ELAS stands at Galatsi *(right)*.

Left: The National Republican Greek League (Ethnikos Dimokratikos Ellinkos Syndemos, EDES) was also founded in September 1941 and was led by Napoleon Zervas. *Right:* Initially called the Supreme Committee of Cretan Struggle (AEAK), it was the first armed resistance group but it was dissolved and became the umbrella unit for all the non-EAM groups on the island, being

renamed The National Organisation of Crete (Ethniki Organosi Kritis, EOK). And they did not just have male members as we saw with the Bouboulina group. The third of the main resistance groups was the National and Social Liberation (Ethniki kai Koinoniki Apelrftherosis, EKKA) which came together later in 1942 only to be bloodily put down by ELAS in 1944.

In fact, it was the first and only time that the country's two major guerilla forces co-operated militarily, as soon there was open conflict between them. The combined force numbered 150, the SOE team being dropped by parachute. They carried out the actual demolition while the guerillas provided cover and neutralised the guard posts on the bridge. The first explosion heavily damaged the central pier, collapsing two spans, and a second charge brought down the remaining span. The line was disrupted for seven weeks before the Germans repaired it.

CURRENCY

In the Italian-held areas, the Italian lira and Albanian franc were introduced as an additional currency by the proclamation of the Duce of June 21,1941. According to this order, 100 drachma were to be equivalent to 12.50 lire and to 2 Albanian francs. Later on the Italians issued the liretta in the Ionian Islands and the Mediterranean drachma on the mainland of Greece.

The communists were able to organise the first armed groups in the summer of 1942 with the purpose of defending farmers from tax collectors checking on the delivery of their crops, but tensions arose between the guerillas and the farmers as the former looked on the crops as food but to the farmers it was their livelihood. Although the Italians made efforts to contain such acts against their forces, they were unable to halt the creation of 'liberated' areas in the mountains, including even some towns. The destruction of the Gorgopotamos Bridge in central Greece by a combined team of Special Operations Executive (SOE) operatives and Greek guerillas on November 25, 1942 marked the real beginning of permanent British involvement with Greek resistance. Operation 'Harling' was devised to try to stem the flow of supplies through Greece to the port of Piraeus for shipment to North Africa. Lieutenant-Colonel Eddie Myers of the Royal Engineers was to lead a 12-man SOE demolition team to be joined by 86 members of the National Liberation Front (ELAS) and 52 from the National Republican Greek League (EDES).

Ironically the Germans destroyed it before they evacuated Greece in October 1944.

Immediately after the occupation, the Germans started to requisition all food and fruits. A special arrangement was made for German soldiers to be permitted to send air-mail packages of food to their homes. Food production since the beginning of the occupation was directed toward the needs of the German war economy. For example, in May 1942, all the milk production was requisitioned for making into cheese and butter to be sent to Germany. Later fresh fruit was also requisitioned.

One of the main problems of German administration consisted in recruiting labour and preventing sabotage. All males between 16 and 50 years of age were liable for labour conscription for work in Greece or in Germany. Strikes and lock-outs were outlawed and severe penalties threatened for anyone resorting to such action, and those organising or directing a strike were liable to the death penalty. Strikers as well as saboteurs were tried by military courts. For the prevention of sabotage, the Germans resorted very widely to their practice of taking hostages. They also introduced the death penalty for any attempt to sabotage the postal, telegraph and telephone services.

THE AREA OF THE GREEK PUPPET GOVERNMENT

The Greek mainland, Thessaly and the Peloponnesos, representing a total of 60,263 square kilometres, with a population of 3,546,185 people, was administered by a Greek puppet government established by the Axis in Athens and controlled by them.

The Italians occupied the major part of Greece — some two-thirds of the country — including the majority of the islands in the Aegean of which around 200 were inhabited. The Third Reich occupied the northern islands, primarily for military and security reasons but Samos, the ninth largest and just a mile from Turkey, lay in the Italian zone. From the very first moment of their arrival on the island on May 8, 1941, the Italians had the objective of completely demoralising the national spirit of the Samiots to accept its annexation together with the smaller neighbouring islands of Ikaria and Furni. The islands produce was confiscated for the needs of the 'glorious' Italian armed forces leading to a serious problem of starvation during the winter of 1941-42. At the same time a number of prominent residents were ordered to leave, thus depriving the populace of its spiritual and intellectual leaders, while others fled to Turkey. As a result, the population decreased from 83,000 to less than 60,000. A steady process of Italianisation led to the instruction of the Italian language and history in schools and a cultural institution called the Casa di Dante was established in the islands capital Vathi *(above)*. This de-Hellenisation of the islands led to resistance on a scale unparalled in any other Greek island save for Crete.

The architecture of Vathi has seen little change in the intervening period.

229

From 1942 the partisans received their arms from the SOE base established on the Cesme Peninsula at Agrilla in Turkey.

Left: A typical target: Italian vessels moored in Samos's Pythagorio harbour in 1943. *Above:* A peaceful village today.

ADMINISTRATION

Although the former ministries still functioned, special German and Italian plenipotentiaries maintained offices in Athens where they acted as representatives of the Reich and of Italy to the Greek puppet government. A considerable authority was given to the Minister of Finance who was virtually an economic dictator having control over the Ministries of Agriculture, Food and Labour. The Minister of Finance had the right to supervise these ministries; to determine their jurisdiction and control their services; to create or abolish positions, and to supervise trade, supplies, prices and rationing. Even the so-called 'soup kitchens' were within his jurisdiction.

The two main resistance groups on the island called themselves the National Guerilla Corps of Samos comprising of around 400 men. Due to their small size the guerillas could not engage the Italians in open battle but had to be content with sabotage and ambushes.

On July 10, 1943, Allied armies landed on the shores of Axis-held Sicily, an event that was to lead to King Victor Emmanuel forcing Mussolini to resign two weeks later. It was the beginning of the end for the Axis partnership. With the Duce under arrest, the King appointed a new non-fascist Prime Minister, Marshal Pietro Badoglio, although his first communiqué stated: 'the war goes on'. Meanwhile, on Samos, two Blackshirt battalions of 1,200 ruthless fascists arrived on the island to conduct anti-guerilla operations and 17 young men of the village of Kastania were rounded up on August 30 and shot. Another ten people were murdered in the surrounding area. This memorial was dedicated in 1981 to honour the memory of the fallen.

Three days after the murders, Italy surrendered. The King and his entourage with Badoglio and his government fled leaving a country and its army bereft of leadership. The armistice on September 8 drastically changed the situation in the Aegean. While the Germans took immediate steps to counter the defection of their former ally, the British sought to step into the vacuum and land on the more-important islands. Samos became the first Greek territory to be liberated when British forces under Major-General Allan Arnold, accompanied by two battalions of the Royal West Kents, arrived on September 9. Apart from having to deal with the Blackshirts, the situation on the island was chaotic and Arnold also had to accept that the guerillas were the heroes of the moment. Here they are pictured marching to a church parade in Vathi on October 31 to celebrate the liberation of the island.

Much of Vathi remains unchanged: this is the main square *(above)* with Saint Nicholas Church *(below)*.

However, the euphoria was short-lived. When the island of Leros was captured from the British on the evening of November 16 (see *After the Battle* No. 90), an attack on Samos seemed inevitable. General Henry Wilson, the C-in-C Middle East, informed Churchill that there were no forces on Samos able to put up a strong defence and the following day the British pulled out, much to the indignation and dissatisfaction of the Greek government-in-exile who had been kept totally in the dark. Consequently, the Germans now took over Samos, remaining until October 4, 1944. Following the signing of the armistice, Lieutenant-General Antonio Gandin *(left)*, the commander of the Acqui Division on Cephalonia, the largest of the Ionian group of islands, received confusing orders. Initially, the Italian War Office told him to treat the Germans as enemies, but then a second message from his superior said that his troops were to 'cede' their weapons to the Germans who would transport the men back to Italy.

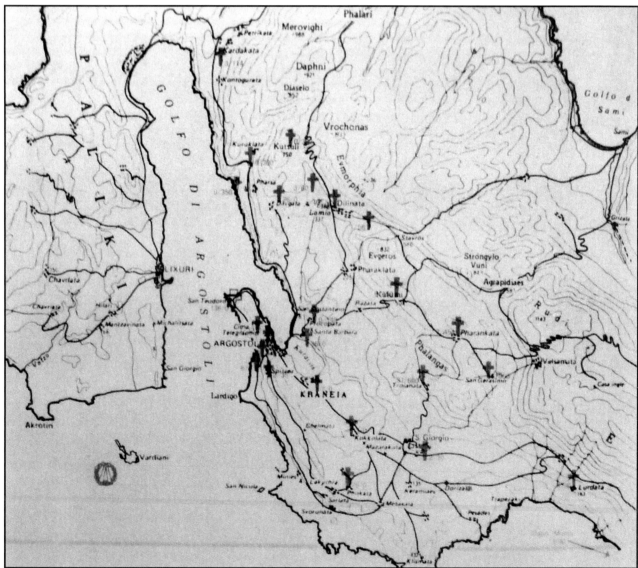

Matters came to a head when one of his artillery captains, without consulting him, gave orders to open fire on two German vessels approaching the port of Argostoli. The Germans considered this 'an act of hostility' and ordered the Acqui Division to immediately lay down their arms. However, Gandin's men were now in favour of opposing the Germans but, after fighting on for eight days, with ammunition now almost totally exhausted, they were forced to surrender. Infuriated, Hitler now ordered that all the Italian soldiers who had fought on Cephalonia be shot. General Hubert Lanz *(top right)*, the commander of the XXII. Gebirgs-Armeekorps, issued the appropriale orders and over 3,300 met their deaths at over 25 different locations.

By far the largest killing on the island took place in this stone-walled field at Troianata where over 600 were mown down.

The scene of the massacre today, although no memorial marks the spot.

General Gandin and his staff officers were the first to die at the Casetta Rossa (the Red House). Their bodies were thrown in two nearby pits. After the war the remains of over 3,000 men were exhumed on Cephalonia for reburial in the Italian War Cemetery at Bari. General Lanz was brought to trial by an American court at Nuremberg but, because no evidence was produced by the Italians, he simply denied that any massacre had taken place. He did admit that General Gandin and some of his staff had been shot but said that this was only after they had been found guilty of mutiny at a court-martial. Lanz was sentenced to 12 years but released after serving only three.

In the absence of a coherent strategy for countering the guerillas, the concept of retribution was a fundamental principle of military justice for the Wehrmacht. The reprisal policy in Greece — as throughout Eastern Europe — was born of the Nazi ideology with the blessing of the Führer himself. We have already seen General Student's unambiguous orders for burning down villages and exterminating the male populations on Crete and Generalfeldmarschall Wilhelm List confirmed the draconian guidelines for mainland Greece. Many units arriving to reinforce the country after the armistice had served on the Eastern Front where reprisals were common practice, and all troops carrying out such measures in Greece were guaranteed judicial immunity. At first, army headquarters issued quotas: 50 to 100 Greeks to be shot for the death of one German soldier, ten if a German was wounded. General Karl von Le Suire was aggressive in carrying out reprisals in the Peloponnese like that at Kalavryta, stating that anti-guerilla actions must offer 'terror for terror'. According to a report by the Greek government-in-exile, by July 1944 over 800 villages had been totally destroyed although the final total given in the caption to this map was 1,170. Greece suffered 35,000 military dead but that figure pales into insignificance when set beside the 171,800 civilian deaths plus the 300,000-600,000 who died from famine and disease. In total, the country lost over ten per cent of its population, only Poland and the Soviet Union losing a greater percentage.

Following the surrender of the Italian Army, large numbers of weapons fell into the hands of the partisans enabling the guerillas to increase their operations. A German report stated that although the northern Peloponnese (mainland Greece) had been virtually free of 'bandits' until October 1943, thereafter there were 5,000-6,000 operating in impassable mountain country. This included 2,000-3,000 in the Kalavryta area (see map on the opposite page). This is how the town looked in December 1944 after it was subjected to one of the worst reprisals carried out in Greece.

Rebuilt after the war, the town is now overshadowed by the memorial to the hundreds who died.

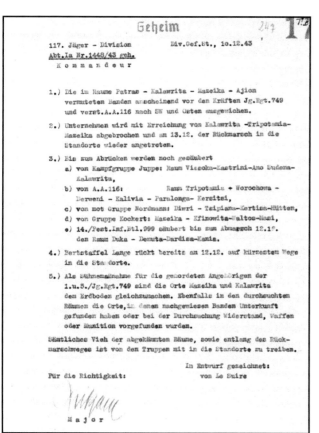

117. Jäger - Division   Div.Gef.St., 10.12.43
Abt.Ia Nr.1468/43 geh.
Kommandeur

1.) Die im Raume Patras - Kalawrita - Mazeika - Ajion
    vermuteten Banden anscheinend vor den Kräften Jg.Rgt.749
    und verst.A.A.116 nach SW und Osten ausgewichen.

2.) Unternehmen wird mit Erreichung von Kalawrita -Tripotamia-
    Mazeika abgebrochen und am 13.12. der Rückmarsch in die
    Standorte wieder angetreten.

3.) Bis zum Abrücken werden noch gesäubert
    a) von Kampfgruppe Juppe: Raum Vissoka-Kastrini-Ano Budena-
       Kalawrita,
    b) von A.A.116:   Raum Tripotamia + Worochowa -
       Derwend - Kalivia - Paralonga- Kersitsi,
    c) von mot Gruppe Nordmann: Diwri - Tsipiana-Kertisa-Hütten,
    d) von Gruppe Kockert: Mazeika - Kfinowita-Waltos-Masi,
    e) 14./Fest.Inf.Btl.999 säubert bis zum Abmarsch 12.12.
       den Raum Duka - Demuta-Dardisa-Kania.

4.) Bertstaffel Lange rückt bereits am 12.12. auf kürzestem Wege
    in die Standorte.

5.) Als Sühnemaßnahme für die gemordeten Angehörigen der
    1.u.5./Jg.Rgt.749 sind die Orte Mazeika und Kalawrita
    dem Erdboden gleichzumachen. Ebenfalls in den durchsuchten
    Räumen die Orte, in denen nachgewiesen Banden Unterkunft
    gefunden haben oder bei der Durchsuchung Widerstand, Waffen
    oder Munition vorgefunden wurden.

Sämtliches Vieh der abgekämmten Räume, sowie entlang des Rück-
marschweges ist von den Truppen mit in die Standorte zu treiben.

                            In Entwurf gezeichnet:
Für die Richtigkeit: von Le Suire

        Major

On October 19, the 5. Kompanie of Jäger-Regiment 749 of the 117. Jager-Division was ambushed at a rail junction, some four kilometres north of Kalavryta. Four Germans were killed and 78 soldiers taken prisoner. The Germans offered to exchange their men for Greeks held in custody but rejected after the partisans insisted on 50 Greeks being released for one German — the ratio the Germans themselves followed in their reprisal policy. Following unsuccessful attempts to find the prisoners, on November 28 the Germans mounted a major search-and-destroy operation using three Kampfgruppen. A detailed log was maintained over the next two weeks which reveals that the Germans discovered that the guerrillas had shot the prisoners on December 7. Two days later a cordon was set up ten kilometres around Kalavryta with this order *(left)* to not let anyone escape; to burn the village down and kill all the male inhabitants. On December 13, the village awoke to find German troops in the streets. Everyone was ordered to the school where the men and women were separated. Several hundred men were marched to a hollow outside the town *(right)* where they were held under guards from Kampfgruppe Ebersberger. During the morning, smoke began to rise from the town and a red flare was the signal for Hauptmann Egon Döhnert to order eight machine guns to open fire. After about five minutes the firing stopped to allow the Germans to minister the coup de grâce to anyone showing signs of life. Just 13 survived to tell what had taken place.

This photograph is purported to have been taken during the operation.

BARTER

Although price regulations were enacted, they were unable in practice to fulfil their purpose because of the complete disintegration of the value of the currency and the pressure of the black market. Therefore, in some instances, currency practically ceased to fulfil its mission of being a measure of value. Goods were exchanged against goods and even government officials were paid sometimes in goods, especially in food provided them by the soup kitchens. Some taxes were paid by farmers in agricultural products. When requisitions failed, the Axis authorities exchanged manufactured objects for agricultural products from the farmers.

FEEDING THE POPULATION

In view of the particularly bad food situation in Greece, the United Nations agreed to make an exception with respect to the blockade and to send food to Greece with the co-operation of the Swedish Government.

A considerable role in feeding the population was played by soup kitchens, which handed out food to the population on the streets. Soup kitchens were

By the end of December LXVIII. Armeekorps reported that its troops had burned 28 villages, shot 918 Greeks (696 being hostages from Kalavryta) and eight monks. These are the burned-out houses on Kernikis Prokopiou Street.

dispersed throughout the country and various professions or groups, such as government employees, bank employees and students, had their own soup kitchens. As already stated, the soup kitchens were controlled by the Ministry of Finance and handled by a Central Soup Kitchen Committee.

Today the rebuilt town is a bustling resort and administrative centre. (For more on Kalavryta, see *After the Battle* No. 83).

The gutted Church of the Assumption of the Virgin Mary.

It was rebuilt leaving the original pillars still standing.

To counter the threat of attack from Bulgaria, a chain of fortifications comprising 21 forts was constructed in the north-east along the Greco-Bulgarian border. Named after the Prime Minister Ioannis Metaxas (see page 218), the Metaxas Line — like the Maginot Line in France — was outflanked when Greece was invaded in April 1941.

BULGARIAN OCCUPATION

Bulgaria annexed Eastern Macedonia, Thrace (Aegean region) and Samothrace, this territory comprising 16,682 square kilometres and including the provinces of Serrai, Drama, Cavalla and Rhodope. The Bulgarians claimed that the Aegean was necessary for their living space, and the sea-coast especially important for their overseas trade. Thus Bulgaria augmented its population by about 590,000 as a result of the annexation of Greek territory.

ADMINISTRATION

The Greek administrative agencies were abolished and Bulgarian institutions introduced instead. The provincial administration of the occupied areas was headed by Bulgarian governors.

For purposes of colonisation, special additional agencies were created: (1) a regional director for colonisation in every region; (2) a central committee for land grants (the activities of this committee are described below).

The personnel of the administration was Bulgarised completely, a procedure which followed the well-established Balkan pattern of changing all officials upon taking over new territories. This appeared to be justified because of the national antagonisms that had always been rife in the Balkans. During the war, former Greek officials were replaced by Bulgarian officials to a larger extent than in any other occupied country in Europe. In order to enable these Bulgarian public servants to live

At the outbreak of the war, Bulgaria under the Prime Minister Georgi Kyoseivanov declared the country's neutrality, but after the failure of the Italian invasion of Greece, Hitler demanded that Bulgaria permit German troops to have free passage across the country for its attack on Greece. Tsar Boris III, pictured here with Hitler, signed the Tripartite Pact for Bulgaria to join the Axis, and on April 30 Bulgarian forces entered Greece having invaded Yugoslavia with Germany a few days earlier. On May 14, Bulgaria officially annexed territory it had lost after the First World War and an immediate programme was begun to wipe out all traces of it ever having belonged to Greece. The YVE/PAO resistance group was formed specially to bring the war to the Bulgarians in northern Greece and Macedonia but later on it was attacked by ELAS and dissolved.

However, the attempt to 'Bulgarianise' the area led to an uprising that began in the city of Drama in Eastern Macedonia. Although no official data has been made available, it is believed that the uprising was sparked off in the early hours of September 29, 1941, when armed men kidnapped the Bulgarien mayor in Drama — the Bulgarian flag flies over the Town Hall *(above)*. Led by the Communist Party, the revolt quickly spread to other towns and clashes broke out with the occupying forces. The following day Bulgarian troops entered the nearby town of Doxato to ruthlessly supress the insurrection, rounding up all the males between 18 and 45. The old men, women and children were locked inside the school while 270 others were killed. Executions continued in more than two dozen other towns and villages as the authorities embarked on a revengeful clamp-down to prevent similar insurgencies taking place in the future.

A parade is held each year at Doxato on which day petals are scattered on the memorial to remember the dead.

ΔΩΡΕΑ ΓΕΩΡΓΙΟΥ ΙΩΑΝΝΗ ΚΟΤΖΑΓΙΩΡΓΗ

It was reported that over 3,000 were executed in Drama alone, and it is estimated that 15,000 Greeks were killed over the next few weeks with entire villages being looted, machine-gunned and destroyed. Bulgarien reprisals continued long after the suppression of the uprising so that by the end of 1941, over 100,000 Greeks had fled from the Bulgarian occupation zone into the German zone. Panels stand alongside the memorial as a visual reminder of those who lost their lives.

239

Despite the alliance with the Axis, and the presence of Germans in the capital Sofia, and along the railway line leading to Greece, Tsar Boris of Bulgaria was not willing to give full co-operation to Germany. After Hitler invaded the Soviet Union, Boris refused to send troops to fight on the Eastern Front, or to accede to Nazi demands to deport its Jews. Instead he told an irritated Hitler that all able-bodied Jewish men were needed for labour to build roads and railways within Bulgaria, a subterfuge that saved at least 50,000 from extermination. Inspecting Bulgarian Red Cross personnel, Boris is pictured here with his wife Giovanna von Savoyen. In 1943, shortly after a meeting with Hitler, Tsar Boris III died on August 28, and, according to Oberstleutnant Carl-August von Schoenebeck, the German attaché in Sofia, it was believed he was poisoned. With his death, his six-year-old son took the throne as Tsar Simeon II with former Prime Minister Bogdan Filov, Prince Kyril and Lieutenant-General Nikola Mihov as Regents. Between 1943 and 1944 Bulgaria was really just a German-sponsored puppet state.

permanently in the Aegean region with their families, land and houses were granted, at the start only on a temporary basis. The temporary grant lasted up to the completion of three years' uninterrupted service in the Aegean region. After the servant had completed this, the grant became permanent.

TRANSFER OF POPULATION

The policy pursued by the Bulgarians in Eastern Macedonia was entirely different from the one adopted in the Aegean region. Whereas in Macedonia a policy of rehabilitation was followed — the Macedonians being considered by the occupant as of Bulgarian origin 'freed from the Greeks' — a real genocide policy was applied to the Greeks in the Aegean region. Greek churches and schools were closed and Bulgarian was made the official language. These measures were aimed at changes in the composition of the population in accordance with the German pattern. First of all, those Greeks who had come as immigrants from Anatolia and settled in Greece after the exchange of populations in 1922-23 were expelled from Thrace into that part of the Greek territory which was left under a Greek puppet government.

Various other devices were also used in order to compel the Greeks to leave including the introduction of a general licencing system for trades and professions. No one could engage in trades who had not received a special licence from the Bulgarian Chamber of Commerce and Trade. The refusal of such a licence was equivalent to condemning the applicant to starvation. Again, the property of the wealthier classes was confiscated. Furthermore, pre-invasion bank deposits were not returned to Greeks (see below). Consequently, many of the Greeks preferred to leave the territory rather than to starve. More than 100,000 Bulgarians were brought from Bulgaria proper to Thrace for purposes of colonisation, mainly in the areas between the Struma and Mesta rivers.

On June 10, 1944, just as SS-Panzergrenadier-Regiment 4 of the 2. SS-Panzer-Division was about to wreak vengeance on Oradour-sur-Glane in France (see page 196), so a police unit from the Waffen-SS were carrying out its revenge on Distomo (left), 105 kilometres north-west of Athens. In overall command of the 4. SS-Polizei-Panzergrenadier-Division was SS-Standartenführer Karl Schümers who already had a reputation for ordering or carrying out mass executions like 277 persons at Kleisoura on April 5 and 368 children at Pyrgoi on April 24. Leading the 2. Kompanie that day was SS-Hauptsturmführer Fritz Lautenbach (right). According to survivors, the SS 'bayoneted babies in their cribs, stabbed pregnant women, and beheaded the village priest'. The Germans reported that they had come under attack by Greek partisans from the direction of Distomo, killing 40 of their men. Lautenbach said that he ordered his troops to execute 12 people they had taken hostage on their way to the village, but at a subsequent military investigation he accepted that he had gone beyond his standing orders having massacred 214 men, women and children.

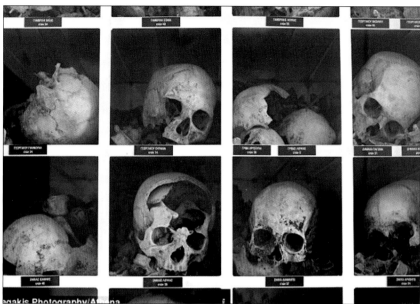

In the autumn of 1942, a decree was issued whereby 'all private estates indispensable for the building of residences for immigrants in the Aegean province are to be expropriated'. The immigrant colonists in this region received credits, land and houses. The colonisation and the granting of land and houses was handled by regional directors in the respective regions and by a central committee for land grants. A deficiency budget of 12 million leva was appropriated by the Sobranje (Parliament) for the construction and repair of dwelling-houses for colonists in the Aegean region.

On October 9, 1942, the Council of Ministers issued a decision establishing the conditions for granting lands and dwelling-houses to Bulgarian officials moving in from Bulgaria, such as the mayors of villages, agents of the police, guards of the fields, janitors, and super-

A Red Cross team arriving from Athens a few days later found bodies still lying around and others dangling from ropes in the street. The dead were later exhumed, their bones now resting in a mausoleum standing on a hill overlooking the village.

visors of breeding stations. According to this decision, lands were not granted to unmarried officials or public servants who did not have families at the place of their employment, nor were they granted to married functionaries whose families were not living at the place of their employment. By thus replacing officials, from higher officials down to janitors, the Bulgarian occupying force intended to achieve an additional goal, namely, to increase the numbers of the Bulgarian population in the occupied areas. The Bulgarian officials were summoned to Thrace with their families, and if they brought their families along, they were entitled to receive land grants and houses.

FINANCE

In accordance with the decision of the Council of Ministers of May 26, 1941, all private persons and firms with domicile and residence in territories occupied by the Bulgarian authorities heretofore belonging to Greece, namely Western Thrace and Eastern Macedonia, were ordered to declare to agencies of the Bulgarian National Bank, or branches of the Bulgarian Agricultural and Co-operative Bank, all drachma in their possession in banknotes of 100 drachma and higher denominations. Declaration of banknotes of less than 100 drachma denomination was not required. The drachma was then declared invalid after June 19, 1941, and the deposits changed

The only reason that the investigation by the Germans took place is that a Geheime Feldpolizei agent, Georg Koch, had been with the troops that day and his report contradicted the one submitted by Lautenbach. Koch revealed that the men had been ambushed several kilometres from Distomo and it was only after the 'bandits' had retreated that the 2. Kompanie retraced **their route back to the village where they killed everyone that they could find. Lautenbach was exonerated in that 'military necessity' justified the use of arms, Schümers asking the court to let him admonish Lautenbach himself. Schümers was killed on August 18 when his vehicle detonated a land mine placed by the resistance but Lautenbach was never tried for the war crime.**

In August 1944, the Bulgarian Fatherland Front began a successful armed rebellion against the government, driving out the German troops by the end of the month. On September 8 Bulgaria formally changed sides and declared war on Germany at which point Soviet forces were welcomed into the country. *Left:* Guerillas parade through the streets of the liberated capital Sofia. *Right:* This is Lege Street today with the imposing building of the Bulgarian National Bank in the background.

into leva. Moreover, the Bulgarian National Bank was entrusted with the collection in leva or drachma of the claims of the Greek Bank and the Greek National Bank against private persons and firms in Western Thrace and Eastern Macedonia.

As to bank deposits dating from the pre-invasion period, the Bulgarian authorities in occupied Greece proceeded in the same way as in that part of Yugoslavia occupied by Bulgaria. The same decision of the Council of Ministers settled the problem of bank deposits in both the Yugoslav and Greek areas under Bulgarian occupation. Accordingly, all accounts existing and all amounts collected by the National Bank of Greece, the Bank of Greece and the Agricultural Bank of Greece were to be centralised in the central account of the Ministry of Finance with the Sofia branch of the Bulgarian National Bank. Payments to depositors of the above-mentioned institutions could be made only to persons of Bulgarian origin who had not emigrated from these regions during 1941. Most of these payments, however, could take place only in instalments. Thus, for amounts up to 2,000 leva, payment was permitted in full, but for amounts above that figure the payments could only be made at the rate of 2,000 leva monthly. By this procedure the Greek population was deprived of all its bank deposits.

RAPHAEL LEMKIN, 1944

This memorial to the partisans stands in a small park in Tran in western Bulgaria, not far from the border with Serbia.

Three years of being occupied by the Axis had led to almost non-stop guerilla activity which was carried out at an horrendous cost in human suffering. Every operation by the partisans resulted in merciless retaliation against the civilian population, which in turn led to counter-reprisals against the occupiers, and so on. Although the Germans (seen here laying a wreath on the tomb of the Unknown Soldier in Athens) had gone by the end of 1944, sadly the fighting was not over as Greece was then in turmoil through power struggles between the rival factions of the resistance. Yet through it all the words of Winston Churchill still rang true: 'Henceforth we will not say that Greeks fight like heroes, but that heroes fight like Greeks'.

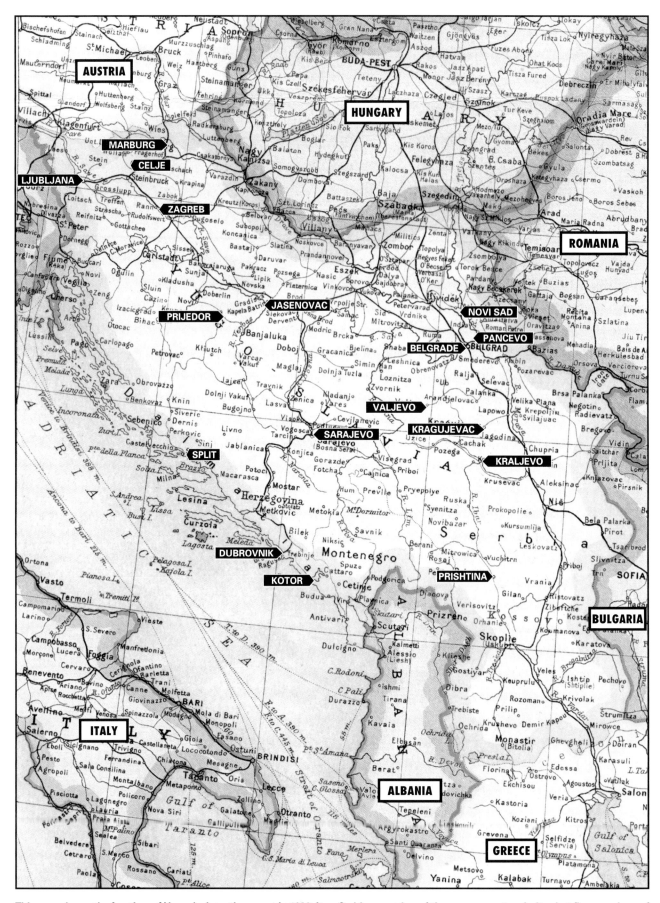

This map shows the frontiers of Yugoslavia as they were in 1938. It had been formed in 1918 following the collapse of the Austro-Hungarian and Ottoman Empires by amalgamating Croatia and Serbia, Bosnia and Herzegovina, Montenegro and Macedonia, an already deeply-divided collection of nationalities. The new country was called the Kingdom of Serbs, Croats and Slovenes. In June 1928 a Serbian member of the government majority shot five members of the Croation Peasant Party, including their leader Stjepan Radic, and, as a result of the political crisis that followed the shooting, on January 6, 1929 King Alexander abolished the constitution and introduced a personal dictatorship. In October that year he changed the official name of the country to the Kingdom of Yugoslavia.

Yugoslavia

Of all the countries occupied by the Axis, Yugoslavia was the most dismembered having been divided into the greatest number of administrative units, its territory being occupied by Germany, Italy, Bulgaria, Hungary and Albania. Parts of its territories were also formed into the new puppet state of Croatia. Even the idea of the pre-Versailles state of Montenegro was revived, although the country was not set up in a definite form.

This dismemberment of Yugoslavia served, not only the immediate political purposes of the occupying powers, but also to disintegrate and divide the political forces in the occupied areas in order to make it difficult in the future to achieve the unification of all the political elements within the framework of one state.

In the process of dismemberment, Germany and Italy took advantage of the fact that the country already had difficult population problems. The inhabitants consisted of three main national groups. Slovenes were living in the north-west, Croats in the central northern part, and Serbs in the east and south. Also smaller groups such as Moslems (in Bosnia-Herzegovina); Macedonians (in the part of Macedonia which was taken in previous wars from Bulgaria and incorporated into the Kingdom of the Serbs, Croats and Slovenes by the Treaty of Neuilly in 1919); Germans living in the so-called Banat and scattered in other parts of Slovenia; Italians scattered over Dalmatia and near Fiume, plus Jews, Albanians and a number of gypsies.

Among these groups there were many differences and conflicts, the relations between the Serbs and Croats being especially hostile. The Croatian grievances were mainly that the Treaty of Versailles created a Kingdom of Serbs, Croats and Slovenes, implying in this name the idea of a three-nation

Just seconds after this picture was taken on October 9, 1934, King Alexander of Yugoslavia (left) was assassinated on a state visit to France. Several cameramen were filming his arrival in Marseilles as he took his place beside the French Foreign Minister Louis Barthou.

state, whereas, according to the Croats, the Serbs had unilaterally endeavoured to create an integrated Yugoslav state under Serbian leadership without granting the Croats equal representation in the government. The Croats referred particularly to the Geneva Agreement of 1918 between them and the Serbs to the effect that the Croats should have equal representation in the government with the Serbs, and they maintained that the terms of this agreement had not been observed by the Serbs. In addition, the Croats asserted that the constitution which had been adopted in 1921 was not patterned along federative lines, and that the Croatian population was not duly represented in the making of this constitution. Furthermore, the fact that the constitution was changed by King Alexander in 1929 by means of a coup d'état augmented the Croatian griev-

ances. And then when the King changed the name of the Kingdom of Serbs, Croats and Slovenes to 'Yugoslavia', the Croats saw in this change of name a new pattern for political homogeneity and a danger to their own national aspirations.

The Croatian political parties at the time differed in their policies. The Peasant Party under Stjepan Radic, and later under Vladko Macek, opposed the centralising tendencies of the Belgrade government, and Radic visited the capitals of the Allies in order to try to win them over to the Croatian cause. When a pro-Serbian radical party, created in Zagreb in 1929, approved the changes in the constitution, the Croats claimed that this party represented only a slight minority of the Croatian population, 95 per cent being organised in the opposition or Peasant Party. Upon Radic's

As the King was being driven from the old port in an open-top car, Vlado Chernozemski, a member of a Macedonian revolutionary organisation that wanted to secede from Yugoslavia, stepped forward with a 7.65mm 'broomhandle' Mauser — then the preferred weapon used by anarchists — and opened fire, killing the King and his driver. Barthou was mortally wounded although he was possibly shot by a French policeman in the confusion. Chernozemski also did not survive as he was cut down by a cavalryman's sword before he was beaten to death by the crowd.

Reportedly, the King's final words were 'Save Yugoslavia and the friendship with France' as back in 1927, as a counter to growing Italian expansionism under Mussolini, Yugoslavia had signed an agreement of friendship with Britain and France. The country had already formed the 'Little Entente' with Czechoslovakia and Romania to prevent Hungary regaining territories she had lost after the First World War, and a 'Balkan Entente' alliance followed with Greece, Romania and Turkey to try to maintain an equilibrium in the Balkans. Then, in September 1940, Germany,

Italy and Japan signed the Tripartite Pact, a defensive military alliance later joined by Hungary (November 20), Romania (November 23), Slovakia (November 24), Bulgaria (March 1, 1941), followed by Yugoslavia on March 25. This provoked a coup d'état in the capital Belgrade whereupon Germany and Italy used it as an excuse to invade Yugoslavia on April 6 with Hungary joining the attack five days later. The military commanders were Walther von Brauchitsch *(left)* for Germany, Vittorio Ambrosio *(centre)* for Italy, and Elemér Gorondy-Novák for Hungary *(right)*.

return to Zagreb after his unsuccessful political mission abroad, he and other members of the Peasant Party made an arrangement with the Serbs for participation in the Parliament. However, in 1928 Radic was shot during one of the sessions of the Parliament by an extremist Serb nationalist deputy.

About the same time, another Croatian party called the 'Ustasa' or Croatian Liberation Movement, was developing its activities along more-radical and more-revolutionary lines. Whereas Radic had endeavoured to win the Allies of 1914-18 for the Croatian cause, the leaders of the Ustasa movement — Ante Pavelic and Dido Kvaternik — collaborated with the countries dissatisfied with the Versailles and Trianon treaties, namely, Germany, Hungary, the Macedonian Irredenta and especially Italy, which had made claims on the Adriatic coast and was pursuing expansionist policies in the Balkans. These countries gave their support to the separatist programme of Ustase. In Italy, Pavelid and Kvaternik were given every support in training Ustase men for future military and terrorist action.

In 1934, King Alexander of Yugoslavia was assassinated in Marseilles by members of the Ustase while on a state visit to France. The gunman was beaten to death by the onlookers.

In 1938, the Croats participated in elections to the Belgrade Skupstina (parliament) but subsequently the Croatians who were elected refused to enter the Parliament, the elections having been used only for the purpose of displaying the political strength of the Croatian Nationalist Party.

The Ustasa leaders, who were collaborating with the Axis Powers, took over the organisation of Croatia as a puppet state when the Axis invaded Yugoslavia. On April 8, 1941, in the course of the invasion, Ante Pavelic, broadcasting from abroad, issued an appeal to the Croats to secede from the Serbs and to support Germany and Italy. The manner in which the Axis proceeded to divide up Yugoslavia is shown in the following sections.

When King Alexander declared his dictatorship in 1929 and banned all political parties, the Croatian politician Ante Pavelic left the country to plot with the Internal Macedonian Revolutionary Organisation against Yugoslavia. As a result, he was tried and sentenced to death in absentia. He then founded Ustasa, a Croatian movement founded on the principles of racialism and intolerance, with the aim of creating an independent Croatia by any means, which included the killing of King Alexander. For this murder, the French also sentenced Pavelic to death in absentia. Following the invasion, the Axis victory was swift with Yugoslav forces surrendering after less than ten days. Pavelic returned to Yugoslavia and took control of a puppet government in Croatia where he created a political system similar to that in Nazi Germany. Here he is pictured on an official visit to Hitler at the Berghof on June 9, 1941. At the meeting Hitler impressed on Pavelic that he needed to maintain a policy of 'national intolerance' for 50 years and to accept Slovenian immigrants while deporting Serbs from the country to Serbia.

THE DIVISION OF SLOVENIA

Slovenia, with a population of about two million Slovenes, was divided between Germany and Italy in accordance with an agreement signed in Berlin on July 8, 1941 by the Italian Ambassador Dino Alfieri and Ernst von Weiszäcker, the German State Secretary for Foreign Affairs. Hungary was also given a few small towns and villages with less than 100,000 inhabitants. Under the agreement between Germany and Italy, Germany annexed approximately three-fourths of Slovenia, an area with a population of about 900,000 inhabitants, these parts being incorporated into Germany as a special district called Südsteiermark and including Lower Styria, parts of Carinthia, and Upper Carniola. Italy annexed the province of Ljubljana, with about 350,000 inhabitants. The Slovenes, being the immediate neighbours of Greater Germany and of Italy (the Slovenes also resided in Trieste and Fiume), were considered by both countries as creating a natural barrier to their expansion in the Balkans. The division of this highly cultured Slavic nation had, especially with respect to German policy, a definite genocide purpose.

Yugoslavia was literally carved up by the Axis so that a country already beset with huge ethnic issues was now subjected to forced transfers, expulsions . . . and worse. Photograph shows a meeting of German and Italian forces on the frontier of the Slovenian district referred to by the Germans as Südsteiermark.

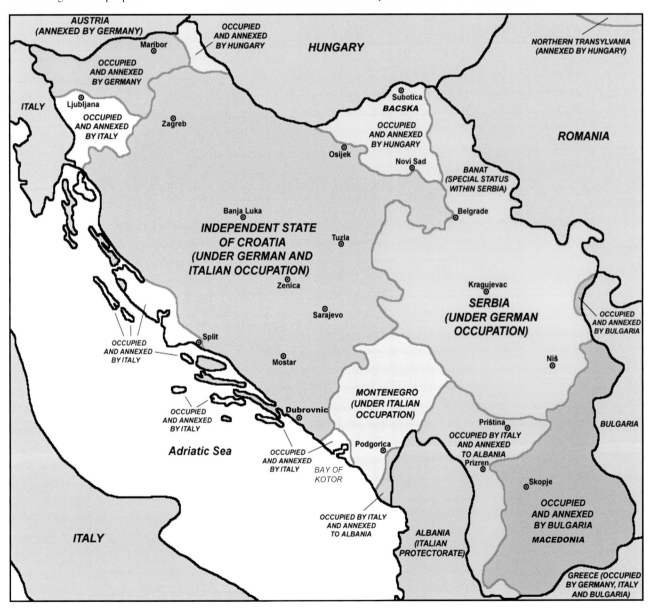

247

Hitler could not wait to visit his latest acquisition. Here he is pictured with Siegfried Uiberreither, the new Chief of the Civil Administration of Lower Styria, inspecting the Old Bridge, also named the State or Drava Bridge, which had been blown on the Drava river at Marburg, the second-major city in Slovenia. German troops had marched in at 9 p.m. on April 8, Hitler arriving on April 26. During the First World War the inhabitants were predominently Austrian with the Slovenian minority being suspected as being enemies of the state, but after the demise of the Austro-Hungarian Empire in 1918, Marburg was claimed by both sides. In 1919 it was recognised as part of the Kingdom of Slovenes, Croats and Serbs at which point most of the Austrian Germans left the country; hence when Hitler arrived he proclaimed that he wanted to 'make this land German again'. Now it was the Slovenes who were expelled or imprisoned, the Nazi goal being to re-Germanise the population.

For expediency, engineers built a timber bridge across the river and it was not until 1998 that the main road bridge was finally rebuilt.

mans Heimholung (Bringing into the Homeland), the Germans claiming that these territories belonged to the German living space. A special bureau (Gaugrenzlandamt) saw to it that the vacated farms, after removal of the Slovenes, were colonised by German peasant families that were politically reliable.

German teachers, together with other administrative personnel, were put in charge of Slovenian schools and introduced teaching methods in harmony with the principles of National Socialism. In their endeavours to destroy all traces of Slovenian culture, the Germans demanded the surrender of Slovenian books, including even prayer books.

The Slovenians had developed an efficient system of financial co-operatives that carried on activities in agriculture and trade. The co-operatives had improved the standard of living for the Slovenians and provided means for the creation of national cultural institutions. Hence the Slovenians cherished them as an instrument of social and national

LOWER STYRIA, CARINTHIA AND CARNIOLA
(German Occupation)

Immediately after the occupation began the Germans proceeded with the destruction of the national Slovenian way of life in the occupied area. The German language was proclaimed as the only official language, and all Slovenian signs on offices and principal buildings were removed and replaced with German signs. The names and surnames of the population were permitted to be used only in the German form, both in speech and in writing. A great number of Slovenes were removed to Croatia and other parts of Yugoslavia in order to make room for German colonists. The latter were recruited from the Reich and from Germans who had been removed to Germany from Romania (Bessarabia and Dobruja), from Italy (Southern Tyrol), and from Italian-occupied Slovenia. The process of colonisation was called by the Ger-

The occupation of Yugoslavia was marked by an horrific loss of life with upwards of a million casualties. Military deaths are estimated at 237,000, partisans and collaborators at 209,000, while 581,000 civilians died including 57,000 Jews. Losses in the various republics are believed to be 316,000 for Bosnia, Serbia 273,000, Croatia 271,000, Slovenia 33,000, Montenegro 27,000, and Macedonia 17,000. The reasons for the high human toll can be explained by the fact that military operations involved the three Axis countries plus the Ustasa organisation and Yugoslav partisans; that Hitler ordered special vengeance against the Serbs whom he considered as 'Untermenschen'; that there were deliberate acts of reprisal and the execution of hostages; and due to the systematic extermination of large numbers of people for political, religious or racial reasons. Himmler visited the Slovenian town of Celje in April 1941 and, apart from Stari Prison being used to torture inmates, the yard was used for six mass executions during which 325 men and 49 women were put to death. This picture was taken on July 22, 1942 when 100 were shot.

progress. However, realising the importance of these co-operatives in strengthening the national spirit, one of the first steps by the Germans was to liquidate them. As early as May 19, 1941, a decree was issued in Lower Styria closing all co-operatives, savings banks and agricultural associations. German banking institutions alone were allowed to function. In fact, only the Creditanstalt-Bankverein A.G. and the Länderbank in Vienna were permitted to open branches in Marburg and Celje. A number of German savings banks were established but these also had a political mission, i.e. the exercise of political discrimination in granting credits and withholding the repayment of deposits. Special political commissioners were entrusted with the business of those institutions.

It was stated in the decree of June 5, 1941 that the repayment of deposits made prior to occupation was dependent upon the orders of the Chief of Civil Administration. When one realises how the Germans handled bank deposits in other countries, especially Poland, one can see in this order that it was an instrument of racial discrimination and political oppression, which meant that the Germans were privileged and the Slovenians underprivileged in receiving their deposits.

Not only the banking system but also the monetary system was Germanised. German currency was introduced by the decree of May 28, 1941, effective as of June 1, 1941 in Lower Styria. As to Carinthia and Carniola, German currency was introduced as legal tender by the decree of May 23, 1941, to become effective on June 1, 1941. The rate of exchange for the dinar was established as one dinar to 0.05 Reichsmark.

Thus it was plain that the Germans were pursuing a policy of genocide in Slovenia being evident not only from the measures taken but also from public statements. The *Stajerski Gospodar*, a German newspaper which was published in the Slovenian language in order to promote the policies of Germanism, stated on April 11, 1942: 'The most-important task has been to prove that the inhabitants of Lower Styria are not Slovenes but Styrian patriots and thus [are] qualified to be an integral part of the Greater German national community and able to graduate as perfect Germans. When in the near future Lower Styrians are serving in the German army, they will be yet one step nearer the supreme ideal of becoming totally German.'

At the end of the war, any German-speakers remaining in the city were expelled. The Yugoslav Department of National Security then set out to eliminate all potential political opposition and it is estimated that the post-war authorities executed upwards of 5,000 in a purge of Croatians, Serbians and Slovenians deemed to have collaborated with the Germans or opposed the Communist regime. In 1965 the old prison at Celje (see the map on page 244) was opened as a memorial site to victims of Nazi violence, although the wall used by the Germans as a back-stop had by then collapsed. It stood on the left of this photo where the prison workshop with the barbed wire now stands. However, it was not until 1991, when Slovenia split from Yugoslavia, that it became possible to discuss openly what had taken place there.

The Italian Armed Forces occupied the south-western part of Slovenia, this column marching across Congress Square in the capital Ljubljana (see the map on page 244). On May 3, 1941, the city was made the capital of the Provincia di Lubiana.

LJUBLJANA
(Italian Occupation)

Of the remaining Slovenian areas, the major part was organised as the province of Ljubljana, while some of the smaller areas in the neighbourhood of the province of Fiume were incorporated directly into that province.

The province of Ljubljana was annexed to Italy by Royal Decree of May 3, 1941. The decree envisaged autonomy for this province and was to take 'into consideration the racial characteristics of the population, the geographical position of the territory, and its special local needs'. The powers of the Italian government were exercised by a High Commissioner appointed by a Royal Decree on the motion of Benito Mussolini, and it was further provided that the High Commissioner should be assisted by a council consisting of 14 representatives chosen from among the 'productive' classes of the Slovenian population. As the decree stated that the annexed territory has a 'uniformly Slovene population', the Slovenian language was made 'obligatory' in the elementary schools, while in secondary and higher education, instruction in Italian was made optional. All official documents had to be printed in both languages. Although a slight freedom was permitted in the cultural field (such as schools and language), in the economic field a system of exploitation was embarked upon. An illustration of this tendency was evident in the decree-law introduced on May 19, 1941 establishing a monopoly for Italian services in this province.

> ### ITALIAN LAWS OF OCCUPATION BEFORE THE DIVISION OF YUGOSLAVIA
>
> **Proclamation by the Duce on Measures concerning the Administration of Justice in the Territories Formerly Forming Part of the Yugoslav State and Occupied by the Italian Armed Forces, April 24, 1941**
>
> The legislation in force in the territories of the former Kingdom of Yugoslavia occupied by the Italian armed forces in matters of civil, commercial, exchange and penal law shall continue in effect, except as may be otherwise established by special regulations issued by the Italian authorities.
>
> MUSSOLINI

As regards the legal system, the original courts were retained essentially unchanged, but appeals from these courts, in so far as they were directed previously to the Court of Appeals of Zagreb (the capital of Croatia), were transferred to the Court of Appeals in Fiume on Italian territory. However, because cases arising in Slovenia required a particular knowledge of local law, a special branch for the appeal of cases from the province of Ljubljana was set up within the Court of Appeals in Fiume.

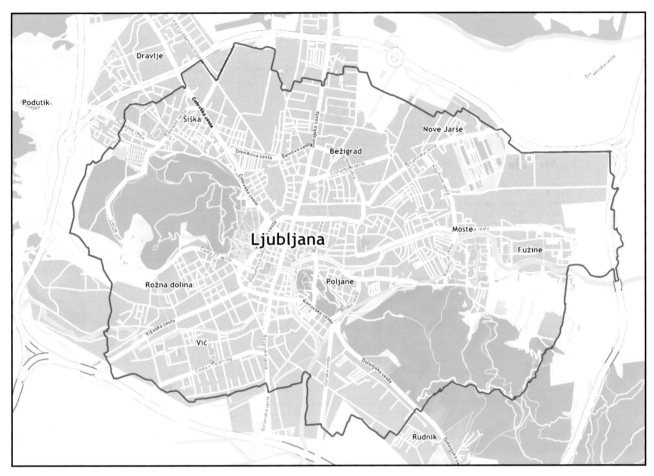

The following year, in a desperate attempt to prevent contact between the resistance movement that operated both inside and outside Ljubljana, the Italians erected a barbed-wire fence, some 30-odd kilometres long, surrounding the city with fortified bunkers at intervals. Each year since 1957, on the weekend closest to May 9, a traditional 'March along the Wire' has been held to mark the liberation of the city, and in 1974 it was decided to formalise this as the 'Trail of Remembrance and Comradeship'. Completed in 1985, the pathway is marked by signposts and information boards with 102 octagonal memorial stones marking the former positions of the bunkers. Alongside the four-metre-wide path, 7,400 trees have been planted for what is now a protected nature monument. Because of the expansion of the city since 1945, some stretches of the path now pass through built-up areas. Those who walk the entire distance of 34 kilometres can collect stamps at eight checkpoints and receive a memorial badge and a medal.

The avenue of birches in the Rudnik district.

Remains of one of the Italian bunkers in Siska.

251

With the Albanian coastline already under Italian control, the harbour at Kotor (see map page 244), further north up the Dalmation coast, was an important prize. Rivalling Dubrovnik and Venice, the large sheltered Bay of Kotor, French at the beginning of the 19th century, passed through the hands of Montenegro before being annexed by the Austrians in 1815. In 1918 it became part of the Kingdom of Slovenes, Croats and Serbs, coming under Italian occupation in April 1941. This Italian motor torpedo boat, pictured shortly after they had taken over, is the *Generali Antonio Cantore,* named after the country's first high-ranking commander to be killed in World War I (when Italy was fighting on the side of the Allies). The vessel hit a mine off Tobruk on August 22, 1942.

DALMATIA
(Italian Occupation)

The territories along the Adriatic known as Dalmatia, as well as most of the Adriatic islands, with the exception of Pag, Brac and Hvar, were annexed by Italy. Dalmatia was organised as a province with the capital in Zadar (Zara). Following the proclamation by Mussolini of July 11, 1941, a governorship for Dalmatia was created with Giuseppe Bastianini, the Italian Under-Secretary of Foreign Affairs, as the first governor, directly responsible to the Duce. Italian currency and various Italian economic laws were gradually introduced into Dalmatia.

On annexation, the former Croat administrative authorities were replaced by Italians. All municipal councils were dismissed and Italian commissioners appointed instead. Croat schools were gradually changed into Italian with Italian teachers imported from Italy. In the political, social and economic field, Fascist institutions were introduced, Italian policy in Dalmatia being based upon the idea of keeping both shores of the Adriatic under control of elements upon which Italy could rely.

A proclamation by the Duce on April 29, 1941 declared that tariffs and customs laws in force at the time of occupation remained unchanged, but that this provision refered only to trade other than that between the occupied territories and the Italo-Albanian Customs Union. No customs duties were levied on goods originating in, and shipped from the area of, the Italo-Albanian Union into the occupied territories, or on goods shipped from those territories into the area of the Italo-Albanian Union, or into the free zones of Carnaro and Zara.

On May 18, 1941, Italy formally annexed large parts of Dalmatia of which Split was a strategic asset. However the Italians met heavy opposition from the Croat population and the city became the centre of anti-fascist activity in Yugoslavia. Ten Italian officials were soon assassinated.

Split has now become known as one of Europe's top holiday destinations.

On April 6 the marines of the San Marco Regiment of the Italian Navy landed at Zara, the capital of Dalmatia, and practically captured the entire Yugoslav navy. Five days later the San Marco Marines captured Croatia's largest island, Krk. Parts of Dalmatia were annexed by Italy as the Governatorate di Dalmatia, the local population thereafter being subjected to forced italianisation by the fascist authorities. Then in September Mussolini ordered the military occupation of the entire Dalmatian coast, including Dubrovnik. His plans were initially opposed by Ante Pavelic of the adjoining Independent State of Croatia but its islands of Pago, Brazza and Lesino were still occupied by the Italian army. The province of Zara remained Italian right up until 1945, even after the armistice in September 1943 when the Germans took over all the territory formally occupied by Italy. These Italian troops were pictured marching along Stradun in Dubrovnik.

Left: On June 19, 1941, the fascist politician Serafino Mazzolini was appointed the civil High Commissioner for Montenegro, and on July 25 Mussolini gave Generale Alessandro Pirzio Biroli *(right)*, the Commander of the Italian Ninth Army, military powers. At first the Italians had intended that Montenegro would become an independent state, closely allied to Italy, but forced transfers of the population quickly led to grievances which were seized upon by the communists. On July 13 a general uprising broke out, triggered by a proclamation the previous day concerning the restoration of the Kingdom of Montenegro to be headed by an Italian regent. The rebels seized control of several towns and villages. The extent of the fighting worried the Italians and Generale Biroli directed his forces to crush the revolt. Dozens of villages were burned down, hundreds killed and thousands interned, but within six weeks the Italians had regained control. In December Mazzolini's position was abolished and Biroli appointed Governor with responsibility for both civil and military matters.

MONTENEGRO
(Italian Occupation)

Montenegro, or Crna Gora, which existed as a separate state before and during the First World War, was absorbed by Yugoslavia (then known as the Kingdom of the Serbs, Croats and Slovenes) after 1918. When the Italian forces occupied Montenegro, it was planned that this area should receive special treatment, involving not only military aspects but diplomatic aspects as well which became obvious when Mussolini issued a proclamation appointing a High Commissioner for the territory. The commissioner, in his exercise of civilian authority, was to communicate directly with the Italian Minister of Foreign Affairs. Two underlying factors no doubt had a bearing on these arrangements. On the one hand, there had existed traditionally well-established relations between King Nicholas of Montenegro and the Royal House of Savoy because Victor Emmanuel III had married the daughter of Nicholas; and, on the other hand, the fact that Montenegro had been abolished as a state and absorbed into the Kingdom of Yugoslavia was sufficient to cause the Italians to treat it in a more favourable way.

For these reasons, there was a certain hesitancy in the policy of the Italians towards Montenegro. At the beginning the tendency was not to apply to Montenegro the basic Italian decree on military occupation of May 17, 1941. In particular, the decree of July 26, 1941 provided that the Supreme Command could, for the territory of Montenegro, refrain from establishing a civil

Resistance against foreign occupation soon sprang up in the form of two guerrilla movements. *Left:* One was the Chetniks, the Royalist and mostly Serbian guerrillas under Colonel Draza Mihailovic (seen wearing the glasses conferring with his men), an officer of the pre-war Yugoslav army. *Right:* The other was the communist and pan-Slavic 'partisans' under their charismatic leader Josip Broz-Tito, the secretary-general of the Yugoslav Communist Party. The two movements had completely different strategies and aims. Mihailovic's approach was to mostly abide his time in the mountains to await an Allied invasion after which his troops would come out to restore the Serb monarchy. Tito's strategy was to strike at the Germans whenever and wherever he could, regardless of the risks or the inevitable reprisals, and, once victorious, to create a Communist-led people's republic of Yugoslavia. The political divergence quickly led to internal strife. The Chetniks, who had initially been fighting the Germans, soon changed their focus to destroying the communist partisans and the struggle quickly devolved into a state of civil war. In their fervour to annihilate the Partisans, the Chetniks even engaged in secret or open collaboration with the Germans and Italians and with the Croat Ustase. Once the nationalists in Montenegro heard about the split between the Chetniks and the Partisans, it gave them increased impetus to collaborate with the Italian occupation forces.

commissioner as provided for in other territories. However, a later decree of October 3, 1941 created a governorship for Montenegro, the Governor being empowered to establish a civil commissariat headed by a civil commissioner. Thus the organisation of Montenegro in the terms of the latter decree meant that the Governor reported on political, civil and administrative matters to the Minister of Foreign Affairs (which indicated that Montenegro represented special political aspects). The handling of these matters was entrusted to the civil commissioner who reported to the Governor in Cetinje. Concerning military matters, the Governor communicated directly with the Supreme Command.

By a proclamation of October 6, 1941, Italian legal tender was introduced and dinars were exchanged by a special committee at the rate of 38 lire for 100 dinars.

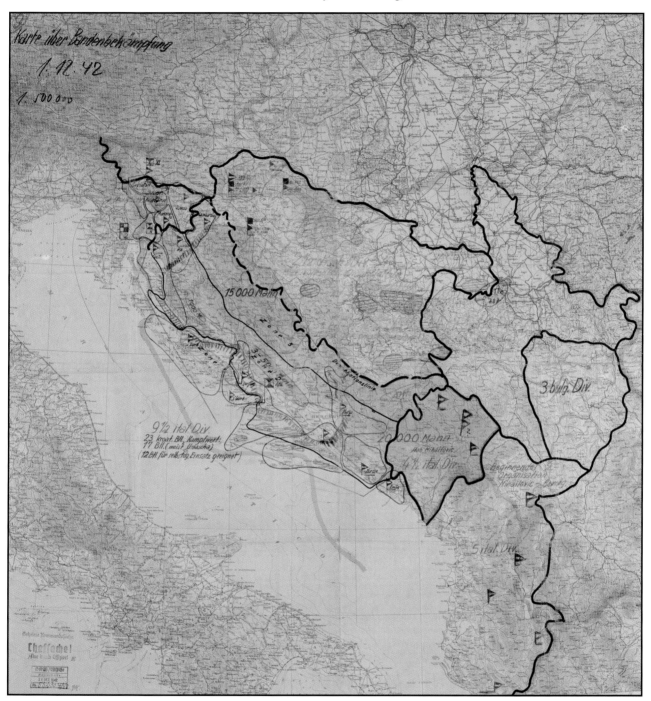

The Western Allies, notably Britain, initially supported Mihailovic, sending in weapons, supplies and money to the Chetniks. However, after agents of the Special Operations Executive (SOE) parachuted into Yugoslavia reported in early 1943 that Tito's partisans were doing most of the fighting against the Germans, Britain changed sides and the bulk of the support thereafter went to the communists. Between 1941 and 1944 the Axis armies launched six big offensives aimed at encircling and destroying the growing partisan army. However, each time Tito, his staff and large bodies of partisans managed to escape from every trap and all efforts to annihilate them came to nothing. On the contrary, when Italy capitulated in September 1943, the partisans captured huge amounts of arms and equipment from the Italian divisions stranded in Yugoslavia, enabling them to set up several new divisions of what was by then known as the National Liberation Army of Yugoslavia. By the spring of 1944 the NLA had grown to more than 300,000 men, organised in 11 army corps with 39 divisions and several independent brigades. While the German forces held the towns and cities with strong garrisons and guarded the major roads and railways, the partisans were masters of large tracts of the rugged and mountainous countryside, which in effect could be seen as 'liberated territory'. The Germans regularly produced maps like this one dated December 1, 1942 to record their progress — or lack of it — in dealing with the huge problem of partisan activity in Yugoslavia.

The Axis forces enacted brutal reprisals, public hangings being deemed a deterrent. Here two Serbian partisans hang from gallows in the main square in Kraljevo.

SERBIA
(German Occupation)

As a result of the process of disintegration, Serbia was left with 4,500,000 inhabitants — 28 per cent of the population of the original Kingdom of Yugoslavia — and was subjected to German military occupation. In this German-controlled territory, a Serbian puppet government was established under General Milan Nedic who acted through his ministers (called commissarial directors) and the local Serbian authorities.

The German administration was in the hands of a German military commander and local military commanders. The German military commander supervised the Serbian Government and local authorities, with the German occupation authorities legislating extensively, aiming at the complete political, economic and social subordination of Serbia. The Serbian puppet government also issued orders and decrees.

Law

As the territory was never completely subdued as the army of General Draza Mihailovic continued to fight as partisans, the Germans attempted to meet this resistance by the creation of a semi-legal system of terror, and German military courts with vast powers were introduced. In one of the first decrees promulgated by the German Commander-in-Chief of the Army in the *Verordnungsblatt* (the official gazette) for the occupied Yugoslav territories, it was stated: 'Any person who commits an act punishable according to German law and is brought to trial before courts of the armed forces, shall be subject to German criminal law'. Thus a foreign legal code of the greatest complexity was introduced in the first days of occupation, and it took effect immediately without giving the

Time marches on but the memory of what once took place on this spot remains.

256

on the occupant force for a determination of the consequences of their actions. The Hague Regulations (see page 261) endeavoured to create a rule of law to be applied in occupied territories but instead the Germans established legal channels as an instrument of administrative coercion. This was a flagrant violation of both the letter and spirit of the Hague Regulations.

Property

An order concerning the confiscation of property for activities hostile to the state, dated December 22, 1941, gave the chief of the administrative staff of the German military commander in Serbia the right to 'decide by order, without formal judicial procedure: (a) on the penalty of confiscation, (b) on the use to be made of the property thus confiscated'. Not only was the property of the defendant liable to confiscation but also the property of the members of his family, a procedure that punished persons without establishing their individual guilt.

Anti-Guerrilla Legislation

Anti-guerrilla legislation was introduced to cope with the partisans and with the Chetniks of General Draza Mihailovic. As the guerrillas used cornfields extensively as hiding places, the German military commander issued an order on October 9,1941 for the early harvesting of the corn. Not only the persons in possession of the cornfields and their owners but also the mayors having jurisdiction in the respective localities were made responsible for the early harvesting of the crops. Non-compliance with this order was punishable by death or, under extenuating circumstances, by hard labour.

Genocide Legislation

As in other occupied countries, legislation regarding racial discrimination was introduced. The fate of the Jews was shared in Yugoslavia by the gypsies, both being excluded from practising professions. The liquidation of the Jews

Putting villages to the torch or executing people by firing-squad were everyday occurences. The precise locations for these two photographs — one German and one Italian — are not given.

population any opportunity to become acquainted with it. In this connection, one must distinguish between the promulgation of a particular order issued in the language of the local population, and a reference made in a specific order to the legal code of the home country of the occupying force which is unknown to the population of the occupied country. Whereas in the first case it is possible for the population to become acquainted with the law and act accordingly, in the second case the population has no opportunity to obtain exact knowledge of what is right and what is wrong under the code.

Moreover, the above-mentioned order also gave the German courts jurisdiction to impose punishment for acts committed before the German occupation, prosecution of such offences to be 'at the discretion of the prosecuting authorities'. Thus the occupant created a state of legal uncertainty and constant fear among the local inhabitants now completely dependent

In response to an attack on the 6. Kompanie of Landesschützen-Bataillon 920 by Chetnik resistance fighters in the town of Gorni Milanovac on September 28, 1941, the Wehrmacht commander in Serbia at the time, General Franz Böhme *(left)*, sent German troops to the area to carry out reprisal actions. Böhme boasted a profound hatred of Serbs and encouraged his predominantly Austrian-born troops to exact 'vengeance' against them. His primary grievances were the assassination of Archduke Franz Ferdinand and subsequent Austro-Hungarian military defeats at the hands of the Royal Serbian Army that he thought could only be rectified by the reprisal shooting of Serbian civilians. 'Your objective', Böhme declared, 'is to be achieved in a land where, in 1914, streams of German blood flowed because of the treachery of the Serbs, men and women. You are the avengers of those dead. One of the participating units was the I. Bataillon of Infanterie-Regiment 724, under the command of Major Paul König. Stationed temporarily in the town of Kragujevac, 150 kilometres south of Belgrade (see map on page 244), König ordered a 'comprehensive reprisal' for the loss of ten German dead and 26 wounded. On October 19 several villages in the vicinity of Groznice were burned to the ground and 422 people were shot. The following day operations continued in Kraguje-vac as German soldiers collected 2,300 men and boys for execution *(right)*. The Serbs were held overnight on a public plaza and shot just outside of the town on October 21 by the I. Bataillon of Infantrie-Regiment 724. Böhme went on to other appointments in Austria, then back to the Balkans, before ending the war as the C-in-C Norway. Following his capture, he was charged with war crimes in Serbia where he killed 50 for every German wounded and a 100 for every German killed. On May 29, 1947, when extradition to Yugoslavia was imminent, he committed suicide.

— an essential element of German policy — was of primary importance in Serbia. Accordingly, the Serbs were forbidden to help Jews by an order of December 22, 1941 that provided the death penalty for sheltering or hiding Jews or for accepting from them objects of value of any description, such as furniture and money, or even for purchasing such objects from them. Jewish accounts in the banks were also blocked.

Finance

By the decree of May 29, 1941, the military commander in Serbia ordered the liquidation of the National Bank of the Kingdom of Yugoslavia, and the German Plenipotentiary for Economic Affairs in Serbia was entrusted with the execution of this liquidation decree. Two days later a decree was published establishing a new Serbian National Bank with an initial capital of 100 million Serbian dinars, divided into 10,000 shares of 10,000 Serbian dinars each. It was stated in this decree that the shares should be paid up at least 50 per cent at the time of subscription. As in other banks of issue created under German occupation, it was provided in this decree that the clearing debts in favour of Serbia should serve also as one of the cover items for the new issue. The creation of huge clearing debts through the over-importation from occupied countries was one of the exploitation devices of the Germans.

The German Plenipotentiary for Economic Affairs was given a decisive role in the organisation of the new bank. He was to appoint the Governor of the bank and his deputies, as well a governing board consisting of ten persons. The German commissioner appointed by the economic plenipotentiary was attached to the administration.

The new currency, called the Serbian dinar, was divided into 100 para. In addition the bank was permitted to issue a subsidiary currency in the form of coins not exceeding 20 Serbian dinars. It was stated that the total amount of the subsidiary currency must not exceed 250 dinars per head of the population.

A national holiday is held each year at Kragujevac on October 21 to remember the dead.

Stjepan Filipovic was born in Opuzen, then in Austria-Hungary but today in Croatia. In 1937, Filipovic joined the local workers' movement in Kragujevac and was arrested and sentenced to a year in prison. In 1940 he joined the Communist Party of Yugoslavia and was in the city of Valjevo, 75 kilometres south-west of Belgrade, when the Nazi invasion took place. He joined the Kolubara troops of the Valjevo partisan detachment in July which led to his appointment as a commanding officer of a Tam-navsko-Kolubarski unit, but on December 24 the Chetniks captured him and handed him over to the Gestapo in Belgrade. After being interrogated over several weeks he still refused to co-oper-ate (his file being marked 'Impossible case') and he was returned to Valjevo to be executed on the gallows in the main square. On May 22, 1942, Filipovic was dragged through the streets to the central square, while all the time he was shouting vigorously: 'Long live the liberators of the people! Down with the Fascists and the quisling collaborators! Long live communism!' *Left:* While standing on the scaffold and with the noose around his head, he held his arms high and delivered his final words to the surrounding crowd: 'What are you waiting for? Why are you allowing this? Grab those rusty rifles and free your country from this scum! Long live our liberating army and our allies!'

The photo of Filipovic was taken by 17-year-old girl, Slobodanka Vasić, who worked in a photographic studio in Valjevo. The pic-ture of Filipovic with his hands held high sparked a lot of interest among locals who visited the studio to buy copies but as the Ger-man HQ was located across the street, the activity at the Foto Kosare shop led them to raid the studio and seize all the photos. Slobodanka spent two weeks in prison where she was interro-gated on whose order she was taking those photos and whether was she working with the partisans. However, one copy found its way to Branko Kesler, the local doctor, who worked for the parti-san resistance. The Nazis trusted him and one officer decided to show Kesler the confiscated photos. Taking advantage of the opportunity, Kesler surreptitiously dropped one and with the tip of his foot pushed it under the rug. Through this photo, Stjepan Filipovic became the Yugoslav symbol of anti-Fascism and of the fight for freedom. The post-war regime adopted it to commemo-rate both his victory and also the communist victory in the revo-lution. *Right:* A huge statue — the 'Monument to the Fighters of the Revolution' — was erected on the site of an old cemetery on a hill overlooking the town. Floodlit at night, it dominates Valjevo. (A second statue erected in Filipovic's home town of Opuzen in Croatia was demolished in the civil war of the 1990s.)

Hanging from the same gallows are Steven Borota and Yossipe Mayer, two Serbian partisans executed by Croatian collaborators.

A stone slab marks the exact spot where the scaffold stood on the transformed square, an obelisk being added in 1976.

THE BANAT
(German Occupation)

A part of the Danube Province with a considerable German population, many who were descendants of those who had come as immigrants from the Rhine provinces, from Bavaria and from Alsace under Maria Theresa, was organised by the Germans as a separate administrative unit called the Banat. As the Banat formed only a part of the territory of the Danube Province, it was headed by a Vice-Governor, with the title of Vize-Banus ('Banus' being the title of the Governor). The office of the Vice-Governor was formally subordinated to the Ministry of the Interior within the puppet government in Belgrade.

The Banat was divided into the following administrative districts: Pancevo, Vrsac, Bela Crkva, Kovin, Jasa Tomic, Veliki Beckerek, Velika Kikinda, Novi Becej, Nova Kanjiza, Kovacica and Alibunar, as well as the city of Pancevo. The higher officials in the Banat were appointed by the puppet government in Belgrade on the recommendation of the Vice-Governor.

The administration of the Banat was mainly in the hands of local Germans, from the Vice-Governor down to the lower officials. The requirements of the existing Civil Service Code were lowered in order to enable great numbers of local Germans to procure civil service appointments. Judges and notaries public were also German.

The administration of posts, railways and finance was also in the hands of local Germans. Taxes and revenues in the territory of the Banat went to the central Treasury in Serbia, but the revenues from provincial taxes and duties were used for the needs of the provin-

The Banat region of Serbia (see the map on page 247) began life back in October 1918 when there were five ethnic groups occupying the region: Romanian, Hungarian, German, Jewish and Serb. An autonomous republic was proclaimed but although Hungary recognised its independence, Romania did not. In the end the region was divided primarily between Romania and the Kingdom of Serbs, Croats and Slovenes. In November 1941, it was reported in the publication *Free Europe* that Hitler intended to create a Donaustaat (Danube State) in which he would settle German minorities living in Hungary, Romania and Croatia. The whole of the Banat, including the Romanian part, would then become a kind of Balkan East Prussia. On March 1, 1942, a new mountain division — the Freiwilligen-Gebirgs-Division — was formed from those Volksdeutsche residing in the Banat region. Over 20,000 of these ethnic Germans from Serbia joined the unit which was later renamed the 7. SS-Freiwilligen-Gebirgs-Division 'Prinz Eugen'. Its task was specifically to fight the Partisans.

cial administration. As the major part of the population of the Banat was Serbian, both German and Serbian were the official languages.

The division operated under the V. SS-Freiwilligen-Gebirgs-Korps whose commander was SS-Obergruppenführer Friedrich-Wilhelm Krüger (left). He already had a career of brutal killings and atrocities as Himmler's Higher SS and Police Leader in the General Government area of Poland (see page 84). He committed suicide in 1945.

ANNEX TO THE CONVENTION RESPECTING THE LAWS AND CUSTOMS OF WAR ON LAND

Section III.— Military Authority over the Territory of the Hostile State.

ARTICLE 42

Territory is considered occupied when it is actually placed under the authority of the hostile army. The occupation extends only to the territory where such authority has been established and can be exercised.

ARTICLE 43

The authority of the legitimate power having in fact passed into the hands of the occupant, the latter shall take all the measures in his power to restore, and ensure, as far as possible, public order and safety, while respecting, unless absolutely prevented, the laws in force in the country.

ARTICLE 44

A belligerent is forbidden to force the inhabitants of territory occupied by it to furnish information about the army of the other belligerent, or about its means of defence.

ARTICLE 45

It is forbidden to compel the inhabitants of occupied territory to swear allegiance to the hostile Power.

ARTICLE 46

Family honour and rights, the lives of persons, and private property, as well as religious convictions and practice, must be respected. Private property cannot be confiscated.

ARTICLE 47

Pillage is formally forbidden.

ARTICLE 48

If, in the territory occupied, the occupant collects the taxes, dues, and tolls imposed for the benefit of the State, he shall do so, as far as is possible, in accordance with the rules of assessment and incidence in force, and shall in consequence be bound to defray the expenses of the administration of the occupied territory to the same extent as the legitimate Government was so bound.

ARTICLE 49

If, in addition to the taxes mentioned in the above Article, the occupant levies other money contributions in the occupied territory, this shall only be for the needs of the army or of the administration of the territory in question.

ARTICLE 50

No general penalty, pecuniary or otherwise, shall be inflicted upon the population on account of the acts of individuals for which they cannot be regarded as jointly and severally responsible.

ARTICLE 51

No contribution shall be collected except under a written order, and on the responsibility of a Commander-in-Chief. The collection of the said contribution shall only be effected as far as possible in accordance with the rules of assessment and incidence of the taxes in force. For every contribution a receipt shall be given to the contributors.

ARTICLE 52

Requisitions in kind and services shall not be demanded from municipalities or inhabitants except for the needs of the army of occupation. They shall be in proportion to the resources of the country, and of such a nature as not to involve the inhabitants in the obligation of taking part in military operations against their own country. Such requisitions and services shall only be demanded on the authority of the commander in the locality occupied. Contributions in kind shall as far as possible be paid for in cash; if not, a receipt shall be given and the payment of the amount due shall be made as soon as possible.

ARTICLE 53

An army of occupation can only take possession of cash, funds, and realisable securities which are strictly the property of the State, depots of arms, means of transport, stores and supplies, and, generally, all movable property belonging to the State which may be used for military operations.

All appliances, whether on land, at sea, or in the air, adapted for the transmission of news, or for the transport of persons or things, exclusive of cases governed by naval law, depots of arms, and, generally, all kinds of ammunition of war, may be seized, even if they belong to private individuals, but must be restored and compensation fixed when peace is made.

ARTICLE 54

Submarine cables connecting an occupied territory with a neutral territory shall not be seized or destroyed except in the case of absolute necessity. They must likewise be restored and compensation fixed when peace is made.

ARTICLE 55

The occupying State shall be regarded only as administrator and usufructuary of public buildings, real estate, forests, and agricultural estates belonging to the hostile State, and situated in the occupied country. It must safeguard the capital of these properties, and administer them in accordance with the rules of usufruct.

ARTICLE 56

The property of municipalities, that of institutions dedicated to religion, charity and education, the arts and sciences, even when State property, shall be treated as private property. All seizure of, destruction or wilful damage done to institutions of this character, historic monuments, works of art and science, is forbidden, and should be made the subject of legal proceedings.

Although The Hague Regulations signed by all the belligerants in 1907 covering the 'Rules of War' did not specifically outlaw the taking and execution of civilian hostages, Article 47 banned pillage and Article 50 clearly stated that no penalty should be given to an individual for an act for which he or she was not responsible. The widespread policy adopted by the Axis forces in the Second World War towards the taking of hostages, officially approved by Feldmarschall Wilhelm Keitel in September 1941, resulted in the deaths of tens of thousands. This led to the establishment of the International Convention against the taking of hostages adopted by the United Nations in December 1979, it being somewhat ironical that it was first proposed by West Germany which stated that hostage-taking for any purpose was 'abhorrent and inhuman', and 'absolutely intolerable and incompatible with universally accepted standards of human conduct'.

In this photo a soldier from the mountain troops is kicking a man to death during the 'cleansing' of the Macva region. Third from the left is a Ustasa officer.

On April 22, 1941, German Wehrmacht photographer Gerhard Gronefeld attended what he regarded as the 'most terrible scene which I ever photographed'. This was the mass hanging and shooting of Serbian civilians by the German army in Pancevo, the capital of Banat 20 kilometres north-east of Belgrade (see the map on page 244). Thirty-six Serbian civilians were rounded up at random and executed by German occupation forces, the Grossdeutschland Regiment under Oberstleutnant Wilhelm-Hunert von Stockhausen, in revenge for the killing of two SS officers by Serbian partisans.

Gerhard Gronefeld (left) began working in 1935 for Heinrich Hoffmann who was the official photographer of the Nazi Party. During the war, he was assigned to a propaganda company and was a war photographer and correspondent in Belgium, France, Poland, the Soviet Union, Yugoslavia, Serbia and the Balkans. Gronefeld rode on German patrol boats off the coast of England, photographed triumphant German troops after they marched into Paris, and accompanied Wehrmacht units as they invaded the Soviet Union. His wartime pictures appeared in German publications to illustrate army victories. Using a Carl Zeiss Ikon Contax camera, he documented not only the events of the war, but also Wehrmacht retaliatory measures against civilians, hostages and guerrillas, which is how he came to be present at the executions of Serbian civilians in Pancevo. Gronefeld regarded the photos that he took as the most important of his career, and the ones that had the most impact on him personally. In an interview three years before his death, he revealed that his memory of the pleading eyes of the Serb victims — 35 men and one woman — 'those eyes will always pursue me . . . they will never give me peace'.

In March 1997, 11 of his photographs of the reprisal massacre in Pancevo were part of a travelling exhibit documenting atrocities committed in the Balkans and the Soviet Union by Germany's regular armed forces. The exhibit caused a furore during its stop in Munich when the governing party of Bavaria called it an insult to the Wehrmacht, and about 5,000 neo-Nazis marched through the city to protest. The exhibit was intended to confront Germans with a fact many would rather not admit: that ordinary soldiers, not just special units like the Nazi SS, killed Jews and other civilians. The German army destroyed most of the evidence of its involvement in the Holocaust and other atrocities. Suspecting that his photos of the killings would likely be destroyed, Gronefeld never turned them over to his superiors, nor was he asked for the photos. Gronefeld says he kept the pictures because he wanted to someday tell the world what happened at Pancevo.

The executions were also filmed in colour by Gottfried Kessel of the propaganda company belonging to the Infanterie-Regiment 'Grossdeutschland'. He filmed the executions and hangings as well as the funerals of the SS soldiers killed earlier. Gronefeld said the execution at Pancevo was the only atrocity he witnessed. He photographed the civilians being taken to the cemetery, where they were made to stand on chairs while nooses were placed over their heads. The chairs on which they stood were then kicked away. 'In their eyes before they died, I saw their last appeal for mercy', Gronefeld recalled. After 18 died on the gallows, the remainder were taken outside to be lined up against the cemetery wall and executed by firing-squad. Gronefeld also pictured a soldier who drew his pistol and finished off a wounded victim. 'They were completely innocent of any wrongdoing', he said.

A memorial plaque has since been mounted on the cemetery wall.

Of all the assassinations that have taken place since Julius Caesar was struck down in Rome in March 44 BC *(left)*, none have

surpassed the worldwide repercussions that followed the death of the Archduke Franz Ferdinand in Bosnia in June 1914 *(right)*.

Left: Amazingly it was only in October 2016 that it was announced that archaeologists had pinpointed the exact spot where Caesar had been stabbed to death. A team from the Spanish National Research Council reported that they had found a structure that had been erected by Augustus, Caesar's adopted son and successor, over the place where the attack took place on the steps of the Theatre of Pompey sometimes used for meetings of the Senate, now the Torre Argentina excavation site.

Right: Bosnia-Herzegovina with Slovenia and Croatia were then part of the Habsburg Empire having been occupied by the Austrians since 1876. This fermented discontent with the Serbians who felt betrayed by losing territory they believed was theirs by right. A young Bosnian Serb, Gavrilo Princip, carried out the murder of the Archduke, who was heir to the Austro-Hungarian throne, during an official visit to the Bosnian capital Sarajevo. *Right:* This was Princip's view as he fired at the car. (For more on the assassination, see *After the Battle* 164.)

After the invasion, Bosnia and Herzegovina were absorbed into Croatia. Pictured on one of the bridges spanning the River Drina in April/May 1942 are (L-R) Dido Kvaternik, Jure Francetic and Mladen Lorkovic. Kvaternik was a Croatian Ustasa lieutenant-general and chief of the Internal Security Service. He instituted a reign of terror against Croatian Serbs, Jews and gypsies and other enemies of the state but fell out of favour with Ante Pavelic, the Croatian dictator in 1943. He fled to Argentina where he died in a car crash in 1962. Francetic was the Ustasa Commissioner for the Bosnia and Herzegovina regions and also the commander of the 1st Ustasa Regiment of the Ustasa militia. As a member of Pavelic's inner circle he was considered as a possible successor but died of wounds suffered when captured by Partisans in December 1942. Another close associate was Lorkovic who served as the Croatian Foreign Minister and Minister of the Interior. In 1944 he was suspected with others of a conspiracy to change sides and was executed in April 1945.

THE STATE OF CROATIA

When German troops entered Zagreb three days after the broadcast by Ante Pavelic on April 8, 1941 (see page 246). Dido Kvaternik proclaimed Croatia as a free and independent state. This state had a population of around six and a half million, including about two million Serbs.

Establishment of the State

On April 11, 1941, Kvaternik, as Deputy Chief of State, ordered that until the government of the State of Croatia had been established, its administrative affairs would be 'discharged by the divisional offices of the Provincial Government of Croatia'. In the meantime, Pavelic arrived in Zagreb and, after issuing a proclamation as chief of the new state

(Poglavnik), he established the first Croatian government by decree of April 16, 1941. This government consisted of Pavelic as presiding minister and at the same time Minister of Foreign Affairs; of a Vice-President, a Commander of the Armed Forces, and Minister of Defence (Kvaternik, who was also appointed Deputy Chief of State). In the same decree, offices were created for Ministers of Justice, of the Interior, of Public Health, of National Economy, of Religion and Education, of Forestry and Mines, and of Corporations. In addition, the decree established a Legislative Committee with a president appointed by Pavelic.

International Relations

On April 15, Germany and Italy granted recognition to Croatia. The

Croatian State was subsequently recognised by Hungary and Slovakia (April 16), Bulgaria (April 22), Romania (May 7), and Japan (June 7).

On May 18, 1941, three agreements were signed in Rome by Italy and Croatia: a treaty fixing the frontiers between Croatia and Italy; a military agreement, and a treaty of guaranty and collaboration that was to last 25 years. By the terms of the latter, Italy guaranteed the political independence and territorial integrity of Croatia, while in order to safeguard the 'protective' rights of Italy, Croatia accepted that it was not to contract any obligations incompatible with such guaranties. The treaty also stressed the aim of both parties to enter into fuller and closer relationship in customs and currency affairs, and provided for future

Head of the military in Croatia was Kvaternik's father, Slavko, seen here on parade in front of the Strossmayer

Gallery, opened in 1880 in Zrinevac Park, Zagreb, the capital of Croatia.

Then . . . then . . . and now! *Left:* Back in 1914, just before he was killed, the Archduke attended a reception in the Sarajevo Town Hall, taken over by the Germans in 1941 *(right)* for their headquarters.

agreements on other matters of mutual interest. It would seem, however, that the military clauses, taken in conjunction with the military agreement of the same date, were actually the provisions of a determining character in the treaty; in fact the intent of those provisions was to put the 'independent' Croatian State in a position of complete military dependence on Italy. In Article 3 of the treaty, the Croatian Government declared that it would use Italians in the organisation and instruction of its armed forces as well as in the establishment of the military defences of the country. The military agreement provided that the Dalmatian shore and islands of the Croatian State were not to be fortified (Article 1), which meant that, in military matters, Italy was to have a free hand in relation to Croatia. This presumption was strengthened by the provision in the agreement that Croatia was not to have a navy (except for specialised units necessary for police and customs services), and that Italy should have the right of military transit across Croatian territory.

Following the signing of the treaties on May 18, King Victor Emmanuel III, at the request of Pavelic, designated his nephew, Aimone Savoy-Aosta, Duke of Spoleto, to be King of Croatia, and in Rome the latter was proclaimed King in the presence of Pavelic and a hundred Croat delegates. However, he never actually assumed his functions.

Council of State

The Council of State was created as a substitute for parliament. The decree on its establishment, dated January 24, 1942, was based upon two premises:

(1) That although the Croatian State was dissolved centuries ago, the national traditions had lasted throughout the centuries and there was a historical constitutional law which afforded a basis for the present constitution of the Independent State of Croatia.

(2) That not only the Ustase movement but also other political groups and persons which were active in the cause of Croatian independence were responsible for the activities of the Council of State.

Apparently the rulers of Croatia wished to be able to present evidence in the future that the creators of independant Croatia were acting not on a narrow but on a broader national level, particularly in the formation of the first Council of State. In this broader basis of the Croatian Council of State, it was deemed necessary to include surviving Croat representatives of the last Croatian Diet of 1918; surviving Croat representatives of the Skupstina (parliament in Belgrade) elected in 1938; the

founders and life members of the Central Committee of the former Croatian Agrarian Party, and members of the council of the former Party for the Acquisition of Rights for the Croats, elected in 1919.

Because of Axis affiliations, representatives of the German national minority were accorded the right to send their representatives to the first Council of State. According to Section 5 of the decree, members of the Council of State enjoyed rights of immunity. By including this provision, it endeavoured to create the impression that the Council of State was a parliament in the strict sense of the word. (The president of the Supreme Court was charged with the execution of the decree in Section 7.)

The impressive building in a psuedo-Moorish style was completed in 1896 and was known as the Vijecnica. It served as the Town Hall until 1949 when it was handed over to the University Library of Bosnia and Herzegovina. During the siege of Sarajevo, on the night of August 25/26, 1992, Bosnian-Serb artillery shells set it on fire, completely destroying the library. The repair took over 20 years with contributions towards the restoration coming from around the world.

Monoparty System

The main political feature of the new state was the monoparty system and the exclusion of all other parties. The only party entitled to represent the political idea of Croatia was the Ustase Party that proclaimed the independence of Croatia by revolutionary means. It was a radical, nationalistic movement with socialistic inclinations. Labour was proclaimed as a basis for any reward. While the party consisted of adult members and special youth groups, two additional elements were involved: the union of professional organisations and special party guards of Ustase troops which represented the executive element of the party.

Church

The religion of the predominant part of the Croat population was Roman Catholic, while the Serbs included within the boundaries of the new state belonged to the Serbian Orthodox Church. Before the dismemberment of Yugoslavia, all Serbs belonging to the Orthodox faith were united in the Eastern Orthodox Church with its headquarters in Belgrade. After the creation of the new state, the Croatian authorities looked unwillingly on the fact that their own citizens might seek religious leadership in a foreign country, and hence they were eager to sever relations between their new citizens and the Eastern Orthodox Church in Belgrade. Therefore a Croatian Orthodox Church was established in the territory of Croatia by a law of April 3, 1942.

A little later a special statute was enacted for the new Croatian Orthodox Church declaring that the Croatian Orthodox Church was indivisible in its unity, that it was autocephalous, and that it would be guided dogmatically and canonically by the principles of the Holy Eastern Orthodox Church. The new church was given the status of a patriarchy, with its seat at Zagreb.

The language of the Eastern Orthodox Church of Yugoslavia since 1918 — and in former times back to the earliest days — had been Serbian. The lettering in its literature and other written materials had also been Serbian using the Cyrillic alphabet. Despite this, the

German soldiers and members of the Ustasa militia lead a group of Serbian villagers from the Kozara region of Bosnia to a concentration camp, most probably the one at Jasenovac.

statute declared that the official language as well as the official lettering of the Croatian Orthodox Church should be Croatian, which, in the existing circumstances, was felt by the Serbs to be an infringement upon their religion.

In order to connect the new church officially and visually with the new state, it was provided that the flag of the church should have the colours of the Croatian state (red, white and blue).

As already noted, it was officially declared in the statute that the new church is autocephalous, but this autonomy was illusory when one considers the complete subordination of the clergy to the state in matters of appointments as well as for financial support. Thus, as regards the procedure for appointments, a Council of Electors was established which comprised all the bishops of the new church; a government official (the Chief of the Eastern Orthodox Division in the Ministry of Justice); the Dean of the Orthodox Faculty of the University of Zagreb, and five members of the Eastern Orthodox Church appointed by the Chief of the State, upon the recommendation of the

Ministry of Justice. The bishops themselves were to be appointed by the Chief of the State, upon the recommendation of the Minister of Justice, from among three candidates presented by the Synod of Bishops. In order to elect the Patriarch of the church, the Council of Electors had to nominate three candidates from among the bishops, it being the Chief of the State who had the final decision in the matter. According to Section 116, the Chief of the State appointed the first Patriarch and the first bishops.

As to the financial status of the church, the religious officers of the church were paid by the state in the same manner as government officials and their civil service ratings were determined in accordance with the general principles of the Croatian Civil Service. The money for the expenses of the church was collected by local tax authorities from parishes of the Croatian Orthodox Church, and the Treasury passed on the receipts to the church authorities. Thus the new church was also made financially dependent on the Croatian State.

Left: **These people are being marched through Prijedor (see map page 244) on their way to the Jasenovac camp, a journey** **of some 50 kilometres.** *Right:* **The same mosque still stands on Kralja Petra I Oslobodioca.**

After seizing power, the Ustasa authorities erected numerous concentration camps in Croatia, the largest being the Jasenovac complex comprising a string of five camps on the bank of the Sava river, about 100 kilometres south of Belgrade. In late August 1941, the Croat authorities established the first two camps — Krapje and Brocica — but these were closed four months later. The other three camps in the complex were Ciglana, established in November 1941 and dismantled in April 1945; Kozara, established in February 1942 and terminated in April 1945, and Stara Gradiška. *Left:* Miroslav Filipovic-Majstorovic (centre) was a Croatian Catholic priest and member of the Ustasa who served as commandant at Jasenovac and Stara Gradiška. He was ordained in 1939 and then became a chaplain to an Ustasa brigade which massacred over 2,200 Serbian villagers in Drakulic, Motika and Sargovac. Accused of inciting this mass murder of Bosnian Serbs, he was court-martialled and brought before a German military court. The papal legate Ramiro Marcone suspended him after the massacres but, through the intervention of Vjekoslav Luburic, the head of administration of Croatia's concentration camps, he was appointed commandant of Jasenovac on June 10, 1942. Conditions in the Jasenovac camps were horrendous. Prisoners received minimal food, shelter and sanitary facilities were totally inadequate and the guards cruelly tortured, terrorised and murdered prisoners at will. Between its establishment in 1941 and its evacuation in April 1945, Croat authorities murdered thousands of people at Jasenovac. Among the victims were: between 45,000 and 52,000 Serb residents of the so-called Independent State of Croatia; between 8,000 and 20,000 Jews; between 8,000 and 15,000 gypsies, and between 5,000 and 12,000 ethnic Croats and Muslims, who were political and religious opponents of the regime. The Croat authorities murdered between 330,000 and 390,000 ethnic Serb residents of Croatia and Bosnia during the period of Ustasa rule; more than 30,000 Croatian Jews were killed either in Croatia or at Auschwitz-Birkenau. Between 1941 and 1943, Croat authorities deported Jews from throughout the so-called Independent State to Jasenovac and shot many of them at the nearby killing sites of Granik and Gradina.

Courts

When the territory of Croatia was a part of the Yugoslav Kingdom, the Supreme Court of Yugoslavia was the highest court of the whole kingdom. After the creation of the Independent State of Croatia, a Supreme Court for the entire Croatian territory was established in Bania Luca. At the same time, the office of a national Attorney General was established in Bania Luca, as well as offices for state attorneys in Zagreb and Sarajevo. The Supreme Court in Bania Luca had the final jurisdiction in civil and criminal cases as well as in non-trial cases. This court comprised a president, a vice-president and an appropriate number of judges. The president (or in his absence the vice-president) was vested with power to suspend any decision by individual benches in civil cases, 'if such decision is in contradiction to previous important or basic decisions of the Supreme Court' or 'in obvious contradiction to the contents of the record in the case, or if it is in obvious violation of the law'. The same decree stated that 'whenever

the president exercised this right, the case has be brought before the plenary session of the Supreme Court'. However, there was no statement to the effect that the plenary session could overrule the president.

Penal Law

On July 20, 1942, a law was published concerning the suppression 'of violent crimes against the state, individuals and property'. This law provided for special treatment of political and certain common criminals. It did not, however, define in a detailed manner the offences for which especially harsh treatment was the penalty, but spoke only generally of persons 'who violate public order and safety or threaten the peace and quiet of the Croatian people, or who undertake some violent crime against the state, individuals or property'. For such crimes two types of treatment were introduced:

Confinement in a concentration camp for a period of not less than three months nor more than three years.

Confiscation of property.

Although the law provided for deprivation of liberty and property, this was not carried out by way of judicial procedure but merely by a division of the Ministry of the Interior designated as 'Administration of Public Order and Safety'. A particular provision stated that if the culprits had fled, members of their families could be confined in concentration camps and their property confiscated, a provision that was in direct contradiction to the principle of individual responsibility under modern criminal law.

However, the most drastic penal law was published on April 17, 1941. This imposed the death penalty for the most serious political crimes. However, the acts for which that sentence could be imposed were defined quite vaguely, simply as harm done 'to the honour and vital interests of the Croatian nation' or for acts endangering the 'existence of the Independent State of Croatia or its government authorities'. Such cases were tried by extraordinary People's Courts consisting of three judges applying a summary procedure.

Left: **Having been rounded up, Serbs and gypsies are marched to Jasenovac concentration camp, the first camp used for** extermination by the Ustase. *Right:* **On arrival they were stripped of any personal possessions.**

Filipovic admitted that he had personally killed about 100 prisoners and had attended mass executions of many more. He estimated that under his command some 20,000 to 30,000 prisoners were liquidated at the main Jasenovac camp which became known as the 'Yugoslav Auschwitz'. However, unlike the sophisticated extermination mechanisms installed at the death camp in Poland, Filipovic said that his prisoners would often just be made to stand in prepared trenches where each was then killed with a blow from a sledgehammer.

Genocide

Genocide policy was directed predominantly against Jews and Serbs. Even in the first stage of the formation of the state, a differentiation in treatment of the population was introduced in accordance with the racial principles laid down in the German Nuremberg legislation. According to German criteria, nationality was divided into two classifications. The higher type created a full right of relationship between individual and state and was granted only to persons of Aryan origin. The inferior type of nationality did not confer rights to participate in political life but gave

certain protection to the person involved, such as the right to be granted a passport and the right to participate in economic activities within certain limitations. This latter type of nationality was granted to Jews and even to non-Jews who were not considered as completely reliable politically.

In Croatia all Jewish property was seized. By a decree of April 14, 1941, all transactions between Jews and between Jews and third parties entered into within two months before the independence of the State of Croatia was proclaimed, were to be declared null and void if the value exceeded 100,000

dinars. This law was later made applicable to legal transactions entered into after independence was proclaimed.

Several other limitations relating to the exercise of professions and economic activities reduced the Jewish population in Croatia to a state of degradation.

The Serbian population living in Croatia was affected mainly in its political and cultural aspects as its national pattern was destroyed by genocide legislation. Since the main difference between the Serbian and Croatian languages consists in the use by the Croats of the Roman lettering and by the Serbs of the Cyrillic lettering, the use of the latter was prohibited. By this measure the Serbs were obliged to use the Croatian language in writing and when one considers that Cyrillic lettering was an essential part of the ritual of the Eastern Orthodox Church, this directive to use the Roman lettering amounted to interference with religion.

Labour

The labour legislation of Croatia stressed the importance of labour in society. The law regulating labour relations proclaimed that 'it is the right and duty of every citizen to work, and work alone should be the basis of his existence and the measure of his usefulness'. The state had the right to supervise not only the nature of work but also wages. Moreover, penalties were imposed for workers' failures in accomplishment and for actions making work impossible or difficult. Both employers and employees were called upon to conduct their mutual relations primarily 'upon the principle of the welfare of the nation and the state as a whole', and only secondarily 'with regard to individual profit'. However, collective bargaining was permitted.

The camp was dismantled in 1945, this flower monument by Vladimir Kulic being erected as a striking symbol to remember those murdered here. Since the war the total number killed has been a contentious issue, mainly for political reasons, but it is now believed that around 100,000 died in Jasenovac camp. In 1946 Filipovic was put on trial in Belgrade and sentenced to death. He was hanged wearing the robes of the Franciscan Order.

The Croat authorities had established Stara Gradiška as an independent holding centre for political prisoners in the summer of 1941 and converted it in the winter of 1942 into a concentration camp for women and children, but still within the Jasenovac system. At his post-war trial Filipovic described his tenure in command. 'I was at Stara Gradiška from the end of October 1942 until March 27, 1943. During that time mass liquidations were performed, usually outside the camp, for instance in Mlaka and Jablanac, but some were sent off to Jasenovac too. Such large transports for liquidations were carried out by the order of Matković Ivica and in this way 2,000 to 3,000 people were sent away. I know that at the end corpses of prisoners from Gradiška were being exhumed and burned, in order to cover up traces of what had been done.'

The Croatian Union of Workers was established as a professional organisation of workers covering all fields of labour in Croatia. According to its statute, this union was a part of the Ustasa liberation movement. It embraced all workers and their societies and all trade unions, the highest office of the union being that of the leader who was appointed by the government. Thus the workers were controlled politically by the Ustasa Party and in an administrative way by their leader who was a government appointee. As all trades and economic activities were controlled by the government, it was possible for the government to exercise a decisive control over both employers and employees and to decide their disputes by fiat.

Control of Trades
On April 18, 1942, a Fascist corporate system was introduced. The purpose of this decree was to seize and develop the national resources; to organise and protect trades, and to eliminate competition in economic activities. The underlying aim was to strengthen the nation and the state. The decree provided for the establishing of chambers of handicrafts, industry, commerce, banking and insurance, throughout the country, all to be supervised by the Minister of Handicrafts, Industry and Commerce. No person could engage in economic activity without having a trade licence or membership of a particular chamber. Even government enterprises, and establishments and enterprises belonging to the local government, had to be members of the respective chambers. The chambers were required to organise a regular association under the title of 'Representatives of Croatian Trade Chambers' to serve as a consultative body to the government.

Besides the trade chambers, professional associations were also to be established under this law. The Minister of Handicrafts, Industry and Commerce and the Minister of Finance were charged with its execution, and were authorised 'to amend, change, correct, abolish and interpret' all rules and regulations issued thereunder, and to issue new ones.

Finance
By the decree of May 10, 1941, a Croatian State Bank was established in Zagreb. A new monetary unit was introduced for Croatia, namely the kuna. The kuna contains 100 banica. It was stated that the value of the kuna should be 17,921 milligrams of fine gold.

The staff included the Ustasa Sergeant Ante Vrban who tested methods of killing using sulphur dioxide gas, Zyklon B crystals, and carbon monoxide exhaust fumes. The treatment of the inmates was so horrific that on the night of August 29/30, 1942, bets were laid among the prison guards as to who could kill the largest number of inmates. Peter Brzica won having reportedly cut the throats of 1,360 prisoners with a butcher's knife. Partisans liberated the camp in April 1945 and it was used in later years by the Yugoslav regime. It has now fallen into disrepair but the names of 12,790 individuals have now been confirmed as having been put to death at Stara Gradiška.

After much searching for us, Ardit Bicaj found the former prison at Prishtina (see the map on page 244) still standing on Zejnel Salihu Street, now used by the Kosova Statistics Agency.

KOSOVO, DIBRANO AND STRUGA (Albanian Occupation)

On June 9, 1940, King Victor Emmanuel III promulgated a Royal Decree to the effect that the Kingdom of Albania considered itself at war with those states with which the Kingdom of Italy was at war. By the same decree, the Albanian Fascist Militia and Forestry Militia and the Armed Police Force and all other Albanian armed units were put under the orders of the Supreme Commander of the Italian Armed Forces. Thus Albania was automatically involved in the war with Yugoslavia when Italy started military action. It received for itself a part of the spoils of Yugoslavia.

The proclamation by Mussolini of June 29, 1941 declared that in the territories of Kosovo, Dibrano and Struga occupied by Italian forces in Yugoslavia, the rights of the military occupant were 'transferred to the Albanian Government'. These territories were later annexed by the Albanian Government under the law of September 12, 1942 when Albanian administration was introduced into them.

A special Ministry for Redeemed Territories was created in Tirana, the capital of Albania, although this was later abolished.

On July 22, 1942, the Vicegerent published a decree establishing offices for public works in the redeemed territories at Prishtina, Peja, Dibrano and Tetova. In these areas a genocide policy in relation to Serbs was carried out. Yugoslav schools were closed (with the exception

In 1938, Mosa and Gabriela Mandil moved from Belgrade to Novi Sad, where Mosa opened a photo studio (his father-in-law had been the royal photographer of King Alexander in Belgrade). After the German invasion in April 1941, the family fled south to the Italian-controlled province of Kosovo. There they were imprisoned for ten months along with several other Jewish families in the city of Prishtina. In prison, Mosa became friendly with Majer and Mimi Altarac, another refugee family from Serbia, and he took this photo *(left)* of them with young Jasa posing outside the prison. Majer's family home in Sarajevo had been destroyed in a German bombing raid in which his mother and daughter were killed. When the city was occupied by German troops the Altarac family returned in July to Belgrade. There they had to register with the police, and Majer was detailed for forced labour. Majer's business partner applied for permission for the family to move to the Italian-occupied zone of Yugoslavia but when these documents were late in coming, the Altaracs fled without them. They went to Skopje in Macedonia but their stay was cut short when Majer was recognised one day on the street. Fearful of being reported to the police for his illegal presence in the city, Majer fled with his family to Prishtina in Italian-occupied Kosovo. However, the situation there soon changed for the worse as the Italian authorities came under increased pressure from their German allies to turn over the growing numbers of Jewish refugees in the city. First they were placed in an abandoned school, and later transferred to the city's main prison, where they met the Mandils. While prison life was unpleasant for the refugees, it was far better than living under German occupation. During the day they could stay in the prison courtyard, which provided a place for the children to play. Mosa ingratiated himself with his Italian captors by volunteering to take their pictures. After being incarcerated for some time the Jewish families complained about the overcrowded prison conditions. Their complaints were conveyed by Italian prison officials to their German allies who, in response, executed half of the prisoners. Fearful that the others would also be killed, Mosa appealed to the Italians whom he had befriended to save the remaining Jews. The Italians obliged and on July 8 they decided to disperse the remainder of the Jewish prisoners in several locations around Albania. The Mandil and Altarac families were among a group of 18 prisoners (from five families) that was sent by truck to Kavaja where they were given limited freedom. There, the Jewish families were required to report to the police station every day, but otherwise were left alone. In September 1943, the Altaracs decided to move to Tirana in Albania. While they were travelling by taxi to the capital they witnessed the capitulation of the Italians and the immediate occupation of Albania by the Germans. Following the liberation of Tirana in 1944, the Altaracs returned to Belgrade, where they remained until their immigration to Palestine in 1948. After the war the Mandils returned to Novi Sad, where they re-opened their photo studio but in 1948, after the consolidation of the communist regime in Yugoslavia and the founding of the Jewish State, the Mandils also decided to emigrate to Israel.

of some schools belonging to Serbian religious bodies) and in their place Albanian schools were opened. Those pupils of Albanian nationality who had previously attended the discontinued Yugoslav schools were given every opportunity to continue their studies in the new Albanian schools. The Minister of Education was empowered to take possession of the buildings and equipment, archives and all scientific endowments of the former Yugoslav schools. By so doing, the occupant violated Articles 46 and 56 of the Hague Regulations (see page 261), which prohibit the seizure of property of institutions dedicated to education and science. The discontinuance of the Yugoslav schools was also an encroachment upon the right to education, which is protected by customs of international law and by the principles of humanity which form part of the Hague Regulations.

The Albanian franc was made legal tender, and Yugoslav dinars were exchanged at the rate of 6.08 Albanian francs for 100 dinars. For transactions in connection with conversion of currency, a special committee was set up comprising a president chosen by the Italian civil commissioner, a member appointed by the National Bank of Albania, and a civilian elected from among the population.

As the Serbian population in the annexed territories displayed a hostile attitude toward the Albanian occupation, drastic measures were applied. There existed in Albania a law dating from 1930 that provided for severe collective penalties for members of families of offenders who were in hiding.

These penalties included the internment of families, sequestration of property, and setting fire to the houses of culprits. This law had a special practical importance in these areas, where taking refuge in the mountains was prevalent. The penalties imposed upon the innocent members of families were intended to cause the culprits to leave their hiding places. The Albanian occupation forces proceeded to promulgate this law on collective penalties in the occupied areas but the introduction of such a provision in occupied territory was a violation of the Hague Regulations. Article 50 prohibited the inflicting of collective penalties upon the population because of the acts of individuals for which the population cannot be regarded as jointly and severally responsible.

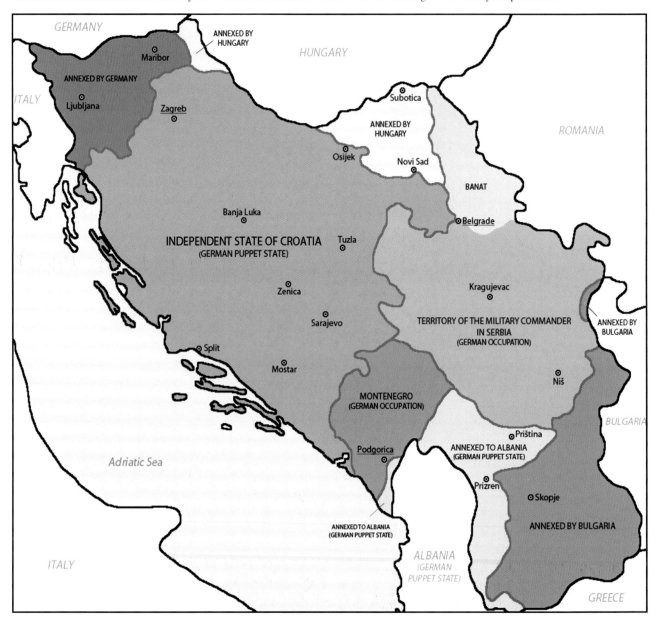

The sudden capitulation of Italy in September 1943 came when 35 Italian divisions (around 600,000 men) were stationed in the Balkans, of which approximately 380,000 were on occupation duties in Slovenia, Dalmatia and Montenegro (see map page 247). The surrender had the effect of redrawing the occupation map of Yugoslavia as depicted here. The Germans moved swiftly to fill the vacuum. Some Italian soldiers chose to continue to fight with the Axis while about 400,000 were sent to Germany for forced labour or to be killed. Others, like we have seen at Cephalonia (pages 232-233) were just wiped out on the spot. Apart from the Germans taking over, another consequence was that the resistance movement suddenly recruited 150,000 additional fighters for the Partisans' People's Liberation Army of Yugoslavia, together with a huge amount of armaments.

Hungarian occupation troops prepare for public executions in Novi Sad (now called Vojvodina). The history of this region is quite complicated. Back in August 1921, the Serb-Hungarian Baranya-Bačka Republic was proclaimed having been decided by the Treaty of Trianon. It included northern parts of the Baranya and Bačka regions, which were assigned to Hungary. The southern Yugoslav part of the region was part of Novi Sad county between 1918 and 1922, part of Bačka Oblast between 1922 and 1929, and in 1929 it was included into the Danube Banovina, a province of the Kingdom of Yugoslavia. In 1941, Yugoslav Baranya was occupied by Hungary, but it was returned to Yugoslavia in 1944. In 1944-1945, Yugoslav Baranya became part of the Autonomous Province of Vojvodina, while in 1945 it was assigned to the People's Republic of Croatia. During the war in 1991, it came under control of the Serbian Autonomous Oblast Eastern Slavonia, Baranja and Western Srem, which became part of the Republic of Serbian Krajina. After the war ended in 1995, it was peacefully integrated into Croatia in 1998, by the Erdut Agreement. According to the agreement, it was administered by the United Nations from 1996 to 1998, after which it was returned to the full sovereignty of Croatia.

BARANJA, BACKA, PREKOMURJE AND MEDZUMURJE
(Hungarian Occupation)

After the Treaty of Trianon in 1920, Hungary claimed a revision of its frontiers with Yugoslavia, not only with a view to restoring Hungarian ethnographic regions but also to regain the 'Southern Territories' that had belonged to Hungary in the past such as Croatia. Here again, the doctrine of the Holy Crown (see page 31) was invoked.

Therefore, during the intervening years, the relations between the two countries were greatly strained and Hungary was often accused by Yugoslavia of fostering separatist movements in Yugoslavia. In particular, charges were brought that the Hungarians were training Croatian terrorists in Hungary. A change in the relations of the two countries occurred on December 12, 1940, when their respective foreign ministers met in Belgrade and signed a

The execution of Djordje Radujkov, Rudolf Klaus, Ivan Koci, Pal Karas and Djula Varga took place on October 15, 1941 in the barracks on Vojvode Bojovic Street, then occupied by the Hungarian occupying army. Nikola Jelenkovic took this comparison for us.

In early 1942, thousands of residents of Novi Sad were murdered by the Hungarians in one of the most awful massacres. The pogrom against Serbian and Jewish families began on January 21 with inhabitants being rounded up. Those not killed in the streets or their homes were taken in trucks to the riverbank of the Danube that was frozen at the time.

All were stripped naked — men, women and children — and then shot and thrown on the ice. The killing spree lasted for three days by which time over 4,000 had been slaughtered. Today this poignant memorial stands beside the river where so many died — the contrast between then and now could not be greater.

Although Yugoslav Bačka was occupied by the Axis powers and attached to Horthy's Hungary, it was still internationally recognised as part of Yugoslavia. Before the occupation, the census determined that the region had 784,896 inhabitants, of whom there were 284,865 Yugoslavs, 268,711 Hungarians and 169,858 Germans. The Hungarian occupation authorities expelled several thousands of Serbs from the region and settled ethnic Hungarians from other parts of Central Europe in their place. More than 4,000 Jews lived in Novi Sad before the Second World War, out of a total population of 80,000. Their synagogue was the fifth to be erected at the same location on Jevrejska (Jewish) Street since the 18th century. In 1944 the interior was desecrated and (above) used to assemble Jews before they were transported to concentration camps. During the occupation, Hungarian troops killed about 20,000 Serbs, Jews and gypsies, and only about 1,000 Jews survived the annexation of Bačka region by Hungary. When the occupation ended in 1944, members of the Yugoslav Partisan army killed several thousands of inhabitants of German, Hungarian and Serb ethnic origin. Yugoslav Bačka became part of the new Democratic Federal Yugoslavia (later the Socialist Federal Republic of Yugoslavia).

Administration

In the beginning these territories were administered by Hungarian military commanders of the occupying forces but later Hungarian civil administration was extended to them. The Hungarian authorities introduced a policy of genocide by endeavouring to impose a Hungarian pattern upon these territories. As Prekomurje and Medzumurje were inhabited also by Slovenes and Croats, the genocide policy affected both those races, and in Backa and Baranja it affected the Serbs and Jews.

On May 6, 1942, the Yugoslav Government in London delivered a memorandum to the Allied Governments concerning the mass destruction of the Serbian population in the occupied territories. In addition to the details concerning the many atrocities that had taken place under Hungarian occupation, the memorandum stated that concentration camps had been established in every town, the largest being in Subotica, Novi Sad, Pechuj and Baja. The one at Novi Sad contained about 13,000 men, women and children, Serbs and Jews. The memorandum further charged that churches had been looted and destroyed.

Citizenship

According to the Law XX, the inhabitants of the incorporated Southern Territories were given the right to re-acquire Hungarian citizenship as from April 11, 1941, providing that they were Hungarian citizens on July 26, 1921 under Hungarian law and had become citizens of the Kingdom of the Serbs, Croats and Slovenes by virtue of the Treaty of Trianon. However, such persons must have lived continuously in the incorporated Southern Territories for ten years, i.e. from June 1, 1931 to June 1, 1941.

treaty of friendship (the Hungaro-Yugoslav Treaty of Amity). Article I of this treaty expressly provided that 'Permanent peace will reign and eternal friendship will exist between the Kingdom of Yugoslavia and the Kingdom of Hungary', and Article II stated: 'The Signatory parties agree to consult on all problems which, in their opinion, affect their mutual relations'.

Four months later, during the German invasion of Yugoslavia in April 1941, Hungarian troops marched into Yugoslavia and occupied the regions of Medzumurje, Prekomurje, Baranja and Backa. This occupation coincided with the proclamation of Croatia as an 'independent' state.

Incorporation

On December 27, 1941, the territories so occupied, referred to as the 'Southern Territories' were formally incorporated into Hungary by law. As was the case with the Highland Territories and Sub-Carpathia (see also page 31), the law referred to the Hungarian Holy Crown as the legal entity into which the Southern Territories were incorporated, and thus an official document gave expression again to the doctrine of the Holy Crown.

Representation in Parliament

Law XX of 1941 provided for representation in Parliament of the incorporated Southern Territories. However, during the period when the citizens' electors could not choose representatives 'by normal procedure', the members of the Upper House were to be nominated on a motion of the Prime

Minister by the Parliament, both houses concurring. Law XXI of 1942 further provided that the county assemblies should elect representatives to the Upper House, the number of such members for every county and autonomous city in the Southern Territories being fixed in advance.

While the synagogue in Novi Sad is no longer used for religious ceremonies, it is used for many cultural concerts and events. In 1991 the building was added to the list of Spatial Cultural-Historical Units of Great Importance and it is protected by the Republic of Serbia.

MACEDONIA, MORAVA, SKOPJE AND BITOLIA
(Bulgarian Occupation)

A considerable part of Yugoslavia was occupied also by Bulgaria. The occupied areas included the long-disputed territory of western Macedonia and the regions of Skopje, Bitolia and parts of the Morava regions, different policies being adopted by the Bulgarians for each of the respective regions.

Macedonia, which had been claimed by Bulgaria for many years, was considered as Bulgarian territory being returned to the homeland. Therefore a policy of rehabilitation and reconstruction was adopted there in relation to the Macedonians who were considered by the Bulgarians as of Bulgarian origin. As to the other ethnic groups of the population, especially Serbs, a policy of national oppression was adopted and 120,000 Serbs were removed from Macedonia to Old Serbia. Yugoslav administration was abolished and Bulgarian administration introduced in its stead. Because of an old feud between the Serbs and the Bulgarians in this region, most of the officials were replaced by Bulgarians.

As far as currency was concerned, the Yugoslav dinar was replaced by the Bulgarian lev. By Decision No. 2012 of the Council of Ministers, all private persons and firms with domicile and residence in Macedonia, Morava and the western regions, were ordered to deposit, within 14 days as from June 6, 1941, in the respective agencies of the Bulgarian National Bank, notes of 100 dinars and higher denominations. Dinars would thereafter cease to be legal tender.

An unidentified village in Macedonia is put to the torch.

Bulgaria entered the Second World War in 1941 as a member of the Axis but declined to participate in Operation 'Barbarossa' and saved its Jewish population from deportation to concentration camps. However, the sudden death of Boris III in the summer of 1943 pushed the country into political turmoil as the war turned against Germany and the communist guerrilla movement gained momentum. Bulgaria did not comply with Soviet demands to expel German forces from its territory, resulting in a declaration of war and invasion by the USSR in September 1944. The communist-dominated Fatherland Front took power, ended participation in the Axis, and joined the Allied side. In this photo Macedonian partisans of the People's Liberation Army of Macedonia (part of the larger National Liberation Army) and Partisan Detachments of Yugoslavia march through the streets of Skopje together with units of the newly-Allied Bulgarian People's Army in November 1944. The left-wing uprising that September led to the abolition of monarchic rule, but it was not until 1946 that a one-party people's republic was established. This became a part of the Soviet sphere of influence under the leadership of Georgi Dimitrov who laid the foundations for a Stalinist state which was also highly repressive with thousands of dissidents being executed.

The Baltic States

The three Baltic States, Lithuania, Latvia and Estonia, granted Russia military bases on their own territories in November and December 1939. (After the occupation of Poland by Germany and the Soviet Union in September 1939, Russia turned over to Lithuania the Polish city of Wilno together with the western part of that province.) In June 1940, the three states were occupied and incorporated into the Union of Soviet Socialist Republics as autonomous soviet republics of Lithuania, Latvia and Estonia. A communist regime was gradually introduced into these countries up to the date of their occupation by Germany.

GERMAN ADMINISTRATION

After Germany occupied the Baltic States in June and July 1941, during the course of the war with Russia, each of these states was organised as a general commissariat, with headquarters in the capital of the respective state. Thus there was a General Commissariat for Lithuania with headquarters in Kaunas; a General Commissariat for Latvia with headquarters in Riga, and a General Commissariat for Estonia with headquarters in Tallinn. These three general commissariats, together with a fourth called General Commissariat for White Russia, composed one Reich Com-

On September 21, 1939, Reinhard Heydrich held a meeting to clarify occupation policy in the newly conquered Polish territories. Concerning the Jews, he was quite explicit: 'The Jews are to be concentrated in ghettos in cities in order to facilitate a better possibility of control and later expulsion'. Heydrich stressed that 'it was urgent that the Jew disappears from the countryside' and that 'this must be carried out within the next three to four weeks'. Opposition from the military, which was opposed at such a hasty demographic upheaval at such a time, forced Heydrich to backtrack a week later, but the die was still cast. The first of the Eastern Europe ghettos was set up in Poland, 40 kilometres south-east of Lodz at Piotrkow Trybunalski. This was an 'open' ghetto, i.e. without walls or fences, the first truly closed version being this one set up between February and April 1940 at Lódz (Litzmannstadt) holding over 162,000 Jews.

This is where the pedestrian bridge once crossed the 'Aryan' street (Ul. Zgierska), known to the Germans as Hohensteiner Strasse on Plac Koscielni (Kirchplatz).

George Hirsch, born in 1922, was given a Voigtlander camera for his tenth birthday. On June 15, 1941, when Soviet forces invaded Lithuania, George was ready with his camera and, through a spyhole in the paper that was used to cover this window *(above)*, he pictured Red Army tanks driving through the capital Kaunas. *Right:* The armour was pictured passing the Cathedral Basilica of St Peter and St Paul. Later that year George was confined in Kovno ghetto and then to a number of labour camps but he still managed to retain his camera and photographs. However, on the night of July 9/10, 1944, before trying to escape from the Kedainiai labour camp near Kaunas, he was worried that he might lose his precious photos and negatives so he handed them over to his father who was then working at the camp as a cook. He wrapped them in waxed paper and buried them in a canister under the kitchen.

Then, using a pair of pliers, George cut a hole through the barbed-wire fence surrounding the camp and escaped, along with his father and another companion. One month later, after the German retreat, he returned to Kedainiai and managed to retrieve his photographs which he found undamaged.

In 1952, having changed his surname in the meantime to Birman, George emigrated to America with his photo collection which is now in the archive of the US Holocaust Memorial Museum in Washington. This is the junction of Alexsoto with Karaliaus Mindaugo — then and now.

Left: **Alfred Rosenberg, one of the pioneers of the Third Reich, had led the National Socialist party during the period that Hitler was in prison following the Munich Beer Hall putsch. He was also a key instigator of the Nazi Party's ideological creeds, including its racial policy of the persecution of the Jews for whom he adopted the term 'Untermenschen' after the title of a book published in 1925. Following the invasion of the USSR, Rosenberg was appointed head of the Reich Ministry for the Occupied Eastern Territories (Reichsministerium für die besetzten Ostgebiete). He presented Hitler with his plan for the organisation of the conquered Eastern territories, suggesting the establishment of new administrative districts, to replace the previously Soviet-controlled territories with new Reichskommissariats. These would be: Ostland (Baltic countries and Byelorussia); Ukraine (Ukraine and nearest territories); Kaukasus (Caucasus area), and Moskau (Moscow metropolitan area and the rest of nearest Russian European areas).** *Right:* **At Nuremberg he was sentenced to death and executed by hanging for war crimes and crimes against humanity.**

missariat for the Ostland, with headquarters in Riga. The Reich Commissariat Ostland, as well as other territories occupied in Russia, was supervised by a specially-created Ministry for the Occupied Territories in the East, with headquarters in Berlin. Alfred Rosenberg was named Reich Minister for the Occupied Territories in the East.

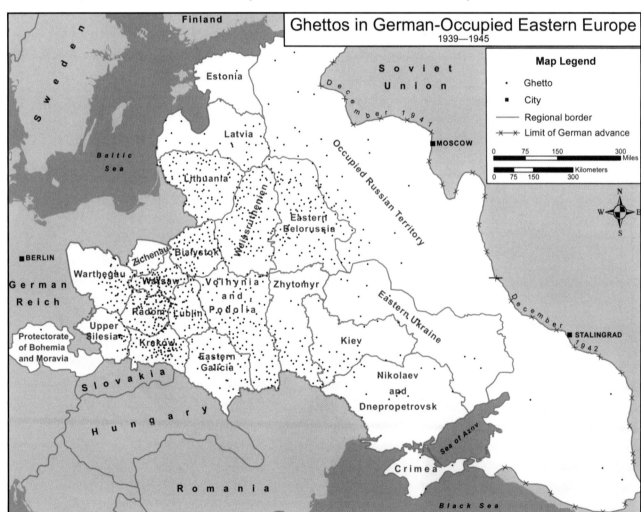

The Germans established at least 1,100 ghettos in German-occupied or annexed Eastern Europe, 600 in Poland, 250 in the Soviet Union and 130 in the Baltic states alone. There were also three types of ghettos: open ghettos, i.e. unfenced but still with severe penalties for entering or leaving; closed ghettos sealed off with walls and fences, and then those designed specifically as killing ghettos. The largest by far was at Warsaw which was sealed on November 1940.

PROCLAMATION OF JULY 28, 1941

By a decree of July 17, 1941, the Führer of the Greater German Reich, Adolf Hitler, has appointed me Reich Commissioner for the Ostland. In this area the former free state of Lithuania is also included.

By a decree of the same date the Führer has likewise appointed Herr Dr Adrian von Renteln as Commissioner General for the former free state of Lithuania. Commissioner General Dr von Renteln shall be responsible to me, as the representative of the Reich Government for the Reich Commissariat of the Ostland, for the execution in Lithuania of all decrees and orders issued by the Reich Government or by myself. His own decrees and orders shall likewise be obeyed in every instance within this territory.

I first address to the inhabitants of the territories south of the Dvina and as far as the boundaries of the former free state of Lithuania, inclusive, the appeal to co-operate uniformly and with all their energy in carrying out the task assigned to me, namely, to restore order and work in these territories.

Bolshevism was threatening all Europe. It was on the march to attack Germany, and it has also inflicted most terrible wounds upon you. If this world enemy had been rampant among you a few more years, nothing would have been left to you of your property and people. The Bolshevik leaders would have carried you off to Siberia, robbed, and murdered you.

At the cost of their blood, the armed forces of the German people have overthrown the Bolshevik universal enemy; and so everyone will understand that this German people has therefore now assumed the duty and the right to make such arrangements that never again will a similar danger be able to threaten anew the traditions of the people of Europe, and indeed their whole existence.

Those who in the past 20 years promised you so much freedom believed themselves under the necessity of following a policy based upon playing off the Soviet Union against the German Reich. But the moment the German Reich, in view of an English attack, renounced certain territories in the east as its sphere of interest, this attitude, so fraught with consequences for you all, was revealed in its true form. The Soviet Union was able to fall upon you without opposition.

In spite of everything which has been done to injure Germans and the attacks which have been made upon the National Socialist German Reich, the Reich Government will take pains, in the interest of your welfare, to assure you work, bread and continued development. However, the German administration must demand that its orders be unconditionally obeyed, for they serve only this single purpose: the safety of the country and security of your lives. The German administration will call upon your representatives in the communities and in the cities for collaboration. It will in case of necessity appoint deputies from your people through whom your wishes may be transmitted to the Reich Commissioner, the Commissioner General, and the district commissioners, and it will permit you to form police organisations for the security of your work and your lives.

I expect the entire population to obey my directions, in order to heal the grave wounds which the universal Bolshevik enemy has inflicted upon you also. Only then will culture and well-being again be established in the future; only then will you all be able to live in peace. The German Reich offers you the opportunity. It is now for you to make use of this opportunity.

Kaunas, July 28, 1941
LOHSE, REICH COMMISSIONER FOR THE OSTLAND

The German administration had barely got into gear in the Baltic countries — and even before Rosenberg's deputy Hinrich Lohse *(above)*, the Reich Commissioner for the Ostland, had given his welcome address — than the massacres began, incited by SS-Brigadeführer Franz Stahlecker of Einsatzgruppe A. *Centre:* On June 27, 68 Jews were rounded up in Kaunas by the nationalist Lithuanian Activist Front and beaten to death with iron bars in front of the Lietukis Garage on Vytautas Street. Some victims were even subjected to inhumane treatment inflicted from high-pressure water hoses, all while a crowd of bystanders cheered the murderers on. In more recent years, the massacre even became an event that was looked on with a patriotic light, instead of one of the blackest pages in the country's history. (In 1948, Lohse was sentenced to ten years in prison but was released due to illness in 1951. He died on February 25, 1964.)

Finally, in July 2015, a monument was erected to the massacre but instead of it being sited where it happened, it was tucked out of the way in a play area entered from Misko Street.

Ghettos in the Lithuania Region
1941 - 1943

Map Legend

● Ghetto

◎ **GEBIET CENTER AND GHETTO**

–·–·– Regional border

――― Gebiet border

– – – Rayon border

0 10 20   40
Miles

Kilometers
0   20   40

Ghettoisation of Lithuania began within a few days of the German occupation and, by the end of September, there were more than 80 ghettos and holding camps in the country. The three main ones were at Wilno, Kaunas and Siauliai.

In the Baltic States the administration was in the hands of the Reich Commissioner for the Ostland. In each Baltic state there was also a Commissioner General who handled the administration in each individual state, chief commissioners who supervised administration of special regions or special branches, and district commissioners who were responsible for the administration in the smaller territorial units. However, the former administrative division was not continued but in its stead larger administrative districts or regions (Gebiete) were created with a chief commissioner at the head of each region. Thus in Lithuania the country's 27 administrative districts were grouped in six larger Gebiete.

Adrian von Renteln, the Generalkommissar for Lithuania, on an inspection tour with his local adviser General Petras Kobilienas. The ghetto in Kaunas provided forced labour for the German military, the Jews being employed primarily at various sites outside the ghetto, especially in the construction of a military aerodrome in Aleksotas. The Jewish Council hoped the Germans would not kill Jews who were producing for the army but in early July 1941, German Einsatzgruppe (mobile killing unit) detachments and their Lithuanian auxiliaries began systematic massacres of Jews. Thousands of men, women and children were shot, and within six months of the German occupation, half of all the Jews in the city had been murdered. Between July and August 15, 1941, the Germans concentrated the remaining Jews — some 29,000 people — in a ghetto established in Kaunas' Slobodka district, an area of small primitive houses and no running water.

The ghetto had two parts, called the 'small' and 'large' ghetto, separated by Paneriu Street. The Germans continually reduced the ghetto's size, forcing Jews to relocate several times. The small ghetto was destroyed on October 4, 1941, with almost all of its inhabitants being slaughtered at the Ninth Fort. Later that same month, on October 29, 1941, the Germans staged what became known as the 'Great Action' when, in a single day, they shot 9,200 Jews at the Ninth Fort. By January 1942 over 150,000 Jews had been murdered. On October 26, 1943, the SS deported more than 2,700 people from the main ghetto which had now taken on the role of a concentration camp. Those deemed fit to work were sent to labour camps in Estonia, and children and the elderly were deported to Auschwitz.

ADMINISTRATION BY THE LOCAL POPULATION

To a certain extent the local population was called upon to participate in the administration. Administration by the local population (Landeseigene Verwaltung) was headed in each of the states by a group of department chiefs who had the title of general councillors in Lithuania but general directors in Latvia and Estonia. These departmental chiefs were appointed by the commissioners general in conjunction with the Reich Commissioner for the Ostland. The departmental chiefs received directions from and were strictly supervised by the Office of the Commissioner General in each state. The participation of the local population in the lower echelon, i.e. in the districts, was effected by district elders (Einheimische Kreisälteste). These district elders were appointed from the local population by the Commissioner General in each country on the recommendation of the departmental chiefs. Just as the departmental chiefs received directions from and were supervised by the German commissioners general, the district elders received their instructions from and were supervised by the German district commissioners.

Administration in the urban and rural communities was carried out by special leaders who were assisted in towns by town councillors (Stadträte) and in the rural communities by parish councillors (Gemeinderäte).

COURTS

The German courts in the Baltic States applied German criminal law to the same extent as in other occupied countries. As the principle criminal law was introduced in the German Criminal Code in 1935, no legal guaranties were given to the local population as to previous knowledge of the criminal nature of an act. This provision regarding German criminal law, in conjunction with the limitations regarding review and

On July 8, 1944, the Germans evacuated the camp, deporting most of the remaining Jews to the Dachau concentration camp in Germany or to the Stutthof camp, near Danzig, on the Baltic coast (see *The Nazi Death Camps Then and Now*). Three weeks before the Soviet army arrived in Kaunas, the Germans razed the ghetto to the ground with grenades and dynamite. As many as 2,000 people burned to death or were shot while trying to escape. The Soviet army liberated Kaunas on August 1, 1944.

In the Latvian capital Riga, the Maskavas Forstate suburb was chosen for the establishment of a large ghetto. All the non-Jewish residents were evicted from the area and on October 25, 1941, every Jew living in the city was relocated there having been previously registered with a Jewish Council (Judenrat). The ghetto was fenced with barbed wire and anyone approaching too close was shot by Latvian guards, working under the German police. The ghetto itself had only been in existence for 37 days when Higher SS and Police Leader Ostland Friedrich Jeckeln ordered almost half of the inhabitants — more than 11,000 people — to be taken by units of the German Order Police to the Rumbula forest ten kilometres away. There, they were shot and buried in pre-dug pits. On the same date, November 30, 1941, the first transport of 1,000 Jews from Berlin arrived in Riga, so Jeckeln decided to kill these individuals as well, but, on his own authority, without waiting for orders from Berlin.

After this massacre a 'small ghetto', divided into male and female sections, was provided for the remaining Jews while the original larger ghetto was allocated to Jews arriving from Germany.

defence, created a state of lawlessness and placed the population completely at the mercy of the German administration.

A German Superior Court for all of the Ostland was established at the headquarters of the Reich Commissioner, and at the headquarters of each Commissioner General a German court was established for his jurisdictional district. In addition, a special court was associated with each German court. These courts had jurisdiction over all criminal cases except when these had been referred to another court for judgment.

(They had civil jurisdiction when a German citizen or a German by descent (Volkszugehöriger) was a party to the case.) The Reich Commissioner could also, at his discretion, expressly define the jurisdiction of the German tribunals. From decisions made by the lower German courts in the occupied areas, appeals were to be heard by the German Superior Court. The special courts had such jurisdiction as was expressly defined in the laws of the Reich or in the laws of the Ostland. According to established principles, the jurisdiction of special courts was always

defined by the decree that determined the penalties. There were also courts-martial having the normal jurisdiction of a German court-martial.

In the German court, as described above, only one judge was required for decisions, but in the German Superior Court there were three judges, except as otherwise prescribed. The special courts had one presiding judge and two associates, these associates to be 'as far as practicable with qualifications for the office of judge'. However, the insertion of the phrase 'as far as practicable' in the legislation made it obvious that

The sign reads: 'Persons crossing the fence or attempting to contact the ghetto through it will be shot at without warning'.

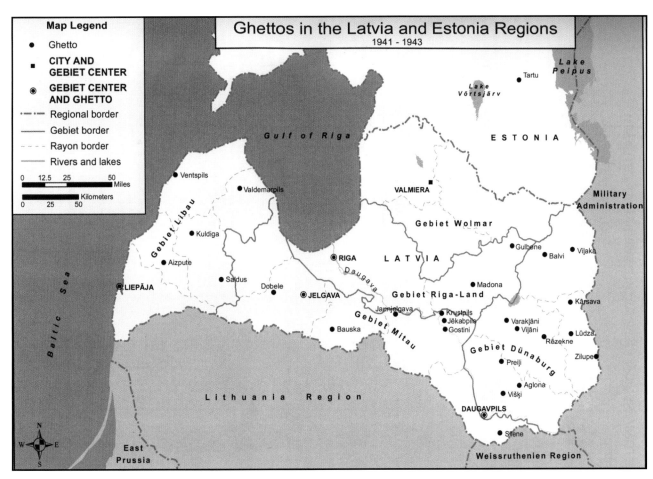

Ghettos in the Latvia and Estonia Regions
1941 - 1943

Map Legend

- • Ghetto
- ▪ **CITY AND GEBIET CENTER**
- ◉ **GEBIET CENTER AND GHETTO**
- ·—··—· Regional border
- ——— Gebiet border
- - - - - Rayon border
- ——— Rivers and lakes

Miles: 0 12.5 25 50
Kilometers: 0 25 50

ESTONIA

Lake Peipus

Lake Võrtsjärv

Tartu

Gulf of Riga

Baltic Sea

VALMIERA

Military Administration

Gebiet Wolmar

Gebiet Libau

Ventspils

Valdemarpils

Kuldiga

Aizpute

Saldus

LIEPĀJA

Dobele

JELGAVA

◉ RIGA

Daugava

LATVIA

Gulbene

Balvi

Viļaka

Madona

Gebiet Riga-Land

Kārsava

Gebiet Mitau

Jaunjelgava

Bauska

Krustpils

Jēkabpils

Gostini

Varakļāni

Viļāni

Rēzekne

Lūdza

Zilupe

Gebiet Dünaburg

Preiļi

Aglona

Višķi

DAUGAVPILS

Sīlene

Lithuania Region

East Prussia

Weissruthenien Region

N W E S

---

this qualification was not an absolute prerequisite. The Commissioner General appointed associates for one year from the ranks of German citizens or Germans by descent resident in the district of the special court. In some cases, the presiding judge of the Superior Court could decide without oral process. Also representation by counsel was not compulsory: any Reich German or German by descent who 'offers surety for an adequate defence' could be admitted as defence counsel. The right of appeal was limited. In criminal cases it was allowed only when a penalty of more than one month's imprisonment or 500 marks' fine had been imposed.

Amazingly, the wooden building still stands — looking south along Daugavpils–Iela.

In 1941 the Nazi Party established the Einsatzstab Reichsleiter Rosenberg or ERR, an organisation dedicated to appropriating cultural property from the occupied countries. Led by Rosenberg from within the NSDAP Office of Foreign Affairs, the ERR was initially a project of the Hohe Schule der NSDAP, a Nazi-oriented elite university. Rosenberg wanted it to be a research institute filled with cultural material on the opponents of the Nazi ideology. These included Jewish, Masonic, Communist and democratic organisations material, and between 1940 and 1945, the ERR operated throughout the German-occupied countries in Europe including the territory of the Reichskommissariat Ostland and Reichskommissariat Ukraine. In this picture, wagons are being loaded with books and other artefacts which were being removed from Estonia's oldest and most-renowned University of Tartu.

SEIZURE OF PROPERTY

The problem of the ownership of property was complicated because of the imposition of special regulations that were introduced in the Baltic States after their incorporation into the USSR. Since the bulk of property under the communist regime belongs to the state, or to collective economic associations, it was possible for the Germans to immediately seize a large number of properties already held in special forms of economic concentration of combines or trusts.

By an order of August 18, 1941, the Reich Commissioner for the Ostland declared that 'the German Civil Administration takes over all of the real and personal property situated in the territories administered by the Reich Commissioner for the Ostland which belongs to the Union of Soviet Socialist Republics, its member states, public corporations, associations, and partnerships, including all claims, investments, rights and interests of all kinds as of June 20, 1941'. These properties were put under the administration of special trustees but, because of the great number of trustees involved, an elaborate system of control became necessary. Special public records were established in which the names of the trustees were entered for the information of the public. For the duration of the sequestration of property, no legal processes for the benefit of the creditors of any specific property were permitted. Severe penalties, including the death penalty, were imposed for any persons interfering with the administration of the sequestrated properties.

As some private property had survived to a certain extent in the Baltic States, the Germans first gave attention to Jewish owners. An order was issued on October 13, 1941 to the effect that Jewish property would be subject to sequestration, trustee administration, and confiscation. Only the following were exempted from seizure: household furniture which was used for essential personal needs, and cash, bank, and savings credits up to a total of 100 Reichsmarks.

RETURN TO PRIVATE PROPERTY

In June 1941 when the German Army occupied territory held by the Soviet Union, Lithuania, Latvia and Estonia had been under a communist regime for a year — from June 1940 to June 1941 — while the eastern Polish territories had been under Russian administration since September 1939. The remainder of the territories in the east captured by Germany had been communist since 1917 and 1918 so it was obvious that communism would be more deeply entrenched in those areas.

In his first proclamation to the population, Hinrich Lohse, the Reich Commissioner for the Ostland, denounced the communist system, stating in his address on July 28, 1941 that 'Bolshevism was threatening all Europe. If this world enemy had been rampant among you a few more years, nothing would have been left to you of your property and people.' Lohse also stated that the Germans had made a sacrifice of their blood in order to overthrow 'the Bolshevik universal enemy' and that the German people have 'therefore now assumed the duty and the right to make such arrangements that never again will a similar danger be able to threaten anew the traditions of the people of Europe, and indeed their whole existence'.

Rosenberg was able to get full authority from Hitler to be the only official art procurement organisation acting in the occupied countries. In a Führer Directive of July 5, 1940, Hitler authorised the ERR to confiscate precious manuscripts and books from national libraries and archives; important artefacts of ecclesiastical authorities and Masonic lodges, and all valuable cultural property belonging to Jews. The ERR central administration was transferred to Berlin on March 1, 1941 where it became a formal sub-division of the German Foreign Office. Most of the looted Jewish property, especially books, was sent to Rosenberg's Institut zur Erforschung der Judenfrage in Frankfurt. The Institute served as the core research library for the planned Hohe Schule, but other research institutes that received looted books included the Institut für Biologie und Rassenlehre in Stuttgart, the Institut für Religionswissenschaft and the Institut für Deutsche Volkskunde.

It was not until 1943, when Germany was losing the oil fields near the Caspian Sea, that the oil-shale industry in Estonia became of vital importance. On June 21 that year, Himmler ordered the closure of the remaining ghettos in the Baltic states and the transfer of the inmates to newly formed concentration camps. The main camp in Estonia — and one of the last to be established in Europe — was at Vaivara, supported by around 20 satellites, one of which was Klooga (see *The Nazi Death Camps Then and Now*). Himmler, seen here smoking a cigar, visited Estonia on an inspection tour with his deputy Reinhard Heydrich (third from left) so the photo must have been taken before the latter's death on June 4, 1942. The Third Reich accorded Heydrich a hero's grave in Berlin's Invaliden Cemetery (see page 47). However, Himmler, responsible for the deaths of countless millions, committed suicide upon his capture in May 1945 and four British Army soldiers were detailed to take his body out to bury it in a secret grave near Lüneburg (see *After the Battle* Nos. 14 and 17).

This proclamation therefore encouraged the hope on the part of the local population that their private properties would be restored to them. However, in the first executive regulation concerning the re-organisation of handicrafts, small industry and the retail trade issued on December 23, 1941, the Commissioner General in Riga announced that in order to avoid excessive upheaval to normal economic life, the abolition of the Bolshevik system would only take place step by step. The reason for the change in attitude would appear to be that the communist system now seemed of benefit to the German war economy since it provided a concentration of resources and wealth in a centralised form of control. The existing institutions such as collective farms (Kolhozy) and state farms (Sovhozy) and industrial associations such as combines, cartels and trusts, were considered by the Germans as ideal for immediately taking over the whole economy of the area.

The return of small industrial concerns and retail trade outlets was envisaged to a certain extent only in the Baltic States, but was still made dependent upon two principles: it must be in the 'public interest' and the owner must be personally and professionally qualified to manage the business. Properties that were likely to lose efficiency and output in the hands of a private owner, or by redistribution between or among the several owners, were not to be handed back to those to whom they rightfully belonged.

The procedure for the return of property required a formal and detailed application. Then, in the event of a favourable decision, the permit for restoration of the property specified a date on which the property in question was to be separated from the collective or state institution.

RAPHAEL LEMKIN, 1944

Soviet forces entered the sub-camp at Klooga on September 28, 1944 and found hundreds of unburied bodies, with evidence that attempts had been made to destroy the corpses by burning. German prisoners were brought in to dig mass graves and bury the dead.

In August 1939, while outwardly negotiating a German-Soviet Commercial Agreement, Joachim von Ribbentrop, the German Foreign Minister, and Vyacheslav Molotov, his Soviet counterpart, agreed secret non-aggression protocols that divided Poland between Germany and the USSR (see map page 83). Eleven days after the Soviet invasion of Poland, the secret protocol in the Pact was modified by the German–Soviet Treaty of Friendship, Co-operation and Demarcation, allotting Germany a larger part of Poland and transferring the majority of Lithuania to the Soviets. On January 10, 1941, both then signed an further agreement modifying the 'Secret Additional Protocols' of the German–Soviet Boundary and Friendship Treaty. This ceded a strip of Lithuanian territory to the Soviet Union in exchange for 31.5 million Reichsmarks, and formally set the border between Germany and the Soviet Union between the Igorka river and the Baltic Sea.

The Union of Soviet Socialist Republics

The Reich Ministry for the Occupied Territories in the East, which was created in Berlin shortly after the war with the Soviet Union started in June 1941, extended its control to the territories of the USSR to the east of the eastern borders of the Baltic States, Poland and Romania as they existed at the outbreak of the war in 1939. (The part of Russia between the Rivers Dniester and Lower Bug was under Romanian occupation, see page 304.)

In the 1980s, the date of August 23 began to be used by refugees from those countries still occupied by the Soviet Union to protest against the Pact that gave Stalin a free hand in Eastern Europe. On August 23, 1986, 'Black Ribbon Day' demonstrations, as they became called, were held in 21 western countries. Today August 23 has been officially made the European Day of Remembrance for Victims of Stalinism and Nazism.

GERMAN –SOVIET NON-AGGRESSION PACT

The Government of the German Reich and The Government of the Union of Soviet Socialist Republics desirous of strengthening the cause of peace between Germany and the USSR, and proceeding from the fundamental provisions of the Neutrality Agreement concluded in April 1926 between Germany and the USSR, have reached the following Agreement:

ARTICLE I. Both High Contracting Parties obligate themselves to desist from any act of violence, any aggressive action, and any attack on each other, either individually or jointly with other Powers.

ARTICLE II. Should one of the High Contracting Parties become the object of belligerent action by a third Power, the other High Contracting Party shall in no manner lend its support to this third Power.

ARTICLE III. The Governments of the two High Contracting Parties shall in the future maintain continual contact with one another for the purpose of consultation in order to exchange information on problems affecting their common interests.

ARTICLE IV. None of the High Contracting Parties shall participate in any grouping of Powers whatsoever that is directly or indirectly aimed at the other party.

ARTICLE V. Should disputes or conflicts arise between the High Contracting Parties over problems of one kind or another, both parties shall settle these disputes or conflicts exclusively through friendly exchange of opinion or, if necessary, through the establishment of arbitration commissions.

ARTICLE VI. The present Treaty is concluded for a period of ten years, with the proviso that, in so far as one of the High Contracting Parties does not advance it one year prior to the expiration of this period, the validity of this Treaty shall automatically be extended for another five years.

ARTICLE VII. The present treaty shall be ratified within the shortest possible time. The ratifications shall be exchanged in Berlin. The Agreement shall enter into force as soon as it is signed.

[The section below was not published at the time.]

Secret Additional Protocol.

ARTICLE I. In the event of a territorial and political rearrangement in the areas belonging to the Baltic States (Finland, Estonia, Latvia, Lithuania), the northern boundary of Lithuania shall represent the boundary of the spheres of influence of Germany and USSR In this connection the interest of Lithuania in the Vilna area is recognised by each party.

ARTICLE II. In the event of a territorial and political rearrangement of the areas belonging to the Polish state, the spheres of influence of Germany and the USSR shall be bounded approximately by the line of the rivers Narev, Vistula and San.

The question of whether the interests of both parties make desirable the maintenance of an independent Polish States and how such a state should be bounded can only be definitely determined in the course of further political developments.

In any event both Governments will resolve this question by means of a friendly agreement.

ARTICLE III. With regard to South-eastern Europe attention is called by the Soviet side to its interest in Bessarabia. The German side declares its complete political disinterestedness in these areas.

ARTICLE IV. This protocol shall be treated by both parties as strictly secret.

Moscow, August 23, 1939.

For the Government of the German Reich v. Ribbentrop Plenipotentiary of the Government of the USSR V. Molotov

---

As far as Hitler was concerned, the Pact was a tactical manoeuvre to allow him to invade Poland without the fear of Soviet intervention so his message to Stalin on August 25 was somewhat two-faced: 'On the occasion of your 60th [sic] anniversary, please accept my sincerest congratulations. With this I want to pass my best wishes, good health personally to you, and also happy future to the people of friendly Soviet Union.' Stalin replied: 'To the head of the State of Germany, Mr Adolf Hitler. Please accept my appreciation for your congratulations and for your kind wishes to the people of Soviet Union.'

On September 17, Vasily Chuikov's Fourth Army received the order to cross the Polish border. Three days later, and 20 days after the German invasion of Poland, advance units of the Soviet 29th Tank Brigade, led by Brigadier-General Semyon Krivoshein, encountered General Heinz Guderian's forces of the XIX. Armeekorps moving in the direction of Brest-Litovsk. Upon approaching the city, at the confluence of the Bug and Mukhavets rivers on the morning of September 22, Krivoshein realised that German troops were in occupation and that Guderian had already established his headquarters there. During his meeting with Krivoshein, Guderian proposed a joint parade of Soviet and German troops, including a line-up of soldiers from both armies on the central square. However, because the Soviet troops were tired after a long march, Krivoshein declined but promised to supply a military band and a few battalions and agreed to Guderian's request that they both stand together to review the parade.

The square was named Adolf-Hitler-Platz during the Nazi occupation but after 1945, with Brest ending up in Byelorussia, it became Lenin Square.

ADMINISTRATION

The territories occupied by Germany in Russia were included partly in the General Commissariat for White Russia, the headquarters of which was in Minsk, and partly in the Reich Commissariat for the Ukraine. Both commissariats also included the Polish territory to the west of the Polish-Russian border as it existed in 1939. The eastern parts of the Polish provinces — Nowogródek, Wilno and Polesie — were included in the General Commissariat for White Russia, while the main part of the Polish province of Luck, as well as the southern part of the Polish province of Polesie, was included in the Reich Commissariat for the Ukraine.

The General Commissariat for White Russia formed part of the Reich Commissariat for the Ostland, which had its headquarters in Riga, and was supervised by the Ministry for the Occupied

Territories in the East with headquarters in Berlin. It consisted of ten regional districts (Landgebiete): Minsk-Land, Wilejka, Glebokie, Borisow, Sluck, Lida, Slonim, Baranowicze, Nowo-

gródek and Hancewicze. The first five districts were grouped in the general region of Minsk (Hauptgebiet Minsk), and the other five districts in Baranowicze (Hauptgebiet Baranowicze).

Brest (the name was shortened in 1945) has gone down in the history books as the place where the Treaty of Brest-Litovsk was signed on March 3, 1918 between the new Bolshevik government of Soviet Russia and the Central Powers (Germany, Austria-Hungary, Bulgaria and the Ottoman Empire) that ended Russia's participation in the First World War, although the treaty was superseded in November 1918 when Germany surrendered to the Allies. How-

ever, it was the memory of the joint German-Soviet victory parade held in 1939 that led one Russian commentator to state recently that 'in Soviet history there were many disgraceful events that Soviet historians never acknowledged officially. One of these shameful pages was the Soviet-Fascist parade in Brest.' *Right:* On the podium (L-R): Generalleutnant Mauritz von Wiktorin, commander of the 20. Infanterie-Division, Guderian and Krivoshein.

From the beginning of operational planning for the attack on the USSR, Germans intended to wage a war of annihilation against the Communist state as well as the Jews of the Soviet Union whom they characterised as forming the racial basis for the Soviet state. Officials of the Army High Command (Oberkommando des Heeres — OKH) and the Reich Security Main Office (Reichssicherheitshauptamt — RSHA) prepared for the deployment of mobile killing units behind the front lines to physically annihilate Jews, communists, and other persons deemed to be dangerous to establishment of long-term German rule on Soviet territory. These Einsatzgruppen were special squads from the Security Police and the Security Service (Sicherheitsdienst — SD). As the German army advanced deep into Soviet territory, the Einsatzgruppen followed with the Wehrmacht providing logistical support, including supplies, transportation, housing and occasionally manpower to guard and transport prisoners. At first the Einsatzgruppen shot primarily Jewish men but by the late summer of 1941 they also killed Jews without regard for age or sex. The commander of Einsatzgruppe A was SS-Brigadeführer and Generalmajor der Polizei Franz Stahlecker (left) and in a report of October 15, 1941 he wrote that 'considering that the population of the Baltic countries had suffered very heavily under the government of Bolshevism and Jewry while they were incorporated in the USSR, it was to be expected that after the liberation from that foreign government, they would render harmless most of the enemies left behind after the retreat of the Red Army. During the first pogrom on the night of June 25/26, the Lithuanian partisans did away with more than 1,500 Jews, set fire to several synagogues or destroyed them by other means, and burned down a Jewish dwelling district consisting of about 60 houses. During the following nights about 2,300 Jews were made harmless in a similar way.'

The Reich Commissariat for the Ukraine, with headquarters in Równe, was divided into six general commissariats: Zitomir, Kiev, Nikolajev, Tshernigov, Dnepropetrovsk and Crimea, and was also supervised from Berlin by the Ministry for Occupied Territories.

The areas under the General Commissariat for White Russia and the Reich Commissariat for the Ukraine were in the hands of German non-military administrators, while those areas to the east of these commissariats, approaching the zone of military operations, were in the hands of military commanders.

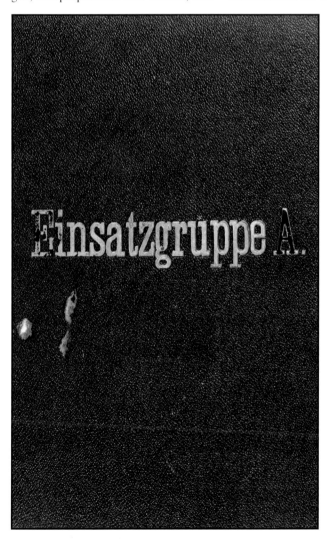

In November Stahlecker advised Berlin that Einsatzgruppe A had murdered some 249,420 Jews, which resulted in his promotion to Höhere SS- und Polizeiführer of Reichskommissariat Ostland at the end of the month. His report with charts, maps and illustrations was submitted to the Reich Security Main Office in Berlin in February 1942 and when it was discovered after the war, it was used as incriminating evidence in the Einsatzgruppen trial at Nuremberg (see page 298). (Stahlecker was killed by Soviet partisans near Krasnogvardeysk, Russia, on March 23, 1942.)

Victims were marched or transported by truck to the site chosen for the execution where trenches had already been prepared. In some cases, the people were made to dig their own graves (see

page 298). After they had handed over their valuables and had undressed, men, women and children were shot, either standing before the open trench, or lying face down in the prepared pit.

One of the first large-scale mass murders in the Reichskommissariat Ukraine took place under its head for the southern region, SS-Obergruppenführer Friedrich Jeckeln (we already met him in

Latvia on page 282), at Kamianets-Podilskyi in south-west Ukraine on August 27-28, 1941 when 23,600 Jews were massacred. (Jeckeln was publically hanged in Riga on February 3, 1946.)

After the war, Jews from the town tried in several ways to commemorate their relatives who had been murdered and in August 1946 an attempt was made to hold a meeting to remember the fifth anniversary of their deaths. However, the local authorities categorically banned such a meeting. In July 1948 members of the Jewish community petitioned Nikolai Shvernik, the Chairman of the Presidium of the Supreme Council of the USSR, and Nikita Khrushchev, the Chairman of the Council of Ministers of

the Ukrainian SSR, to allow them to publicly commemorate the Jewish victims, but still to no avail. Nevertheless, local Jews later succeeded in erecting several monuments at the crime scenes. Two were placed at the site of the former munitions depot where thousands had been murdered, with inscriptions in Russian and Yiddish, and in recent years further memorials have been dedicated. Jews living in Kamianets-Podilskyi still gather annually in remembrance of those who lost their lives.

The slaughter of the innocents at Babi Yar, the largest mass killing during the campaign in the Soviet Union. Little Mania Halef *(left)* was just one of the 33,000 victims.

PROPERTY

In the territories occupied in Russia that were part of the USSR in accordance with the frontier of 1939, the problem of private property presented various problems. In the first stage of the occupation, the Germans maintained the communist status of ownership. Collective farms were continued but since the knowledgeable heads of these farms had fled with the Russian Army, the Germans were faced with a serious situation as the land had to provide food for the army. Also the farms were unproductive because of the scarcity of implements and sometimes even of manpower. The task of reorganising and supervising these farms was entrusted to German agricultural leaders (Landwirtschaftsführer), specially trained in Germany. In order to increase their authority, they were vested with some administrative powers, and with the right to punish farmers for not carrying out the agricultural programme.

The Germans were reluctant to return to the system of private property in those areas because such a redistribution of land would require capital and implements, with a great many technical and legal formalities (such as measurements and recording by courts). Difficulties would also arise in tracing titles of former owners, particularly with city property. The problem of finding criteria for establishing new property titles had also to be solved. In order to instil fear, the Germans simply relied on the principle of collective responsibility in Russian cities and farms, a principle that found its natural basis in the institution of Soviet collective ownership and work among the Russian people. For example, if a collective farm failed to deliver its products, all the members of the farm would be punished collectively.

However, apparently for propaganda purposes, a change in the forms of ownership was envisaged by the decree of Reich Minister Rosenberg issued on February 28, 1942, which was designed to 'guide the agricultural population back to individual farming'. The decree stated

It was orchestrated by Generalmajor Kurt Eberhard *(left)*, the military governor of Kiev, together with Jeckeln and the Einsatzgruppe C commander, SS-Brigadeführer Otto Rasch. The Einsatzgruppen in the Soviet Union were composed of four battalion-sized operational groups. Einsatzgruppe A fanned out from East Prussia across Lithuania, Latvia and Estonia toward Leningrad, and massacred Jews in Kaunas, Riga and Vilna. Einsatzgruppe B started out from Warsaw and moved across Byelorussia toward Smolensk and Minsk, carrying out massacres in Grodno, Minsk, Brest-Litovsk, Slonim, Gomel and Mogilev, among other places. Einsatzgruppe C began operations from Krakow and then across the western Ukraine toward Kharkov and Rostov-on-Don. Its personnel directed massacres in Lvov, Tarnopol, Zolochev, Kremenets, Kharkov, Zhitomir and Kiev where in late September 1941 units of the Einsatzgruppe's detachment 4a massacred 33,771 Kiev Jews in the ravine at Babi Yar *(right)*. Einsatzgruppe D operated in the southern Ukraine and the Crimea, especially in Nikolayev, Kherson, Simferopol, Sevastopol, Feodosiya and in the Krasnodar region. (Eberhard was captured by American forces in November 1945 but committed suicide while in captivity on September 8, 1947. Rasch died November 1, 1948 while in custody.)

Walther von Reichenau (right) was the son of a Prussian general and served in the Prussian Army in the First World War. He became an ardent supporter of Nazism, served in Poland in 1939 and on the Western Front in 1940, being promoted to Field Marshal in June. Although he opposed the invasion of the Soviet Union, nevertheless he commanded the 6. Armee in its drive through the Ukraine in 1941. His unequivocal order issued on October 10 that year *(below)* came in the wake of the Babi Yar massacre of September 29-30. In an attempt to keep fit, Reichenau used to go on a daily cross-country run, and on January 12, 1942, he ran several kilometres in temperatures well below minus 20 degrees Fahrenheit. When he returned, he complained of feeling unwell and later that day he suffered a severe heart attack. After being unconscious for five days, it was decided to fly him back to Germany but he died on January 17 when the plane carrying him to Leipzig crash-landed. He was given a state funeral and interred in the Invalidenfriedhof in Berlin.

that collective farms (Kolhozy) were to be transformed into joint-farming establishments (Gemeinwirtschaften). The latter were considered, according to the decree, to be of a merely transitional nature. From this an individual farming system was to be developed to combine the principle of co-operative farming with that of individual farming. The following organisations were adopted by the Germans for farming in the territory they occupied in Russia.

The Joint-Farming Establishment (Gemeinwirtschaft). The members of a joint-farming establishment were peasant farmers employed in the labour of plowing, sowing and harvesting, and they received wages. Full property rights in the small plots surrounding their houses were granted them whereas, in the collective system, the farmers had individual use of the plots only as long as they were members of the collective farm.

The main difference between a joint farming establishment and a collective farm was that with the latter, income in kind or in cash was distributed on the basis of so-called 'labour days' which were not actually working days but abstract accounting units used to calculate the amount of work performed by individual workers. In a joint-farm the farmers received wages. Also the right to breed cattle was now granted to managers of joint-farm establishments.

ORDERS FOR CONDUCT IN THE EAST

Army Headquarters, October 10, 1941
Subject: Conduct of Troops in Eastern Territories.

Regarding the conduct of troops towards the Bolshevistic system, vague ideas are still prevalent in many cases. The most essential aim of war against the Jewish-Bolshevistic system is a complete destruction of their means of power and the elimination of Asiatic influence from the European culture. In this connection the troops are facing tasks that exceed the one-sided routine of soldiering. The soldier in the Eastern territories is not merely a fighter according to the rules of the art of war but also a bearer of ruthless national ideology and the avenger of bestialities which have been inflicted upon German and racially related nations.

Therefore, the soldier must have full understanding for the necessity of a severe but just revenge on sub-human Jewry. The Army has to aim at another purpose, i.e. the annihilation of revolts in the hinterland, which, as experience proves, have always been caused by Jews.

Combating the enemy behind the front line is still not being taken seriously enough. Treacherous, cruel partisans and degenerate women are still being made prisoners of war, and guerilla fighters dressed partly in uniform or plain clothes and vagabonds are still being treated as proper soldiers and sent to prisoner of war camps. In fact, captured Russian officers talk even mockingly about Soviet agents moving openly about the roads and, very often, even eating at German field kitchens.

Such an attitude of the troops can only be explained by complete thoughtlessness so it is now high time for the commanders to clarify the meaning of the pressing struggle.

The feeding of the natives and of prisoners of war who are not working for the armed forces from Army kitchens is an equally misunderstood humanitarian act as is the giving of cigarettes and bread. Things which the people at home can spare under great sacrifices and things that are being brought by the command to the front under great difficulties should not be given to the enemy by the soldier even if they originate from booty. It is an important part of our supply.

When retreating, the Soviets have often set buildings on fire. The troops should be interested in extinguishing fires only as far as it is necessary to secure sufficient numbers of billets. Otherwise, the disappearance of symbols of the former Bolshevistic rule, even in the form of buildings, is part of the struggle of destruction. Neither historic nor artistic considerations are of any importance in the Eastern territories. The command issues the necessary directives for the securing of raw material and plants vital to the war economy.

The complete disarming of the civilian population in the rear of the fighting troops is imperative considering the long, vulnerable lines of communications. Where possible, captured weapons and ammunition should be stored and guarded. Should this

be impossible because of the battle situation, the weapons and ammunition will be rendered useless. If isolated partisans are found using firearms in the rear of the army, drastic measures are to be taken. These measures will be extended to that part of the male population who were in a position to hinder or report the attacks. The indifference of numerous apparently anti-Soviet elements, which originates from a 'wait and see' attitude, must give way to a clear decision for active collaboration. If not, no one can complain about being judged and treated a member of the Soviet system.

The fear of German counter-measures must be stronger than threats of the wandering Bolshevistic remnants. Regardless of all future political considerations, the soldier has to fulfil two tasks:

1. Complete annihilation of the false Bolshevist doctrine of the Soviet state and its armed forces.

2. The pitiless extermination of foreign treachery and cruelty and thus the protection of the lives of military personnel in Russia.

This is the only way to fulfill our historic task to liberate the German people once and for all from the Asiatic-Jewish danger.

Commander-in-Chief
VON REICHENAU
Feldmarschall

The Lazebniks lived in the town of Lenin (in Poland but named after the original estate owner, not the communist revolutionary). Their son Moishe ran the family photographic business and his sister Faigel learned photography from her brother. After the start of the war, Lenin fell under Soviet control and they ordered that all inhabitants have a valid identification card so Faigel was kept busy taking photographs for the whole town and surrounding villages. On May 10, 1942, the Nazis created a ghetto in Lenin but on August 14 they rounded up the ghetto's Jews and placed them in an open truck. They were taken to three trenches outside the town where they were shot, 1,850 being killed including Faigel's parents, sisters and younger brother. Faigel was spared along with six essential workers. The Nazis took pictures of the killing and ordered Faigel to develop the prints. Two weeks later, when a group of partisans burst into the town, Faigel fled to the forests with them. She joined the Molotov Brigade, a partisan group composed mostly of escaped Soviet POWs. Though she did not have a weapon or military training, she was accepted because the partisans knew that her brother-in-law had been a doctor and assumed that she could work as nurse.

The Farming Association (Landbau-Genossenschaft). This was an association of individual farmers who received merely the usufruct of the land. They were engaged in collective labour for only part of the year, for example, for plowing, sowing and harvesting. Members did not receive wages. The crops they harvest were divided among them, after deduction of compulsory deliveries to the German administration. Here, as well as in the joint-farming system, the prospect was held out to the members that the land might in the future be conveyed to them in full ownership.

For the next two years Faigel lived with the partisans serving as a nurse and also participating in their raids. Later in 1942, the Molotov Brigade conducted a second raid on Lenin. Faigel went along with the group and fortunately succeeded in recovering her old photographic equipment and family pictures. During the next two years, she took over a hundred photographs and developed them in primitive darkrooms made from blankets. These are just two of the photographs she took. After the war, Faigel worked as a photographer in Pinsk before she later emigrated to North America. *Above:* Pictured from left to right are M. I. Gerasimov, commander of the Molotov Brigade, Pinsk region; S. I. Sikorskiy, secretary of the underground regional committee of the Communist Party of the Brest region, and N. V. Bobkov, commander of the Soviet Byelorussian partisan detachment, Brest region. *Left:* Members of the Molotov Brigade.

The ultimate price should a partisan be captured was death and, according to the caption, this is believed to be one of the first public executions after the invasion of the USSR. Three Byelorussian partisans — one woman and two men — were hanged by troops of the 707. Infanterie-Division on Karl Marx Street in Minsk in front of the National Academy of Science of Byelorussia on October 26, 1941. The woman was identified as Olga Shcherbatsevich whose son was hanged on the gate of the Minsk yeast generator plant the same day (see overleaf). The bodies were left to hang for several days to serve as a warning to would-be resistors, the notice reads: 'We are partisans and have shot at German soldiers'.

Individual farms (Einzelwirtschaft). Individual farming was permitted only in exceptional cases by the German authorities. Such farms were granted as a reward for co-operation with the Germans against Soviet guerrillas as well as for demonstrated efficiency in farming.

State farms (Sovhozy) were taken over and maintained under German administration. In this, the role played by the tractor stations in the Soviet system was a vital factor as the depots were the central point in the organisation of Soviet agriculture. The stations held the monopoly of mechanised equipment and leased it to collective farms. The services of tractor stations was paid for in kind in grain, sunflower seed, etc., at rates fixed by the government for different types of operations. By monopolising mechanised implements, the Soviet Government was enabled to control and impose its will upon the collective farms. The Germans took over this system completely because it served the German war economy for the supply of essential produce for the military, as well as political control. Under such a system, the counterpart for reward was punishment which was applied extensively to Russian and Ukrainian peasants who were reluctant to co-operate with the Germans.

The following month Hinrich Lohse (we met him on page 279) published this proclamation concerning partisan activity.

JUSTICE

The problem of organising justice in the Ukraine created many difficulties. The local courts (so-called 'People's Courts'), based upon the principles of communist justice, obviously could not be used for political reasons. On the other hand, because of the fact that the communist regime was retained in its essential features, the need for courts to deal with civil matters was not so urgent as it would be in a country which allowed private ownership. The Germans resolved the problem of civil justice by setting up an institution of local arbitrators (Einheimische Schlichter) to take care of civil disputes arising between members of the local population. These arbitrators were appointed by the Reich Commissioner for the Ukraine upon the recommendation of the respective district commissioners. For criminal cases German courts were patterned along the same lines as those for the other occupied countries.

GENOCIDE AND RESISTANCE

Since the beginning of the occupation, the Russian population was engaged in constant guerrilla fighting with the Germans. Widespread collective penalties were inflicted in the form of mass execu-

---

UNION OF SOVIET SOCIALIST REPUBLICS
Proclamation, November 15, 1941

In the interest of the safety of the country and the security of the property of the inhabitants, the combatting of terroristic bands and groups will be carried out by the authorities with all intensity.

The people are urged to give their active co-operation to this effort.

1. Anyone who observes suspicious elements, particularly parachute jumpers, escaped Soviet Russian officers or soldiers, spies or saboteurs, Soviet Russian officials, etc., or members of their families, or who has or obtains knowledge of their appearance or places to which they resort, must report this information immediately to the nearest German or non-German public agency.

2. Anyone who fails to make such a report or gives these enemies any kind of aid (maintenance, care or any other assistance) will be shot.

3. Any member of a non-German public agency who does not immediately transmit a report made to him to the nearest German officer will be shot.

4. For information leading to the prevention of disruptions of public security and order, or to the apprehension of the offender, a reward to the amount of 5,000 rubles may be granted by the District Commissioner. Informers shall be assured that if they wish their names will be kept secret.

5. The residents of communities shall be collectively responsible for the security of communication lines passing in their vicinity — roads, railways, wires and all other German installations. For neglect of this responsibility drastic proceedings will be taken against the residents, particularly against the responsible elders of communities, counties and districts.

Riga, November 15, 1941.

LOHSE
Reich Commissioner for the Ostland

---

tions and mass destruction of property. The scorched-earth policy carried out by the retiring German armies increased the extent of destruction. In implementing the decisions of the Moscow Conference to the effect that war criminals should be tried by local courts of the countries where the crimes were perpetrated, the Government of the USSR ordered the first trials of German war criminals in December 1943. These trials revealed a gruesome picture of war atrocities.

At the yeast factory, 12 members of the Communist underground in Minsk were hanged in four groups of three. Of the four only one group was photographed. This consisted of Olga's son Volodya, Masha Bruskina and Kiril Trus. Bruskina was a 17-year-old Jewish girl who had resided in the Minsk ghetto during the summer of 1941. She was living as a non-Jew on the Aryan side when she was captured. In the months before her arrest she had worked as a medical assistant in a hospital that the German army had converted into a prison camp for wounded Soviet POWs. In league with resistance groups operating near Minsk, she smuggled in civilian clothing and false documents for escaping Soviet officers. Following her arrest by German troops she was imprisoned and tortured. Unable to make her yield, the Germans then paraded Masha and her two Byelorussian colleagues through the streets of Minsk wearing placards before an officer of the 707. Infanterie-Division publically executed them.

A ghetto had been created soon after Minsk was captured and the Germans lost no time in wiping out 1,000 Jews, a total that rose to over 20,000 once Einsatzgruppe B got to work. In March 1942, 5,000 were killed on this spot on the corner of Melnikayte and Zaslavskaya Streets. When a memorial, dubbed 'The Pit', was proposed in 1947, no machinery was used and all work was carried out by hand, a process that took eight years. Then in 2000 a bronze sculpture was added of a column of doomed martyrs walking down the steps into the pit.

LABOUR

Russian workers were used to a great extent by the Germans in the occupied territories where an especially severe regime was established. Any reluctance to work, or inefficiency in work, was punished, such punishment ranging from flogging to the death penalty.

Special provisions regarding wages were made for workers transferred to Germany from the Reich Commissariat for the Ukraine, from the General Commissariat for White Russia, and from the territory further east. Thus, according to a decree issued on June 30, 1942 by Hermann Göring, President of the Council of Ministers for the Defence of the Reich, the workers imported from these eastern territories were given a special employment status.

RAPHAEL LEMKIN, 1944

Above: Situated at Pinsk, some 220 kilometres south-west of Minsk, was one of the largest ghettos in the Soviet Union, and in October 1942 Himmler was conducting a fact-finding tour in the area. He was pictured there on the 27th with Higher SS and Police Leader SS-Obergruppenführer Hans Prützmann (on the extreme left) who he had just instructed to kill all the residents of the ghetto. *Right:* Between October 29 and November 1 over 16,000 were murdered at Pinsk. The inhabitants were marched to Dobrovalia, a village five kilometres from the ghetto, where local peasants had been made to dig a huge pit, 40 metres long and four deep. The people were ordered to strip and walk into the pit and lie down on those already dead to wait to be shot in the head. At the end of the war, Prützmann was captured by the British but committed suicide on May 21, 1945. SS-Gruppenführer Ludolf von Alvensleben (second from the left), who was co-responsible for the massacre, was also apprehended by British forces but escaped and fled to Argentina, never to be brought to justice.

Krasnodar, 1300 hours, July 18, 1943: summary justice on the city square. 'Deliberating in open court from the 14th to the 17th of July, the Military Tribunal of the North Caucasus Front has examined the matter of the atrocities of the German Fascist invaders and their supporters on the territory of the City of

Krasnodar and Krasnodar region. The Military Tribunal has sentenced Ivan Kladov, Mikhail Lastovina, Georgi Misan, Yakov Naptsok, Vassily Pavlov, Nikolai Pushkarev, Vladimir Tischenko and Gregori Tuchkov to death by hanging. The sentence is final and no appeals will be heard.'

'Comrade Colonel, carry out the sentence.' Still from a cine film showing the hanging of Russians who had collaborated with the Nazis.

Interviewer: 'Christina Ivanovna, please tell us what I heard you telling us earlier. Which of them do you know well?' Christina: 'This one in the pink shirt, Pushkarev. There was a building here at the new bazaar and in the basement were 300 people who had been arrested. And certainly he was guarding them. He was armed and when the building caught fire, well of course there was a great cry. It was horrible. The people were going to be burned.' Interviewer: 'Who was shouting?' Christina: 'The

arrestees . . . our Soviet people. And the neighbours could not stand it and they ran there to that building and went down on their knees and begged him.' Interviewer: 'Who were they begging?' Christina: 'This Puskarev here. Please open the doors, we will give you money. How much do you want? And they offered him a lot of money and he said "Get out of here or I'll shoot you". And of course we couldn't do anything to help the people, and so they all burned and we couldn't stop it.'

Right: The old town hall overlooked the main square in Krasnodar where the executions took place in 1943. *Above:* Today, beautifuly landscaped, a striking new town hall dominates Theatre Square. *Below:* On May 9, 2015, Krasnodar celebrated the victory of the Soviet Union in the Great Patriotic War. The Governor Veniamin Kondratiev addressed 384 veterans in the Grandstand of Honour: 'Dear veterans, respectable compatriots! Today is the ninth of May. It is the main date for Russia and it is the day of national triumph and a holiday for every family. No other country in the world has made such an awful sacrifice for the sake of peace. Krasnodar Region was among the first which faced the enemy's attack, and a great deal of hardship was experienced by Krasnodar where the fascists martyred thousands citizens in gas-vans. We remember all this and bow to the heroic feat of Soviet soldiers; our life itself is entirely your Victory. Respectable veterans, thank you so much for the possibility of being proud of your feat. Hats off to you.'

The Largest Murder Trial in History

As early as November 1943, the Allied leaders Winston Churchill, Franklin Roosevelt and Joseph Stalin explicitly warned the German government that at the end of the war 'all those who have taken a consenting part in atrocities, massacres and executions of innocent people will be pursued to the uttermost ends of the earth and will be delivered to their accusers in order that justice may be done'. This statement became known as 'The Moscow Declaration on German Atrocities' and under its terms, the Allies agreed that perpetrators would be returned to the location of their crimes so that they could be punished accordingly by the local authorities. However, the Allied Control Council Law No. 10 of December 20, 1945 allowed the Allies to hold trials independent of one another. Robert Jackson, the US Supreme Court Justice appointed by President Truman in May 1945 to prosecute the most-prominent Nazi war criminals, was instrumental in the planning and preparation on the International Military Tribunal to be held in Nuremberg. It was his negative experiences, particularly with the Soviets, that led him to conclude that the United States should not participate in a second trial conducted by the Four Powers. Instead he favoured that each occupation authority pursue justice in their own zones against prisoners in their custody.

Brigadier Telford Taylor, the American lawyer in charge of organising what became known as the Nuremberg Military Trials (NMT), drew up a list for 12 separate trials, each one covering a particular facet of the Nazi regime. Bearing in mind that eight million Germans were members of the Nazi Party in May 1945, the number of potential war crimi-

nals was staggering so a short list had to be drawn up of 100 (revised to between 200-500) persons who were considered major war criminals. In the end the Americans tried fewer that 200 individuals in the 12 trials but, because of their scope, they have been adjudged as the single most concerted prosecution effort against Nazi criminals in the post-war period. Case No. 9 was to be for the leaders of the Einsatzgruppen responsible for the mass murder of Soviet Jewry.

There was no end to the killing in the Soviet Union and one could go on and on with further nauseating descriptions of hundreds of massacres at thousands of locations across the occupied USSR. It is difficult to put precise numbers to those killed by each Einsatzgruppe unit but by the end of 1941 alone, Einsatzgruppe A reported a total of 125,000; Einsatzgruppe B over 45,000; Einsatzgruppe C 95,000 by the beginning of December, and Einsatzgruppe D 76,000 by start of the New Year. These men, forcing victims to dig their own grave, most probably belonged to Einsatzgruppe A, and are believed to be at work in Siauliai, Lithuania.

EINSATZGRUPPEN COMMANDERS

Commanders	Dates of Command
Einsatzgruppe A	
Walter Stahlecker	June 22, 1941-March 23, 1942
Heinz Jost	March 23, 1942-June 15, 1942
Humbert Achamer-Pifrader	June 15, 1942-September 5, 1943
Friedrich Panzinger	September 5, 1943-May 6, 1944
Wilhelm Fuchs	May 6, 1944-October 17, 1944
Einsatzgruppe B	
Arthur Nebe	June 1, 1941-November 16, 1941
Erich Naumann	November 16, 1941- March 1, 1943
Horst Böhme	March 1, 1943-August 28, 1943
Erich Ehrlinger	August 28, 1943-April 28, 1944
Heinz Seetzen	April 28, 1944-August 11, 1944
Horst Böhme	August 11, 1944-August 28, 1944
Einsatzgruppe C	
Emil Otto Rasch	June 1, 1941-October 4, 1941
Max Thomas	October 4, 1941-August 28, 1943
Horst Böhme	September 6, 1943-March 1944
Einsatzgruppe D	
Otto Ohlendorf	June 4, 1941-July 30, 1942
Walther Bierkamp	July 30, 1942-July 15, 1943

The Einsatzgruppen, comprising approximately 3,000 men of the SS, were responsible for a death toll that was later estimated to be at least one million.

Left: One of the principal defendants was to be SS-Brigade-führer Otto Ohlendorf, the former head of Einsatzgruppe D who was arrested by the British at Admiral Karl Dönitz's headquarters in Flensburg on the Danish border. He freely admitted the he and his unit had killed 90,000 people. At the London Cage — the POW interrogation centre in Kensington Palace Gardens — he gave the first evidence linking Heydrich and Himmler to the implementation of the so-called 'Final Solution'

to the Jewish question. The Americans requested his extradition and he was taken to the main US military prison at Landsberg on October 18, 1945. So prolific was Ohlendorf's testimony that the subsequent trial was given the official title: 'The United States of America versus Otto Ohlendorf et al'. *Right:* On July 7, 1947, Colonel Charles Mays, the Marshal of the Military Tribunal, hands out the indictments to (L-R) Otto Ohlendorf, Heinz Jost, Erich Naumann and Erwin Schulz.

Several of those accused were extradited from the British and French zones but none from the USSR as the Soviets just ignored the request. In September 1947, 24 members of the Einsatzgruppen, including the heads of the four groups, were put on trial by the US Nuremberg Military Tribunal sitting in the same courtroom in the Palace of Justice that had been used a year earlier by the International Military Tribunal to try the top Nazi hierarchy. It was the only trial that dealt exclusively with the Hitler's plan for the Final Solution, and one which became a testing ground for the term 'genocide'

(coined by Raphael Lemkin in 1944, see page 6) — a crime that had yet to be legally codified. Also, unlike the earlier IMT in which many witnesses were called to give their testimony, the evidence for the NMT was provided by excerpts from operational reports by the Einsatzgruppen and the sworn affidavits of the defendants. Although it transpired that ideology was an important motivator to commit the murders, none of the defendants accepted any responsibility for their actions, and none showed any remorse or was willing to apologise for what they had done.

EINSATZKOMMANDO LEADERS

Group	Kommando	Leaders	Dates of Command
EG A	Sonderkommando 1a	Martin Sandberger	June 1941-August 1, 1943
		Bernhard Baatz	August 1, 1943-October 15, 1944
	Sonderkommando 1b	Erich Ehrlinger	June 1941- February 24, 1942
		Walter Hofmann	February 24, 1942-March 13,1942
		Eduard Strauch	March 13,1942-June 30, 1943
		Erich Isselhorst	June 30, 1943-October 1943
	Einsatzkommando 2	Rudolf Batz	June 1, 1941-November 4, 1941
		Eduard Strauch	November 4, 1941-December 3, 1941
		Rudolf Lange	December 3, 1941 March 2, 1944
	Einsatzkommando 3	Karl Jäger	June 1, 1941-September 15, 1943
		Wilhelm Fuchs	September 15, 1943-May 11, 1944
		Hans Joachim Böhme	May 11, 1944-January 1, 1945
	After re-organisation in June 1942:		
	Einsatzkommando 1a	Martin Sandberger	June 1942-Autumn 1942
	(later Einsatzkommando 1)	Karl Tschierschky	Autumn 1942
		Erich Isselhorst	November 13, 1942-June 30, 1943
		Bernhard Baatz	August 1, 1943-October 15, 1944
	Einsatzkommando 1b	Hermann Hubig	June 1942-October 1942
	(later Einsatzkommando 2)	Manfred Pechau	October 1942-March 26, 1943
		Reinhard Breder	March 26, 1943-September 1943
		Oswald Poche	September 1943-early 1944
	Einsatzkommando 1c	Kurt Graaf	August 1, 1942-November 28, 1942
	(later Einsatzkommando 3)	Kurt Traut	November 28, 1942-May (?) 1943
EG B	Sonderkommando 7a	Walter Blume	June 1, 1941-September 7, 1941
		Eugen Steimle	September 7, 1941-December 10, 1941
		Kurt Matschke	December 10, 1941-February 29, 1942
		Albert Rapp	February 29, 1942-January 28, 1943
		Helmut Looss	January 28, 1943-June 3, 1944
		Gerhard Bast	June 3, 1944-November 28,1944
	Sonderkommando 7b	Günther Rausch	June 1, 1941-February 15, 1942
		Adolf Ott	February 15, 1942-January 21, 1943
		Josef Auinger	January 21, 1943-January 27, 1943
		Georg Raabe	January 27, 1943-October 14, 1944
		Rudolf Hotzel	October 1944-???
	Vorkommando Moscow	Franz Six	June 20, 1941-August 22, 1941
	(Sonderkommando 7c	Waldemar Klingelhöfer	August 22, 1941-October 1, 1941
	from January 1942)	Erich Körting	October 1, 1941-December 1941
		Wilhelm Bock	December 1941-June 2, 1942
		Rudolf Schmücker	June 2, 1942-August 29, 1942
		Wilhelm Bluhm	August 29,1942-July 22, 1943
		Hans Eckard	July 22, 1943-December 27, 1943
	Einsatzkommando 8	Otto Bradfisch	June 1, 1941-January 21, 1942
		Heinz Richter	January 21, 1942-September 8, 1942
		Erich Isselhorst	September 8, 1942-November 13, 1942
		Hans Schindhelm	November 13, 1942-October 11, 1943
		Alfred Renndorfer	October 11, 1943-April 26, 1944
	Einsatzkommando 9	Alfred Filbert	June 1, 1941-October 20, 1941
		Oswald Schäfer	October 20, 1941-February 7, 1942
		Wilhelm Wiebens	February 7, 1942-January 19, 1943
		Friedrich Buchardt	January 19, 1943-October 10, 1943
		Werner Kämpf	October 10, 1943-March 16, 1944
EG C	Sonderkommando 4a	Paul Blobel	June 1, 1941-January 13, 1942
		Erwin Weinmann	January 13, 1942-July 27, 1942
		Eugen Steimle	July 27, 1942-January 9, 1943
		Friedrich Schmidt	January 9, 1943-January 15, 1943
		Theodor Christensen	January 15, 1943-August 28, 1943
	Sonderkommando 4b	Günther Hermann	June 1, 1941-October 1, 1941
		Fritz Braune	October 1, 1941-March 21, 1942
		Walter Haensch	March 21, 1942-July 6, 1942
		August Meier	July 6, 1942-November 17, 1942
		Friedrich Suhr	November 17, 1942-August 12,1943
		Waldemar Krause	August 12, 1943-January 7, 1944
	Einsatzkommando 5	Erwin Schulz	May 12, 1941-September 5, 1941
		August Meier	September 5, 1941-January 6, 1942
	Einsatzkommando 6	Erhard Kroeger	June 1, 1941-November 18, 1941
		Robert Mohr	November 18, 1941-September 5, 1942
		Ernst Biberstein	September 5, 1942-November 19, 1942
		Friedrich Suhr	November 19, 1942-August 5, 1943
EG D	Sonderkommando 10a	Heinz Seetzen	June 1, 1941-August 1, 1942
		Kurt Christmann	August 1, 1942-July 11, 1943
	Sonderkommando 10b	Alois Persterer	May 12, 1941-February 13, 1943
		Eduard Jedamzik	February 13, 1943-May 7, 1943
	Sonderkommando 11a	Paul Zapp	June 1, 1941-July 5, 1942
		Rolf Maurer	July 5, 1942-November 17, 1942
		Gerhard Bast	November 17, 1942-December 6, 1942
		Werner Hersmann	December 6, 1942-May 12, 1943
	Sonderkommando 11b	Hans Unglaube	June 1, 1941-July 21,1941
		Bruno Müller	July 21, 1941-October 23, 1942
		Werner Braune	October 23, 1941-September 16, 1942
		Paul Schultz	September 16, 1942-February 23, 1943
	Einsatzkommando 12	Gustav Nosske	June 1, 1941-March 1, 1942
		Erich Müller	March 1, 1942-October 24, 1942
		Günther Hermann	October 24, 1942-March 1, 1943

The four Einsatzgruppen were subdivided into a dozen numbered Einsatzkommandos, some of which were further split into two, sometimes three Sonderkommandos. As the campaign progressed some of the mobile units settled down in permanent stations and their commanders became the equivalent of Kommandeure der Sipo und des SD (KdS, Commanders of Security Police and Security Service) in their region, although the task of the unit remained the same. Einsatzgruppe A was re-organised in the summer of 1942.

In its judgement the NMT declared that the facts were so beyond the experience of normal man and the range of man-made phenomena that only the most complete judicial inquiry could verify and confirm them. This was 'a crime of such unprecedented brutality and of such inconceivable savagery that the mind rebels against its own thought image and the imagination staggers in the contemplation of a human degradation beyond the power of language to adequately portray. The number of deaths resulting from the activities with which these defendants have been connected and which the prosecution has set at one million is but an abstract number. One cannot grasp the full cumulative terror of murder one million times repeated. It is only when this grotesque total is broken down into units capable of mental assimilation that one can understand the monstrousness of the things we are in this trial contemplating. One must visualise not one million people but only ten persons — men, women, and children, perhaps all of one family — falling before the executioner's guns. If one million is divided by ten, this scene must happen one hundred thousand times, and as one visualises the repetitive horror, one begins to understand the meaning of the prosecution's words: "It is with sorrow and with hope that we here disclose the deliberate slaughter of more than a million innocent and defenseless men, women and children".'

In May 1949 the Federal Republic of Germany was established in the British, French and US Zones of West Germany, one of its tenets being the ending of the death penalty. This resulted in a groundswell by politicians, the clergy, abolitionists, and others to close down the military prison at Landsberg where several Nazi prisoners still faced execution. In the latter half of 1950 and into 1951, thousands of Germans took part in protest demonstrations outside the prison calling for pardons to be given to all war criminals. Media coverage was overwhelmingly on the side of the condemned who were now depicted as innocent victims of American justice. Matters turned violent on January 7, 1951 when a group of Jewish protesters arrived at Landsberg demanding the execution of the remaining prisoners. Those demonstrating for an amnesty began chanting the Nazi cry of 'Juden raus!' and clashes broke out as the Jews were beaten up. One German politician even went as far as comparing the suffering of the condemned prisoners with that of the deaths of six million Jews. The West German Chancellor, Konrad Adenauer, met with John McCloy and argued that to execute the remaining prisoners would ruin the co-operation of the two countries. McCloy was also put under extreme pressure by German public opinion to review the sentences that had been handed down at the Nuremberg and also the Dachau trials and, as a result, 21 of the remaining 28 prisoners under sentence of death were reprieved. However, execution of seven others — described as 'the worst of the worst' — was confirmed.

SENTENCES

Defendant	Original Sentence	Advisory Board	McCloy
Blobel, Paul	Death	Death	Death
Biberstein, Ernst	Death	15 years	Life
Blume, Walter	Death	20 years	25 years
Braune, Werner	Death	Death	Death
Fendler, Lothar	10 years	Time served	8 years
Haensch, Walter	Death	15 years	15 years
Jost, Heinz	Life	10 years	10 years
Klingelhöfer, Waldemar	Death	Death	Life
Naumann, Erich	Death	Death	Death
Nosske, Gustav	Life	10 years	10 years
Ohlendorf, Otto	Death	Death	Death
Ott, Adolf	Death	Death	Life
Radetzky, Waldemar von	20 years	Time served	Time served
Rühl, Felix	10 years	Time served	Time served
Sandberger, Martin	Death	Death	Life
Schubert, Heinz	Death	Time served	10 years
Schulz, Erwin	20 years	10 years	15 years
Seibert, Willy	Death	Time served	15 years
Six, Franz	20 years	Time served	15 years
Steimle, Eugen	Death	15 years	20 years

With the International Military Tribunal there was no provision for an appeal against the sentences that were handed down on October 1, 1946. Consequently, those sentenced to death were speedily executed within two weeks but not so with the NMT. After the sentences were announced in April 1948, there followed a lengthy appeals process. This table shows how the original sentences were modified by the Advisory Board on Clemency and then changed further by John J. McCloy, the US High Commissioner in Germany.

And the absolute worst of the worst has to be Paul Blobel. As leader of Sonderkommando 4a in Einsatzgruppe C, he had been responsible for the notorious massacre at Babi Yar near Kiev (see page 290). According to one witness, Blobel lost patience with the pace of the killing and yelled at his men to speed it up. A year after the massacre, he returned to the ravine and when he saw strange movements of the earth he just laughed: 'Here live my thirty thousand Jews!' His role in the massacre earned him a nomination by Heydrich for the War Service Cross and it enhanced his reputation as the most efficient killer of Jews. At his interrogation, it was reported that even among the defendants he was hated and reviled and two of his fellow defendants told the Americans that Blobel was 'a bloodhound, brutal, without any inhibition and not very well liked'. He was first on the gallows on June 7, 1951, followed by Braune, Naumann and Ohlendorf. Although he denied so many thousands a known grave, the Americans buried him in the prison cemetery at Spöttinger.

Left: **Corneliu Codreanu was the founder and charismatic leader of the Romanian Iron Guard, a fascist and violently anti-Semitic faction outlawed by the authorities yet managing to continue its activities underground. Codreanu advocated an alliance with Germany but the rivalry with the more-moderate King Carol *(right)* led to the Iron Guard leader's imprisonment and subsequent assassination in November 1938. In September 1939, King Carol declared his country neutral but, with the war going in Germany's favour, in May 1940 he changed his mind and re-aligned his foreign policy with the Axis which had great need of Romanian oil. At the same time the King made peace with the Iron Guard inviting its then leader Horis Sima, in exile in Germany, to return to Romania to join the government. In August the King signed an economic treaty with Germany that finally assured them of the oil that would be needed to mount the subsequent attack on the USSR.**

Romania

BESSARABIA, BUKOVINA, AND TRANSNISTRIA

Romania joined Germany in its attack on Russia in June 1941 as a result of an internal transformation of the state under German influence. The attack was also as a result of specific relations with Russia which had developed since 1940 when Romania was compelled to cede North Bukovina and Bessarabia to the Soviet Union.

For several years, Hitler had endeavoured to penetrate Romanian political and economic life, because Romania occupied such a strategic position, and also because it was a country rich in raw materials. Through his agents, he fostered the Romanian Fascist Iron Guard and organised it as his fifth column against King Carol. At first, Carol resisted these influences by the execution in 1938 of Corneliu Codreanu, the Chief of the Iron Guard, and his assistants while 'attempting to escape' from Bucharest one morning at dawn. The King was, however, undermined by Hitler, who forced him to give up a part of Transylvania to Hungary under the Vienna 'arbitration' award rendered by Germany and Italy on August 30, 1940 (see page 31).

The popularity of King Carol was also weakened by two other losses of territory. In June 1940, as stated above, he had ceded North Bukovina and Bessarabia to Russia, when the latter, having mobilised, made a request for these territories. Bessarabia had constituted part of Russia until the end of the First World War when it became incorporated into Romania. Under the treaty of September 7, 1940, Romania had also ceded Southern Dobruja to Bulgaria. In the same month, King Carol was forced to abdicate by the new leader of the Iron Guard, Marshal Ion Antonescu, who declared himself Leader of the Romania, the state being organised on Fascist lines. Antonescu placed King Carol's son Michael on the throne and forced Carol to leave the country and to go into exile.

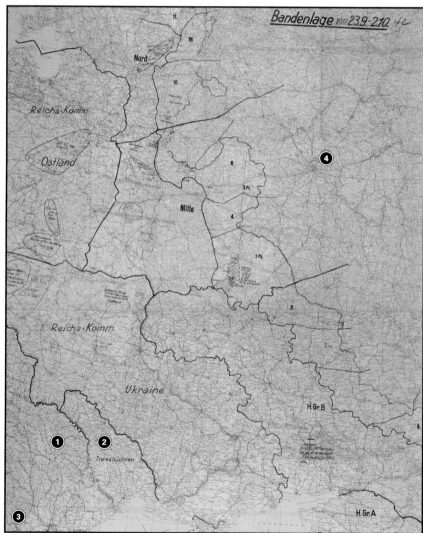

In June 1940, The Soviet Union submitted an ultimatum demanding that Romania hand over Bessarabia [1] which had been Russian until 1918, and the northern part of Bukovina (which had never been Russian). King Carol appealed to Germany for help but was told to agree to Stalin's demands. His acquiescence quickly led to the Bulgarians demanding the return of territory they lost in 1913 while the Hungarians stepped in to ask for Transylvania (see also page 31). Ironically reminiscent of earlier promises made by the German leader, Hitler offered the King a guarantee of no more territorial losses. When Germany invaded Russia, Transnistria [2] was administered by Romania [3], implementing a process of Romanianisation. This German map of the period shows the number of partisans killed (1,357), south of Slonim [4], between September 23 and October 2, 1942.

Ion Antonescu was a Romanian army officer who initially sympathised with the fascist Iron Guard, although his extreme political views brought him into conflict with the King. During the political crisis in 1940 he established the National Legionary State and, once the country was allied to Germany, he eliminated the Iron Guard. Soon after joining the Axis in the attack on the USSR in Operation 'Barbarossa', which Antonescu claimed was a holy war or crusade against the Soviet Union, Romania recovered Bessarabia and Northern Bukovina. When he met Hitler on August 6, 1941 in the Ukrainian city of Berdychiv, he was awarded the Knight's Cross of the Iron Cross — the first Romanian to be so decorated — and two weeks later was promoted by royal decree to Marshal of Romania in recognition of his restoration of the country's eastern frontier. Antonescu ordered the expulsion of all Jews from Bessarabia and Bukovina, three concentration camps being set up to receive them near the villages of Bogdanovka, Domanevka and Akhmetchetka in the Golta area [1] of Transnistria.

NORTH BUKOVINA AND BESSARABIA

Bessarabia and Bukovina were occupied by Romania and Germany in the first weeks of the war. After a short period of military administration, the Leader of State, Ion Antonescu, introduced civil administration in the form of two governorships, one for each province. To each were attached directorates for various administrative services to be co-ordinated by a special committee of the directorates concerned. Specific importance was attached to the Directorate for Romanianisation, Colonisation and Inventorisation, which had been given the right to have its own special budget. The governorship was divided into districts, with heads of administration called prefects.

Romanian administration was faced with many difficulties because of the sudden territorial changes, but again the main attention of the government was directed toward Romanianisation. The proclamation of July 25, 1941 by the Presidency of the Council of Ministers, provided for a return of refugees to Bessarabia and Bukovina. However, only Romanians and Germans by origin could obtain permission to return to these provinces. In order to strengthen the Romanian element, Romanian agriculturalists received 80 per cent tax exemptions and Romanian businessmen and industrialists were completely freed from taxation until March 31, 1943. Jews were expressly excluded from the benefits of this law.

A decree-law of May 26, 1942, restored Romanian citizenship in principle to the inhabitants of Bessarabia and Northern Bukovina providing that they were Romanian citizens under the provisions of the revised law on citizenship of June 28, 1940. Such citizenship was denied to three categories of persons:

1. Persons who requested permission to return from Romania to Bessarabia when it was occupied by Russia, with the exception of demobilised soldiers who were returning home.

2. Persons who after June 28, 1940 acquired another citizenship than that of one of the republics of the Soviet Union.

3. Persons who left the territory occupied by Russia before it was re-occupied by Romania. However, Romanians by origin were not denied citizenship even if they came within this latter category.

By the end of 1941 the camps held over 50,000 but by March 1943 only a few hundred persons remained, all having been massacred by Romanian gendarmerie and Ukrainian police, aided by Volksdeutsche Einsatzgruppe personnel. The pitiful remains were disinterred after the war and today a memorial marks the site of the killing at Bogdanovka.

303

Odessa, which became Antonescu's headquarters, was attacked by Romanian and German troops in August 1941, the Red Army holding out until the city fell on October 16. Six days later a time-bomb, placed by the Soviets in the Romanian headquarters, exploded killing 67 people including the commander and 17 Romanian officers and four Germans. Blaming the Jews who made up 30 per cent of the population, and also communists, Antonescu let his troops loose on a killing spree and 5,000 civilians were shot out of hand, a further 19,000 being taken to warehouses that were then set on fire.

He wanted another hundred hanged in city squares and Odessa's mayor Gherman Pantea awoke 'to a frightful sight; in all the main streets and at intersections, groups of four to five people were hanging'. Unaware of who was behind it, he asked who was responsible 'for this barbaric deed, this disgrace, of which we will never be absolved by the civilised world'. Over the following days more mass killings followed, the official report stating that up to March 1942, the Romanians had killed upwards of 25,000 and deported over 35,000, although other sources put the figure higher.

TRANSNISTRIA

Transnistria was the name of the Russian territory lying between the pre-June 1940 Russo-Romanian border and the Lower Bug. This was delimited on the western side by the Dniester river and on the eastern side by the Lower Bug. The northern boundary was determined by a line running approximately from Zhmerinka to Mogilev Podolsk, while the Black Sea marked the southern extent. This territory was handed over by the Germans to Romania for administration purposes. A Romanian governor was appointed by Marshal Antonescu with his headquarters in Odessa. German advisers were delegated to his staff by German authorities. The area was divided into territorial districts and 64 counties corresponding approximately to Soviet administrative divisions. Romanian prefects were put in charge of the districts. At the head of the counties were two higher officials, one Romanian and one from the local population.

After the introduction of Romanian currency (the lei), the following exchange rate was established: 60 lei equalled ten roubles of Reichskreditkassenschein.

In this territory, which had been subject to the communist property system since the Russian Revolution, the rules covering property under Romanian administration were not changed to any great extent. Land ownership was only granted for the most part as a reward for pro-Romanian activities and zealous work.

This territory became a large centre to which Romanian Jews were deported in the same way that Poland was made a centre for west European Jews. Several hundred thousand Romanian Jews of both sexes above 15 years of age were deported to Transnistria from Bessarabia and North Bukovina, being forced to work under inhumane conditions in labour camps.

Odessa was subject to Romanian rule until it was recaptured by Soviet forces on April 10, 1944. In August, King Michael (who had taken the Romanian throne after his father had been forced to abdicate in September 1940) led a successful coup against the Axis and, with the support of most of the army, was able to depose Antonescu. On August 23 the King announced a cease–fire and proclaimed that henceforth Romania would join the Allies. His army was now ordered to oppose the Germans but this created a precarious situation as Romanian units were integrated within German lines and it was not clear which units were still loyal to the Axis and which to the Soviets.

Transformed from war to peace: Bolharska Street in Moldavanka, a suburb of Odessa.

The Romanians then fought the remainder of the war alongside the Red Army. In 1945 Odessa was awarded the title of 'Hero City' along with Leningrad, Sevastopol and Stalingrad. These are troops of General Chuikov's Eighth Guards Army, which liberated the city.

The Romanian Opera and Ballet Theatre lay at the end of Lanzheronivska Street.

On August 24 German troops attempted to seize Bucharest and suppress the coup instigated by King Michael but they were repulsed by loyal forces. Meanwhile the Red Army was advancing at speed towards the capital which was entered on August 30, welcomed by massed crowds. This column is approaching along Ion C. Bratianu Boulevard, passing Baratia Church on the right.

The armistice signed three weeks later reflected terms favourable to the Soviet Union. While Romania unconditionally surrendered to the USSR, the terms of the agreement signed on September 12 stated that 'an Allied Control Commission will be established which will undertake until the conclusion of peace, the regulation and control over the execution of the present terms under the general direction and orders of the Allied (Soviet) High Command acting on behalf of the Allied Powers'. The Romanian army now continued fighting the Germans alongside the Red Army, suffering heavy casualties in the process.

Special decrees were promulgated concerning these deportees. Conditions in Transnistria being very difficult for them, they were able to escape in some cases to Romania. However, a special law published by Marshal Antonescu fixed the death penalty for Jewish deportees who returned illegally to Romania, and persons who helped them to escape were to be punished by imprisonment up to 25 years.

Another law brought in severe penalties for using secret mails and packages in communications with Transnistria, because the deportees, under Romanian regulations, were to be completely isolated from their homes and friends in Romania.

Moral debasement in the administration of justice was illustrated by the decree of July 9, 1941 that awarded the death penalty even for such minor offences as non-declaration of property left by the retreating enemy. Trial and execution had to take place within 24 hours. Unparalleled in legal legislation was the following paragraph of the above-mentioned law: 'In case of flagrante delicto, the culprit shall be executed on the spot'.

In 1945 Odessa was a devastated port on the Black Sea but now it is a popular destination for the massive cruise ships of another century.

ROMANIANISATION

Property, and the most important branches of economic life such as businesses, professions and other occupations, could only be enjoyed by persons of Romanian ethnic origin. Two aspects paved the way for this process: the anti-Jewish trend, which became accentuated in Romania several years before the war, and the territorial changes which brought into Romania masses of Romanian refugees from Transylvania, Dobruja, Bessarabia and Northern Bukovina. Faced with this situation, the Romanian government introduced measures to provide for the acquisition of properties and businesses from Jews and distributing them among Romanians. The first important laws of this nature were promulgated on October 4 and November 12, 1940. The law of October 4 introduced the institution of 'Romanianisation' commissioners in Jewish enterprises, and the November law ordered the ousting of Jewish employees from private concerns. On May 2, 1941, two further decrees were published which established a new organisational framework under which an Undersecretariat for Romanianisation, Colonisation and Inventorisation was created and established in connection with the presidency of the Council of Ministers. It was a central body that laid down policies concerning colonisation of Romanian refugees and the re-allocation of property in Romania. The second law of this date established a National Centre for Romanianisation. This was an operational agency for taking over and distributing principally Jewish properties.

RAPHAEL LEMKIN, 1944

The Mussolini family residence was the Villa Torlonia situated in parkland off the Via Nomentana in Rome's north-eastern suburbs. Abandoned since 1945, the Villa Torlonia has now been restored and opened as a museum.

Italy

Benito Mussolini had thrust Italy into the Second World War on June 10, 1940, his intention being to share in the plunder of a virtually prostrate France and to defeat Britain in the Mediterranean and North Africa. Three years and one month later, on July 10, 1943, the Allies landed in Sicily, and nine days on, bombed Rome for the first time. Both events came hard on the heels of a long list of Italian military disasters and severely shook the nation's remaining confidence in its leader who, up to then, had remained in complete charge of events.

The Mussolinis had lived in Rome in a huge and monumental villa belonging to Prince Torlonia, scion of one of the main Roman aristocratic families. Villa Torlonia, for which the Duce paid a peppercorn rent, was set in a huge park that he used for his daily horse rides.

Mussolini and his wife Rachele lived in two separate suites on the first floor of the house and the rest of his family — his son Vittorio and his family, and the widow of his other son Bruno (killed in a plane crash in August 1941) with her daughter Marina — lived in the many smaller buildings scattered around the park. In July 1943, his other son, Romano, and daughter, Anna Maria, although usually resident at Villa Torlonia, were on holiday at Riccione in Mussolini's native Romagna.

The only member of his immediate family who did not live close by was Edda, Mussolini's fiery eldest daughter who was married to Count Galeazzo Ciano and who lived in a penthouse in the up-market Roman quarter of Parioli. Ciano had been Italy's Foreign Minister until February 1943, but by July

was a mere Ambassador to the Holy See. The Duce's mistress Clara Petacci spent most of her day in an apartment that had been converted especially for her use in the rear of the Palazzo Venezia, Mussolini's administrative headquarters in the heart of Rome.

Mussolini had always maintained an uneasy relationship with his Gerarchi (senior officials of the Fascist Party). On the one hand he surrounded himself with sycophants of limited intelligence such as Achille Starace who was responsible, as Party Secretary in the 1930s for most of the choreography of fascism and for spreading the myth of an infallible Duce. The more intelligent and capable Gerarchi such as Dino Grandi (former Foreign Minister and Ambassador to the Court of St James) and Giuseppe Bottai (the one true intellectual of the

Mussolini pictured at the villa with his two sons Vittorio (right) and Bruno who was killed on a test-flight in 1941.

Following the Duce's demise, Rome Council let it fall into decay and it was fenced off after a child was killed by falling masonry.

fascist movement) had become increasingly critical of the management of the war effort and secretly of Mussolini himself.

Consequent upon the scarcity of good advice and the constant adulation, the Duce not surprisingly had become detached from reality and by the end of June 1943 had appeared increasingly hesitant and withdrawn — a shadow of his former self. This apparent loss of concentration had coincided with a recurrence of the dictator's stomach troubles from which he had suffered on and off since before the First World War. To treat the pain of what was thought to be a duodenal ulcer, Mussolini followed a very strict diet of milk and butter derivatives and had given up tobacco and alcohol. His home life was also not as good as the regime propaganda portrayed it.

On July 14, Mussolini received a delegation of Gerarchi in his large study at the Palazzo Venezia. It comprised officials who had been ordered by the Duce through Carlo Scorza, the secretary of the Fascist Party, to speak out in favour of the war at a variety of meetings throughout the country. Many of them, like Tullio Cianetti, the Minister for the Corporations (the guilds upon which the fascist state was supposedly based), found it difficult to obey the order seeing that when Mussolini made the decision to enter the war he never bothered to consult them. It was at this meeting that a request was first put forward to the Duce for the summoning of the Gran Consiglio del Fascismo (Grand Council of Fascism). This was an advisory body of the regime and last assembled in December 1939, made up of 28 of the most senior Gerarchi and chaired by the Duce himself. Its function had always been a minor one, and had been a way to get the party to rubber-stamp Mussolini's decisions. A further peculiarity of the Gran Consiglio was that it started work at 5 p.m. Since the proceedings consisted of interminable monologues by Mussolini or the Party Secretary the proceedings always ended late at night.

The Palazzo Venezia, formerly the Palace of St Mark, stands just north of the Capitoline Hill. Dating from the 15th century, it originally consisted of a modest medieval house intended as the residence of the cardinals appointed to the church of San Marco but in 1469, having undergone a massive extension, it became a residential papal palace. It was later used as the embassy for the Republic of Venice. During the First World War it was used by the Austrian ambassador to the Vatican but was then seized by Italy in 1916. Mussolini took the building over, the balcony overlooking the Piazza Venezia being used to deliver many of his speeches to crowds gathered in the square below.

Mussolini listened to the complaints and ended the meeting with a vague promise to summon the Gran Consiglio as by law only he had the power to do so. However, nothing happened. The following day at the Palazzo Venezia, the Duce chaired the meeting that was to be his last military conference as head of the Italian government. Present were General Vittorio Ambrosio (Chief of the Italian General Staff, i.e. of all three Services) and Feldmarschall Albert Kessel-

ring, German C-in-C in Italy. Although the Allies were fast advancing into the heart of Sicily, Mussolini appeared strangely detached, only mildly insisting that more German divisions cross the Messina Strait to shore up the disintegrating Italian Army. Although earlier on he had correctly recognised that using the still-powerful Italian fleet was the key to weakening the Allies, Mussolini appears not to have had any intention of ordering it to sea.

The Duce used the huge Sala del Mappamondo for his office which remains unchanged having retained the fascist 'fasces' symbol inlaid in the mosaic floor with the date when it was

laid: the fifth year of the fascist state, i.e. 1927. The building currently houses the National Museum of the Palazzo Venezia although Mussolini's office is closed to public view.

The meeting between Mussolini and Hitler — the 13th and last of their careers — took place at a villa in the foothills of the Dolomites, some 80 kilometres south of the border with Austria. However, the reason behind its choice as a venue has never been reliably explained as to get there the two leaders had to follow a roundabout route. They both flew to the airfield at Treviso, near Venice, then set off north by train to Feltre, a town nearly half-way back to the Austrian border, from where they had a further hour's journey by open-top cars in sweltering heat to reach the Villa Gaggia at Belluno. The meeting began at 11 a.m. and we are told that Hitler monopolised the conversation by speaking for the three hours, trying to bolster up his ally, yet in the end it was to no avail.

On July 19, Mussolini met Hitler at Feltre on the Austrian-Italian border for an important meeting to discuss strategy. Although urged by General Ambrosio and by Giuseppe Bastianini, Under-Secretary to the Foreign Ministry, to try and decouple Italy from Germany, Mussolini made no effort to warn the Führer that Italy was in no state to continue the fight, confining himself to listening to one of Hitler's long monologues. His passive attitude at this meeting was a major trigger for the events which followed. The Duce's timidity in facing up to Hitler was soon common knowledge among the Gerarchi, and caused consternation among them because the Feltre meeting had been seen by the more-sensible members as possibly the last chance to save Italy and the regime.

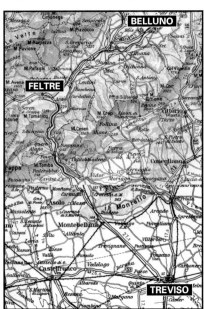

The conference chamber in the Palazzo Venezia that was the scene of the decisive meeting of the Fascist Grand Council on July 24, 1943. No photographs appear to have been taken on that day, this picture showing an earlier meeting in April 1939.

The Gerarchi's agitation and alarm continued to grow with the worsening strategic situation. A consensus for either 'embalming' Mussolini or replacing him came out in the open amongst them during this period, although many were still under the spell of the dictator. Then, on the 20th and quite unexpectedly, Mussolini agreed to summon the Council to meet at 5 p.m. on Saturday, July 24.

In the days preceding the meeting, three different alignments within the Fascist Party emerged. The first, championed by Roberto Farinacci, one of the most violent of the Gerarchi, was to seek a closer collaboration with the Germans which would mean letting them take over the running of the Italian war effort. The second, proposed by Party Secretary Carlo Scorza, was to seek a rallying of the party. The third, initially championed by Dino Grandi, Speaker of the Chamber of Deputies, Giuseppe Bottai, Minister for Education, and Luigi Federzoni, President of the Italian Academy, was to implore King Victor Emmanuel III to take over the command of the armed forces from Mussolini to whom it had been delegated at the beginning of the war. The common ground between these three approaches was that there would be a change of role for the Duce. All three were formally submitted as motions to be discussed at the meeting.

Mussolini was made aware of the contents of all three motions and appears to have been in no doubt as to what was in store for him if the Grandi motion was accepted, his wife and mistress having both warned him of impending danger.

On the afternoon of the 24th, the mood of most of those involved was maudlin, only Bottai and Grandi, and perhaps Ciano, appearing to have fully understood what was at stake.

That afternoon, as the Gerarchi arrived one by one in the courtyard of the Palazzo Venezia, they were met by an ominously heavily-armed company of blackshirts. Grandi, for one, had the feeling of having walked into a trap.

THE NIGHT OF THE FASCIST GRAND COUNCIL

At 5.15 p.m., Mussolini, in the uniform of Consul General of the Militia, followed by Scorza, entered the council chamber from his study and opened the meeting with a 45-minute speech on the military situation. In particular he accused his troops and generals of cowardice. This brought Marshal Emilio De Bono to his feet to defend the Army and express his contempt for the Germans who according to him, and to most of the Gerarchi present, were the real traitors as they had not consulted their allies before invading Poland.

De Bono was interrupted angrily by Roberto Farinacci, champion of the Axis, who discussed the content of his pro-German motion and smeared the realistic attitude of Chief-of-Staff General Vittorio Ambrosio as defeatism. De Bono, Federzoni, Bottai and Cesare Maria De Vecchi, the Governor of the Italian Aegean Colonies, all then spoke against Farinacci.

Around 7 p.m., after the discussions had been under way for almost two hours, Grandi rose for the first time and explained the substance of his motion, asking for support and reminding the Duce and Scorza that they both had seen the motion 48 hours previously. Gaetano Polverelli, Minister for Popular Culture, Carlo Alberto Biggini, Minister of Education, and Farinacci then stood to oppose the motion while Federzoni, Alfredo De Marsico, Justice Minister, Alberto De Stefani of the Italian Academy, Bottai, Annio Bignardi (President of the Italian Farmers Confederation) and Ciano all expressed their support for Grandi.

At 11.30 p.m., after a menacing speech by the hard-line General Italo Galbiati, Chief-of-Staff to the Militia, Grandi won a 20-minute break. During the interval, although fearing imminent arrest, Grandi and his comrades managed to secure 20 signatures for the motion (one man, Count Giacomo Suardo, President of the Senate, later abstained). After the meeting reassembled, the discussion raged on until 3 a.m. when the voting on the Grandi motion began. Unbelievably, Scorza had withdrawn his motion and Farinacci's gained only one vote, that of its author.

Grandi's motion was accepted and the meeting broke up at 3.30 a.m. when the Duce informed the Gerarchi that he would go to the Villa Savoia (the royal residence) to brief the King the next day.

Still no photography allowed in the room, this picture dating from 20 years ago.

ENTER THE KING

Italy's diminutive King had been in contact with Grandi since 1940 and the Gerarca had expressed all his doubts and misgivings to his sovereign. The King had always told his retinue that in order to get rid of the Duce he needed a vote against Mussolini by one of the regime's own internal organs such as the Grand Council. This was a somewhat unlikely event in a dictatorship and one that only took place after thousands of Italian lives had been lost. These scruples were euphemistically termed 'constitutional' by the King's advisers. At their last meeting on June 4, Victor Emmanuel had told Grandi he would act when the time was ripe. Grandi kept him informed of his plans through Minister D'Acquarone but despaired of the King's apparent inertia. He felt, probably rightly, that the King's scruples should long ago have been overcome by events.

After the Council had broken up, Grandi had briefed D'Acquarone on the outcome and he in turn informed the King who, with uncharacteristic decision, set about preparing a trap for the Duce.

After a brief sleep, Mussolini had spent July 25 at his desk and had been informed by Scorza that Cianetti had withdrawn his signature and support for the Grandi motion. The Duce had tried frantically to shore up his position by trying to demonstrate that the vote was meaningless, as, according to him, the Gran Consiglio was only a consultative body and, under Italy's pre-fascist constitution, the King could disregard the outcome of the previous night's proceedings.

On the following day Mussolini drove to the Royal residence in the Villa Savoia for an audience with King Victor Emmanuel III. Also known as the Villa Ada, this was located four kilometres north of the Palazzo Venezia in a secluded park on the Via Salaria. In the hours since the meeting, and after much soul-searching, the King had made up his mind to appoint Marshal Pietro Badoglio as the new head of government, and had agreed to have Mussolini arrested. A Carabinieri colonel with 50 men had already arrived and taken up positions when the Duce arrived shortly after 5 p.m. The King listened to Mussolini's version of what had taken place the previous evening but, totally disagreeing with Mussolini belittling the vote of no confidence against him, the King curtly cut him short and asked for his resignation. Silenced by the forceful response from his monarch, Mussolini accepted the inevitable and, as he descended the front steps, he was arrested.

At five o'clock that afternoon the Duce was driven with his secretary, Nicolo De Cesare, to meet the King, fully confident that Victor Emmanuel would confirm him as head of government. This misjudgment was to cost him and his family dear. During the meeting, which lasted half an hour, the King listened to Mussolini without comment before forcing him to resign as head of the government. As the Duce and De Cesare walked down the steps of Villa Savoia's front entrance, they were greeted by Lieutenant-Colonel Giovanni Frignani, Chief Constable Morazzini, Captains Paolo Vigneri and Raffaele Aversa, three policemen armed with sub-machine guns, three senior NCOs and 50 men of the Carabinieri, a somewhat large body of people to simply arrest one man. When the officers informed Mussolini that he was under arrest, he meekly allowed them to put him in a waiting ambulance which drove to the Podgora Carabinieri Barracks. There he was to remain until transferred to the island of Ponza and then Maddalena off the northern Sardinian coast and eventually to the Gran Sasso.

At 10.45 p.m. that night, the Italians were informed in a broadcast that Mussolini had been arrested, and that the King had appointed a new Prime Minister, Marshal Pietro Badoglio, who had now formed the first non-fascist government since 1922. No member from any of Mussolini's Cabinets had been included. Grandi recalls walking exhaustedly in the centre of Rome as the news broke and witnessing scenes of delirious joy as the populace thought that this meant the end of the war. Few had read Badoglio's first communiqué that contained the famous phrase 'the war goes on' (as allies of Germany).

Italy continued the war against the Allies until the armistice was signed at Cassibile on September 3. News of the armistice was broadcast five days later whereupon the Germans invaded Italy. Overnight the former ally had turned into an occupation force. The King and his entourage, with Badoglio and his government, fled to Bari leaving behind an army without orders or leadership. It was soon disarmed by the Germans and part of it was interned in Germany.

MAJOR TOM JEFFERSON, 1992

On September 8, King Victor Emmanuel announced the signing of an armistice with the Allies and the setting up of the Italian Co-Belligerent Army under the Badoglio government. Four days later Mussolini was freed from his mountaintop prison (see *After the Battle* No. 22) and reinstated by the Germans in northern Italy. In a precision operation, SS-Sturmbannführer Otto Skorzeny led a gliderborne attack on the Hotel Campo Imperatore on the Gran Sasso mountain range in central Italy. Mussolini was rescued unharmed from his Italian captors and flown off the nearby plateau in a Fieseler Storch.

Since the war, an extension lobby has been added in front of the old entrance to the hotel.

THE AXIS DISINTEGRATES

The overthrow of Mussolini took the Germans completely by surprise. Hitler, when he received the news, was furious and at the daily conference at his 'Wolfsschanze' headquarters in Rastenburg openly expressed his mistrust of the new Italian leadership and the King.

Hitler had long since begun to entertain misgivings about Italy's reliability as an ally, fearing fascism might collapse or the country defect from the alliance. These worries increased significantly after the Axis defeat in North Africa in May 1943. Considering political stability in Italy and retention of the country, especially the northern part of it, as vital for the defence of Germany, Hitler had ordered the Oberkommando der Wehrmacht (OKW, Armed Forces High Command) to make contingency plans for the eventuality of Italy withdrawing from the war or Mussolini being toppled from power, the idea being to have German units in Italy take over the country by force.

The initial plan, which was issued on May 22 and code-named 'Alarich', provided for a German occupation of northern Italy, coupled with evacuation by German troops of the rest of the Italian boot. The operation was to be carried out by Heeresgruppe B, under Generalfeldmarschall Erwin Rommel, initially with six or seven divisions to be withdrawn from the Eastern Front, later revised to eight divisions from the OB West command in France.

On receiving the news of Mussolini's fall on July 25, Hitler's first inclination was to strike back with lightning speed: seize Rome with the 3. Panzergrenadier-Division (from Lake Bolsena) and the 2. Fallschirmjäger-Division (to be flown in to the Rome area from France); kidnap the King, Badoglio and his cabinet ministers, and find and liberate Mussolini as a first step to reinstating the Fascist regime.

However, Rommel and others recommended a more cautious approach, advising instead to withdraw all German forces from Sicily, Sardinia and southern Italy, but retain and defend

With Mussolini now out of the picture, the new Italian leader was Marshal Pietro Badoglio *(left)*, former Italian Chief-of-Staff. Chief of the Supreme Command (Comando Supremo) was General Vittorio Ambrosio *(centre)*. General Albert Kesselring *(right)*, the Oberbefelshaber Süd, was the overall German commander in the Mediterranean theatre.

northern Italy. Kesselring, more optimistic by nature, took a different view. Having been assured by Badoglio and Ambrosio, the Comando Supremo chief, that Italy would continue the war on Germany's side, he advised Hitler to feel out the Italian government on their willingness to receive further German divisions. With these, Kesselring believed he could defend all of Italy and the Balkans.

The result of all this was that Hitler decided to suspend the immediate seizure of Rome. Instead, he instructed Kesselring to put all his effort in persuading the Comando Supremo to allow the maximum number of German troops into northern Italy. However, this was not because he trusted the Italians. Hitler was still certain that the Badoglio government was planning to betray him, and he ordered the OKW to draw up a new contingency plan to meet that possibility, but now with the intention of seizing control of the whole country. The new German forces entering Italy were ostensibly to reinforce the Axis troops fighting in Sicily but in reality they also formed part of Hitler's plan to counter an Italian double-cross.

While telling the Germans that the war goes on, the Italians began secret negotiations with the Allies early in August. (L-R): Brigadier Kenneth Strong, Chief of Intelligence (G-2) at Allied Forces Headquarters (AFHQ); Generale Giuseppe Castellano in civilian clothes, the emissary from the Badoglio government; Major General Walter Bedell Smith, the AFHQ Chief-of-Staff, and the interpreter Franco Montanari.

THE ITALIAN ARMISTICE

Hitler's distrust of the Italians was well founded. Almost immediately after the ousting of Mussolini, the new Badoglio government, with the blessing of the King, began to secretly explore the possibilities of an armistice with the Allies, all the while reassuring the Germans of their good faith and willingness to continue the war. The secret negotiations with Allied top diplomatic, political and military officials were protracted and complicated but finally, on September 3 (the same day the British Eighth Army crossed the Strait of Messina and landed at Reggio di Calabria in the toe of Italy), in a tent at 15th Army Group headquarters at Cassibile near Syracuse on Sicily, Generale di Brigata Guiseppe Castellano, as emissary of the Italian government (and himself strongly anti-German), signed the armistice terms that, in theory at least, put Italy out the war.

The agreement stipulated that General Dwight D. Eisenhower, the Allied Commander-in-Chief in the Mediterranean, and Badoglio would simultaneously announce the armistice over the radio at 1830 hours on the evening preceding the Allied main invasion on the Italian mainland by the US Fifth Army. This would ensure that Italian units would not oppose these landings. However, for obvious security reasons the place and date of the invasion — at Salerno, 200 kilometres south of Rome, on September 9 — could not be disclosed to the Italians.

However, Badoglio now renounced the armistice terms signed by Castellano, saying that it would provoke an immediate seizure of Rome by the Germans, and he therefore refused to broadcast the armistice that night as had been agreed.

On receipt of the news, Eisenhower was understandably furious about the Italian turnabout. He radioed Badoglio a blistering message, which reached Rome at 1730, stating that he would proceed with the public announcement of the armistice at 1830 that evening as had been agreed.

Bedell Smith signs the Armistice for the Allies at 1715 hours on September 3. Standing around are (L-R) Commodore Royer Dick, Chief-of-Staff to Admiral Sir Andrew Cunningham, commander of Allied Naval Forces; Major General Lowell Rooks, AFHQ G-3 (Chief of Operations); Captain Deane, Brigadier Strong's adjutant, serving as interpreter; Castellano; Strong (behind Castellano) and interpreter Montanari. General Dwight D. Eisenhower, the Allied Commander-in-Chief, was present at the ceremony but he left the actual signing of what he regarded as a 'crooked deal' to his Chief-of-Staff.

At 1830 hours Radio Algiers transmitted Eisenhower's recorded announcement: 'This is General Dwight D. Eisenhower, Commander-in-Chief of the Allied Forces. The Italian government has surrendered its armed forces unconditionally. As Allied Commander-in-Chief I have granted a military armistice, the terms of which have been approved by the governments of the United Kingdom, the United States and the Union of Soviet Socialist Republics. Hostilities between the armed forces of the United Nations and those of Italy terminate at once.'

Meanwhile, faced with Eisenhower's fait accompli, the Italian government had no other choice but to comply. With Badoglio still unable to make up his mind, the King took a decision: Italy could not change sides again but was committed to the armistice. At 1945 hours — over one hour late —speaking from the EIAR radio studios in Via Asiago, Badoglio read out the announcement of the armistice, following exactly the text approved by AFHQ.

The news of a separate peace between Italy and the Allies spread quickly through the international news agencies. Within minutes, German Foreign Minister Joachim von Ribbentrop was telephoning Rudolf Rahn, the German Ambassador in Rome, asking about the truth of the news picked up from a Reuters dispatch. Rahn called the Italian Foreign Ministry, which categorically refuted it claiming that 'the report from New York is a barefaced lie of British propaganda'.

Left: Marshal Badoglio broadcast the news of the armistice from the studio of the radio station Ente Italiano per le Audizioni Radiofoniche (EIAR) located at No. 10 Via Asiago in Rome. Here members of the fascist police force, the Polizia d'Africana Italiana (PAI), guard the building after the capitulation. *Right:* The building is still in use by the successor of the EIAR station, the state broadcasting company Radio Audizioni Italiane (RAI).

FIRST GERMAN MOVES

The news of the Italian double-cross did not come unexpected to Hitler and the OKW. Three days before, on September 5, the OKW had warned Kesselring to be ready for any emergency. On the 7th, at the suggestion of General-oberst Alfred Jodl, Hitler had begun preparing an ultimatum to Badoglio demanding that the Italians unequivocally rally on the German side or else he would take control of the country and its government. It was to be delivered on September 9, but the armistice announcement precipitated all that. Hitler was told the news as he returned from a visit to the Eastern Front. Very irritated, he immediately instructed the OKW to call Kesselring and implement Plan 'Achse'.

At that moment, the Germans had 17 divisions in Italy. Spread out over central and southern Italy was the 10. Armee under General der Panzertruppe Heinrich von Vietinghoff with eight divisions, six in the south and two in the Rome area. In northern Italy, Heeresgruppe B, commanded by Rommel, had another nine divisions. According to Hitler's orders, the latter were to remain where they were so, for the moment, the 10. Armee was on its own to fend off the Anglo-American invasion at Salerno and confront the insurrection of the Badoglio forces.

The dispersion and strength of troops in and around Rome showed a significant disparity in favour of the Italians. Ever since Mussolini's overthrow, the Comando Supremo had been surreptitiously strengthening the forces guarding the capital and the Italians could now muster six divisions under three corps headquarters, with two more divisions on the way. Against this the Germans could only field two divisions.

Along with their combat actions, the Germans skilfully exploited the confusion and lack of clear instructions on the Italian side. Making smart use of this, they arranged local truces and appealed to the honour of Italian soldiers that the war was over and they might go home if they wished and many of the Italian soldiers simply abandoned their weapons and disappeared in the countryside.

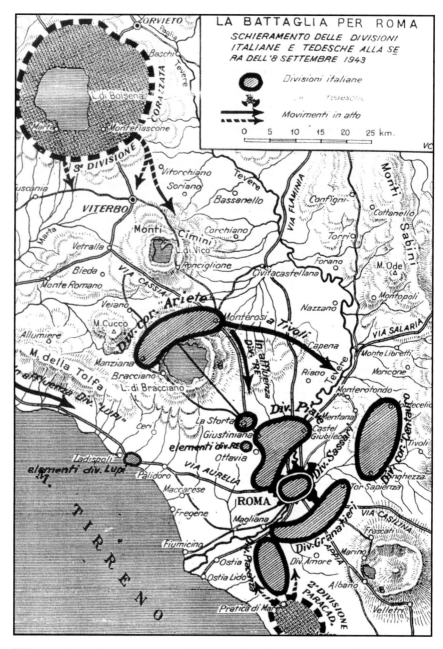

This map shows the deployment of the six Italian divisions around the city with the 3. Panzergrenadier-Division 75 kilometres away to the north and the 2. Fallschirm-jäger-Division 20 kilometres to the south.

Left: **An Italian Semovente 75/18 self-propelled gun knocked out by German anti-tank fire on the Via Ostiense — the ancient route running 30 kilometres west to the port of Ostia Antica. This particular vehicle belonged to the Lancieri di Montebello,** the armoured reconnaissance regiment of the 'Ariete' Division, which was brought in to the city as a reinforcement on September 9. *Right:* **It was knocked out here on the corner with the Via dei Conciatori.**

FLIGHT OF THE KING AND THE HIGH COMMAND

In the early hours of September 9, as various reports of encounters with German units came in, Army Chief-of-Staff Mario Roatta became aware that the Germans were making a concentric approach to Rome from several directions. Appreciating that the city was about to be surrounded, he realised that the only escape route still open to the Royal Family was the Via Tiburtina (Route 5), leading out of the city to the east. From here it was still possible to reach Pescara on the Adriatic coast and embark for the south, towards territory in Anglo-American hands. When he reported this to Ambrosio shortly after 0400, the latter took two far-reaching decisions: firstly, the King and the government would leave Rome immediately; secondly, all military forces in and around Rome were to withdraw from the city and concentrate near Tivoli, along Route 5 some 30 kilometres to the east.

Thus, around 0500, eight cars carrying the King, Queen, Crown Prince Umberto, Badoglio and four military aides hastily left Rome, motoring first to Pescara on the Adriatic coast and then to Ortona, boarding an Italian Navy cruiser for Brindisi, in the south and in Allied hands.

Before he left, the King had given instructions that Ambrosio, the three service Chiefs-of-Staff and the three service ministers leave Rome as well and join him at Pescara. Thus, shortly after 0600, the complete Italian high command — Comando Supremo chief Ambrosio; Army Chief-of-Staff Roatta; Navy Chief-of-Staff Ammiraglio di Squaddra Raffaele de Courten; Air Force Chief-of-Staff Generale di Divisione Aerea Renato Sandalli and several other key officers — all departed from the capital. Before he left, Roatta turned over command of all the forces defending Rome to General Giacomo Carboni, commander of the Motorised Corps, directing him to withdraw his forces to the Tivoli area according to Ambrosio's decision.

Right: **Today, the Villa Wolkonsky no longer houses the German Embassy but — in an ironic twist of history — serves as the official residence of the British Ambassador! After the liberation of Rome in 1944, the Italian government sequestrated the property and it was placed under the Allied Control Commission. For a short time the building was occupied by the Swiss Legation, then by the Italian Red Cross. Then, after the clandestine militant Zionist group Irgun blew up the British Embassy at Porte Pia on October 31, 1946, the Italian government made the Villa Wolkonsky available to the United Kingdom as temporary embassy and ambassadorial residence. After the embassy moved back to the newly completed premises at Porte Pia in 1971, the villa remained in use as ambassador's dwelling. When Germany re-established diplomatic relations with Italy in June 1951, it had to find a new address for its embassy. First it was in Via Don Giovanni Verità, then from 1957 in Via Po, and from 1998 at No. 4 Via San Martino della Battaglia.**

As the King and his retinue made their preparations to escape from Rome, together with Ambrosio and the three service chiefs, Rudolf Rahn, the German Ambassador, and his staff were hastily burning secret diplomatic papers at the German Embassy fearing its capture by the Italians. They evacuated the premises during the night of September 8/9, the Italian authorities having issued them with special passes permitting them to leave the city.

This photograph was taken some time later once the Germans were back in control with members of the PAI police.

Left: The 2. Fallschirmjäger-Division launched its main penetrations into Rome along the Via Ostiense and the Via Laurentina, the two main thoroughfares leading into the city from the south-west. Here they were confronted by troops of the Italian 'Granatieri di Sardegna' Division. The junction of the two roads in the suburb of Montagnola saw a violent clash between the paratroopers and the 1st Infantry Regiment 'Granatieri'. In the course of the skirmish, the Fallschirmjäger knocked out two Italian armoured cars, both of which burst into flames. While the Italian vehicles burned, the Fallschirmjäger set up no less than three of their anti-tank guns to cover the road junction. At least two German Propaganda-Kompanie photographers and a cine cameramen were present and were able to record the fighting here, this picture being taken by PK photographer Reuschler. *Right:* The Forte Ostiense, another of the strongholds of the 'Granatieri' Division during the battle, lies a kilometre or so further down the Via Ostiense, away to the left.

BATTLE FOR ROME

Meanwhile, events followed one another quickly. During the morning of September 9 lead elements of the 3. Panzergrenadier-Division met outposts of the Ariete Division at Manziana on the Via Claudia Braccianese, and at Monterosi on the Via Cassia near Monterosi Lake, and ordered them to give way. The Italians refused. When the Germans tried to rush tank columns through the Italian strong points, which were protected by well-placed mines and well-directed artillery fire, they were rebuffed. At Monterosi, the bridge over which the Germans had to pass was blown by a courageous Italian 2nd lieutenant, Sottotenente Ettore Rosso, who was killed in the act. The Germans halted, regrouped, brought up infantry and threatened an attack.

In the south, at the Cecchignola military complex, some 200 Italian troops, mostly cadets from an officer and NCO training course, still refused to give in against the veteran 2. Fallschirmjäger-Division. This unexpected opposition led the Germans to bypass the position and head directly towards the city. However, it gave many Italian soldiers the time and opportunity to turn up and report at their stations to participate in the defence of the city.

The 800 paratroopers of the II. Bataillon of Fallschirmjäger-Regiment 6 (under Major Walter Gericke) sent to Monterotondo north of Rome to capture the Italian Army commander and general staff in the Palazzo Orsini had more trouble. Taking off from Foggia airfield and parachuting from 52 Junkers Ju 52 aircraft around 0700, they ran into tenacious opposition from Italian soldiers, assisted in many cases by civilians. They captured some 2,500 troops, but by the time they seized the Army headquarters, they found that General Roatta and his staff had gone.

On the morning of September 9, the Italian Army General Staff began setting up a new headquarters at the carabinieri barracks at Tivoli. Carboni, who had been placed in command of all the forces around Rome, arrived there at 0900 but he found no orders waiting for him as he had expected. At 1300 he took command. His first act was to start the withdrawal to the Tivoli area of the two most-reliable motorised divisions, the Ariete and the Piave. The Ariete had just that morning given the 3. Panzergrenadier-Division a bloody nose at Manziana and Monterosi, forcing the Germans to halt and regroup. During this interval, the Ariete and Piave Divisions withdrew, and were replaced in the line by the Re Division. Unaware of the change-over, the German division commander, Generalleutnant Fritz-Hubert Gräser, maintained his threatening attitude but refrained from launching an attack.

Men of Fallschirm-Panzerjäger-Abteilung 2, the divisional anti-tank unit, have set up a 5cm PaK 38 gun on a corner of the Via Ostiense, close to the Mercati Generali marketplace compound which dates from 1912.

The old market building survives in a dilapidated state. Since 2005, plans are underway to reinvigorate the whole Mercati Generali complex into a modern civic and entertainment centre.

The most-important clash of the 1943 battle for Rome took place at the Porta San Paolo, where the Via Ostiense enters the old city through one of the ancient gates in the Aurelian Walls. Here troops from all over Rome and civilians willing to take up the fight in defence of their city rallied with soldiers of the 'Granatieri' Division in a desperate and bloody fight that lasted throughout September 10. Here a field gun has been set up on the square in front of the gate, its barrel pointing towards the Via delle Cave Ardeatine.

In other areas, however, the confusion was still great and fighting continued. In the south-west, at the Ponte della Magliana, a false order issued by the Germans at 1600 hours instructed the Italians to abandon their positions and head towards the city centre. At first it seemed strange, but then the soldiers began to dismantle their roadblocks and move in accordance with the directions received. By the time the deception became clear, the main positions had been irretrievably lost.

South of the Tiber, fighting between the Fallschirmjäger and the Granatieri Division intensified. Exerting the strongest pressure against strong points guarding the Via Ostiense and the Via Laurentina, the paratroopers late in the afternoon knocked out several Italian artillery batteries. The Italians pulled back slightly but maintained a solid front. Carboni telephoned the division commander, Generale di Brigata Gioacchino Solinas, and encouraged him to continue the fight.

Towards midnight of September 9/10, the Granatieri Division attacked to recapture the Ponte della Magliana. By dawn, despite heavy losses, they had almost succeeded. At this point, however, the fighting was again interrupted to initiate further negotiations, the Germans requesting passage in order to proceed to the south to counter the Allied landings. The Italians accepted, but as soon as they came over the bridge to allow the Germans to move, the latter resumed firing. The situation became critical and the Italians were forced to fall back along the Via della Magliana towards the junction with the Via Ostiense, where they received orders to retreat to the EUR. Here, however, the German paratroopers had in the meantime infiltrated, sniping from the roofs of nearby buildings.

Now the last obstacle facing the Germans was the imposing Porta San Paolo, the city gate in the Aurelian walls, with its embattled towers and walls of over four metres thick. This is where the most-decisive and bloody clash of the two-day battle for Rome took place. Here, spontaneously or on orders from young and courageous junior officers, soldiers congregated from the military barracks in Rome, as well as civilians who wished to help out in defence of their city. In the vast square, bounded by the Pyramid of Cestius on the left and the Ostiense Railway Station on the right, the hardest clashes occurred, in which the Germans also made use of mortars. A few light tanks and armoured cars from an Italian motorised cavalry platoon arrived to support the position, but they had no armour to resist the German anti-tank guns, and so one vehicle after another was destroyed by accurate German fire.

The Porta San Paolo Station in the background remains as a link with the past.

319

Two officers of the 'Sassari' Division and a captain from an Alpini unit are being led into the German lines blindfolded to discuss a possible truce with officers of the 2. Fallschirmjäger-Division. The German officer on the right is most likely Oberstleutnant Wolfgang Meder-Eggebert, acting commander of Fallschirmjäger-Regiment 6 and, in the absence of Generalleutnant Hermann-Bernhard Ramcke, acting division commander.

SURRENDER NEGOTIATIONS

While all this was happening, the Germans continued their appeals to the Italian divisions to cease fighting their former comrades. These petitions had little effect on the Granatieri Division, which fought stubbornly and well. But they did find a receptive audience in the Centauro Division, which had thus far taken no part in the fighting.

At 1700 on September 9, a German parliamentary, Hauptmann Hans Schacht, presented himself at the Centauro Division headquarters at Bagni Acque Albule, some 20 kilometres east of Rome, bringing an oral appeal from General Kurt Student to the division commander, General Giorgio Calvi di Bergolo. This declared confidence in the division's friendly attitude towards the German troops and requested that the division treat the German troops as friendly. It was not quite clear whether this represented a demand for surrender, an offer of honourable capitulation, or a request to let the German forces pass unmolested to the north.

In reply, Calvi di Bergolo sent his Chief-of-Staff, Tenente Colonello Leandro Giaccone, to Kesselring's headquarters at Frascati to learn exactly what terms the Germans would offer. Arriving there with a lieutenant interpreter at 2100, Giaccone carried out a long-drawn-out discussion with Kesselring, his Chief-of-Staff General Siegfried Westphal and Student. He from his side proposed that the Germans continue to respect the 'open city' status of Rome (which the Italians had declared on August 14) and evacuate the capital; that one Italian division (the Piave Division) and the police force be allowed to stay in the city; that other Italian troops lay down their arms and be sent home; and that the Italians be permitted to surrender honourably. Against that, Kesselring insisted on having German troops occupy the German Embassy, the telephone exchange and the radio station; that the Italian division remaining

in Rome was to have no artillery; that the Italian officer appointed as commander of the city was to give him, Kesselring, a daily report; and that the Italian soldiers, after their discharge, were to have the alternative of taking up military or labour service with the Germans.

Meanwhile, Maresciallo d'Italia Enrico Caviglia had on his own accord taken over the command of all civil and military forces in the capital. His chief priority was to save Rome and its population from the destruction of battle so he immediately began efforts to pacify the Germans. However, the staff at the German Embassy had gone, and Kesselring's headquarters at Frascati proved hostile to his attempts at negotiation. To tranquillise the population, he directed the Minister of Propaganda, Carlo Galli, to broadcast radio messages and put up posters calling on the people to stay calm and assuring them

that negotiations were underway with the Germans. These public announcements, when they appeared early on the 10th, only served to further demoralise the civil population and the troops, thus undermining Carboni's plan for continued resistance.

At the same time, Carboni made contact with members of the Resistance in order to promote popular insurrection against the Germans, even committing to provide weapons and ammunition to the men of the clandestine Comitato di Liberazione Nazionale' (CLN, Committee of National Liberation). Four days earlier — on September 6 — Carboni had acquired and set aside 500 rifles, 400 pistols and 15,000 hand-grenades for distribution to the people of Rome. Luigi Longo, chief of the Communist Party, had taken charge of the distribution and when he reported to Carboni on the morning of the 10th, the latter encouraged him to get civilian fighters to reinforce the Granatieri troops south of Rome. Around noon, Carboni sent Dr. Eduardo Stolfi to the CLN to tell them that the moment had come to arm the population and have it rise against the Germans. However, the committee refused to take action and in the end only few civilians joined and fought with the military. The Romans were disillusioned and tired of the war, and most of them preferred to follow Caviglia's radio and poster appeals to stay calm rather than Carboni's call to fight.

Meanwhile, Lieutenant-Colonel Giaccone had arrived back at Kesselring's headquarters at 0700 to confirm that the Italian command had accepted the conditions drafted the night before. However he was confronted with a nasty surprise when Kesselring told him that the Allied landing at Salerno, far to the south, meant that the Italians in Rome were on their own and that he therefore had a new set of terms, much sterner than the one agreed on earlier. He now demanded complete capitulation, and if the Italians did not comply before 1700, he would send the Luftwaffe to bomb Rome.

The men are standing on what is today the Circonvallazione Ostiense, the side street off the Via Ostiense. The warehouse on the right belongs to the the Mercati Generali complex. The industrial buildings in the left background are those of the gas works.

Prisoners from the 'Piave' Division being rounded up by Fallschirmjäger in the Piazza di Santa Costanza, a few hundred metres south of the Via Asmara.

New development has transformed the piazza but the two apartment blocks in the background survive unchanged. This is Via Bolzano from its junction with Piazza di Santa Costanza.

When the news of the surrender reached the Porta San Paolo, Italian resistance weakened and the defenders were pushed back towards Monte Testaccio and the Viale Aventino, where many surrendered to the Germans. Although news of the surrender spread quickly, sporadic fighting continued for a few hours in many areas of the city. Clashes occurred in the Via Appia, in Piazza Vittorio, in Via Merulana, in Via Gioberti, in Via Cavour and at the large military barracks of Castro Pretorio, while the Piazza Esedra, where the wounded were assembled, increasingly resembled an enormous open air field hospital. The last clashes occurred in the Piazza dei Cinquecento, in front of the Stazione Termini (main railway station). Italian soldiers, backed by some railway workers, attempted a desperate final stand around an Army train, which ended at 2030.

The Wehrmacht quickly took control of all of Rome. The Fallschirmjäger speedily occupied the ministries and the most-important public buildings; anti-tank guns and machine guns were placed at the major crossroads and many other points all over the city, while the first posters signed by Kesselring and communicating the new rules to the people of Rome appeared on the walls. The gates of the Vatican, which for reasons of safety had been closed during the fighting, were re-opened. However, German sentries respected the dividing line between Italy and the neutral Vatican State. The following afternoon, September 11, the 3. Panzergrenadier-Division entered Rome, parading in along the Via Veneto with its armoured columns.

Like in Rome, the disarming of the Italian Army in the rest of Italy and the occupied territories proceeded without problems. Isolated groups of Italian soldiers continued sporadic resistance here and there, but they were quickly overwhelmed by the better organised and efficient German forces and subjected to the inevitable retaliation. When everything finally came to an end, the Italian Army had completely disintegrated.

MARCO MARZILLI, 2011

Thus Rome became a German-occupied city. Generalmajor Reiner Stahel was appointed Stadtkommandant (City Commandant). The German command confiscated large hotels in the Via Veneto and isolated the area with barbed wire and sentries yet the sanctity of the Vatican was observed. These Fallschirmjäger stand on the edge of the Piazza San Pietro.

The boundary is now denoted by a line of bollards.

The Massacre at the Ardeatine Caves

In March 1944 the ancient capital of Rome was awaiting its liberation by the Allies who had already landed in Italy three times during the previous six months. In July 1943, Fascism had been deposed and Mussolini had been arrested only to be later rescued and reinstated by the Nazis. When the new government of King Victor Emmanuel sued for an armistice, by the time the Italian government decided to accept the unconditional surrender terms offered in return, German forces had taken over the defence of Italy. Nevertheless, Italians hoped that Rome, the Eternal City, would be spared the ravages of war and so, by and large, it was by both the Germans and the Allies. It was a third force, the Comitato di Liberazione Nazionale, the CLN, a clandestine amalgamation of anti-Fascist resistance movements, which was, indirectly, to bring the full horrors of war to the people of Rome.

When German forces occupied Rome they agreed to respect an earlier proclamation that Rome would be an 'open city', but since

the Anzio landings the number of military movements had tripled, the Swiss correspondent of *The New York Times* reporting that: 'On the Ponte Milvio, which is perpetually clogged throughout the hours of darkness, down the Via Flaminia and the Corso in the heart of Rome proper, the stream pours in unending waves of tanks, motorised artillery and trucks loaded with munitions which filter through the maze of streets to disappear into the Pontine Plains or southward to the escarpments of Cassino. During the daytime, of course, none of this is visible for there is the perpetual danger of American aerial machine-gunning along the roads north and south of the capital.'

'Open city' status was never recognised as such by the Allies and, after President Roosevelt declared at a Washington press conference that 'Germany has used the Holy City of Rome as a military center', Allied air attacks were launched against targets on the south and east of the city. Pope Pius XII protested vigorously but his action in turning a blind eye

to Hitler's violation of his earlier assurances was to cause a bitter controversy in later years over the partiality of Vatican policy.

Since the landings at Anzio in January, Italian partisans had already engaged in attacking the German forces, their supply routes and depots, although some felt that these pinpricks were hardly the way to win a decisive victory. It was the arrival in Rome of the III. Bataillon of SS-Polizeiregiment Bozen in February 1944 that gave the partisans the opportunity to mount the operation that was to have such far-reaching repercussions. The regiment, posted under the command of SS-Obergruppenführer Karl Wolff, head of the SS in Italy, had arrived to provide an additional force to help keep the people of Rome under strict Fascist control. The 2. Kompanie, comprising 156 men, was assigned to Rome and their regular daily 'show the flag' march through the streets of Rome to the Macao Barracks in the Castro Pretorio gave the Roman 'partigiani' the idea of striking directly at the enemy.

Both events, coming after a series of Italian military disasters, severely shocked the nation and before the month was out Benito Mussolini had been deposed by the Fascist Grand Council following a vote of no confidence. A request for an armistice with the Allies was not long delayed but the Germans were alive to the possibility of Italy changing sides and quickly moved to establish authority. Although these photos of a column of Sturmgeschütze moving through Rome are undated, it is significant that they are travelling north on the Via del Tritone, a main avenue which lies just west of the Via Rasella (see map opposite).

March 23, 1944, was the 25th anniversary of the day that Mussolini had formed his Fascist Party in 1919 and, while the dictator could not be present, the anti-Fascist Comitato di Liberazione Nazionale (CLN) were planning a spectacular operation for that particular day. The III. Bataillon of SS-Polizei-regiment Bozen had arrived in Rome in February and its 2. Kompanie carried out a daily 'show the flag' march through the capital. Part of the route to the Macao Barracks led up a small side street — the Via Rasella — and it was there that he CLN planned to explode a bomb hidden in a dust-cart in the front of the marching column. This still re-enacts the march in the 1972 film *Massacre in Rome* based on the book by Robert Katz *Death in Rome*. Robert told us that the filming was not carried out in the actual street where it happened.

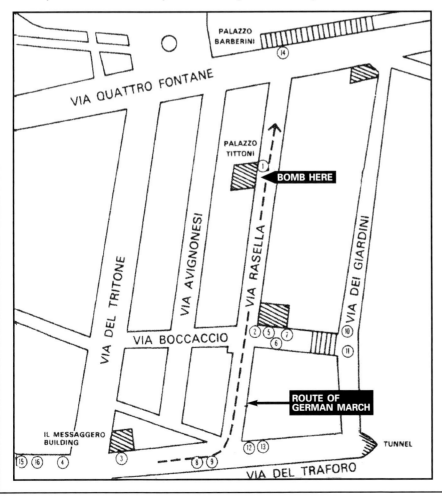

The road-sweeper's handcart was to be parked two-thirds of the way up the hill, outside the Palazzo Tittoni. A young physicist, Giulio Cortini, and his wife were to prepare the explosives; 12 kilogrammes of TNT in a steel canister, itself surrounded with more TNT packed with pieces of iron tubing to increase the shrapnel effect. The bomb was to be detonated by a 50-second delay fuse. This timing was established by test runs up the street so that if the fuse was lit as the first Germans reached the Via Boccaccio crossroads, the bomb would detonate as the column was abreast of it. In all 16 partisans would be required for the attack, dispersed in the positions indicated on the plan. No. 1, Rosario Bentivegna, would light the fuse on a signal from No. 2, Franco Calamandrei. No. 3, Carla Capponi, Bentivegna's fiancée, was to initially take up a position outside the *Il Messaggero* building on the corner of the Via del Traforo and Via del Tritone. On a signal from No. 4, Pasquale Balsamo, that the Germans were approaching, she would walk ahead, up the Via Rasella to the corner of Via Quattro Fontane, as a sign to all that it was time to get ready. As soon as the bomb exploded, Partisans 5, 6 and 7 would lob Brixia shells at the rear of the column, or what was left of it, before escaping southwards down the steps to the Via dei Giardini. Meanwhile Nos. 8, 9, 12 and 13 would converge on the bottom of the Via Rasella to attack any Germans who tried to escape that way. Partisans 10 and 11 would first guard the rear of the men in the Via Boccaccio and then move west down the Via dei Giardini to protect 8, 9, 12 and 13. Bentivegna would be guarded by No. 14, positioned at the gates of the Palazzo Barberini, so that he could look straight down the street. Nos. 15 and 16 would be in the Via due Macelli.

Using a system of visual signals, the 16-man team of partisans had carefully planned the attack, timing the march up the steep hill so that their fuse would be of the correct length with a 50-second delay. The bomb exploded at 3.45 p.m. and blasted a huge hole in the roadway, killing 26 men instantly.

Each of the six CLN political parties had military commands theoretically under the jurisdiction of an overall Military Junta although, in reality, operations against the Germans were conducted individually. (Only after Rome was liberated did the CLN fight as a uniformed resistance army in support of the Allies in northern Italy.) The underground movement — the 'macchia' — in the centre of Rome came under the Communist-led Gruppi di Azione Patriottica and it was a member of that group, Mario Fiorentini, who had kept watch on the daily march of the SS police. He reported to his commander, Carlo Salinari, code-named 'Spartaco', that when the Germans reached the narrow, steep Via Rasella at around 2 p.m. each day, they provided an ideal target. Fiorentini proposed that three partisans could be positioned at the top of the street where they would be able to look down on the approaching column. From there they could hurl grenades at the troops and could easily escape in the confusion. However, although the plan was accepted and mounted early one afternoon in the second week of March, on this very day the march had been suspended and the partisans had to abandon the attempt.

March 23 was an historic date in the Fascist calendar: the day that Mussolini had formed his movement in 1919. Thus 1944 was the 25th anniversary of the creation of the ideology which had even inspired Hitler and so a day-long series of celebrations was planned by the Roman diehards.

The Germans, on the other hand, felt the proposals were inopportune with little popular support by the Italian people at that stage of the war, and they sought to play down what they felt might turn out to be a useless provocation. The views of SS-Standartenführer Eugen Dollmann, Himmler's personal representative in Rome, were that the ceremonies should be curtailed, a view reinforced by his opposite number in the SD (the Sicherheitsdienst or Security Service of the SS, by now indistinguishably merged with the Gestapo), SS-Obersturmbannführer Herbert Kappler. As a result, the Italian Fascists were instructed to cancel their plans, save for a church service.

However, having read of the proposed anniversary parades in the Fascist-controlled newspaper *Il Messaggero*, the partisans were also planning to celebrate March 23 although not quite in the same way. To strike a blow on the very day sacred to Fascism would add immeasurably to the propaganda effect and thus plans were laid once again to attack the police column which had meanwhile resumed its daily march up the Via Rasella.

On the morning of the 23rd, a Thursday, as the Fascist chiefs gathered in the church of Santa Maria della Pieta to attend a Mass to honour all those who had lost their lives in the Fascist cause, the partisans were making their own last-minute preparations. Their base was at No. 42 Via Marco Aurelio, just two kilometres from the Via Rasella, where a stolen rubbish cart had been stored overnight. Now Giulio Cortini installed the device in one of the two dustbin containers while Rosario Bentivegna donned a street cleaner's uniform. He planned to light the fuse from his pipe.

With the temperature already in the eighties, Bentivegna, escorted at a discreet distance by two of the party, set out on the strenuous journey to push the unwieldly barrow across central Rome. His route followed the Via Claudia, past the Colosseum, and along the Via dell'Impero flanked by the ruins of the Roman Forum. Then across the Piazza Venezia, scene of so many of Mussolini's public speeches, past the Quirinal Palace to the Via Quattro Fontane (see plan). From here it was not far to the top of the Via Rasella, from where he could drop down to the chosen spot outside the Palazzo Tittoni. Once in position, he wedged the cart

against the curb to stop it rolling down the steep hill and waited. It was ten minutes to two.

A few hundred metres away, Carla Capponi had arrived at the *Il Messaggero* building. Unfortunately the two plain-clothes bodyguards of the newspaper proprietor were standing outside and they soon became suspicious of the girl hanging about, seemingly with no purpose. Although she managed to 'flirt' her way out of a difficult situation, by 2.20 p.m. the Germans had still not arrived and she knew she would not be able to stall their interest indefinitely. Then Pasquale Balsamo came up unexpectedly and whispered something she could not catch before hurrying away. Assuming it was the signal for the approach of the Germans, she began her walk to the top of the Via Rasella but almost immediately sensed that Balsamo's hurried departure was nothing to do with the arrival of the Germans. Turning round she saw to her horror that the two bodyguards were following close behind. She kept going but she dare not stop or signal to the waiting partisans that it was a false alarm. Passing her fiance outside No. 156, by deliberately not looking at him she hoped he would realise something was wrong.

The tell-tale repair in the cobble-stones outside the Palazzo Tittoni is still visible today.

As she paused for breath on reaching the Palazzo Barberini, the men following her came up and asked why she was carrying a man's raincoat. Explaining that it was her boyfriend's, she was saved further questioning when she saw a friend of her mother fortuitously coming down the street. Rushing up to her, the lady greeted her in true Italian style with a flurry of words with the result that the two men moved some distance away although still watching Carla suspiciously.

By now it was half past three and still the Germans had not arrived. Bentivegna had already lit his pipe three times only to extinguish it when nothing happened; now he was out of tobacco except for odd shreds and pieces of paper which he crumpled into the bowl as a last resort. Convinced that the Germans had abandoned their march and that the operation should be abandoned, he was not looking forward to having to push the cart back across Rome. Five minutes later Balsamo came by with a message that if the Germans failed to appear in the next ten minutes, they would abort the attempt.

The dead were collected together and laid out at the top of the street.

Bentivegna was on the point of making a move when the sound of singing and marching boots heralded the approach of the Germans. He lit his pipe. Now, as the column of 156 men in battle kit escorted by a command vehicle turned into the Via Rasella, the partisans tensed for action. As the SS reached the crossroads, Franco Calamandrei crossed the street in front of them, raising his cap. Seeing the signal, Bentivegna put his pipe to the fuse, placing his own cap on the rubbish cart to signal that everything was in order before walking back up the hill.

At 3.45 p.m., as the police column neared the top of the street, the bomb exploded, the sound reverberating throughout the centre of Rome. Twenty-six men were killed instantly as the cart disintegrated, sending lethal shards scything through the ranks, wounding another 60, 16 of them grievously. As soon as they heard and felt the explosion, the three partisans sheltering from the blast around the corner in the Via Boccaccio hurled their bombs, one failing to explode. Those Germans still on their feet opened fire indiscriminately, assuming they were under attack from the buildings overlooking the street, and in the confusion all the partisans escaped safely.

Marty Morgan of Slidell, Louisiana, sent us this comparison that he took in 2013.

With more explosions from hand-thrown bombs, surviving members of the troop take cover while scanning windows.

The opening on the crossroads of the Via Boccaccio is where several of the partisans were stationed.

REPRISALS

That lunchtime the German Commandant in Rome, General Kurt Mälzer, had been dining with Kappler at the Hotel Excelsior. Mälzer had already drunk too much and the explosion gave him a rude awakening. Arriving at the Via Rasella somewhat the worse for wear, the scene of carnage which greeted him made him livid with rage. Sporadic shooting was still taking place, any movement at a window inviting a fusillade of shots. Mälzer was beside himself with anger, bellowing for every man, woman and child living on the street to be rounded up. As his men began their work Dollmann arrived. 'Everywhere there were large puddles of blood', he recalled after the war, 'the air was full of groans and cries and shots still rang out.' Mälzer came up 'raving like a madman, crying in a voice choked with tears', shrieking for revenge, shouting that he was going to blow up the whole street.

By now some 200 people had been lined up in front of the gates of the Palazzo Barberini, including Donna Bice from No. 156. The scene was indescribable, with the road littered with rubble, human remains, pieces of furniture and other household items, and covered in glass, with the water from a broken main cascading through the bloody mess.

When the German Consul, Eitel Möllhausen, drove up with the Fascist Minister of the Interior, Guido Buffarini, he was stunned by what he saw, Mälzer having 'lost all control of himself' and also still under the influence of alcohol. As engineers prepared boxes of explosives to blow up the street, an argument immediately broke out between the two Germans. Dollmann tried to intervene, as a heated shouting match took place before the assembled company of German and Italian soldiers and civilians.

Meanwhile Kappler had heard the explosions on his return to his office in Gestapo headquarters in the Via Tasso. Summoned urgently by telephone to the scene, he met Möllhausen's car coming the opposite way. The Consul, in a state of excitement, explained what had taken place and what Mälzer was planning. Kappler then proceeded to see for himself. When he arrived at the Via Rasella, a scene he later described as a 'terrible picture', he found the General in a lather on the corner of the Via Rasella. Dollmann stood nearby. The Gestapo chief soon sized up the situation and suggested that he should take charge, urging Mälzer to return

to his headquarters. The overwrought General conceded and was assisted to his car as Kappler's SD detachment under SS-Sturmbannführer Borante Domizlaff began a thorough house to house search. The civilians, whom Mälzer had ordered must be shot, were turned over temporarily to the Italian authorities.

Around 4.15 p.m., Möllhausen arrived back at the Embassy. He was still in a foul mood and immediately telephoned Generalfeldmarschall Kesselring's headquarters just outside Rome. The Commander-in-Chief of German Forces in Italy was out of his office visiting the front when the call came through

Bullet holes can still be seen on the building opposite.

Meanwhile, a wholesale round-up began with innocent people just plucked from the streets. Here some 200 are lined up on the Via Quattro Fontaine in front of the gates to the Palazzo Barberini at the top of Via Rasella. Hostages were to be selected and executed at the ratio of ten Italians for every one German killed.

but the news of the terrorist attack was immediately relayed on to OKW headquarters at Rastenburg. When Hitler was informed he was furious and within 15 minutes a call came back from East Prussia with orders to shoot 30 to 50 Italians for every German police officer killed.

Events moved fast. At a meeting in Mälzer's office, the General received instructions from his immediate superior. General Eberhard von Mackensen, commander of the 14. Armee, who thought the Führer's demands excessive and set the ratio at ten Italians for every German. Kappler, who was present, advised von Mackensen that he had already prepared contingency plans for just such an eventuality in that they should choose 'Todeskandidaten', that is people already held under sentence of death.

Although the order for the executions was still to be confirmed, Kappler immediately set to work drawing up a list of those held in German and Italian jails in Rome, the total German dead now having risen to 28. On his return to his HQ, Kesselring ordered that the executions should take place within 24 hours.

It soon became clear to Kappler that he could not possibly make up the total of 280 out of genuine Todeskandidaten and he called his chief, the head of the SD in Italy, SS-Gruppenführer Wilhelm Harster, for advice. Harster advised that the total could easily be met by including as many Jews as needed, and that it was imperative that the list be completed on time.

Kappler worked on throughout the night to make up his total, having sought and obtained permission from the German Military Tribunal in Rome to include people awaiting trial for capital crimes and others already convicted but serving terms of imprisonment. He also called for a list of those civilians rounded up in the Via Rasella to check the names against police files for possible suspects. As the hours passed his task was made increasingly difficult as more of the wounded policemen died, and before the night was out it had risen to 32, necessitating an additional 40 names. By 3 a.m. he had built up a figure of 270 but still 50 short of the total he required. Having exhausted every possibil-

ity of those prisoners held under German jurisdiction, he resolved that the balance would have to be supplied by the Italian police. Early next morning the Italians were told they had until 1 p.m. to produce 50 suitable candidates.

This was the best Marty could do with the street constantly lined with parked cars.

SS-Obersturmbannführer Herbert Kappler (left) went to inspect the cave system which had been suggested to him. Right: It lay three kilometres south of Rome on the Via Ardeatina with a large off-road area suitable for unloading the vehicles with the hostages.

THE EXECUTIONS

When Kappler arrived back in his office on Friday morning he began to plan the second part of the operation — the actual executions. If Hitler's deadline were to be observed, the job would have to be completed that afternoon and a meeting was held to discuss with his men the practical means by which 300-odd people could be killed in the shortest possible time. Having already decided that only SD men of German nationality should carry out the executions, he had available 74 men including himself. As this total was 'much less than the number who had to be shot,' Kappler later described how 'I calculated the number of minutes necessary for the killing of each of the 320. I had the arms and ammunition computed. I figured the total amount of time I had. I divided my men into small platoons, which would function alternately. I ordered that each man fire only one shot. I specified that the bullet enter the victim's brain from the cerebellum in order that there be no wasted firing and that death be effected instantaneously.'

Then came the problem as to where the executions should take place. Normally the death penalty in Rome was carried out in Forte Bravetta, the victim being tied to a chair according to Italian custom. 'As we did not have time for these formalities', Kappler coldly explained, 'I thought of creating a kind of large, natural death chamber'. One of his officers said that he was familiar with a network of caves not three kilometres away beside the Via Ardeatina, near the complex of Christian catacombs of St Callixtus, and Kappler instructed the officer, SS-Hauptsturmführer Gerhard Köhler, to go immediately to the site to investigate its suitability and also to examine the ways and means of subsequently sealing off the entrances to create a sepulchre.

When Köhler reported back favourably, Kappler decided to personally inspect the site. Just before he left, news came in that a further policeman had died, necessitating another ten people being added to the list, but Kappler quickly solved the problem by including ten Jews who had just been brought in that morning.

A few minutes before two o'clock Kappler and Kohler set out for the caves. As the SD chief left his headquarters his men had already begun shepherding the prisoners held in the Gestapo jail into covered lorries parked in the Via Tasso, the first truckload of Italians departing at precisely 2 p.m. escorted by their executioners.

After passing through the Roman wall at the ancient Appian Gate (the latter-day Porta San Sebastino), the route lay south along what must be the world's most historic road — the old Via Appia.

A few hundred metres beyond the railway bridge the road forks. To the left the Via Appia Antica continues south while to the right the Via Ardeatina, another of Imperial Rome's highways, branches off to the port of Ardea. Here, with a grinding of gears, the loaded trucks turned off, but to the prisoners, if they perceived the route or caught a glimpse of the outside world through the canvas, the road ahead only led to the battle-front at Anzio. However those of the Christian faith, who perhaps by now had realised that this was no ordinary ride, would have drawn comfort from this spot, for here, nearly 2,000 years before, Peter the Apostle is said to have seen a vision of the Risen Christ: 'Domine Quo Vadis?' 'Lord whither goest thou?', the sacred place now marked by the little chapel named after the event.

After a further kilometre the lorries slowed and turned into the open clearing in front of the caves that lay on the right-hand side of the road. There were three entrances. Kappler had already chosen the spot where two tunnels intersected (see plan) as the execution chamber and instructed that the victims be escorted there via the central entrance in groups of five, each accompanied by his executioner. Kappler had already given his men a pep talk and demonstrated the method to be used — a single shot in the back of the head of each victim as he knelt. He reminded his men that if any flinched from the task, which had been ordered by the Führer, that man would himself be lined up and shot.

The scene was lit by flashlights held by soldiers lining the tunnel. Even so the light was poor and Sturmbannführer Domizlaff said later that 'one scarcely saw the target against which one had to shoot'. Off to one side stood SS-Hauptsturmführer Erich Priebke with the list of names. It was still short but the killings would have to begin if they were to be completed by 8 p.m. when the 24-hour deadline expired. SS-Hauptsturmführer Carl-Theodor Schütz stood by to give the order to fire.

The caves had been constructed during the mining of volcanic dust used for making concrete duirng the great rebuilding era of the Fascist regime but by 1944 they had been exhausted and were abandoned. All the roads in the vicinity were sealed off while troops patrolled the ground above the caves to keep out any curious locals.

By now it was 3.30 p.m. Other prisoners had already arrived outside the caves brought from the Regina Coeli prison. The first five Germans selected an Italian whose hands were tied behind their backs. After each man had been asked to identify himself, and names ticked off, the five were led to the rear of the central tunnel, forced to their knees and told to face the wall. None protested.

Kappler felt that he and his officers had to set an example to the men so he personally led the next group. 'I went to a nearby truck', he later testified, 'and I took a victim with me, whose name was crossed out by Priebke from his copy of the list. Four other officers did the same. We led the victims to the same place and, in the same way, a little behind the first five, they were shot.'

Leaving his men to continue their grisly task Kappler retired to his office whereupon he despatched more of his staff to take their turn in the execution squads. At the same time he was annoyed to find that the Fascist authorities had still not come up with their

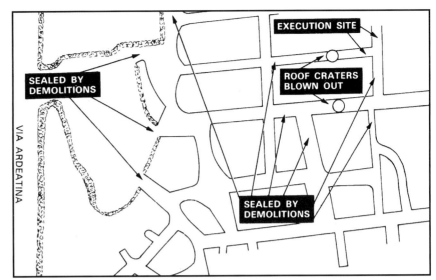

share of prisoners to make up the required number. To expedite matters he sent SS-Obersturmführer Heinrich Tunnat direct to Regina Coeli with orders to get the 50 by 4.30 p.m. at the latest. When the deadline was reached, and with still no list, Tunnat decided to wait no longer. A truck was backed up and the Germans began taking prisoners at random, driving off with some 30 men. Shortly afterwards the list arrived spec-

ifying the detainees by name. Eleven of these did not coincide with those taken by the Germans but arbitrary deletions were made to the list to try to make the numbers tally.

Meanwhile Kappler had received a telephone call from the officer he had left in charge of the executions reporting that one officer, SS-Obersturmführer Reinhold Wetjen, had refused to take his turn. He decided to deal with the man personally and drove

Bearing in mind the actual caves are now a sacred national shrine, 'another location was found in Rome which virtually duplicated the original site', wrote Robert Katz to us in response to our query over the film re-enactment of the massacre.

back to the caves. When he arrived he then found that his plans for an orderly operation were already faltering. Some prisoners had resisted and had had to be beaten to their knees, others had been shot singly and bodies were strewn haphazardly for some 25 metres down the tunnel and at this rate the corpses would soon extend out into the open. The horror of the massacre was also having a debilitating effect on his men and once again he decided to set an example. With an arm round his waist, he led the mutinous officer into the caves and stood beside him as they both shot two Italians. He then ordered a rest period, passing round a bottle of brandy, advising his men to get drunk.

From now on the victims were made to climb on top of the dead and, as the corpses piled ever higher, so the executioners themselves had to climb on top of the bodies. As night fell the orgy of killing continued, the drunken executioners becoming ever more sloppy in their work, needing more and more shots to kill each victim. The horrific scene defies written description and can hardly even be imagined . . . the flickering torches . . . the distorted shadows of the executioners . . . the muffled shots . . . the acrid pistol fumes mingling with the smell of death . . . the screams and cries of the dying . . .

By 8 p.m. it was all over and engineers moved in with boxes of explosives to seal the tunnel. The first two charges were fired that evening, and the following day they returned to complete the sealing of the outer entrances. Believing that all traces of the crime were now eliminated the troops departed and silence at last descended on the Via Ardeatina.

German engineers attempted to blow up the entrances to seal the bodies inside but in two places the charge penetrated the roof.

THE AFTERMATH

SS-Obersturmbannführer Kappler was not pleased. Only now did he learn that an additional five Italians had been shot, over and above the specified 330, due to the last-minute mix-up to make up the numbers, and he was also made aware of the fact that his orders from General Mälzer specified only 320 people; thus the additional ten names he had added at the last moment were technically unauthorised. In their public communiqué announcing reprisals, the Germans avoided any mention of Kappler's double mistake although it was agreed that, if questioned, responsibility for the error must be his alone.

The German engineers had also bungled the demolitions and in two places the explosions had been too powerful, blowing right through the tunnel roof to the surface, leaving the interior open to the outside air. When an awful overpowering stench began to pervade the district Kappler's solution was to dump refuse from the city around the entrances supposedly trying to mask one odour with another!

During the following week priests from the nearby catacombs visited the caves several times seeking a way in but it was not until some boys, scavenging the area for anything of value, came across the hole in the roof swarming with hundreds of bloated flies that one was found. The boys informed the priests and two of their number returned with them and climbed down a ladder into the hole. 'At about two metres from the opening we stumbled upon a pile of corpses', Don Valentini later recounted. 'Six were plainly visible although they lay face down covered with a thick mould. The tunnel extending behind them was completely filled by cadavers lying in awkward positions.'

The priests immediately informed the authorities at the Vatican; another party came to investigate the discovery the following day, and on Friday, March 31, Don Valentini reported in person to the Holy See. Meanwhile the Germans had learned that the bodies had been found and immediately sent engineers to fill in the hole. Later that afternoon more explosions were heard, the rotting corpses now being effectively buried under piles of sand.

As soon as American forces entered Rome on Sunday, June 4, an immediate call came for an investigation and a commission was set up headed by Dr Attilio Ascarelli, a forensic scientist at the University of Rome. Dr Ascarelli's investigation team entered the tunnels at the beginning of July.

'At the entrance to the caves there were numerous wreaths, and the walls were decorated with writings and relics placed there out of compassion by the people.

'Entering those sombre tunnels, the visitor was overcome with a sense of coldness and, even worse, by an offensive odour, which was difficult to tolerate — a stench that was so nauseating it made one vomit. There was no one who having once entered that place of sadness and martyrdom did not experience an unforgettable sense of horror, of pity for the victims, and of execration for the murderers. The members of the commission were terrified. They inspected the caves, passing through the sloping tunnels by the light of torches, and arrived at the sacred site of the massacre.

'To give an exact idea and a representative description of the appearance of those two piles of human remains is something I do not know how to express in words. The sense of horror and of pity that gripped the visitor is beyond any imagination. Two enormous, shapeless heaps of cadavers, from which arose an unbelievable smell of rottenness, of rancid and decomposed fat. It penetrated and permeated one's clothes to the point that it became necessary to take precautions by wearing special garments, gloves and boots, and to shield the respiratory tract with gauze masks soaked in deodorant. And even that was not enough.

'Little could be seen of the bodies, but through the mixture of volcanic dust, soil and the decomposed cadaverous fat that covered the corpses there emerged a foot, here and there a pair of shoes, there a skull, whole or crushed, now a limb, now a piece of tattered clothing. Insects swarmed among the scattered limbs. Myriads of larvae fed on the rotting flesh. Numerous large rats darted from the unburied and unguarded remains, and even from the fragmented heads.'

At the beginning of June American forces entered Rome (see *After the Battle* No. 152) and an immediate investigation was set in motion. The following month the entrance was uncovered revealing a scene too awful to describe.

The United States Army Information and Education Branch, in co-operation with the Italian government, had this notice prepared for visitors to the cave system which lies alongside the ancient Appian Way of Roman times. The photographs *(below)* were taken in November 1946 when coffins of the dead still lined the tunnels.

Families were spared the agonies of visual identification and instead questionnaires listing personal details and personal effects were used by the team which in the end succeeded in identifying 322 of the 335 victims. A huge mausoleum, 50 metres by 25 metres, was constructed nearby with the remains laid to rest in individual named sarcophagi, and on March 24, 1949, the fifth anniversary of the massacre, Le Fosse Ardeatine was dedicated as a Memorial Cemetery and National Monument open daily for visitors.

Every year, on the anniversary of the massacre, and in the presence of senior officials of the Italian Republic a solemn commemoration is held at the Fosse Ardeatine Monument to the Fallen.

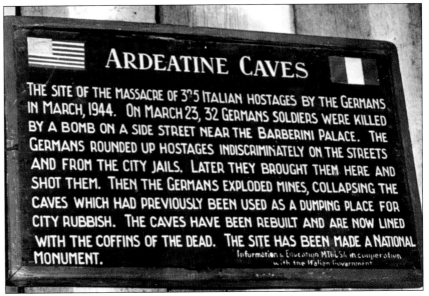

ARDEATINE CAVES

THE SITE OF THE MASSACRE OF 3?5 ITALIAN HOSTAGES BY THE GERMANS IN MARCH, 1944. ON MARCH 23, 32 GERMANS SOLDIERS WERE KILLED BY A BOMB ON A SIDE STREET NEAR THE BARBERINI PALACE. THE GERMANS ROUNDED UP HOSTAGES INDISCRIMINATELY ON THE STREETS AND FROM THE CITY JAILS. LATER THEY BROUGHT THEM HERE AND SHOT THEM. THEN THE GERMANS EXPLODED MINES, COLLAPSING THE CAVES WHICH HAD PREVIOUSLY BEEN USED AS A DUMPING PLACE FOR CITY RUBBISH. THE CAVES HAVE BEEN REBUILT AND ARE NOW LINED WITH THE COFFINS OF THE DEAD. THE SITE HAS BEEN MADE A NATIONAL MONUMENT. Information & Education MTbUSh in cooperation with the Italian Government

In the end, 322 of the 335 victims were identified and a huge mausoleum, 50 metres by 25 metres, was constructed nearby where the remains were laid to rest in stone sarcophagi. It was dedicated on the fifth anniversary of the massacre on March 24, 1949 when the Fosse Ardeatine was inaugurated as a national monument.

Coincidentally with Dr Ascarelli's investigation, a new Italian judicial system installed in Rome by the Allies began its work into 'Fascist crimes'. The first person connected with the atrocity to be put on trial was Pietro Caruso, the Italian police chief of Rome who had prepared the supplementary list of 50 names. His trial on September 20 lasted a single day; the following morning he met his end at Forte Bravetta.

The German participants, or those who could be traced in Allied custody at the end of the war, were taken back for trial in Italy. Generals Mackensen and Mälzer faced a British military tribunal in Rome in November 1946, were found guilty and sentenced to death, later commuted to life imprisonment. Mälzer died in jail while Mackensen was released in 1952.

Albert Kesselring also faced a British military court in February the following year in Venice. He too was sentenced to death but reprieved two months later and sentenced to life imprisonment which was, in turn, reduced to a term of 21 years. After having served five years in the British military prison at Werl, Germany, he was released.

Under the terms of the Moscow Declaration on German Atrocities, war criminals were to be sent 'back to the scene of their crimes to be judged on the spot by the peoples whom they have outraged', and Herbert Kappler, held by the British, was turned over to the post-war Italian government. His trial, together with co-defendants Hans Clemens, Borante Domizlaff, Johannes Quapp, Carl Schütz and Karl Wiedner, opened before the Tribunale Militare di Roma on May 3, 1948. During his eight-day testimony, Kappler not only argued that he was acting under Hitler's orders, but sought to justify the reprisals as a legitimate act of 'collective repression' in response to the illegal action in the Via Rasella. The verdict when it came graphically demonstrated the inequality liable to occur when defendants accused of the same crime are brought to trial separately by different nations. The Italian court decided that the ten-fold reprisal was perfectly legal and Kappler was found not guilty of murder in the case of 330 of the Italians and, but for the mistake of killing the extra people, he may well

Summary justice for the Italian police chief Pietro Caruso for providing 50 Italians to be massacred by the Nazis. He was executed at Fort Bravetta by a firing-squad comprising 16 Rome policemen.

have been acquitted. As it was, he was found guilty only in respect of the excess five. The other defendants were all found not guilty.

As the Code of Justice for the new Italian republic renounced the death penalty, Kappler was sentenced to life imprisonment. A series of appeals prolonged the issue until his final plea was turned down by the Supreme Court in December 1953. Four years later, from his prison cell at Gaeta on the coast between Anzio and Naples, he addressed an appeal to the Italian State for a pardon. It was denied. In 1959, by then a reportedly devout Christian, Kappler sent a request to the Italian President that he might be permitted to visit the shrine at Ardeatine as 'pilgrimage of penitence to render homage'. This too was denied. A year later a further appeal to the highest Italian Military Court for an amnesty was also rejected.

In 1972 he was allowed to marry a West German nurse, Anneliese Wenger, but four years later he had to be transferred from prison to a hospital in Rome suffering from stomach cancer. The following month, March 1976, his wife appealed to President Giovanni Leone to allow her husband to die at home in Germany and although it was reported that his life sentence had been suspended, it was stated that the German was now too ill to be moved.

Nothing more was heard of Kappler until the morning of Tuesday, August 16, 1977 when headlines around the world screamed of his escape from hospital, aided by his wife who had concealed him in a wardrobe suitcase.

Every Thursday Frau Kappler was in the habit of flying to Rome to visit her sick husband in Celio Military Hospital and on the

Generaloberst Eberhard von Mackensen *(left)*, the former commander of the 14. Armee in Italy, and Generalleutnant Kurt Mälzer *(centre)*, the Ortskommandant in Rome, faced a British Military Tribunal in November 1946, both being sentenced to death. Having been reprieved, in January 1947 they were sent to the British Military Prison at Werl, a small provincial town 30 kilometres east of Dortmund (see *After the Battle* No. 118). Mälzer died in jail in March 1952, von Mackensen being released in October that year.

Generalfeldmarschall Albert Kesselring *(left)* was tried in Venice in 1947 for the atrocities committed under his command as former C-in-C Italy. Condemned to death, he was also reprieved and joined the others at Werl, being released with von Mackensen in October 1952.

Left: **Herbert Kappler was apprehended by British forces in 1945 having tried to seek refuge in the Vatican. He was turned over to the Italians and put on trial in 1948** *(right).* **By that time Italy had abolished the death penalty so instead he was sentenced to life imprisonment to be served in the military prison at Gaeta.**

Monday night had gone to his private room around 1 a.m. Claiming that she had acted completely on her own, she smuggled Kappler from his room, leaving a 'do not disturb before 10 o'clock' notice on the door. By the time the authorities realised what had happened the Bonn Government had received word that Herbert Kappler was now safely in Germany. Reporters immediately descended on the Kappler home in Soltau where Frau Kappler said that she freed her husband 'because in desperation he wanted to take his own life'.

An immediate request was sent from Italy to the German government for his extradition but as Article 16 of the West German constitution prohibited the extradition of any German to a foreign country, the request was denied. As Kappler had become to many Italians the ultimate personification of the evils of Nazism, it was said that a 'hit squad' had already been despatched to Germany to either capture or kill him. Retaliation from pro-Kappler supporters led to bombs being exploded outside the Italian embassy in Paris and the Ardeatine caves themselves.

Six months later the legal impasse was finally at an end when Herbert Kappler died of cancer in February 1978.

AFTER THE BATTLE, 1986

Kappler's wife divorced him but in 1972 the Italian authorities permitted him to marry Anneliese Wenger within the prison *(above).* In 1975, he was diagnosed with terminal cancer and moved to the military hospital in Rome. On a prison visit in August 1977, his wife managed to carry him out in a large suitcase (he weighed about 47kg) and returned with him to West Germany. He died at Soltau on February 9, 1978, the funeral *(left)* being attended by over 700 people. The man giving the Hitler salute was arrested and fined 9,600 Deutschmarks in court at Lüneburg, although he claimed he was merely giving the 'official salute of the Wehrmacht'. *Right:* **SS-Hauptsturmführer Erich Priebke, who had helped compile the list of those to be executed, was being held in a British prison camp in Italy pending his trial when he escaped in 1946. He reached Argentina where he lived as a free man until 1994 when American journalists from ABC News tracked him down. Priebke was extradited to Italy but amid huge protests, he was released in August 1996 only to be re-arrested and put under house arrest. He died in Rome on October 11, 2013.**

Hungary

One of the most significant repercussions of the First World War was the extent to which the victors redrew national boundaries in Europe. Germany and her allies were each affected to varying degrees but none worse than Hungary which, as a result of the Treaty of Trianon in June 1920, lost more than two-thirds of its territory. Reduced from 125,641 square miles in the pre-1914 days of the Austro-Hungarian Empire, it shrank to a mere 92,962 square kilometres — Romania, Czechoslovakia and Yugoslavia taking the lion's share with lesser fragments going to Austria, Poland and Italy. As a result, Hungary's pre-war population decreased from more than 20 million to 7½ million, a losing in the process over three million Magyars of the mother tongue. The treaty also provided for unspecified reparations and strictly limited the size of the armed forces.

Just as Germany — even more so after the emergence of Hitler — despised the so-called injustices of the Treaty of Versailles, so Hungarians angered under the Trianon Treaty that had effectively destroyed their country. The inter-war period was one of extreme confusion, unrest and bitterness. Not only was the country saddled with the burden of half-a-million refugees from the successor states but the people were split over the rightful position of King Charles following his declaration of a republic in November 1918. An interim measure was to elect a regent as provisional head of state and Admiral Miklos Horthy took office in March 1920.

A treaty of friendship signed with Italy in 1927 presaged a gradual shift into the Axis camp, accelerated by the rejection of Hungarian claims over Czechoslovakia by the Western Allies in 1938. On the other hand, Germany and Italy ceded Hungary the southern fringe of Slovakia and a second 'Vienna Award' in August 1940 covered Northern Transylvania (see page 31).

Miklós Horthy *(left)* served in the Austro-Hungarian Navy in the First World War, attaining the rank of Vice-Admiral. From March 1920 to October 1944, he acted as Regent of the Kingdom of Hungary, leading the national government in the inter-war years. However, his foreign policy led him to enter an uneasy alliance with Germany, which led to Horthy giving support for its attack on the Soviet Union. Also, as we have seen, when Germany and Italy agreed the return of Northern Transylvania in the Second Vienna Award, Hungary thereby recovered territory given to the Kingdom of the Serbs, Croats and Slovenes by the Allies after the First World War. *Right:* Here on September 5, 1940, Horthy enters Szatmárnémeti (now Satu Mare in Romania) in triumphant style.

Although Horthy had tried to keep his country out of the war, and had refused Germany permission to move its forces across Hungarian soil during the attack on Poland the previous year, now he relented and allowed German troops to cross into Romania. The signing of the Tripartite Pact in November was yet another step down the slippery slope as was the ill-fated Treaty of Eternal Friendship made with Yugoslavia. When the Yugoslav government was overturned in favour of a pro-Western one in March 1941, Hitler called on Hungary to join him in an invasion. Once again Hungary receded from the ultimate decision and merely allowed passage across its territory but when Germany attacked Russia in June, Hungary agreed to supply a token force for what they thought would be yet another quick German conquest.

Finally committed to the Axis cause, the strength of Soviet resistance resulted in Hitler forcing the Hungarians to throw in its entire armed forces at the beginning of 1942. With Great Britain allied to the USSR against the common enemy having declared war on Hungary the month before, and the latter reciprocating against the United States, the Hungarians were now well and truly committed.

The procession passed along Strada Stefan cel Mare having just crossed Aleea Aurora. The large building on the right is now occupied by the Democrat Socialist Party.

Nevertheless, Horthy refused to succumb to Hitler's demands for harsher measures towards the Jews and by 1944, with the Axis losing the war and the Soviet Armies on Hungary's border, the Admiral was looking for a way to leave the alliance with Germany. He was already putting out feelers to the Allies about an unconditional surrender. As a result, on March 18, 1944, Horthy was summoned by Hitler for a meeting at Schloss Klessheim. Located just west of Salzburg in Austria, this had always been a convenient location as Hitler's residence on the Obersalzberg lay just 40 kilometres away, and it was an ideal venue for conferences and for hosting official guests. Today it is a casino but in the past Mussolini, Ion Antonescu, Josef Tiso and Ante Pavelic among others had all visited Hitler there. Now it was the turn of Admiral Miklós Horthy.

Horthy, however, still believed that the Allies would, in the end, be victorious and he was anxious to leave a lifeline open to the West. With the appointment of Miklos Kallay as Prime Minister, a man who shared the same views, for two years Hungary successfully walked the tightrope. With the Hungarians soundly defeated in the East at Voronezh in January 1943, Kallay let it be known in the West that he would surrender unconditionally when Allied troops reached his borders.

With Germany's defeats on the Soviet front mounting, Hitler was increasingly concerned over the loyalty of his dubious ally on his southern flank. By March 1944 Hitler could tolerate the situation no longer and on the 18th he met with Horthy to offer him a straight choice: either he co-operate fully with Germany or Hungary would be occupied as if an enemy country. In reality Hitler's offer of a choice was a sham as he had already issued instructions for the German take-over to begin in the early hours of the following day. So swift was the operation that by the time Horthy reached Budapest, just before noon on the 19th, he found a German honour guard all lined up at the station to greet him!

The conference was a ruse to get Horthy out of the way while the Wehrmacht invaded his country. Hitler warned Horthy that German troops were going to invade Hungary the very next day and that he could only stay in office if he agreed to the installation of a pro-Nazi government with complete power to deport the Jewish population. Horthy immediately gave in although by the time he arrived back in Budapest at midday on the 19th, his attitude had hardened against this demand. He appointed his ambassador to Germany, General Dome Sztojay, as Prime Minister, as he felt that he would be sympathetic, but his hopes were dashed as the deportations of his country's Jews began on May 14 at a rate of 12-14,000 per day and continued until July 24.

335

As a show of strength a German Guard of Honour were at the station ready to greet Horthy although the bloodless take-over of Hungary did not get underway until the morning of March 26. Here a convoy from the 16. SS-Panzergrenadier-Division crosses the Margaret Bridge. The trams were still running normally.

Seven months later, as Soviet forces approached, the Germans had prepared the bridges over the Danube for demolition. However, in the case of the Margaret Bridge, German engineers set off the charges by mistake when several cars, lorries and a tram were still on the bridge.

Operation 'Margarethe' — the code-name for the German plan for military occupation — had, in fact, been conceived the previous autumn when Hungary appeared to be a likely candidate for desertion from the German camp. It was executed under the responsibility of the Oberbefehlshaber Südost (the Commanding General South-East), Generalfeldmarschall Maximilian von Weichs.

As the overall forces allocated to 'Margarethe' were insufficient to cover the entire country, the aim was to occupy only the vital western part as far as the Tisza river which would become a line of defence against Hungarian troops garrisoned in the east. The invasion was to be launched from four directions simultaneously, each by motorised troops as speed would be a critical factor.

To deal with any reaction from the Hungarian government (or the Hungarian Army), it was important to occupy the key points in Budapest in the early hours of the first day. For that purpose, a special operation had been organised with the concept of the Trojan Horse. Troops that to all intents and purposes were in transit through Hungary would by chance find themselves in Budapest on the eve of the operation and thus already in place to take over the city. Aptly named Operation 'Trojanisches Pferd', it was planned under the command of Generalmajor Alexander von Pfuhlstein, commander of the famous Brandenburg Division.

One convoy would leave Belgrade north for Germany with the bulk of the 4. Regiment Brandenburg while another would leave Vienna eastwards for Romania with elements of the Panzer-Lehr-Division. Both convoys would arrive in Budapest area by the evening of March 18. At the same time, the paratroopers of Fallschirmjäger-Bataillon Brandenburg, operating from Brunn near Vienna, would seize the airfield at Budaors either by landing their Ju 52s or by parachuting in.

To ensure efficient communications between the various units, a small signals unit from the division had travelled by train to Budapest, together with their radio apparatus, and by March 16 was already set up for work in a hotel room!

Meanwhile Admiral Horthy had had several hours for Hitler's ultimatum to sink in yet by the time his train reached Budapest, the Regent's attitude had hardened. Nevertheless, with a welcome home committee of German troops to greet him when he arrived back in his capital, Horthy had no option but to bow to German pressure and install a collaborationist government under Dome Sztojay, the Hungarian Minister in Berlin. By March 25 the roads to the city had been sealed off and troops had arrived in Budapest in a show of strength.

The impositions of the new government carried all the usual hallmarks of the Nazi dictatorship: political parties, trades unions and the Press were all repressed, and the Jews, who until then had been more or less left unharmed in Hungary, began to receive harsh treatment. General mobilisation was proclaimed to provide additional forces to bolster the German cause in the East and by the end of the summer the Hungarian army comprised 12 divisions.

Germany's problems in the East were not helped by the shaky allegiance of Romania and the declared neutrality of Bulgaria. With the Soviet offensive in the summer of 1944, the former changed sides declaring war on Germany on August 25 and the latter, with Russian troops already on its soil, did likewise on September 8. Both countries entered the battle alongside the

The convoy proceeded via Erzsébet körút and Rákóczi útca to Kálvin tér . . . a street that has seen little change.

advancing Soviet army which during September was pushing into Hungary towards Budapest. Following the capture of Arad on the 21st, the German military plenipotentiary in Budapest reported that the Hungarian High Council had completely lost its nerve.

Hitler had already received disturbing reports on the internal situation in Hungary (Dome Sztojay had been replaced by Géza Lakatos on August 29) and a meeting with the chief of the Hungarian General Staff, General Voros Janos, on September 12 did nothing to allay his suspicions. (Peace feelers had in fact already been put out to the Allies by Horthy.) Ever distrustful of his so-called ally, Hitler summoned to the his 'Wolfs-schanze' headquarters in the east at Rastenburg someone whose loyalty he could count on, and the man whose daring had already been proved a year before in the mountains of Italy: Otto Skorzeny.

When Skorzeny reached Hitler's headquarters on September 10, he was ordered to attend some important conferences on the situation in the southeastern theatre as an important assignment was under consideration for him in that area. The overall position was crystal clear: if Hungary, Germany's last ally, should go under, 70 divisions — more than a million men — would go with her and the war would be irretrievably lost. Hitler told Skorzeny that he was aware of Horthy's secret overtures to both the West and the Russians: 'You', Skorzeny later wrote in his autobiography, 'must be prepared to seize the Citadel of Budapest by force if he betrays his alliance with us'.

Hitler explained that General Ulrich Kleemann was in Hungary at that very moment putting together a new IV. Panzerkorps, from what remained of

the IV. Armeekorps that had been decimated in the Soviet offensive, ready for the defence of Budapest. He said that while Skorzeny would be subordinate to General Kleeman, he [Skorzeny] would be given carte blanche for whatever assistance he needed for the task.

With the written orders signed by Hitler in his pocket, requiring all political and military authorities everywhere to give Skorzeny all the assistance he needed, he travelled to Budapest. There, under the guise of 'Doktor Wolff' he lived, together with his aides, for three weeks in the luxurious flat of a pro-German Hungarian, seeking out the lie of the land.

The first problem they had to deal with was Admiral Horthy's younger son

Miklós whom they dubbed 'Mickey Mouse' after his nickname 'Nicky'. (The Admiral's elder son, Stefan, had been named Vice-Regent but had been killed in an aircraft crash in August 1942.) Now Miklós Jr. was implicated in the Hungarian peace negotiations with the Soviet Union being conducted through Yugoslav emmissaries loyal to Marshal Tito. The German intelligence service had managed to infiltrate one of its Croation agents into the negotiations and thus SS-Obergruppenführer Otto Winckelmann, head of German security forces in Hungary, was aware of every development.

JEAN PAUL PALLUD, 1983

In August 1944, when Romania withdrew from the Axis, it prompted Horthy to oust Prime Minister Sztojay and to halt the deportations. At the same time, he renewed peace feelers with the Soviets, terms of an armistice being agreed on October 11. The previous day, both Horthys, father and son Miklós Junior *(left)*, were observed attending a meeting with Soviet representatives so SS-Obergruppenführer Otto Winckelmann,
the Higher SS and Police Leader in Hungary, was instructed to arrest the son before the next meeting. *Right:* Hitler had great faith in the abilities of SS-Sturmbannführer Otto Skorzeny, who had successfully rescued Mussolini for him the previous September, so Hitler had already despatched him to Budapest to lead a coup de main assault on the Burgberg, the seat of government, and also to capture Horthy's son.

The German Take-over of Budapest

October 15, 1944, was a bright Sunday. The streets were empty at the time appointed for the rendezvous. My company was in a side street in covered trucks. Hauptsturmführer Adrian von Fölkersam, my aide, kept me in touch with them as obviously I could not show myself in uniform that day. If I was to appear on the stage, so to speak, I must be inconspicuous. My driver and another man, both Luftwaffe personnel, were taking the air on a seat in the little garden which occupied most of the square.

I drove up in my own car shortly before the meeting began. When I entered the square, I noticed a Hungarian military lorry and a private car, which was presumably Horthy's, stationed in front of the building of which we had been told. It took me no time to make up my mind and park my own car right in the path of these vehicles so that they could not get away in a hurry. The floor above the offices in this building had been occupied the day before by policemen who had taken lodgings nearby. Others were to

enter it from the street about 10.10 a.m., and make the arrests.

Three Honved [Hungarian army] officers were sitting in the covered lorry, but could not be seen from the street. Two others were lounging on benches in the gardens. I was standing by my car, pretending to be fiddling with the engine, when the curtain rose on the drama.

The first German policeman had hardly entered the building when there was a burst of machine-pistol fire from the lorry, and the second fell to the ground with a wound in the stomach. The two other Hungarian officers came running out of the gardens, firing their revolvers. I had just time to take cover

Hitler had anticipated Horthy's surrender move so Miklós Jr. was to be held as a bargaining chip: his life for the father's acquiescence. Felix Bornemisza, the director of the Danube Steamship Company, was acting as an intermediary with the Soviets, and on the morning of October 15, as Miklós arrived at
his office on Galamb Street, Skorzeny and his men were ready and waiting in Marcius 15 ter — March 15 Square *(above)*. 'My driver and another man, both Luftwaffe personnel, were taking the air on a seat in the little garden. I was standing by my car pretending to be fiddling with the engine.'

'We hurled a number of grenades in the doorway, thereby bringing down the door and some marble slabs which temporarily blocked the entrance.' *Left:* Back in 1983, when Jean Paul Pallud ventured behind the Iron Curtain to take this photograph, the doorway facing the square still showed signs of the damage from Skorzeny's attack, but today all has been repaired *(right)*.

behind my car when its open door was drilled. Things were getting really hot! Honved soldiers appeared at the windows and on the balconies of houses. The moment the first shots rang out, my driver and his companion rushed up to me, assuming that I had been hit. The driver was shot through the thigh, but could still walk. I gave the agreed signal to my detachment and we three defended ourselves with our weapons as best we could against the rain of fire from the enemy. It was a most uncomfortable situation, though it only lasted a few minutes.

By then my car was not much more than a sieve. Bullets ricocheting from walls passed unpleasantly near and we could only put our noses out of cover for long enough to have pot shots at the enemy and keep them at least 10 to 15 metres away.

Then I heard my men running out of the side street in our direction. Fölkersam had taken the situation in at a glance and posted the first section at the corner of the square, while the others swept through the gardens and began firing at the house-fronts. My first assailants now withdrew to the shelter of a nearby house which was occupied by Hungarians in some strength. I observed that these men were lining up for an assault and quick thinking inspired us to hurl a number of grenades in the doorway, thereby bringing down the door and some marble slabs which temporarily blocked the entrance. With that the fighting ceased. It may have lasted five minutes.

Our policemen now came down from the upper floor bringing four prisoners with them. The two Hungarians, 'Micky Mouse' [Miklós Horthy, the Admiral's son] and his comrade Felix Bornemisza were bundled into one of our trucks. To conceal their identity, our fellows had tried to roll them up in carpets, with only partial success, I observed, noting the effort required to get the refractory prisoners into the vehicle.

The lorry moved off and my company withdrew. I was anxious to avoid further scuffles, which were only too likely when the enemy recovered from his surprise.

The Burgberg, some 3,000 metres long and 600 wide, on the top of Castle Hill, was the centre of political life in Hungary and Horthy governed from there. Around midday on October 15 it was occupied by Honved troops and the gates and roads leading to it closed to traffic, thus isolating inside several German organisations, amongst them the embassy. At 2 p.m. Hungarian radio broadcast an announcement by Admiral Horthy in which he made public his intention of agreeing an armistice with the Soviets. Consequently, the Germans set the wheels in motion to install their own man, Ferenc Szálasi of the Nazi Arrow Cross Party, broadcasting a counter-proclamation. The Germans waited no longer and, without further ado, orders for Operation 'Panzerfaust' were issued. During the afternoon German troops occupied the railway station and other important buildings and the Burgberg was surrounded.

Some instinct prompted me to follow the truck. Another car and driver were available for me. Barely a hundred metres from the square, under the Erzsebet bridge, I saw three Honved companies approaching at the double. If they got any nearer, they could easily find themselves involved in a mix-up with my men, an eventuality I was determined to prevent at all costs. Time must be gained somehow but bluff was my only resource. I told my driver to pull up, and ran towards the officer who appeared to be in command. 'Halt your men quick!' I yelled. 'There's a hell of a mix-up going on up there! No one knows what's happening! You'd better find out for yourself first!'

The trick came off. The troops halted and the officer seemed undecided what to do. It was lucky for me that he knew some German as otherwise he might not have understood me. The short pause was vital from my point of view. By now, my own men must have got away in their trucks. 'I must get on!' I called to the Hungarian officer, jumped into my car and made for the aerodrome. When I arrived, the two Hungarians were in a plane, and two minutes later they were on their way to Vienna.

It was known that the Hungarians had been taking military precautions at the Citadel and the German military attaché told us that it was now occupied by Honved troops and the gates and roads were closed to traffic.

Just before 2 o'clock we were told to stand by for a special announcement on the Hungarian wireless. A message from the Regent, Admiral Horthy, came through: 'Hungary has concluded a separate peace with Russia!'

Our counter-measures now had to be carried out at once and at a conference late in the afternoon it was decided that Operation 'Panzerfaust' should be carried out early in the morning of the 16th. I fixed on 6 a.m. for zero hour.

I projected a concentric assault that should have a focal point in the centre which I intended to be a detachment approaching from Vienna Street. The factor of surprise would be of greatest effect. I hoped to rush the Vienna Gate with little resistance and without too much noise, and suddenly emerge in the square facing the Citadel. A rapid decision should follow automatically. If we could quickly force our way into the presumed centre of the Hungarian resistance, the action would soon be over with a minimum of casualties on both sides.

The Vienna Gate is one of the main entrances. Skorzeny entered here at 6 a.m. on October 16 to capture the seat of government.

Just before 5.30 a.m., when it was beginning to get light, I took my place in my truck at the head of the column. Behind me, I had two [*sic*] Tigers, followed by a platoon of the Goliath company, and the rest of the unit in their trucks. Automatics were set at safety. Most of the men had slumped in their seats and were enjoying a quiet nap. They had the hardened warriors' gift of snatching a bit of sleep when a really tough job lay ahead.

I took the precaution of sending my second-in-command to Corps Headquarters, to ascertain whether there had been any change in the situation, but the answer was in the negative, so zero-hour was adhered to.

In my truck I had Fölkersam and Ostafel, as well as five NCOs who had been in the Gran Sasso show. I considered them my personal assault group. Each was armed with a machine-pistol, a few hand-grenades, and the new panzerfaust. We were wondering what the Hungarian tanks in the Citadel would do. If necessary, our tanks and panzerfausts would have to look after them.

At one minute before 6 o'clock, I waved my arm as the signal to switch on. Then I stood up in my truck and pointed upwards several times, whereupon we started off, rather slowly, as it was uphill. I could only hope that none of our vehicles struck a mine, which would have blocked our advance and upset our plan. The Vienna Gate emerged out of the half-light — the way was open! A few Hungarian soldiers stared curiously at us. We were soon at the top. 'Gradually accelerate', I whispered to my driver.

On our right was a Honved barracks. 'Nasty if we get fired on from the flank', murmured Fölkersam at my side. There were two machine guns behind sandbags in front of the barracks but nothing happened. No sound could be heard but the rumble of the Tigers behind.

I chose the side street on the right in which the German Embassy was situated. We could now travel at a good pace without losing the rest of the column. The tanks were doing a good 35 to 40 kilometres to the hour, and the Citadel was not more than a thousand metres away and a substantial part of our task had been accomplished.

Left: Szent György útca leads to the square outside the Royal Palace — the Valpalota. This Tiger is covering the entry into the street. *Right:* Much of this part of the Burgberg was destroyed during the subsequent battle for Budapest as the coup d'etat brought only a brief respite to the Germans. By the end of 1944 Budapest was encircled by the Red Army with the city under siege conditions, pounded by artillery. Although the Germans tried to keep the city supplied from the air, and made an effort to break through on the ground, they were vain attempts. Wavering Hungarian troops were hardly the best allies and many deserted to the Soviets so that by February 12 it was all over.

Left: **With the bulky silhouette of Skorzeny on the right side of the turret, one of the four Tigers smashes through a barricade** **after leaving the inner yard of the Palace.** *Right:* **The obstacle had been set up in the Lions Gate.**

Now the great detached mass of the War Ministry appeared to the left and we heard the distant sound of two heavy explosions. Our men must have forced their way through the tunnel. The critical moment was at hand. We were past the War Ministry and in the square in a flash. Three Hungarian tanks faced us but as we drew level the leading one tilted its gun skywards as a signal that they would not fire.

A barricade of stones had been placed in front of the gate of the Citadel. I told my driver to draw aside and signalled to the leading Tiger to charge it. We left our truck and ran behind while the barricade collapsed under the weight of the 30-ton monster. Levelling its gun at the centre of the courtyard, it found itself faced with a battery of six anti-tank guns.

We leapt over the debris of the barricade and burst through the shattered gate. A colonel of the guard got out his revolver to stop us but Fölkersam knocked it out of his hand. On our right was what appeared to be the main entrance, and we took it at the run, almost colliding with a Honved officer, whom I ordered to lead us straight to the Commandant. He immediately complied, and at his side we rushed up the broad staircase, not failing to notice the elegant red carpet.

On reaching the first floor we turned left into a corridor and I left one of my men behind to cover us. The officer pointed to a door and we went into a small ante-room where a table had been drawn up to the open window and a man was lying on it firing a machine gun into the courtyard. Unterscharführer Hans Holzer, a short, stocky NCO, clasped the gun in his arms and flung it out of the window. The gunner was so surprised that he fell off the table.

I saw a door on my right, knocked and walked straight in. A Honved major-general got up and came towards me. 'Are you the Commandant?' I asked. 'You must surrender the Citadel at once! If you don't, you will be responsible for any bloodshed. You must decide immediately!' As we could hear shots outside, including bursts of machine-gun fire, I added: 'You can see that any resistance is hopeless. I have already occupied the Citadel.'

The Hungarian major-general was not long in making up his mind: 'I surrender the Citadel and will order the cease-fire at

once'. We shook hands and soon arranged that a Hungarian officer and one of ours should inform the troops fighting in the Citadel gardens of the cease-fire. After ten minutes had passed, no noise of battle could be heard.

Accompanied, at my request, by two Hungarian majors to serve as interpeters, I went along the corridor to have a look round. We came to the rooms adjoining the Regent's reception room. I was astonished to find that he was not there and learned that he had left shortly before six o'clock. It transpired later that he had been escorted by SS-Obergruppenführer Karl Pfeffer-Wildenbruch to his residence on the Citadel hill. The presence of Horthy would have made no difference to our plans, which were not concerned with him personally, but confined to controlling the seat of government.

While we were looking out of the window a few bullets whistled past. Werner Hunke, my Ia, subsequently explained that it had proved impossible to notify the cease-fire to some of the Hungarian posts on the Danube

side of the Citadel gardens. Two rounds from a panzerfaust soon convinced them that it would be wiser to abandon resistance.

The whole operation had not taken more than half an hour before peace returned to the city. I rang up Corps Headquarters and could almost hear the sigh of relief at the other end. Apparently they had considered the success of my coup as somewhat problematic.

Shortly afterwards, the reports came in from the War Ministry (where there had been a short, sharp action), and the Ministry for Home Affairs, and one by one the commanders of the different groups turned up to relate their experiences. Our casualties had been agreeably low, not more than four killed and about 12 wounded. The only serious fighting had been in the gardens. I asked the Commandant about the Hungarian casualties and was told that they amounted to three killed and 15 wounded.

SS-STURMBANNFÜHRER
OTTO SKORZENY, 1977

Skorzeny crosses Szent György Square with SS-Hauptsturmführer Adrian von Fölkersam, his Chief-of-Staff, and SS-Untersturmführer Walter Girg, a platoon commander with SS-Jäger-Bataillon 502. The building in the background is the Royal Palace that was virtually razed to the ground in the subsequent fighting.

Ferenc Szálasi, the new ruler after the Skorzeny coup, with the new Minister of War Karoly Beregfy (with moustache). After the war, both were tried as traitors by the People's Tribunal and hanged in March 1946.

Together with detachments from his own special units, SS-Jagdverband Mitte and SS-Fallschirmjäger-Bataillon 600, Skorzeny had at his disposal various units already near Budapest or discreetly brought up for the action. By midnight on October 15 these troops had been positioned behind the cordon drawn around the Burgberg by elements of the 22. SS- Freiwilligen-Kavallerie-Division during the afternoon. South of the Burgberg, a battalion formed from officer cadets of the Kriegsakademie at Wiener-Neustadt was to get into the gardens of the Palais after having blown open an access through the iron gates and then keep the Hungarian troops positioned there pinned down. On the east, where the Burgberg overlooked the Danube river, a company of SS paratroopers had to capture an underground passage leading from the bank of the river up to the War Ministry while on the northern side, the main detachment would drive up to the Burgberg along two parallel roads until reaching Szent Gyorgy ter and the Palais. That detachment was composed of a company from SS-Jagdverband Mitte backed by some Tiger IIs from schwere Panzer-Abteilung 503 and a platoon of engineers with some Goliath remote-controlled demolition vehicles.

Following the German coup d'etat, the Red Army began their assault on the city on December 26, the 50-day siege lasting until February 13, 1945. Less than 2,000 Germans and Hungarians managed to break out and reach friendly lines now some 30 kilometres to the west.

Budapest was in ruins, 35,000 German and Hungarian troops had been killed and an equal number made prisoner. An estimated 60,000 civilians had lost their lives inside the city alone, and, altogether, its alliance with Germany cost Hungary more than 136,000 soldiers killed. However, the ultimate irony came long after the fighting had ceased when, on February 10, 1947, the country was once again reduced to its 1920 frontiers by the Treaty of Paris.

The ornate frieze identifies the building — once boarded up as a ruin — as the beautifully restored Office of the President of Hungary.

Admiral Horthy had been taken into custody by the Germans on the day of the coup. He was allowed back to the Palace to collect personal belongings at which point Premier Géza Lakatos handed him a statement to sign. This said that the Admiral was retracting his declaration of an armistice and that he was abdicating in favour of the Arrow Cross leader Ferenc Szálasi. At first Horthy was reluctant to sign but when it was pointed out that his son was being held as a hostage, he capitulated although he later explained that 'I neither resigned nor appointed Szálasi Premier. I merely exchanged my signature for my son's life. A signature wrung from a man at machine-gun point can have little legality.' Horthy was then escorted by Skorzeny to Schloss Hirschberg near Weilheim in Upper Bavaria where he remained under SS guard until the Americans reached the area. On May 1, 1945, General Alexander Patch, commander of the US Seventh Army, visited Horthy and told him he was to be treated as a prisoner of war as Hungary was looked upon as being in the Axis camp. Held in Nuremberg as a witness for the trials, he was released in December 1945.

Admiral Horthy had been given a solemn promise that his son would be released after he signed the document but this never happened and Miklós Junior remained held in Mauthausen concentration camp, under the cover name 'Maus' (Mouse), until the end of the war. He was reunited with his father at Nuremberg.

Meanwhile in Hungary, the post-war communist regime was anxious to extradite Horthy, then residing with his family in Germany, for trial as Marshal Tito, the new ruler of Yugoslavia, had asked for the former regent to be charged with complicity with the massacre of Serbian and Jewish civilians by Hungarian troops in 1942. Although Horthy appeared at Nuremberg in March 1948 to testify at the Ministries Trial (one of the 12 US-run trials, see page 298), the Americans did not indict him for war crimes.

The Germans kept Admiral Horthy under guard in the castle at Hirschberg, 30 kilometres south-west of Munich. He was held there until liberated on May 1, 1945. By then the other leaders of the Axis were either mouldering in their graves like Hitler and Mussolini or in line for the firing-squad like Ion Antonescu in Romania. As Hungary was considered by the Allies to be part of the Axis, Horthy was soon arrested and moved through several detention centres before arriving at Nuremberg in September 1945 — the Allied prison where the top Nazi heirarchy were being held. He was asked to provide evidence to the International Military Tribunal but did not testify in person. While there he was reunited with his son and also Otto Skorzeny. In his post-war memoirs Skorzeny describes how they 'had a pleasant conversation for more than two hours at the end of which we were good friends. I had been able to satisfy him that Operation "Panzerfaust" was not directed against him personally and he told me that his policy towards Germany had always been friendly, but had been thwarted by difficulties which became insurmountable towards the end of the war.'

In 1950 the Horthy family found a home in Portugal and seven years later he died in Estoril. In his will, he specified that his body was not to be returned to Hungary 'until the last Russian soldier has left'. This request was honoured and in 1993, two years after Soviet troops had left, his remains were returned to be interred in the family tomb in his home town of Kenderes.

AFTER THE BATTLE, 2017

In 1993, news of the repatriation of the remains of Miklós Horthy from Portugal was received in Hungary with considerable controversy. He had always wanted to be buried in Hungary but not until the last Soviet soldier had departed. So now it was time to carry out his dying wish and return the Admiral to his homeland. The funeral took place on September 4.

Displaced Persons in Europe

French slave labourers, freed by the US Ninth Army, prepare for their journey home to France.

With the defeat of Germany, one huge problem facing the Allies was the resettlement of the many millions who had been subjected to the extensive movements of whole populations that had taken place throughout Europe. Some people had been removed from their homes to be used as forced labourers while others had fled the advancing armies. Hundreds of thousands more were imprisoned in concentration camps. For administrative purposes the military authorities defined those found within their own country as refugees while those found outside were to be known as displaced persons, or 'DPs'. In all, in May 1945 it was estimated that there were at least 11 million refugees or displaced persons in France, Belgium, Luxembourg, Holland, Denmark, Norway, Poland, Czechoslovakia and Germany.

In the case of enemy refugees and displaced persons, it was the Allied policy to place the responsibility for their care and repatriation on the shoulders of the Germans themselves, but that Allied nationals would be handled by Allied military commanders until the United Nations Relief and Rehabilitation Administration (UNRRA) could take over.

When the Allied armies entered the concentration camps it was realised that the camp records would be vital in trying to reunite broken families right across Europe and fortunately the Nazis had kept quite meticulous files on their prisoners. Those records which had escaped destruction were first taken to Höchst in the American Zone 40 kilometres south of Frankfurt, but moved in January 1946 to a former school at Bad Arolsen — a spa town west Kassel con-

veniently situated near the junction of the US, British and French Zones. Here the tremendous task of trying to reunite families began, the work being shared between the German Red Cross, working on behalf of German nationals, and for other nations by the Central Tracing Bureau set up under UNRRA.

Initially there were only about 50,000 Jewish survivors and those from eastern Europe did not want to return to their countries of origin. A report to President Harry Truman in August 1945 supported the assertion that the Jewish DPs were non-repatriable. It stated that instead they should be considered as Jews, rather than nationals

of their native countries, and that 100,000 immigration certificates to Palestine should be provided for them through the Jewish Agency. These recommendations were accepted by the military government in the US Zone, where there was the highest concentration of Jewish DPs, and separate camps were set up by UNRRA. The first Jewish DP camp was located at Feldafing but by February 1947 the total number of Jewish DPs had risen to 184,000. Two months later the American authorities barred any further infiltration of refugees into the US Zone (the British Zone had been closed off in December 1945).

Photo taken of a group of Greek-Jewish Displaced Persons (DPs) at the camp at Feldafing, Bavaria, by Samuel Zisman who served as a district commander with the United Nations Relief and Rehabilitation Administration (UNRAA) from 1945 to 1947. Six million DPs in Europe were repatriated to their home countries but nearly two million refused, the majority wanting instead to go to the promised land in Palestine.

Of the many hundreds of DP camps that were established, some dealt specifically with the needs of unaccompanied children, and on July 11, 1945 the first DP Children's Centre to be set up in the American Zone was located in the Kloster Indersdorf convent near Dachau concentration camp. Here orphaned and displaced children of various nationalities were cared for, many coming from families in central and eastern Europe.

The first international DP children's centre in the American Zone of Germany was set up on July 11, 1945 in a former convent at Indersdorf, 16 kilometres from the concentration camp at Dachau. UNRAA Team 182 sheltered and processed more than 1,000 orphan children from here for a new life overseas.

The team — pictured (below) **in front of the Schneiderturm — published photographs in an attempt to locate surviving relatives.**

345

In July/August 1946, this centre was moved to Prien on the Chiemsee lake after which Kloster Indersdorf was used exclusivly for Jewish children being prepared for a new life in Palestine. Following the formal creation of the state of Israel in 1948, this centre was closed.

The International Children's Center at Prien was located in a former German sanatorium in extensive grounds on the edge of the lake. Under Dr

Now this is the Strand Hotel but then it was the International Children's Centre in Prien on Lake Chiemsee. We are told that discipline was lax and a lack of teachers and educational materials did not help. Also the children tended to keep together according to nationality despite constant efforts by the staff to integrate the different national groups. Furthermore, there were conflicts between the Jewish and non-Jewish children.

Alexander Stern, children attended compulsory classes, only limited by the available teachers and educational materials. They had swimming and rowing classes in the summer and skiing in winter, and those destined for resettlement in Canada were given extra tuition in English.

As the children at Prien were destined for Canada, they were given additional English language classes for life in North America.

AMERICAN JOINT DISTRIBUTION COMMITTEE
c/o PC IRO Area 3 , Sub-HQ Ansbach,

FROM : Childrens Nutrition Center STRÜTH

SUBJECT : Monthly Report MAY 1948

Week ending:	0-1	2-5	6-13	14-17	18-45 male	18-45 female	45 & over male	45 & over female
1 May	3	6	9	4	25	28	1	7
8 May	4	12	93	25	26	29	1	7
15 May	4	12	93	25	26	29	1	7
22 May	4	12	93	25	26	29	1	7
AVERAGE for MAY :	4	12	72	15	26	29	1	7

MONTHLY :	Pregn. women	Nursing women	Deaths	Births	Hospital
	1	1	---	---	1

From July 1945 Millicent Diamond *(above left)* **worked at Prien (where this picture was taken) before moving on to the sanatorium at Strüth near Ansbach in Bavaria.** *Right:* **This is her monthly report for May 1948.**

The building taken over for the Strüth DP camp still stands with its facade unchanged, although it is now occupied by the Rangau Clinic. The two main buildings then housed around 300 children.

One young boy, Rafi Ben Zur, described how he came to end up in another DP camp for children at Strüth near Ansbach:

'My story begins when the ghetto in Budapest was freed by Russian troops on January 18, 1945. I was 14 and my brother 13, both totally alone in the middle of chaos, not knowing what to do. We just followed bigger children, running away from the fighting; later, we were found by the Dror Habonim movement that was looking for lonely, hungry children. At the time we knew nothing of Zionism or Palestine, all it meant to us was food and shelter, someone to wash you, and give you clothes and shoes.

'The organisation took us to the southern part of Hungary. Our father, who had been on a forced-labour brigade, found us and took us home and tried to rebuild what was left of our family but it was inpossible. Everything around us reminded us of the past, the humiliation, discrimination, hatred and the killing. We wanted to start a new life in a new homeland where we could live as free people.

'In December 1945 we were on the move again, this time to Germany. We were taken to the sanatorium at Strüth. A team of American soldiers and local professional staff ran the camp efficiently. We built roads, milked cows, and did all the cleaning jobs, learning to respect work itself. We started to learn the basic Hebrew language but we had to wait a whole year until our turn came to join "Aliyah Bet" in southern France.'

The largest DP camp in Germany was located at Bergen-Belsen in the British Zone. After the concentration camp was liberated on April 15, 1945, the survivors were taken to the nearby Wehrmacht barracks where they received medical treatment. Then in June separate living areas were established for the Polish and Jewish DPs with each section catering for up to 10,000 individuals. In September 1946, the British military authorities disbanded the Polish camp as around two-thirds of the DPs had returned to Poland or gone to the USA or Canada. The remaining DPs were dispersed to other camps in the British Zone. The problem with the Jewish inmates was that the majority had come from central and eastern Europe and the very idea of returning was unthinkable. In September 1945, a small Jewish camp organisation became the official Central Committee of Liberated Jews in the British Zone. This body called for 'Zionism' — the movement to return to the Jewish homeland — with unimpeded emigration to Palestine.

'Aliyah Bet' was the code-name given to the clandestine immigration to Palestine between 1934 and 1948. Since 1923, Britain had been responsible for administering the Mandated Territory of Palestine (carved out of Ottoman Syria). In 1939, Britain set an economic limit of 75,000 Jews to be accepted over the next five years into what was intended to be a future Jewish national home. However, as the persecution of the Jews intensified in Europe during the Nazi era, the urgency led to the establishment of organisations working to circumvent the quota system, and immigration continued throughout the war. In 1945 the journey from the DP camps started in the US Zone at two collection points: Bad Reichenhall and Leipheim. American, French and Italian officials turned a blind eye to the movement of individuals to ports on the Mediterranean. Several UNRRA staff also facilitated the emigration of Jews, but the British government was vehemently opposed, mounting armed naval patrols to prevent illegal immigrants from landing in Palestine.

The problem was that Palestine was still administered by Britain under a Mandate awarded by the League of Nations after the First World War. In 1945 the British reaffirmed the pre-war policy of restricting Jewish immigration which had been put in place following the influx of 250,000 Jews fleeing the rise of Nazism in the 1930s. This had been an anathema to the Palestinians and had already led to the Arab revolt in 1936-39. Meanwhile, the Jewish Brigade Group, formed as a unit within the British Army in late 1944, worked with former partisans to help organise the exodus of tens of thousands of Jewish refugees across closed borders. In 1946, the British prevented any more DPs entering the camp, handing over administration to the UNRRA in March. Bergen-Belsen DPs, like other Jewish DPs in the British Zone, continually protested at the United Kingdom's refusal to allow them into Palestine, and the Haganah, the Jewish military force in Palestine, sent agents to hold clandestine military training in the camp. The British authorities forbade free departure from the camp until 1949, the last DPs leaving in August 1951.

The code-name for the illegal immigration of Jews to Palestine was 'Aliyah Bet' and over 100,000 attempted the journey by sea, even though many of the ships were boarded by the Royal Navy and turned back. The first successful sailing was from Italy on August 28, 1945, but the navy blockade intercepted many of the vessels that followed over the next few months. While the United Nations deliberated over the creation of the State of Israel by the controversial partition of Palestine, on July 18, 1947 the largest batch of DPs departed from Sète on the Mediterranean coast of France aboard the former US steamer SS *President Warfield*, now flying the flag of Honduras and renamed by the Haganah: *Exodus*.

Most of the ships intercepted by the Royal Navy were escorted to Cyprus where the Jews were held in camps but the *Exodus* had almost reached the Palestinian coast when intercepted. She was taken to the port at Haifa where the passengers were transferred to three more seaworthy ships for the return voyage to France. However, on reaching Marseilles, the DPs began a hunger strike and refused to disembark. After much soul-searching, the British government concluded that the DPs would have to be returned to Germany — something that was bound to result in a huge uproar in the press — and sure enough by the time they reached Hamburg they were in a defiant mood. After being held in various camps, many managed to reach Palestine by various means, and in time for the Israeli Declaration of Independence in May 1948. The remainder were finally released in January 1949 when Britain formally recognised the new State of Israel.

Over 100,000 people attempted the journey in over 140 sailings by 120 ships, over half of which were intercepted and stopped by the Royal Navy. (Those immigrants found aboard were mostly interned in camps in Cyprus.) One crucial incident came with sailing of the SS *Exodus* in July 1947. She was carrying 4,515 immigrants and was intercepted off Haifa by the cruiser HMS *Ajax* and a flotilla of destroyers. She was rammed, boarded and turned around, and the passengers returned to DP camps in Germany — the resulting publicity causing great embarrassment to the British government.

UNRRA, which had set up the Central Tracing Service, was wound up in 1947, being superseded by the International Refugee Organisation. In 1955 the decision was taken by the Allied High Commission for Germany to hand over the day-to-day running of its records archive located at Bad Arolsen to the International Committee of the Red Cross (ICRC). Under a new name — the International Tracing Service (ITS) — by 1965 over a quarter of a million cases had been investigated and 127,000 German children had been traced out of the 300,000 missing at the end of the war. By 1968 the archive comprised 28 million index cards covering around seven million individuals with all the problems of names being duplicated or mis-spelt.

Under the Bonn Agreements of 1955, access to the archive was restricted with a total ban on the publication of any data that might harm the former victims or their families. However, as a result of pressure being brought to bear by both families and researchers, following high-level negotiations in Washington between the German Justice Minister and the director of United States Holocaust Memorial Museum, in May 2006

the 11-member countries of the International Commission decided that the ITS archive, then covering 26 kilometres of shelving, should be made available for public inspection.

With the passing of the years, and the inevitable decline in the number of formal requests for tracing, the ICRC acknowledged that the original purpose of the archive had changed. Consequently, in May 2011, the International Committee of the Red Cross decided that it would withdraw from the management of the International Tracing Service from December 31, 2012. In future the ITS was to work in conjunction with German Federal Archives marking the evolution of Bad Arolsen from a purely tracing service to a documentation centre for research and education.

AFTER THE BATTLE, 2018

As the American Zone in southern Germany was totally landlocked, Bremen, and the port of Bremerhaven on the River Weser, had been designated part of an American enclave in order to provide the US occupation army with a seaport to supply its zone. It remained in American hands until the creation of the German Federal Republic in September 1949. This ceremony marking the departure from there of the 50,000th DP destined for the New World took place on July 13, 1949.

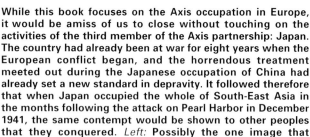

While this book focuses on the Axis occupation in Europe, it would be amiss of us to close without touching on the activities of the third member of the Axis partnership: Japan. The country had already been at war for eight years when the European conflict began, and the horrendous treatment meeted out during the Japanese occupation of China had already set a new standard in depravity. It followed therefore that when Japan occupied the whole of South-East Asia in the months following the attack on Pearl Harbor in December 1941, the same contempt would be shown to other peoples that they conquered. *Left:* Possibly the one image that demonstrates this more than any other is this one showing the beheading of an Allied soldier. The photograph was taken at the request of the executioner, the negative being discovered in the belongings of a dead Japanese. It received considerable publicity, although the identity of the soldier was not known and often misrepresented. However, in 1945, the Australian casualty branch correctly named him as Sergeant Len Siffleet, a commando serving with the Second Australian Imperial Force. *Right:* The execution took place on the beach at Atape in New Guinea where this memorial was dedicated in May 2015 (for more see *After the Battle* No. 169).

Japan

According to Japanese historians, the principles of 'Hakko Ichiu' and 'Kodo'— the former meaning simply, making the world one big family, and the second that this could be obtained solely through loyalty to the Emperor — date from the time of the foundation of the Empire of Japan over 2,600 years ago.

These two estimable concepts, harmless in themselves, were responsible for the militaristic expansionist policy of Japan in the 20th century, and were exploited and misused by those in Japan who urged a policy of territorial acquisition. Those who made military aggression the national policy of Japan turned it into a moral issue by invoking the names of Hakko Ichiu and Kodo to this aim.

Although neither country had much in common with the other, Japan, like Hitler's Germany, was engaged in preparations for a war of aggression. The country had been at war with China since 1931 and both had designs on the Soviet Union, as the Anti-Comintern

Pact of 1936 testified (see page 103). However, Japan wanted something more, a military alliance, and on the day after the Munich agreement was concluded, the Japanese Minister of War sent a message to Hitler congratulating him on his handling of the Sudeten question in Czechoslovakia: 'May Germany's national fortunes continue to rise', he wrote, 'and the friendship of the German and Japanese Armies, united on the Anti-Comintern front, be strengthened more than ever.'

Then in July 1940 a great historic opportunity arrived in Japanese history. Great Britain, France and the Netherlands had, in their eyes, been defeated. Japan would, therefore, seize all British, French, Dutch and Portuguese possessions in East and South-East Asia and the Pacific. These ambitious objectives included Hong Kong, French Indo-China, Thailand, Malaya, the Netherlands East Indies, the Philippines, New Guinea, all territory lying between Eastern India and Burma on the one hand, and Australia and New Zealand on the other. It was not Japan's intention to intervene in Europe, but to assist

Germany in conquering Great Britain by every means short of a declaration of war, and by undermining her position in the Far East and aiding and abetting nationalism in India and Burma.

Simultaneously the terms and scope of the Tripartite Alliance began to be discussed in detail. It became clear that Germany was thinking in terms of a military alliance directed, at least in part, against the Western powers. At that time her appreciation of the international situation was as follows. War with the Soviet Union was inevitable, Hungary and Czechoslovakia were potential allies, and Romania would remain neutral. It would not be possible to drive a wedge between France and England, and if it came to war between those countries and Germany, the USA would probably give them financial but not military aid.

Meanwhile the relations between the Western powers and Japan had been gradually worsening for in China attacks were still being made on British and American subjects and their property, and before the end of the month the Japanese Cabinet had resigned.

The signing of the Tripartite Pact took place in the New Reich Chancellery in Berlin on September 27, 1940. The signatories were (L-R) Saburo Kurusu, Imperial Japan's Ambassador to Germany, Galeazzo Ciano for Italy and Adolf Hitler for Germany.

The Army, and the military faction in the Government, had been working for this for some months. The foreign policy of the new Cabinet envisaged a rapprochement with Germany and Italy, a successful settlement of the war in Indo-China, and full national mobilisation. At the same time the possibility of intervention by the United States in the European war would be reduced by Japan's actions that would constitute a threat to that country in the Far East.

The new Japanese Foreign Minister lost no time in putting this idea to the German Ambassador in Tokyo and simultaneously to the Foreign Ministry in Berlin. It now appeared to the Germans that it could be in their interest to collaborate with Japan so they replied that 'Germany desires to end the European War quickly, and does not at present require Japan's military assistance,

but she would be glad if Japan would restrain and prevent the United States from entering the war. Germany and Italy themselves would do everything possible to restrain the United States and would supply Japan with such war equipment as they could reasonably spare. Germany recognised and respected Japan's political leadership in East Asia and would assist in bringing about a rapprochement between her and the Soviet Union.'

On September 27, 1940 the ten-year Tripartite Alliance between Germany, Japan and Italy was signed in Berlin. Also popularly referred to as the Berlin-Tokyo-Rome Axis, in an Imperial Japanese Rescript it was hailed as 'an instrument of peace' that would enable each nation 'to have its proper place in the world'. However the Japanese Lord Keeper of the Privy Seal

understood its full significance as he told the Emperor that if it was concluded, a supreme effort would have to be made to end the war in China, for sooner or later Japan would have to reckon with Great Britain and America, and would be involved in war with France, the Netherlands and all the countries of the British Commonwealth.

Immediately after the conclusion of the Tripartite Pact, a 'Tentative Plan for the Southern Regions' was prepared by the Japanese Foreign Office. Its primary objectives were to seize and occupy Singapore, Malaya and the Dutch East Indies without becoming involved in war with Russia or America. Should war break out between Japan and the United States, further objectives would include the Philippines, Guam and other American possessions in the Pacific.

The shortcomings of the 1907 Hague Convention concerning prisoners of war were addressed at a conference in Geneva in July 1929 when 41 states signed the 'International Convention Relative to the Treatment of Prisoners of War'. Japan signed but had not formally ratified it when she went to war. In 1942, the Japanese Foreign Minister Shigenori Togo gave formal assurance to the Western powers that although Japan was not bound by the Convention, Japan would apply it to all American, Australian, British, Canadian and New Zealand prisoners of war. It turned out that this assurance meant nothing and the cruel ill-treatment of Allied prisoners needs no elaboration here. Lord Russell, our author for this chapter, explains that the uncivilised treatment of prisoners of war by the Japanese was

the natural outcome of the code of Bushido, which was indoctrinated into the Japanese soldier as part of his basic training. The concept to fight to the death and never surrender undoubtedly led to the Japanese soldier feeling absolute contempt towards those of the Western Allies who surrendered to Japanese forces. As such they had lost their honour and so were not entitled to any respect. Prisoners were worked to death, killed out of hand, or even used for target and bayonet practice. Captured aircrews were tortured by the Kempei Tai (the equivalent of the Gestapo) before being executed; many thousands of innocent civilians murdered, and the inhabitants of villages wiped out. It was a ghastly record, mirroring what took place in Europe.

It was accepted that there was no possible way of bringing to trial all those responsible for crimes committed across the Far East, China and the Pacific Islands. Instead, like at Nuremberg, the International Military Tribunal for the Far East shortlisted 28 'Class A' defendants to set an example, and heading the list was General Hideki Tojo, the Minister of War and Prime Minister at the time of Pearl Harbor. Flanked by the three Axis flags, Tojo is seen here introducing a ceremony held in Tokyo on September 27, 1942 to mark the second anniversary of the signing of the Tripartite Pact. After he was arrested he made a botched attempt to shoot himself but he survived and was able to attend the trial that began on May 3, 1946.

JAPANESE WAR CRIMINALS

The task of identifying, locating and apprehending the many thousands of suspected Japanese war criminals was a colossal undertaking, for which an elaborate Allied war crimes machinery had to be developed. The main burden of this task fell upon the British and American military authorities and each country set up a special war crimes organisation, the British in Singapore and the Americans in Tokyo.

Although their primary function was to deal with all cases in which war crimes had been committed against their own nationals, they co-operated with all the other nations concerned, and the information and evidence which they gathered together was made available to all.

UNITED STATES

A directive of the United States Joint Chiefs-of-Staff ordered the investigation, apprehension and detention of all persons suspected of war crimes, and made provision for handing over war criminals wanted by other nations. It also empowered General Douglas MacArthur, the Supreme Commander of the Allied Powers, to set up special international courts and prescribe rules of procedure for them.

By the same directive the military commanders of any nation taking part in the occupation of Japan were authorised to set up military courts for the trial of war criminals.

In pursuance of the directive two war crimes offices were established. The first, which was for the prosecution of Japanese major war criminals, was called the 'International Prosecution Section'. The other office was for the investigation of all other war crimes and the apprehension and prosecution of all those responsible for them.

The first branch of this office was opened as the War Crimes Branch of the United States General Headquarters, Army Forces Pacific, and two regional branches were set up, one in Yokohama and the other in Manila.

In addition to these agencies, three more United States war crimes organisations were set up in China, India and the Pacific Ocean islands.

This vast network covering an immense space performed outstanding achievements. It identified, located, apprehended and brought to trial thou-

Left: **The prisoners were held in Sugamo Prison in Tokyo, and transported each day in a blacked-out coach, escorted by Jeeps, to the courtroom that had been constructed in the**

Japanese Imperial Army Headquarters *(right)* **known as Ichigawa Heights. Both buildings have now been demolished, see** *After the Battle* **No. 81.**

Between 1946 and 1951, the United States, the United Kingdom, China, the Soviet Union, Australia, New Zealand, Canada, France, the Netherlands and the Philippines all held military tribunals to try Japanese indicted for 'Class B' and 'Class C' war crimes. Class B defendants were accused of having committed such crimes themselves; 'Class C' defendants, mostly senior officers, were accused of planning, ordering or failing to prevent them *Left:* Some 5,600 Japanese personnel were prosecuted in more than 2,200 trials outside Japan, this one taking place in Singapore. *Right:* Due to the huge logistical dificulties of having witnesses attend, unsworn statements were accepted from prisoners of war who were shown mug-shots of thousands of prisoners in custody for identification. The Chinese communists also held a number of trials for Japanese personnel. In the end, more than 4,400 Japanese personnel were convicted and about 1,000 were sentenced to death.

sands of Japanese war criminals. Thus, the Investigation Division investigated nearly 3,000 cases. The investigations covered the following theatres of war: Burma, Siam, French Indo-China, Malaya, Singapore, Sumatra, Java, Borneo and the Celebes.

Another important case investigated was that of the Burma-Siam Railway on which some 640 United States Army, Navy and Marine prisoners of war were employed.

Many cases of the illegal execution of American airmen in Burma and French Indo-China were also investigated, and the perpetrators brought to trial, many of them before British military courts.

GREAT BRITAIN

The investigation and trial of those who had committed war crimes against British nationals became the responsibility of General Headquarters, Allied Land Forces, South-East Asia, which had to operate over a very large area: Singapore, Malaya, Siam, French Indo-China, Burma, Hong Kong, Tientsin, Shanghai, British North Borneo, the Netherlands East Indies, the Andaman and Nicobar Islands. A War Crimes Group was formed comprising a number of investigation teams, a registry section, a co-ordinating section and a legal section.

The entire organisation was eventually brought under the control of the Judge Advocate General's Branch directly responsible to the Military Deputy of the Judge Advocate General in London.

When Japan surrendered, the Japanese forces in South-East Asia passed into the hands of the Allies, and with them the staff of prisoner of war camps, whose brutality was notorious.

Photographs were taken of all these men, and the prints were circulated, particularly to Allied ex-prisoners of war at home, who then made affidavits concerning the treatment they had received. The person making the affidavit would be shown about six prints, one of which was of the person concerned in the charge, and from this photographic identification parade the individual photographs were identified. More than 10,000 of such photographs were taken and, when identified, were sent with the affidavits to the Registry at Singapore from where they were sent out to the investigation teams.

These teams operated throughout the whole area, sometimes in areas of comparative civilization and sometimes deep in the jungle. With the help of

photographs, affidavits, local evidence and sometimes of voluntary statements made by the accused, they were able to build up cases which were sent to the Legal Section of the War Crimes Group.

Where a primafacie case was proved to exist the Legal Section brought the accused to trial. Ex-prisoners from England attended the trial as witnesses but where their presence was not practicable, the affidavits made at home were used in evidence. All cases were not so simple and many suspects remained untraced owing to their having been transferred to another theatre prior to the capitulation, but efforts to trace them proceeded successfully.

By February 1948, 931 Japanese war criminals had been tried by British military courts.

The only trial to be held in Australia took place at Emery Point (now Larrakeyah Barracks) in Darwin in 1946.

Ten Japanese were charged with ill-treating prisoners of war in Timor. One man received the death penalty, Lieutenant Yutani

Yujiro being taken to face a firing-squad at Rabaul in Papua New Guinea.

AUSTRALIA

The first information received by the Australian military authorities regarding the commission of war crimes by the Japanese forces against the Australian forces was after the Japanese invasion of New Britain in January 1942. This came from survivors who escaped to the mainland.

Details of other atrocities committed by the Japanese in Amboina was also brought to Australia by soldiers who had managed to escape capture.

As a result of this, action was taken to obtain statements from all serving officers and men who were able to give information regarding breaches by the Japanese of the rules of warfare.

In June 1944 the Australian Government appointed a commissioner to enquire into war crimes perpetrated by the Japanese against Australian military personnel. The commissioner appointed was Sir William Webb, Chief Justice of the Supreme Court of Queensland, who was subsequently appointed President of the International Military Tribunal for the Far East which tried the major Japanese war criminals at Tokyo.

After the Japanese surrender in 1945 much further evidence of the commission of war crimes by the Japanese was obtained from liberated prisoners of war and ex-internees, which resulted in the apprehension and identification of many alleged war criminals.

Shortly after the Japanese capitulation, a War Crimes Act was passed in the Commonwealth under which the power to convene military courts under the Act was delegated by the Governor-General in council to certain military commanders and senior staff officers in the field, and a special staff was set up at Australian Army Headquarters to deal with war crimes. A number of War Crimes Sections were set up by this Headquarters, two of which co-operated with the British in Singapore and the Americans in Tokyo. The other section operated in New Guinea, and a number of other Pacific territories.

The Australian War Crimes Section in Singapore dealt mainly with cases in Malaya, on the Burma-Siam Railway, and the Netherlands East Indies, and worked in close co-operation with the British war crimes investigation authorities in Singapore, and with the Dutch military authorities in Java.

Many Australian military courts were set up for the trial of alleged war criminals and others were tried by British military courts upon which an Australian officer sat as a member. This network of investigation covered a very wide area, Malaya, Burma, Java, New Guinea, New Britain, the Celebes, Timor, the Ceram Islands, including Amboina, British and Dutch Borneo and a number of other territories.

Altogether over 800 Japanese war criminals were tried, of whom slightly less than one third were acquitted.

In March 1946, Hideki Tojo, the former Japanese Prime Minister and military leader, made this statement.

'Since the end of the war I have read about the inhumane acts committed by the Japanese Army and Navy. These were certainly not the intention of those in authority, namely the General Staff, or the War or Navy Departments or myself. We did not even suspect that such things had happened. The Emperor especially, because of his benevolence, would have had a contrary feeling. Such acts are not permissible in Japan, the character of the Japanese people is such that they believe that neither Heaven nor Earth would permit such things. It will be too bad if people in the world believe that these inhumane acts are the result of Japanese character.'

Regarding Tojo's statement that the Japanese war leaders did not even suspect that atrocities and other war crimes were being committed, the International Military Tribunal at Tokyo said this in its judgment: 'During a period of several months the Tribunal heard evidence from witnesses who testified in detail to atrocities committed in all theatres of war on a scale so vast, yet following so common a pattern that only one conclusion is possible. The atrocities were either secretly ordered or wilfully permitted by the Japanese Government or individual members thereof, and by the leaders of the armed forces.'

Throughout the Sino-Japanese and Pacific wars, in every theatre of operations, unspeakable cruelties and merciless tortures were inflicted upon thousands of Allied prisoners of war and innocent civilians by all ranks of the Japanese armed forces, without any compunction and, for the most part, without any feelings of compassion whatsoever.

LORD RUSSELL
OF LIVERPOOL, 1958

At the trial of the major Japanese war criminals in Tokyo, the defence contended that the Tripartite Alliance which created the Berlin—Tokyo—Rome Axis, was 'an instrument of peace'. Dealing with this contention in its judgment, the Tribunal stated that 'the decisions of the leaders of Japan show that the conspirators were determined to extend the domination of Japan over a huge area and population and to use force, if necessary, to accomplish their aims. They show by plain admission that their purpose in entering into the Tripartite Pact was to secure support for the accomplishment of these illegal aims.' The Tribunal wholly refuted the contention that the purpose of the Tripartite Pact was to promote the cause of peace.

And so the leaders of the Axis triumvirate paid the ultimate price. First to fall was Benito Mussolini, shot by communist agents on April 28, 1945, his body being displayed for all to see in the Piazzale Loretto in Milan. At the same time in Berlin, Adolf Hitler was planning his own demise, shooting himself in the early hours of April 30 in his study in the Führerbunker.

General MacArthur, as the Supreme Allied Commander, had already decided to exonerate Emperor Hirohito from any wrong-doing to preserve the throne as a symbol of continuity and cohesion for the Japasese people. Instead, seven of the Japanese military hierarchy died in his place. Apart from General Tojo, they were General Kenji Doihara, Chief of the Intelligence Services in Manchukuo; Koki Hirota, Prime Minister (later Foreign Minister); General Seishiro Itagaki, War Minister; General Heitaro Kimura, Commander, Burma Area Army; Lieutenant-General Akira Muto, Chief-of-Staff, 14th Area Army, and General Iwane Matsui, Commander, Shanghai Expeditionary Force and Central China Area Army. MacArthur, afraid of embarrassing and antagonising the Japanese people, defied the wishes of President Truman and barred photography of any kind at the executions which took place in Sugamo Prison on December 23, 1948. Instead, he brought in four members of the Allied Council to act as official witnesses. This boulder now marks the site of the gallows. The message is simple: 'Pray for Eternal Peace'.

INDEX

COMPILED BY PETER GUNN

Note: Page numbers in *italics* refer to illustrations. There may also be textual references on these pages.

Memorial to the Ukrainian partisan groups that fought below the city of Odessa during the Second World War.

POLAND